S0-AHA-684

Readings in ————————
SOCIAL PSYCHOLOGY

General, Classic, and Contemporary Selections

SIXTH EDITION

WAYNE A. LESKO
Marymount University

PEARSON

Boston New York San Francisco
Mexico City Montreal Toronto London Madrid Munich Paris
Hong Kong Singapore Tokyo Cape Town Sydney

With love to Marlaine and Matt
for the many ways you have enriched my life
and for the wonders yet to come

Executive Editor: Susan Hartman
Series Editorial Assistant: Therese Felser
Marketing Manager: Pam Laskey
Production Editor: Won McIntosh
Editorial-Production Service: Communicáto, Ltd.
Composition Buyer: Linda Cox
Manufacturing Buyer: JoAnne Sweeney
Electronic Composition: Cabot Computer Services
Cover Designer: Kristina Mose-Libon

For related titles and support materials, visit our online catalog at www.ablongman.com

Copyright © 2006, 2003, 2000, 1997, 1994, 1991 Pearson Education, Inc.

All rights reserved. No part of the material protected by this copyright notice may be reproduced or utilized in any form or by any means, electronic or mechanical, including photocopying, recording, or by any information storage and retrieval system, without written permission from the copyright owner.

To obtain permission(s) to use material from this work, please submit a written request to Allyn and Bacon, Permissions Department, 75 Arlington Street, Boston, MA 02116 or fax your request to 617-848-7320.

Between the time website information is gathered and then published, it is not unusual for some sites to have closed. Also, the transcription of URLs can result in typographical errors. The publisher would appreciate notification where these errors occur so that they may be corrected in subsequent editions.

Library of Congress Cataloging-in-Publication Data

Readings in social psychology : general, classic, and contemporary
    selections / [compiled by] Wayne A. Lesko. — 6th ed.
        p. cm.
    Includes bibliographical references and index.
    ISBN 0-205-45439-9
    1. Social psychology.   I. Lesko, Wayne A.

HM1033.R43 2005
302—dc22

                                                                                2005046480

Printed in the United States of America

10   9   8   7   6   5   4   3   2   1   HAM   09   08   07   06   05

Brief Contents

Contents

Preface

THE TYPICAL SOCIAL psychology class ranges from sophomore through graduate levels, and the members may include majors who are required to take the course as well as non-majors who have elected to do so. Regardless of the level or the audience, many instructors—myself included—feel that a collection of readings is a valuable means of promoting an understanding of the discipline.

Most collections of readings typically fall into two categories: professional articles from journals in the field or popular articles reprinted from such magazines as *Psychology Today*. The category of professional readings may include contemporary articles, classic articles, or a combination of the two. These articles provide excellent insight into the core of social psychology by describing not only the research outcomes but also the detailed methodology for how the results were obtained. Popular articles, on the other hand, lack the scientific rigor of journal articles but often present a broad overview of a number of findings pertaining to a particular topic. Clearly, both types of readings have advantages and disadvantages associated with them, depending on the particular level at which the course is taught.

In over three decades of teaching social psychology at both the undergraduate and graduate levels, I have found that students seem to respond best to a variety of reading formats. Popular articles are easy to understand and provide a good overview, while also generating critical thinking about an issue. Research articles provide insight into the methodological issues in social psychology and help the student develop a critical attitude in evaluating research contributions and conclusions. Classic research articles familiarize the student with early research that has had a lasting impact on social psychology, while contemporary works illustrate issues currently being studied and the methods used to investigate them.

Like the first five editions, this sixth edition of *Readings in Social Psychology: General, Classic, and Contemporary Selections* is designed to provide exactly that breadth of exposure to the different sources of information available in the field. In response to feedback about the last edition of the book and to keep current with trends in the field of social psychology, this edition has taken two applied chapters and expanded them into three. The book now includes separate chapters on business psychology, forensic psychology, and health psychology, thus adding three readings.

As in the previous editions, each chapter begins with an introduction to the topic, which is followed by three articles: one general (popular), one classic, and one contemporary. Each article begins with a short introduction that sets the stage, or provides a context for the article. Each article is followed by a set of Critical Thinking Questions, which ask the student to examine critically some part of the article presented, to speculate about generalizations and implications of the research, and, in some cases, to suggest new studies based on the information in the article. Each classic article is also followed by a list of Additional Related Readings for students who may wish to examine more contemporary articles on the same topic. New to this edition is a section called Chapter Integration Questions, which has been added at the end of each chapter. These questions are intended to link the three chapter articles, usually by identifying a theme or themes common to all of them. As with the Critical Thinking Questions, these questions can be used in their entirety or in part, as best meets the needs of the instructor.

The topical organization of *Readings in Social Psychology: General, Classic, and Contemporary Selections* (sixth edition) directly parallels that of many social psychology textbooks. As such, it can be adapted readily for use with any text or used in lieu of a text, depending on how the course is taught. Likewise, the book can be used with classes of varying levels, by structuring which articles will be emphasized and in how much detail they will be examined.

Finally, all articles are presented verbatim, in their entirety, since it is my firm belief that one valuable skill gained by students from reading research articles is the ability to abstract pertinent information from an original source. The only exception to this, necessitated by copyright ownership, is found in Table 1 of Article 14, which is an abbreviation of the Bem Sex Role Inventory.

Because the articles are presented in their original forms, some of them, especially the contemporary articles, may be difficult to understand. However, I selected these particular articles for a variety of reasons. First, the topic of each of these articles is one that not only represents the type of research being conducted on this topic today but that also usually has interest to the reader. Second, these contemporary articles were selected to give the reader a broad exposure to the different types of professional publications in the field. Most of the more difficult articles are from journals published by the American Psychological Association (APA). In fact, if only less complex articles were included in this book, then APA publications virtually would be excluded. This would be a disservice to the reader, from my view.

For even the most complex contemporary articles, I have found that users without much background in psychology (e.g., sophomores with little or no prior research exposure) can read them effectively with the proper guidance. In addition to the guidance provided by the instructor, students will benefit by reading A Note to the Reader, which follows this Preface. That section provides some useful suggestions for how to read a research article without getting lost in all of the statistics and technical detail.

At this point, perhaps some notice is in order about several of the articles. Understandably, everything is representative of the time in which it was written, both in terms of the ideas presented and the language used. Some of the classic articles in this collection were written 40 or more years ago and are out of step with current language style. Moreover, some of the descriptions made and observations offered would be considered condescending and even offensive by today's standards. Please keep this in mind, and consider the context in which each of the articles was written.

ACKNOWLEDGMENTS

At Allyn and Bacon, I would like to thank Susan Hartman, Executive Editor, and Therese Felser, Series Editorial Assistant, for their guidance and help with the format of the book. I likewise wish to extend my gratitude to Sue Freese, of Communicáto, Ltd., for her excellent copyediting of this book. Thanks also go to Robert A. Baron, Rensselaer Polytechnic Institute, and Donn Byrne, State University of New York–Albany, who provided input about the organization and content of the various editions. In particular, I would like to thank the following individuals, who reviewed this edition: Kim Duff, Cerritos College; Mary Dzindolet, Cameron University; and Colleen Sinclair, University of Missouri at Columbia.

I am especially indebted to my graduate and undergraduate students in social psychology at Marymount University, whose honest feedback on the contents of the first five editions helped me create a new, improved book of readings.

I also want to thank the various friends, colleagues, and graduate assistants who helped me and provided encouragement and advice over the many editions of this collection of readings. Without their input, this work would not have been possible.

Last but not least, I thank all of the authors and publishers of the articles contained in this book for their permission to reprint these materials. Their fine work in advancing the field of social psychology is literally what made this book possible.

W. L.

A Note to the Reader

As YOU EMBARK on your study of social psychology, you will soon discover that the field is broad indeed. You will encounter many different topics, but they all are related by the common thread that defines social psychology—namely, the study of individual behavior in social situations.

As a collection of readings, this book is designed to expose you to some of the most important areas of study within social psychology. Just as the topics found in the area of social psychology are diverse, so, too, are the ways in which social psychological knowledge is disseminated. If you are new to the field, most likely you have encountered one common source of information: articles in nonprofessional sources. For example, newspaper and magazine articles may present the information from some study in social psychology. Typically nontechnical pieces directed to the general public, these articles summarize a number of studies on a given topic and are fairly easy to comprehend. Each of the 15 chapters that comprise this book begins with such an article—what I have termed a *general* reading.

A second source of information is actually the backbone of social psychology: articles that appear in professional journals of the field. These articles are the primary means by which new ideas and the results of research are shared with the professional community. While they tend to be more technical and difficult to read compared to the general works, professional articles have the advantage of providing readers with sufficient detail to draw their own conclusions, rather than be forced to rely on someone else's interpretation of the information. Some of these articles represent research that has stood the test of time and are generally regarded as *classics* in the field; the second reading found in each chapter is such an article.

Finally, the last type of article found in each chapter is labeled *contemporary*. These articles are fairly recent examples of research currently being conducted in social psychology. As noted in the Preface, these articles can be particularly challenging to read but are significant in terms of what they represent about the field of social psychology.

The format of each chapter is the same. Each opens with a brief introduction to the chapter topic; one general, one classic, and one contemporary article are then presented, in that order. Each article begins with an introduction written by me, which serves to focus your perspective before reading. Every article is then followed by Critical Thinking Questions. In some cases, these questions directly refer to information contained in the articles; in others, the questions are more speculative, asking you to go beyond the data presented. The classic articles also contain Additional Related Readings. The references included here are either recent articles that address the same issues discussed in the classic article (a way of updating the current status of research on the topic) or a topic similar to the one discussed in the original. In either case, the interested student can use these references to find more information on the topic. Finally, each chapter concludes with a section called Chapter Integration Questions. These questions relate the articles to one another, usually by having you identify a theme or themes that cut across them. Considering these questions provides another way of seeing the articles in the larger context of the topic, rather than as isolated pieces of research.

Before reading the articles in this book, it might be worthwhile to review the fundamentals of research tactics. Having such a basic understanding will help you understand even the most complex articles.

Research studies in social psychology (or indeed, in any scientifically based discipline) fall into two broad categories: correlational studies and experimental studies. A *correlation* is a finding that two variables are somehow related; that is, as one variable changes, so does the other one. For example, consider the relationship between the amount of violent content that children watch on television and their subsequent aggressive behavior. A correlation may show that the more aggressive programs a child watches, the more aggressive he or she is in playing with other children. Would such a correlation mean that watching the aggressive shows makes children more aggressive? Not necessarily. The children may be more aggressive for other reasons (e.g., maybe they eat too much candy while watching the shows), or perhaps children who are innately more aggressive are more attached to violent programs. In short, all that a correlation tells us is that two variables are related. It does *not* tell us that one variable causes the other one.

What, then, is the value of a correlation if it does not allow us to make cause-effect connections? One major value is that a correlation allows us to *predict*. That is, knowing that two variables are correlated allows us to predict the value of one when we only know the other is present. Again, using the violent programs example, if we know that there is a strong correlation between the amount of time children spend watching violent television and their subsequent aggressive behavior, then simply knowing how much violent television a child watches will allow us to predict the likelihood of his or her being aggressive.

In addition to making predictions, sometimes we want research to determine *why* something happens. In other words, we may want to determine a cause-and-effect relationship. The established way to do so is to use *experimental* research. The goal of all experimental research is to determine causation. No matter how complex a study's research design, the underlying logic of experimental research is fundamentally the same and fairly straightforward.

To understand the logic behind experimental research, along with its commonly used terms, let's look again at the example of aggressive television programming and children's behavior. Suppose we want to determine if exposure to violent television makes children more aggressive. First of all, we will need two groups of children—one watching violent television and the other watching something else—so that we can compare one group to another. But how will we form the two groups of children? We could ask the children which type of programming they prefer to watch and then group them accordingly. The problem with this approach is that we will not know if children already prone to aggression are more likely to prefer watching violent television programs.

The solution to this problem is actually quite simple: We will use *random assignment* to put the children into the groups. In other words, we will use pure chance, such as the results of a coin toss, to determine to which group each child is assigned. Why? By using chance, we are essentially creating two equal groups at the beginning of the study. For each child who is aggressive and is assigned to the one group, by chance, there will be another aggressive child assigned to the other group. In other words, individual differences cancel themselves out when we use random assignment.

Let's get back to our study design. Suppose we start out with, say, 100 children of the same age and randomly assign them to the two groups. Half of these children are assigned to a group that will watch violent television programs. This group is called the *experimental group,* since it involves the variable we are investigating—namely, exposure to violent programs. The other half of the children are assigned to a group that will watch nonviolent programs. This latter group is called the *control group,* and it will be our comparison group.

Another term you need to understand is *independent variable*. The independent variable is what the researcher is manipulating. In our example, the independent variable is whether or not the child is exposed to violent television programs. It is called *independent* because the experimenter is free to manipulate it as he or she wishes.

Let's pause for a second to look at the design of our experiment thus far. We started out with a group of children and randomly assigned them to two groups. Doing so resulted in our starting out with two equal groups. Next, we treated the two groups the same except for one thing: the independent variable. That is, half the children watched violent shows, and the other half watched nonviolent shows. Next, following exposure to the independent variable, we need some sort of way to measure the children's aggression. This outcome measure is known as the *dependent variable*. The two groups were identical to begin with (due to our random assignment), but what if we now find they are different after exposure to the independent variable? The answer is that the difference must be due to the only difference between the two groups—namely, exposure to the independent variable. Thus, a cause-and-effect relationship can be established, demonstrating that exposure to violent television programming causes children to become more aggressive.

No matter how complex a study's research design is (and you will encounter some very complex designs in the studies that follow), the logic of experimental research is the same as outlined in our experiment: Identical groups are created through random assignment, they are exposed to different conditions (the independent variable), and the outcomes are measured (the dependent variable). If a difference is observed in the dependent variable, then it must be due to the different treatments that the subjects received.

The reality of conducting research and drawing warranted conclusions obviously is a bit more complicated than our discussion would indicate. Nonetheless, if you keep in mind the basics of experimental design, you will find it easier to understand the studies that you read.

All of the articles in this collection are reprinted in their entirety. Not a word has been abridged or altered. (Again, the only exception is Article 14, which has been abbreviated due to a copyright restriction.) For the general articles, this should not be a problem for anyone. However, if this is the first time that you are reading journal articles from their primary sources, some assistance might be in order. First of all, do not allow yourself to be overwhelmed or intimidated. New students often are confused by some of the terminology that is used and are left totally dumbfounded by the detailed statistics that are usually part of such articles. Approached in the right way, these articles need not be intimidating and should be comprehensible to any reader willing to expend a little effort.

In reading a research article, I would like to make the following suggestions:

■ Most articles begin with an Abstract or end with a Summary. If these are provided, begin by carefully reading them; they will give you an overview of why the study was conducted, what was done, and what the results were.

■ Next, read the Introduction fairly carefully; this is where the authors describe previous research in the area and develop the logic for why they are conducting the experiment in the first place.

■ The Methods section describes in detail the techniques used by the researchers to conduct their study; read this section thoroughly in order to understand exactly what was done.

■ The next section, Results, is where the authors describe what was found in the study. This is often the most technically difficult part of the article; from your standpoint, you might want to skim over this part, focusing only on the sections that verbally describe what the results were. Do not worry about the detailed statistical analyses that are presented.

■ Finally, you might want to read the Discussion section in some detail; here, the authors discuss the findings and implications of the study and perhaps suggest avenues for further study.

To summarize: Each article is fairly straightforward to comprehend, provided that you do not allow yourself to get too bogged down in the details and thus frustrated. The journey may seem difficult at times, but the end result—an appreciation and understanding of the complex issues of human social behavior—will be worth it. Enjoy!

W. L.

Chapter One

THE FIELD OF SOCIAL PSYCHOLOGY

AN INTRODUCTION TO a course such as social psychology often includes a section on research methods. Nonmajors confronting this topic often wonder why they need to know about research methods when in all likelihood they will never actually conduct research. Whether you are majoring in psychology or not, familiarity with research methods will benefit you, for several reasons.

First, it will help you understand the studies that make up the knowledge base of social psychology. Familiarity with methodology will allow you to make informed decisions about the conclusions drawn by various studies. Second, and perhaps more important, some knowledge of research issues will allow you to be an intelligent consumer of research information. Results of studies often are reported to the general public in newspapers and magazines. Knowing something about the methods used to produce these results will better prepare you to decide whether the conclusions drawn are warranted. Finally, it is useful to fully appreciate why the results of experimental data are needed instead of just relying on common sense. Article 1, "Folk Wisdom: Was Your Grandmother Right?" shows how folk wisdom (i.e., common sense) often is contradictory and hence not very useful as a guideline for behavior.

Research is the basic underpinning of psychological science. Given the subject matter of social psychology, it is often difficult, if not impossible, to get unbiased results if subjects know what is being observed. For that reason, psychologists, in general, and social psychologists, in particular, often have relied on deception as a means of obtaining naive subjects. But what ethical issues are involved in the use of deception? And what if deception is so widely used that subjects expect to be deceived whenever they participate in a research study? What, if any, are the alternatives to the use of deception? These are some of the questions addressed in Article 2, "Human Use of Human Subjects: The Problem of Deception in Social Psychological Experiments."

Finally, Article 3 gives a good first-hand account of what it is like to actually conduct research in social psychology. When you read research articles in this book or elsewhere, all that you often see is the final result of the research. What you often do not see, however, are all of the false starts, unforeseen problems, and other practical issues that may have influenced the final design and outcome of the study. "Lessons Learned from a Lifetime of Applied Social Psychology Research" looks at what it is really like to undertake applied research problems.

ARTICLE 1 _____

At the heart of all the articles you will read in this book is *research methodology.* Given a question you want to investigate, how do you go about actually collecting data?

There are a number of different ways of conducting social psychological research. One broad distinction is between *experimental methods* and *correlational (nonexperimental) methods.* Each method has potential advantages and disadvantages. One is not necessarily better than the other; it depends on what you are investigating.

Students encountering research methods literature for the first time are often surprised at the difficulty of designing and conducting a good piece of research. It is not as easy as it might seem on the surface. Numerous artifacts that can affect the outcome of a study need to be accounted for and controlled. An examination of the introductory chapters of most social psychology texts will give you a better understanding of some of these issues.

Sometimes, a study obtains results that are quite unexpected and surprises readers. Other times, however, readers may feel that the outcome of a study was totally expected— indeed, that it was just common sense. The reaction to such an article often is to question why it is even necessary to test the obvious.

The only problem with common sense is that it is often contradictory. For example, to whom are people most attracted: people like themselves or people different from themselves? Common sense would predict that "Birds of a feather flock together"; on the other hand, "Opposites attract." So which is it? As it turns out, common sense is not such a good predictor of actual behavior. The only way to know for sure is to go out and empirically test the concept.

The following article by Robert Epstein examines a number of common-sense ideas that have been passed down to us in light of what current research tells us about their validity. The article underscores the necessity of testing ideas empirically and why even supposedly obvious notions must be exposed to scientific scrutiny.

Folk Wisdom
Was Your Grandmother Right?
■ Robert Epstein

The table next to me at Fillipi's restaurant was a noisy one. Two men and two women in their 20s and 30s were arguing about a relationship issue. One of the men—call him Male #1—would soon be leaving the country for six months. Would the passion he shared with his beloved survive? The exchange went something like this:

Female #1 (probably the girlfriend): "When you really love someone, being apart makes you care even more. If someone is good to you, you sometimes take that for granted when the person is around every day. But when he's gone, all that good treatment is gone, too, and you realize just how much you had. You really start to yearn for him."

Male #2 (looking lustfully at Female #1, even though he seemed to be with the other woman): "That's right. The same thing happens when your parents die. You really start to miss and appreciate them.

Reprinted from *Psychology Today,* 1997 (November/December), *30,* 46–50, 76. Reprinted with permission from *Psychology Today* magazine. Copyright © 1997 (Sussex Publishers, Inc.).

You even rewrite the past, forgetting the bad things and focusing on the good times and the kindness they showed you."

Female #1 (starting to look lovingly at Male #2): "Exactly. Everyone knows that absence makes the heart grow fonder."

Then Male #1, the one probably on his way to Thailand, spoke up. "Well, but . . ." He faltered, thinking hard about going on. All eyes were on him. He took a deep breath.

And then he said, slowly and deliberately, "But don't we also say, 'Out of sight, out of mind'?"

This was not good for anyone's digestion. Female #1's face turned the color of marinara sauce. Male #2 smiled mischievously, presumably imagining himself in bed with Female #1. Female #2 looked back and forth between her date and Female #1, also apparently imagining them in bed together. And Male #1, not wanting to face the carnage, lowered his eyes and tapped out a strange rhythm on the table top with his fork. Was he thinking about the classy Thai brothels he had read about on the Internet?

TRUTH OR POPPYCOCK?

"Absence makes the heart grow fonder" and "Out of sight, out of mind" are examples of folk wisdom—folk psychology, you might say. All cultures pass along wisdom of this sort—sometimes in the form of proverbs; sometimes through songs (remember Paul Simon's "Fifty Ways to Leave Your Lover"?), rhymes (Mother Goose), or stories (Aesop's fables); sometimes through laws and public information campaigns ("Stay alive, don't drink and drive"); and always through religion ("Do unto others as you would have them do unto you").

But folk wisdom is an unreliable, inconsistent kind of wisdom. For one thing, most proverbs coexist with their exact opposites, or at least with proverbs that give somewhat different advice. Does absence truly make the heart grow fonder, or are loved ones out of mind when they're out of sight? And isn't variety the spice of life? (If Male #1 had come up with *that* one, he might have been murdered on the spot.)

Do opposites attract, or do birds of a feather flock together? Should you love the one you're with, or

would that be like changing horses in midstream? We all know that he who hesitates is lost, but doesn't haste make waste, and isn't patience a virtue, and don't fools rush in, and aren't you supposed to look before you leap?

And, sure, money is power, but aren't the best things in life supposed to be free? And since time is money, and money is power, and power corrupts, does that mean time also corrupts? Well, maybe so. After all, the Devil finds work for idle hands.

I've only covered a few well-known proverbs from the English-speaking world. Each culture passes along its own wisdom, which is not always meaningful to outsiders. In India, for example, people say, "Call on God, but row away from the docks," and Romanians advise, "Do not put your spoon into the pot that does not boil for you." In Bali they say, "Goodness shouts and evil whispers," while in Tibet the message is, "Goodness speaks in a whisper, but evil shouts."

You get the idea. Proverbs that relay wisdom about how we're supposed to live do not necessarily supply useful or reliable advice. In fact, proverbs are sometimes used merely to justify what we already do or believe, rather than as guidelines for action. What's more, we tend to *switch* proverbs to suit our current values and ideals. A young man might rationalize risky action by pointing out that "You only live once"; later in life—if he's still around—he'll probably tell you, "Better safe than sorry."

Is the situation hopeless? Can we glean any truths at all from the wisdom of the ages?

The behavioral sciences can help. Science is a set of methods for testing the validity of statements about the world—methods for getting as close to "truth" as we currently know how to get. Psychologists and other scientists have spent more than a century testing the validity of statements about human behavior, thinking, and emotions. How well does folk psychology stand up to scientific inquiry? What do we find when we test a statement like "Absence makes the heart grow fonder"? If, as I do, you sometimes rely on folk wisdom to guide your actions or teach your children, this is a question well worth considering.

Here's how five common proverbs measure up to behavioral research.

CONFESSION IS GOOD FOR THE SOUL

Psychologists don't study the soul, of course. But, says psychologist James W. Pennebaker, Ph.D., "If we define 'soul' loosely as who you are, how you feel about yourself, and how healthy you are, then confession is good for the soul." Pennebaker, a researcher at the University of Texas at Austin, is one of several behavioral scientists who have looked carefully at the results of "self-disclosure"—talking or writing about private feelings and concerns. His research suggests that for about two-thirds of us, self-disclosure has enormous emotional and physical benefits. Pennebaker's newly revised book, *Opening Up: The Healing Power of Expressing Emotion,* summarizes 15 years of compelling research on this subject.

Self-disclosure, as you might expect, can greatly reduce shame or guilt. In fact, studies of suspected criminals showed that they acted far more relaxed after confessing their crimes—despite the fact that punishment now awaited them. Self-disclosure may also provide the power behind talk therapy. "The fact that self-disclosure is beneficial," says Pennebaker, "may explain why all forms of psychotherapy seem to be helpful. Whether the therapy is behavioral or psychoanalytic, in the beginning the clients tell their stories."

Perhaps most intriguing are the physical effects of "confession." Pennebaker has found that self-disclosure may actually boost the immune system, spurring production of white blood cells that attack invading microorganisms, increasing production of antibodies, and heightening the body's response to vaccination.

But what about those other proverbs that advise us to keep our mouths shut? "Let sleeping dogs lie." "Least said is soonest mended." "Many have suffered by talking, few by silence." Can self-disclosure do harm? According to Pennebaker, self-disclosure is not likely to be beneficial when it's forced. University of Notre Dame psychologist Anita Kelly, Ph.D., has suggested, moreover, that revealing secrets may be harmful if the confidant is likely to be judgmental. And a 1989 study conducted by Maria Sauzier, M.D., of Harvard Medical School, showed that people often regret disclosures of child abuse. Sauzier found that nearly half of the parents whose children had disclosed sexual abuse (usually to the other parent or a therapist) felt that both the children and the families were harmed by the disclosures. And 19 percent of the adolescents who confessed that they had been abused regretted making the disclosures. In general, however, confession seems to be a surprisingly beneficial act.

ALL WORK AND NO PLAY MAKES JACK A DULL BOY

To me, the most frightening scene in the movie *The Shining* was the one in which actress Shelley Duvall, concerned that her husband (Jack Nicholson) was going crazy, approached the desk at which he had spent several months supposedly writing a novel. There she found hundreds of pages containing nothing but the sentence, "All work and no play makes Jack a dull boy" typed thousands of times on a manual typewriter. I've always wondered who did all that typing! And I've also wondered about the truth of the proverb. Once again, we're also faced with contradictory bits of folk wisdom that urge us to work until we drop: "Rest makes rusty." "Labor warms, sloth harms." "Labor is itself a pleasure."

Is too much work, without the balance of leisure activity ("play"), actually harmful? Research suggests that the answer is yes, with one possible exception: if you love your work—in other words, if you've been able to make your *avocation* your *vocation*—then work may provide you with some of the benefits of play.

In the 1940s, anthropologist Adam Curle pointed out that the distinction between work and leisure seems to be an unfortunate product of modern society. In many traditional cultures, he wrote, "there is not even a word for work." Work and play "are all of a piece," part of the integrated structure of daily living. But modern society has created the need for people to earn a living, an endeavor that can be difficult and can easily get out of hand. Hence, the modern pursuit of "leisure time" and "balance"—correctives for the desperate measures people take to pay their bills.

Study after study confirms the dangers of overwork. It may or may not make you a dull person, but it clearly dulls your mind. For example, recent research on fire fighters by Peter Knauth, Ph.D., shows that long work shifts increase reaction time and lower alertness. And studies with emergency room physicians show that overwork increases errors and impedes judgment. Indeed, a Hollywood cameraman, coming off an 18-hour work shift, made news recently when he lost control of his car and died in a crash.

Conversely, leisure activities have been shown in numerous studies by researchers Howard and Diane Tinsley, Virginia Lewis, and others, to relieve stress, improve mood, increase life satisfaction, and even boost the immune system.

Curiously, the hard-driven "type A" personalities among us are not necessarily Dull Jacks. According to a recent study of more than 300 college students by Robert A. Hicks, Ph.D., and his colleagues, type-A students claim to engage in considerably more leisure activities than their relaxed, type-B counterparts. Type As may simply live "more intensely" than type Bs, whether they're on the job or goofing off.

The distinction between work and play is, to some extent, arbitrary. But it's clear that if you spend too much time doing things you don't want to do, your performance, health, and sense of well-being will suffer.

BOYS WILL BE BOYS

The widely held (though politically incorrect) belief that boys are predisposed from birth to feel, learn, and perform differently from girls is strongly supported by research. For example, boys are, on average, considerably more aggressive than girls. They are left-handed more frequently than girls and tend to be better at math and at spatial rotation tasks. Girls, meanwhile, may perform certain kinds of memory tasks better. They also start talking earlier than boys, and, at the playground, they're more likely to imitate boys than boys are to imitate girls. And boys tend to listen more with their right ear, while girls tend to listen with both ears equally. These findings generally hold up cross-culturally, which suggests that they are at least somewhat independent of environmental influences. Upbringing plays an important role in gender differences, of course—even in the first days after birth, parents treat boy babies differently from girls—but converging evidence from psychology, neuroscience, and evolutionary biology suggests that many gender differences are actually programmed from birth, if not from conception.

Since the brain is the mechanism that generates behavior, where we find behavioral differences, we should also find neurological differences. Indeed, recent research suggests a host of differences between male and female brains. For example, although, on average, male brains are larger than female brains, the hemispheres of the brain seem to be better connected in females, which may help explain why females are more sensitive and emotional than males.

Behavior is also driven by hormones. Here, too, there are significant gender differences. From birth, testosterone levels are higher in males, which helps to account for males' aggressiveness. June Reinisch, Ph.D., then at Indiana University, studied boys and girls whose mothers had been exposed to antimiscarriage drugs that mimic testosterone. Not surprisingly, she found that these children of both sexes were considerably more aggressive than their counterparts with normal testosterone levels. But even among the exposed children, the boys were more aggressive than the girls.

So boys will indeed be boys (and, by implication, girls will be girls). But this is only true "on average." Male and female traits overlap considerably, which means that a particular male could be more emotional than most females and a particular female could be better at math than most males. To be fair, you have to go case by case.

EARLY TO BED, AND EARLY TO RISE, MAKES A MAN HEALTHY, WEALTHY, AND WISE

This proverb, often attributed to Ben Franklin, actually seems to have originated in the late 1400s, and Franklin may have lifted it from a collection of adages published in 1656. Historical trivia aside, research on sleep suggests that the proverb gives sound advice— but only because our culture is out-of-synch with the biology of nearly half the population.

Here's how it works: it's long been known that the body has natural rhythms. Those that occur on a 24-hour cycle are called "circadian" and include cycles of temperature change, wakefulness, and eating. For most people, these cycles are highly resistant to change. This much you probably have heard, but what you might not know is that there are two distinctly different circadian rhythm patterns. "Larks"— who show what researchers call "morningness" (honest!)—are people whose cycles peak early in the day. Not surprisingly, larks awaken early and start the day strong. "Owls"—people inclined toward "eveningness"—peak late in the day. In both cases, the peaks are associated with better performance on memory tasks, quicker reaction times, heightened alertness, and cheerful moods. Some people are extreme larks or owls, others are moderates, and a few fit neither category.

There's a problem here, especially if, like me, you're an extreme owl. The trouble is that many important human activities—business meetings, job interviews, weddings, classes, and so on—are conducted during daylight hours, when larks have a distinct advantage. Not surprisingly, owls spend much of their time griping about how out-of-synch they seem to be. A 1978 study of college students by Wilse B. Webb, Ph.D., and Michael H. Bonnet, Ph.D., of the University of Florida, paints a grim picture for people like me: "Larks reported waking up when they expected to, waking up feeling more rested, and waking up more easily than the owls." Larks also reported having "fewer worries" and getting "more adequate sleep," and they awakened feeling physically better than owls. The differences were even greater, moreover, when owls tried to adapt to the lark sleep pattern. What's more, these problems can impair not only owls' sense of restedness but also their bank account; a study of Navy personnel suggests that people who sleep well make considerably more money than people who sleep poorly.

The long and short of it is that if your biorhythms allow you easily to "go to bed with the lamb and rise with the lark" (another old proverb), you may indeed end up with more money, better health, and more life satisfaction—but only because your internal clock is more in-synch with the stock exchange.

SPARE THE ROD AND SPOIL THE CHILD

A recent headline in my local newspaper proclaimed, "Spanking Backfires, Latest Study Says." I cringe when I see stories like this, because I believe they ultimately harm many children. People have come to confuse discipline with "abuse," which is quite a different beast. "Discipline"—whether in the form of "time outs," reprimands, or spankings—is absolutely

necessary for parenting. Extensive research by psychologist Diana Baumrind, Ph.D., and others, has shown that permissive parenting produces children who can't handle independence and are unable to behave in a socially responsible manner. A great many social problems that we face today may be the inadvertent product of a generation of well-meaning, misinformed, overly-permissive parents.

However, if all you provide is discipline, without affection and emotional support—the "authoritarian" parenting style—you can damage your children. Offspring of authoritarian parents tend to be hostile and defiant, and, like the victims of permissive parents, they too have trouble with independence.

The most effective parenting style involves both a high level of discipline and ample affection and support. That's the best approach for producing children who are self-reliant, socially responsible, and successful in their own relationships, research shows.

In the latest anti-spanking study, published in August by University of New Hampshire sociologist Murray Straus, Ph.D., children between the ages of 6 to 9 who were spanked more than three times a week displayed more misbehavior two years later. Doesn't this show that spanking causes misbehavior? Not at all. Correlational studies are difficult to interpret. Perhaps without those spankings, the kids would have been even worse off. It's also possible that many of these spankings were unnecessary or excessive, and that it was this inappropriate discipline that sparked the later misbehavior.

Conversely, at least eight studies with younger kids show that spanking can indeed improve behavior. The age of the child, in fact, is probably important. Children under the age of six seem to regard spanking as a parent's right. But older kids may view it as an act of aggression, and in such cases spanking's effects may not be so benign.

Punishment, verbal or physical, applied in moderation and with the right timing, is a powerful teaching tool. It should not be the first or the only tool that a parent uses, but it has its place.

TRUTH À LA CARTE

But what about the restaurant debate? Does absence make the heart grow fonder or not? Alas, not enough research has been conducted to shed much light on this question. We do know that "out of sight, out of mind" is true when we're fresh from the womb; young babies will behave as if a toy has vanished into thin air when the toy is moved out of sight. But our memories quickly improve. Research conducted by Julia Vormbrock, Ph.D., and others, shows that children grow more fond of their caregivers when they're separated from them—at least for a few days. After two weeks of separation, however, most children become "detached," reports Vormbrock.

Psychologist Robert Pelligrini, Ph.D., once asked 720 young adults about separation, and two-thirds said that "absence makes the heart grow fonder" seemed more true than "out of sight, out of mind." A poll, however, doesn't tell us much about the truth of the matter. To settle things, we'll need an experiment. Hmmm. First we'll need 100 couples, whom we'll give various tests of "fondness." Then we'll assign, at random, half of the couples to a Control Group and half to an Absence Group. Next we'll separate the partners in each couple in our Absence Group by, say, 1,000 miles for six months—somehow providing jobs, housing, and social support for every person we relocate. Finally, we'll readminister our fondness tests

---

Rating the Proverbs

Here's a quick rundown on how well some other common proverbs measure up to research findings:

★★★★★	Looks good
★★★★	Some evidence supports it
★★★	Not clear
★★	Some evidence casts doubt
★	Scrap heap

"Once bitten, twice shy." Behind almost every dog or cat phobia, there's a bite or scratch. ★★★★★

"Practice makes perfect." Even the brain-injured can often learn new material with sufficient repetition. ★★★★

"Misery loves company." Depressed people often shun company, which unfortunately is part of the problem. ★★

"Two heads are better than one." Teams or groups typically produce better solutions than individuals do. ★★★★

"Cold hands, warm heart." Cold hands, poor circulation. See your physician. ★

"Every cloud has a silver lining." Not really, but therapy techniques like cognitive restructuring can get you to think so, and that can get you through the day. ★★★

"Old habits die hard." When we fail at a task, we tend to resort to old behavior patterns, even those from childhood. ★★★★

"You can't teach an old dog new tricks." You'll feel better, think more clearly, and may even live longer if you keep learning throughout life. ★★

"Familiarity breeds contempt." People tend to like what's familiar. ★

"Blood will tell." For better or worse, genes really do set limits on both physical characteristics and behavior. ★★★★

"A woman's place is in the home." Only when artificial barriers keep her there. ★

"When the cat's away, the mice will play." Kids and employees tend to slack off when their parents or supervisors are out of sight. ★★★★

"There's no accounting for tastes." Until you look at upbringing, biochemistry, evolutionary influences, and so on. ★★

to all 100 couples. If we find significantly greater levels of fondness in the separated couples than in the unseparated couples, we'll have strong support for the idea that absence makes the heart grow fonder.

Any volunteers? What? You would never subject yourself to such an absurd procedure? Well, fortunately, no one would ever conduct such research, either.

And that's the bottom line: the behavioral sciences can provide useful insights about how we should lead our lives, but there are limits to the kind of research that can be conducted with people. Folk wisdom may be flawed, but, in some instances, it's all we've got or will ever have. So don't put all you eggs in one basket.

CRITICAL THINKING QUESTIONS

1. A number of proverbs are rated in the box at the end of the article. Select one of the proverbs, and design a study that would test its validity.
2. Select one of the proverbs referred to in Question 1, and find a study that has been conducted on the topic. Summarize the results.
3. In addition to the folk wisdom mentioned in the article, what are other examples of common-sense ideas that contradict one another?
4. Many people rely on folk wisdom to guide their actions or explain certain situations. Is doing so ineffective or even dangerous? Or does folk wisdom (or common sense) still play a useful role in helping people manage their lives? Summarize the pros and cons of relying on folk wisdom as a guide to behavior.

ARTICLE 2 _____

Have you ever participated in a social psychology experiment? What were you thinking while you were participating? Were you accepting of the situation and the explanation you were given by the researcher, or were you trying to figure out the real purpose of the experiment? If you were doing the latter, you would be in good company, as many people have come to associate psychological research (and in particular, social psychology research) with the use of deception.

Deception has always been a staple in the research conducted in the field. But what exactly is *deception*? Is it simply another term for *lying*? In practice, deception in research can be located on a continuum from simply withholding from the subjects the true nature of the experiment to actively creating a cover story to try to keep the subjects from determining the actual purpose of the study. Deception is largely based on the assumption that if subjects knew the true nature of the experiment (the hypothesis being tested, that is), then they would not act naturally and hence contaminate the results.

This next classic article by Herbert C. Kelman explores the use of deception in social psychological experiments. After discussing some of the ethical issues involved in the use of deception, Kelman goes on to suggest how the use of deception should be handled, as well as alternatives to deception. In the years since the publication of this article in 1967, many changes in the ethical guidelines for the treatment of human subjects have been made. For example, it is now standard policy for institutions to have ethical review boards for the approval of any study involving human subjects. Nonetheless, deception in one form or another is still a common feature in social psychological research.

Human Use of Human Subjects
The Problem of Deception in Social Psychological Experiments[1]
■ Herbert C. Kelman

Though there is often good reason for deceiving Ss in social psychological experiments, widespread use of such procedures has serious (a) ethical implications (involving not only the possibility of harm to S, but also the quality of the E-S relationship), (b) methodological implications (relating to the decreasing naïveté of Ss), and (c) implications for the future of the discipline. To deal with these problems, it is necessary (a) to increase active awareness of the negative implications of deception and use it only when clearly justified, not as a matter of course; (b) to explore ways of counteracting and minimizing negative consequences of deception when it is used; and (c) to develop new experimental techniques that dispense with deception and rely on S's positive motivations.

In 1954, in the pages of the *American Psychologist*, Edgar Vinacke raised a series of questions about experiments—particularly in the area of small groups—in which "the psychologist conceals the true purpose and conditions of the experiment, or positively misinforms the subjects, or exposes them to painful, embarrassing, or worse, experiences, without the subjects' knowledge of what is going on [p. 155]." He summed up his con-

Reprinted from *Psychological Bulletin,* 1967, *67,* 1–11. Copyright © 1967 by the American Psychological Association. Reprinted with permission.

cerns by asking, "What . . . is the proper balance between the interests of science and the thoughtful treatment of the persons who, innocently, supply the data? [p. 155]." Little effort has been made in the intervening years to seek answers to the questions he raised. During these same years, however, the problem of deception in social psychological experiments has taken on increasingly serious proportions.[2]

The problem is actually broader, extending beyond the walls of the laboratory. It arises, for example, in various field studies in which investigators enroll as members of a group that has special interest for them so that they can observe its operations from the inside. The pervasiveness of the problem becomes even more apparent when we consider that deception is built into most of our measurement devices, since it is important to keep the respondent unaware of the personality or attitude dimension that we wish to explore. For the present purposes, however, primarily the problem of deception in the context of the social psychological experiment will be discussed.

The use of deception has become more and more extensive, and it is now a commonplace and almost standard feature of social psychological experiments. Deception has been turned into a game, often played with great skill and virtuosity. A considerable amount of the creativity and ingenuity of social psychologists is invested in the development of increasingly elaborate deception situations. Within a single experiment, deception may be built upon deception in a delicately complex structure. The literature now contains a fair number of studies in which second- or even third-order deception was employed.

One well-known experiment (Festinger & Carlsmith, 1959), for example, involved a whole progression of deceptions. After the subjects had gone through an experimental task, the investigator made it clear—through word and gesture—that the experiment was over and that he would now "like to explain what this has been all about so you'll have some idea of why you were doing this [p. 205]." This explanation was false, however, and was designed to serve as a basis for the true experimental manipulation. The manipulation itself involved asking subjects to serve as the experimenter's accomplices. The task of the "accomplice" was to tell the next "subject" that the experiment in which he had just participated (which

was in fact a rather boring experience) had been interesting and enjoyable. He was also asked to be on call for unspecified future occasions on which his services as accomplice might be needed because "the regular fellow couldn't make it, and we had a subject scheduled [p. 205]." These newly recruited "accomplices," of course, were the true subjects, while the "subjects" were the experimenter's true accomplices. For their presumed services as "accomplices," the true subjects were paid in advance—half of them receiving $1, and half $20. When they completed their service, however, the investigators added injury to insult by asking them to return their hard-earned cash. Thus, in this one study, in addition to receiving the usual misinformation about the purpose of the experiment, the subject was given feedback that was really an experimental manipulation, was asked to be an accomplice who was really a subject, and was given a $20 bill that was really a will-o'-the-wisp. One wonders how much further in this direction we can go. Where will it all end?

It is easy to view this problem with alarm, but it is much more difficult to formulate an unambiguous position on the problem. As a working experimental social psychologist, I cannot conceive the issue in absolutist terms. I am too well aware of the fact that there are good reasons for using deception in many experiments. There are many significant problems that probably cannot be investigated without the use of deception, at least not at the present level of development of our experimental methodology. Thus, we are always confronted with a conflict of values. If we regard the acquisition of scientific knowledge about human behavior as a positive value, and if an experiment using deception constitutes a significant contribution in such knowledge which could not very well be achieved by other means, then we cannot unequivocally rule out this experiment. The question for us is not simply whether it does or does not use deception, but whether the amount and type of deception are justified by the significance of the study and the unavailability of alternative (that is, deception-free) procedures.

I have expressed special concern about second-order deceptions, for example, the procedure of letting a person believe that he is acting as experimenter or as the experimenter's accomplice when he is in fact serving as the subject. Such a procedure undermines the relationship between experimenter and subject even further than simple misinformation about the purposes of the experiment; deception does not merely take place *within* the experiment, but encompasses the whole definition of the relationship between the parties involved. Deception that takes place while the person is within the role of subject for which he has contracted can, to some degree, be isolated, but deception about the very nature of the contract itself is more likely to suffuse the experimenter-subject relationship as a whole and to remove the possibility of mutual trust. Thus, I would be inclined to take a more absolutist stand with regard to such second-order deceptions—but even here the issue turns out to be more complicated. I am stopped short when I think, for example, of the ingenious studies on experimenter bias by Rosenthal and his associates (e.g., Rosenthal & Fode, 1963; Rosenthal, Persinger, Vikan-Kline, & Fode, 1963; Rosenthal, Persinger, Vikan-Kline, & Mulry, 1963). These experiments employed second-order deception in that subjects were led to believe that they were the experimenters. Since these were experiments about experiments, however, it is very hard to conceive of any alternative procedures that the investigators might have used. There is no question in my mind that these are significant studies; they provide fundamental inputs to present efforts at reexamining the social psychology of the experiment. These studies, then, help to underline even further the point that we are confronted with a conflict of values that cannot be resolved by fiat.

I hope it is clear from these remarks that my purpose in focusing on this problem is not to single out specific studies performed by some of my colleagues and to point a finger at them. Indeed, the finger points at me as well. I too have used deception, and have known the joys of applying my skills and ingenuity to the creation of elaborate experimental situations that the subjects would not be able to decode. I am now making active attempts to find alternatives to deception, but still I have not forsworn the use of deception under any and all circumstances. The questions I am raising, then, are addressed to myself as well as to my colleagues. They are questions with which all of us who are committed to social psychology must come to grips, lest we leave their resolution to others

who have no understanding of what we are trying to accomplish.

What concerns me most is not so much that deception is used, but precisely that it is used without question. It has now become standard operating procedure in the social psychologist's laboratory. I sometimes feel that we are training a generation of students who do not know that there is any other way of doing experiments in our field—who feel that deception is as much de rigueur as significance at the .05 level. Too often deception is used not as a last resort, but as a matter of course. Our attitude seems to be that if you can deceive, why tell the truth? It is this unquestioning acceptance, this routinization of deception, that really concerns me.

I would like to turn now to a review of the bases for my concern with the problem of deception, and then suggest some possible approaches for dealing with it.

IMPLICATIONS OF THE USE OF DECEPTION IN SOCIAL PSYCHOLOGICAL EXPERIMENTS

My concern about the use of deception is based on three considerations: the ethical implications of such procedures, their methodological implications, and their implications for the future of social psychology.

1. *Ethical implications.* Ethical problems of a rather obvious nature arise in the experiments in which deception has potentially harmful consequences for the subject. Take, for example, the brilliant experiment by Mulder and Stemerding (1963) on the effects of threat on attraction to the group and need for strong leadership. In this study—one of the very rare examples of an experiment conducted in a natural setting—independent food merchants in a number of Dutch towns were brought together for group meetings, in the course of which they were informed that a large organization was planning to open up a series of supermarkets in the Netherlands. In the High Threat condition, subjects were told that there was a high probability that their town would be selected as a site for such markets, and that the advent of these markets would cause a considerable drop in their business. On the advice of the executives of the shopkeepers' organizations, who had helped to

arrange the group meetings, the investigators did not reveal the experimental manipulations to their subjects. I have been worried about these Dutch merchants ever since I heard about this study for the first time. Did some of them go out of business in anticipation of the heavy competition? Do some of them have an anxiety reaction every time they see a bulldozer? Chances are that they soon forgot about this threat (unless, of course, supermarkets actually did move into town) and that it became just one of the many little moments of anxiety that must occur in every shopkeeper's life. Do we have a right, however, to add to life's little anxieties and to risk the possibility of more extensive anxiety purely for the purposes of our experiments, particularly since deception deprives the subject of the opportunity to choose whether or not he wishes to expose himself to the risks that might be entailed?

The studies by Bramel (1962, 1963) and Bergin (1962) provide examples of another type of potentially harmful effects arising from the use of deception. In the Bramel studies, male undergraduates were led to believe that they were homosexually aroused by photographs of men. In the Bergin study, subjects of both sexes were given discrepant information about their level of masculinity or femininity; in one experimental condition, this information was presumably based on an elaborate series of psychological tests in which the subjects had participated. In all of these studies, the deception was explained to the subject at the end of the experiment. One wonders, however, whether such explanation removes the possibility of harmful effects. For many persons in this age group, sexual identity is still a live and sensitive issue, and the self-doubts generated by the laboratory experience may take on a life of their own and linger on for some time to come.

Yet another illustration of potentially harmful effects of deception can be found in Milgram's (1963, 1965) studies of obedience. In these experiments, the subject was led to believe that he was participating in a learning study and was instructed to administer increasingly severe shocks to another person who after a while began to protest vehemently. In fact, of course, the victim was an accomplice of the experimenter and did not receive any shocks. Depending on the conditions, sizable proportions of the subjects obeyed the experimenter's instructions and continued to shock the other person up to the maximum level, which they believed to be extremely painful. Both obedient and defiant subjects exhibited a great deal of stress in this situation. The complexities of the issues surrounding the use of deception become quite apparent when one reads the exchange between Baumrind (1964) and Milgram (1964) about the ethical implications of the obedience research. There is clearly room for disagreement, among honorable people, about the evaluation of this research from an ethical point of view. Yet, there is good reason to believe that at least some of the obedient subjects came away from this experience with a lower self-esteem, having to live with the realization that they were willing to yield to destructive authority to the point of inflicting extreme pain on a fellow human being. The fact that this may have provided, in Milgram's (1964) words, "an opportunity to learn something of importance about themselves, and more generally, about the conditions of human action [p. 850]" is beside the point. If this were a lesson from life, it would indeed constitute an instructive confrontation and provide a valuable insight. But do we, for the purpose of experimentation, have the right to provide such potentially disturbing insights to subjects who do not know that this is what they are coming for? A similar question can be raised about the Asch (1951) experiments on group pressure, although the stressfulness of the situation and the implications for the person's self-concept were less intense in that context.

While the present paper is specifically focused on social psychological experiments, the problem of deception and its possibly harmful effects arises in other areas of psychological experimentation as well. Dramatic illustrations are provided by two studies in which subjects were exposed, for experimental purposes, to extremely stressful conditions. In an experiment designed to study the establishment of a conditioned response in a situation that is traumatic but not painful, Campbell, Sanderson, and Laverty (1964) induced—through the use of a drug—a temporary interruption of respiration in their subjects. "This has no permanently harmful physical consequences but is nonetheless a severe stress which is not in itself painful . . . [p. 628]." The subjects' reports confirmed that this was a "horrific" experience for them. "All the subjects in the standard series said that they thought they were dying [p. 631]." Of course the subjects, "male alcoholic patients who volunteered for the experiment when they were told that it was connected with a possible therapy for alcoholism [p. 629]," were not warned in advance about the effect of the drug, since this information would have reduced the traumatic impact of the experience.[3] In a series of studies on the effects of psychological stress, Berkun, Bialek, Kern, and Yagi (1962) devised a number of ingenious experimental situations designed to convince the subject that his life was actually in danger. In one situation, the subjects, a group of Army recruits, were actually "passengers aboard an apparently stricken plane which was being forced to 'ditch' or crash-land [p. 4]." In another experiment, an isolated subject in a desolate area learned that a sudden emergency had arisen (accidental nuclear radiation in the area, or a sudden forest fire, or misdirected artillery shells—depending on the experimental condition) and that he could be rescued only if he reported his position over his radio transmitter, "which has quite suddenly failed [p. 7]." In yet another situation, the subject was led to believe that he was responsible for an explosion that seriously injured another soldier. As the authors pointed out, reactions in these situations are more likely to approximate reactions to combat experiences or to naturally occurring disasters than are reactions to various laboratory stresses, but is the experimenter justified in exposing his subjects to such extreme threats?

So far, I have been speaking of experiments in which deception has potentially harmful consequences. I am equally concerned, however, about the less obvious cases, in which there is little danger of harmful effects, at least in the conventional sense of the term. Serious ethical issues are raised by deception per se and the kind of use of human beings that it implies. In our other interhuman relationships, most of us would never think of doing the kinds of things that we do to our subjects—exposing others to lies and tricks, deliberately misleading them about the purposes of the interaction or withholding pertinent information, making promises or giving assurances that we intend to disregard. We would view such behavior as a violation of the respect to which all fellow humans are entitled and of the whole basis of our

relationship with them. Yet we seem to forget that the experimenter-subject relationship—whatever else it is—is a *real* interhuman relationship, in which we have responsibility toward the subject as another human being whose dignity we must preserve. The discontinuity between the experimenter's behavior in everyday life and his behavior in the laboratory is so marked that one wonders why there has been so little concern with this problem, and what mechanisms have allowed us to ignore it to such an extent. I am reminded, in this connection, of the intriguing phenomenon of the "holiness of sin," which characterizes certain messianic movements as well as other movements of the true-believer variety. Behavior that would normally be unacceptable actually takes on an aura of virtue in such movements through a redefinition of the situation in which the behavior takes place and thus of the context for evaluating it. A similar mechanism seems to be involved in our attitude toward the psychological experiment. We tend to regard it as a situation that is not quite real, that can be isolated from the rest of life like a play performed on stage, and to which, therefore, the usual criteria for ethical interpersonal conduct become irrelevant. Behavior is judged entirely in the context of the experiment's scientific contribution and, in this context, deception—which is normally unacceptable—can indeed be seen as a positive good.

The broader ethical problem brought into play by the very use of deception becomes even more important when we view it in the light of present historical forces. We are living in an age of mass societies in which the transformation of man into an object to be manipulated at will occurs "on a mass scale, in a systematic way, and under the aegis of specialized institutions deliberately assigned to this task [Kelman, 1965]." In institutionalizing the use of deception in psychological experiments, we are, then, contributing to a historical trend that threatens values most of us cherish.

2. *Methodological implications.* A second source of my concern about the use of deception is my increasing doubt about its adequacy as a methodology for social psychology.

A basic assumption in the use of deception is that a subject's awareness of the conditions that we are trying to create and of the phenomena that we wish to study would affect his behavior in such a way that we could not draw valid conclusions from it. For example, if we are interested in studying the effects of failure on conformity, we must create a situation in which the subjects actually feel that they have failed, and in which they can be kept unaware of our interest in observing conformity. In short, it is important to keep our subjects naïve about the purposes of the experiment so that they can respond to the experimental inductions spontaneously.

How long, however, will it be possible for us to find naïve subjects? Among college students, it is already very difficult. They may not know the exact purpose of the particular experiment in which they are participating, but at least they know, typically, that it is *not* what the experimenter says it is. Orne (1962) pointed out that the use of deception "on the part of psychologists is so widely known in the college population that even if a psychologist is honest with the subject, more often than not he will be distrusted." As one subject pithily put it, "'Psychologists always lie!'" Orne added that "This bit of paranoia has some support in reality [pp. 778–779]." There are, of course, other sources of human subjects that have not been tapped, and we could turn to them in our quest for naïveté. But even there it is only a matter of time. As word about psychological experiments gets around in whatever network we happen to be using, sophistication is bound to increase. I wonder, therefore, whether there is any future in the use of deception.

If the subject in a deception experiment knows what the experimenter is trying to conceal from him and what he is really after in the study, the value of the deception is obviously nullified. Generally, however, even the relatively sophisticated subject does not know the exact purpose of the experiment; he only has suspicions, which may approximate the true purpose of the experiment to a greater or lesser degree. Whether or not he knows the *true* purpose of the experiment, he is likely to make an effort to figure out its purpose, since he does not believe what the experimenter tells him, and therefore he is likely to operate in the situation in terms of his own hypothesis of what is involved. This may, in line with Orne's (1962) analysis, lead him to do what he thinks the experimenter wants him to do. Conversely, if he resents the experimenter's attempt to deceive him, he may try to throw a monkey wrench into the works; I would not be surprised if this kind of Schweikian game among subjects became a fairly well-established part of the culture of sophisticated campuses. Whichever course the subject uses, however, he is operating in terms of his own conception of the nature of the situation, rather than in terms of the conception that the experimenter is trying to induce. In short, the experimenter can no longer assume that the conditions that he is trying to create are the ones that actually define the situation for the subject. Thus, the use of deception, while it is designed to give the experimenter control over the subject's perceptions and motivations, may actually produce an unspecifiable mixture of intended and unintended stimuli that make it difficult to know just what the subject is responding to.

The tendency for subjects to react to unintended cues—to features of the situation that are not part of the experimenter's design—is by no means restricted to experiments that involve deception. This problem has concerned students of the interview situation for some time, and more recently it has been analyzed in detail in the writings and research of Riecken, Rosenthal, Orne, and Mills. Subjects enter the experiment with their own aims, including attainment of certain rewards, divination of the experimenter's true purposes, and favorable self-presentation (Riecken, 1962). They are therefore responsive to demand characteristics of the situation (Orne, 1962), to unintended communications of the experimenter's expectations (Rosenthal, 1963), and to the role of the experimenter within the social system that experimenter and subject jointly constitute (Mills, 1962). In any experiment, then, the subject goes beyond the description of the situation and the experimental manipulation introduced by the investigator, makes his own interpretation of the situation, and acts accordingly.

For several reasons, however, the use of deception especially encourages the subject to dismiss the stated purposes of the experiment and to search for alternative interpretations of his own. First, the continued use of deception establishes the reputation of psychologists as people who cannot be believed. Thus, the desire "to penetrate the experimenter's inscrutability and discover the rationale of the experiment [Riecken, 1962, p. 34]" becomes especially strong. Generally, these efforts are motivated by the subject's desire to meet the expectations of the experimenter and of the situation. They may also be motivated, however, as I have already mentioned, by a desire to outwit the experimenter and to beat him at his own game, in a spirit of genuine hostility or playful one-upmanship. Second, a situation involving the use of deception is inevitably highly ambiguous since a great deal of information relevant to understanding the structure of the situation must be withheld from the subject. Thus, the subject is especially motivated to try to figure things out and likely to develop idiosyncratic interpretations. Third, the use of deception, by its very nature, causes the experimenter to transmit contradictory messages to the subject. In his verbal instructions and explanations he says one thing about the purposes of the experiment; but in the experimental situation that he has created, in the manipulations that he has introduced, and probably in covert cues that he emits, he says another thing. This again makes it imperative for the subject to seek his own interpretation of the situation.

I would argue, then, that deception increases the subject's tendency to operate in terms of his private definition of the situation, differing (in random or systematic fashion) from the definition that the experimenter is trying to impose; moreover, it makes it more difficult to evaluate or minimize the effects of this tendency. Whether or not I am right in this judgment, it can, at the very least, be said that the use of deception does not resolve or reduce the unintended effects of the experiment as a social situation in which the subject pursues his private aims. Since the assumptions that the subject is naïve and that he sees the situation as the experimenter wishes him to see it are unwarranted, the use of deception no longer has any special obvious advantages over other experimental approaches. I am not suggesting that there may not be occasions when deception may still be the most effective procedure to use from a methodological point of view. But since it raises at least as many methodological problems as any other type of procedure does, we have every reason to explore alternative approaches and to extend our methodological inquiries to the question of the effects of using deception.

3. *Implications for the future of social psychology.* My third concern about the use of deception is based on its long-run implications for our discipline and combines both the ethical and methodological considerations that I have already raised. There is something disturbing about the idea of relying on massive deception as the basis for developing a field of inquiry. Can

one really build a discipline on a foundation of such research?

From a long-range point of view, there is obviously something self-defeating about the use of deception. As we continue to carry out research of this kind, our potential subjects become more and more sophisticated, and we become less and less able to meet the conditions that our experimental procedures require. Moreover, as we continue to carry out research of this kind, our potential subjects become increasingly distrustful of us, and our future relations with them are likely to be undermined. Thus, we are confronted with the anomalous circumstance that the more research we do, the more difficult and questionable it becomes.

The use of deception also involves a contradiction between our experimental procedures and our long-range aims as scientists and teachers. In order to be able to carry out our experiments, we are concerned with maintaining the naïveté of the population from which we hope to draw our subjects. We are all familiar with the experimenter's anxious concern that the introductory course might cover the autokinetic phenomenon, need achievement, or the Asch situation before he has had a chance to complete his experimental runs. This perfectly understandable desire to keep procedures secret goes counter to the traditional desire of the scientist and teacher to inform and enlighten the public. To be sure, experimenters are interested only in temporary secrecy, but it is not inconceivable that at some time in the future they might be using certain procedures on a regular basis with large segments of the population and thus prefer to keep the public permanently naïve. It is perhaps not too fanciful to imagine, for the long run, the possible emergence of a special class, in possession of secret knowledge—a possibility that is clearly antagonistic to the principle of open communication to which we, as scientists and intellectuals, are so fervently committed.

DEALING WITH THE PROBLEM OF DECEPTION IN SOCIAL PSYCHOLOGICAL EXPERIMENTS

If my concerns about the use of deception are justified, what are some of the ways in which we, as experimental social psychologists, can deal with them? I would like to suggest three steps that we can take:

increase our active awareness of the problem, explore ways of counteracting and minimizing the negative effects of deception, and give careful attention to the development of new experimental techniques that dispense with the use of deception.

1. *Active awareness of the problem.* I have already stressed that I would not propose the complete elimination of deception under all circumstances, in view of the genuine conflict of values with which the experimenter is confronted. What is crucial, however, is that we always ask ourselves the question whether deception, in the given case, is necessary and justified. How we answer the question is less important than the fact that we ask it. What we must be wary of is the tendency to dismiss the question as irrelevant and to accept deception as a matter of course. Active awareness of the problem is thus in itself part of the solution for it makes the use of deception a matter for discussion, deliberation, investigation, and choice. Active awareness means that, in any given case, we will try to balance the value of an experiment that uses deception against its questionable or potentially harmful effects. If we engage in this process honestly, we are likely to find that there are many occasions when we or our students can forego the use of deception—either because deception is not necessary (that is, alternative procedures that are equally good or better are available), because the importance of the study does not warrant the use of an ethically questionable procedure, or because the type of deception involved is too extreme (in terms of the possibility of harmful effects or of seriously undermining the experimenter-subject relationship).

2. *Counteracting and minimizing the negative effects of deception.* If we do use deception, it is essential that we find ways of counteracting and minimizing its negative effects. Sensitizing the apprentice researcher to this necessity is at least as fundamental as any other part of research training.

In those experiments in which deception carries the potential of harmful effects (in the more usual sense of the term), there is an obvious requirement to build protections into every phase of the process. Subjects must be selected in a way that will exclude individuals who are especially vulnerable; the potentially harmful manipulation (such as the induction of stress) must be kept at a moderate level of intensity; the experimenter must be sensitive to danger signals in the reactions of his subjects and be prepared to deal with crises when they arise; and, at the conclusion of the session, the experimenter must take time not only to reassure the subject, but also to help him work through his feelings about the experience to whatever degree may be required. In general, the principle that a subject ought not to leave the laboratory with greater anxiety or lower self-esteem than he came with is a good one to follow. I would go beyond it to argue that the subject should in some positive way be enriched by the experience, that is, he should come away from it with the feeling that he has learned something, understood something, or grown in some way. This, of course, adds special importance to the kind of feedback that is given to the subject at the end of the experimental session.

Postexperimental feedback is, of course, the primary way of counteracting negative effects in those experiments in which the issue is deception as such, rather than possible threats to the subject's well-being. If we do deceive the subject, then it is our obligation to give him a full and detailed explanation of what we have done and of our reasons for using this type of procedure. I do not want to be absolutist about this, but I would suggest it as a good rule of thumb to follow: Think very carefully before undertaking an experiment whose purposes you feel unable to reveal to the subjects even after they have completed the experimental session. It is, of course not enough to give the subject a perfunctory feedback, just to do one's duty. Postexperimental explanations should be worked out with as much detail as other aspects of the procedure and, in general, some thought ought to be given to ways of making them meaningful and instructive for the subject and helpful for rebuilding his relationship with the experimenter. I feel very strongly that to accomplish these purposes, we must keep the feedback itself inviolate and under no circumstance give the subject false feedback or pretend to be giving him feedback while we are in fact introducing another experimental manipulation. If we hope to maintain any kind of trust in our relationship with potential subjects, there must be no ambiguity that the statement "The experiment is over and I shall explain to you what it was all about" means precisely that and nothing else. If subjects have reason to suspect even that statement, then we have lost the whole basis for a decent human relationship with our subjects and all hope for future cooperation from them.

3. *Development of new experimental techniques.* My third and final suggestion is that we invest some of the creativity and ingenuity, now devoted to the construction of elaborate deceptions, in the search for alternative experimental techniques that do not rely on the use of deception. The kind of techniques that I have in mind would be based on the principle of eliciting the subject's positive motivations to contribute to the experimental enterprise. They would draw on the subject's active participation and involvement in the proceedings and encourage him to cooperate in making the experiment a success—not by giving the results he thinks the experimenter wants, but by conscientiously taking the roles and carrying out the tasks that the experimenter assigns to him. In short, the kind of techniques I have in mind would be designed to involve the subject as an active participant in a joint effort with the experimenter.

Perhaps the most promising source of alternative experimental approaches are procedures using some sort of role playing. I have been impressed, for example, with the role playing that I have observed in the context of the Inter-Nation Simulation (Guetzkow, Alger, Brody, Noel, & Snyder, 1963), a laboratory procedure involving a simulated world in which the subjects take the roles of decision-makers of various nations. This situation seems to create a high level of emotional involvement and to elicit motivations that have a real-life quality to them. Moreover, within this situation—which is highly complex and generally permits only gross experimental manipulations—it is possible to test specific theoretical hypotheses by using data based on repeated measurements as interaction between the simulated nations develops. Thus, a study carried out at the Western Behavioral Sciences Institute provided, as an extra, some interesting opportunities for testing hypotheses derived from balance theory, by the use of mutual ratings made by decision-makers of Nations A, B, and C, before and after A shifted from an alliance with B to an alliance with C.

A completely different type of role playing was used effectively by Rosenberg and Abelson (1960) in their studies of cognitive dilemmas. In my own research program, we have been exploring different kinds of role-playing procedures with varying degrees of success. In one study, the major manipulation consisted in informing subjects that the experiment to which they had just committed themselves would require them (depending on the condition) either to receive shocks from a fellow subject, or to administer shocks to a fellow subject. We used a regular deception procedure, but with a difference: We told the subjects before the session started that what was to follow was make-believe, but that we wanted them to react as if they really found themselves in this situation. I might mention that some subjects, not surprisingly, did not accept as true the information that this was all make-believe and wanted to know when they should show up for the shock experiment to which they had committed themselves. I have some questions about the effectiveness of this particular procedure. It did not do enough to create a high level of involvement, and it turned out to be very complex since it asked subjects to role-play subjects, not people. In this sense, it might have given us the worst of both worlds, but I still think it is worth some further exploration. In another experiment, we were interested in creating differently structured attitudes about an organization by feeding different kinds of information to two groups of subjects. These groups were then asked to take specific actions in support of the organization, and we measured attitude changes resulting from these actions. In the first part of the experiment, the subjects were clearly informed that the organization and the information that we were feeding to them were fictitious, and that we were simply trying to simulate the conditions under which attitudes about new organizations are typically formed. In the second part of the experiment, the subjects were told that we were interested in studying the effects of action in support of an organization on attitudes toward it, and they were asked (in groups of five) to role-play a strategy meeting of leaders of the fictitious organization. The results of this study were very encouraging. While there is obviously a great deal that we need to know about the meaning of this situation to the subjects, they did react differentially to the experimental manipulations and these reactions followed an orderly pattern, despite the fact that they knew it was all make-believe.

There are other types of procedures, in addition to role playing, that are worth exploring. For example, one might design field experiments in which, with the full cooperation of the subjects, specific experimental variations are introduced. The advantages of dealing with motivations at a real-life level of intensity might well outweigh the disadvantages of subjects' knowing the general purpose of the experiment. At the other extreme of ambitiousness, one might explore the effects of modifying standard experimental procedures slightly by informing the subject at the beginning of the experiment that he will not be receiving full information about what is going on, but asking him to suspend judgment until the experiment is over.

Whatever alternative approach we try, there is no doubt that it will have its own problems and complexities. Procedures effective for some purposes may be quite ineffective for others, and it may well turn out that for certain kinds of problems there is no adequate substitute for the use of deception. But there *are* alternative procedures that, for many purposes, may be as effective or even more effective than procedures built on deception. These approaches often involve a radically different set of assumptions about the role of the subject in the experiment: They require us to *use* the subject's motivation to cooperate rather than to bypass it; they may even call for increasing the sophistication of potential subjects, rather than maintaining their naïveté. My only plea is that we devote some of our energies to active exploration of these alternative approaches.

REFERENCES

Asch, S. E. Effects of group pressure upon the modification and distortion of judgments. In H. Guetzkow (Ed.), *Groups, leadership, and men.* Pittsburgh: Carnegie Press, 1951. Pp. 117–190.

Baumrind, D. Some thoughts on ethics of research: After reading Milgram's "Behavioral Study of Obedience." *American Psychologist,* 1964, **19**, 421–423.

Bergin, A. E. The effect of dissonant persuasive communications upon changes in a self-referring attitude. *Journal of Personality,* 1962, **30**, 423–438.

Berkun, M. M., Bialek, H. M., Kern, R. P., & Yagi, K. Experimental studies of psychological stress in man. *Psychological Monographs,* 1962, **76**(15, Whole No. 534).

Bramel, D. A dissonance theory approach to defensive projection. *Journal of Abnormal and Social Psychology,* 1962, **64**, 121–129.

Bramel, D. Selection of a target for defensive projection. *Journal of Abnormal and Social Psychology,* 1963, **66**, 318–324.

Campbell, D., Sanderson, R. E., & Laverty, S. G. Characteristics of a conditioned response in human subjects during extinction trials following a single traumatic conditioning trial. *Journal of Abnormal and Social Psychology,* 1964, **68**, 627–639.

Festinger, L., & Carlsmith, J. M. Cognitive consequences of forced compliance. *Journal of Abnormal and Social Psychology,* 1959, **58**, 203–210.

Guetzkow, H., Alger, C. F., Brody, R. A., Noel, R. C., & Snyder, R. C. *Simulation in international relations.* Englewood Cliffs, N.J.: Prentice-Hall, 1963.

Kelman, H. C. Manipulation of human behavior: An ethical dilemma for the social scientist. *Journal of Social Issues,* 1965, **21**(2), 31–46.

Milgram, S. Behavioral study of obedience. *Journal of Abnormal and Social Psychology,* 1963, **67**, 371–378.

Milgram, S. Issues in the study of obedience: A reply to Baumrind. *American Psychologist,* 1964, **19**, 848–852.

Milgram, S. Some conditions of obedience and disobedience to authority. *Human Relations,* 1965, **18**, 57–76.

Mills, T. M. A sleeper variable in small groups research: The experimenter. *Pacific Sociological Review,* 1962, **5**, 21–28.

Mulder, M., & Stemerding, A. Threat, attraction to group, and need for strong leadership. *Human Relations,* 1963, **16**, 317–334.

Orne, M. T. On the social psychology of the psychological experiment: With particular reference to demand characteristics and their implications. *American Psychologist,* 1962, **17**, 776–783.

Riecken, H. W. A program for research on experiments in social psychology. In N. F. Washburne (Ed.), *Decisions, values and groups.* Vol. 2. New York: Pergamon Press, 1962. Pp. 25–41.

Rosenberg, M. J., & Abelson, R. P. An analysis of cognitive balancing. In M. J. Rosenberg et al., *Attitude organization and change.* New Haven: Yale University Press, 1960. Pp. 112–163.

Rosenthal, R. On the social psychology of the psychological experiment: The experimenter's hypothesis as unintended determinant of experimental results. *American Scientist,* 1963, **51**, 268–283.

Rosenthal, R., & Fode, K. L. Psychology of the scientist: V. Three experiments in experimenter bias. *Psychological Reports,* 1963, **12**, 491–511. (Monogr. Suppl. 3-V12)

Rosenthal, R., Persinger, G. W., Vikan-Kline, L., & Fode, K. L. The effect of early data returns on data subsequently obtained by outcome-biased experimenters. *Sociometry,* 1963, **26**, 487–498.

Rosenthal, R., Persinger, G. W., Vikan-Kline, L., & Mulry, R. C. The role of the research assistant in the mediation of experimenter bias. *Journal of Personality,* 1963, **31**, 313–335.

Vinacke, W. E. Deceiving experimental subjects. *American Psychologist,* 1954, **9**, 155.

ENDNOTES

1. Paper read at the symposium on "Ethical and Methodological Problems in Social Psychological Experiments," held at the meetings of the American Psychological Association in Chicago, September 3, 1965. This paper is a product of a research program on social influence and behavior change supported by United States Public Health Service Research Grant MH-07280 from the National Institute of Mental Health.

2. In focusing on deception in *social* psychological experiments, I do not wish to give the impression that there is no serious problem elsewhere. Deception is widely used in most studies involving human subjects and gives rise to issues similar to those discussed in this paper. Some examples of the use of deception in other areas of psychological experimentation will be presented later in this paper.

3. The authors reported, however, that some of their other subjects were physicians familiar with the drug; "they did not suppose they were dying but, even though they knew in a general way what to expect, they too said that the experience was extremely harrowing [p. 632]." Thus, conceivably, the purposes of the experiment might have been achieved even if the subjects had been told to expect the temporary interruption of breathing.

CRITICAL THINKING QUESTIONS

1. Which of the studies mentioned in the article involves the greatest ethical issues? Why? Select one of the studies cited in this article, and suggest an alternative to the type of deception that was employed.

2. Should the use of deception be banned? Why or why not? If not, under what conditions should it be allowed? What impact would such a limitation have on social psychological research? Defend your position.

3. Who should determine what constitutes an ethically appropriate experiment? Professors? Students? Outside laypeople? Explain your answer. What would be the ideal composition of a board charged with reviewing research proposals? Why?

4. Obtain a copy of the current "American Psychological Association Guide for the Ethical Treatment of Human Subjects." Review these guidelines, considering how comprehensive they are. What criteria should be used in determining what is in the best interests of the subjects of an experiment?

5. What do you think of Kelman's position on "second-order" deception? Do you agree that it is of even greater concern than standard ("first-order") deception practices? Why or why not?

6. What do you think of Kelman's suggestions for the development of new experimental techniques as an alternative to deception? Find a research study that tried such a technique in lieu of deception. Alternatively, find a research study reported in this book of readings and suggest an alternative to the deception that was used. In either case, what might be lost and what might be gained by not deceiving subjects? Explain your answer.

ADDITIONAL RELATED READINGS

Kimmel, A. J. (2001). Ethical trends in marketing and psychological research. *Ethics and Behavior, 11*(2), 131–149.

Nosek, B. A., Banaji, R., & Greenwald, A. G. (2002). E-Research: Ethics, security, design, and control in psychological research on the Internet. *Journal of Social Issues, 58*(1), 161–176.

ARTICLE 3 _____

Social psychology can be defined as the "scientific field of study that investigates how people's feelings, thoughts, and behaviors are influenced by other people." Given this rather broad definition, the scope of what comes under the heading of social psychology is large, indeed. Think, for a second, about your own life. What aspects of your life are truly independent of social influences? Obviously, when you are with other people, social factors are likely operating. But what about when you are alone?

To take an extreme example, suppose you were stranded on a deserted island. Would your behavior still be influenced by social factors? The answer is yes and no: No, because no one would be around to have an immediate impact on your behaviors, thoughts, and feelings. But yes, because you already would have acquired your beliefs, your emotional responses to the world, and your tendency to act in certain ways. The fact is, we are social creatures, and what we are now is the product of all the social encounters that we have experienced in the past.

Given that the domain of social psychology is the whole realm of human social interaction, what questions should the discipline address? For example, social psychology could investigate obvious social phenomena, such as the tendency for people to be more attracted to physically appealing individuals. Or at the other extreme, social psychology could investigate aspects of social phenomena that are obscure and even superfluous, such as why people tend to be more willing to believe their own lies if someone gives them $1 for telling the lie than if they are given $20 for telling the same lie. Thus, social psychology can address questions that range from the trivial to the critically important.

A basic distinction that can be made about research methods is between *basic* (or *pure*) research and *applied* research. While the two general approaches are not necessarily incompatible, basic research generally tends to examine variables and possibly uncover cause-and-effect relationships without necessarily trying to address a real-world problem. For example, studying why people help in certain circumstances but not in others or what factors may be involved in our initial attraction to other people may provide important insights into the what and why of human behavior, enlightening us as to the reasons we act the way that we do. However, such studies may or may not have relevance to real-world problems. The majority of studies in social psychology tend to fall into this basic or pure research category.

However, social psychology often is called on to answer questions about real-world problems. This applied research often has as its goal the answering of questions with direct implications for the behaviors and/or policies of people. While basic and applied research share similar methodologies, the latter often is conducted with more limitations due to the constraints of working in the real world. As such, choosing a methodology and drawing conclusions from the data are both many times more difficult in applied settings.

The following article by Abraham S. Ross presents an interesting perspective on the challenges and issues facing researchers in applied settings. When reading research articles (such as the ones in this book of readings), we often only see the finished product. What we don't necessarily see are the dead ends, the trial and error, and the other issues that came up before execution of the final study. This article provides insights into the kinds of learning that occur in the process of applied research and how such learning, in turn, helps to shape future research.

Lessons Learned from a Lifetime of Applied Social Psychology Research

■ Abraham S. Ross

ABSTRACT

I started life as an experimental social psychologist but migrated to applied social psychology research. Each time I have been involved in a major applied project I have learned things that have helped in subsequent projects. Most of the time the lesson has been about research design (e.g., you must know how the study should be done before you deal with the reality of how it has to be done). Examples of other lessons include using appropriate research technology, and the importance of program planner awareness of psychological research. In this paper I describe some of the major studies in which I was the investigator and the lesson(s) I learned from each. I also touch on the relevance of the scientist/practitioner model for the applied researcher.

Phil Zimbardo, in his introduction to Plous (1993) wrote:

> In recent years, the field of social psychology has emerged as central in psychology's quest to understand human thought, feeling, and behavior. Thus, we see the inclusion-by-hyphenation of social psychology across diverse fields of psychology, such as social-cognitive, social-developmental, social-learning, and social-personality, to name but a few recent amalgamations.
>
> In their role as the last generalists in psychology, nothing of individual and societal concern is alien to social psychological investigation—from psychophysiology to peace psychology, from students' attributions for failure to preventive education for AIDS. . . . Indeed since the days when George Miller, former president of the APA called upon psychologists to "give psychology back to the people," social psychologist have been at the forefront. (p. xi)

I would add to Phil's comments that social psychologists are also the best general methodologists in psychology. One of the things we have to "give back to

the people" is a method of learning about the world, studying problems, and suggesting solutions. The core of what we do is to try to ascertain causal relationships beyond the attributions made as part of the normal human attribution process.

Arla Day (2003), in her column in *The Canadian Industrial and Organizational Psychologist,* wrote about the scientist/practitioner model in I/O. Until I had read her column I had thought that the s/p model was relevant to clinical practitioners, not to social psychologists. After reading Arla's column, I realized that the model was relevant and that I am a s/p. The difference between my work and that of a clinical practitioner is that in the work I do there is usually a "proper" or ideal way to conduct the studies, whereas in clinical work there is not always a "proper" treatment. However, in applied social research the ideal study is not often possible so we must work as best we can and be aware of the threats to our conclusions.

I am not an artist but I have always understood that in order to be able to draw like Picasso, you first have to know the ways to accurately represent the physical world in your pictures. Only then can you deviate to indicate the way the world "really looks" to you.

Research methods are like art in that you have to know how it should be done to determine causality before you can deviate from the straight and narrow. For instance, you must know what threats you are introducing to your ability to ascertain causality (in other words, the validity of your results and conclusions) when you do not randomly assign people to experimental conditions.

Luckily for me, I started as an experimental social psychologist, working with Judson Mills and Elliot Aronson, both of whom trained me to do proper experimental research. I do not remember when I first

Reprinted from *Canadian Psychology,* 2004, *45*(1), 1–8. Copyright 2004, Canadian Psychological Association. Reprinted with permission.

came across Campbell and Stanley's little book, *Experimental and Quasi-experimental Designs for Research* (1963), but it was truly enlightening. It lists all of the threats to internal and external validity—and theirs was probably the first (and only) explanation of "regression toward the mean" that I have ever understood. For me the enlightening aspect of Campbell and Stanley was their section on quasi-experimental designs. They drew attention to the problems of deviating from the straight and narrow.

Indeed, I was so indoctrinated into the experimental framework that when I was first approached to do some applied research, while still in Toronto, I turned it down. Gilovich and Medvac (1995) found that in the short run, people regret acts of commission (things they did that they wish they had not) more than acts of omission (things they did not do that they wish they had). In the long run, however, people come to regret acts of omission more than acts of commission. This was true in my case—as time passed, I regretted having turned down the request to do applied research. A few years later, after I moved to Memorial, I was in my office one day when someone from the provincial government came looking for a person to assess the impact of a proposed government project. This was the opportunity for me to overcome my regret.

JOHN HOWARD SOCIETY

Soon after I got to St. John's, in the mid-seventies, we learned that the John Howard Society was seeking city council approval for a half-way house for ex-offenders. The formal name, by the way, is Community Residential Centre (CRC). Ted Hannah had a contract with the Solicitor General (Canada) to look at the impact of a CRC on a neighbourhood. At that time, and continuing today, people were not and are not keen on having a CRC in their neighbourhood. Today we even have an acronym for it, "NIMBY" (Not in my backyard). Amongst other claims were the ones that property values would go down and crime would go up. Solicitor General Canada asked Ted Hannah, Malcolm Grant, and me to find out what really happens.

At the time we first became involved, the news that a CRC was proposed in a local neighbourhood had already reached the media and the furor had started. We knew that we needed some kind of baseline to assess any changes in attitudes we discovered but clearly it was too late to get any "premeasures."

We decided to use successive random samples of the neighbourhood (Experimental condition) and the city at large (Control condition). The sampling followed what Campbell and Stanley (1963) refer to as "The separate-sample pretest-posttest control group design."

Quantitative Results

The only result that was significant (and it was marginal) was a three-way interaction on one of the factors on one of our three measures. In the first draft of the report we simply presented these results and in the discussion section related them to the theories. By the way, I should mention that for me this was a transitional study—in the Introduction we presented relevant theories and then related the results to these theories in the discussion section. (I have subsequently discovered that in most cases people who need research done are not usually interested in theory.)

At any rate, simply presenting the results and relating them to the theories did not go over very well with our contact at Solicitor General. The department's position was that we had been working on this project for three years and they asked, "Was this all we could tell them?" They asked us what we "thought" about what was going on. We were pushed to speculate beyond the .05 level—which we did and with which they were satisfied. However, we felt uncomfortable relying on our experience rather than the data.

Lesson: When you do applied research for an organization that has to make decisions and take actions, they want recommendations. Simply reporting p levels is not enough.

I also learned some incidental lessons. I attended several of the meetings conducted by the St. John's city council when the CRC proposal was presented. Residents voiced their concerns and the John Howard Society responded. I heard residents expressing affective concerns. For instance, "'They will rape my daughter." On the other hand, I heard cognitive responses being made. For instance, "The statistics are that rate of crimes . . ." I realized that at that time

95% of social psychology was cognitive. The Zajonc/Lazarus argument about emotion versus cognition was just beginning.

Lesson: I also learned to listen to people and to hear what they were saying.

Listening led me to the hypothesis that you may have to respond to affective arguments with affective data. Unfortunately, I never had time to follow this up in the lab.

At one session, the John Howard Society presented data from our random sample of the neighbourhood showing that most people were either in favour or had no objection to the CRC. However, one resident presented a petition against the CRC with the affective argument, "They have the numbers but we have the names." We suggested to the JHS that they circulate their own petition getting signatures of people who supported the CRC in their neighbourhood. Based on our random sample survey responses, they would get many more signatures than the other petition. We were right and the JHS petition was presented to the city council. We were a bit nervous about suggesting the petition because it could have backfired. We were forced to put our reputation where our mouth was and learned to trust a good random sample.

A final confession about this study. It was early computer days and it was the first report we had ever done on a computer. It turned out that this was a big advantage because when we neared the final version, the government complained that the report was too long (I have got that complaint often since then). We dealt with that complaint by changing the page margins to get the total length down to where they wanted it without removing any text. This would not have been possible before word processing.

Incidentally, we never did find an answer to the question that started it all, whether or not property values went down in the neighbourhood. Anecdotally, we heard that crime actually goes down in the neighbourhood because people do not want to muddy their own stream bed.

UNIFIED FAMILY COURT

The concept of a Unified Family Court (UFC; 1974) was developed by the Law Reform Commission in response to problems experienced by the public and by professionals in dealing with the conventional court system in the area of family law. The UFC brought together family matters that would previously have been dealt with in two or three other courts. For instance, before the UFC, two people who were getting divorced might have to go to the provincial court, to the Supreme Court, and to the old Family Court. They would have to repeat the same information each time and pay a lawyer for his or her time. The other major innovation was that the UFC had a social arm that provided services in the areas of intake, counselling, conciliation, and investigation. The St. John's UFC started operation in 1979.

As in much of the applied work I have done, the problem we faced here was a suitable comparison group. We were asked to do an evaluation once the planning was well underway. We did not have much information about the final form the court would take nor their objectives to devise a suitable outcome measure. So, we could not collect premeasures. When we looked for other cities to use as a baseline, it was clear that any city we chose would differ in important ways and would add considerably to the cost of the study.

So, we ended up doing a case study in which we interviewed people who had been through the court after the UFC started. We also had questions for people who used the UFC and who had also been through the old court system. What conclusions could we draw under these circumstances? Fortunately for us, St. John's was one of four UFC pilot projects. There were three similar but somewhat different pilot projects taking place at the same time: Saint John, NB, Saskatoon, SK, and London, ON all had UFC pilot projects. Each UFC pilot project had an evaluator with a different background. In Saint John, the evaluator was a sociologist, in Saskatoon, the evaluator was a person who had both a social work and a law degree, and in London, the evaluator was a person with a master's degree in psychology.

At all four locations, we found that there was friction between the court administrator and the person responsible for the social arm. The goals of the two were quite different: one was efficient and expedient operation; the other was satisfactory resolution of human relations problems (which do not necessarily lend themselves to efficient and expedient operation).

Lesson: When you have the same finding in several case studies, each of which is flawed in a different way, you can probably draw some conclusions about causality and there is probably good external validity.

Quite early in the study we were under pressure to tell the steering committee how the court was doing. We explained that we could not give them information because the court had not been functioning long enough for us to have reliable data. For instance, any problems might just have been the results of starting up and "growing pains." After we assured them that we would tell them if we saw anything catastrophic in the offing, they were willing to give us a bit of a respite.

Lesson: An important part of any applied social research project is educating the people for whom or with whom you are doing the study.

I have subsequently modified my approach, moving away from the model of the "objective outsider," being more willing to give advice, make suggestions, and involve the parties in the study. Other research in the area indicates that recommendations are more likely to be followed when there is "buy-in" by the parties. Buy-in occurs when they are more involved in the study.

WOMEN INTERESTED IN SUCCESSFUL EMPLOYMENT

The Women Interested in Successful Employment (WISE) project had three objectives, (1) assisting women in career decision-making and returning to the work force, (2) raising participants' level of awareness of nontraditional careers, and (3) increasing participants' self-confidence. Our evaluation indicated that the project was very successful at assisting women in decision-making, returning to the work force, and at increasing women's self-confidence. While it was clear that the program was successful, we had to question the internal validity. In other words, what caused the results? Was it the program itself or would you get the same result if you just brought together 20 women of the same age, with the same experience, and set them up with information about writing resumes, and so forth? In fact, the government funds projects that do just that, they are called "Job Clubs." We actually presented Employment Canada (as it was known then) with a true experimental design to compare the two approaches, random assignment included. However, they were not interested in funding the experiment.

Lesson: Funding agencies often are not interested in knowing "why" a project works, they just want to know whether or not it worked.

The one goal the project did not achieve was getting the women to consider nontraditional careers. After the first few groups, they realized that "raising awareness" might not lead women to choose nontraditional careers. To find out why, I met with the women in the program and asked them (for me at this time, this was a radical approach). They explained that (a) because of their age, they were having problems getting even traditional "female" jobs, (b) men had trouble getting jobs in areas the women were being encouraged to consider (for example, welding) so (c) they, the women, would be even less likely to get jobs. However, the program was having an impact because the women who had daughters all said that they were passing the message on to their daughters and were going to see that they considered nontraditional jobs.

Lesson: Do not underestimate the importance of qualitative/subjective information in understanding a process and/or result.

Another finding that was very interesting was from the one group that went through the program and expressed extreme dissatisfaction with it. At one point in the program, a fish plant in the province closed. The government decided that since the WISE program was so successful, they would send a group of the female plant workers to the program for them to be exposed to new career alternatives, job hunting skills, etc. When I met with the women at the end of the program, they were quite vocal in their dissatisfaction. Surprisingly, their questionnaire responses were not as negative as their comments at our meeting. I got some insight into the problem the next day when I got a phone call from one of the participants who had not been at the discussion. She explained that she had not come to the meeting because she would have been afraid to speak her mind. She, and several others, were very satisfied with the WISE program but a few of the more powerful women in the group were quite unhappy. (Remember that all of these women had worked together and all lived in the same small community.)

Lesson: Do not underestimate the importance of knowing about the background of the participants and the importance of group dynamics. This also reinforced my awareness that any group is really an *N* of 1 when you analyze results.

PRIMARY HEALTH CARE

In the Primary Health Care study, the Association of Registered Nurses of Newfoundland and Labrador proposed a "stand alone" project in which two nurses were put in each of several communities. The object was to improve population health (by prevention of disease) and reduce medical costs by having the salaried nurses perform tasks that are usually done by a physician who is billing for his/her time, such as measuring blood pressure. The province questioned the external validity of any project that was not integrated into the existing health care system. (They did not use the term "external validity.") It was only well after the project was underway that we discovered that the geographic region and towns were selected by a person working for the provincial government who wanted to improve health care in his or her home region. So, on the one side, we had a proposal for what we might call a controlled environment project that would have little external validity. On the other side, we had a bureaucrat refusing to do this (for legitimate reasons) and then putting it in an area where neighbours, friends, and family would benefit!

These motives did not become clear until the second year when the project was ready to put nurses into the communities. At that time, there was what can only be described as a power struggle between the parties involved to control the project.

Had we just come along toward the end of the project with questionnaires and health measures, we would have missed all of the growing pains that might very well have influenced the success or failure of the project.

Lesson: Be aware of the process involved, not just the end result. I also learned that applied social psychology often takes place in a political (small "p") environment where many of the parties involved in a project have their own covert or hidden agendas.

When the health economists in Denmark (the other project site) were asked to be involved in the three-year evaluation, they refused saying that there would be no visible impact in less than 10 years. What were our options in this situation? Do we refuse to do the study, as the economists did? Our choice was to develop what we called "milestone measures." We examined behaviours that are supposed to predict health, such as changes in exercise, stopping smoking, and looked for changes over the three years of the study.

Lesson: Sometimes you have to use dependent measures that are less than perfect or not do the study at all.

One of the things that I have always liked about contract research, as opposed to grant research, is that you can negotiate with the funding agency. When we first submitted the proposal to evaluate this project to Health and Welfare Canada, they flew to Newfoundland with three reviewers and we discussed the proposal we had submitted. They pointed out areas that had not been previously researched and helped us create a better proposal, which was eventually funded by Health and Welfare Canada for around $300,000.

ANTI-VIOLENCE FRAMEWORK

In 1991, the Newfoundland Government established a Committee to Develop a Provincial Strategy Against Violence. The end result was an *Action Plan* (Women's Policy Office, 1995) with two goals, (1) prevention of violence, and (2) improved service delivery to the victims of violence. There were four targeted areas: legislation, service delivery, education, and research/data collection/evaluation. Each targeted area had objectives and strategies.

We developed a framework to be used to evaluate whether the program was achieving its goals. To develop this framework we used program logic modelling (see Figure 1) and theories of human behaviour to clarify causal links. (This was the first time I had ever used a logic model to analyze a program.) This enabled us to see where there were weak causal links and to make recommendations to make the program "evaluable," that is, possible to evaluate.

A logic model looks simple to us as social scientists but is a very useful tool when talking with a nonscientist. My interpretation of the logic model is that social science theories are relevant to the arrows between the boxes. For instance, why do we expect an activity to lead to a particular output and outcome? One of the outcomes of the strategy was, "To raise awareness about the extent and nature of violence against women, children and elderly and dependent adults." The activity was to, "Develop a plan for a multi-phased, multi-year information campaign . . ." In this case, the link from the activity to the objective is straightforward—an information campaign should lead to raised awareness. The outputs are also specified, "'Develop six 30-second television and radio advertisements targeting youth, adults and seniors." The time frame is specified, "Implement and evaluate the campaign over a four-year time." The intended short-term outcome is clear: raising awareness. However, the link to the long-term outcomes, the goal of reducing violence, is not clear. Why, or how, should raising awareness lead to either the goal of prevention or improved service delivery?

Developing the program theory also makes clearer the theories of human behaviour assumed in the model. In the present case, the implicit and naive theory of human behaviour is a common one in programs aimed at changing behaviour. The naive theory might be diagrammed as a series of causal assumptions:

- If we give people information, then they will know about a topic.
- If they know about the topic, it will change their attitudes.
- If their attitudes change, then their behaviour will change.

However, as we are all aware, there is ample psychological theory and research that suggest that these are questionable causal assumptions.

Lesson: It is important to educate people about program logic and causality and also about the importance of social science research in *planning and developing* programs, not just in studying them once they are implemented.

CANADIAN MENTAL HEALTH ASSOCIATION PILOT FOR HOME-CARE

This was part of a pilot study on home-care services for mental health consumers. It was one of three pilot projects across Canada. As a member of the research committee of the Newfoundland Chapter of the Canadian Mental Health Association, I was involved in the evaluation of the local pilot study. Luckily for me, by now I had learned to listen to others, even those who were not psychologists. Anyway, the Newfoundland research committee was made up of strong minded people who were not going to let me get too quantitative.

In one of the three pilot locations in Canada, the evaluators, in my opinion, moved too quickly to quantification. With around only 20 consumers, they used structured interview questions like the following:

On a scale with response options: daily, weekly, monthly, annually, never—How often do you have contact with

Friends
Drop-in centres
Support groups
Social or recreational activities

FIGURE 1 / Program Logic Model

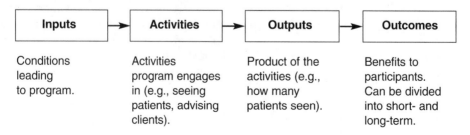

Inputs	Activities	Outputs	Outcomes
Conditions leading to program.	Activities program engages in (e.g., seeing patients, advising clients).	Product of the activities (e.g., how many patients seen).	Benefits to participants. Can be divided into short- and long-term.

General physician
Psychiatrist

And

Which of the following home care services do you require (examples from list given to "consumer"):

Meal preparation
Help preparing meals
Help planning meals
Help preparing a shopping list
Washing floors
Washing dishes
Sweeping
Cleaning windows
Cleaning bathroom
Dusting
Help getting laundry ready
Help sorting laundry
Other

In Newfoundland, we agreed that with the small number of people we had, it would be reasonable to use open interviews with probes. We asked questions like:

What kinds of things have you been doing in the last week?
How have you been feeling recently?
How has it been living [on your own or with your family]?
How is it working out with the home support worker?

The quantitative study results indicated findings like:

Meal preparation: 65% wanted assistance
Shopping: 60% wanted assistance
Sweeping: 60% wanted assistance

These are the kinds of results you would expect—even when you include "other" in a list, few people seem to use it. On the other hand, we found that the services mental health consumers needed from home support workers were quite different from the traditional services. We categorized services needed in three types of activities.

Traditional
House cleaning—I really don't like dirt. I feel better about myself.

Social
Playing games—[worker] is not judgmental and she loves to play Scrabble with me.
Conversation—The girl always asks you how you are feeling. Sometimes you can't always tell the doctors what is troubling you.
Mental Health—Pills help so much but you have to help yourself too. You can use "the girl" to help you do this.

Enabling
Riding bus to work with consumer—I need a shove to go places. I need someone to go places with me.

Yes, they did need some traditional service, but they also needed what we called "social" and "enabling" services. Our results were an eye-opener for me and for the other members of the research committee, some of whom had been working with, and on behalf of, mental health consumers for years. The Director of the Newfoundland Chapter of the Canadian Mental Health Association actually called it an "epiphany" for her.

Lesson: I learned the importance of appropriate research methods. Jumping in to detailed quantitative design may not be the way to do research in the early stages of a project, particularly one with a small N (6).

NURSING HOME

Our most recent research was the evaluation of a pilot project for a Provincial Private Partnership (PPP) in a home for seniors. In Newfoundland, long-term care residential accommodations for seniors are currently provided by both personal care homes and by nursing homes. Personal care homes represent a private-for-profit industry that offers care and accommodations for persons with low care needs. On the other hand, nursing homes are primarily publicly owned and operated. They provide services to persons with high care needs. There are seven nursing homes in the St. John's region. One of these was the focus of this evaluation.

All residents in the study initially entered the nursing home as individuals needing low-level care. As some of them exhausted their personal funds, they sought assistance, through public funds, to remain at the nursing home. These individuals applied for, and received, home support subsidies. However, the care needs of many of the residents in the study subsequently changed from low to high. Thus, they now required nursing home level care but still wished to stay at the nursing home. At that time there were no private nursing homes only private personal care homes. All parties had to determine how best to provide these individuals with higher level care and be respectful of their desire to remain at the nursing home. The solution arrived at was to enter into a one-year pilot project with the nursing home for the provision of nursing home care to 30 residents.

Thus, in October 2001, the Department of Health and Community Services, the nursing home, and the St. John's Nursing Home Board entered into an agreement to conduct a one-year pilot project for the provision of 30 subsidized beds for Levels III and IV care at the nursing home. Included in the pilot project was the provision of nursing home subsidies for these 30 beds. This project was to be retroactive to April 1, 2001, and continue until March 31, 2002.

Our job was to assess the pilot project. Among several factors, we were asked to:

Analyze the quality of the care received by the residents.

Assess the residents' quality of life and satisfaction levels.

Look at the cost effectiveness of the project.

Happily for me, the two people who were carrying the main burden for the "psychological" research were Colin Perrier and Nancy Carter, both graduates of our Master's of Applied Social Psychology program. (The person looking after the cost effectiveness was a consultant who had also submitted a proposal. Ours was weak on cost effectiveness and his was not as strong as ours on the psychological side.) Colin and Nancy drafted the proposal, which included getting ethical approval for the project. This was a bit ahead of its time because the province still does not have an ethics review board. However, the university (Social Science) ethics review board agreed to look at our proposal even though they were not sure that it really fit with the tri-council definition of "research." They agreed to do this because of the vulnerable nature of the population being studied.

After we started on the study, we learned that virtually all of the residents were cognitively impaired. This meant that we were faced with two problems, 1) the ethical one of getting informed consent to include the residents' data in the study, and 2) ascertaining their quality of life. For the first, we would have to go to the person who had power of attorney. For the second, we knew that we could use the "Person Most Knowledgeable" (PMK) as a source of information but did not know if any protocols have been developed to clearly define who the PMK is. Assuming that we were not the first researchers to face this problem, I posted an inquiry on a list-server to which I subscribe. We received invaluable information and suggestions, based on people's experience. They came from Texas, Missouri, the UK, and eventually circled back to researchers in Ontario.

Lesson: One problem in applied research is that the studies are often done for government and the private sector and do not get published. Solution—the Internet is a great way to find out who is doing what and where.

Back to the ethics review. In the submission we made it clear that we were asking for guidance on the research, not on the pilot project itself. That is, we did not ask if the pilot itself would have received ethics approval. The review board had a few minor suggestions and some complimentary remarks about the lengths to which we were going to protect the residents.

Unfortunately, the families of the residents were not so complimentary. To be charitable, they were very concerned about the future of their parent(s) who were living in the nursing home. They envisioned them being "put out on the street" if the pilot received a poor evaluation. There were two issues. First, they had not been apprised that this was to be a pilot study. This had nothing to do with us; this was done long before we came on the scene. And to be fair to the provincial government, they had come up with what they thought was a creative solution to the original problem. The second concern did have more to do with us—when you conduct a study you have to make it clear to the participants what potential harm there might be. The families claimed that the results of our study might mean that their family member would be moved out of the nursing home. They thought that this implication had not been made clear to the Ethics Review Board. (Indeed, some wrote to the Board complaining about this. A letter of complaint from a participant in a study was a first for the Review Board.) On the other hand, the provincial government had been quite explicit at our meetings, that our results were merely one piece of evidence they would take into account in making their decision. Thus, the final decision did not stand or fall based on our recommendations. Given that a decision was going to be made, we wondered how the families would prefer that the decision be made. Would they prefer that it be made with no evidence whatsoever?

Lesson: Although we sometimes complain about having to get an ethics review for a study, in our case having the ethics review gave us a level of comfort we might not have had in dealing with the residents and in dealing with their families.

There you have it. I have chosen a few of the applied social psychology studies in which I have been involved over the last 25 years from which I have learned important research lessons. There are a few other lessons I have learned that I would like to impart but which are not tied to any particular study.

It is important to be able to work with an interdisciplinary team—I have learned to work with nurses, social workers, economists, and mental health professionals. All bring a different perspective to the research.

In applied social psychological research, unlike experimental work, you have virtually no control over the variables of interest. Further, you go where the problems are. You do not get to do a program of research where there are consistent theoretical issues that you can pursue.

If you want your results taken seriously, and attention paid to your recommendations, write for the audience—they are usually not psychologists.

Related to this, never underestimate the value of reporting means and percentages and using chi-square tests.

Do not underestimate the importance of your own observations but at same time know the importance of validating conclusions or pointing out limitations to your reader.

And finally,

Never forget the importance of knowing the threats to the statistical, internal, construct, and external validity of your research.

I owe a large debt to John Evans, the Head of the Psychology department at MUN who allowed me a lighter teaching load while I was President of CPA. Amongst other things this allowed me more time to work on this address. I also owe a huge debt to my social psychology colleagues who are constantly challenging me intellectually at our weekly research meetings and who keep me in good humour all of the time. Finally, a special thanks to Cathryn Button who has carried so much of the burden for the Applied Social Psychology (Co-op) program at MUN. Thanks John, Malcolm, Ted, and Cathryn.

REFERENCES

Campbell, D. T., & Stanley, J. C. (1963). *Experimental and quasi-experimental designs for research*. Rand McNally: USA.

Day, A. (2003, January). Comments from the Chair. *The Canadian Industrial and Organizational Psychologist, 19,* 1.

Gilovich, T., & Medvec, V. H. (1995). The experience of regret: What, when, and why. *Psychological Review, 102,* 379–395.

Law Reform Commission of Canada. (1974). *Working Paper No. 1. The Family Court*. Ottawa, ON: Information Canada.

Plous, S. (1993). *The psychology of judgement and decision making*. Toronto, ON: McGraw Hill.

Women's Policy Office. (1995). Towards the year 2000: The provincial strategy against violence. An action plan. Newfoundland and Labrador: Office of the Queen's Printer.

CRITICAL THINKING QUESTIONS

1. Applied research, as described in this article, focuses on a real-world problem and attempts to provide an answer. Design an experimental study using at least one of the applied studies described by the author of this article as your starting point. In other words, design a study to address the *theoretical issues* involved, not necessarily the specifics of a given real-world problem.

2. *External validity* refers to how generalizable the results of one particular study are to other settings. The author discusses the problems associated with the generalizability of results in applied settings. What, however, are the limitations of generalizability in more traditional experimental methods? For example, a majority of experimental studies use college students as subjects. Is this a problem? Why or why not?

3. Develop a list of what you consider the most important questions that social psychology should try to answer. As you go through the course, keep track of which of these questions have been investigated and what the findings were. If a question you listed has not been investigated, why do you think that may be the case?

4. Select a real-world problem in which you think obtaining research data might be useful in determining what to do. Then design an applied study that attempts to address this problem. What do you see as the potential issues in or limitations of such a study? What do you see as the potential advantages of such a study compared to experimental, nonapplied studies on the same topic?

5. Discuss the advantages and disadvantages of applied versus experimental research.

CHAPTER INTEGRATION QUESTIONS

1. All three articles in this chapter relate to aspects of research: why relying on common sense is not always accurate, the problems of deception in research, and unforeseen lessons learned from working in the area of applied social psychology research. Identify one or more themes common to all three articles.

2. Based on these articles, what are the major issues confronting an individual embarking on a career in social psychology research?

3. In *How to Lie with Statistics,* Darrell Huff states, "Statistics are like people. Torture them enough and they will tell you anything." What does this quotation mean to you? Do you agree or disagree with it? Why?

Chapter Two

SOCIAL PERCEPTION

HOW DO WE form impressions of other people? What information do we use in forming those impressions? How important are first impressions? How do we make judgments about why people act the way they do? These are some of the questions addressed by the readings in this chapter on social perception.

When we interact with another person, we are literally bombarded with information. What the person looks like, what he or she is saying, and how he or she is acting comprise but a fraction of the information available to us that we may use in forming an impression of the individual. One judgment we may make about another individual concerns his or her overall character. In other words, we want to know how honest, trustworthy, likeable, or good the person is. But exactly what are we looking for? And are some of us better than others at making accurate judgments?

One topic of study in this area is how long it takes for us to form an impression of someone. Do we do so almost immediately, or do we hold off until we know more about him or her? Furthermore, how accurate are our first impressions? Is a first impression formed after less than a minute of interaction with a stranger any less accurate than an impression formed after knowing someone for a much longer period of time? These and other questions pertaining to the power of first impressions are examined in Article 4, "The Once-Over: Can You Trust First Impressions?"

Another topic of interest is whether all the information available about someone is equally relevant in forming our impressions of him or her. In other words, are some factors more important than others? Article 5, "The Warm-Cold Variable in First Impressions of Persons," examines some of the important factors that influence our judgments of other people. This classic article is a fine example of the power of first impressions and the impact that they have on how we relate to others.

Finally, Article 6, "Detecting True Lies: Police Officers' Ability to Detect Suspects' Lies," offers a contemporary look at research on one particular aspect of impression formation: the ability to detect when someone is lying. The article examines variables and techniques that may be important in accurately detecting deception. Moreover, the article answers a very important practical question: Are police officers any better than the rest of us at detecting deception?

ARTICLE 4 _____

What information do we use in forming impressions of other people? When meeting someone for the first time, we rely on a variety of information, such as how he or she acts, looks, and dresses, and what he or she says. Some of this information is nonverbal. We pay a lot of attention to facial expressions, for example, as well as body postures and movements. Most of us have some sort of intuitive rules for decoding nonverbal behavior. For example, what does it mean when someone is standing upright with his or her arms folded across the chest? Is that person being defensive? Not very warm and open? Some popularizations of psychology maintain that certain nonverbal cues have specific meanings, such as in the example just given. However, the example used also might mean nothing more than that the person was cold or that he or she habitually stands that way. Regardless of any supposedly clearcut meanings of nonverbal behavior, we all have our own intuitive means for making judgments about the people we meet.

Although we may have confidence in our own judgments, the concept known as the *fundamental attribution error* suggests that we only see what we want to see. According to this concept, we have a basic tendency to make global, personality generalizations based upon observations made in specific situations. For example, if we meet someone at a party who seems warm, outgoing, and confident, we assume that this is what his or her personality is like in other situations, as well. In other words, we think that we know the real person and ignore or downplay the fact that he or she may act quite differently in other situations. Worse yet, once we form this initial impression, it may be hard to change, since we may persist in only seeing what is consistent with our initial judgment.

So, how long does it take for us to make a judgment about someone? An hour? Fifteen minutes? Two seconds? The following article by Carlin Flora discusses research that shows that people make judgments about others in a remarkably short period of time. Furthermore, these quick judgments tend to be amazingly similar to those made by people interacting over a much longer time period or even by trained interviewers. But the question is: How accurate are the judgments made by *any* of these people?

The Once-Over

Can You Trust First Impressions?

■ Carlin Flora

Bill and Hillary Clinton often tell the story of how they met: They locked eyes across Yale's law library, until Hillary broke the silent flirtation and marched straight over to Bill. "Look, if you're going to keep staring at me, and I'm going to keep staring back, we might as well be introduced. I'm Hillary Rodham. What's your name?" Bill has said he couldn't remember his own name. It was quite a first impression, one so powerful that it sparked a few chapters of U.S. history.

Initial encounters are emotionally concentrated events that can overwhelm us—even convince us that the room is spinning. We walk away from them with a first impression that is like a Polaroid picture—a

Reprinted from *Psychology Today,* 2004 (May/June), *37,* 60–66. Reprinted with permission from *Psychology Today* magazine. Copyright © 2004 (Sussex Publishers, Inc.).

head-to-toe image that develops instantly and never entirely fades. Often, that snapshot captures important elements of the truth.

Consider one study in which untrained subjects were shown 20- to 32-second videotaped segments of job applicants greeting interviewers. The subjects then rated the applicants on attributes such as self-assurance and likability. Surprisingly, their assessments were very close to those of trained interviewers who spent at least 20 minutes with each applicant. What semblance of a person—one with a distinct appearance, history and complex personality—could have been captured in such a fleeting moment?

The answer lies in part in how the brain takes first-impression Polaroids—creating a composite of all the signals given off by a new experience. Psychologists agree that snap judgments are a holistic phenomenon in which clues (mellifluous voice, Rolex watch, soggy handshake, hunched shoulders) hit us all at once and form an impression larger than their sum.

We do search for one particular sign on a new face: a smile. "We can pick up a smile from 30 meters away," says Paul Ekman, professor of psychology at the University of California Medical School in San Francisco, and a pioneer of research on facial expressions. "A smile lets us know that we're likely to get a positive reception, and it's hard not to reciprocate."

By the time we flash that return grin, our Polaroid shutter will have already closed. Just three seconds are sufficient to make a conclusion about fresh acquaintances. Nalini Ambady, professor of psychology at Tufts University in Medford, Massachusetts, studies first impressions carved from brief exposure to another person's behavior, what she calls "thin slices" of experience. She says humans have developed the ability to quickly decide whether a new person will hurt or enrich us—judgments that had lifesaving ramifications in an earlier era.

She believes that thin slices are generated in the most primitive area of the brain, where feelings are also processed, which accounts for the emotional punch of some first encounters. Immediate distrust of a certain car salesman or affinity for a prospective roommate originates in the deepest corners of the mind.

The ability to interpret thin slices evolved as a way for our ancestors to protect themselves in an eat-or-be-eaten world, whereas modern-day threats to survival often come in the form of paperwork (dwindling stock portfolios) or intricate social rituals (impending divorce). The degree to which thin slices of experience help us navigate modern encounters—from hitchhikers to blind dates—is up for debate.

Ekman says that people excel at reading facial expressions quickly, but only when a countenance is genuine. Most people cannot tell if someone is feigning an emotion, he says, "unless their eyes have been trained to spot very subtle expressions that leak through." Consider anger: When we are boiling mad, our lips narrow—an expression we can't make on demand when we're pretending.

And the accuracy of a snap judgment always depends on what exactly we're sizing up. Ekman doesn't think we can use a thin slice of behavior to judge, say, if someone is smart enough to be our study partner or generous enough to lend us a bus token. "But we can pretty easily distinguish one emotion from another, particularly if it's on the face for a second or more." Spending more time with a genuine person, he says, won't yield a more accurate sense of that person's emotional state.

First impressions are not merely hardwired reactions—we are also taught how to judge others, holding our thin slices up to the light of social stereotypes. Brian Nosek, professor of psychology at the University of Virginia, studies the implicit attitudes that enter into our calculations. Just because someone carries an ACLU membership card or makes a point to invite their senior-citizen friends to dance-club outings doesn't mean they don't have prejudices bubbling under the surface. Nosek and colleagues administer a quick online test that reveals the beliefs people either can't or won't report.

Called the Implicit Association Test, it asks participants to pair concepts, such as "young" with "good," or "elderly" with "good." If, in some part of his mind, "old" is more closely related to "bad" than to "good," the test taker will respond more quickly to the first pairing of words than to the second. In versions of these tests, small differences in response times are used to determine if someone is biased toward youth over the elderly, African-Americans over Caucasians or for President Bush over President Kennedy. "When I took the test," says Nosek, "I showed a bias toward whites.

Street-Corner Psychologists: From Store Manager to Police Officer, Certain Professions Rely on Making the Right Snap Judgment

—Jeff Grossman, Neil Parmar, Jammie Salagubang, and Susan A. Smith

Jeff Ayers, novelty-store manager
To spot a thief, check for eye contact, says New York-based Ayers. Persistent looking around or eyes that dart from left to right should raise suspicion. Ayers also watches people with "forced body language." They pace purposefully up and down aisles. "Sometimes the best-dressed [are the culprits]; they're on a shopping spree with someone else's credit card. The ones I can't [pick out] are those I've been friendly with. One guy would jibber-jabber, then bend down to tie his shoes and stick $300 worth of stuff in his bag."

Gerald Scott, police officer
Scott has been a New York City police officer for 10 years. He says he can easily spot bad apples on the street because they "tend to stay in a certain space for long periods of time. They're not really doing anything, they're just watching everybody. They're never reading the paper or anything. They're worried about everything going on around them. Just look at their eyes. There's a lot of nervousness. You can tell they're trying to figure out if you're a cop or not."

Eric McMullen, cardsharp
In the gritty gambling locales of Harlem, McMullen is better known as "DOC," or the Dealer of Cards. "If I don't cheat, I don't eat," says the amateur magician turned master cardsharp. "Amateurs have shifty eyes. They look around the table and try to talk to everyone. Let's say the sharp wants to switch the whole deck. He'll get a little fidgety—that's a telltale sign for cheating." Subtlety is the secret behind flawless moves. "Always make gestures and jokes, look people in the eye and don't look at the deck."

John Breen, retired detective
"I'm not claiming to be Sherlock Holmes, but there are a number of behavioral interviewing techniques taught in the police academy that can help tell you when someone is lying," says Breen, a former police lieutenant in Arizona. "A suspect might put her hand up to her mouth or she may cross her arms over her chest. Whereas someone who is more receptive, open and forthcoming won't cross her arms. But you can't take that as gospel. You have to [measure up] the individual and determine what her normal reactions might be."

Sudha Chinniah, high-end salesperson
"You can never tell who's going to spend on clothing," says Chinniah, who works at the Bergdorf Goodman department store in New York. But "how you look is an extension of [how you feel]. The wealthiest guy may be dressed casually, but he carries himself with confidence. A customer's wallet, watch and shoes approximate her financial background. Right now there's a trend toward slim shoes with elongated toes, which defines a customer who's absolutely current."

David Boyle, county prosecutor
Every nuance counts for a trial lawyer, who must quickly convince a group of strangers that his version of the facts is the truth. "Everything you do is being judged—the way you dress, the way you talk," says Boyle, a prosecutor in Walton County, Georgia. If he wants jurors to listen to a friendly witness, Boyle positions himself at the far end of the jury box, forcing the witness to look straight at the jury and speak loud enough for everyone to hear. During harmful testimony, he'll study his files or consult with his partner to indicate complete disinterest.

I was shocked. We call it unconsciousness-raising, in contrast to the consciousness-raising of the 1960s."

As subtle as implicit attitudes are, they can cause serious real-world damage. If an angry person stumbles upon someone of a different race or religion, he is likely to perceive that person negatively, according to recent research. Anger incites instinctive prejudiced responses toward "outsiders," a finding that has

How to Make a Great First Impression

Curb Conversational Narcissism

He's talking about his new Subaru, which reminds you of the battle you waged—and won—with that smarmy Hertz-rental-car dealer in Miami last month. This "faux segue" is a big no-no, says psychologist and business consultant Valerie White. "We are tempted to share impressive things about ourselves, but the one idea you should keep in mind is 'How am I making the other person feel?'" Actively encourage others to talk about themselves, and respond genuinely—without bringing it back to you.

Don't Betray Your Anxiety

"If you're not quick-witted or well-versed in certain subjects, you can still make a great impression," White says. Just focus on the other person. This in turn will take the pressure off you. However, avoid interrogating a new acquaintance. If you're jittery, control movements such as leg twitching. And remember to speak slowly—nervousness makes us talk too fast.

Fake a Sunny Mood

"Be yourself" is solid first-impression advice from cognitive scientists and self-help gurus alike. But it's worth suppressing a bad mood when you meet someone new. While you know you are just experiencing a momentary state, a new acquaintance will take you for a full-time complainer. "There is a contagion effect," says White. "A bad mood will bring the other person down, too. Try to start off well, and then share what's bothering you."

The Eyes Have It

If you want to get to know a stranger, break with body language conventions by catching her eye for more than a second. When you first meet someone, author and lecturer Nicholas Boothman says, focus on your eye contact, your smile and your posture. "If you notice somebody's eye color, and you say 'great' to yourself, you will actually be smiling, and you will give off a super mood."

Get in Sync

Adjusting your posture, voice, words and gestures to match those of a new acquaintance is critical, says Boothman, because we are attracted to others who are just like us. "People respond when you speak at their pace," agrees White. To establish an instant rapport, mirror your new friend's head nods and tilts.

Use Flattery, Sparingly

"People like to be flattered," says White. "Even if they suspect you are brownnosing, they still like it." But use flattery judiciously—focus on the other person's accomplishments or achievements. This works best when a person believes you don't say ingratiating things to just anyone.

The Do-Over

You arrive at a party fuming over a parking ticket. A cheery guest introduces herself, but you brush her off and head for the bar. You've made a bad impression, but you can recover if you demonstrate self-awareness, says White. Pull her aside and say, "I wasn't myself earlier." Show your sense of humor: "I see you met my evil twin." And remember to cut others slack if they make a bad impression on you.

important implications for people in law enforcement and security.

Certain physical features consistently prompt our brains to take first-impression Polaroids with a distorting filter. People who have a "baby face," characterized by a round shape, large eyes and small nose and chin, give off the impression of trustworthiness and naiveté—on average, a false assumption. A pretty face also leads us astray: Our tendency is to perceive beautiful people as healthier and just plain better than others.

Leslie Zebrowitz, professor of psychology at Brandeis University in Massachusetts, argues that we overgeneralize in the presence of baby mugs and homely visages. Humans are hardwired to recognize a baby as an innocent, weak creature who requires protection. By the same token, mating with someone who is severely deformed, and thereby unattractive, may keep your DNA from spreading far and wide. But we overgeneralize these potentially helpful built-in responses, coddling adults with babyish miens who in fact don't need our care and shunning unattractive people who may not meet our standards of beauty but certainly don't pose an imminent threat to our gene pool.

Zebrowitz has found that many baby-faced grown-ups, particularly young men, overcompensate for misperceptions by cultivating tougher-than-average personalities in an attempt to ward off cheek-pinching aunts. Think of the sweet-faced rapper Eminem, who never cracks a smile, or the supermodel-juggling, hard-partying actor Leonardo DiCaprio.

Not every observer is equally likely to draw unwarranted conclusions about a smooth-cheeked man or a woman with stunning, symmetrical features. People who spend time cultivating relationships are more likely to make accurate snap judgments.

"A good judge of personality isn't just someone who is smarter—it's someone who gets out and spends time with people," says David Funder, a professor of psychology at the University of California at Riverside, who believes in the overall accuracy of snap judgments. Funder has found that two observers often reach a consensus about a third person, and the assessments are accurate in that they match the third person's assessment of himself. "We're often fooled, of course, but we're more often right."

On the other side of the equation, some people are simpler to capture at first glance than others. "The people who are easiest to judge are the most mentally healthy," says Randy Colvin, associate professor of psychology at Northeastern University in Boston. "With mentally healthy individuals," Colvin theorizes, "exterior behavior mimics their internal views of themselves. What you see is what you get."

LEARN MORE ABOUT IT

First Impressions Valerie White and Ann Demarais *(Bantam, 2004)*

Emotions Revealed: Recognizing Faces and Feelings to Improve Communication and Emotional Life Paul Ekman *(Times Books, 2003)*

How to Make People Like You in 90 Seconds or Less Nicholas Boothman *(Workman, 2000)*

Implicit Association Test (https://implicit.harvard.edu.implicit/)

CRITICAL THINKING QUESTIONS

1. In everyday situations, what can be done to help minimize the power of first impressions? Or is it even possible not to *form* first impressions? Defend your position with data regarding impression formation and impression management.

2. What advice have you received from others about how to make a good first impression? How consistent (or inconsistent) is that advice with the information contained in this article?

3. How might the findings in this article about the power of first impressions be applicable to jury trials? Dating situations? Job interviews? Is the process involved in forming a first impression fundamentally the same in all situations, or does it depend on the context in which the impression is being made? Defend your position.

4. Is it feasible to teach people to be more aware of the first impressions they make? Is it possible to teach people how to interpret such impressions more accurately? How might either or both of these goals be accomplished? Explain your answers.

5. "You cannot *not* communicate." Discuss what this statement means in terms of impression formation.

ARTICLE 5 _____

A variety of sources of information may be available for use in forming an impression of a person. However, that does not mean that all of the information will be used or hold equal value. Some sources of information may carry more weight than others. For example, we may notice how the person acts, or we may have heard something about him or her from someone else. How do we use this information to develop an impression of the person?

Building on the classic work of S. E. Asch, Harold H. Kelley examines what can be called a *central organizing trait,* one that is important in influencing the impressions that we form. By examining the effect of changing just one adjective in describing a person (i.e., *warm* versus *cold*), the study demonstrates that this initial difference influenced how the subjects actually rated the person. Even more interesting is that these differences in initial impression carried over into how the subjects interacted with the person. The implication is that perhaps our initial impressions lead us to act in certain ways toward others, perhaps creating a self-fulfilling prophecy by giving us what we expected to see in the first place.

The Warm-Cold Variable in First Impressions of Persons
■ Harold H. Kelley

This experiment is one of several studies of first impressions (3), the purpose of the series being to investigate the stability of early judgments, their determinants, and the relation of such judgments to the behavior of the person making them. In interpreting the data from several nonexperimental studies on the stability of first impressions, it proved to be necessary to postulate inner-observer variables which contribute to the impression and which remain relatively constant through time. Also some evidence was obtained which directly demonstrated the existence of these variables and their nature. The present experiment was designed to determine the effects of one kind of inner-observer variable, specifically, *expectations* about the stimulus person which the observer brings to the exposure situation.

That prior information or labels attached to a stimulus person make a difference in observers' first impressions is almost too obvious to require demonstration. The expectations resulting from such preinformation may restrict, modify, or accentuate the

impressions he will have. The crucial question is: What changes in perception will accompany a given expectation? Studies of stereotyping, for example, that of Katz and Braly (2), indicate that from an ethnic label such as "German" or "Negro," a number of perceptions follow which are culturally determined. The present study finds its main significance in relation to a study by Asch (1) which demonstrates that certain crucial labels can transform the entire impression of the person, leading to attributions which are related to the label on a broad cultural basis or even, perhaps, on an autochthonous basis.

Asch read to his subjects a list of adjectives which purportedly described a particular person. He then asked them to characterize that person. He found that the inclusion in the list of what he called *central* qualities, such as "warm" as opposed to "cold," produced a widespread change in the entire impression. This effect was not adequately explained by the halo effect since it did not extend indiscriminately in a positive or negative direction to all characteristics. Rather, it dif-

Reprinted from *Journal of Personality,* 1950, *18,* 431–439. Copyright © 1950 by Blackwell Publishers, Ltd. Reprinted with permission of Blackwell Publishers.

ferentially transformed the other qualities, for example, by changing their relative importance in the total impression. Peripheral qualities (such as "polite" versus "blunt") did not produce effects as strong as those produced by the central qualities.[1]

The present study tested the effects of such central qualities upon the early impressions of *real* persons, the same qualities, "warm" vs. "cold," being used. They were introduced as preinformation about the stimulus person before his actual appearance; so presumably they operated as expectations rather than as part of the stimulus pattern during the exposure period. In addition, information was obtained about the effects of the expectations upon the observers' behavior toward the stimulus person. An earlier study in this series has indicated that the more incompatible the observer initially perceived the stimulus person to be, the less the observer initiated interaction with him thereafter. The second purpose of the present experiment, then, was to provide a better controlled study of this relationship.

No previous studies reported in the literature have dealt with the importance of first impressions for behavior. The most relevant data are found in the sociometric literature, where there are scattered studies of the relation between choices among children having some prior acquaintance and their interaction behavior. For an example, see the study by Newstetter, Feldstein, and Newcomb (8).

PROCEDURE

The experiment was performed in three sections of a psychology course (Economics 70) at the Massachusetts Institute of Technology.[2] The three sections provided 23, 16, and 16 subjects respectively. All 55 subjects were men, most of them in their third college year. In each class the stimulus person (also a male) was completely unknown to the subjects before the experimental period. One person served as stimulus person in two sections, and a second person took this role in the third section. In each case the stimulus person was introduced by the experimenter, who posed as a representative of the course instructors and who gave the following statement:

Your regular instructor is out of town today, and since we of Economics 70 are interested in the general problem of how various classes react to different instructors, we're going to have an instructor today you've

never had before, Mr. ____. Then, at the end of the period, I want you to fill out some forms about him. In order to give you some idea of what he's like, we've had a person who knows him write up a little biographical note about him. I'll pass this out to you now and you can read it before be arrives. Please read these to yourselves and don't talk about this among yourselves until the class is over so that he won't get wind of what's going on.

Two kinds of these notes were distributed, the two being identical except that in one the stimulus person was described among other things as being "rather cold" whereas in the other form the phrase "very warm" was substituted. The content of the "rather cold" version is as follows:

Mr. ____ is a graduate student in the Department of Economics and Social Science here at M.I.T. He has had three semesters of teaching experience in psychology at another college. This is his first semester teaching Ec. 70. He is 26 years old, a veteran, and married. People who know him consider him to be a rather cold person, industrious, critical, practical, and determined.

The two types of preinformation were distributed randomly within each of the three classes and in such a manner that the students were not aware that two kinds of information were being given out. The stimulus person then appeared and led the class in a twenty-minute discussion. During this time the experimenter kept a record of how often each student participated in the discussion. Since the discussion was almost totally leader-centered, this participation record indicates the number of times each student initiated verbal interaction with the instructor. After the discussion period, the stimulus person left the room, and the experimenter gave the following instructions:

Now, I'd like to get your impression of Mr. ____. This is not a test of you and can in no way affect your grade in this course. This material will not be identified as belonging to particular persons and will be kept strictly confidential. It will be of most value to us if you are completely honest in your evaluation of Mr. ____. Also, please understand that what you put down will not be used against him or cause him to lose his job or anything like that. This is not a test of him but merely a study of how different classes react to different instructors.

The subjects then wrote free descriptions of the stimulus person and finally rated him on a set of 15 rating scales.

RESULTS AND DISCUSSION

1. *Influence of warm-cold variable on first impressions.* The differences in the ratings produced by the warm-cold variable were consistent from one section to another even where different stimulus persons were used. Consequently, the data from the three sections were combined by equating means (the S.D.'s were approximately equal) and the results for the total group are presented in Table 1. Also in this table is presented that part of Asch's data which refers to the qualities included in our rating scales. From this table it is quite clear that those given the "warm" preinformation consistently rated the stimulus person more favorably than those given the "cold" preinformation.

Summarizing the statistically significant differences, the "warm" subjects rated the stimulus person as more considerate of others, more informal, more sociable, more popular, better natured, more humorous, and more humane. These findings are very similar to Asch's for the characteristics common to both studies. He found more frequent attribution to his hypothetical "warm" personalities of sociability, popularity, good naturedness, generosity, humorousness, and humaneness. So these data strongly support his finding that such a central quality as "warmth" can greatly influence the total impression of a personality. This effect is found to be operative in the perception of real persons.

This general favorableness in the perceptions of the "warm" observers as compared with the "cold" ones indicates that something like a halo effect may have been operating in these ratings. Although his data are not completely persuasive on this point, Asch was convinced that such a general effect was *not* operating

TABLE 1 / Comparison of "Warm" and "Cold" Observers in Terms of Average Ratings Given Stimulus Persons

Item	Low End of Rating Scale	High End of Rating Scale	Average Rating Warm N = 7	Cold N = 28	Level of Significance of Warm-Cold Difference	Asch's Data: Per Cent of Group Assigning Quality at Low End of Our Rating Scale* Warm	Cold
1	Knows his stuff	Doesn't know his stuff	3.5	4.6			
2	Considerate of others	Self-centered	6.3	9.6	1%		
3†	Informal	Formal	6.3	9.6	1%		
4†	Modest	Proud	9.4	10.6			
5	Sociable	Unsociable	5.6	10.4	1%	91%	38%
6	Self-assured	Uncertain of himself	8.4	9.1			
7	High intelligence	Low intelligence	4.8	5.1			
8	Popular	Unpopular	4.0	7.4	1%	84%	28%
9†	Good natured	Irritable	9.4	12.0	5%	94%	17%
10	Generous	Ungenerous	8.2	9.6		91%	08%
11	Humorous	Humorless	8.3	11.7	1%	77%	13%
12	Important	Insignificant	6.5	8.6		88%	99%
13†	Humane	Ruthless	8.6	11.0	5%	86%	31%
14†	Submissive	Dominant	13.2	14.5			
15	Will go far	Will not get ahead	4.2	5.8			

*Given for all qualities common to Asch's list and this set of rating scales.

†These scales were reversed when presented to the subjects.

in his study. Closer inspection of the present data makes it clear that the "warm-cold" effect cannot be explained altogether on the basis of simple halo effect. In Table 1 it is evident that the "warm-cold" variable produced differential effects from one rating scale to another. The size of this effect seems to depend upon the closeness of relation between the specific dimension of any given rating scale and the central quality of "warmth" or "coldness." Even though the rating of intelligence may be influenced by a halo effect, it is not influenced to the same degree to which considerateness is. It seems to make sense to view such strongly influenced items as considerateness, informality, good naturedness, and humaneness as dynamically more closely related to warmth and hence more perceived in terms of this relation than in terms of a general positive or negative feeling toward the stimulus person. If first impressions are normally made in terms of such general dimensions as "warmth" and "coldness," the power they give the observer in making predictions and specific evaluations about such disparate behavior characteristics as formality and considerateness is considerable (even though these predictions may be incorrect or misleading).

The free report impression data were analyzed for only one of the sections. In general, there were few sizable differences between the "warm" and "cold" observers. The "warm" observers attributed more nervousness, more sincerity, and more industriousness to the stimulus person. Although the frequencies of comparable qualities are very low because of the great variety of descriptions produced by the observers, there is considerable agreement with the rating scale data.

Two important phenomena are illustrated in these free description protocols, the first of them having been noted by Asch. *Firstly,* the characteristics of the stimulus person are interpreted in terms of the precognition of warmth or coldness. For example, a "warm" observer writes about a rather shy and retiring stimulus person as follows: "He makes friends slowly but they are lasting friendships when formed." In another instance, several "cold" observers described him as being, ". . . intolerant: would be angry if you disagree with his view. . ."; while several "warm" observers put the same thing this way: "Unyielding in principle, not easily influenced or swayed from his original attitude." *Secondly,* the preinformation about

the stimulus person's warmth or coldness is evaluated and interpreted in the light of the direct behavioral data about him. For example, "He has a slight inferiority complex which leads to his coldness," and "His conscientiousness and industriousness might be mistaken for coldness." Examples of these two phenomena occurred rather infrequently, and there was no way to evaluate the relative strengths of these countertendencies. Certainly some such evaluation is necessary to determine the conditions under which behavior which is contrary to a stereotyped label resists distortion and leads to rejection of the label.

A comparison of the data from the two different stimulus persons is pertinent to the last point in so far as it indicates the interaction between the properties of the stimulus person and the label. The fact that the warm-cold variable generally produced differences in the same direction for the two stimulus persons, even though they are very different in personality, behavior, and mannerisms, indicates the strength of this variable. However, there were some exceptions to this tendency as well as marked differences in the *degree* to which the experimental variable was able to produce differences. For example, stimulus person A typically appears to be anything but lacking in self-esteem and on rating scale 4 he was generally at the "proud" end of the scale. Although the "warm" observers tended to rate him as they did the other stimulus person (i.e., more "modest"), the difference between the "warm" and "cold" means for stimulus person A is very small and not significant as it is for stimulus person B. Similarly, stimulus person B was seen as "unpopular" and "humorless," which agrees with his typical classroom behavior. Again the "warm" observers rated him more favorably on these items, but their ratings were not significantly different from those of the "cold" observers, as was true for the other stimulus person. Thus we see that the strength or compellingness of various qualities of the stimulus person must be reckoned with. The stimulus is not passive to the forces arising from the label but actively resists distortion and may severely limit the degree of influence exerted by the preinformation.[3]

2. Influence of warm-cold variable on interaction with the stimulus person. In the analysis of the frequency with which the various students took part in the discussion led by the stimulus person, a larger proportion of those given the "warm" preinformation participated than of those given the "cold" preinformation. Fifty-six per cent of the "warm" subjects entered the discussion, whereas only 32 per cent of the "cold" subjects did so. Thus the expectation of warmth not only produced more favorable early perceptions of the stimulus person but led to greater initiation of interaction with him. This relation is a low one, significant at between the 5 per cent and 10 percent level of confidence, but it is in line with the general principle that social perception serves to guide and steer the person's behavior in his social environment.

As would be expected from the foregoing findings, there was also a relation between the favorableness of the impression and whether or not the person participated in the discussion. Although any single item yielded only a small and insignificant relation to participation, when a number are combined the trend becomes clear cut. For example, when we combine the seven items which were influenced to a statistically significant degree by the warm-cold variable, the total score bears considerable relation to participation, the relationship being significant as well beyond the 1 per cent level. A larger proportion of those having favorable total impressions participated than of those having unfavorable impressions, the bi-serial correlation between these variables being .34. Although this relation may be interpreted in several ways, it seems most likely that the unfavorable perception led to a curtailment of interaction. Support for this comes from one of the other studies in this series (3). There it was found that those persons having unfavorable impressions of the instructor at the end of the first class meeting tended less often to initiate interactions with him in the succeeding four meetings than did those having favorable first impressions. There was also some tendency in the same study for those persons who interacted least with the instructor to change least in their judgments of him from the first to later impressions.

It will be noted that these relations lend some support to the autistic hostility hypothesis proposed by Newcomb (7). This hypothesis suggests that the possession of an initially hostile attitude toward a person leads to a restriction of communication and contact with him which in turn serves to preserve the hostile attitude by preventing the acquisition of data which could correct it. The present data indicate that a restriction of interaction is associated with unfavorable preinformation and an unfavorable perception. The data from the other study support this result and also indicate the correctness of the second part of the hypothesis, that restricted interaction reduces the likelihood of change in the attitude.

What makes these findings more significant is that they appear in the context of a discussion class where there are numerous *induced* and *own* forces to enter the discussion and to interact with the instructor. It seems likely that the effects predicted by Newcomb's hypothesis would be much more marked in a setting where such forces were not present.

SUMMARY

The warm-cold variable had been found by Asch to produce large differences in the impressions of personality formed from a list of adjectives. In this study the same variable was introduced in the form of expectations about a real person and was found to produce similar differences in first impressions of him in a classroom setting. In addition, the differences in first impressions produced by the different expectations were shown to influence the observers' behavior toward the stimulus person. Those observers given the favorable expectation (who, consequently, had a favorable impression of the stimulus person) tended to interact more with him than did those given the unfavorable expectation.

REFERENCES

1. Asch, S. E., Forming impressions of personality. *J. Abnorm. Soc. Psychol.*, 1946, 41, 258–290.
2. Katz, D., and Braly, K. W. Verbal stereotypes and racial prejudice. In Newcomb, T. M. and Hartley, E. L. (eds.), *Readings in social psychology.* New York: Holt, 1947. Pp. 204–210.
3. Kelley, H. H. First impressions in interpersonal relations. Ph.D. thesis, Massachusetts Institute of Technology, Cambridge, Mass. Sept., 1948.
4. Krech, D., and Crutchfield, R. S. *Theory and problems of social psychology.* New York, McGraw-Hill, 1948.
5. Luchins, A. S. Forming impressions of personality: A critique. *J. Abnorm. Soc. Psychol.*, 1948, 43, 318–325.

6. Mensch, I. N., and Wishner, J. Asch on "Forming impressions of personality": further evidence. *J. Personal.*, 1947, 16, 188–191.

7. Newcomb, T. M. Autistic hostility and social reality. *Hum. Relations.*, 1947, 1, 69–86.

8. Newstetter, W. I., Feldstein, M. H., and Newcomb, T. M. *Group adjustment: A study in experimental sociology.* Cleveland: Western Reserve University, 1938.

ENDNOTES

1. Since the present experiment was carried out, Mensch and Wishner (6) have repeated a number of Asch's experiments because of dissatisfaction with his sex and geographic distribution. Their data substantiate Asch's very closely. Also, Luchins (5) has criticized Asch's experiments for their artificial methodology, repeated some of them, and challenged some of the kinds of interpretations Asch made from his data. Luchins also briefly reports some tantalizing conclusions from a number of studies of first impressions of actual persons.

2. Professor Mason Haire, now of the University of California, provided valuable advice and help in executing the experiment.

3. We must raise an important question here: Would there be a tendency for "warm" observers to distort the perception in the favorable direction regardless of how much the stimulus deviated from the expectation? Future research should test the following hypothesis, which is suggested by Gestalt perception theory (4, pp. 95–98): If the stimulus differs but slightly from the expectation, the perception will tend to be *assimilated* to the expectation; however, if the difference between the stimulus and expectation is too great, the perception will occur by contrast to the expectation and will be distorted in the opposite direction.

CRITICAL THINKING QUESTIONS

1. Reread the information that was presented to the subjects to manipulate the warm-cold variable. The manipulation obviously produced a significant effect on the subjects' subsequent evaluations of the teacher. Do you feel that the manipulation was realistic? For example, how realistic is it to have a guest teacher described as "rather cold" in a brief biographical sketch? Could this particular manipulation have resulted in any experimental demand characteristics? Address the issue of the relative importance of experimental versus mundane realism as it pertains to this study.

2. How long lasting do you think first impressions are? For example, would they persist over the course of a semester or even longer? How could you test this?

3. What are the practical implications of this study? If you were working in a setting where you were interviewing and hiring applicants for a job, how could you use this information to help you make better, more accurate decisions?

4. The warm-cold information was provided by the instructor of the course, a person who presumably had high credibility. Do you think the credibility of the source of the information would affect how influenced the individuals were? How could you test this?

ADDITIONAL RELATED READINGS

Evans, D. C., Hart, A. J., & Hicks, J. C. (2003). Are race and gender central or peripheral traits? Examining evaluative amplification of personality impressions in the classic Asch paradigm. *Current Research in Social Psychology, 9*(7), 1–13.

Pontari, B. A., & Schlenker, B. R. (2004). Providing and withholding impression management support for romantic partners: Gender of the audience matters. *Journal of Experimental Social Psychology, 40*(1), 41–51.

ARTICLE 6 _____

As discussed in Article 4 on first impressions, we use a variety of information in forming judgments of other people. Yet this process also seems to occur quite quickly. In fact, as that article points out, we often draw conclusions about people we meet in as little as three seconds!

Some of the information that we use in forming initial impressions of people is based on stereotypes of what they look like or whom they remind us of, but even more information is obtained from watching their nonverbal cues. Why is this the case? Simply put, many of the things that people do are under their direct control. For example, the words that we choose to speak are subject to our conscious influence and hence can be readily manipulated. But our nonverbal behavior, such as the body movements that accompany our words, are somewhat less under conscious control. Furthermore, while we are better able to select the words we speak, we may be less aware of—and thus able to control— changes in our speech patterns (known as *paralanguage*), such as pausing, pitch of voice, and rate of speech. An observer may give the nonverbal and paralanguage cues more weight than what we actually say because those cues may seem a more honest reflection of what we are really all about.

One obvious practical application of the use of nonverbal and paralanguage cues is to detect deception. Being able to tell when someone is lying to us has real advantages. Research suggests that lying is a fairly common part of human interaction. Occasionally, these falsehoods take the form of bold-faced lies, such as making up a story to get out of trouble for something we have done. More commonly, however, we use so-called white lies to skirt the truth and perhaps not hurt someone's feelings ("Yes, dear, I really loved the vacuum cleaner you gave me for Christmas").

But how accurate are most of us in detecting such deceptions? Furthermore, are trained professionals, such as police and customs agents, better at detecting deception than the average person? A good deal of research suggests that most people, including law-enforcment professionals, are not particularly accurate in determining when someone is lying. However, most of this research was conducted in a laboratory or experimental setting. As such, it may have some limitations that make generalizing its findings to the real world difficult. The following article by Samantha Mann, Aldert Vrij, and Ray Bull overcomes these limitations by assessing the lie-detecting ability of police officers who are exposed to actual videotapes of confessions. From this research, the authors make corresponding implications for the real world of police work.

Detecting True Lies
Police Officers' Ability to Detect Suspects' Lies

■ Samantha Mann, Aldert Vrij, and Ray Bull

Ninety-nine police officers, not identified in previous research as belonging to groups that are superior in lie detection, attempted to detect truths and lies told by suspects during their videotaped police interviews. Accuracy rates were higher than those typically found in deception research and reached levels similar to those obtained by specialized lie detectors in previous research. Accuracy was positively correlated with perceived experience in interviewing suspects and with mentioning cues to detecting deceit that relate to a suspect's story. Accuracy was negatively correlated with popular stereotypical cues such as gaze aversion and fidgeting. As in previous research, accuracy and confidence were not significantly correlated, but the level of confidence was dependent on whether officers judged actual truths or actual lies and on the method by which confidence was measured.

OVERVIEW

Police manuals give the impression that experienced police detectives make good lie detectors (Inbau, Reid, Buckley, & Jayne, 2001), though this claim has not been supported by previous research. The present study is unique, as we tested police officers' ability to distinguish between truths and lies in a realistic setting (during police interviews with suspects), rather than in an artificial laboratory setting. This provides us with a more valid test of Inbau et al.'s claim. Apart from testing truth and lie detection ability, we also examined what characterizes good and poor lie detectors. On the basis of the available deception research, we argue that paying attention to cues promoted in police manuals (gaze aversion, fidgeting, etc.) actually hampers ability to detect truths and lies.

Accuracy Rates and Their Relationships with Background Characteristics

In scientific studies concerning the detection of deception, observers are typically given videotaped or audiotaped statements from a number of people who are either lying or telling the truth. After each statement, observers are asked to judge whether the statement is true or false. In a review of all the literature available at the time, Kraut (1980) found an accuracy rate (percentage of correct answers) of 57%, which is a low score because 50% accuracy can be expected by chance alone. (Guessing whether someone is lying or not gives a 50% chance of being correct.) Vrij (2000a) reviewed an additional 39 studies that were published after 1980 (the year of Kraut's publication) and found an almost identical accuracy rate of 56.6%. In a minority of studies, accuracy in detecting lies was computed separately from accuracy in detecting truth. Where this did occur, results showed a *truth bias;* that is, judges are more likely to consider that messages are truthful than deceptive and, as a result, truthful messages are identified with relatively high accuracy (67%) and deceptive messages with relatively low accuracy (44%). In fact, 44% is below the level of chance, and people would be more accurate at detecting lies if they simply guessed. One explanation for the truth bias is that in daily life, most people are more often confronted with truthful than with deceptive statements and so are therefore more inclined to assume that the behavior they observe is honest (the so-called availability heuristic; O'Sullivan, Ekman, & Friesen, 1988).

Both reviews (Kraut, 1980; Vrij, 2000a) included studies in which college students tried to detect lies and truths in people they were not familiar with. It could be argued that college students are not habitually called on to detect deception. Perhaps professional lie catchers, such as police officers or customs officers, would obtain higher accuracy rates than laypersons. In several studies, professional lie catchers were exposed to videotaped footage of liars and truth tellers and their ability to detect lies was tested (see Vrij & Mann, 2001b, for a review). Three findings emerged from these studies. First, most total accuracy rates were sim-

Reprinted from *Journal of Applied Psychology,* 2004, *89*(1), 137–149. Copyright © 2004 by the American Psychological Association. Reprinted with permission.

ilar to those found in studies with college students as observers, falling in the 45%–60% range. DePaulo and Pfeifer (1986), Meissner and Kassin (2002), and Vrij and Graham (1997) found that police officers were as (un)successful as university students in detecting deception (accuracy rates around 50%). Ekman and O'Sullivan (1991) found that police officers and polygraph examiners obtained similar accuracy rates to university students (accuracy rates around 55%). Second, some groups seem to be better than others. Ekman's research has shown that members of the Secret Service (64% accuracy rates), Central Intelligence Agency (73% accuracy rates), and sheriffs (67% accuracy rates) were better lie detectors than other groups of lie detectors (Ekman & O'Sullivan, 1991; Ekman, O'Sullivan, & Frank, 1999). Third, the truth bias, consistently found in studies with students as observers, is much less profound, or perhaps even lacking, in studies with professional lie catchers (Ekman et al., 1999; Meissner & Kassin, 2002; Porter, Woodworth, & Birt, 2000). Perhaps the nature of their work makes professional lie catchers more wary about the possibility that they are being lied to.

In summary, even the accuracy rates for most professional lie catchers are modest, raising serious doubt about their ability to detect deceit. However, these disappointing accuracy levels may be the result of an artifact. In typical deception studies, including those with professional lie catchers, observers detect truths and lies told by college students who are asked to lie and tell the truth for the sake of the experiment in university laboratories. Perhaps in these laboratory studies the stakes (negative consequences of being caught and positive consequences of getting away with the lie) are not high enough for the liar to exhibit clear deceptive cues to deception (Miller & Stiff, 1993), which makes the lie detection task virtually impossible for the observer.

To raise the stakes in laboratory experiments, participants are offered money if they successfully get away with their lies (Vrij, 1995), or participants (e.g., nursing students) are told that being a good liar is an important indicator of success in a future career (Ekman & Friesen, 1974; Vrij, Edward, & Bull, 2001a, 2001b). In some studies, participants are told that they will be observed by a peer who will judge their sincerity (DePaulo, Stone, & Lassiter, 1985b). In a series of experiments in which the stakes were manipulated, researchers found that such "high-stakes" lies were easier to detect than low-stakes lies (Bond & Atoum, 2000; DePaulo, Kirkendol, Tang, & O'Brien, 1988; DePaulo, Lanier, & Davis, 1983; DePaulo, LeMay, & Epstein, 1991; DePaulo et al., 1985b; Feeley & deTurck, 1998; Forrest & Feldman, 2000; Heinrich & Borkenau, 1998; Lane & DePaulo, 1999; Vrij, 2000b; Vrij, Harden, Terry, Edward, & Bull, 2001).

In an attempt to raise the stakes even further, participants in Frank and Ekman's (1997) study were given the opportunity to "steal" $50. If they could convince the interviewer that they had not taken the money, they could keep all of it. If they took the money and the interviewer judged them as lying, they had to give back the $50 in addition to their $10 per hour participation fee. Moreover, some participants faced an additional punishment if they were found to be lying. They were told that they would have to sit on a cold metal chair inside a cramped, darkened room ominously labeled *XXX,* where they would have to endure anything from 10 to 40 randomly sequenced, 110-decibel starting blasts of white noise over the course of 1 hr.

A deception study like this probably borders on unethical, and yet the stakes are still not comparable with the stakes in real-life situations in which professional lie catchers operate, such as during police interviews. Therefore, one might argue that the only valid way to investigate police officers' true ability to detect deceit is to examine their skills when they detect lies and truths that are told in real-life criminal investigation settings. Vrij and Mann (2001a, 2001b) were the first researchers to do this. Vrij and Mann (2001a) exposed police officers to fragments of a videotaped police interview with a man suspected of murder. However, that study had two limitations. First, fragments of only one suspect were shown, and second, the police officers could not understand the suspect because he spoke a foreign language (suspect and police officers were of different nationalities). Vrij and Mann (2001b) later exposed judges to videotaped press conferences of people who were asking the general public for help in finding either their missing relatives or the murderers of their relatives. They all lied during these press conferences, and they were all subsequently found guilty of having killed the "missing person" themselves. This study had limitations as well.

First, the judges were only subjected to lies, and, second, again the lie detectors and liars spoke in different languages, as they were from different nationalities.

We overcame these limitations in the present experiment. We exposed British police officers to fragments of videotaped real-life police interviews with English-speaking suspects and asked them to detect truths and lies told by these suspects during these interviews. We expected truth and lie accuracy rates to be significantly above the level of chance (which is 50%), and, as a consequence of this, expected lie accuracy rates to be significantly higher than those typically found in previous research (44%; Hypothesis 1). In view of the fact that police officers in the present study were assessing the veracity of suspects, a group that is likely to arouse heightened skepticism in a police officer (Moston, Stephenson, & Williamson, 1992), a truth bias is unlikely to occur.

We also expected individual differences, with some police officers being more skilled at detecting truths and lies than others. We predicted that the reported experience in interviewing suspects would be positively correlated with truth and lie accuracy (Hypothesis 2). This background characteristic has not been examined in deception research before, but we expected it to be related to accuracy, as it is this particular aspect of police work that gives police officers experience in detecting lies and truths. Previous research has focused on the relationship between length of service/years of job experience and accuracy, and a significant relationship between the two was not found (Ekman & O'Sullivan, 1991; Porter et al., 2000; Vrij & Mann, 2001b). This is not surprising, as an officer who has served in the police force for many years will not necessarily have a great deal of experience in interviewing suspects, and vice versa. Other background characteristics, such as age and gender, have generally not been found to be related to accuracy (DePaulo, Epstein, & Wyer, 1993; Ekman & O'Sullivan, 1991; Ekman et al., 1999; Hurd & Noller, 1988; Köhnken, 1987; Manstead, Wagner, & MacDonald, 1986; Porter et al., 2000; Vrij & Mann, 2001b).

Cues Used to Detect Deceit

We asked lie detectors to indicate which verbal and nonverbal cues they typically use to decide whether someone is lying, so-called beliefs about cues associated with deception (DePaulo, Stone, & Lassiter, 1985a; Zuckerman, DePaulo, & Rosenthal, 1981). We expected good lie detectors to mention speech-related cues significantly more often than poor lie detectors (Hypothesis 3). In part, this is because research has shown that the intellectual ability of suspects who are interviewed by the police is often rather low. Gudjonsson (1994) measured intellectual functioning with three subtests of the Wechsler Adult Intelligence Scale–Revised (WAIS–R; Wechsler, 1981)—Vocabulary, Comprehension, and Picture Completion—and found a mean IQ of 82, with a range of 61–131. It might well be that people with a low IQ will find it hard to tell a lie that sounds plausible and convincing (Ekman & Frank, 1993). Moreover, in their review of detection of deception research, DePaulo et al. (1985a) found that lie detectors who read transcripts only (and are therefore "forced" to focus on story cues) are typically better lie detectors than those who are exposed to the actual person (speech, sound, and behavior; see also Wiseman, 1995).

Stereotypical views typically held among professional lie catchers (and also laypersons) is that liars look away and fidget (Akehurst, Köhnken, Vrij, & Bull, 1996; Vrij & Semin, 1996). These cues, however, are unrelated to deception (see DePaulo, Lindsay, Malone, Muhlenbruck, Charlton, & Cooper, 2003; Vrij, 2000a, for reviews about nonverbal and verbal cues to deceit). We therefore expected negative correlations between mentioning such cues and accuracy rates; in other words, the more of these cues the officers reported to look at, the lower their accuracy rates would become (Hypothesis 4).

In their influential manual about police interviewing, *Criminal Interrogation and Confessions,* Inbau, Reid, and Buckley (1986; a new edition was recently published; Inbau et al., 2001) described in detail how, in their view, liars behave. As evidence, the authors included showing gaze aversion, displaying unnatural posture changes, exhibiting self-manipulations, and placing the hand over the mouth or eyes when speaking. None of these behaviors have been found to be reliably related to lying in deception research. It is therefore not surprising that participants in a deception detection study by Kassin and Fong (1999), who were trained to look at the cues Inbau and colleagues claim to be related to deception, actually performed worse than naive observers who did not receive any information about deceptive behavior. In the present study, we expected negative correlations between reporting "Inbau cues" and accuracy. In other words, the more of these Inbau cues that police officers mentioned that they use to detect deceit, the worse we expected them to be at distinguishing between truths and lies (Hypothesis 5).

We also examined whether the cues lie detectors used to make their veracity judgments were related to the behaviors shown by the suspects in the videotape (so-called cues to perceived deception; Zuckerman et al., 1981).[1] We predicted that poor lie detectors would be significantly more guided by invalid cues, such as gaze aversion, than good lie detectors (Hypothesis 6).

Accuracy–Confidence Relationship

Studies investigating lie detectors' confidence in their decision making typically reveal three findings. First, there is usually no significant relationship between confidence and accuracy (see DePaulo, Charlton, Cooper, Lindsay, & Muhlenbruck, 1997, for a meta-analysis). Second, confidence scores among professional lie catchers are typically high (Allwood & Granhag, 1999; DePaulo & Pfeifer, 1986; Strömwall, 2001; Vrij, 1993), and police officers are sometimes found to be more confident than laypersons (Allwood & Granhag, 1999; DePaulo & Pfeifer, 1986). Furthermore, DePaulo et al. (1997) found an "overconfidence effect"; that is, judges' confidence is typically higher than their accuracy. Third, observers tend to have higher levels of confidence when judging truthful statements than when judging deceptive statements, irrespective of whether they judge the statement as a truth or a lie (DePaulo et al., 1997).

In the present study, confidence was investigated in two different ways. First, it was investigated in the traditional way, by asking observers after each veracity judgment how confident they were of their decision. Second, we also asked participants at the end of the lie detection experiment how well they thought they had done at the task. This latter method of measuring confidence may well result in more accurate confidence levels (less prone to an overconfidence effect), because at that stage lie detectors have insight into their overall performance and are asked to judge this overall per-

formance. For this reason the latter method may even result in a positive relationship between accuracy and confidence. This issue was explored in the present study.

METHOD

Participants

Ninety-nine Kent County Police Officers (Kent, England) participated. Of these, 24 were women and 75 were men. Ages ranged from 22 years to 52 years, with a mean average of 34.3 years (*SD* = 7.40 years). Seventy-eight participants were from the Criminal Investigation Department (CID), 8 were police trainers, 4 were traffic officers, and the remaining 9 were uniform response officers. Although different groups of police officers participated, none of these groups are the specialized groups that are identified by Ekman and his colleagues as particularly good lie detectors (Ekman & O'Sullivan, 1991; Ekman et al., 1999). As some of the group sizes are rather small, differences between groups are not discussed in the main text.

Length of service on the job ranged from 1 year to 30 years, with a mean average of 11.2 years (*SD* = 7.31 years). The distribution of this variable differed significantly from a normal distribution (*z* = 1.83, *p* < .01, skewness = .94, *Mdn* = 9 years).

Materials

Participants in this study were asked to judge the veracity of people in real-life high-stakes situations. More specifically, participants saw video clips of 14 suspects (of whom 12 were men, 4 of whom were juvenile, and 2 were women) in their police interviews. The interview rooms were fitted with a fixed camera, which produces the main color picture and is aimed at the suspect's chair, and a small insert picture, produced by a wide lens camera. The picture in the small insert was not of good quality and displayed the whole interview room from the view taken at the back of the suspect. The purpose of the wide lens insert is to show how many people are present in the room and any larger movements made by any person present (therefore proving or disproving that the officers might have physically threatened or coerced the suspect in some way).[2] The quality of the main picture was good enough to code the occurrences of eye blinks, but not good enough to see subtler facial changes. Sound quality was good in all interviews. The positioning of the cameras varied slightly, depending on which interview room the interview was conducted, but in all cases the suspect's upper torso could be seen. However, in some cases the lower torso could not be seen, hence leg and foot movements were not analyzed.[3] In the main picture only the suspect was visible. Crimes about which the suspects were being interviewed included theft (9), arson (2), attempted rape (1), and murder (2). Cases had been chosen in which other sources (reliable, independent witness statements and forensic evidence) provided evidence that the suspect told the truth and lied at various points within the interview. Once a case had been selected, only those particular clips in which each word was known to be a truth or a lie were selected. The truths that were selected were chosen so as to be as comparable as possible in nature to the lies (e.g., a truthful response to an easy question such as giving a name and address is not comparable to a deceitful response regarding whether the suspect had committed a murder. Video footage about names and addresses were therefore not included as truths in this study). The following account is an example of one of the cases used: The suspect (a juvenile) spent the night in a derelict building with a friend. With the friend, he shot at windows of a neighboring house with his air rifle and then stole items from a local shop. The suspect denied involvement in any of those activities and provided an alibi. His friend (the alibi), however, immediately admitted to both his and the suspect's part in the offenses. The suspect's alibi fell through, and so the suspect confessed to the crimes and told police of the whereabouts of the stolen goods, his gun, and from where he purchased it. The suspect admitted guilt and was charged accordingly. Lies included in clips were the initial denials of any involvement in the crimes. It is important to point out that, rather than take the form of a straightforward "No, I didn't do it" and "Yes, I did do it," all clips used in this study contained story elements that were true and false. So in the above example, in the denial the suspect gave an alternative story of the events of the day to those that actually occurred (that he went over to another friend's house, etc.), and in the confession he gave a

true version of events, not all of which was necessarily incriminating. Therefore, a participant watching the clips, who does not know the facts of the case, would not easily be able to tell what are snippets of denial and what are snippets of confession. See Mann, Vrij, and Bull (2002) for further details.[4]

The length of each clip unavoidably varied considerably (from 6 s to 145 s). There were 54 clips total (23 truthful clips and 31 deceptive clips), and the number of clips for each suspect varied between a minimum of 2 and a maximum of 8 clips (each suspect with at least one example of a truth and a lie). The total length of the video clips of all 14 suspects was approximately 1 hr. Clearly it would be impossible to show each participant all the clips because of logistical constraints and fatigue. Therefore, the clips were divided between four tapes of roughly equal length, and 24–25 participants saw each clip. As mentioned above, the length of the clips varied, and so each of the four tapes contained between 10 and 16 clips (Clip 1: $n = 15$, 6 truths and 9 lies; Clip 2: $n = 16$, 6 truths and 10 lies; Clip 3: $n = 10$, 5 truths and 5 lies; Clip 4: $n = 13$, 6 truths and 7 lies). Those suspects for whom there were several clips may have had clips spread over several of the tapes. However, for each suspect there was always at least one example of a lie and a truth present on each tape on which they appeared. Clips were presented on the tapes in random order so that the same suspect did not appear in consecutive clips. Two analyses of variance (ANOVAs), with tape as the between-subjects factor and lie accuracy and truth accuracy as dependent variables were conducted to examine possible differences in accuracy between the four tapes. Neither of the two ANOVAs were significant for truth accuracy, $F(3, 95) = 0.20$, *ns*, $\eta^2 = .00$; or for lie accuracy, $F(3, 95) = 1.57$, *ns*, $\eta^2 = .05$. Hence, the fact that participants did not all judge exactly the same clips was not considered an issue, and accuracy scores were collapsed over the four tapes in all subsequent analyses.

Procedure

Permission to approach police officers was granted by the Chief Constable in the first instance, and then by appropriate superintendents. Participants were recruited on duty from either the training college where they were attending courses or various police stations within Kent. Participants were approached and asked whether they would participate in a study about police officers' ability to detect deception and informed that their participation would be anonymous. Participants completed the deception detection task individually. Before attempting the task, participants filled out a questionnaire. This included details such as age, gender, length of service, division, perceived level of experience in interviewing suspects (1 = *totally inexperienced*, 5 = *highly experienced; M* = 3.75, *SD* = 0.85), and the verbal or nonverbal cues they use to decide whether another person is lying or telling the truth. After completion of this section, each participant was then read the following instructions: "You are about to see a selection of clips of suspects who are either lying or telling the truth. The clips vary considerably in length, and the suspects may appear on several occasions. This is irrelevant. They will be either lying the whole length of the clip or truth-telling for the length of the clip. After viewing each clip I would like you to indicate whether you think the suspect is lying or telling the truth (measured with a dichotomous scale), and how confident you are of your decision, on a seven-point scale. If you recognize any of the suspects please bring it to my attention." (This latter point was not an issue.) Participants were not informed of how many clips they were going to see, or of how many instances of lies and truths they would see.

After completing the task, participants answered a remaining few questions on the questionnaire. These included questions about what behaviors they had used to guide them in making veracity judgments and questions measuring their confidence. Depending on the participant, participation time lasted between 45 and 90 min. After each veracity judgment, participants were shown each clip again and were asked several questions about the clip. This (time-consuming) part of the experiment is beyond the scope of this article and is therefore not addressed further (see Mann, 2001, for further details about this aspect of the study). The variation in participation time was the result of several factors. Some participants took longer than others to complete their forms; some participants took slightly longer to reach a decision, but the largest time range was in the amount of time taken, and

detail given, in responding to the questions that were asked about each clip after the veracity judgment had been given.

Dependent Variables

The dependent variables for this study were the accuracy scores, the behaviors that participants associated with deception before and after the task, cues to perceived deception, and their confidence scores during and after the task.

Accuracy was calculated by assigning a score of 1 when the participant correctly identified a truth or a lie, and assigning a score of 0 when the participant was incorrect. The lie accuracy score was calculated by dividing the number of correctly classified lies by the number of lies shown on the tape, and the truth accuracy score was calculated by dividing the number of correctly classified truths by the number of truths shown on the tape.

The behaviors that participants typically use to detect deception were investigated with the open-ended question, "What verbal or nonverbal cues do you use to decide whether another person is lying or telling the truth?" The behaviors that participants said they used in the present lie detection task were investigated with the open-ended question, "What verbal or nonverbal cues did you use in this task to decide whether the people on the screen were lying or telling the truth?" In other words, cues to deception both prior to and after the deception task were investigated. A similar procedure was used by Ekman and O'Sullivan (1991). Asking this question twice enabled us to explore whether, in our deception task, the police officers paid attention to cues they typically consider they pay attention to. In case they did, the answers they would give to the "prior" and "after" questions would be similar, whereas the answers would be different in case they did not. We expected similar responses. We had no reason to believe that the police officers would find the responses of the suspects atypical (they were a random sample of suspects' responses in connection with serious crimes), nor did we think that officers would change their mind about beliefs about deception on the basis of a single lie detection task. We return to this issue in the Discussion section. These two open-ended questions were coded by two coders into 30 different cues. Appendix A shows the list of 30 cues.

This list was the result of sorting and tallying all participants' comments into various groups and combining them as much as possible within specific headings to make the system as manageable as possible. Once the coding system was created, the creator coded for each participant every behavior that they mentioned on the questionnaire before and after the task. Another independent coder then used the coding system also to code each behavior mentioned by participants on the questionnaires to determine the reliability of the coding system. For each participant, each code was used a maximum of one time before the task and one time after the task. So, for example, if a participant said before the task "eyes looking up, looking away from interviewer, high-pitched voice, vocally loud," then just the codes gaze and voice would be recorded, even though, in effect, the participant mentioned two aspects of gaze and two aspects of voice. For the 99 participants, 677 behaviors mentioned on the questionnaires before and after completing the task were coded. Hence, each participant mentioned a mean of 6.84 behaviors. In 651 (96.2%) of the 677 mentioned behaviors, the two coders agreed; any disagreements were resolved by discussion. Twenty-nine of those categories could be clustered into four categories: story, vocal, body, and conduct (see the second column of Appendix A). Those four categories have been introduced by Feeley and Young (2000). The total number of times each participant mentioned behaviors in each group was calculated. So, for example, if a participant mentioned gaze aversion and movements, that participant would obtain a score of 2 for the body category. As a result, the scores for story cues could range from 0 to 6, the scores for vocal cues from 0 to 5, the scores for body cues from 0 to 14, and the scores for conduct cues from 0 to 4. One cue, gut feeling, could not be included in any of these categories, and we therefore analyze the data for this cue separately.

To compare good and poor lie detectors, we followed Ekman and O'Sullivan's (1991) procedure and divided the lie detectors into two ability groups. Good lie detectors ($n = 27$) were those who had scored above the mean for lie clips (66.16%, see the Results section) and above the mean for truth clips (63.61%, see the

Results section). Poor lie detectors ($n = 72$) were those who remained, who may well have scored very well on either truth clips or lie clips, but did not score above the mean for both.

To test Hypothesis 4, we constructed new variables: "Popular stereotypical beliefs" (one variable was created for cues mentioned before the task and one for cues mentioned after the task). These variables included three cues (gaze, fidget, and self-manipulation) and could range from 0 to 3.

To test Hypothesis 5, two further new variables were created: Inbau cues (again, separate variables were created for cues mentioned before the task and cues mentioned after the task). Inbau cues included the following five cues: posture, cover, gaze, fidget, and self-manipulation; they could range from 0 to 5.

To examine cues to perceived deception, 13 behaviors of the suspects in the clips were scored by two independent coders with a coding scheme used previously by Vrij and colleagues (Vrij, 1995; Vrij et al., 2001a, 2001b; Vrij, Edward, Roberts, & Bull, 2000; Vrij, Semin, & Bull, 1996; Vrij & Winkel, 1991). An overview of these behaviors and the interrater agreement rates between the two coders (Pearson correlations) are reported in Appendix B. Differences between truth tellers and liars regarding these behaviors have been discussed elsewhere in detail (Mann et al., 2002). To summarize the findings, liars blinked less and included more pauses in their speech.

Confidence was measured in two ways. First, participants indicated after each veracity judgment how confident they were in their decision (1 = *not at all confident*, and 7 = *very confident*). Second, after completing the lie detection task, the participants were also asked to answer the open-ended question, "What percentage of answers do you think you answered correctly?"

RESULTS

Accuracy Rates and Their Relationships with Background Characteristics

For the whole sample, the mean lie accuracy was 66.16% ($SD = 17.0$), and the mean truth accuracy was 63.61% ($SD = 22.5$). The difference between lie and truth accuracy was not significant, $t(98) = 0.87$, *ns, d* = 0.09; neither were lie and truth accuracy *t*(98) significantly correlated with each other, *r*(99) = .08, *ns*.[5]

Both accuracy rates were significantly higher than the level of chance, which is 50%; truth accuracy, *t*(98) = 6.02, *p* < .01, *d* = 0.60; lie accuracy, *t*(98) = 9.43, *p* < .01, *d* = 0.95. (See Clark-Carter, 1997, for conducting *t* tests when the standard deviation of the sample is unknown.) Moreover, the lie accuracy rate was significantly higher than the average lie accuracy rate that was found in Vrij's (2000a) review of previous research (lie accuracy: *M* = 66.16% vs. 44.00%), *t*(98) = 12.93, *p* < .01, *d* = 1.30. Truth accuracy did not differ significantly from what has previously been found (63.61% vs. 67.00%), *t*(98) = 1.50, *ns, d* = 0.15. This supports Hypothesis 1.

Pearson correlations revealed that experience in interviewing, however, was significantly correlated with truth accuracy, *r*(99) = .20, *p* < .05. The correlation with lie accuracy was *r*(99) = .18, *p* = .07. These positive correlations indicate that the more experienced the police officers perceived themselves to be in interviewing suspects, the better they were in the lie detection task. This supports Hypothesis 2. Age and length of service were unrelated to lie accuracy, *r*(99) = −.09, *ns*, and *r*(99) = −.04, *ns*, respectively; and truth accuracy, *r*(99) = .01, *ns*, and *r*(99) = −.07, *ns*, respectively. Age and length of service were strongly correlated, *r*(99) = .80, *p* < .01; whereas age and experience in interviewing, *r*(99) = .34, *p* < .01, and experience in interviewing and length of service, *r*(99) = .46, *p* < .01, were moderately correlated.

Men were significantly better at detecting truths (*M* = 66.61%, *SD* = 21.9) than women (*M* = 54.22%, *SD* = 22.3), *t*(97) = 2.40, *p* < .05, *d* = 0.56; but no differences were found for detecting lies, *t*(97)= .41, *ns, d* = 0.09 (*M* = 66.56%, *SD* = 17.0 vs. *M* = 64.92%, *SD* = 17.7).[6]

Cues Used to Detect Deceit

Appendix A shows how many police officers mentioned that they use the cues to detect deceit before and after the task. The most frequently mentioned cue was gaze, with 73% of the officers (*n* = 72) mentioning the cue before the task and 78% (*n* = 77) after the task. The second most frequently mentioned cue was

movements, which was mentioned by 25 police officers before the task and by 31 officers after the task. Also vagueness, contradictions, miscellaneous speech (a category for speech-related cues that does not fit into other categories, e.g., pleading/minimizing offense or uncertain replies; all story cues), and fidgeting were relatively frequently mentioned.

ANOVAs comparing how many cues were mentioned in each category (ANOVA, with cue category—story, vocal, body, and conduct—as the single within-subjects factor) showed significant differences in the number of cues mentioned, both before the task, *F*(3, 96) = 58.56, *p* < .01, η^2 = .65; and after the task, *F*(3, 96) = 85.61, *p* < .01, η^2 = .73. Before the task, police officers mentioned a mean of 1.84 body cues (*SD* = 1.05; see also Table 1). Tukey's honestly significant difference test revealed that this is significantly more than any of the other three categories of cues. They also mentioned significantly more story cues than conduct and vocal cues before the task. The latter two categories did not differ significantly from each other. Exactly the same pattern emerged for cues mentioned after the task.

To compare the number of cues mentioned before and after the task, we conducted a multivariate analysis of variance (MANOVA), with time (before or after) as the within-subjects factor and the four categories of cues as dependent variables. At a multivariate level, the test revealed a nonsignificant effect, *F*(4, 95) = 1.91, *ns*, η^2 = .07. In other words, the lie detection task did not influence the police officers' ideas about which cues to attend to in order to detect deceit.

TABLE 1 / Overview of the Total Number of Times Each Participant Mentioned Story, Vocal, Body, and Conduct Cues Before and After the Task

Cue	Before the Task		After the Task	
	M	*SD*	*M*	*SD*
Story	0.68b	0.62	0.78b	0.72
Vocal	0.40a	0.59	0.48a	0.61
Body	1.84c	1.05	2.01c	0.96
Conduct	0.32a	0.49	0.28a	0.50

Note: Only mean scores in the columns with a different subscript differ significantly from each other.

However, if we look at individual cues (see Appendix A), rather than the categories, differences emerged regarding some cues. Sharp increases in cues mentioned (between before and after the task) occurred for self-corrections, miscellaneous speech, hand movements and head movements; and sharp decreases were found for contradictions, evidence, facial cues and physiological cues; the latter findings might be the result of the experimental setting. For example, noticing physiological cues might be difficult when watching a tape, hence, in this lie detection task, participants did not look for such cues to detect deceit.

To investigate and compare behaviors mentioned by good and poor lie detectors, we conducted ANOVAs, with skill (good or poor lie detector) as the between-subjects factor and the four cue categories as dependent variables. As predicted in Hypothesis 3, good lie detectors were more inclined to claim that they focused on story cues ($M = .89$, $SD = .60$) than poor lie detectors ($M = .60$, $SD = .60$), $F(1, 97) = 4.50$, $p < .05$, $\eta^2 = .04$; although this effect only occurred for the story cues mentioned before the task. All other effects were not significant.[7]

For the remaining cue, gut feeling, we used chi-square analyses to compare responses from good and poor lie detectors. After the lie detection task, none of the 72 poor lie detectors said that they had relied on gut feeling, whereas 11% ($n = 3$) of the good lie detectors claimed to have relied on such intuitive feelings, $\chi^2(1, N = 99) = 8.05$, $p < .01$, $\phi = .29$. The analysis for mentioning gut feeling before the task was not significant, $\chi^2(1, N = 99) = 2.63$, ns, $\phi = .17$.[8]

ANOVAs further revealed that good and poor lie detectors did not differ significantly from each other

on the newly created variables popular stereotypical beliefs and Inbau cues. A disadvantage of using a dichotomization procedure (i.e., dividing the lie detectors into two groups) is a loss in data measurement, because many participants are treated alike in a dichotomy when in fact they are different. An alternative method is to keep the continuous lie and truth accuracy scores. Pearson correlations (see Table 2) revealed that mentioning popular stereotypical beliefs and Inbau cues (both before and after the task) were negatively correlated with accuracy. This supports Hypotheses 4 and 5.[9]

To investigate cues to perception, we conducted multiple stepwise regression analyses. The units of analysis were the 54 different clips. The criterion was the percentage of police officers who judged the suspect in the clip as lying. The predictors were the behaviors displayed by the suspects (13 behaviors were entered, see the Method section), the veracity of the suspects' statements, and age (adult or juvenile) and gender of the suspects. Different analyses were carried out for good and poor lie detectors. The analysis for good lie detectors revealed two predictors, which explained 61% of the variance, $F(2, 51) = 40.16$, $p < .01$; these were veracity of the clip ($R = .76$, $\beta = .74$), $t(53) = 8.48$, $p < .01$, and illustrators ($R = .02$, $\beta = -.19$), $t(53) = 2.18$, $p < .05$. Participants were most likely to judge the clip as deceptive if the clip was in fact a lie, and the fewer illustrators the suspects made, the more likely it was that they were judged as deceptive.

The analysis for poor lie detectors revealed four predictors, which explained 51% of the variance, $F(4, 49) = 12.60$, $p < .01$. These were gender of the suspect ($R = .38$, $\beta = .57$), $t(53) = 5.14$, $p < .01$; veracity of the

TABLE 2 / Pearson Correlations between Popular Stereotypical Beliefs and Inbau Cues with Truth Accuracy and Lie Accuracy

Variable	Before the Task		After the Task	
	Truth Accuracy	Lie Accuracy	Truth Accuracy	Lie Accuracy
Popular stereotypical beliefs	−.21*	−.02	−.22*	−.08
Inbau cues	−.23*	−.06	−.23*	−.05

Note: *$p < .05$.

clip (R = .18, β = .42), t(53) = 4.06, p < .01; gaze aversion (R = .10, β = .41), t(53) = 4.02, p < .01; and head nods (R = .04, β = .25), t(53) = 2.28, p < .05. Participants were most likely to judge the clip as deceptive if the suspect was a man and if the clip was in fact a lie. Moreover, the more gaze aversion and the more head nods the suspects made, the more likely it was that they were judged as deceptive.

The correlation between displaying gaze aversion and judging the person as deceptive was significant for poor lie detectors, r(54) = .39, p < .01, but not significant for good lie detectors, r(54) = .06, *ns*. These two correlations differed significantly from each other (z = 1.78, p < .05, one-tailed). This supports Hypothesis 6 (poor lie detectors would be more guided by gaze aversion than good lie detectors).

Accuracy–Confidence Relationship

Participants were significantly more confident after they saw a truthful clip (M = 4.55, SD = 0.92) than after watching a deceptive clip (M = 4.38, SD = 0.95), t(98) = 3.08, p < .01, d = 0.18. Those two confidence measures were significantly correlated with each other, r(99) = .82, p < .01. The police officers estimated their percentage of correct answers ("posttask estimated accuracy," measured after the lie detection task) very modestly (M = 49.98%, SD = 15.08). This percentage was significantly lower than the actual truth accuracy (M = 63.61, SD = 22.50), t(98) = 5.65, p < .01, d = 0.52, and lie accuracy (M = 66.16, SD = 17.05), t(98) = 7.05, p < .01, d = 0.74, obtained in the lie detection task.

Neither the truth accuracy–truth confidence correlation, r(99) = .10, nor the lie accuracy–lie confidence correlation, r(99) = .03, were significant. Neither was the posttask estimated accuracy significantly correlated with the actual lie accuracy, r(99) = −.07, or actual truth accuracy, r(99) = .17. Age, length of service, and experience in interviewing suspects were not significantly correlated with truth confidence, lie confidence, or posttask estimated accuracy. Neither were there significant differences found between men and women on any of these three variables, although the difference between men and women for posttask estimated accuracy was marginally significant, t(97) = 1.93, p = .056, d = 0.47 (women were more skeptical about their performance, M = 44.38%, SD = 13.21, than men, M = 51.12%, SD = 15.35).[10]

DISCUSSION

Accuracy Rates and Their Relationships with Background Characteristics

In the present study, 99 police officers, who did not belong to a group that has been identified as specialized in lie detection, attempted to detect lies and truths told by suspects during their police interviews. Regarding accuracy, two main findings emerged. First, truth accuracy and lie accuracy were both around 65% in this study, which was higher than was found in most previous deception detection studies. It is also the highest accuracy rate ever found for a group of "ordinary" police officers. The accuracy rates found in this sample of ordinary police officers were comparable to those found among specialized groups of lie detectors in previous studies (Ekman & O'Sullivan, 1991; Ekman et al., 1999). In other words, ordinary police officers might well be better at detecting truths and lies than was previously suggested. Although the accuracy rates were significantly higher than the average accuracy scores obtained by laypersons (mostly college students) in previous research, we cannot conclude that police officers are actually better lie detectors than laypersons, because the latter were not included in this study. Had they been included as participants, it is possible that laypersons would have scored similarly to police officers. Unfortunately, inclusion of a group of laypersons was not possible, as (understandably) the police would not give us permission to show the highly sensitive stimulus material (fragments of real-life police interviews) to laypersons.

Second, findings showed a modest but significant relationship between experience in interviewing suspects and truth accuracy, with the more experience police officers reported in interviewing suspects (a self-report measure), the higher truth accuracy scores they obtained. This finding suggests that experience does make police officers better able to distinguish between truths and lies, a finding typically not found in deception studies with professionals as observers (DePaulo & Pfeifer, 1986; Ekman & O'Sullivan, 1991; Porter et al., 2000). We believe that this finding is affected by the way we measured experience. Other researchers use length of service/years of job experience as a measurement for experience (DePaulo & Pfeifer, 1986; Ekman & O'Sullivan, 1991; Porter et al., 2000). Such a measurement is unfortunate, as it says little about the officers' actual experience in situations in which they will attempt to detect deceit such as interviewing suspects. There is little reason to suggest that a police officer who had worked for many years in a managerial or administrative position within the police force would be a better lie detector than someone with a similar position outside the police force. Therefore, perhaps unsurprisingly, the present study also did not reveal significant correlations between length of service and accuracy. In other words, experience may benefit truth and lie detection only if the relevant experience is taken into account. Perhaps a weakness of our experience measure is that it is a self-report rather than an objective measure. It would be interesting to see whether an objective measure of experience in interviewing suspects (e.g., the number of suspect interviews a police officer has conducted) would correlate with accuracy as well. This would strengthen our argument. Unfortunately, the police do not record objective measures of experience with interviewing suspects.

The findings further revealed that men were better at detecting truths than women. We discuss this further below.

Theoretically, the higher than usual accuracy rates obtained in this study could be explained in several ways. First, as previously discussed in the introduction, the stakes for liars and truth tellers were higher in this study than in previous studies, and high-stakes lies were easier to detect than low-stakes lies. Second, the police officers were exposed to truths and lies told by the sort of people they are familiar with, namely police suspects, and familiarity with this group of people might have increased the accuracy rates. Third, police officers were exposed to truths and lies in a setting that is familiar to them, namely during police interviews, and familiarity with the setting might have increased accuracy rates. Probably all three factors contributed to the high accuracy rates found in this study. Therefore, these explanations have two theoretical implications. First, the obtained findings might well be situation and person specific and we therefore cannot guarantee that exposing police officers to high-stakes lies in situations that they are not familiar with (such as lies told by businesspeople in negotiations, by salespersons to clients, by politicians during interviews, or between romantic partners, etc.) would lead to similar accuracy rates as those found in this study. Similarly, we cannot guarantee that police officers will be any good at detecting low-stakes lies told by suspects. Second, to obtain insight into police officers' skills to detect deceit, exposing them to ecologically valid material (high-stakes lies told by suspects in police interviews) is crucial. This ecologically valid argument also applies to the measurement of relevant background variables, such as measuring police officers' experience with interviewing suspects.

Cues Used to Detect Deceit

The majority of police officers claimed that looking at gaze is a useful tool to detect deceit. This discovery was in agreement with previous findings (Akehurst et al., 1996; Vrij & Semin, 1996). On the one hand, this finding is surprising given that deception research has convincingly demonstrated that gaze behavior is not related to deception (DePaulo et al., 2003; Vrij, 2000a). Nor was gaze related to deception in the present stimulus material (Mann et al., 2002). On the other hand, this finding is not so surprising given that police manuals, including Inbau's manual, which is widely used, claim that suspects typically show gaze aversion when they lie (Gordon & Fleisher, 2002; Hess, 1997; Inbau et al., 1986, 2001). In other words, police officers are taught to look for these incorrect cues.

Several (modest) relationships occurred between cues mentioned by the officers as useful to detect deceit and their accuracy in truth and lie detection. First, good lie detectors mentioned story cues more often than poor lie detectors. Second, the more popular stereotypical belief cues participants mentioned (gaze, fidget, and self-manipulations), and the more they endorsed Inbau's view on cues to deception (liars show gaze aversion, display unnatural posture changes, exhibit self-manipulations, and place the hand over the mouth or eyes when speaking), the worse they became at distinguishing between truths and lies. In other words, looking at Inbau et al.'s (1986, 2001) cues is counterproductive. This is not surprising, as deception research has not supported Inbau's views (DePaulo et al., 2003; Vrij, 2000a). Female participants claimed to look more at Inbau cues than male participants, which might explain why female participants were poorer at detecting truths than male participants.

When we, by means of a regression analysis, compared the veracity judgments made by good and poor lie detectors with the behaviors actually shown by the suspects in the stimulus material (so-called cues to perceived deception), we found that poor lie detectors associated an increase in gaze aversion and an increase in head nods with deception. However, good lie detectors associated a decrease in illustrators with deception. Research has demonstrated that a decrease in illustrators is a much more valid cue to deception than gaze aversion or head nods (Ekman & Friesen, 1972; see DePaulo et al., 2003, and Vrij, 2000a, for reviews of such literature). The regression analysis further showed that poor lie detectors were guided by the gender of the suspect: Female suspects were considered less suspicious than male suspects. Obviously, such a generalized approach has nothing to do with sophisticated truth and lie detection.

Police officers were asked both prior to and after the lie detection task which cues they pay attention to in order to detect deceit. The results revealed that, with a few exceptions, the officers mentioned the same cues before and after the task. The exceptions are easy to explain. For example, officers mentioned physiological cues more often prior to the task. This is unsurprising, as such cues are difficult to notice when someone watches a videotape. Moreover, they mentioned looking for facts more often prior to the task than after. This is also unsurprising, as facts about the cases were not made available to the lie detectors in this study. The fact that a big overlap emerged between cues mentioned before and after the task has a theoretical implication. It suggests that the cues police officers rely on are more general rather than idiosyncratic. Moreover, these general views could then be used to predict police officers' lie detection ability in future situations. Our results support this idea. Mentioning popular stereotypical beliefs and mentioning Inbau's cues prior to the task was negatively correlated with accuracy.

Finally, apart from relying on different cues, the results revealed one further difference between poor and good lie detectors. For poor lie detectors, a significant negative correlation emerged between lie and truth accuracy, whereas such a significant correlation did not emerge for good lie detectors. This implies that for poor lie detectors, increased success at one aspect of the task (success at either lie detection or truth detection) hampers success at the other aspect of the task.

Accuracy–Confidence Relationship

Our analyses regarding the accuracy–confidence relationship revealed three major findings. First, as many researchers before us (see DePaulo, et al., 1997, for a review), we did not find a significant relationship between accuracy and confidence. Even our alternative method of measuring confidence (measuring confidence after completing the whole lie detection task instead of after each veracity judgment) did not lead to any significant relationships. Second, participants were more confident when they were rating actual truths compared with when they were rating actual lies. This same effect has been found before (DePaulo et al., 1997), including in several recent studies (Anderson, Ansfield, & DePaulo, 1999; Vrij & Baxter, 2000; Vrij et al., 2001). However, the reason for this is unclear. Possibly, when judges observe lies, there is something going on in the presentation that raises their doubts. Perhaps there is not enough to indicate the person as a liar, but enough to raise doubts about their subsequent judgment.

Most important, participants' estimated performance in the lie detection task (investigated after the task was completed) was significantly lower than their actual performance. This contradicts the overconfidence effect typically found in deception studies (DePaulo et al., 1997). Perhaps the overconfidence is an artifact. People are typically asked to express their confidence after each veracity judgment they make. One might argue that this is a very difficult task that could easily lead to overconfidence. Participants may believe that some veracity judgments they make during a lie detection task are correct. They then will probably give themselves confidence levels of above 50% for these judgments. For each judgment in which they are uncertain, they will probably give themselves a 50% chance of being correct, because why would they think that they have less than a 50% chance of being correct for each individual judgment? A confidence score above 50% is the likely result of this strategy.

Methodological Issues

Two methodological issues merit attention. First, police officers were exposed to an unbalanced number of truths and lies. This made it impossible to calculate a total accuracy score (accuracies of truths and lies combined) in this study, as that score cannot be unambiguously interpreted. For example, if an observer thinks that everyone was lying, that person would have a high total accuracy score in the event that he or she watched Tape 1 because that tape included nine lies and six truths. However, in this example, there would be no lie detecting ability, only a lie bias. We overcame this problem in two different ways, first by calculating truth and lie accuracy scores separately. The results showed that the difference between lie and truth accuracy was not significant, indicating that the sample as a whole did not show a truth or lie bias. We found that experience in interviewing was positively correlated with both truth accuracy and lie accuracy (although the latter correlation was only marginally significant). The fact that both correlations were positive indicates that experienced officers were most accurate and rules out the consideration that they were more biased. If they had a lie bias, then the experience–truth accuracy correlation would have been negative and vice versa; if they had a truth bias, then the experience–lie accuracy correlation would have been negative. The same reasoning applies to the other correlational findings. For example, mentioning Inbau et al.'s (1986, 2001) cues was negatively correlated with both truth and lie accuracy (although the latter correlation was not significant), hence, looking at those cues makes observers less accurate and not more biased. Moreover, we found that men were significantly better at detecting truths than women, whereas no significant gender difference emerged for detecting lies. Again, this demonstrates that men were more accurate at detecting truths and not more biased. In other analyses, in which the group of police officers were divided into two ability groups (poor lie detectors and good lie

detectors), good lie detectors were those who scored both above the mean for lie clips (66.16%) and above the mean for truth clips (63.61%). This rules out that any of the good lie detectors could have been biased, as a lie bias would have resulted in a low truth accuracy score and a truth bias would have resulted in a low lie accuracy score.

Second, although the lie detection task was very realistic, it still differs in some aspects from real-life lie detection in police interviews. For example, normally the police officers would conduct the interview, and not just watch it. However, research has shown that conducting the interview is not necessarily advantageous in lie detection. Several researchers compared the accuracy scores of observers who actually interviewed potential liars with those who passively observed the interviews but did not actually interview the potential liars (Buller, Strzyzewski, & Hunsaker, 1991; Feeley & deTurck, 1998; Granhag & Strömwall, 2001). In all three studies, researchers found that passive observers were more accurate in detecting truths and lies than were interviewers. These findings suggest that merely observing is actually an advantage, not a disadvantage, in detecting deceit.

Moreover, ordinarily the police officer would see a much larger section, if not the whole interview(s), than they were exposed to in this experiment. Showing the whole interview would not have worked in this experiment, because without cutting out the majority of the interview, the footage would contain a huge amount of information that the experimenter could not be sure was true or false. Additionally, the experimenters were not asking participants to determine whether the suspect was guilty, as the truth–lie did not necessarily specifically relate to whether the suspect committed the crime under investigation, as mentioned earlier.

Also, in real life, officers may know some facts of the case. Although we could have provided our participants with the available evidence facts, we found this undesirable, as it would have made detecting some lies (those of which the suspect's statement contradicts the available evidence) too easy.

Finally, although participants on the whole were very willing to participate in the task, and keen to achieve high accuracy levels, this experiment does not have the same motivating consequences for them that judging the veracity of suspects in real life has. However, DePaulo, Anderson, and Cooper (1999) demonstrated that motivation does not improve performance in a lie detection task.

CONCLUSION

Police manuals typically give the impression that police officers who are experienced in interviewing suspects are good lie detectors (Inbau et al., 1986, 2001). Although previous research could not support this view whatsoever, our study, superior in terms of ecological validity over previous research, revealed that these claims are true to a limited extent. Police officers can detect truths and lies above the level of chance, and accuracy is related to experience with interviewing suspects. However, the results also revealed serious shortcomings in police work. First, accuracy rates, although above the level of chance, were far from perfect, and errors in truth–lie detection were frequently made. Second, police officers had a tendency to pay attention to cues that are not diagnostic cues to deceit, particularly body cues, such as gaze aversion. There may be various reasons why these nondiagnostic cues are so popular, one of which may be the discussion of these cues as diagnostic cues to deception in popular police manuals, such as the manual published by Inbau and colleagues. In fact, our research revealed that the more police officers followed their advice, the worse they were in their ability to distinguish between truths and lies.

REFERENCES

Akehurst, L., Köhnken, G., Vrij, A., & Bull, R. (1996). Lay persons' and police officers' beliefs regarding deceptive behaviour. *Applied Cognitive Psychology, 10*, 461–471.

Allwood, C. M., & Granhag, P. A. (1999). Feelings of confidence and the realism of confidence judgments in everyday life. In P. Juslin & H. Montgomery (Eds.), *Judgment and decision making: Neo-Brunswikian and process-tracing approaches* (pp. 123–146). Mahwah, NJ: Erlbaum.

Anderson, D. E., Ansfield, M. E., & DePaulo, B. M. (1999). Love's best habit: Deception in the context of relationships. In P. Philippot, R. S. Feldman, & E. J. Coats (Eds.), *The social context of nonverbal behavior* (pp. 372–409). Cambridge, England: Cambridge University Press.

Anderson, D. E., DePaulo, B. M., Ansfield, M. E., Tickle, J. J., & Green, E. (1999). Beliefs about cues to deception: Mindless stereotypes or untapped wisdom? *Journal of Nonverbal Behaviour, 23*, 67–89.

Bond, C. F., & Atoum, A. O. (2000). International deception. *Personality and Social Psychology Bulletin, 26*, 385–395.

Buller, D. B., Strzyzewski, K. D., & Hunsaker, F. G. (1991). Interpersonal deception II: The inferiority of conversational participants as deception detectors. *Communication Monographs, 58*, 25–40.

Clark-Carter, D. (1997). *Doing quantitative psychological research: From design to report.* Hove, England: Psychology Press.

DePaulo, B. M., Anderson, D. E., & Cooper, H. (1999, October). *Explicit and implicit deception detection.* Paper presented at the Society of Experimental Social Psychologists, St. Louis, MO.

DePaulo, B. M., Charlton, K., Cooper, H., Lindsay, J. L., & Muhlenbruck, L. (1997). *Personality and Social Psychology Review, 1*, 346–357.

DePaulo, B. M., Epstein, J. A., & Wyer, M. M. (1993). Sex differences in lying: How women and men deal with the dilemma of deceit. In M. Lewis & C. Saarni (Eds.), *Lying and deception in everyday life* (pp. 126–147). New York: Guilford Press.

DePaulo, B. M., Kirkendol, S. E., Tang, J., & O'Brien, T. P. (1988). The motivational impairment effect in the communication of deception: Replications and extensions. *Journal of Nonverbal Behavior, 12*, 177–201.

DePaulo, B. M., Lanier, K., & Davis, T. (1983). Detecting the deceit of the motivated liar. *Journal of Personality and Social Psychology, 45*, 1096–1103.

DePaulo, B. M., LeMay, C. S., & Epstein, J. A. (1991). Effects of importance of success and expectations for success on effectiveness at deceiving. *Personality and Social Psychology Bulletin, 17*, 14–24.

DePaulo, B. M., Lindsay, J. L., Malone, B. E., Muhlenbruck, L., Charlton, K., & Cooper, H. (2003). Cues to deception. *Psychological Bulletin, 129*, 74–118.

DePaulo, B. M., & Pfeifer, R. L. (1986). On-the-job experience and skill at detecting deception. *Journal of Applied Social Psychology, 16*, 249–267.

DePaulo, B. M., Stone, J. L., & Lassiter, G. D. (1985a). Deceiving and detecting deceit. In B. R. Schenkler (Ed.), *The self and social life* (pp. 323–370). New York: McGraw-Hill.

DePaulo, B. M., Stone, J. I., & Lassiter, G. D. (1985b). Telling ingratiating lies: Effects of target sex and target attractiveness on verbal and nonverbal deceptive success. *Journal of Personality and Social Psychology, 48,* 1191–1203.

Ekman, P., & Frank, M. G. (1993). Lies that fail. In M. Lewis & C. Saarni (Eds.), *Lying and deception in everyday life* (pp. 184–201). New York: Guilford Press.

Ekman, P., & Friesen, W. V. (1972). Hand movements. *Journal of Communication, 22,* 353–374.

Ekman, P., & Friesen, W. V. (1974). Detecting deception from the body or face. *Journal of Personality and Social Psychology, 29,* 288–298.

Ekman, P., & O'Sullivan, M. (1991). Who can catch a liar? *American Psychologist, 46,* 913–920.

Ekman, P., O'Sullivan, M., & Frank, M. G. (1999). A few can catch a liar. *Psychological Science, 10,* 263–266.

Feeley, T. H., & deTurck, M. A. (1998). The behavioral correlates of sanctioned and unsanctioned deceptive communication. *Journal of Nonverbal Behavior, 22,* 189–204.

Feeley, T. H., & Young, M. J. (2000). The effects of cognitive capacity on beliefs about deceptive communication. *Communication Quarterly, 48,* 101–119.

Forrest, J. A., & Feldman, R. S. (2000). Detecting deception and judge's involvement: Lower task involvement leads to better lie detection. *Personality and Social Psychology Bulletin, 26,* 118–125.

Frank, M. G., & Ekman, P. (1997). The ability to detect deceit generalizes across different types of high-stake lies. *Journal of Personality and Social Psychology, 72,* 1429–1439.

Gordon, N. J., & Fleisher, W. L. (2002). *Effective interviewing and interrogation techniques.* San Diego, CA: Academic Press.

Granhag, P. A., & Strömwall, L. A. (2001). Detection deception based on repeated interrogations. *Legal and Criminological Psychology, 6,* 85–101.

Gudjonsson, G. H. (1994). Psychological vulnerability: Suspects at risk. In D. Morgan & G. M. Stephenson (Eds.), *Suspicion and silence: The right to silence in criminal investigations* (pp. 91–106). London: Blackstone.

Heinrich, C. A., & Borkenau, P. (1998). Deception and deception detection: The role of cross-modal inconsistency. *Journal of Personality, 66,* 687–712.

Hess, J. E. (1997). *Interviewing and interrogation for law enforcement.* Reading, England: Anderson Publishing Co.

Hurd, K., & Noller, P. (1988). Decoding deception: A look at the process. *Journal of Nonverbal Behavior, 12,* 217–233.

Inbau, F. E., Reid, J. E., & Buckley, J. P. (1986). *Criminal interrogation and confessions* (3rd ed.). Baltimore: Williams & Wilkins.

Inbau, F. E., Reid, J. E., Buckley, J. P., & Jayne, B. C. (2001). *Criminal interrogation and confessions* (4th ed.). Gaithersburg, MD: Aspen Publishers.

Kassin, S. M., & Fong, C. T. (1999). "I'm innocent!": Effects of training on judgments of truth and deception in the interrogation room. *Law and Human Behavior, 23,* 499–516.

Köhnken, G. (1987). Training police officers to detect deceptive eyewitness statements. Does it work? *Social Behaviour, 2,* 1–17.

Kraut, R. E. (1980). Humans as lie detectors: Some second thoughts. *Journal of Communication, 30,* 209–216.

Lane, J. D., & DePaulo, B. M. (1999). Completing Coyne's cycle: Dysphorics' ability to detect deception. *Journal of Research in Personality, 33,* 311–329.

Mann, S. (2001). *Suspects, lies and videotape: An investigation into telling and detecting lies in police/suspect interviews.* Unpublished doctoral dissertation, University of Portsmouth, Portsmouth, England.

Mann, S., Vrij, A., & Bull, R. (2002). Suspects, lies, and videotape: An analysis of authentic high-stake liars. *Law and Human Behavior, 26,* 365–376.

Manstead, A. S. R., Wagner, H. L., & MacDonald, C. J. (1986). Deceptive and nondeceptive communications: Sending experience, modality, and individual abilities. *Journal of Nonverbal Behavior, 10,* 147–167.

Meissner, C. A., & Kassin, S. M. (2002). "He's guilty!": Investigator bias in judgments of truth and deception. *Law and Human Behavior, 26,* 469–480.

Miller, G. R., & Stiff, J. B. (1993). *Deceptive communication.* Newbury Park, CA: Sage.

Moston, S., Stephenson, G. M., & Williamson, T. M. (1992). The effects of case characteristics on suspect behaviour during police questioning. *British Journal of Criminology, 32,* 23–40.

O'Sullivan, M., Ekman, P., & Friesen, W. V. (1988). The effect of comparisons on detecting deceit. *Journal of Nonverbal Behaviour, 12,* 203–216.

Porter, S., Woodworth, M., & Birt, A. R. (2000). Truth, lies, and videotape: An investigation of the ability of federal parole officers to detect deception. *Law and Human Behavior, 24,* 643–658.

Strömwall, L. A. (2001). *Detecting deception: Moderating factors and accuracy.* Unpublished doctoral dissertation, University of Gothenburg, Gothenburg, Sweden.

Vrij, A. (1993). Credibility judgments of detectives: The impact of nonverbal behavior, social skills, and physical characteristics on impression formation. *Journal of Social Psychology, 133,* 601–610.

Vrij, A. (1995). Behavioral correlates of deception in a simulated police interview. *Journal of Psychology, 129,* 15–28.

Vrij, A. (2000a). *Detecting lies and deceit: The psychology of lying and the implications for professional practice.* Chichester, England: Wiley.

Vrij, A. (2000b). Telling and detecting lies as a function of raising the stakes. In C. M. Breur, M. M. Kommer, J. F. Nijboer, & J. M. Reintjes (Eds.), *New trends in criminal investigation and evidence II* (pp. 699–709). Antwerpen, Belgium: Intersentia.

Vrij, A., & Baxter, M. (2000). Accuracy and confidence in detecting truths and lies in elaborations and denials: Truth bias, lie bias and individual differences. *Expert Evidence: The International Digest of Human Behaviour, Science and Law, 7,* 25–36.

Vrij, A., Edward, K., & Bull, R. (2001a). People's insight into their own behaviour and speech content while lying. *British Journal of Psychology, 92,* 373–389.

Vrij, A., Edward, K., & Bull, R. (2001b). Stereotypical verbal and nonverbal responses while deceiving others. *Personality and Social Psychology Bulletin, 27,* 899–909.

Vrij, A., Edward, K., Roberts, K. P., & Bull, R. (2000). Detecting deceit via analysis of verbal and nonverbal behaviour. *Journal of Nonverbal Behaviour, 24,* 239–263.

Vrij, A., & Graham, S. (1997). Individual differences between liars and the ability to detect lies. *Expert Evidence: The International Digest of Human Behaviour, Science and Law, 5,* 144–148.

Vrij, A., Harden, F., Terry, J., Edward, K., & Bull, R. (2001). The influence of personal characteristics, stakes and lie complexity on the accuracy and confidence to detect deceit. In R. Roesch, R. R. Corrado, & R. J. Dempster (Eds.), *Psychology in the courts: International advances in knowledge* (pp. 289–304). London: Routledge.

Vrij, A., & Mann, S. (2001a). Telling and detecting lies in a high-stake situation: The case of a convicted murderer. *Applied Cognitive Psychology, 15,* 187–203.

Vrij, A., & Mann, S. (2001b). Who killed my relative? Police officers' ability to detect real-life high-stake lies. *Psychology, Crime, & Law, 7,* 119–132.

Vrij, A., & Semin, G. R. (1996). Lie experts' beliefs about nonverbal indicators of deception. *Journal of Nonverbal Behaviour, 20,* 65–80.

Vrij, A., Semin, G. R., & Bull, R. (1996). Insight into behavior displayed during deception. *Human Communication Research, 22,* 544–562.

Vrij, A., & Winkel, F. W. (1991). Cultural patterns in Dutch and Surinam nonverbal behavior: An analysis of simulated police/citizen encounters. *Journal of Nonverbal Behavior, 15,* 169–184.

Wechsler, D. (1981). Manual for the Wechsler Adult Intelligence Scale–Revised (WAIS–R). New York: Psychological Corporation.

Wiseman, R. (1995). The megalab truth test. *Nature, 373,* 391.

Zuckerman, M., DePaulo, B. M., & Rosenthal, R. (1981). Verbal and nonverbal communication of deception. In L. Berkowitz (Ed.), *Advances in experimental social psychology, Volume 14* (pp. 1–57). New York: Academic Press.

ENDNOTES

1. Investigating *beliefs about cues associated with deception* provides insight into which cues people think they use when detecting deceit, but it does not necessarily mean that they actually use these cues when they try to detect deceit. For example, people may indicate that they use gaze aversion as a cue for deceit, but it still may be the case that they subsequently judge someone who shows gaze aversion to be truthful. Investigating *cues to perceived deception* provides insight into which cues lie detectors actually use to indicate deception, but it is not certain whether they actually realize this. For example, when there is a tendency among lie detectors to judge those who moved a great deal as more deceptive than those who made few movements, it can be concluded that they used making movements as a cue to detect deception. It is, however, unclear whether lie detectors realized that they used making movements as a cue to detect deceit. The combination of those two methods therefore provides the most complete insight.

2. The picture in the small insert was not clear enough to enable the viewer to see any detail like, for example, the expressions of the interviewer. It is therefore unlikely that the participants paid any attention to this small insert picture (nobody mentioned that they did), and so it is unlikely that participants have been guided by the behavior or demeanor of the interviewer when judging the veracity of the suspects. (When the participants were asked afterward to indicate what made them decide whether the suspect on the screen was lying, nobody mentioned that they had been influenced by the interviewer.)

3. Although it is unfortunate that sometimes the lower torso could not be seen, this is not atypical for detection of deception research, as in many studies, including Ekman et al. (1999), only the head and shoulders are visible.

4. Mann et al. (2002) examined the behaviors of 16 suspects. However, 2 of those suspects were omitted for the purpose of this study. Those 2 were too well-known to show the clips to participants, as they were higher profile cases that received some media attention. We did not want participants to know the cases that they were seeing, as obviously this would give them an advantage, and they may score high accuracy, not on the merits of the task, but purely on facts that they already knew.

5. Separate analyses for poor and good lie detectors showed that the truth–lie accuracy correlation was significant for poor lie detectors, $r(72) = -.35$, $p < .01$, but not for good lie detectors, $r(27) = -.21$, *ns*. A negative correlation means that the better poor lie detectors were at detecting truths, the worse they were at detecting lies, and vice versa. However, truth and lie accuracy did not differ significantly from each other for poor lie detectors (truth accuracy: $M = 57.61$, $SD = 22.7$; lie accuracy: $M = 61.37$, $SD = 16.6$), $t(71) = 0.97$, *ns*, and good lie detectors (truth accuracy: $M = 79.61$, $SD = 11.5$; lie accuracy: $M = 78.94$, $SD = 10.4$), $t(26) = 0.20$, *ns*.

6. A 2 (veracity) × 2 (gender of suspect) × 2 (gender of observer) ANOVA, with a mixed factorial design (the first two factors were within-subjects factors), was carried out to investigate the

gender issue in more detail. In this analysis, only 74 participants (58 men and 16 women) were included because on one tape, no female suspects appeared. Apart from a significant gender of observers effect, $F(1, 72) = 5.51$, $p < .05$, $\eta^2 = .07$ (indicating that male accuracy was superior, $M = 68\%$, $SD = .13$, to female accuracy, $M = 58\%$, $SD = .20$), a Deception × Gender of Suspect effect occurred, $F(1, 72) = 15.09$, $p < .01$, $\eta^2 = .17$. In male suspects, lies ($M = 72.00$, $SD = 19.11$) were more easily detected than truths ($M = 59.73$, $SD = 24.44$), whereas in female suspects, truths ($M = 79.73$, $SD = 40.48$) were more easily detected than lies ($M = 52.03$, $SD = 43.44$). However, participants only saw three deceptive clips of female suspects (and six truthful clips), so conclusions have to be drawn with caution. A significant difference between the four groups was found for detecting lies, $F(3, 95) = 4.44$, $p < .01$, $\eta^2 = .12$.

The 4 traffic officers who participated were highly accurate ($M = .95$, $SD = .58$), and Tukey's honestly significant difference test revealed that they were more accurate than any of the other three groups of participants (which did not differ significantly from each other). Because only 4 traffic officers participated, it would be presumptuous to assume that this sample is representative of all traffic officers and claim that all officers in this area of specialty would be more accurate at detecting deception. However, reasons why traffic officers may be more accurate than officers from other divisions include that they are more used to making snap judgments (e.g., highway patrol officers) about whether a person is drinking, or is lying about their involvement in a crash, and so on. Also they may speak to more people on a daily basis, because many traffic offenses are fairly quick to deal with, and hence traffic officers are more practiced in making veracity judgments than officers in other departments.

7. These findings are available from Aldert Vrij.

8. Following Anderson, DePaulo, Ansfield, Tickle, and Green (1999), who found gender differences in cues mentioned, we conducted ANOVAs and chi-square analyses, with gender as the between-subjects factor and the four categories and gut feeling as dependent variables. We only found one significant difference: Before the task, female participants mentioned more body cues ($M = 1.72$, $SD = 1.18$) than male participants ($M = 1.72$, $SD = .98$), $F(1, 97) = 4.08$, $p < .05$, $\eta^2 = .04$.

9. To explore gender differences in how often popular stereotypical beliefs and Inbau cues were mentioned, ANOVAs were carried out, with gender as the between-subjects factor and popular stereotypical beliefs and Inbau cues as dependent variables. Before the task, women mentioned popular stereotypical beliefs significantly more often ($M = 1.29$, $SD = 0.69$) than men ($M = 0.89$, $SD = 0.65$), $F(1, 97) = 6.65$, $p < .05$, $\eta^2 = .06$. Also after the task, women mentioned these cues more often ($M = 1.17$, $SD = 0.76$) than men ($M = 0.88$, $SD = 0.59$); although the difference was borderline significant, $F(1, 97) = 3.69$, $p = .058$, $\eta^2 = .03$.

Before the task, women mentioned Inbau cues significantly more often ($M = 1.46$, $SD = 0.78$) than men ($M = 1.00$, $SD = 0.72$), $F(1, 97) = 7.13$, $p < .01$, $\eta^2 = .07$. No gender differences emerged regarding the mention of Inbau cues after the task (men: $M = 1.09$, $SD = 0.74$; women: $M = 1.38$, $SD = 0.82$), $F(1, 97) = 2.50$, *ns,* $\eta^2 = .03$.

10. Differences between the four groups (Criminal Investigation Department, police trainers, traffic officers, and uniform response officers) were not found on any of the three (truth confidence, lie confidence, and posttask estimated accuracy) confidence scores (all *ps* > .32).

This study was sponsored by Economic and Social Research Council Grant R00429734727.

APPENDIX A

Cue Categories, Descriptions and Frequency of Cues Mentioned Before and After the Task, and Number of Participants to Mention Each Cue

Cue	Group	Examples (including antonyms)	Before Task	After Task
Vagueness	Story	Vague reply/lots of detail	19	20
Contradictions	Story	Contradictions in story/consistent	18	10
Speech content	Story	Story content/specific words	9	15
Self-corrections	Story	Corrected self/corrected officer	0	7
Repetitions	Story	Repeating the question/buying time	3	1
Misc. speech	Story	Anything about speech that does not fit into "speech content," e.g., pleading/minimizing offense or "uncertain replies"	10	22
Evidence	Story	Facts of the case	8	2
Hesitance/pauses	Vocal	Hesitation/pauses in speech/fluent speech	16	27
Voice	Vocal	Voice pitch/volume/harshness/soft	15	16
Stammering	Vocal	Stammered/stuttered	4	0
Speech fillers	Vocal	Lots of "ems" and "ahs"/no "ems"	2	1
Response length	Vocal	Lengthy reply/one-word reply	3	4
Gaze	Body	Averting gaze/eye contact	72	77
Movements	Body	Body language and movements	25	31
Posture	Body	Upright posture/slouched	6	13
Fidgeting	Body	Fidgeting/nervous movements/twiddling	19	11
Covering face	Body	Hands over face/hiding mouth	6	8
Hands	Body	Hand movements/still hands	9	28
Self-manipulation	Body	Touching/fiddling with self—excluding nails	7	6
Facial	Body	Facial expression/smiling/frowning	5	1
Props	Body	Playing with other things, e.g., cup/cigarette	3	2
Nail-biting	Body	Biting the nails/chewing fingers	2	2
Head movements	Body	Shaking/nodding/moving head	0	9
Physiological	Body	Sweating/blushing/blinking	15	5
Emotion	Body	Crying/upset/happy	6	1
Changes	Body	Changes in behavior/attitude	7	5
Demeanor	Conduct	Demeanor/relaxed/attitude	9	10
Defensive	Conduct	Sitting defensively/legs or arms crossed	12	9
Confidence	Conduct	Confidence/nervousness	11	9
Gut feeling	Other	Gut feeling/intuition	1	3
Total			322	355

Note: Misc. = miscellaneous.

APPENDIX B

Descriptions of the Coded Behaviors Displayed by the Suspects in the Stimulus Material and the Interrater Agreement Scores between the Two Coders (Pearson Correlations)

1. Gaze aversion: number of seconds in which the participant looked away from the interviewer (two coders, $r = .86$).
2. Smiles: frequency of smiles and laughs ($r = .98$).
3. Blinking: frequency of eye blinks ($r = .99$).
4. Head nods: frequency of head nods for which each upward and downward movement was counted as a separate nod ($r = .93$).
5. Head shakes: frequency of head shakes. Similar to head nods, each sideways movement was counted as a separate shake ($r = .98$).
6. Other head movements: head movements that were not included as head shakes or head nods (e.g., tilting the head to the side, turning the face, etc.; $r = .95$).
7. Shrugs: frequency of where one or both shoulders is briefly raised in an "I don't know" type gesture ($r = .99$).
8. Self-manipulations: frequency of scratching the head, wrists, etc. (touching the hands was counted as hand/finger movements rather than self-manipulations; $r = .99$).
9. Illustrators: frequency of arm and hand movements which were designed to modify and/or supplement what was being said verbally ($r = .99$).
10. Hand and/or finger movements: any other movements of the hands or fingers without moving the arms ($r = .99$).
11. Speech fillers: (speech fillers and speech errors were scored on the basis of a typed verbatim text) frequency of saying "ah" or "mmm," etc., between words ($r = .98$).
12. Speech errors: frequency of word and/or sentence repetition, sentence change, sentence incompletion, stutters, etc. ($r = .97$). Deviations from the official English language (e.g., local dialects such as saying "it weren't me" rather than "it wasn't me") were not included as speech errors.
13. Pauses: number of seconds in which there is a noticeable pause in the monologue of the participant ($r = -.55$).

CRITICAL THINKING QUESTIONS

1. Compare the conclusions in this article with those presented in Article 4. What similarities do you see in their findings? What differences? Can any of the information presented in this article (Article 6) be generalized to the issues of impression formation presented in Article 4 or vice versa? Explain your answer.
2. What implications does the information presented in this article have for situations such as therapy sessions and courtroom proceedings? For instance, is it feasible to teach people to be more aware of the nonverbal and verbal messages they send when they are lying or telling the truth? Can people learn how to interpret such messages more accurately? How might either or both of these goals be accomplished? Explain your answers.
3. From the information contained in this article, develop a list of specific cues that are associated with detecting deception. Which commonly assumed correlates of lying are not really useful in detecting deception?
4. How useful are the findings from the present study for detecting deception in real-world settings (e.g., when you do not have a videotape of an event to review)? Include in your answer the implications for police settings as well as non–law enforcement settings.
5. This study found that men were better than women at detecting deception. However, previous research (in nonpolice settings) has suggested that women are generally better than men in interpreting nonverbal behaviors. What might account for these gender effects? Be specific in your answer.

CHAPTER INTEGRATION QUESTIONS _____

1. Do any common themes emerge from the three articles in this chapter? If so, what are they?

2. Using the information from these articles, what advice could you give on how to make the most positive first impression on others? Also, how can we more accurately form first impressions of other people?

3. Spanish philosopher Santayana wrote, "People often see what they believe rather than believe what they see." What does this quotation mean to you? Do you agree or disagree with it? Why?

4. How can you relate the Santayana quotation to the chapter themes that you identified in Question 1?

Chapter Three

SOCIAL COGNITION

THE WORLD AROUND us presents a complex array of information. Due simply to sheer volume, it is humanly impossible to pay attention to all the information available to us. So, given all of this information, how do we make sense of it? This chapter on social cognition examines some of the ways that people process information about themselves and others in order to make judgments.

A major interest of social psychologists is how people mentally process the information they receive. Decisions are not always based on a thorough analysis of the information at hand. Instead, people sometimes rely on mental shortcuts or intuition in reaching decisions. These mental shortcuts, or *heuristics,* are commonly employed strategies that people use for making sense of the world. The problem is, these mental strategies often get us into trouble by shading how we interpret events in the world around us. Article 7, "Some Systematic Biases of Everyday Judgment," examines how heuristics and other forms of cognitive bias may hinder effective decision making.

Social cognition also deals with how we make sense of ourselves. One interesting line of research has addressed the relationship between cognition and emotion. Specifically, do our mental processes influence what we feel, or do our feelings shape our mental processes? Article 8, "Cognitive, Social, and Physiological Determinants of Emotional State," is a classic investigation of the relationship between thought processes and emotion. The methods and findings of the study make interesting reading, but its implications are even more important: Is it possible to change the emotions we experience simply by changing the cognitive labels that we attach to them?

Finally, the last article in this chapter returns to the question of how we try to make sense of the world. Specifically, Article 9, "The Fundamental Attribution Error in Detecting Deception: The Boy-Who-Cried-Wolf Effect," explores how a common attribution error may be responsible for our accuracy (or lack thereof) in determining when someone is lying or telling the truth. Like Article 6 in the previous chapter, this article also examines the issue of detecting deception. However, it seeks to discover the underlying cognitive mechanisms involved in doing so.

ARTICLE 7 _____

Social cognition is concerned with the processes that people use to make sense of the social world. One finding from research in this area is that people tend to be *cognitive misers;* that is, all things being equal, people prefer to think as little as possible in reaching decisions. To help them achieve this goal, they employ cognitive strategies such as *heuristics* (i.e., mental shortcuts for understanding the world).

For example, why are some people afraid of flying? If you asked them whether they know that statistics show that airplane travel actually is safer than other modes of transportation, the majority undoubtedly would say that yes, they know that. Yet their fear persists. Why? One contributing factor may be the *availability heuristic,* a mental shortcut that involves judging the probability of something happening by how easily it comes to mind. We all can vividly recall the images of airplane crashes that appear in the media every time an accident occurs. The pictures are terrifying, so they readily come to mind. Even though automobile accidents are more common, how often do we see detailed (and repeated) images of car crashes? Rarely. So even though airplane crashes occur much less frequently than fatal automobile accidents, it is easier to recall images of the former. Hence, we have a greater tendency to fear them, as well.

We use many types of heuristics to help us explain and understand our world. What all of these mental shortcuts do, however, are create biases in how we interpret the events around us. Many of these biases involve inconsequential events, and no harm comes from believing them. But in other situations, using this biased information processing to make important decisions about our lives may lead to problems.

The following article by Thomas Gilovich examines some of the biases in everyday judgment that cloud our ability for accurate, critical thinking.

Some Systematic Biases of Everyday Judgment

■ Thomas Gilovich

Skeptics have long thought that everyday judgment and reasoning are biased in predictable ways. Psychological research on the subject conducted during the past quarter century largely confirms these suspicions. Two types of explanations are typically offered for the dubious beliefs that are dissected in *Skeptical Inquirer*. On one hand, there are motivational causes: Some beliefs are comforting, and so people embrace that comfort and convince themselves that a questionable proposition is true. Many types of religious beliefs, for example, are often explained this way. On the other hand, there are cognitive causes: faulty processes of reasoning and judgment that lead people to misevalu-

ate the evidence of their everyday experience. The skeptical community is convinced that everyday judgment and reasoning leave much to be desired.

Why are skeptics so unimpressed with the reasoning abilities and habits of the average person? Until recently, this pessimism was based on simple observation, often by those with a particularly keen eye for the foibles of human nature. Thus, skeptics often cite such thinkers as Francis Bacon, who stated:

> . . . *all superstition is much the same whether it be that of astrology, dreams, omens, retributive judgment, or the like . . . [in that] the deluded believers*

Reprinted from *The Skeptical Inquirer,* March 13, 1997, *21*(2), p. 31. Copyright © 1997, CSICOP, Inc. www.CSICOP.org. Reprinted with permission.

observe events which are fulfilled, but neglect or pass over their failure, though it be much more common. (Bacon 1899/1620)

John Stuart Mill and Bertrand Russell are two other classic scholars who, along with Bacon, are often quoted for their trenchant observations on the shortcomings of human judgment. It is also common to see similar quotes of more recent vintage—in *Skeptical Inquirer* and elsewhere—from the likes of Richard Feynman, Stephen Jay Gould, and Carl Sagan. During the past twenty-five years, a great deal of psychological research has dealt specifically with the quality of everyday reasoning, and so it is now possible to go beyond simple observation and arrive at a truly rigorous assessment of the shortcomings of everyday judgment. In so doing, we can determine whether or not these scholars we all admire are correct. Do people misevaluate evidence in the very ways and for the very reasons that Bacon, Russell, and others have claimed? Let us look at the research record and see.

THE "COMPARED TO WHAT?" PROBLEM

Some of the common claims about the fallibility of human reasoning stand up well to empirical scrutiny. For example, it is commonly argued that people have difficulty with what might be called the "compared to what" problem. That is, people are often overly impressed with an absolute statistic without recognizing that its true import can only be assessed by comparison to some relevant baseline.

For instance, a 1986 article in *Discover* magazine (cited in Dawes 1988) urges readers who fly in airplanes to "know where the exits are and rehearse in your mind exactly how to get to them." Why? The article approvingly notes that someone who interviewed almost two hundred survivors of fatal airline accidents found that ". . . more than 90% had their escape routes mentally mapped out beforehand." Good for them, but note that whoever did the study cannot interview anyone who perished in an airplane crash. Air travel being as scary as it is to so many people, perhaps 90 percent or more of those who died in airline crashes rehearsed their escape routes as well. Ninety percent sounds impressive because it is so close to 100 percent. But without a more pertinent comparison, it really does not mean much.

Similarly, people are often impressed that, say, 30 percent of all infertile couples who adopt a child subsequently conceive. That is great news for that 30 percent to be sure, but what percentage of those who do not adopt likewise conceive? People likewise draw broad conclusions from a cancer patient who goes into remission after steadfastly practicing mental imagery. Again, excellent news for that individual, but might the cancer have gone into remission even if the person had not practiced mental imagery?

This problem of failing to invoke a relevant baseline of comparison is particularly common when the class of data that requires inspection is inherently difficult to collect. Consider, for example, the commonly expressed opinion, "I can always tell that someone is wearing a hairpiece." Are such claims to be believed, or is it just that one can tell that someone is wearing a hairpiece . . . when it is obvious that he is wearing a hairpiece? After all, how can one tell whether some have gone undetected? The goal of a good hairpiece is to fool the public, and so the example is one of those cases in which the confirmations speak loudly while the disconfirmations remain silent.

A similar asymmetry should give pause to those who have extreme confidence in their "gaydar," or their ability to detect whether someone is gay. Here, too, the confirmations announce themselves. When a person for whatever reason "seems gay" and it is later determined that he is, it is a salient triumph for one's skill at detection. But people who elude one's gaydar rarely go out of their way to announce, "By the way, I fooled you: I'm gay."

At any rate, the notion that people have difficulty invoking relevant comparisons has received support from psychological research. Studies of everyday reasoning have shown that the logic and necessity of control groups, for example, is often lost on a large segment of even the educated population (Boring 1954; Einhorn and Hogarth 1978; Nisbett and Ross 1980).

THE "SEEK AND YE SHALL FIND" PROBLEM

Another common claim that stands up well to empirical research is the idea that people do not assess hypotheses even-handedly. Rather, they tend to seek out confirmatory evidence for what they suspect to be true, a tendency that has the effect of "seek and ye shall find." A biased search for confirmatory information frequently turns up more apparent support for a hypothesis than is justified.

This phenomenon has been demonstrated in numerous experiments explicitly designed to assess people's hypothesis-testing strategies (Skov and Sherman 1986; Snyder and Swann 1978). But it is so pervasive that it can also be seen in studies designed with an entirely different agenda in mind. One of my personal favorites is a study in which participants were given the following information (Shafir 1993):

> *Imagine that you serve on the jury of an only-child sole-custody case following a relatively messy divorce. The facts of the case are complicated by ambiguous economic, social, and emotional considerations, and you decide to base your decision entirely on the following few observations. To which parent would you award sole custody of the child?*
>
> **Parent A:**
> *average income*
> *average health*
> *average working hours*
> *reasonable rapport with the child*
> *relatively stable social life*
>
> **Parent B:**
> *above-average income*
> *minor health problems*
> *lots of work-related travel*
> *very close relationship with the child*
> *extremely active social life*

Faced with this version of the problem, the majority of respondents chose to award custody to Parent B, the "mixed bag" parent who offers several advantages (above-average income), but also some disadvantages (health problems), in comparison to Parent A. In another version of the problem, however, a different group is asked to which parent they would deny custody of the child. Here, too, a majority selects Parent B. Parent B, then, is paradoxically deemed both more and less worthy of caring for the child.

The result is paradoxical, that is, unless one takes into account people's tendencies to seek out confirming information. Asked which parent should be awarded the child, people look primarily for positive qualities that warrant being awarded the child—looking less vigilantly for negative characteristics that would lead one to favor the other parent. When asked which parent should be denied custody, on the other hand, people look primarily for negative qualities that would disqualify a parent. A decision to award or deny, of course, should be based on a comparison of the positive and negative characteristics of the two parents, but the way the question is framed channels respondents down a narrower path in which they focus on information that would confirm the type of verdict they are asked to render.

The same logic often rears its head when people test certain suppositions or hypotheses. Rumors of some dark conspiracy, for example, can lead people to search disproportionately for evidence that supports the plot and neglect evidence that contradicts it.

THE SELECTIVE MEMORY PROBLEM

A third commonly sounded complaint about everyday human thought is that people are more inclined to remember information that fits their expectations than information at variance with their expectations. Charles Darwin, for example, said that he took great care to record any observation that was inconsistent with his theories because "I had found by experience that such facts and thoughts were far more apt to escape from the memory than favourable ones" (cited in Clark 1984).

This particular criticism of the average person's cognitive faculties is in need of revision. Memory research has shown that often people have the easiest time recalling information that is inconsistent with their expectations or preferences (Bargh and Thein 1985; Srull and Wyer 1989). A little reflection indicates that this is particularly true of those "near misses" in life that become indelibly etched in the brain. The novelist Nicholson Baker (1991) provides a perfect illustration:

> *[I] told her my terrible story of coming in second in the spelling bee in second grade by spelling keep "c-e-e-p" after successfully tossing off microphone, and how for two or three years afterward I was pained every time a yellow garbage truck drove by on Highland Avenue and I saw the capitals printed on it, "Help*

Keep Our City Clean," with that impossible irrational K that had made me lose so humiliatingly. . . .

Baker's account, of course, is only an anecdote, possibly an apocryphal one at that. But it is one that, as mentioned above, receives support from more systematic studies. In one study, for example, individuals who had bet on professional football games were later asked to recall as much as they could about the various bets they had made (Gilovich 1983). They recalled significantly more information about their losses—outcomes they most likely did not expect to have happen and certainly did not prefer to have happen (see Figure 1).

Thus, the simple idea that people remember best that which they expect or prefer needs modification. Still, there is something appealing and seemingly true about the idea, and it should not be discarded prematurely. When considering people's belief in the accuracy of psychic forecasts, for example, it certainly seems to be fed by selective memory for successful predictions. How then can we reconcile this idea with the finding that often inconsistent information is better recalled? Perhaps the solution lies in considering when an event is eventful. With respect to their capacity to grab attention, some events are one-sided and others two-sided. Two-sided events are those that stand out and psychologically register as events regardless of how they turn out. If you bet on a sporting event or an election result, for example, either outcome—a win or a loss—has emotional significance and is therefore likely to emerge from the stream of everyday experience and register as an event. For these events, it is doubtful that confirmatory information is typically better remembered than disconfirmatory information.

In contrast, suppose you believe that "the telephone always rings when I'm in the shower." The potentially relevant events here are one-sided. If the phone happens to ring while showering, it will certainly register as an event, as you experience great stress in deciding whether to answer it, and you run dripping wet to the phone only to discover that it is someone from AT&T asking if you are satisfied with your long-distance carrier. When the phone does not ring when you are in the shower, on the other hand, it is a non-event. Nothing happened. Thus, with respect to the belief that the phone always rings while you are in the shower, the events are inherently one-sided: Only the confirmations stand out.

Perhaps it is these one-sided events to which Bacon's and Darwin's comments best apply. For one-sided events, as I discuss below, it is often the outcomes consistent with expectations that stand out and are more likely to be remembered. For two-sided events, on the other hand, the two types of outcomes are likely to be equally memorable; or, on occasion, events inconsistent with expectations may be more memorable.

But what determines whether an event is one- or two-sided? There are doubtless several factors. Let's consider two of them in the context of psychic predictions. First, events relevant to psychic predictions are inherently one-sided in the sense that such predictions are disconfirmed not by any specific event, but by their accumulated failure to be confirmed. Thus, the relevant comparison here is between confirmations and non-confirmations, or between events and non-events. It is no surprise, surely, that events are typically more memorable than non-events.

In one test of this idea, a group of college students read a diary purportedly written by another student, who described herself as having an interest in the prophetic nature of dreams (Madey 1993). To test whether there was any validity to dream prophecy, she decided to record each night's dreams and keep a record of significant events in her life, and later determine if there was any connection between the two.

FIGURE 1 / Gamblers' Recall of Information about Bets Won and Lost. (From Gilovich 1983.)

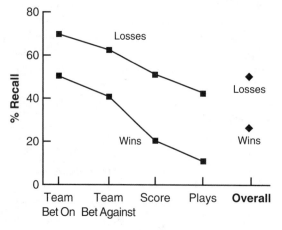

Half of the dreams (e.g., "I saw lots of people being happy") were later followed by events that could be seen as fulfilling ("My professor cancelled our final, which produced cheers throughout the class"). The other half went unfulfilled.

After reading the entire diary and completing a brief "filler" task, the participants were asked to recall as many of the dreams as they could. As figure 2 shows, they recalled many more of the prophecies that were fulfilled than those that were not (see Figure 2). This result is hardly a surprise, of course, because the fulfillment of a prophecy reminds one of the original prediction, whereas a failure to fulfill it is often a non-event. The relevant outcomes are therefore inherently one-sided, and the confirmations are more easily recalled. The end result is that the broader belief in question—in this case, dream prophecy—receives spurious support.

The events relevant to psychic predictions are one-sided in another way as well. Psychic predictions are notoriously vague about when the prophesied events are supposed to occur. "A serious misfortune will befall a powerful leader" is a more common prophecy than "The President will be assassinated on March 15th." Such predictions are temporally unfocused, in that there is no specific moment to which interested parties are to direct their attention. For such predictions, con-

firmatory events are once again more likely to stand out because confirmations are more likely to prompt a recollection of the original prophecy. The events relevant to temporally unfocused expectations, then, tend to be one-sided, with the confirmations typically more salient and memorable than disconfirmations.

Temporally focused expectations, on the other hand, are those for which the timing of the decisive outcome is known in advance. If one expects a particular team to win the Super Bowl, for example, one knows precisely when that expectation will be confirmed or refuted—at the end of the game. As a result, the events relevant to temporally focused expectations tend to be two-sided because one's attention is focused on the decisive moment, and both outcomes are likely to be noticed and remembered.

In one study that examined the memory implications of temporally focused and unfocused expectations, participants were asked to read the diary of a student who, as part of an ESP experiment, was required to try to prophesy an otherwise unpredictable event every week for several weeks (Madey and Gilovich 1993). The diary included the student's weekly prophecy as well as various passages describing events from that week. There were two groups of participants in the experiment. In the temporally unfocused condition, the prophecies made no mention of when the prophesied event was likely to occur ("I have a feeling that I will get into an argument with my Psychology research group"). In the temporally focused condition, the prediction identified a precise day on which the event was to occur ("I have a feeling that I will get into an argument with my Psychology research group on Friday"). For each group, half of the prophecies were confirmed (e.g., "Our professor assigned us to research groups, and we immediately disagreed over our topic") and half were disconfirmed (e.g., "Our professor assigned us to research groups, and we immediately came to a unanimous decision on our topic"). Whether confirmed or disconfirmed, the relevant event was described in the diary entry for the day prophesied in the temporally focused condition. After reading the diary and completing a short distracter task, the participants were asked to recall as many prophecies and relevant events as they could.

Knowing when the prophesied events were likely to occur helped the respondents' memories, but only for

FIGURE 2 / Participants' Recall of Dream Prophecies That Were Either Confirmed or Unconfirmed. (Adapted from Madey 1993.)

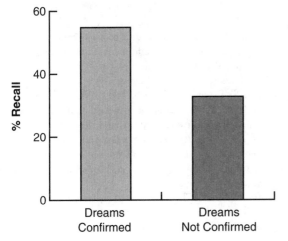

those prophecies that were disconfirmed (see Figure 3). Confirmatory events were readily recalled whether temporally focused or not. Disconfirmations, on the other hand, were rarely recalled unless they disconfirmed a temporally focused prediction. When one considers that most psychic predictions are temporally unfocused, the result, once again, is that the evidence for psychic predictions can appear more substantial than it is.

CONCLUSION

There is, of course, much more psychological research on the quality of everyday judgment than that reviewed here (see, for example, Baron 1988; Dawes 1988; Gilovich 1991; Nisbett and Ross 1980; Kahneman, Slovic, and Tversky 1982). But even this brief review is sufficient to make it clear that some of the reputed biases of everyday judgment turn out to be real, verifiable shortcomings. Systematic research by and large supports the suspicions of much of the skeptical community that everyday judgment is not to be trusted completely. At one level, this should not come

as a surprise: It is precisely because everyday judgment cannot be trusted that the inferential safeguards known as the scientific method were developed. It is unfortunate that those safeguards are not more widely taught or more generally appreciated.

REFERENCES

Bacon, F. 1899. *Advancement of Learning and the Novum Organum* (rev. ed.). New York: Colonial Press. (Original work published 1620).

Baker, N. 1991. *Room Temperature.* New York: Vintage.

Bargh, J. A., and R. D. Thein. 1985. Individual construct accessibility, person memory, and the recall-judgment link: The case of information overload. *Journal of Personality and Social Psychology* 49: 1129–1146.

Baron, J. 1988. *Thinking and Deciding.* New York: Cambridge University Press.

Boring, E. G. 1954. The nature and history of experimental control. *American Journal of Psychology* 67: 573–589.

Clark, R. W. 1984. *The Survival of Charles Darwin: A Biography of a Man and an Idea.* New York: Random House.

Dawes, R. M. 1988. *Rational Choice in an Uncertain World.* San Diego, Calif.: Harcourt Brace Jovanovich.

Einhorn, H. J., and R. M. Hogarth. 1978. Confidence in judgment: Persistence in the illusion of validity. *Psychological Review* 85: 395–416.

Gilovich, T. 1983. Biased evaluation and persistence in gambling. *Journal of Personality and Social Psychology* 44: 1110–1126.

———.1991. *How We Know What Isn't So: The Fallibility of Human Reason in Everyday Life.* New York: Free Press.

Kahneman, D., P. Slovic, and A. Tversky. 1982. *Judgment under Uncertainty: Heuristics and Biases.* Cambridge: Cambridge University Press.

Madey, S. F. 1993. Memory for expectancy-consistent and expectancy-inconsistent information: An investigation of one-sided and two-sided events. Unpublished doctoral dissertation, Cornell University.

Madey, S. F., and T. Gilovich. 1993. Effect of temporal focus on the recall of expectancy-consistent and expectancy-inconsistent information. *Journal of Personality and Social Psychology* 65: 458–468.

Nisbett, R. E., and L. Ross. 1980. *Human Inference: Strategies and Shortcomings of Social Judgment.* Englewood Cliffs, N.J.: Prentice-Hall.

Shafir, E. 1993. Choosing versus rejecting: Why some options are both better and worse than others. *Memory and Cognition* 21: 546–556.

FIGURE 3 / Participants' Recall of Prophecies That Were Confirmed or Disconfirmed, as a Function of Whether or Not the Prophecies Specified When the Critical Events Were to Occur. (Adapted from Madey and Gilovich 1993.)

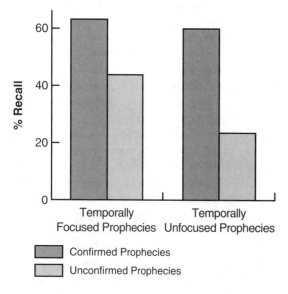

Skov, R. B., and S. J. Sherman. 1986. Information-gathering processes: Diagnosticity, hypothesis-confirmatory strategies, and perceived hypothesis confirmation. *Journal of Experimental Social Psychology* 22: 93–121.

Synder, M., and W. B. Swann. 1978. Hypothesis-testing processes in social interaction. *Journal of Personality and Social Psychology* 36: 1202–1212.

Srull, T. K., and R. S. Wyer. 1989. Person memory and judgment. *Psychological Review* 9: 58–83.

CRITICAL THINKING QUESTIONS

1. Find sources from various media that illustrate the "compared to what" problem discussed in the article. Discuss how your examples illustrate erroneous reasoning.

2. The article states that "Studies of everyday reasoning have shown that the logic and necessity of control groups, for example, is often lost on a large segment of even the educated population." Explain what is meant by the "logic and necessity of control groups."

3. Do you agree or disagree with the concept expressed in the quote in Question 2 that many people have poor critical-thinking skills? If you agree, what suggestions do you have for how people can handle life's issues most effectively? If you disagree, defend your position.

4. Give a personal example of some sort of biased thinking that you have witnessed. What bias or biases were involved?

5. Check your horoscope at the beginning of the day to see what it says is in store for you. Then record events at the end of the day that either confirm or disconfirm the predictions in your horoscope. Use the information contained in the article to discuss your findings.

*ARTICLE 8*_____

How do you know what emotion you are experiencing? Ask that question of someone who has just learned that he or she has won the lottery, and the answer would undoubtedly be "thrilled," "excited," "overjoyed," or some such adjective to describe a very positive emotional state. Ask if it is actually anger that the winner is feeling, and he or she probably would look at you as if you were crazy. But how does that person *know* what emotion he or she is feeling?

The work that follows by Schachter and Singer is a classic study that addresses what determines a person's emotional state. Briefly, the authors' findings suggest that what we call *emotion* is partly due to some sort of physiological arousal. However, what we feel is also determined by the cognitive label that we attach to that physiological arousal. According to this approach, a person who experiences some sort of physiological arousal might subjectively experience one of two very different emotional states, either anger or euphoria, depending on how he or she labeled the experience. The article discusses the process as well as some of the conditions that result when this process occurs.

While reading the article, think of its implications: Is cognition a necessary part of emotion? Without it, what (if anything) would we feel? What about newborn children? Since their cognitive abilities are not yet fully developed, does that mean that they don't experience emotions?

Cognitive, Social, and Physiological Determinants of Emotional State[1]

■ Stanley Schachter and Jerome E. Singer

The problem of which cues, internal or external, permit a person to label and identify his own emotional state has been with us since the days that James (1890) first tendered his doctrine that "the bodily changes follow directly the perception of the exciting fact, and that our feeling of the same changes as they occur *is* the emotion" (p. 449). Since we are aware of a variety of feeling and emotion states, it should follow from James' proposition that the various emotions will be accompanied by a variety of differentiable bodily states. Following James' pronouncement, a formidable number of studies were undertaken in search of the physiological differentiators of the emotions. The results, in these early days, were almost uniformly negative. All of the emotional states experimentally manipulated were characterized by a general pattern of excitation of the sympathetic nervous system but there

appeared to be no clear-cut physiological discriminators of the various emotions. This pattern of results was so consistent from experiment to experiment that Cannon (1929) offered, as one of the crucial criticisms of the James-Lange theory, the fact that "the same visceral changes occur in very different emotional states and in non-emotional states" (p. 351).

More recent work, however, has given some indication that there may be differentiators. Ax (1953) and Schachter (1957) studied fear and anger. On a large number of indices both of these states were characterized by a similarly high level of autonomic activation but on several indices they did differ in the degree of activation. Wolf and Wolff (1947) studied a subject with a gastric fistula and were able to distinguish two patterns in the physiological responses of the stomach wall. It should be noted, though, that for many

Reprinted from *Psychological Review,* 1962, *69,* 379–399.

months they studied their subject during and following a great variety of moods and emotions and were able to distinguish only two patterns.

Whether or not there are physiological distinctions among the various emotional states must be considered an open question. Recent work might be taken to indicate that such differences are at best rather subtle and that the variety of emotion, mood, and feeling states are by no means matched by an equal variety of visceral patterns.

This rather ambiguous situation has led Ruckmick (1936), Hunt, Cole, and Reis (1958), Schachter (1959) and others to suggest that cognitive factors may be major determinants of emotional states. Granted a general pattern of sympathetic excitation as characteristic of emotional states, granted that there may be some differences in pattern from state to state, it is suggested that one labels, interprets, and identifies this stirred-up state in terms of the characteristics of the precipitating situation and one's apperceptive mass. This suggests, then, that an emotional state may be considered a function of a state of physiological arousal[2] and of a cognition appropriate to this state of arousal. The cognition, in a sense, exerts a steering function. Cognitions arising from the immediate situation as interpreted by past experience provide the framework within which one understands and labels his feelings. It is the cognition which determines whether the state of physiological arousal will be labeled as "anger," "joy," "fear," or whatever.

In order to examine the implications of this formulation let us consider the fashion in which these two elements, a state of physiological arousal and cognitive factors, would interact in a variety of situations. In most emotion inducing situations, of course, the two factors are completely interrelated. Imagine a man walking alone down a dark alley; a figure with a gun suddenly appears. The perception-cognition "figure with a gun" in some fashion initiates a state of physiological arousal; this state of arousal is interpreted in terms of knowledge about dark alleys and guns and the state of arousal is labeled "fear." Similarly a student who unexpectedly learns that he has made Phi Beta Kappa may experience a state of arousal which he will label "joy."

Let us now consider circumstances in which these two elements, the physiological and the cognitive, are,

to some extent, independent. First, is the state of physiological arousal alone sufficient to induce an emotion? Best evidence indicates that it is not. Marañon[3] (1924), in a fascinating study (which was replicated by Cantril & Hunt, 1932, and Landis & Hunt, 1932), injected 210 of his patients with the sympathomimetic agent adrenalin and then simply asked them to introspect. Seventy-one percent of his subjects simply reported their physical symptoms with no emotional overtones; 29% of the subjects responded in an apparently emotional fashion. Of these the great majority described their feelings in a fashion that Marañon labeled "cold" or "as if" emotions, that is, they made statements such as "I feel *as if* I were afraid" or "*as if* I were awaiting a great happiness." This is a sort of emotional "déjà vu" experience; these subjects are neither happy nor afraid, they feel "as if" they were. Finally a very few cases apparently reported a genuine emotional experience. However, in order to produce this reaction in most of these few cases, Marañon (1924) points out:

> One must suggest a memory with strong affective force but not so strong as to produce an emotion in the normal state. For example, in several cases we spoke to our patients before the injection of their sick children or dead parents and they responded calmly to this topic. The same topic presented later, during the adrenal commotion, was sufficient to trigger emotion. This adrenal commotion places the subject in a situation of "affective imminence." (pp. 307–308)

Apparently, then, to produce a genuinely emotional reaction to adrenalin, Marañon was forced to provide such subjects with an appropriate cognition.

Though Marañon (1924) is not explicit on his procedure, it is clear that his subjects knew that they were receiving an injection and in all likelihood knew that they were receiving adrenalin and probably had some order of familiarity with its effects. In short, though they underwent the pattern of sympathetic discharge common to strong emotional states, at the same time they had a completely appropriate cognition or explanation as to why they felt this way. This, we would suggest, is the reason so few of Marañon's subjects reported any emotional experience.

Consider now a person in a state of physiological arousal for which no immediately explanatory or appropriate cognitions are available. Such a state could result were one covertly to inject a subject with adrenalin or, unknown to him, feed the subject a sympathomimetic drug such as ephedrine. Under such conditions a subject would be aware of palpitations, tremor, face flushing, and most of the battery of symptoms associated with a discharge of the sympathetic nervous system. In contrast to Marañon's (1924) subjects he would, at the same time, be utterly unaware of why he felt this way. What would be the consequence of such a state?

Schachter (1959) has suggested that precisely such a state would lead to the arousal of "evaluative needs" (Festinger, 1954), that is, pressures would act on an individual in such a state to understand and label his bodily feelings. His bodily state grossly resembles the condition in which it has been at times of emotional excitement. How would he label his present feelings? It is suggested, of course, that he will label his feelings in terms of his knowledge of the immediate situation.[4] Should he at the time be with a beautiful woman, he might decide that he was wildly in love or sexually excited. Should he be at a gay party, he might, by comparing himself to others, decide that he was extremely happy and euphoric. Should he be arguing with his wife, he might explode in fury and hatred. Or, should the situation be completely inappropriate, he could decide that he was excited about something that had recently happened to him or, simply, that he was sick. In any case, it is our basic assumption that emotional states are a function of the interaction of such cognitive factors with a state of physiological arousal.

This line of thought, then, leads to the following propositions:

1. Given a state of physiological arousal for which an individual has no immediate explanation, he will "label" this state and describe his feelings in terms of the cognitions available to him. To the extent that cognitive factors are potent determiners of emotional states, it could be anticipated that precisely the same state of physiological arousal could be labeled "joy" or "fury" or "jealousy" or any of a great diversity of emotional labels depending on the cognitive aspects of the situation.

2. Given a state of physiological arousal for which an individual has a completely appropriate explanation (e.g., "I feel this way because I have just received an injection of adrenalin") no evaluative needs will arise and the individual is unlikely to label his feelings in terms of the alternative cognitions available.

Finally, consider a condition in which emotion inducing cognitions are present but there is no state of physiological arousal. For example, an individual might be completely aware that he is in great danger but for some reason (drug or surgical) remain in a state of physiological quiescence. Does he experience the emotion "fear"? Our formulation of emotion as a joint function of a state of physiological arousal and an appropriate cognition, would, of course, suggest that he does not, which leads to our final proposition.

3. Given the same cognitive circumstances, the individual will react emotionally or describe his feelings as emotions only to the extent that he experiences a state of physiological arousal.[5]

PROCEDURE

The experimental test of these propositions requires (a) the experimental manipulation of a state of physiological arousal, (b) the manipulation of the extent to which the subject has an appropriate or proper explanation of his bodily state, and (c) the creation of situations from which explanatory cognitions may be derived.

In order to satisfy the first two experimental requirements, the experiment was cast in the framework of a study of the effects of vitamin supplements on vision. As soon as a subject arrived, he was taken to a private room and told by the experimenter:

> *In this experiment we would like to make various tests of your vision. We are particularly interested in how certain vitamin compounds and vitamin supplements affect the visual skills. In particular, we want to find out how the vitamin compound called "Suproxin" affects your vision.*
>
> *What we would like to do, then, if we can get your permission, is to give you a small injection of Suproxin. The injection itself is mild and harmless; however, since some people do object to being injected we don't want to talk you into anything. Would you mind receiving a Suproxin injection?*

If the subject agrees to the injection (and all but 1 of 185 subjects did) the experimenter continues with instructions we shall describe shortly, then leaves the room. In a few minutes a physician enters the room, briefly repeats the experimenter's instructions, takes the subject's pulse and then injects him with Suproxin.

Depending upon condition, the subject receives one of two forms of Suproxin—epinephrine or a placebo.

Epinephrine or adrenalin is a sympathomimetic drug whose effects, with minor exceptions, are almost a perfect mimicry of a discharge of the sympathetic nervous system. Shortly after injection systolic blood pressure increases markedly, heart rate increases somewhat, cutaneous blood flow decreases, while muscle and cerebral blood flow increase, blood sugar and lactic acid concentration increase, and respiration rate increases slightly. As far as the subject is concerned the major subjective symptoms are palpitation, tremor, and sometimes a feeling of flushing and accelerated breathing. With a subcutaneous injection (in the dosage administered to our subjects), such effects usually begin within 3–5 minutes of injection and last anywhere from 10 minutes to an hour. For most subjects these effects are dissipated within 15–20 minutes after injection.

Subjects receiving epinephrine received a subcutaneous injection of 1/2 cubic centimeter of a 1:1000 solution of Winthrop Laboratory's Suprarenin, a saline solution of epinephrine bitartrate.

Subjects in the placebo condition received a subcutaneous injection of 1/2 cubic centimeter of saline solution. This is, of course, completely neutral material with no side effects at all.

Manipulating an Appropriate Explanation

By "appropriate" we refer to the extent to which the subject has an authoritative, unequivocal explanation of his bodily condition. Thus, a subject who had been informed by the physician that as a direct consequence of the injection he would feel palpitations, tremor, etc. would be considered to have a completely appropriate explanation. A subject who had been informed only that the injection would have no side effects would have no appropriate explanation of his state. This dimension of appropriateness was manipulated in three experimental conditions which shall be called: Epinephrine Informed (Epi Inf), Epinephrine

Ignorant (Epi Ign), and Epinephrine Misinformed (Epi Mis).

Immediately after the subject had agreed to the injection and before the physician entered the room, the experimenter's spiel in each of these conditions went as follows:

> Epinephrine Informed. *I should also tell you that some of our subjects have experienced side effects from the Suproxin. These side effects are transitory, that is, they will only last for about 15 or 20 minutes. What will probably happen is that your hand will start to shake, your heart will start to pound, and your face may get warm and flushed. Again these are side effects lasting about 15 or 20 minutes.*

While the physician was giving the injection, she told the subject that the injection was mild and harmless and repeated this description of the symptoms that the subject could expect as a consequence of the shot. In this condition, then, subjects have a completely appropriate explanation of their bodily state. They know precisely what they will feel and why.

Epinephrine Ignorant   In this condition, when the subject agreed to the injection, the experimenter said nothing more relevant to side effects and simply left the room. While the physician was giving the injection, she told the subject that the injection was mild and harmless and would have no side effects. In this condition, then, the subject has no experimentally provided explanation for his bodily state.

> Epinephrine Misinformed. *I should also tell you that some of our subjects have experienced side effects from the Suproxin. These side effects are transitory, that is, they will only last for about 15 or 20 minutes. What will probably happen is that your feet will feel numb, you will have an itching sensation over parts of your body, and you may get a slight headache. Again these are side effects lasting 15 or 20 minutes.*

And again, the physician repeated these symptoms while injecting the subject.

None of these symptoms, of course, are consequences of an injection of epinephrine and, in effect, these instructions provide the subject with a completely inappropriate explanation of his bodily feelings. This condition was introduced as a control condition of sorts. It seemed possible that the description of side effects in the Epi Inf condition might turn the subject introspective, self-examining, possibly slightly troubled. Differences on the dependent variable between the Epi Inf and Epi Ign conditions might, then, be due to such factors rather than to differences in appropriateness. The false symptoms in the Epi Mis condition should similarly turn the subject introspective, etc., but the instructions in this condition do not provide an appropriate explanation of the subject's state.

Subjects in all of the above conditions were injected with epinephrine. Finally, there was a placebo condition in which subjects, who were injected with saline solution, were given precisely the same treatment as subjects in the Epi Ign condition.

Producing an Emotion Inducing Cognition

Our initial hypothesis has suggested that given a state of physiological arousal for which the individual has no adequate explanation, cognitive factors can lead the individual to describe his feelings with any of a diversity of emotional labels. In order to test this hypothesis, it was decided to manipulate emotional states which can be considered quite different—euphoria and anger.

There are, of course, many ways to induce such states. In our own program of research, we have concentrated on social determinants of emotional states and have been able to demonstrate in other studies that people do evaluate their own feelings by comparing themselves with others around them (Schachter 1959; Wrightsman 1960). In this experiment we have attempted again to manipulate emotional state by social means. In one set of conditions, the subject is placed together with a stooge who has been trained to act euphorically. In a second set of conditions the subject is with a stooge trained to act in an angry fashion.

Euphoria

Immediately[6] after the subject had been injected, the physician left the room and the experimenter returned with a stooge whom he introduced as another subject, then said:

Both of you have had the Suproxin shot and you'll both be taking the same tests of vision. What I ask you to do now is just wait for 20 minutes. The reason for this is simply that we have to allow 20 minutes for the Suproxin to get from the injection site into the bloodstream. At the end of 20 minutes when we are certain that most of the Suproxin has been absorbed into the bloodstream, we'll begin the tests of vision.

The room in which this was said had been deliberately put into a state of mild disarray. As he was leaving, the experimenter apologetically added:

The only other thing I should do is to apologize for the condition of the room. I just didn't have time to clean it up. So, if you need any scratch paper or rubber bands or pencils, help yourself. I'll be back in 20 minutes to begin the vision tests.

As soon as the experimenter had left, the stooge introduced himself again, made a series of standard icebreaker comments, and then launched his routine. For observation purposes, the stooge's act was broken into a series of standard units, demarcated by a change in activity or a standard comment. In sequence, the units of the stooge's routine were the following:

1. Stooge reaches for a piece of paper and starts doodling saying, "They said we could use this for scratch, didn't they?" He doodles a fish for some 30 seconds, then says:

2. "This scrap paper isn't even much good for doodling" and crumples paper and attempts to throw it into wastebasket in far corner of the room. He misses but this leads him into a "basketball game." He crumples up other sheets of paper, shoots a few baskets, says "Two points" occasionally. He gets up and does a jump shot saying, "The old jump shot is really on today."

3. If the subject has not joined in, the stooge throws a paper basketball to the subject saying, "Here, you try it."

4. Stooge continues his game saying, "The trouble with paper basketballs is that you don't really have any control."

5. Stooge continues basketball, then gives it up saying, "This is one of my good days. I feel like a kid again. I think I'll make a plane." He makes a

paper airplane saying, "I guess I'll make one of the longer ones."

6. Stooge flies plane. Gets up and retrieves plane. Flies again, etc.

7. Stooge throws plane at subject.

8. Stooge, flying plane, says, "Even when I was a kid, I was never much good at this."

9. Stooge tears off part of plane saying, "Maybe this plane can't fly but at least it's good for something." He wads up paper and making a slingshot of a rubber band begins to shoot the paper.

10. Shooting, the stooge says, "They [paper ammunition] really go better if you make them long. They don't work right if you wad them up."

11. While shooting, stooge notices a sloppy pile of manila folders on a table. He builds a tower of these folders, then goes to the opposite end of the room to shoot at the tower.

12. He misses several times, then hits and cheers as the tower falls. He goes over to pick up the folders.

13. While picking up, he notices, behind a portable blackboard, a pair of hula hoops which have been covered with black tape with a few wires sticking out of the tape. He reaches for these, taking one for himself and putting the other aside but within reaching distance of the subject. The stooge tries the hula hoop, saying, "This isn't as easy as it looks."

14. Stooge twirls hoop wildly on arm, saying, "Hey, look at this—this is great."

15. Stooge replaces the hula hoop and sits down with his feet on the table. Shortly thereafter the experimenter returns to the room.

This routine was completely standard, though its pace, of course, varied depending upon the subject's reaction, the extent to which he entered into this bedlam and the extent to which he initiated activities of his own. The only variations from this standard routine were those forced by the subject. Should the subject originate some nonsense of his own and request the stooge to join in, he would do so. And, he would, of course, respond to any comments initiated by the subject.

Subjects in each of the three "appropriateness" conditions and in the placebo condition were submitted

to this setup. The stooge, of course, never knew in which condition any particular subject fell.

Anger

Immediately after the injection, the experimenter brought a stooge into the subject's room, introduced the two and after explaining the necessity for a 20 minute delay for "the Suproxin to get from the injection site into the bloodstream" he continued, "We would like you to use these 20 minutes to answer these questionnaires." Then handing out the questionnaires, he concludes with, "I'll be back in 20 minutes to pick up the questionnaires and begin the tests of vision."

Before looking at the questionnaire, the stooge says to the subject,

I really wanted to come for an experiment today, but I think it's unfair for them to give you shots. At least, they should have told us about the shots when they called us; you hate to refuse, once you're here already.

The questionnaires, five pages long, start off innocently requesting face sheet information and then grow increasingly personal and insulting. The stooge, sitting directly opposite the subject, paces his own answers so that at all times subject and stooge are working on the same question. At regular points in the questionnaire, the stooge makes a series of standardized comments about the questions. His comments start off innocently enough, grow increasingly querulous, and finally he ends up in a rage. In sequence, he makes the following comments.

1. Before answering any items, he leafs quickly through the questionnaire saying, "Boy, this is a long one."

2. Question 7 on the questionnaire requests, "List the foods that you would eat in a typical day." The stooge comments, "Oh for Pete's sake, what did I have for breakfast this morning?"

3. Question 9 asks, "Do you ever hear bells? _____ How often? _____" The stooge remarks, "Look at Question 9. How ridiculous can you get? I hear bells every time I change classes."

4. Question 13 requests, "List the childhood diseases you have had and the age at which you had them"

to which the stooge remarks, "I get annoyed at this childhood disease question. I can't remember what childhood diseases I had, and especially at what age. Can you?"

5. Question 17 asks, "What is your father's average annual income?" and the stooge says, "This really irritates me. It's none of their business what my father makes. I'm leaving that blank."

6. Question 25 presents a long series of items such as "Does not bathe or wash regularly," "Seems to need psychiatric care," etc. and requests the respondent to write down for which member of his immediate family each item seems most applicable. The question specifically prohibits the answer "None" and each item must be answered. The stooge says, "I'll be damned if I'll fill out Number 25. 'Does not bathe or wash regularly'—that's a real insult." He then angrily crosses out the entire item.

7. Question 28 reads: "How many times each week do you have sexual intercourse?" 0–1 _____ 2–3 _____ 4–6 _____ 7 and over _____. The stooge bites out, "The hell with it! I don't have to tell them all this."

8. The stooge sits sullenly for a few moments then he rips up his questionnaire, crumples the pieces and hurls them to the floor, saying, "I'm not wasting any more time. I'm getting my books and leaving" and he stamps out of the room.

9. The questionnaire continues for eight more questions ending with: "With how many men (other than your father) has your mother had extramarital relationships?" 4 and under _____; 5–9 _____; 10 and over _____.

Subjects in the Epi Ign, Epi Inf and Placebo conditions were run through this "anger" inducing sequence. The stooge, again, did not know to which condition the subject had been assigned.

In summary, this is a seven condition experiment which, for two different emotional states, allows us (a) to evaluate the effects of "appropriateness" on emotional inducibility and (b) to begin to evaluate the effects of sympathetic activation on emotional inducibility. In schematic form the conditions are the following:

Euphoria	*Anger*
Epi Inf	Epi Inf
Epi Ign	Epi Ign
Epi Mis	Placebo
Placebo	

The Epi Mis condition was not run in the Anger sequence. This was originally conceived as a control condition and it was felt that its inclusion in the Euphoria conditions alone would suffice as a means of evaluating the possible artifactual effect of the Epi Inf instructions.

Measurement

Two types of measures of emotional state were obtained. Standardized observation through a one-way mirror was the technique used to assess the subject's behavior. To what extent did he act euphoric or angry? Such behavior can be considered in a way as a "semi-private" index of mood for as far as the subject was concerned, his emotional behavior could be known only to the other person in the room—presumably another student. The second type of measure was self-report in which, on a variety of scales, the subject indicated his mood of the moment. Such measures can be considered "public" indices of mood for they would, of course, be available to the experimenter and his associates.

Observation

Euphoria   For each of the first 14 units of the stooge's standardized routine an observer kept a running chronicle of what the subject did and said. For each unit the observer coded the subject's behavior in one or more of the following categories:

Category 1: Joins in activity. If the subject entered into the stooge activities, e.g., if he made or flew airplanes, threw paper basketballs, hula hooped, etc., his behavior was coded in this category.

Category 2: Initiates new activity. A subject was so coded if he gave indications of creative euphoria, that is, if, on his own, he initiated behavior outside of the stooge's routine. Instances of such behavior would be the subject who threw open the window and, laughing, hurled paper basketballs at passersby; or, the subject who jumped on a table and spun one hula hoop on his leg and the other on his neck.

Categories 3 and 4: Ignores or watches stooge. Subjects who paid flatly no attention to the stooge or who, with or without comment, simply watched the stooge without joining in his activity were coded in these categories.

For any particular unit of behavior, the subject's behavior was coded in one or more of these categories. To test reliability of coding two observers independently coded two experimental sessions. The observers agreed completely on the coding of 88% of the units.

Anger   For each of the units of stooge behavior, an observer recorded the subject's responses and coded them according to the following category scheme:

Category 1: Agrees. In response to the stooge the subject makes a comment indicating that he agrees with the stooge's standardized comment or that he, too, is irked by a particular item on the questionnaire. For example, a subject who responded to the stooge's comment on the "father's income" question by saying, "I don't like that kind of personal question either" would be so coded (scored +2).

Category 2: Disagrees. In response to the stooge's comment, the subject makes a comment which indicates that he disagrees with the stooge's meaning or mood; e.g., in response to the stooge's comment on the "father's income" question, such a subject might say, "Take it easy, they probably have a good reason for wanting the information" (scored −2).

Category 3: Neutral. A noncommittal or irrelevant response to the stooge's remark (scored 0).

Category 4: Initiates agreement or disagreement. With no instigation by the stooge, a subject, so coded, would have volunteered a remark indicating that he felt the same way or, alternatively, quite differently than the stooge. Examples would be "Boy I hate this kind of thing" or "I'm enjoying this" (scored +2 or −2).

Category 5: Watches. The subject makes no verbal response to the stooge's comment but simply looks directly at him (scored 0).

Category 6: Ignores. The subject makes no verbal response to the stooge's comment nor does he look at him; the subject, paying no attention at all to the stooge, simply works at his own questionnaire (scored −1).

A subject was scored in one or more of these categories for each unit of stooge behavior. To test reliability, two observers independently coded three experimental sessions. In order to get a behavioral index of anger, observation protocol was scored according to the values presented in parentheses after each of the above definitions of categories. In a unit-by-unit comparison, the two observers agreed completely on the scoring of 71% of the units jointly observed. The scores of the two observers differed by a value of 1 or less for 88% of the units coded and in not a single case did the two observers differ in the direction of their scoring of a unit.

Self-Report of Mood and Physical Condition

When the subject's session with the stooge was completed, the experimenter returned to the room, took pulses and said:

Before we proceed with the vision tests, there is one other kind of information which we must have. We have found, as you can probably imagine, that there are many things beside Suproxin that affect how well you see in our tests. How hungry you are, how tired you are, and even the mood you're in at the time—whether you feel happy or irritated at the time of testing will affect how well you see. To understand the data we collect on you, then, we must be able to figure out which effects are due to causes such as these and which are caused by Suproxin.

The only way we can get such information about your physical and emotional state is to have you tell us. I'll hand out these questionnaires and ask you to answer them as accurately as possible. Obviously our data on the vision tests will only be as accurate as your description of your mental and physical state.

In keeping with this spiel, the questionnaire that the experimenter passed out contained a number of mock questions about hunger, fatigue, etc., as well as questions of more immediate relevance to the experiment. To measure mood or emotional state the following two were the crucial questions:

1. How irritated, angry or annoyed would you say you feel at present?

I don't feel at all irritated or angry	I feel a little irritated and angry	I feel quite irritated and angry	I feel very irritated and angry	I feel extremely irritated and angry
(0)	(1)	(2)	(3)	(4)

2. How good or happy would you say you feel at present?

I don't feel at all happy or good	I feel a little happy and good	I feel quite happy and good	I feel very happy and good	I feel extremely happy and good
(0)	(1)	(2)	(3)	(4)

To measure the physical effects of epinephrine and determine whether or not the injection had been successful in producing the necessary bodily state, the following questions were asked:

1. Have you experienced any palpitation (consciousness of your own heart beat)?

Not at all	A slight amount	A moderate amount	An intense amount
(0)	(1)	(2)	(3)

2. Did you feel any tremor (involuntary shaking of the hands, arms or legs)?

Not at all	A slight amount	A moderate amount	An intense amount
(0)	(1)	(2)	(3)

To measure possible effects of the instructions in the Epi Mis condition, the following questions were asked:

1. Did you feel any numbness in your feet?
2. Did you feel any itching sensation?
3. Did you experience any feeling of headache?

To all three of these questions was attached a four-point scale running from "Not at all" to "An intense amount."

In addition to these scales, the subjects were asked to answer two open-end questions on other physical or emotional sensations they may have experienced during the experimental session. A final measure of bodily state was pulse rate which was taken by the physician or the experimenter at two times—immediately before the injection and immediately after the session with the stooge.

When the subjects had completed these questionnaires, the experimenter announced that the experiment was over, explained the deception and its necessity in detail, answered any questions, and swore the subjects to secrecy. Finally, the subjects answered a brief questionnaire about their experiences, if any, with adrenalin and their previous knowledge or suspicion of the experimental setup. There was no indication that any of the subjects had known about the experiment beforehand but 11 subjects were so extremely suspicious of some crucial feature of the experiment that their data were automatically discarded.

Subjects

The subjects were all male, college students taking classes in introductory psychology at the University of Minnesota. Some 90% of the students in these classes volunteer for a subject pool for which they receive two extra points on their final exam for every hour that they serve as experimental subjects. For this study the records of all potential subjects were cleared with the Student Health Service in order to insure that no harmful effects would result from the injections.

Evaluation of the Experimental Design

The ideal test of our propositions would require circumstances which our experiment is far from realizing. First, the proposition that: "A state of physiological arousal for which an individual has no immediate explanation will lead him to label this state in terms of the cognitions available to him" obviously requires conditions under which the subject does not and cannot have a proper explanation of his bodily state. Though we toyed with such fantasies as ventilating the experimental room with vaporized adrenalin, reality forced us to rely on the disguised injection of Suproxin—a technique which was far from ideal for no matter what the experimenter told them, some subjects would inevitably attribute their feelings to the injection. To the extent that subjects did so, differences between the several appropriateness conditions should be attenuated.

Second, the proposition that: "Given the same cognitive circumstances the individual will react emotionally only to the extent that he experiences a state of physiological arousal" requires for its ideal test the manipulation of states of physiological arousal and of physiological quiescence. Though there is no question that epinephrine effectively produces a state of arousal, there is also no question that a placebo does not prevent physiological arousal. To the extent that the experimental situation effectively produces sympathetic stimulation in placebo subjects, the proposition is difficult to test, for such a factor would attenuate differences between epinephrine and placebo subjects.

Both of these factors, then, can be expected to interfere with the test of our several propositions. In presenting the results of this study, we shall first present condition by condition results and then evaluate the effect of these two factors on experimental differences.

RESULTS

Effects of the Injections on Bodily State

Let us examine first the success of the injections at producing the bodily state required to examine the propositions at test. Does the injection of epinephrine produce symptoms of sympathetic discharge as compared with the placebo injection? Relevant data are presented in Table 1 where it can be immediately seen that on all items subjects who were in epinephrine conditions show considerably more evidence of sym-

pathetic activation than do subjects in placebo conditions. In all epineprine conditions pulse rate increases significantly when compared with the decrease characteristic of the placebo conditions. On the scales it is clear that epinephrine subjects experience considerably more palpitation and tremor than do placebo subjects. In all possible comparisons on these symptoms, the mean scores of subjects in any of the epinephrine conditions are greater than the corresponding scores in the placebo conditions at better than the .001 level of significance. Examination of the absolute values of these scores makes it quite clear that subjects in epinephrine conditions were, indeed, in a state of physiological arousal, while most subjects in placebo conditions were in a relative state of physiological quiescence.

The epinephrine injection, of course, did not work with equal effectiveness for all subjects; indeed for a few subjects it did not work at all. Such subjects reported almost no palpitation or tremor, showed no increase in pulse and described no other relevant physical symptoms. Since for such subjects the necessary experimental conditions were not established, they were automatically excluded from the data and all further tabular presentations will not include such subjects. Table 1, however, does include the data of these subjects. There were four such subjects in euphoria conditions and one of them in anger conditions.

In order to evaluate further data on Epi Mis subjects it is necessary to note the results of the "numbness," "itching," and "headache" scales also presented in Table 1. Clearly the subjects in the Epi Mis condi-

TABLE 1 / Effects of the Injections on Bodily State

Condition	N	Pulse		Self-Rating of				
		Pre	Post	Palpitation	Tremor	Numbness	Itching	Headache
Euphoria								
Epi Inf	27	85.7	88.6	1.20	1.43	0	0.16	0.32
Epi Ign	26	84.6	85.6	1.83	1.76	0.15	0	0.55
Epi Mis	26	82.9	86.0	1.27	2.00	0.06	0.08	0.23
Placebo	26	80.4	77.1	0.29	0.21	0.09	0	0.27
Anger								
Epi Inf	23	85.9	92.4	1.26	1.41	0.17	0	0.11
Epi Ign	23	85.0	96.8	1.44	1.78	0	0.06	0.21
Placebo	23	84.5	79.6	0.59	0.24	0.14	0.06	0.06

tion do not differ on these scales from subjects in any of the other experimental conditions.

Effects of the Manipulations on Emotional State

Euphoria Self-report. The effects of the several manipulations on emotional state in the euphoria conditions are presented in Table 2. The scores recorded in this table are derived, for each subject, by subtracting the value of the point he checks on the irritation scale from the value of the point he checks on the happiness scale. Thus, if a subject were to check the point "I feel a little irritated and angry" on the irritation scale and the point "I feel very happy and good" on the happiness scale, his score would be +2. The higher the positive value, the happier and better the subject reports himself as feeling. Though we employ an index for expositional simplicity, it should be noted that the two components of the index each yield results completely consistent with those obtained by use of this index.

Let us examine first the effects of the appropriateness instructions. Comparison of the scores for the Epi Mis and Epi Inf conditions makes it immediately clear that the experimental differences are not due to artifacts resulting from the informed instructions. In both conditions the subject was warned to expect a variety of symptoms as a consequence of the injection. In the Epi Mis condition, where the symptoms were inappropriate to the subject's bodily state the self-

TABLE 2 / Self-Report of Emotional State in the Euphoria Conditions

Condition	N	Self-Report Scales	Comparison	p
Epi Inf	25	0.98	Epi Inf vs. Epi Mis	< .01
Epi Ign	25	1.78	Epi Inf vs. Epi Ign	.02
Epi Mis	25	1.90	Placebo vs. Epi Mis, Ign, or Inf	ns
Placebo	26	1.61		

All *p* values reported throughout paper are two-tailed.

report score is almost twice that in the Epi Inf condition where the symptoms were completely appropriate to the subject's bodily state. It is reasonable, then, to attribute differences between informed subjects and those in other conditions to differences in manipulated appropriateness rather than to artifacts such as introspectiveness or self-examination.

It is clear that, consistent with expectations, subjects were more susceptible to the stooge's mood and consequently more euphoric when they had no explanation of their own bodily states than when they did. The means of both the Epi Ign and Epi Mis conditions are considerably greater than the mean of the Epi Inf condition.

It is of interest to note that Epi Mis subjects are somewhat more euphoric than are Epi Ign subjects. This pattern repeats itself in other data shortly to be presented. We would attribute this difference to differences in the appropriateness dimension. Though, as in the Epi Ign condition, a subject is not provided with an explanation of his bodily state, it is, of course, possible that he will provide one for himself which is not derived from his interaction with the stooge. Most reasonably he could decide for himself that he feels this way because of the injection. To the extent that he does so he should be less susceptible to the stooge. It seems probable that he would be less likely to hit on such an explanation in the Epi Mis condition than in the Epi Ign condition for in the Epi Mis condition both the experimenter and the doctor have told him that the effects of the injection would be quite different from what he actually feels. The effect of such instructions is probably to make it more difficult for the subject himself to hit on the alternative explanation described above. There is some evidence to support this analysis. In open-end questions in which subjects described their own mood and state, 28% of the subjects in the Epi Ign condition made some connection between the injection and their bodily state compared with the 16% of subjects in the Epi Mis condition who did so. It could be considered, then, that these three conditions fall along a dimension of appropriateness, with the Epi Inf condition at one extreme and the Epi Mis condition at the other.

Comparing the placebo to the epinephrine conditions, we note a pattern which will repeat itself throughout the data. Placebo subjects are less euphoric than either Epi Mis or Epi Ign subjects but somewhat more euphoric than Epi Inf subjects. These differences are not, however, statistically significant. We shall consider the epinephrine-placebo comparisons in detail in a later section of this paper following the presentation of additional relevant data. For the moment, it is clear that, by self-report manipulating appropriateness has had a very strong effect on euphoria.

Behavior.   Let us next examine the extent to which the subject's behavior was affected by the experimental manipulations. To the extent that his mood has been affected, one should expect that the subject will join in the stooge's whirl of manic activity and initiate similar activities of his own. The relevant data are presented in Table 3. The column labeled "Activity index" presents summary figures on the extent to which the subject joined in the stooge's activity. This is a weighted index which reflects both the nature of the activities in which the subject engaged and the amount of time he was active. The index was devised by assigning the following weights to the subject's activities: 5—hula hooping; 4—shooting with slingshot; 3—paper airplanes; 2—

TABLE 3 / Behavioral Indications of Emotional State in the Euphoria Conditions

Condition	N	Activity Index	Mean Number of Acts Initiated
Epi Inf	25	12.72	.20
Epi Ign	25	18.28	.56
Epi Mis	25	22.56	.84
Placebo	26	16.00	.54

p value

Comparison	Activity Index	Initiates
Epi Inf vs. Epi Mis	.05	.03
Epi Inf vs. Ipi Ign	ns	.08
Plac vs. Epi Mis. Ign. or Inf	ns	ns

Tested by χ^2 comparison of the proportion of subjects in each condition initiating new acts.

paper basketballs; 1—doodling; 0—does nothing. Pretest scaling on 15 college students ordered these activities with respect to the degree of euphoria they represented. Arbitrary weights were assigned so that the wilder the activity, the heavier the weight. These weights are multiplied by an estimate of the amount of time the subject spent in each activity and the summed products make up the activity index for each subject. This index may be considered a measure of behavioral euphoria. It should be noted that the same between-condition relationships hold for the two components of this index as for the index itself.

The column labeled "Mean number of acts initiated" presents the data on the extent to which the subject deviates from the stooge's routine and initiates euphoric activities of his own.

On both behavioral indices, we find precisely the same pattern of relationships as those obtained with self-reports. Epi Mis subjects behave somewhat more euphorically than do Epi Ign subjects who in turn behave more euphorically than do Epi Inf subjects. On all measures, then, there is consistent evidence that a subject will take over the stooge's euphoric mood to the extent that he has no other explanation of his bodily state.

Again it should be noted that on these behavioral indices, Epi Ign and Epi Mis subjects are somewhat more euphoric than placebo subjects but not significantly so.

Anger   Self-report.   Before presenting data for the anger conditions, one point must be made about the anger manipulation. In the situation devised, anger, if manifested, is most likely to be directed at the experimenter and his annoyingly personal questionnaire. As we subsequently discovered, this was rather unfortunate, for the subjects, who had volunteered for the experiment for extra points on their final exam, simply refused to endanger these points by publicly blowing up, admitting their irritation to the experimenter's face or spoiling the questionnaire. Though as the reader will see, the subjects were quite willing to manifest anger when they were alone with the stooge, they hesitated to do so on material (self-ratings of mood and questionnaire) that the experimenter might see and only after the purposes of the experiment had been revealed were many of these subjects willing to admit to the experimenter that they had been irked or irritated.

This experimentally unfortunate situation pretty much forces us to rely on the behavioral indices derived from observation of the subject's presumably private interaction with the stooge. We do, however, present data on the self-report scales in Table 4. These figures are derived in the same way as the figures presented in Table 2 for the euphoria conditions, that is, the value checked on the irritation scale is subtracted from the value checked on the happiness scale. Though, for the reasons stated above, the absolute magnitude of these figures (all positive) is relatively meaningless, we can, of course, compare condition means within the set of anger conditions. With the happiness-irritation index employed, we should, of course, anticipate precisely the reverse results from those obtained in the euphoria conditions; that is, the Epi Inf subjects in the anger conditions should again be less susceptible to the stooge's mood and should, therefore, describe themselves as in a somewhat happier frame of mind than subjects in the Epi Ign condition. This is the case; the Epi Inf subjects average 1.91 on the self-report scales while the Epi Ign subjects average 1.39.

Evaluating the effects of the injections, we note again that, as anticipated, Epi Ign subjects are somewhat less happy than Placebo subjects but, once more, this is not a significant difference.

Behavior.   The subject's responses to the stooge, during the period when both were filling out their questionnaires, were systematically coded to provide a behavioral index of anger. The coding scheme and the numerical values attached to each of the categories have been described in the methodology section. To arrive at an "Anger index" the numerical value assigned to a subject's responses to the stooge is summed together for the several units of stooge behavior. In the coding scheme used, a positive value to this index indicates that the subject agrees with the stooge's comment and is growing angry. A negative value indicates that the subject either disagrees with the stooge or ignores him.

The relevant data are presented in Table 5. For this analysis, the stooge's routine has been divided into two phases—the first two units of his behavior (the "long" questionnaire and "What did I have for breakfast?") are considered essentially neutral revealing nothing of the stooge's mood; all of the following units are considered "angry" units for they begin with an irritated remark about the "bells" question and end with the stooge's fury as he rips up his questionnaire and stomps out of the room. For the neutral units, agreement or disagreement with the stooge's remarks is, of course, meaningless as an index of mood and we should anticipate no difference between conditions. As can be seen in Table 5, this is the case.

For the angry units, we must, of course, anticipate that subjects in the Epi Ign condition will be angrier than subjects in the Epi Inf condition. This is indeed the case. The Anger index for the Epi Ign condition is positive and large, indicating that these subjects have

TABLE 4 / Self-Report of Emotional State in the Anger Conditions

Condition	N	Self-Report Scales	Comparison	p
Epi Inf	22	1.91	Epi Inf vs. Epi Ign	.08
Epi Ign	23	1.39	Placebo vs. Epi Ign or Inf	ns
Placebo	23	1.63		

TABLE 5 / Behavioral Indications of Emotional State in the Anger Conditions

Condition	N	Neutral Units	Anger Units
Epi Inf	22	+0.07	−0.18
Epi Ign	23	+0.30	+2.28
Placebo	22[a]	−0.09	+0.79

Comparison for Anger Units	p
Epi Inf vs. Epi Ign	< .01
Epi Ign vs. Placebo	< .05
Placebo vs. Epi Inf	ns

[a]For one subject in this condition the sound system went dead and the observer could not, of course, code his reactions.

become angry, while in the Epi Inf condition the Anger index is slightly negative in value indicating that these subjects have failed to catch the stooge's mood at all. It seems clear that providing the subject with an appropriate explanation of his bodily state greatly reduces his tendency to interpret his state in terms of the cognitions provided by the stooge's angry behavior.

Finally, on this behavioral index, it can be seen that subjects in the Epi Ign condition are significantly angrier than subjects in the Placebo condition. Behaviorally, at least, the injection of epinephrine appears to have led subjects to an angrier state than comparable subjects who received placebo shots.

Conformation of Data to Theoretical Expectations

Now that the basic data of this study have been presented, let us examine closely the extent to which they conform to theoretical expectations. If our hypotheses are correct and if this experimental design provided a perfect test for these hypotheses, it should be anticipated that in the euphoria conditions the degree of experimentally produced euphoria should vary in the following fashion:

$$\text{Epi Mis} \geq \text{Epi Ign} > \text{Epi Inf} = \text{Placebo}$$

And in the anger conditions, anger should conform to the following pattern:

$$\text{Epi Ign} > \text{Epi Inf} = \text{Placebo}$$

In both sets of conditions, it is the case that emotional level in the Epi Mis and Epi Ign conditions is considerably greater than that achieved in the corresponding Epi Inf conditions. The results for the Placebo condition, however, are ambiguous for consistently the Placebo subjects fall between the Epi Ign and the Epi Inf subjects. This is a particularly troubling pattern for it makes it impossible to evaluate unequivocally the effects of the state of physiological arousal and indeed raises serious questions about our entire theoretical structure. Though the emotional level is consistently greater in the Epi Mis and Epi Ign conditions than in the Placebo condition, this difference is significant at acceptable probability levels only in the anger conditions.

In order to explore the problem further, let us examine the experimental factors identified earlier,

which might have acted to restrain the emotional level in the Epi Ign and Epi Mis conditions. As was pointed out earlier, the ideal test of our first two hypotheses requires an experimental setup in which the subject has flatly no way of evaluating his state of physiological arousal other than by means of the experimentally provided cognitions. Had it been possible to physiologically produce a state of sympathetic activation by means other than injection, one could have approached this experimental ideal more closely than in the present setup. As it stands, however, there is always a reasonable alternative cognition available to the aroused subject—he feels the way he does because of the injection. To the extent that the subject seizes on such an explanation of his bodily state, we should expect that he will be uninfluenced by the stooge. Evidence presented in Table 6 for the anger condition and in Table 7 for the euphoria conditions indicates that this is, indeed, the case.

As mentioned earlier, some of the Epi Ign and Epi Mis subjects in their answers to the open-end questions clearly attributed their physical state to the injection, e.g., "the shot gave me the shivers." In Tables 6 and 7 such subjects are labeled "Self-informed." In Table 6 it can be seen that the self-informed subjects are considerably less angry than are the remaining subjects; indeed, they are not angry at all. With these self-informed subjects eliminated the difference between the Epi Ign and the Placebo conditions is significant at the .01 level of significance.

Precisely the same pattern is evident in Table 7 for the euphoria conditions. In both the Epi Mis and the Epi Ign conditions, the self-informed subjects have considerably lower activity indices than do the remaining subjects. Eliminating self-informed subjects, comparison of both of these conditions with the

TABLE 6 / The Effects of Attributing Bodily State to the Injection on Anger in the Anger Epi Ign Condition

Condition	N	Index	Anger p
Self-informed subjects	3	−1.67	*ns*
Others	20	+2.88	*ns*
Self-informed vs. Others			.05

TABLE 7 / The Effects of Attributing Bodily State to the Injection on Euphoria in the Euphoria Epi Ign and Epi Mis Conditions

Epi Ign			
	N	Activity Index	p
Self-informed subjects	8	11.63	ns
Others	17	21.14	ns
Self-informed vs. Others			.05

Epi Mis			
	N	Activity Index	p
Self-informed subjects	5	12.40	ns
Others	20	25.10	ns
Self-informed vs. Others			.10

Placebo condition yields a difference significant at the .03 level of significance. It should be noted, too, that the self-informed subjects have much the same score on the activity index as do the experimental Epi Inf subjects (Table 3).

It would appear, then, that the experimental procedure of injecting the subjects, by providing an alternative cognition, has, to some extent, obscured the effects of epinephrine. When account is taken of this artifact, the evidence is good that the state of physiological arousal is a necessary component of an emotional experience for when self-informed subjects are removed, epinephrine subjects give consistent indications of greater emotionality than do placebo subjects.

Let us examine next the fact that consistently the emotional level, both reported and behavioral, in Placebo conditions is greater than that in the Epi Inf conditions. Theoretically, of course, it should be expected that the two conditions will be equally low, for by assuming that emotional state is a joint function of a state of physiological arousal and of the appropriateness of a cognition we are, in effect, assuming a multiplicative function, so that if either component is at zero, emotional level is at zero. As noted earlier this expectation should hold if we can be sure that there is no sympathetic activation in the Placebo conditions.

This assumption, of course, is completely unrealistic for the injection of placebo does not prevent sympathetic activation. The experimental situations were fairly dramatic and certainly some of the placebo subjects gave indications of physiological arousal. If our general line of reasoning is correct, it should be anticipated that the emotional level of subjects who give indications of sympathetic activity will be greater than that of subjects who do not. The relevant evidence is presented in Tables 8 and 9.

As an index of sympathetic activation we shall use the most direct and unequivocal measure available—change in pulse rate. It can be seen in Table 1 that the predominant pattern in the Placebo condition is a decrease in pulse rate. We shall assume, therefore, that those subjects whose pulse increases or remains the same give indications of sympathetic activity while those subjects whose pulse decreases do not. In Table 8, for the euphoria condition, it is immediately clear that subjects who give indications of sympathetic activity are considerably more euphoric than are subjects who show no sympathetic activity. This relationship is, of course, confounded by the fact that euphoric subjects are considerably more active than non-euphoric subjects—a factor which independent of mood could elevate pulse rate. However, no such factor operates in the anger condition where angry subjects are neither more active nor talkative than calm subjects. It can be seen in Table 9 that Placebo subjects who show signs of sympathetic activation give indications of considerably more anger than do subjects who show no such signs. Conforming to expectation, sympathetic activation accompanies an increase in emotional level.

TABLE 8 / Sympathetic Activation and Euphoria in the Euphoria Placebo Condition

Subjects Whose:	N	Activity Index	p
Pulse decreased	14	10.67	ns
Pulse increased or remained same	12	23.17	ns
Pulse decrease vs. pulse increase or same			.02

TABLE 9 / Sympathetic Activation and Anger in Anger Placebo Condition

Subjects Whose:	N^a	Activity Index	p
Pulse decreased	13	+0.15	ns
Pulse increased or remained same	8	+1.69	ns
Pulse decrease vs. pulse increase or same			.01

[a]N reduced by two cases owing to failure of sound system in one case and experimenter's failure to take pulse in another.

It should be noted, too, that the emotional levels of subjects showing no signs of sympathetic activity are quite comparable to the emotional level of subjects in the parallel Epi Inf conditions (see Tables 3 and 5). The similarity of these sets of scores and their uniformly low level of indicated emotionality would certainly make it appear that both factors are essential to an emotional state. When either the level of sympathetic arousal is low or a completely appropriate cognition is available, the level of emotionality is low.

DISCUSSION

Let us summarize the major findings of this experiment and examine the extent to which they support the propositions offered in the introduction of this paper. It has been suggested, first, that given a state of physiological arousal for which an individual has no explanation, he will label this state in terms of the cognitions available to him. This implies, of course, that by manipulating the cognitions of an individual in such a state we can manipulate his feelings in diverse directions. Experimental results support this proposition for following the injection of epinephrine, those subjects who had no explanation for the bodily state thus produced, gave behavioral and self-report indications that they had been readily manipulable into the disparate feeling states of euphoria and anger.

From this first proposition, it must follow that given a state of physiological arousal for which the individual has a completely satisfactory explanation, he will not label this state in terms of the alternative cognitions available. Experimental evidence strongly supports this expectation. In those conditions in which subjects were injected with epinephrine and told precisely what they would feel and why, they proved relatively immune to any effects of the manipulated cognitions. In the anger condition, such subjects did not report or show anger; in the euphoria condition, such subjects reported themselves as far less happy than subjects with an identical bodily state but no adequate knowledge of why they felt they way they did.

Finally, it has been suggested that given constant cognitive circumstances, an individual will react emotionally only to the extent that he experiences a state of physiological arousal. Without taking account of experimental artifacts, the evidence in support of this proposition is consistent but tentative. When the effects of "self-informing" tendencies in epinephrine subjects and of "self-arousing" tendencies in placebo subjects are partialed out, the evidence strongly supports the proposition.

The pattern of data, then, falls neatly in line with theoretical expectations. However, the fact that we were forced, to some extent, to rely on internal analyses in order to partial out the effects of experimental artifacts inevitably makes our conclusions somewhat tentative. In order to further test these propositions on the interaction of cognitive and physiological determinants of emotional state, a series of additional experiments, published elsewhere, was designed to rule out or overcome the operation of these artifacts. In the first of these, Schachter and Wheeler (1962) extended the range of manipulated sympathetic activation by employing three experimental groups—epinephrine, placebo, and a group injected with the sympatholytic agent, chlorpromazine. Laughter at a slapstick movie was the dependent variable and the evidence is good that amusement is a direct function of manipulated sympathetic activation.

In order to make the epinephrine-placebo comparison under conditions which would rule out the operation of any self-informing tendency, two experiments were conducted on rats. In one of these Singer (1961) demonstrated that under fear inducing conditions, manipulated by the simultaneous presentation of a loud bell, a buzzer, and a bright flashing light, rats injected with epinephrine were considerably more frightened than rats injected with a placebo.

Epinephrine-injected rats defecated, urinated, and trembled more than did placebo-injected rats. In non-fear control conditions, there were no differences between epinephrine and placebo groups, neither group giving any indication of fear. In another study, Latané and Schachter (1962) demonstrated that rats injected with epinephrine were notably more capable of avoidance learning than were rats injected with a placebo. Using a modified Miller-Mowrer shuttle-box, these investigators found that during an experimental period involving 200 massed trials, 15 rats injected with epinephrine avoided shock an average of 101.2 trials while 15 placebo-injected rats averaged only 37.3 avoidances.

Taken together, this body of studies does give strong support to the propositions which generated these experimental tests. Given a state of sympathetic activation, for which no immediately appropriate explanation is available, human subjects can be readily manipulated into states of euphoria, anger, and amusement. Varying the intensity of sympathetic activation serves to vary the intensity of a variety of emotional states in both rats and human subjects.

Let us examine the implications of these findings and of this line of thought for problems in the general area of the physiology of the emotions. We have noted in the introduction that the numerous studies on physiological differentiators of emotional states have, viewed en masse, yielded quite inconclusive results. Most, though not all, of these studies have indicated no differences among the various emotional states. Since as human beings, rather than as scientists, we have no difficulty identifying, labeling, and distinguishing among our feelings, the results of these studies have long seemed rather puzzling and paradoxical. Perhaps because of this, there has been a persistent tendency to discount such results as due to ignorance or methodological inadequacy and to pay far more attention to the very few studies which demonstrate *some* sort of physiological differences among emotional states than to the very many studies which indicate no differences at all. It is conceivable, however, that these results should be taken at face value and that emotional states may, indeed, be generally characterized by a high level of sympathetic activation with few if any physiological distinguishers among the many emotional states. If this is correct, the findings

of the present study may help to resolve the problem. Obviously this study does *not* rule out the possibility of physiological differences among the emotional states. It is the case, however, that given precisely the same state of epinephrine-induced sympathetic activation, we have, by means of cognitive manipulations, been able to produce in our subjects the very disparate states of euphoria and anger. It may indeed be the case that cognitive factors are major determiners of the emotional labels we apply to a common state of sympathetic arousal.

Let us ask next whether our results are specific to the state of sympathetic activation or if they are generalizable to other states of physiological arousal. It is clear that from our experiments proper, it is impossible to answer the question for our studies have been concerned largely with the effects of an epinephrine created state of sympathetic arousal. We would suggest, however, that our conclusions are generalizable to almost any pronounced internal state for which no appropriate explanation is available. This suggestion receives some support from the experiences of Nowlis and Nowlis (1956) in their program of research on the effects of drugs on mood. In their work the Nowlises typically administer a drug to groups of four subjects who are physically in one another's presence and free to interact. The Nowlises describe some of their results with these groups as follows:

> At first we used the same drug for all 4 men. In those sessions seconal, when compared with placebo, increased the checking of such words as expansive, forceful, courageous, daring, elated, and impulsive. In our first statistical analysis we were confronted with the stubborn fact that when the same drug is given to all 4 men in a group, the N that has to be entered into the analysis is 1, not 4. This increases the cost of an already expensive experiment by a considerable factor, but it cannot be denied that the effects of these drugs may be and often are quite contagious. Our first attempted solution was to run tests on groups in which each man had a different drug during the same session, such as 1 on seconal, 1 on benzedrine, 1 on dramamine, and 1 on placebo. What does seconal do? Cooped up with, say, the egotistical benzedrine partner, the withdrawn, indifferent dramamine partner, and the slightly bored lactose man, the seconal subject

reports that he is distractible, dizzy, drifting, glum, defiant, languid, sluggish, discouraged, dull, gloomy, lazy, and slow! This is not the report of mood that we got when all 4 men were on seconal. It thus appears that the moods of the partners do definitely influence the effect of seconal. (p. 350)

It is not completely clear from this description whether this "contagion" of mood is more marked in drug than in placebo groups, but should this be the case, these results would certainly support the suggestion that our findings are generalizable to internal states other than that produced by an injection of epinephrine.

Finally, let us consider the implications of our formulation and data for alternative conceptualizations of emotion. Perhaps the most popular current conception of emotion is in terms of "activation theory" in the sense employed by Lindsley (1951) and Woodworth and Schlosberg (1958). As we understand this theory, it suggests that emotional states should be considered as at one end of a continuum of activation which is defined in terms of degree of autonomic arousal and of electroencephalographic measures of activation. The results of the experiment described in this paper do, of course, suggest that such a formulation is not completely adequate. It is possible to have very high degrees of activation without a subject either appearing to be or describing himself as "emotional." Cognitive factors appear to be indispensable elements in any formulation of emotion.

SUMMARY

It is suggested that emotional states may be considered a function of a state of physiological arousal and of a cognition appropriate to this state of arousal. From this follows these propositions:

1. Given a state of physiological arousal for which an individual has no immediate explanation, he will label this state and describe his feelings in terms of the cognitions available to him. To the extent that cognitive factors are potent determiners of emotional states, it should be anticipated that precisely the same state of physiological arousal could be labeled "joy" or "fury" or "jealousy" or any of a great diversity of emotional labels depending on the cognitive aspects of the situation.

2. Given a state of physiological arousal for which an individual has a completely appropriate explanation, no evaluative needs will arise and the individual is unlikely to label his feelings in terms of the alternative cognitions available.

3. Given the same cognitive circumstances, the individual will react emotionally or describe his feelings as emotions only to the extent that he experiences a state of physiological arousal.

An experiment is described which, together with the results of other studies, supports these propositions.

REFERENCES

Ax, A. F. Physiological differentiation of emotional states. *Psychosom. Med.,* 1953, *15,* 435–442.

Cannon, W. B. *Bodily changes in pain, hunger, fear and rage.* (2nd ed.) New York: Appleton, 1929.

Cantril, H., & Hunt, W. A. Emotional effects produced by the injection of adrenalin. *Amer. J. Psychol.,* 1932, *44,* 300–307.

Festinger, L. A theory of social comparison processes. *Hum. Relat.,* 1954, *7,* 114–140.

Hunt, J. McV., Cole, M. W., & Reis, E. E. Situational cues distinguishing anger, fear, and sorrow. *Amer. J. Psychol.,* 1958, *71,* 136–151.

James, W. *The principles of psychology.* New York: Holt, 1890.

Landis, C., & Hunt, W. A. Adrenalin and emotion. *Psychol. Rev.,* 1932, *39,* 467–485.

Latané, B., & Schachter, S. Adrenalin and avoidance learning. *J. Comp. Physiol. Psychol.,* 1962, *65,* 369–372.

Lindsley, D. B. Emotion. In S. S. Stevens (Ed.), *Handbook of experimental psychology.* New York: Wiley, 1951. Pp. 473–516.

Marañon, G. Contribution à l'étude de l'action émotive de l'adrénaline. *Rev. Francaise Endocrinol.,* 1924, *2,* 301–325.

Nowlis, V., & Nowlis, H. H. The description and analysis of mood. *Ann. N. Y. Acad. Sci.,* 1956, *65,* 345–355.

Ruckmick, C. A. *The psychology of feeling and emotion.* New York: McGraw-Hill, 1936.

Schachter, J. Pain, fear, and anger in hypertensives and normotensives: A psychophysiologic study. *Psychosom. Med.,* 1957, *19,* 17–29.

Schachter, S. *The psychology of affiliation.* Stanford, CA: Stanford Univer. Press, 1959.

Schachter, S., & Wheeler, L. Epinephrine, chlorpromazine, and amusement. *J. Abnorm. Soc. Psychol.,* 1962, *65,* 121–128.

Singer, J. E. The effects of epinephrine, chlorpromazine and dibenzyline upon the fright responses of rats under stress and non-stress conditions. Unpublished doctoral dissertation, University of Minnesota, 1961.

Wolf, S., & Wolff, H. G. *Human gastric function.* New York: Oxford Univer. Press, 1947.

Woodworth, R. S., & Schlosberg, H. *Experimental psychology.* New York: Holt, 1958.

Wrightsman, L. S. Effects of waiting with others on changes in level of felt anxiety. *J. Abnorm. Soc. Psychol.,* 1960, *61,* 216–222.

ENDNOTES

1. This experiment is part of a program of research on cognitive and physiological determinants of emotional state which is being conducted at the Department of Social Psychology at Columbia University under PHS Research Grant M-2584 from the National Institute of Mental Health, United States Public Health Service. This experiment was conducted at the Laboratory for Research in Social Relations at the University of Minnesota.

The authors wish to thank Jean Carlin and Ruth Hase, the physicians in the study, and Bibb Latané and Leonard Weller who were the paid participants.

2. Though our experiments are concerned exclusively with the physiological changes produced by the injection of adrenalin, which appear to be primarily the result of sympathetic excitation, the term physiological arousal is used in preference to the more specific "excitation of the sympathetic nervous system" because there are indications, to be discussed later, that this formulation is applicable to a variety of bodily states.

3. Translated copies of Marañon's (1924) paper may be obtained by writing to the senior author.

4. This suggestion is not new for several psychologists have suggested that situational factors should be considered the chief differentiators of the emotions. Hunt, Cole, and Reis (1958) probably make this point most explicitly in their study distinguishing among fear, anger, and sorrow in terms of situational characteristics.

5. In his critique of the James-Lange theory of emotion, Cannon (1929) also makes the point that sympathectomized animals and patients do seem to manifest emotional behavior. This criticism is, of course, as applicable to the above proposition as it was to the James-Lange formulation. We shall discuss the issues involved in later papers.

6. It was, of course, imperative that the sequence with the stooge begin before the subject felt his first symptoms for otherwise the subject would be virtually forced to interpret his feelings in terms of events preceding the stooge's entrance. Pretests had indicated that, for most subjects, epinephrine-caused symptoms began within 3–5 minutes after injection. A deliberate attempt was made then to bring in the stooge within 1 minute after the subject's injection.

CRITICAL THINKING QUESTIONS

1. In order to conduct the experiment, the researchers deceived the subjects. What ethical issues are involved in this type of research? The obvious deception was not telling the subjects the true nature of the experiment. Does the use of injections of a drug that had a physiological impact on the subjects prompt additional ethical considerations? Explain your answer.

2. This study examines the effects of just one drug, epinephrine, which has excitatory effects on people. Would you expect a similar pattern of results for other classes of drugs? Why or why not? Which ones might be interesting to study?

3. What might the implications of this study be for people who use drugs in a social setting? Would the feelings that they associate with using drugs be due to how others around them responded? Explain your answer. How could you test this possibility?

4. Do you think it is possible to change the emotion you are experiencing by changing the label of the emotion? For example, if you were afraid of public speaking, could you change your emotion from a negative one (fear) to a positive one (excitement) by changing the label given to your physiological arousal? Have you had any personal experience with something like this that may have occurred or a situation when you were aware of how other people influenced how you interpreted the situation? Explain your answer.

ADDITIONAL RELATED READINGS

Lazarus, R. S. (1984). On the primacy of cognition. *American Psychologist, 39,* 124–129.

Zajonc, R. B. (1984). On the primacy of affect. *American Psychologist, 39,* 117–123.

ARTICLE 9 _____

While most of us would like to think that we are fairly rational and logical in how we interpret the world around us, the fact is that we are all prone to certain types of biases and distortions in judgment. Some of these more common biases were addressed in Article 7.

When we see someone acting in a certain way, we can make one of two basic explanations for his or her behavior. On the one hand, we can attribute a person's behavior to his or her *disposition* (or *trait*), which means that we see the behavior as a relatively enduring characteristic of him or her. For example, if someone is acting nice toward us, we can interpret that behavior as being due to his or her trait of being a nice person. On the other hand, we also can attribute a person's behavior to the *situation* (or *state*) that he or she is in at the moment. Thus, we can interpret the behavior of the person acting nice toward us as being due to the present situation, such as him or her being watched by someone else or wanting something from us in return. According to this view, behavior is not tied to personality or disposition.

While we can make either situational or dispositional attributions to explain other people's behavior, the fact is that most of us tend to commit what is known as the *fundamental attribution error*. This error refers to our tendency to overestimate the importance of dispositional factors and to downplay the importance of the situation in which the behavior is being observed. Using the preceding example, if someone is acting kindly, our natural tendency is to assume that that behavior stems from his or her being a nice person (a dispositional attribution), rather than other situational factors. Research suggests that even when we know about this bias toward personality, we are still prone to following it. Thus, the fundamental attribution error is both common and difficult to change.

The following article by Maureen O'Sullivan examines the role that the fundamental attribution error may play in detecting when people are lying. Specifically, O'Sullivan looks at how this cognitive bias may influence people's ability to detect lying—something that most of us cannot do very accurately. Unlike Article 6, which also dealt with lie detection, this article looks at the possible underlying mechanisms involved in detecting deception or truth.

The Fundamental Attribution Error in Detecting Deception
The Boy-Who-Cried-Wolf Effect
■ Maureen O'Sullivan

Most people are unable to detect accurately when others are lying. Many explanations for this inability have been suggested but the cognitive heuristics involved in lie detection have received little attention. The present study offers evidence from two experiments, based on two different groups of observers, judging two different kinds of lies, presented in two different testing situations, that the fundamental attribution error significantly undermines the ability to detect honesty and deception accurately. Trait judgments of trustworthiness were highly correlated with

Reprinted from M. O'Sullivan, *Personality and Social Psychology Bulletin, 29*(10), pp. 1316–1327, Copyright © 2003 by Sage Publications, Inc. Reprinted by permission of Sage Publications, Inc.

state judgments of truthfulness, leading, as predicted, to positive correlations with honest detection accuracy and negative correlations with deception detection accuracy. More accurate lie detectors were significantly more likely than less accurate lie detectors to separate state and trait judgments of honesty. The effect of other biases, such as the halo effect and the truthfulness bias, also are examined. Implications for future research and practice are discussed.

Keywords *deception; social cognition; judgment errors; heuristics; accuracy*

Why can't most people distinguish the honest and deceptive behavior of others (Ekman & O'Sullivan, 1991; Malone & DePaulo, 2001)? Many explanations for this phenomenon have been posited but few researchers have examined the role of cognitive heuristics (Tversky & Kahneman, 1974) in accurately detecting deception. This study will do so by examining the effect of one cognitive heuristic, the fundamental attribution error (FAE) (Ross & Nisbett, 1991), in deciding whether someone is lying or telling the truth. The FAE is the tendency, when forming impressions of others, to overestimate the importance of dispositional factors (e.g., sociability or aggressiveness) in the person being judged and to underestimate the importance of the situation in which the observed behavior is occurring (e.g., a party or a job interview). The ubiquity and power (Yzerbyt, Corneille, Dumont, & Hahn, 2001) of the FAE has been demonstrated in many studies. Variations of the FAE have been studied under the rubric of the correspondence bias (Gilbert & Malone, 1995) or the overattribution bias (Quattrone, 1982). It is surprising, therefore, that the cognitive underpinnings of judging deception, which is so relevant in personal relationships (Burgoon, Buller, White, Afifi, & Buslig, 1999; DePaulo, Kenny, Hoover, & Webb, 1987), business dealings (DePaulo & DePaulo, 1989), law enforcement (Kraut & Poe, 1980; Vrij, Edward, & Bull, 2001; Porter, Woodworth, & Birt, 2000), and political life (Ekman, 2001) have not been studied using what has been learned about cognitive heuristics in other realms.

Why are people so poor at detecting deception? Many reasons for this difficulty in social cognition

have been suggested or can be inferred from the literature. They include the following:

a. underutilization of the nonverbal behaviors involved in the emotional and cognitive reactions to lying; that is, although people attend to a variety of nonverbal behaviors when judging honest behavior, they pay less attention to such cues when judging deceptive behavior (Ekman, Friesen, O'Sullivan, & Scherer, 1980; Ekman, O'Sullivan, Friesen, & Scherer, 1991). When people are forced to attend to nonverbal behavior because of brain pathology, they are more accurate in detecting deception (Etcoff, Ekman, Magee, & Frank, 2000);

b. overreliance on the content of speech (DePaulo, Rosenthal, Rosenkrantz, & Green, 1982; O'Sullivan, Ekman, Friesen, & Scherer, 1985). A paradoxical finding in the deception literature is that observers pay more attention to the content of speech when judging deceptive than honest behavior. This is paradoxical because most people can control what they say better than how they say it;

c. truthfulness or deception biases. Most people tend to judge others as truthful most of the time (O'Sullivan, Ekman, & Friesen, 1988; Zuckerman, DeFrank, Hall, Larrance, & Rosenthal, 1979; Zuckerman, Fischer, Osmun, & Winkler, 1987; Zuckerman, Koestner, Colella, & Alton, 1984). Ekman (2001) described a related deception bias among some law enforcement personnel who frequently rated others as lying;

d. incorrect paradigms about the clues to deception (Zuckerman & Driver, 1985). Most Americans believe that averting eye gaze is one of the signs of deception. Research suggests that, in fact, most liars, being aware of this display rule (Ekman & Friesen, 1969), actually increase eye gaze when they lie. Another example is the Othello error (Ekman, 2001), in which a truthful person's fear of being disbelieved is misinterpreted as evidence of lying;

e. physiognomic (Bond, Omar, Pitre, & Lashley, 1992; Zebrowitz, Voinescu, & Collins, 1996), personality (Riggio, Salinas, & Tucker, 1988), cultural (Bond, Omar, Mahmoud, & Bonser, 1990), and behavioral (Ekman, 2001) characteristics of the liar or truth teller that mislead the observer. Observers tend to misinterpret deviations from the norm as signs of deception; therefore, baby-faced, non-weird, extraverted, and nonidiosyncratic people are more likely to be judged truthful;

f. inadequate sampling of the contexts in which lies occur. Hartshorne and May (1928) found that people's tendency to lie did not generalize across different situations. Although Frank and Ekman (1997) reported a positive correlation in lie detection accuracy across two kinds of lies, the size of the correlation was moderate, suggesting that different kinds of lies may involve different kinds of detection clues;

g. variability in social/emotional intelligence (Riggio, Tucker, & Throckmorton, 1987). It seems reasonable to consider lie detection accuracy is one aspect of social/emotional intelligence. If this is the case, differences in emotional intelligence will affect lie detection ability and this has not been examined in most studies of lie detection accuracy;

h. a lack of evolutionary selection for lie detection. Ekman (1996) has argued that the cost for detecting lies in our evolutionary history was probably so severe that there was no widespread selection for this ability. Bond and his colleagues (Bond, Kahler, & Paolicelli, 1985; Bond & Robinson, 1988) and other evolutionists have argued that humans have developed acute lie detection abilities, but these arguments are not supported by data from the deception literature;

i. socialization practices (Saarni & Weber, 1999). Most societies discourage deception yet encourage politeness and other misleading impression-management strategies. Learning to cooperate in this social choreography, by pretending to believe white lies or overlooking the social mistakes of others, may undermine the skills needed to detect deception;

j. the liability involved in accurate lie detection (DePaulo & Rosenthal, 1979; Fiske, 1992). Accusing someone of lying is an assertive, if not aggressive, social act. It may require further action that could be inconvenient, even dangerous, to the accuser. The rewards for detecting lies rarely compensate for the punishments involved in doing so, as much of the literature on whistle-blowing suggests (Johnson, 2002);

k. a related explanation is "accusatory reluctance." Ekman and his colleagues (Ekman et al., 1980; O'Sullivan et al., 1985) found that observers attended to different sources of information (i.e., face, body, voice, or speech) when rating honest and deceptive people, even though they were not accurate in labeling them as honest or deceptive. More recently, DePaulo (1998) noted that if observers were asked how comfortable or relaxed someone was rather than whether she was lying, accuracy rates rose significantly. These studies suggest a discomfort in describing others as deceptive; and

l. collusion with the liar and other self-deceptions (Ekman, 1988). Examples of this lie detection difficulty range from Chamberlain believing Hitler's incredible protestations to spouses overlooking blatant infidelity (Baumeister, 1993).

The present study offers an additional explanation for why most human lie detectors do such a bad job: the FAE (Ross & Nisbett, 1991) or the inability to recognize when a generally trustworthy person is lying or a generally untrustworthy person is telling the truth. This version of the FAE is called the boy-who-cried-wolf effect after Aesop's (1793) fable about the shepherd boy who lied about a wolf stalking his sheep so often that when the wolf actually attacked, the townspeople did not believe him. Although the point of Aesop's fable is the negative consequences of lying for the liar, I am using it to characterize the consequences for those judging a liar. All the reasons outlined above consider the question of poor lie detection ability from the perspective of the person detecting the lie, that is, the abilities, biases, motivations, or genetic capabilities of the person attempting to distinguish truth and deception.

Other research has focused on the problem from another perspective by examining the characteristics of the liar or truth teller, not the lie catcher. Zuckerman et al. (1979), for example, described a demeanor bias in which characteristic and presumably static features of individuals caused them to be judged as honest or deceitful regardless of whether they actually were truthful or lying. Riggio and Friedman (1983) reported personality differences of individuals whom observers thought were honest as opposed to deceptive, again regardless of the accuracy of the truthfulness judgments. More recently, Frank and Ekman (2002) described a truthfulness generality in which differences in dynamic facial movements distinguish people who are generally credible from those who are not. The present study, however, follows the tradition of examining the difficulty in lie detection from the perspective of the lie catcher and will contribute to that literature by demonstrating a cognitive bias among observers that is not related to actual differences in the credibility or demeanor of those being judged as truthful or deceptive but reflects observers' beliefs about the personal characteristics of the liar and the truth teller.

When observers think positively about someone, believing him to be attractive, likeable, or interesting (i.e., making positive dispositional attributions), they will also tend to believe he is telling the truth. Therefore, positive correlations will be found between dispositional judgments and truth accuracy. These positive attributions, however, will work against the lie catcher when the target person is actually lying. If the observer thinks well of the liar, she will also be inclined to think he is truthful. When the other person is actually lying, accuracy in detecting deception will be deleteriously affected. Therefore, there will be a negative correlation between positive dispositional judgments and deception accuracy.

Hypothesis 1: There is a positive correlation between positive trait judgments and truth accuracy (accurately identifying people who are telling the truth).

Hypothesis 2: There is a negative correlation between positive trait judgments and deception accuracy (accurately identifying those who are lying).

Krull and Erickson (1995), in distinguishing the trait inference and the correspondence bias aspects of the FAE, suggested that the trait inference bias is more likely to be stimulated by strong versus weak situations. Given the difficulty most observers have in labeling someone else as a liar, the present study may be viewed as a strong inferential task, which facilitates the high trait inference aspect of the FAE. Krull, Seger, and Silvera (2001) also argued that in judging others, observers do not ordinarily attend to situations, but they can do so if the situation is made salient. To provide a stronger test of Hypotheses 1 and 2, this experiment will attempt to make the situation salient by alerting observers to the state-trait distinction between being truthful in a particular situation and being a generally honest or trustworthy person.

STUDY 1

Method

The Opinion Deception Judgment Task The lie detection materials used in this study were developed by Frank and Ekman (1997). The description of these materials is taken from their report. The liars and truth tellers shown in the Opinion Deception Judgment Task were 10 college men (18 to 28 years of age) who volunteered to participate in a study of communication. The men included 3 African American, 2 Asian American, and 5 Euro-Americans. Based on the false opinion paradigm suggested by Mehrabian (1971), the men were asked the strength of their opinion on a number of controversial social issues before they were told that the experiment involved lying or telling the truth. The opinion that each man felt most strongly about was the one he was then asked to discuss with an interviewer. Some men described their opinion truthfully, whereas others lied, claiming to believe the opposite of their true opinion. Truth tellers who were believed by the interviewer received a $10 bonus. Liars who were believed received a $50 bonus. Liars or truth tellers who were disbelieved received no money and half of them faced an additional punishment (see Frank & Ekman, 1997, for more details).

To verify that the men actually did manifest different behaviors when lying or telling the truth, their facial muscle movements were analyzed using the Facial Action Coding System (Ekman & Friesen, 1978), which demonstrated that "80% of the participants . . . could be successfully classified as liars or truth tellers on the basis of the presence or absence of fear or disgust'" (Frank & Ekman, 1997, p. 1433).

The Opinion Deception Judgment Task consists of 1-min segments from each of 10 videotaped interviews. Each item shows a different man. The 10 interview segments selected were chosen so as to represent equal numbers of pro and con positions on each of the opinions represented. Half of the interview segments are of men who truthfully described their strongly held opinion, whereas half lied about it. (The opinions discussed were either "Convicted cold-blooded murderers should be executed" or "Smoking should be banned in all public places.") The videotapes showed face and shoulder close-ups with full audio. The interviewer could be heard but not seen.

The merit of this detection task is that each of the interviews contains behavioral and/or verbal content clues to either honesty or deception. The interviewees were highly motivated by money rewards and the threat of a noxious punishment. In addition, they were interviewed about opinions they were passionately interested in. Consequently, the participants displayed emotions consistent or inconsistent with what they were saying, so there were sufficient clues in the videotaped interviews to allow honesty or lying to be detected. (In some lie detection research, the lies told are polite, "white" lies that may not cause any emotional arousal in those telling them, thereby providing few, if any, clues for observers to detect.)

The Observers   The observers were 55 women in a general education course in research design who received class credit for participating. They ranged in age from 18 to 23. None were psychology majors. They were tested in groups of about 10 people each. The observers were given about as much information about the deception scenario as was provided above and were told that about half of the men were lying. Only women were used because the judgments obtained for this study were part of a larger study of women's perception of male attractiveness. In other studies with the Frank-Ekman tapes, no sex difference in deception detection accuracy has been found (Ekman, O'Sullivan, & Frank, 1999).

The Judgments   After each videotaped interview was shown, the observers were asked to circle either LYING or TRUTHFUL on their answer sheet. Then the observers rated how attractive, trustworthy, likeable, friendly, and interesting they found each interviewee using a 6-point Likert-type scale ranging from 1 (*not at all*) to 6 (*extremely*). The difference between being trustworthy (trait) and telling the truth (state) was described on the answer sheet and read aloud by the author as part of the instructions. The answer sheet contained the following:

Most of these characteristics are pretty obvious, but your judgment about each man's general trustworthiness may not be that clear. For example, you may think someone is lying about the particular question he is asked, but he seems like a generally honest or trustworthy person. On the other hand, you might think that someone was telling the truth about his opinion on the videotape, but in general he seemed like an untrustworthy person to you.

These instructions were given so as to emphasize the difference between dispositional (trustworthy) and situational (truthful) attributes and to make as salient as possible the idea that trustworthy people can sometimes lie and that untrustworthy ones can sometimes tell the truth. All observers completed a practice item before beginning the Opinion Deception Judgment Task and were encouraged to ask questions.

To determine whether observers were able to distinguish the trait of trustworthiness from the state of honesty, the observers' dichotomous judgments of lying versus truthful and their 6-point ratings of how trustworthy each man was were correlated using biserial correlations. It was hypothesized that these correlations would be significantly positive.

The lying and truthful judgments were then converted to accuracy scores (0 if incorrect; 1 if correct). Biserial correlations between the accuracy scores and the five trait ratings were calculated across the 55 observers. It was predicted that the correlations between accuracy and trait ratings would be positive for interviewees who were telling the truth (H1) and negative for those who were lying (H2).

To examine the effect of the truthfulness bias, the truthful "call rate" was determined by calculating the percentage of time observers labeled interviewees as truthful, regardless of the accuracy of their judgments. An observer who thought all the men on the videotape were honest would have a truthful call rate of 100% and an honest accuracy score of 100%. But her deception accuracy would be zero and her overall accuracy would be 50%. It is also possible for someone to have 50% truthful call rate, to be completely wrong, and to obtain an honest accuracy score of zero. Truthfulness bias and honest accuracy, although usually positively correlated, are measured differently and are conceptually different.

The interviewees in the Opinion Deception Judgment Task were not selected on the basis of how attractive, trustworthy, likeable, friendly, or interesting they were. However, by chance, the honest and deceptive interviewees might have differed in these respects. To ascertain that they did not differ in terms of personal characteristics, differences in mean trait ratings were assessed.

Results

The top half of Table 1 gives the accuracy scores obtained by the observers in Study 1 on the Opinion Deception Judgment Task. (The bottom half of Table 1 shows data from Study 2, which will be discussed later.) The overall mean of 51% is consistent with most findings in the field, that is, most people are at chance (50%) in their ability to detect deception (DePaulo, 1998).

To determine whether there were any differences in how attractive, trustworthy, likeable, friendly, or interesting the five truth tellers and the five liars were judged to be, a series of correlated *t* tests were performed on the average ratings for each of the five traits between the five truth tellers and the five liars. Table 2 shows that the only significant differences were in ratings for attractive and interesting, and these go in opposite directions. The truthful interviewees were rated as more interesting but less attractive than the lying interviewees. These differences cancel each other out in the average trait ratings so that a correlated *t*

test of the difference between the average overall rating of the five honest and the five deceptive interviewees was not significant.

To determine whether observers were able to distinguish the dispositional and situational aspects of honesty, the dichotomous, situation-based ratings for lying versus truthful were correlated with the 6-point ratings for trustworthy for each of the 10 interviewees. As the first column in Table 3 shows, all of these correlations are significantly positive. If observers thought an interviewee was truthful in the interview situation, they also tended to judge him as generally trustworthy. Note that these correlations do not take into account whether the observers were accurate in describing the interviewee as lying or truthful, only that they circled lying or truthful for a particular interviewee.

Table 4 shows the data relevant to Hypotheses 1 and 2 concerning the relationship between the FAE and accuracy. It lists the biserial correlations between each of the five dispositional ratings and the truth or deception accuracy for each of the 10 interviewees. As predicted, the correlations between the dispositional judgments and truth accuracy are overwhelmingly positive; the correlations between the dispositional judgments and deception accuracy are overwhelmingly negative. To determine the probability of obtaining 23 out of 25 positive correlations for the truthful items and 24 out of 25 negative correlations for the deceptive items, by chance alone, a Runs test was conducted in which positive correlations were coded 1

TABLE 1 / Descriptive Statistics for Two Deception Judgment Tasks in Two Studies

Deception Judgment Task	Total Accuracy	Honest Accuracy	Deception Accuracy
Study 1			
Opinion (*N* = 55)			
Percentage correct	51	60	42
M	5.09	3.00	2.09
SD	1.47	0.98	1.19
Study 2			
Crime (*N* = 34)			
Percentage correct	60	64	56
M	5.97	3.18	2.79
SD	1.51	1.06	0.81

TABLE 2 / Mean Trait Ratings for Truthful and Lying Interviewees in the Opinion Deception Task

	Study 1					
	Truthful Interviewees		Lying Interviewees			
Trait	*M*	*SD*	*M*	*SD*	*t*	*p*
Attractive	2.48	0.72	2.89	0.72	−5.36	.000
Trustworthy	3.53	0.58	3.46	0.59	0.85	.400
Likeable	3.62	0.62	3.58	0.64	0.50	.618
Friendly	3.84	0.54	3.74	0.56	1.60	.116
Interesting	3.51	0.76	3.22	0.71	3.56	.001
Overall *M*	3.40	0.53	3.38	0.33	0.06	.950

TABLE 3 / Correlations between Trait Ratings of Trustworthy and State Judgments of Truthful for Two Deception Judgment Tasks

Interviewees	Opinion Deception Task (Study 1)	Crime Deception Task (Study 2)
A.	.409**	.491**
B.	.474**	.279*
C.	.334**	.219
D.	.529**	.327*
E.	.245*	.111
F.	.580**	.385**
G.	.288*	.506**
H.	.320**	.399**
I.	.311**	.472**
J.	.378**	.299*

Note: Letters A through J identify the ten interviewees.

*p < .05.

**p < .01, one-tailed.

and negative correlations were coded 2. Across the 50 items shown in Table 4, the result was highly significant ($Z = -5.427$, $p < .000$). (Hypotheses 1 and 2 predicted the directions, not the size, of the correlations obtained. Even if the Runs analysis is limited only to statistically significant correlations, the run of 10 positive and 11 negative correlations is still highly significant, $Z = -4.029$, $p < .000$.)

Although the directions of the correlations are as predicted, only for the rating of trustworthy are all 10 of the correlations statistically significant. This suggests that the most difficult rating task for the observers was distinguishing the trait of trustworthiness from the situation-based behavior of truthfulness. Observers showed a slight truthfulness bias. They rated 59% of the participants as truthful, although only half of them were and the observers had been informed of that in the instructions.

STUDY 2

The results of Study 1 raise at least five questions: (a) What is the external validity of these findings? Will they generalize to different observers and a different kind of lie? (b) What is the effect of reactivity, because alerting the observers that some of the men were lying may have changed their impression-formation strategies (Park, Yoon, Kim, & Wyer, 2001)? (c) Can't the

TABLE 4 / Correlations between Item Accuracy and Trait Ratings for the Honest and Deception Items of the Opinion Deception Judgment Task (Study 1)

Trait	Honest Interviewees		Deception Interviewees	
Attractive	A.	−.095	F.	−.347**
	B.	.118	G.	−.137
	C.	.322**	H.	−.076
	D.	.071	I.	−.027
	E.	.272*	J.	.125
Trustworthy	A.	.409**	F.	−.580**
	B.	.473**	G.	−.288*
	C.	.334**	H.	−.320**
	D.	.529**	I.	−.311**
	E.	.245*	J.	−.378**
Likeable	A.	.094	F.	−.243*
	B.	.055	G.	−.110
	C.	.198	H.	−.101
	D.	.345**	I.	−.256*
	E.	.239*	J.	−.177
Friendly	A.	.008	F.	−.320**
	B.	.076	G.	−.027
	C.	.100	H.	−.016
	D.	.264*	I.	−.314**
	E.	.103	J.	−.066
Interesting	A.	.096	F.	−.158
	B.	−.036	G.	−.027
	C.	.163	H.	−.016
	D.	.329**	I.	−.314**
	E.	.104	J.	−.066

Note: Letters A through J identify the ten interviewees.

*p < .05.

**p < .01, one-tailed.

results be more parsimoniously explained as another instance of the "halo effect" (Thorndike, 1920), an overall positive or negative evaluation bias? (d) What is the relative contribution of the truthfulness bias, the FAE, and the halo effect to lie detection accuracy? and (e) If the FAE undermines deception detection accuracy, shouldn't more accurate observers have a different judgment pattern than less accurate observers?

Study 2 addressed these questions as follows: (a) External validity was evaluated by having a different group of observers judge a different kind of lie; (b) reactivity, knowing that some of the people to be judged were lying, was examined by obtaining observers' initial trait judgments before the issue of deception was introduced; (c) the influence of the halo effect was examined by hypothesizing that the correlations between dispositional ratings of trustworthy and accuracy in detecting truth and deception will be significantly different than chance but that correlations between the ratings of other dispositions (halo effect) and lie detection accuracy will not (Hypothesis 3). Furthermore, correlations between detection accuracy and the FAE will be significantly different than those between the halo effect and detection accuracy (Hypothesis 4); and (d) more accurate lie detectors will distinguish state judgments of truthfulness from trait judgments of trustworthiness more often than less accurate lie detectors (Hypothesis 5). They will know that Aesop's lying shepherd boy can sometimes tell the truth. This will be reflected in a greater disjunction between state and trait judgments for more versus less accurate observers.

Method

The Crime Deception Judgment Task   As in Study 1, a deception judgment task developed by Frank and Ekman (1997) was used. Ten different men (not those used in Study 1) lied or told the truth about whether they had stolen $50. As in the deception task used in Study 1, the men received a significant reward if they were believed. If they lied and the interviewer believed their protestations of innocence, they kept the $50 they had stolen. If they were innocent and the interviewer believed them, they received $10. If they were disbelieved, whether they were innocent or stole the money, they did not get to keep the $50 and they were threatened with a noxious punishment (see Frank & Ekman, 1997, for more details). As in the Opinion Deception Judgment Task used in Study 1, the men were highly motivated to succeed at the task, whether it was lying or telling the truth. Those who lied showed visible and measurable behavioral signs of cognitive and emotional arousal. Each man was shown being interviewed for about 1 min. Half of the men were lying and half were telling the truth.

The Observers   The observers were 8 men and 26 women enrolled in a general psychology class. They received class credit for their participation and ranged in age from 18 to 22. All observers were tested in a single session.

The Judgments   The first item in the test questionnaire asked the observers to rate "How good are you at judging other people?" on a 6-point scale from 1 (*not good at all*) to 6 (*extremely good*). Then the observers were asked to rate the 10 men in the Crime Deception Judgment Task on how attractive, trustworthy, likeable, friendly, and interesting they were using a 6-point Likert-type scale ranging from 1 (*not at all*) to 6 (*extremely*). The observers saw but did not hear the 10 men. The videotape was paused and left on the screen while the observers made their judgments. At this point in the study, the observers were not informed that the men they were observing might have been lying, and they were not instructed about the distinction between the trait "trustworthy" and the state "truthful." After rating the 10 men from the Crime Deception Judgment Task, the observers then rated the 10 men from the Opinion Deception Judgment Task in the same way.

The author then read aloud the description of the Crime Deception Judgment Task, which was printed on the observers' test booklets. The observers first rated each of the men in the video as either lying or truthful and then rated them, again, on the five traits indicated above. The instruction distinguishing situational honesty from dispositional trustworthiness (see Study 1) also was printed on the test booklet and read aloud. The crime deception video was then played for the observers, who could both see and hear each of the 10 men being interviewed about whether they had stolen $50. No practice item was given.

Other Measures   To compare the explanatory utility of the FAE and a more generalized halo effect, four of the five trait ratings (excluding trustworthy) were summed into a general "positivity" rating. It was predicted that the median correlation between accurately detecting truth or deception and ratings of trustworthy (FAE) would differ significantly from chance but that the median correlation between detection accuracy scores and general positivity ratings (halo effect) would not (Hypothesis 3).

Hypothesis 4, that the absolute value of the correlations between the FAE (trustworthy rating) and detection accuracy will be significantly higher than correlations between the halo effect (positivity rating) and accuracy for each of the 10 crime deception items, will be evaluated using the Wilcoxon Signed Ranks Test.

More and less accurate observers were identified on the basis of their total accuracy scores. Participants obtaining scores of 60% or higher were classified as more accurate; those obtaining scores of 50% or less were classified as less accurate. This classification follows the procedure suggested by Frank and Ekman (1997). They argued,

> First, the experimental literature reported that observers rarely surpass 60% accuracy when detecting deceit. . . . Second, a series of one-sample t tests that set μ at five items correct showed that six items correct . . . was significantly different at the two-tailed p < .05 level. (p. 1434)

The ability to distinguish state (truthful) and trait (trustworthy) ratings was inferred by examining the conjunctions of these ratings across all items and all observers. Trait judgments of trustworthy were dichotomized so that ratings of 1, 2, or 3 were classified as untrustworthy, whereas ratings of 4, 5, or 6 were classified as trustworthy. It was hypothesized that more accurate observers would rate situational liars (state) as generally (trait) trustworthy and truth tellers as untrustworthy more frequently than less accurate lie detectors (Hypothesis 5). This hypothesis was tested using a 2 × 4 chi-square with more versus less accuracy and four rating categories: (a) observer rated the man as lying but generally trustworthy, that is, rating of 4 or higher; (b) observer rated the man as lying and generally untrustworthy, that is, a rating of 3 or lower; (c) observer rated the man as telling the truth in the situation and as generally trustworthy; and (d) observer rated the man as telling the truth but as generally untrustworthy.

Results

Still versus Moving Presentation of the Opinion Video

The women in Study 1 both saw and heard the men who lied or told the truth about their opinion. They were told that half the men were lying and they were alerted about the difference between the trait of trustworthy and the state of truthfulness. The observers in Study 2 saw, but did not hear, a paused videotape of the same men. They were not informed

that some of them were lying and they were not instructed about the trait-state distinction between trustworthy and truthful. Nonetheless, the rank-order correlation between the mean ratings of the observers in Studies 1 and 2 was extremely high ($\rho = +.936$, $n = 10$, $p < .001$, one-tailed).

In Study 2, there was no significant difference between the male ($n = 8$) and female ($n = 26$) observers in their ratings of the men on either the opinion or the two administrations of the crime videotapes. A series of independent t tests of the difference between means for the 150 ratings (50 ratings for each of the three videotape administrations) was done to determine whether gender influenced the ratings. For 150 t tests, 7.5 significant differences would be expected by chance. Four were found: two for the still crime video (attractive: $t = 2.073$, $p < .046$; friendly: $t = 2.215$, $p < .034$), one for the still opinion video (interesting: $t = -2.336$, $p < .026$), and one for the moving crime video (likeable: $t = -3.093$, $p < .003$). Because fewer differences were found than might be expected by chance alone, and the differences found were not consistently greater for men or women, it is unlikely, with these materials, presented in this format, that gender is a significant factor in the mean level of ratings obtained.

Crime Deception Judgment Task

The bottom half of Table 1 shows that the average accuracy for the Crime Deception Judgment Task was 60%. This mean is significantly higher than the mean obtained by the Study 1 observers who saw the Opinion Deception Judgment Task ($t = 2.674$, $p < .015$). Conversely, the overall mean attribution rating (across all scales and all liars and truth tellers) was significantly lower. (The mean overall attribute rating in Study 1 was 3.39; in Study 2, the mean was 2.80.) Although this difference is statistically significant ($t = 7.96$, $p < .000$), the same pattern of correlations between honest and deception accuracy and dispositional ratings that was found in Study 1 was found in Study 2.

Table 5 gives the biserial correlations between the ratings for trustworthy and the mean ratings across the other four attributes and the truth or deception accuracy for each of the 10 interviewees. As predicted (H1), all of the correlations between the dispositional judgments and truth accuracy are positive; nine of the

TABLE 5 / Correlations between Interviewee Accuracy, Trustworthy Rating (FAE), and the Average of Four Trait Ratings (Halo Effect) for the Honest and Deception Items of the Crime Deception Task (Study 2)

		Ratings	
		Trustworthy (FAE)	Average Positivity[a] (Halo Effect)
Honest interviewees	A.	.491**	.447**
	B.	.279*	.180
	C.	.219	.276*
	D.	.327*	.143
	E.	.070	.106
Deception interviewees	F.	−.385**	.015
	G.	−.506**	−.313*
	H.	−.399**	−.278*
	I.	−.472**	−.195
	J.	−.299*	−.149

Note: FAE = fundamental attribution error. Letters A through J identify the ten interviewees.

[a]represents the average of attractive, likeable, friendly, and interesting.

*$p < .05$.

**$p < .01$, one-tailed.

correlations between the dispositional judgments and deception accuracy are negative (H2), except one, which is zero. To determine the probability of obtaining 10 positive correlations for the truthful items and nine negative correlations with the deception items, by chance alone, a Runs test was conducted in which positive correlations were coded as 1 and negative correlations were coded as 2. The result was significant ($Z = -2.348$, $p < .019$). (If only significant correlations are used, the three positive and five negative correlations yield a Z of -1.854, $p < .064$, *ns*.)

Table 5 also suggests the relative strength of the FAE compared with the halo effect. Although 8 of the 10 correlations between trustworthy (FAE) and accuracy are significant, four of the correlations for the averaged ratings (halo effect) are. Another way to view these data is in terms of median correlations. Disregarding sign, as predicted (H3), the median correlation between trustworthy ratings and accuracy is $\rho = +.362$ ($p < .05$, one-tailed). For the average rating (i.e., halo effect), the median correlation is $\rho = +.187$ (*ns*). These median correlations are not significantly different from one another, but as can be seen below, the correlations they summarize, when compared item by item, are significantly different.

The Wilcoxon Signed Ranks Test was used to compare the FAE versus accuracy and halo effect versus accuracy correlations against one another (H4) as opposed to evaluating each against chance (H3). For each item, the absolute values of the correlations between item accuracy and FAE and item accuracy and halo effect were paired. This analysis showed a significant difference in the paired ranks $Z = -2.395$, $p = .017$, two-tailed). As shown in Table 5, the FAE correlations are larger than the halo effect correlations for 8 of the 10 pairs.

Table 6 shows that the pattern of judgments made by more accurate (total accuracy of 60% or greater) ($n = 20$) and less accurate (total accuracy of 50% or lower) ($n = 14$) observers is significantly different from chance, $\chi^2(3, N = 339) = 13.138$, $p < .01$. More accurate observers more frequently distinguish state ratings of truthfulness from trait ratings of trustworthiness.

TABLE 6 / Frequency of Truthful and Trustworthy Ratings for Two Levels of Deception Detection Accuracy (Crime Deception Judgment Task: Study 2)

State Rating	Lying	Lying	Truthful	Truthful	
Trait Rating[a]	Trustworthy	Untrustworthy	Trustworthy	Untrustworthy	
More accurate observers ($N = 20$)	13 (7)	74 (37)	44 (22)	69 (35)	200 (100)
Less accurate observers ($N = 14$)	18 (13)	48 (35)	45 (32)	28 (20)	139 (100)
Column totals	31	122	89	97	339[b]

Note: Values in parentheses are percentages across each row.

[a]Ratings of 3 or lower were classified as untrustworthy; 4 or higher as trustworthy.

[b]Thirty-four observers rated 10 men; 1 rating was omitted.

More accurate observers are more likely (35%) to decide someone is telling the truth but still give him a low trustworthy rating than less accurate observers (20%), and they are less likely (22%) than less accurate observers (32%) to say truthful people are generally trustworthy. A chi-square of this subset of the four cells involved in judging the men as truthful is significant, $\chi^2(1, n = 186) = 9.163, p < .01$. A chi-square of the four cells involved in judging the men as lying is not significant, $\chi^2(1, n = 153) = 3.532$, *ns*. What this suggests is that all observers, even more accurate ones, are unlikely to rate a liar as a trustworthy person, but more accurate observers are more able to maintain the hypothesis that a truthful person in one situation need not be trustworthy in all situations. The linkage between state and trait judgments of honesty seems to be more durable for less accurate observers.

As in Study 1, a truthfulness bias was observed. Although they had been told that half of the men in the Crime Deception Judgment Task were lying, 55% of the observers' ratings were honest. Truthfulness bias was not significantly correlated with total accuracy ($r = +.238$, *ns*, $N = 34$), nor did it distinguish more and less accurate observers ($t = .976$, *ns*).

Discussion

General Findings Both Studies 1 and 2 provided support for Hypotheses 1 and 2. When observers made judgments about the veracity of men telling the truth or lying about two different situations, observers' dispositional attributions were consistently, but differently, related to their accuracy in detecting truthfulness or deception. If observers attributed positive trait characteristics to the men they were judging, they also tended to rate those men as truthful in a given situation (state), regardless of whether they were. If the men they were judging were actually truthful, then the observers were accurate in judging truthfulness. If the men they were judging were lying, then they were inaccurate. Conversely, positive trait ratings were negatively correlated with accuracy in detecting deception. These findings occurred in two different samples of observers, with two different kinds of lies, told by two different groups of men. The trait characteristics of liars and truth tellers were not, on average, rated differently. Therefore, the findings cannot be ex-

plained by a systematic bias such as the demeanor bias (Zuckerman et al., 1979) in which the truth tellers or the liars are seen as more positive overall, thereby skewing the observers' strategies for forming impressions.

It is also unlikely that these results are better explained by the halo effect. Although almost all of the correlations between the trait ratings of trustworthy and the state ratings of truthful (disregarding accuracy) were significant, fewer than half of the other trait ratings were. The median correlation between the trait ratings of trustworthy and detection accuracy was significantly different from chance, whereas the median correlation between the other ratings and detection accuracy was not (Hypothesis 3). Also, an item-by-item comparison of the correlations between trustworthy ratings (FAE) and accuracy and an average positivity rating (halo effect) and accuracy showed the FAE had a significantly higher level of correlation than did the halo effect (Hypothesis 4). This suggests that although there is a halo effect, its impact is weaker than that of the trait-state confusion between trustworthy and truthful. Although it might be argued that the boy-who-cried-wolf effect is merely a particular variant of the halo effect, the inability of the observers to distinguish trait trustworthiness from state honesty is more predictive of detection accuracy than the halo effect and connects this phenomenon with the extensive research in cognitive heuristics.

The impact of the FAE on lie detection accuracy was examined by comparing the conjunction of state ratings of truthfulness or lying with trait ratings of trustworthiness for more and less accurate lie detectors. As hypothesized (H5), more accurate observers were more likely to have a disjunction between their ratings of truthful and trustworthiness, that is, more accurate observers were more likely to deem a man truthful but to rate him as below average in trustworthiness than were less accurate observers. In other words, the decisions of more accurate observers are less bound by the FAE; they were less bound by state-trait consistency. Another interpretation is that more accurate observers are just more cynical, less naive, than less accurate observers. But total accuracy was not related to the truthfulness bias, so differences in a "see-everyone-as-truthful" world view does not explain the accuracy differences found in this study.

Also of interest is the finding that more and less accurate observers do not differ in the conjunction of their state ratings of lying and trait ratings of untrustworthy. When they judged someone as lying, most observers also rated him as generally untrustworthy. Even the more accurate observers were unable to view those they thought were lying as being generally trustworthy. This finding exemplifies the boy-who-cried-wolf effect very well and may illuminate the phenomena of both the truthfulness bias and accusatory reluctance. Once a person has been labeled as a liar, a threshold seems to be crossed, so that his or her general trustworthiness is no longer assumed. The term "the boy-who-cried-wolf effect" was intended to describe how the FAE functions in lie detection broadly speaking. The findings of this study, however, suggest that it may be particularly difficult to change a negative evaluation of someone's honesty to a positive one. Although more accurate observers can go in the other direction, that is, maintain the possibility that truthfulness in one situation does not necessarily generalize to trustworthiness in all situations, even they are unlikely to maintain open minds about the trustworthiness of liars.

Design Issues   To assess the impact of being told that the people being observed might be lying, the Opinion Deception Judgment Task was administered in two diffferent formats in Studies 1 and 2. In Study 1, the observers were shown a full minute of videotape, were informed that half the men they would see and hear were lying, and were alerted to the difference between the trait of trustworthy and the state of truthful. In Study 2, the observers made their ratings of the men in the Opinion Deception Judgment Task on the basis of a soundless still from the videotaped interview. The observers did not hear the videotape, were not informed that deception was involved, and were not alerted to the state-trait distinction between trustworthy and truthful. Despite these differences, the rank order correlation between the mean trait ratings was almost perfect. The relevance for the present findings is that making the judgment about lying versus telling the truth before making the trait judgments of each man does not seem to have affected the trait ratings made in any appreciable way. Another aspect of this finding is that it suggests that most people form

impressions almost instantaneously (Ambady, Hallahan, & Rosenthal, 1995) and before the inconsistencies that are so important to detecting deception would have had a chance to occur.

Limitations   The present study suffers from several limitations. Although two groups of observers were used, only female observers were used in Study 1 and only 25% of the observers in Study 2 were men. Although no gender differences were found in Study 2, and few sex differences in lie detection accuracy have been reported, the relevance of gender differences to cognitive biases in lie detection needs further exploration. Only two kinds of lies were sampled, both showed only men and sampled high stakes lies. Although it seems likely that the findings of the present study would generalize to women liars and truth tellers, this question should be examined. Also, some might disagree with the operationalization of the FAE and the halo effect used in this study. Hopefully, these limitations can be addressed in future research.

Conclusions   The evidence presented shows that a fundamental attribution heuristic is activated when observers are asked to decide whether someone is lying or telling the truth. The question then is, of what use is this heuristic in social interaction and sociobiological adaptation?

Stapel, Koomen, and van der Pligt (1996) suggested that in judging others, people form a "good enough" impression. The present study is consistent with this suggestion. If one grants that most people live in a world in which most other people are telling the truth most of the time, then the truth accuracy that most observers exhibit is "good enough" for most social interactions in which the base rate of honesty is higher than 50%. Assume, for example, that people are honest 90% of the time. (This includes all kinds of interactions, such as "What time is it?" "What is your name?" or "Where is the car parked?") Given 90% honesty, the best heuristic is to assume that most people are honest most of the time. Then, one is wrong only 10% of the time.

The state-trait confusion described in this study may also serve the ongoing social interactions of most people (Kunda, 1990). Most lies are not significant, in the short term. So, for most people, in most situations, it is a better heuristic to make an accurate overall judgment of a person that will serve as a guide for interactions with them (i.e., a trait-based credibility judgment). The almost perfect correlation found in this study between ratings based on stills and ratings based on viewing a 1-min interaction suggests that such judgments are made almost instantaneously (Ambady et al., 1995). Similar to ratings of extraversion (Levesque & Kenny, 1993), trait credibility judgments may have broad consensus, but as suggested by the present research, consensus about credibility is not accuracy about truthfulness.

In terms of evolutionary adaptation, Ekman (1996) argued that in the course of evolutionary history, the cost of detecting lying was so high that superior lie detection did not evolve as a widespread ability. Clore (personal communication, March 20, 2002) suggested that the trait-based assessment strategy illustrated by the present research might be the result of an adaptation to detect habitual liars, who could then be ostracized, rather than individual acts of lying, which could be ignored in the interest of the common good. The finding that even accurate observers tend not to be able to distinguish state-lying from trait-untrustworthiness suggests that this may, indeed, be the case. It also helps explain why accusatory reluctance, evidenced either in the truthfulness bias or greater accuracy when describing people as comfortable rather than lying (DePaulo, 1998), is so common. But as Aesop's fable about the boy who cried wolf suggests, even liars tell the truth sometimes, and even honest people lie on occasion. So the tendency to judge other people on the basis of enduring traits, rather than situationally relevant states, is one of the reasons most lie catchers are so inaccurate, and adjusting this cognitive heuristic is not easy.

Recent research suggests that the FAE (Yzerbytz et al., 2001) and other cognitive biases (Pronin, Lin, & Ross, 2002) are difficult to change in the short term. Merely alerting observers to their existence can suppress them momentarily, only to have them "rebound" with more vigor at a later time. The present study attempted to diminish the impact of the FAE by alerting observers to its presence and instructing them to differentiate their overall assessment of a man's trustworthiness from their judgment about whether he was lying or telling the truth. This manipulation was re-

soundingly unsuccessful. Most of the correlations between 6-point trait ratings of trustworthiness and a dichotomous state rating of truthfulness were statistically significant in both studies.

O'Sullivan and Ekman have begun an intensive examination of the characteristics of superior lie catchers. Initial results suggest that one strategy for limiting the negative effect of the FAE is not to suppress the tendency to dispositional inference but to develop more accurate, more germane, or more sophisticated dispositional descriptors. These descriptors are not limited to a general trait assessment of the person whose truthfulness is being evaluated but include the many other behavioral factors that have been identified as clues to deception: nonverbal clues, task-relevant behaviors, cognitive inconsistencies, relationship variables, and contextual influences.

One of the purposes of the present study is to encourage cognitive psychologists to examine the role of cognitive heuristics in undermining our ability to judge accurately whether someone is lying or telling the truth. In addition to the FAE, other cognitive heuristics also might be examined as potential sources of inaccuracy in detecting deception. The fact that people have inaccurate information about the appearance of deceptive behavior (Malone & DePaulo, 2001) could be regarded as an instance of a more general representativeness or availability heuristic. Recent research on nonconscious regulation of affect (Bargh & Chartrand, 1999; Pronin et al., 2002; Robinson & Clore, 2001) also may suggest experimentally viable ways of exploring the factors involved in poor lie detection. Understanding the processes involved in judging the truthfulness of others is important in all relationships, from the most intimate to the most international. The present study suggests additional ways in which this important question might be addressed.

REFERENCES

Aesop. (1793). *The fables of Aesop: With a life of the author and embellished with one hundred and twelve plates.* London: John Stockdale.

Ambady, N., Hallahan, M., & Rosenthal, R. (1995). On judging and being judged accurately in zero-acquaintance situations. *Journal of Personality and Social Psychology, 69*(3), 518–529.

Bargh, J. A., & Chartrand, T. L. (1999). The unbearable automaticity of being. *American Psychologist, 54*(7), 462–479.

Baumeister, R. F. (1993). Lying to yourself: The enigma of self-deception. In M. Lewis & C. Saarni (Eds.), *Deception in everyday life* (pp. 166–183). New York: Guilford.

Bond, C. F., Kahler, K. N., & Paolicelli, L. M. (1985). The miscommunication of deception: An adaptive perspective. *Journal of Experimental Social Psychology, 21*(4), 331–345.

Bond, C. F., Omar, A., Mahmoud, A., & Bonser, R. N. (1990). Lie detection across cultures. *Journal of Nonverbal Behavior, 14*(3), 189–204.

Bond, C. F., Omar, A., Pitre, U., & Lashley, B. R. (1992). Fishy-looking liars: Deception judgment from expectancy violation. *Journal of Personality and Social Psychology, 63*(6), 969–977.

Bond, C. F., & Robinson, M. (1988). The evolution of deception. *Journal of Nonverbal Behavior, 12*(4, Pt. 2), 295–307.

Burgoon, J. K., Buller, D. B., White, C. H., Afifi, W., & Buslig, A. L. S. (1999). The role of conversational involvement in deceptive interpersonal interactions. *Personality and Social Psychology Bulletin, 25*(6), 669–685.

DePaulo, B. M. (1998, May). *Deceiving and detecting deceit: Insights and oversights from the first several hundred studies.* Invited address, American Psychological Society, Washington, DC.

DePaulo, B. M., Kenny, D. A., Hoover, C. W., & Webb, W. (1987). Accuracy of person perception: Do people know what kinds of impressions they convey? *Journal of Personality and Social Psychology, 52*(2), 303–315.

DePaulo, B. M., & Rosenthal, R. (1979). Telling lies. *Journal of Personality and Social Psychology, 37*(10), 1713–1722.

DePaulo, B. M., Rosenthal, R., Rosenkrantz, J., & Green, C. R. (1982). Actual and perceived cues to deception: A closer look at speech. *Basic and Applied Social Psychology, 3*(4), 291–312.

DePaulo, P. J., & DePaulo, B. M. (1989). Can deception by salespersons and customers be detected through nonverbal behavioral cues? *Journal of Applied Social Psychology, 19*(18, Pt. 2), 1552–1577.

Ekman, P. (1988). Self-deception and detection of misinformation. In J. S. Lockard & D. L. Paulhus (Eds.), *Self-deception: An adaptive mechanism?* (pp. 229–257). Englewood, NJ: Prentice Hall.

Ekman, P. (1996). Why don't we catch liars? *Social Research, 63*(3), 801–817.

Ekman, P. (2001). *Telling lies: Clues to deceit in the marketplace, politics, and marriage* (3rd ed.). New York: Norton.

Ekman, P., & Friesen, W. V. (1969). Nonverbal leakage and clues to deception. *Psychiatry: Journal for the Study of Interpersonal Processes, 32*(1), 88–106.

Ekman, P., & Friesen, W. V. (1978). *Facial action coding system.* Palo Alto, CA: Consulting Psychologists Press.

Ekman, P., Friesen, W. V., O'Sullivan, M., & Scherer, K. R. (1980). Relative importance of face, body, and speech in judgments of personality and affect. *Journal of Personality and Social Psychology, 38*(2), 270–277.

Ekman, P., & O'Sullivan, M. (1991). Who can catch a liar? *American Psychologist, 46*(9), 913–920.

Ekman, P., O'Sullivan, M., & Frank, M. G. (1999). A few can catch a liar. *Psychological Science, 10*(3), 263–266.

Ekman, P., O'Sullivan, M., Friesen, W. V., & Scherer, K. R. (1991). Invited article: Face, voice, and body in detecting deceit. *Journal of Nonverbal Behavior, 15*(2), 125–135.

Etcoff, N. L., Ekman, P., Magee, J. J., & Frank, M. G. (2000). Lie detection and language comprehension. *Nature, 405*(6783), 139.

Fiske, S. T. (1992). Thinking is for doing: Portraits of social cognition from daguerreotype to laserphoto. *Journal of Personality and Social Psychology, 63*(6), 877–889.

Frank, M. G., & Ekman, P. (1997). The ability to detect deceit generalizes across different types of high-stake lies. *Journal of Personality and Social Psychology, 72*(6), 1429–1439.

Frank, M. G., & Ekman, P. (2002). *Appearing truthful generalizes across different deception situations.* Manuscript submitted for publication.

Gilbert, D. T., & Malone, P. S. (1995). The correspondence bias. *Psychological Bulletin, 117*(1), 21–38.

Hartshorne, H., & May, M. A. (1928). *Studies in deceit. Book I. General methods and results. Book II. Statistical methods and results.* New York: MacMillan.

Johnson, R. A. (2002). *Whistleblowing: When it works and when it doesn't.* Boulder, CO: Lynne Rienner.

Kraut, R. E., & Poe, D. B. (1980). Behavioral roots of person perception: The deception judgments of customs inspectors and laymen. *Journal of Personality and Social Psychology, 39*(5), 784–798.

Krull, D. S., & Erickson, D. J. (1995). Judging situations: On the effortful process of taking dispositional information into account. *Social Cognition, 13*(4), 417–438.

Krull, D. S., Seger, C. R., & Silvera, D. H. (2001). On the profits and perils of guessing right: Effects of situational expectations for emotions on the correspondence of inferences. *Journal of Experimental Social Psychology, 37*(5), 413–418.

Kunda, Z. (1990). The case for motivated reasoning. *Psychological Bulletin, 108*(3), 480–498.

Levesque, M. J., & Kenny, D. A. (1993). Accuracy of behavioral predictions at zero acquaintance: A social relations analysis. *Journal of Personality and Social Psychology, 65*(6), 1178–1187.

Malone, B. E., & DePaulo, B. M. (2001). Measuring sensitivity to deception. In J. A. Hall & F. J. Bernieri (Eds.), *Interpersonal sensitivity: Theory and measurement* (pp. 103–124). Mahwah, NJ: Lawrence Erlbaum.

Mehrabian, A. (1971). Nonverbal betrayal of feeling. *Journal of Experimental Research in Personality, 5*(1), 64–73.

O'Sullivan, M., Ekman, P., & Friesen, W. V. (1988). The effect of comparisons on detecting deceit. *Journal of Nonverbal Behavior, 12*(3, Pt. 1), 203–215.

O'Sullivan, M., Ekman, P., Friesen, W. V., & Scherer, K. R. (1985). What you say and how you say it: The contribution of speech content and voice quality to judgments of others. *Journal of Personality and Social Psychology, 48*(1), 54–62.

Park, J. W., Yoon, S. O., Kim, K. H., & Wyer, R. S., Jr. (2001). Effects of priming a bipolar attribute concept on dimension versus concept-specific accessibility of semantic memory. *Journal of Personality and Social Psychology, 81*(3), 405–420.

Porter, S., Woodworth, M., & Birt, A. R. (2000). Truth, lies, and videotape: An investigation of the ability of federal parole officers to detect deception. *Law and Human Behavior, 24*(6), 643–658.

Pronin, E., Lin, D. Y., & Ross, L. (2002). The bias blind spot: Perceptions of bias in self versus others. *Personality and Social Psychology Bulletin, 28*(3), 369–381.

Quattrone, G. A. (1982). Behavioral consequences of attributional bias. *Social Cognition, 1*(4), 358–378.

Riggio, R. E., & Friedman, H. S. (1983). Individual differences and cues to deception. *Journal of Personality and Social Psychology, 45*(4), 899–915.

Riggio, R. E., Salinas, C., & Tucker, J. (1988). Personality and deception ability. *Personality and Individual Differences, 9*(1), 189–191.

Riggio, R. E., Tucker, J., & Throckmorton, B. (1987). Social skills and deception ability. *Personality and Social Psychology Bulletin, 13*(4), 568–577.

Robinson, M. D., & Clore, G. L. (2001). Simulation, scenarios, and emotional appraisal: Testing the convergence of real and imagined reactions to emotional stimuli. *Personality and Social Psychology Bulletin, 27*(11), 1520–1532.

Ross, L., & Nisbett, R. E. (1991). *The person and the situation: Perspectives of social psychology.* New York: McGraw-Hill.

Saarni, C., & Weber, H. (1999). Emotional displays and dissemblance in childhood: Implications for self-presentation. In P. Philippot (Ed.), *The social context of nonverbal behavior* (pp. 71–105). New York: Cambridge University Press.

Stapel, D. A., Koomen, W., & van der Pligt, J. (1996). The referents of trait inferences: The impact of trait concepts versus actor-trait links on subsequent judgments. *Journal of Personality and Social Psychology, 70*(3), 437–450.

Thorndike, E. L. (1920). A constant error in psychological rating. *Journal of Applied Psychology, 4,* 25–29.

Tversky, A., & Kahneman, D. (1974). Judgment under uncertainty: Heuristics and biases. *Science, 185*(4157), 1124–1131.

Vrij, A., Edward, K., & Bull, R. (2001). Police officers' ability to detect deceit: The benefit of indirect deception detection measures. *Legal and Criminological Psychology, 6,* 185–196.

Yzerbyt, V. Y., Corneille, O., Dumont, M., & Hahn, K. (2001). The dispositional inference strikes back: Situational focus and dispositional suppression in causal attribution. *Journal of Personality and Social Psychology, 81*(3), 365–376.

Zebrowitz, L. A., Voinescu, L., & Collins, M. A. (1996). "Wide-eyed" and "crooked-faced": Determinants of perceived and real honesty across the life span. *Personality and Social Psychology Bulletin, 22*(12), 1258–1269.

Zuckerman, M., DeFrank, R. S., Hall, J. A., Larrance, D. T., & Rosenthal, R. (1979). Facial and vocal cues of deception and honesty. *Journal of Experimental Social Psychology, 15,* 378–396.

Zuckerman, M., & Driver, R. E. (1985). Telling lies: Verbal and nonverbal correlates of deception. In W. A. Siegman & S. Feldstein (Eds.), *Multichannel integration of nonverbal behavior* (pp. 129–147). Hillsdale, NJ: Lawrence Erlbaum.

Zuckerman, M., Fischer, S. A., Osmun, R. W., & Winkler, B. A. (1987). Anchoring in lie detection revisited. *Journal of Nonverbal Behavior, 11*(1), 4–12.

Zuckerman, M., Koestner, R., Colella, M. J., & Alton, A. O. (1984). Anchoring in the detection of deception and leakage. *Journal of Personality and Social Psychology, 47*(2), 301–311.

Author's Note: Portions of this research were presented at the Undergraduate Research Conference in Santa Clara, California, in April 1996 and the International Interrogation Conference in Napa, California, in October 2000. Many thanks to David Balahadia, Norman Brand, Gerald Clore, Paul Ekman, Mark Frank, Randall Harrison, and Michael Suileabahn Wilson for their help in gathering these data or in commenting on the article and to Vicki Helgeson for her careful, persistent, and perceptive editing.

CRITICAL THINKING QUESTIONS

1. What implications does the present study have for the accuracy of lie detecting in personal relationships? Law enforcement? Business? Politics? Defend your answers.

2. Formulate your own explanation of why most people are not accurate in detecting lies. Be sure to include the information in the introduction of this article in formulating your response.

3. This article suggests that once we have caught a person in a lie, it is very difficult for us to change our dispositional attribution of his or her being dishonest to one of being honest. Discuss the practical implications of this statement.

4. The studies reported in this article used only males as liars and mostly females as lie detectors. Would it make a difference if female liars were employed or if more male subjects were used to detect the deception? Why or why not?

5. Let's assume that most of us want to make accurate judgments of other people, especially as to whether or not they are lying. Given that, can the information from this study and/or a general understanding of the role of the fundamental attribution error in detecting lies be used to help us make more accurate judgments of other people? Explain your answer.

CHAPTER INTEGRATION QUESTIONS

1. What do you see as a common theme or themes across all of the articles in this chapter?

2. Mark Twain said, "My life has been filled with terrible misfortunes—most of which never happened. Life does not consist mainly—or even largely—of facts and happenings. It consists mainly of the storm of thoughts that is forever blowing through one's head." What does this quotation mean to you? Do you agree or disagree with it? Defend your answer.

3. Relate the quotation from Twain to the overall theme or themes that you identified for this chapter in Question 1.

Chapter Four

ATTITUDES

THE STUDY OF attitudes is considered by many social psychologists to be the core issue in understanding human behavior. How we act in any given situation is the product of the attitudes that we have formed, which in turn are based on the experiences we have had.

Whether or not we believe that attitudes constitute the core of social psychology, the study of attitudes and attitude change has been prominent in social psychological research from the beginning. Part of this interest has been theoretically driven. How attitudes are formed and how they can be changed, as well as what factors make some attitudes so resistant to change, are but a few of the topics that theorists have studied. However, there is also a more pragmatic, applied reason for this interest in attitudes: Principles of attitude change and attitude measurement have a direct bearing on several major industries and even psychotherapy. For example, survey organizations and advertising agencies focus on attitudes, measuring what they are, how they change over time, as well as how best to change them. Likewise, a major goal of both therapy and health promotion might be viewed as modifying people's dysfunctional or health-endangering attitudes and behaviors. Theoretical research often has provided the foundation for the principles applied by clinicians, health professionals, and advertisers.

The readings in this chapter relate to various aspects of attitudes. Article 10, " Don't Even Think about It!" examines the issue of taboos as being a prime example of deeply held attitudes. How are taboos formed? Why are they maintained? How are they changed?

Article 11, "Cognitive Consequences of Forced Compliance," is a classic demonstration of a powerful theoretical model in social psychology known as *cognitive dissonance*. It is an excellent example of how common-sense predictions often are exactly opposite of what actually occurs.

Finally, Article 12, "I'm a Hypocrite, but So Is Everyone Else: Group Support and the Reduction of Cognitive Dissonance," is a contemporary article that elaborates on the concept of cognitive dissonance presented in Article 11. Article 12 provides insight into the direction dissonance research has gone since it was first presented over 60 years ago and how such a concept is continually tested and refined over time.

ARTICLE 10 _____

Obviously, attitudes are formed in a great variety of ways. Some are the result of direct experience. For instance, we meet someone from a certain country and, based on that limited experience, form an attitude (or stereotype) about people from that country. In other words, we generalize our experience to form an attitude. In many other cases, however, we do not experience the person, situation, or event directly but rather indirectly. These so-called *secondhand attitudes* are the result of information we received from someone else, such as our parents or friends. In fact, this kind of information is a major source of our beliefs.

The number of attitudes that people hold can be virtually limitless; however, some attitudes are held more strongly than others. The strength of these attitudes often can be seen most clearly by their absence. That is, what topics do we never discuss? What would we never admit, or what would we never do? In other words, what are our *taboos?* A taboo involves the three elements that comprise all attitudes: First, there is a *cognitive* or *belief* component, which is what we believe is or should be true. Additionally, there is an *affective* or *emotional* component to the taboo. We not only believe something to be true, we also feel very strongly about it. Just the idea of the taboo being violated may fill us with disgust. Finally, the taboo involves a *behavior tendency;* we strongly tend to avoid doing things that violate our taboo belief and affective components.

Many taboos are shared among people in a culture, while others are unique to individuals. Thus, most people in a given society tend to believe that it is acceptable to eat certain foods while other foods are off limits. Sometimes, taboos are more unique, such as beliefs that certain topics should never be mentioned to certain people. In all cases, taboos serve to set limits (sometimes, severe limits) on what we believe, feel, and do.

The following article by Michael Ventura examines the topic of taboos, including their origins and the impact that they have on our daily lives. After reading the article, you may agree with the author that we are not really as free as we would like to believe, despite the fact that freedom is a central concept in American culture.

Don't Even Think about It!

■ Michael Ventura

Taboos come in all sizes. Big taboos: when I was a kid in the Italian neighborhoods of Brooklyn, to insult someone's mother meant a brutal fight—the kind of fight no one interferes with until one of the combatants goes down and stays down. Little taboos: until the sixties, it was an insult to use someone's first name without asking or being offered permission. Personal taboos: Cyrano de Bergerac would not tolerate the mention of his enormous nose. Taboos peculiar to one city: in Brooklyn (again), when the Dodgers were still at Ebbets Field, if you rooted for the Yankees you kept it to yourself unless you wanted a brawl. Taboos, big or small, are always about having to respect somebody's (often irrational) boundary—or else.

There are taboos shared within one family: my father did not feel free to speak to us of his grandmother's suicide until his father died. Taboos within intellectual elites: try putting a serious metaphysical or

Reprinted from *Psychology Today,* 1998 (January/February), *31,* 32–38, 66, 68. Reprinted with permission from *Psychology Today* magazine, Copyright © 1998 (Sussex Publishers, Inc.).

spiritual slant on a "think-piece" (as we call them in the trade) written for the *New York Times,* the *Washington Post,* or most big name magazines—it won't be printed. Taboos in the corporate and legal worlds: if you're male, you had best wear suits of somber colors, or you're not likely to be taken seriously; if you're female, you have to strike a very uneasy balance between the attractive and the prim, and even then you might not be taken seriously. Cultural taboos: in the Jim Crow days in the South, a black man who spoke with familiarity to a white woman might be beaten, driven out of town, or (as was not uncommon) lynched.

Unclassifiable taboos: in Afghanistan, as I write this, it is a sin—punishable by beatings and imprisonment—to fly a kite. Sexual taboos: there are few communities on this planet where two men can walk down a street holding hands without being harassed or even arrested; in Afghanistan (a great place for taboos these days) the Taliban would stone them to death. Gender taboos: how many American corporations (or institutions of any kind) promote women to power? National taboos: until the seventies, a divorced person could not run for major public office in America (it wasn't until 1981 that our first and only divorced president, Ronald Reagan, took office); today, no professed atheist would dare try for the presidency. And most readers of this article probably approve, as I do, of this comparatively recent taboo: even the most rabid bigot must avoid saying "nigger," "spic," or "kike" during, say, a job interview—and the most macho sexist must avoid words like "broad."

Notice that nearly all of our taboos, big and small, public and intimate, involve silence—keeping one's silence, or paying a price for not keeping it. Yet keeping silent has its own price: for then silence begins to fill the heart, until silence becomes the heart—a heart swelling with restraint until it bursts in frustration, anger, even madness.

The taboos hardest on the soul are those which fester in our intimacies—taboos known only to the people involved, taboos that can make us feel alone even with those to whom we're closest. One of the deep pains of marriage—one that also plagues brothers and sisters, parents and children, even close friends—is that as we grow more intimate, certain silences often become more necessary. We discover taboo areas, both

in ourselves and in the other, that cannot be transgressed without paying an awful price. If we speak of them, we may endanger the relationship; but if we do not speak, if we do not violate the taboo, the relationship may become static and tense, until the silence takes on a life of its own. Such silences are corrosive. They eat at the innards of intimacy until, often, the silence itself causes the very rupture or break-up that we've tried to avoid by keeping silent.

THE CANNIBAL IN US ALL

You may measure how many taboos constrict you, how many taboos you've surrendered to—at home, at parties, at work, with your lover or your family—by how much of yourself you must suppress. You may measure your life, in these realms, by what you cannot say, do, admit—cannot and must not, and for no better reason than that your actions or words would disrupt your established order. By this measure, most of us are living within as complex and strictured a system of taboos as the aborigines who gave us the word in the first place. You can see how fitting it is that the word "taboo" comes from a part of the world where cannibalism is said to be practiced to this day: the islands off eastern Australia—Polynesia, New Zealand, Melanesia. Until 1777, when Captain James Cook published an account of his first world voyage, Europe and colonial America had many taboos but no word that precisely meant taboo. Cook introduced this useful word to the West. Its instant popularity, quick assimilation into most European languages, and constant usage since, are testimony to how much of our lives the word describes. Before the word came to us, we'd ostracized, coerced, exiled, tormented, and murdered each other for myriad infractions (as we still do), but we never had a satisfying, precise word for our reasons.

We needed cannibals to give us a word to describe our behavior, so how "civilized" are we, really? We do things differently from those cannibals, on the surface, but is the nature of what we do all that different? We don't cook each other for ceremonial dinners, at least not physically (though therapists can testify that our ceremonial seasons, like Christmas and Thanksgiving, draw lots of business—something's cooking). But we stockpile weapons that can cook the entire world, and we organize our national priorities around their "necessity," and it's a national political taboo to seriously cut spending for those planet-cookers. If that's "progress," it's lost on me. In China it's taboo to be a Christian, in Israel it's taboo to be a Moslem, in Syria it's taboo to be a Jew, in much of the United States it's still taboo to be an atheist, while in American academia it's taboo to be deeply religious. Our headlines are full of this stuff. So it's hardly surprising that a cannibal's word still describes much of our behavior.

I'm not denying the necessity of every society to set limits and invent taboos (some rational, some not) simply in order to get on with the day—and to try to contain the constant, crazy, never-to-be-escaped longings that blossom in our sleep and distract or compel us while awake. Such longings are why even a comparatively tiny desert tribe like the ancient Hebrews needed commandments and laws against coveting each other's wives, stealing, killing, committing incest. That tribe hadn't seen violent, sexy movies, hadn't listened to rock 'n' roll, hadn't been bombarded with ads featuring half-naked models, and hadn't watched too much TV. They didn't need to. Like us, they had their hearts, desires, and dreams to instruct them how to be very, very naughty. The taboo underlying all others is that we must not live by the dictates of our irrational hearts—as though we haven't forgiven each other, or ourselves, for having hearts.

If there's a taboo against something, it's usually because a considerable number of people desire to do it. The very taboos that we employ to protect us from each other and ourselves, are a map of our secret natures. When you know a culture's taboos (or an individual's, or a family's) you know its secrets—you know what it really wants.

FAVORITE TABOOS

It's hard to keep a human being from his or her desire, taboo or not. We've always been very clever, very resourceful, when it comes to sneaking around our taboos. The Aztecs killed virgins and called it religion. The Europeans enslaved blacks and called it economics. Americans tease each other sexually and call it fashion.

If we can't kill and screw and steal and betray to our heart's desire, and, in general, violate every taboo

in sight—well, we can at least watch other people do it. Or read about it. Or listen to it. As we have done, since ancient times, through every form of religion and entertainment. The appeal of taboos and our inability to escape our longing for transgression (whether or not we ourselves transgress) are why so many people who call themselves honest and law-abiding spend so much time with movies, operas, soaps, garish trials, novels, songs, Biblical tales, tribal myths, folk stories, and Shakespeare—virtually all of which, both the great and the trivial, are about those who dare to violate taboos. It's a little unsettling when you think about it: the very stuff we say we most object to is the fundamental material of what we call culture.

That's one reason that fundamentalists of all religions are so hostile to the arts. But fundamentalists partake of taboos in the sneakiest fashion of all. Senator Jesse Helms led the fight against the National Endowment for the Arts because he couldn't get the (vastly overrated) homosexual art of Robert Mapplethorpe or the most extreme performance artists out of his mind—he didn't and doesn't want to. He, like all fundamentalists, will vigorously oppose such art and all it stands for until he dies, because his very opposition gives him permission to concentrate on taboo acts. The Taliban of Afghanistan will ride around in jeeps toting guns, searching out any woman who dares show an inch of facial skin or wear white socks (Taliban boys consider white socks provocative), and when they find such a woman they'll jail and beat her—because their so-called righteousness gives them permission to obsess on their taboos. Pat Robertson and his ilk will fuss and rage about any moral "deviation," any taboo violation they can find, because that's the only way they can give themselves permission to entertain the taboos. They get to not have their taboo cake, yet eat it too.

We are all guilty of this to some extent. Why else have outlaws from Antigone to Robin Hood to Jesse James to John Gotti become folk heroes? Oedipus killed his father and slept with his mother, and we've been performing that play for 2500 years because he is the ultimate violator of our deepest taboos. Aristotle said we watch such plays for "catharsis," to purge our desires and fears in a moment of revelation. Baloney. Ideas like "catharsis" are an intellectual game, to glossy-up our sins. What's closer to the truth is that we need Oedipus to stand in for us. We can't have changed much in 2500 years, if we still keep him alive in our hearts to enact our darkest taboos for us. Clearly, the very survival of Oedipus as an instantly recognizable name tells us that we still want to kill our fathers and screw our mothers (or vice versa).

A COUNTRY OF BROKEN TABOOS

Taboos are a special paradox for Americans. However much we may long for tradition and order, our longings are subverted by the inescapable fact that our country was founded upon a break with tradition and a challenge to order—which is to say, the United States was founded upon the violation of taboos. Specifically, this country was founded upon the violation of Europe's most suffocating taboo: its feudal suppression (still enforced in 1776, when America declared its independence) of the voices of the common people. We were the first nation on earth to write into law that any human being has the right to say anything, and that even the government is (theoretically) not allowed to silence you.

At the time, Europe was a continent of state-enforced religions, where royalty's word was law and all other words could be crushed by law. (Again: taboo was a matter of enforced silence.) We were the first nation to postulate verbal freedom for everyone. All our other freedoms depend upon verbal freedom; no matter how badly and how often we've failed that ideal, it still remains our ideal.

Once we broke Europe's verbal taboos, it was only a matter of time before other traditional taboos fell too. As the writer Albert Murray has put it, Americans could not afford piety in their new homeland: "You can't be over respectful of established forms; you're trying to get through the wilderness of Kentucky." Thus, from the moment the Pilgrims landed, our famous puritanism faced an inherent contradiction. How could we domesticate the wilderness of this continent; how could peasants and rejects and "commoners" form a strong and viable nation; how could we develop all the new social forms and technologies necessary to blend all the disparate peoples who came here—without violating those same Puritan taboos which are so ingrained, to this day, in our national character?

It can't be over-emphasized that America's fundamental stance against both the taboos of Europe and the taboos of our own Puritans, was our insistence upon freedom of speech. America led the attack against silence. And it is through that freedom, the freedom to break the silence, that we've destroyed so many other taboos. Especially during the last 40 years, we've broken the silence that surrounded ancient taboos of enormous significance. Incest, child abuse, wife-battering, homosexuality, and some (by no means all) forms of racial and gender oppression, are not merely spoken of, and spoken against, they're shouted about from the rooftops. Many breathe easier because of this inevitable result of free speech. In certain sections of our large cities, for the first time in modern history, gay people can live openly and without fear. The feminist movement has made previously forbidden or hidden behaviors both speakable and doable. The National Organization of Women can rail against the Promise Keepers all they want (and they have some good reasons), but when you get a million working-class guys crying and hugging in public, the stoic mask of the American male has definitely cracked. And I'm old enough to remember when it was shocking for women to speak about wanting a career. Now virtually all affluent young women are expected to want a career.

Fifty years ago, not one important world or national leader was black. Now there are more people of color in positions of influence than ever. Bad marriages can be dissolved without social stigma. Children born out of wedlock are not damned as "bastards" for something that wasn't their fault. And those of us who've experienced incest and abuse have finally found a voice, and through our voices we've achieved a certain amount of liberation from shame and pain.

These boons are rooted in our decidedly un-Puritan freedom of speech. But we left those Puritans behind a long time ago—for the breaking of silence is the fundamental political basis of our nation, and no taboo is safe when people have the right to speak.

KEEPER OF YOUR SILENCE

In the process, though, we've lost the sanctity of silence. We've lost the sense of dark but sacred power inherent in sex, in nature, even in crime. Perhaps that is the price of our new freedoms.

It's also true that by breaking the silence we've thrown ourselves into a state of confusion. The old taboos formed part of society's structure. Without them, that structure has undeniably weakened. We are faced with shoring up the weakened parts, inventing new ways of being together that have pattern and order—for we cannot live without some pattern and order—but aren't so restrictive. Without sexual taboos, for instance, what are the social boundaries between men and women? When are they breached? What is offensive? Nobody's sure. Everybody's making mistakes. This is so excruciating that many are nostalgic for some of the old taboos. But once a taboo is broken, then for good or ill it's very hard, perhaps impossible, to reinstate it.

But there is another, subtler confusion: yes, enormous taboos have fallen, but many taboos, equally important, remain. And, both as individuals and as a society, we're strained enough, confused enough, by the results of doing away with so many taboos in so short a time, that maybe we're not terribly eager for our remaining taboos to fall. We may sincerely desire that, but maybe we're tired, fed up, scared. Many people would rather our taboos remain intact for a couple of generations while we get our act together again, and perhaps they have a point. But the price of taboo remains what it's always been: silence and constriction.

What do we see, when we pass each other on the street, but many faces molded by the price paid for keeping the silences of the taboos that remain—spirits confined within their own, and their society's, silences? Even this brief essay on our public and intimate strictures is enough to demonstrate that we are still a primitive race, bounded by fear and prejudice, with taboos looming in every direction—no matter how much we like to brag and/or bitch that modern life is liberating us from all the old boundaries. The word taboo still says much more about us than most prefer to admit.

What is the keeper of your silence? The answer to that question is your own guide to your personal taboos. How must you confine yourself in order to get through your day at the job, or to be acceptable in your social circle? The answer to that is your map of your society's taboos. What makes you most afraid to speak? What desire, what word, what possibility, freezes and fevers you at the same time, making any sincere communication out of the question? What makes you vanish into your secret? That's your taboo, baby. You're still in the room, maybe even still smiling, still talking, but not really—what's really happened is that you've vanished down some hole in yourself, and you'll stay there until you're sure the threat to your taboo is gone and it's safe to come out again. If, that is, you've ever come out in the first place. Some never have.

What utterance, what hint, what insinuation, can quiet a room of family or friends? What makes people change the subject? What makes those at a dinner party dismiss a remark as though it wasn't said, or dismiss a person as though he or she wasn't really there? We've all seen conversations suddenly go dead, and just as suddenly divert around a particular person or subject, leaving them behind in the dead space, because something has been said or implied that skirts a silently shared taboo. If that happens to you often, don't kid yourself that you're living in a "free" society. Because you're only as free as your freedom from taboos—not on some grand abstract level, but in your day-to-day life.

It is probably inherent in the human condition that there are no "last" taboos. Or perhaps it just feels that way because we have such a long way to go. But at least we can know where to look: right in front of our eyes, in the recesses of our speechlessness, in the depths of our silences. And there is nothing for it but to confront the keepers of our silence. Either that, or to submit to being lost, as most of us silently are, without admitting it to each other or to ourselves—lost in a maze of taboos.

In Search of the Last Taboo

There is no "last taboo," according to Michael Ventura. But there certainly are a lot of contenders, scattered like clues in a treasure hunt for the heart of our culture. Here, an assortment of last taboos "discovered" by the media in the past few years.

"What a great story: **Incest**. The last taboo!"—*Esquire,* on Kathryn Harrison's memoir *The Kiss*

"'The very word is a room-emptier,' Tina Brown wrote in her editor's note when, in 1991, Gail Sheehy broke the silence with a story in *Vanity* Fair. . . . **Menopause** may be the last taboo." —*Fort Lauderdale Sun-Sentinel*

"The last taboo for women is not, as Gail Sheehy would have it, menopause, but **facial hair.**" —*New York Times*

"At a time when this is the last taboo, Moreton depicts **erections.**"—*Sunday Telegraph,* describing sculptor Nicholas Moreton's work

"Virtually no representations of **faith** are seen on television, it's the last taboo."—*Columbus Dispatch*

"Anything with **sex with underage kids** is the last taboo."—*Toronto Star*

"The last taboo: an openly **homosexual** actor playing a **heterosexual** lead."—*Boston Globe*

"With sexual mores gone the way of Madonna, **picking up the tab** has become the last taboo for women."—*Philadelphia Inquirer*

"Most Americans, if they think about **class** at all (it may be our last taboo subject), would surely describe themselves as middle class regardless of a petty detail like income."—*Los Angeles Times Syndicate*

"The Last Taboo Is **Age**: Why Are We Afraid of It?"—headline in the *Philadelphia Inquirer*

"Smash the last taboo! [Timothy] Leary says he's planning the first . . . **interactive suicide.**" —*Washington Post*

"**Money** is the last taboo."—*Calgary Herald*

"**Menstruation** may be the last taboo."—*Manchester Guardian Weekly*

"The real last taboo is that of **privacy and dignity.**"—*Montreal Gazette*

"And then there's **bisexuality,** the last taboo among lesbians."—*Los Angeles Times*

"I think **personal smells** are one of the last taboos."—*The Observer*

"Television's last taboo, long after f-words and pumping bottoms became commonplace, was the **full-frontal vomit.** Now, even that last shred of inhibition has gone, and every drama . . . [has] a character heaving his guts all over the camera."—*The (London) Mail*

"**Tanning.** The last taboo. If you're tan, then your IQ must be lower than the SPF of the sunscreen you'd be using if you had any brains."—*Los Angeles Times*

CRITICAL THINKING QUESTIONS

1. What do you believe are the five strongest and most universally held taboos in your culture? What would be the sanctions for someone who violated these taboos? Why do these taboos remain so strong, and what function may each serve? Explain your answers.

2. Discuss two beliefs or behaviors that have been considered taboo in your lifetime but are not any longer. When and why did each of these taboos disappear? Is there any particular reason each disappeared when it did rather than, say, 50 years before? Explain your answers.

3. Name two current taboos that you do not believe will be considered taboos 20 years from now. What will it take to eliminate each of these taboos? In your opinion, what are the effects of eliminating taboos? Discuss the positive versus negative effects.

4. Do you hold any personal taboos (as opposed to cultural taboos)? For example, are there certain topics that you cannot discuss or things that you cannot do with certain people yet can with others? Discuss what you believe are the origins, functions, and impacts of these personal taboos on you and on the people affected by them.

ARTICLE 11 ⎯⎯⎯⎯⎯⎯⎯⎯⎯⎯⎯⎯⎯⎯⎯⎯⎯⎯

Suppose someone asked you to publicly say something that contradicted your privately held beliefs and then offered you either a small reward (say, $1) or a large reward ($20) for doing so. Under which of those conditions would you be most likely to actually change your privately held belief to bring it more into the realm of what you just said? If you guessed that would be most likely to happen in the $20 condition, you would have guessed wrong.

A major theory in social psychology is known as *cognitive dissonance*. Briefly stated, this theory says that people feel a tension when they are aware of an inconsistency either between two attitudes or between an attitude and a behavior. Moreover, the theory asserts that such tension produces some type of change to reduce the state of dissonance. The resulting outcome often is counterintuitive to what common sense would predict. The exact conditions under which cognitive dissonance operates and how it is reduced have been investigated in many experiments over the years.

The following article by Leon Festinger and James M. Carlsmith is *the* classic study on dissonance theory. The hypothesis being tested is a simple yet powerful and nonobvious one. Aside from the outcomes, of particular interest is the elaborate design of the experiment. While reading the article, put yourself in the shoes of the subjects and try to imagine how their thinking might account for the obtained results.

Cognitive Consequences of Forced Compliance
■ Leon Festinger and James M. Carlsmith

What happens to a person's private opinion if he is forced to do or say something contrary to that opinion? Only recently has there been any experimental work related to this question. Two studies reported by Janis and King (1954; 1956) clearly showed that, at least under some conditions, the private opinion changes so as to bring it into closer correspondence with the overt behavior the person was forced to perform. Specifically, they showed that if a person is forced to improvise a speech supporting a point of view with which he disagrees, his private opinion moves toward the position advocated in the speech. The observed opinion change is greater than for persons who only hear the speech or for persons who read a prepared speech with emphasis solely on elocution and manner of delivery. The authors of these two studies explain their results mainly in terms of mental rehearsal and thinking up new arguments. In this way, they propose, the person who is forced to improvise a speech convinces himself. They present some evidence, which is not altogether conclusive, in support of this explanation. We will have more to say concerning this explanation in discussing the results of our experiment.

Kelman (1953) tried to pursue the matter further. He reasoned that if the person is induced to make an overt statement contrary to his private opinion by the offer of some reward, then the greater the reward offered, the greater should be the subsequent opinion change. His data, however, did not support this idea. He found, rather, that a large reward produced less subsequent opinion change than did a smaller reward. Actually, this finding by Kelman is consistent with the theory we will outline below but, for a number of reasons, is not conclusive. One of the major weaknesses of the data is that not all subjects in the experiment made an overt statement contrary to their private opinion in order to obtain the offered reward. What is

Reprinted from *Journal of Abnormal and Social Psychology,* 1959, *58,* 203–210.

more, as one might expect, the percentage of subjects who complied increased as the size of the offered reward increased. Thus, with self-selection of who did and who did not make the required overt statement and with varying percentages of subjects in the different conditions who did make the required statement, no interpretation of the data can be unequivocal.

Recently, Festinger (1957) proposed a theory concerning cognitive dissonance from which come a number of derivations about opinion change following forced compliance. Since these derivations are stated in detail by Festinger (1957, Ch. 4), we will here give only a brief outline of the reasoning.

Let us consider a person who privately holds opinion "X" but has, as a result of pressure brought to bear on him, publicly stated that he believes "not X."

1. This person has two cognitions which, psychologically, do not fit together: one of these is the knowledge that he believes "X," the other the knowledge that he has publicly stated that he believes "not X." If no factors other than his private opinion are considered, it would follow, at least in our culture, that if he believes "X" he would publicly state "X." Hence, his cognition of his private belief is dissonant with his cognition concerning his actual public statement.

2. Similarly, the knowledge that he has said "not X" is consonant with (does fit together with) those cognitive elements corresponding to the reasons, pressures, promises of rewards and/or threats of punishment which induced him to say "not X."

3. In evaluating the total magnitude of dissonance, one must take account of both dissonances and consonances. Let us think of the sum of all the dissonances involving some particular cognition as "D" and the sum of all the consonances as "C." Then we might think of the total magnitude of dissonance as being a function of "D" divided by "D" plus "C."

Let us then see what can be said about the total magnitude of dissonance in a person created by the knowledge that he said "not X" and really believes "X." With everything else held constant, this total magnitude of dissonance would decrease as the number and importance of the pressures which induced him to say "not X" increased. Thus, if the overt behavior was brought about by, say, offers of reward or threats of punishment, the magnitude of dissonance is maximal if these promised rewards or threatened pun-

ishments were just barely sufficient to induce the person to say "not X." From this point on, as the promised rewards or threatened punishment become larger, the magnitude of dissonance becomes smaller.

4. One way in which the dissonance can be reduced is for the person to change his private opinion so as to bring it into correspondence with what he has said. One would consequently expect to observe such opinion change after a person has been forced or induced to say something contrary to his private opinion. Furthermore, since the pressure to reduce dissonance will be a function of the magnitude of the dissonance, the observed opinion change should be greatest when the pressure used to elicit the overt behavior is just sufficient to do it.

The present experiment was designed to test this derivation under controlled, laboratory conditions. In the experiment we varied the amount of reward used to force persons to make a statement contrary to their private views. The prediction [from 3 and 4 above] is that the larger the reward given to the subject, the smaller will be the subsequent opinion change.

PROCEDURE

Seventy-one male students in the introductory psychology course at Stanford University were used in the experiment. In this course, students are required to spend a certain number of hours as subjects (Ss) in experiments. They choose among the available experiments by signing their names on a sheet posted on the bulletin board which states the nature of the experiment. The present experiment was listed as a two-hour experiment dealing with "Measures of Performance."

During the first week of the course, when the requirement of serving in experiments was announced and explained to the students, the instructor also told them about a study that the psychology department was conducting. He explained that, since they were required to serve in experiments, the department was conducting a study to evaluate these experiments in order to be able to improve them in the future. They were told that a sample of students would be interviewed after having served as Ss. They were urged to cooperate in these interviews by being completely frank and honest. The importance of this announcement will become clear shortly. It enabled us to measure the opinions of our Ss in a context not directly connected with our experiment and in which we could reasonably expect frank and honest expressions of opinion.

When the S arrived for the experiment on "Measures of Performance" he had to wait for a few minutes in the secretary's office. The experimenter (E) then came in, introduced himself to the S and, together, they walked into the laboratory room where the E said:

> This experiment usually takes a little over an hour but, of course, we had to schedule it for two hours. Since we have that extra time, the introductory psychology people asked if they could interview some of our subjects. [Offhand and conversationally.] Did they announce that in class? I gather that they're interviewing some people who have been in experiments. I don't know much about it. Anyhow, they may want to interview you when you're through here.

With no further introduction or explanation the S was shown the first task, which involved putting 12 spools onto a tray, emptying the tray, refilling it with spools, and so on. He was told to use one hand and to work at his own speed. He did this for one-half hour. The E then removed the tray and spools and placed in front of the S a board containing 48 square pegs. His task was to turn each peg a quarter turn clockwise, then another quarter turn, and so on. He was told again to use one hand and to work at his own speed. The S worked at this task for another half hour.

While the S was working on these tasks, the E sat, with a stop watch in his hand, busily making notations on a sheet of paper. He did so in order to make it convincing that this was what the E was interested in and that these tasks, and how the S worked on them, was the total experiment. From our point of view the experiment had hardly started. The hour which the S spent working on the repetitive, monotonous tasks was intended to provide, for each S uniformly, an experience about which he would have a somewhat negative opinion.

After the half hour on the second task was over, the E conspicuously set the stop watch back to zero, put it away, pushed his chair back, lit a cigarette, and said:

> O.K. Well, that's all we have in the experiment itself. I'd like to explain what this has been all about so you'll have some idea of why you were doing this. [E pauses.] Well, the way the experiment is set up is this. There are actually two groups in the experiment. In one, the group you were in, we bring the subject in and give him essentially no introduction to the experiment. That is, all we tell him is what he needs to know in order to do the tasks, and he has no idea of what the experiment is all about, or what it's going to be like, or anything like that. But in the other group, we have a student that we've hired that works for us regularly, and what I do is take him into the next room where the subject is waiting—the same room you were waiting in before—and I introduce him as if he had just finished being a subject in the experiment. That is, I say: "This is so-and-so, who's just finished the experiment and I've asked him to tell you a little of what it's about before you start." The fellow who works for us then, in conversation with the next subject, makes these points: [The E then produced a sheet headed "For Group B" which had written on it: It was very enjoyable, I had a lot of fun, I enjoyed myself, it was very interesting, it was intriguing, it was exciting. The E showed this to the S and then proceeded with his false explanation of the purpose of the experiment.] Now, of course, we have this student do this, because if the experimenter does it, it doesn't look as realistic, and what we're interested in doing is comparing how these two groups do on the experiment—the one with this previous expectation about the experiment, and the other, like yourself, with essentially none.

Up to this point the procedure was identical for Ss in all conditions. From this point on they diverged somewhat. Three conditions were run, Control, One Dollar, and Twenty Dollars, as follows:

Control Condition

The E continued:

> Is that fairly clear? [Pause.] Look, that fellow [looks at watch] I was telling you about from the introductory psychology class said he would get here a couple of minutes from now. Would you mind waiting to see if he wants to talk to you? Fine. Why don't we go into

the other room to wait? [The E left the S in the secretary's office for four minutes. He then returned and said:] O.K. Let's check and see if he does want to talk to you.

One and Twenty Dollar Conditions

The *E* continued:

Is that fairly clear how it is set up and what we're trying to do? [Pause.] Now, I also have a sort of strange thing to ask you. The thing is this. [Long pause, some confusion and uncertainty in the following, with a degree of embarrassment on the part of the E. The manner of the E contrasted strongly with the preceding unhesitant and assured false explanation of the experiment. The point was to make it seem to the S that this was the first time the E had done this and that he felt unsure of himself.] The fellow who normally does this for us couldn't do it today—he just phoned in, and something or other came up for him—so we've been looking around for someone that we could hire to do it for us. You see, we've got another subject waiting [looks at watch] who is supposed to be in that other condition. Now Professor _____, who is in charge of this experiment, suggested that perhaps we could take a chance on your doing it for us. I'll tell you what we had in mind: the thing is, if you could do it for us now, then of course you would know how to do it, and if something like this should ever come up again, that is, the regular fellow couldn't make it, and we had a subject scheduled, it would be very reassuring to us to know that we had somebody else we could call on who knew how to do it. So, if you would be willing to do this for us, we'd like to hire you to do it now and then be on call in the future, if something like this should ever happen again. We can pay you a dollar (twenty dollars) for doing this for us, that is, for doing it now and then being on call. Do you think you could do that for us?

If the *S* hesitated, the *E* said things like, "It will only take a few minutes," "The regular person is pretty reliable; this is the first time he has missed," or "If we needed you we could phone you a day or two in advance; if you couldn't make it, of course, we wouldn't expect you to come." After the *S* agreed to

do it, the *E* gave him the previously mentioned sheet of paper headed "For Group B" and asked him to read it through again. The *E* then paid the *S* one dollar (twenty dollars), made out a hand-written receipt form, and asked the *S* to sign it. He then said:

O.K., the way we'll do it is this. As I said, the next subject should be here by now. I think the next one is a girl. I'll take you into the next room and introduce you to her, saying that you've just finished the experiment and that we've asked you to tell her a little about it. And what we want you to do is just sit down and get into a conversation with her and try to get across the points on that sheet of paper. I'll leave you alone and come back after a couple of minutes. O.K.?

The *E* then took the *S* into the secretary's office where he had previously waited and where the next *S* was waiting. (The secretary had left the office.) He introduced the girl and the *S* to one another saying that the *S* had just finished the experiment and would tell her something about it. He then left saying he would return in a couple of minutes. The girl, an undergraduate hired for this role, said little until the *S* made some positive remarks about the experiment and then said that she was surprised because a friend of hers had taken the experiment the week before and had told her that it was boring and that she ought to try to get out of it. Most *S*s responded by saying something like "Oh, no, it's really very interesting. I'm sure you'll enjoy it." The girl listened quietly after this, accepting and agreeing to everything the *S* told her. The discussion between the *S* and the girl was recorded on a hidden tape recorder.

After two minutes the *E* returned, asked the girl to go into the experimental room, thanked the *S* for talking to the girl, wrote down his phone number to continue the fiction that we might call on him again in the future and then said: "Look, could we check and see if that fellow from introductory psychology wants to talk to you?"

From this point on, the procedure for all three conditions was once more identical. As the *E* and the *S* started to walk to the office where the interviewer was, the *E* said: "Thanks very much for working on those tasks for us. I hope you did enjoy it. Most of our subjects tell us afterward that they found it quite interesting. You get a chance to see how you react to the tasks and so forth." This short persuasive communication was made in all conditions in exactly the same way. The reason for doing it, theoretically, was to make it easier for anyone who wanted to persuade himself that the tasks had been, indeed, enjoyable.

When they arrived at the interviewer's office, the *E* asked the interviewer whether or not he wanted to talk to the *S*. The interviewer said yes, the *E* shook hands with the *S*, said good-bye, and left. The interviewer, of course, was always kept in complete ignorance of which condition the *S* was in. The interview consisted of four questions, on each of which the *S* was first encouraged to talk about the matter and was then asked to rate his opinion or reaction on an 11-point scale. The questions are as follows:

1. Were the tasks interesting and enjoyable? In what way? In what way were they not? Would you rate how you feel about them on a scale from −5 to +5 where −5 means they were extremely dull and boring, +5 means they were extremely interesting and enjoyable, and zero means they were neutral, neither interesting nor uninteresting.

2. Did the experiment give you an opportunity to learn about your own ability to perform these tasks? In what way? In what way not? Would you rate how you feel about this on a scale from 0 to 10 where 0 means you learned nothing and 10 means you learned a great deal.

3. From what you know about the experiment and the tasks involved in it, would you say the experiment was measuring anything important? That is, do you think the results may have scientific value? In what way? In what way not? Would you rate your opinion on this matter on a scale from 0 to 10 where 0 means the results have no scientific value or importance and 10 means they have a great deal of value and importance.

4. Would you have any desire to participate in another similar experiment? Why? Why not? Would you rate your desire to participate in a similar experiment again on a scale from −5 to +5, where −5 means you would definitely dislike to participate, +5 means you would definitely like to participate, and 0 means you have no particular feeling about it one way or the other.

As may be seen, the questions varied in how directly relevant they were to what the *S* had told the girl. This point will be discussed further in connection with the results.

At the close of the interview the *S* was asked what he thought the experiment was about and, following this, was asked directly whether or not he was suspicious of anything and, if so, what he was suspicious of. When the interview was over, the interviewer brought the *S* back to the experimental room where the *E* was waiting together with the girl who had posed as the waiting *S*. (In the control condition, of course, the girl was not there.) The true purpose of the experiment was then explained to the *S* in detail, and the reasons for each of the various steps in the experiment were explained carefully in relation to the true purpose. All experimental *S*s in both One Dollar and Twenty Dollar conditions were asked, after this explanation, to return the money they had been given. All *S*s, without exception, were quite willing to return the money.

The data from 11 of the 71 *S*s in the experiment had to be discarded for the following reasons:

1. Five *S*s (three in the One Dollar and two in the Twenty Dollar condition) indicated in the interview that they were suspicious about having been paid to tell the girl the experiment was fun and suspected that that was the real purpose of the experiment.
2. Two *S*s (both in the One Dollar condition) told the girl that they had been hired, that the experiment was really boring but they were supposed to say it was fun.
3. Three *S*s (one in the One Dollar and two in the Twenty Dollar condition) refused to take the money and refused to be hired.
4. One *S* (in the One Dollar condition), immediately after having talked to the girl, demanded her phone number saying he would call her and explain things, and also told the *E* he wanted to wait until she was finished so he could tell her about it.

These 11 *S*s were, of course, run through the total experiment anyhow and the experiment was explained to them afterwards. Their data, however, are not included in the analysis.

Summary of Design

There remain, for analysis, 20 *S*s in each of the three conditions. Let us review these briefly: 1. *Control condition.* These *S*s were treated identically in all respects to the *S*s in the experimental conditions, except that they were never asked to, and never did, tell the waiting girl that the experimental tasks were enjoyable and lots of fun. 2. *One Dollar condition.* These *S*s were hired for one dollar to tell a waiting *S* that tasks, which were really rather dull and boring, were interesting, enjoyable, and lots of fun. 3. *Twenty Dollar condition.* These *S*s were hired for twenty dollars to do the same thing.

RESULTS

The major results of the experiment are summarized in Table 1 which lists, separately for each of the three experimental conditions, the average rating which the *S*s gave at the end of each question on the interview. We will discuss each of the questions on the interview separately, because they were intended to measure different things. One other point before we proceed to examine the data. In all the comparisons, the Control condition should be regarded as a baseline from which to evaluate the results in the other two conditions. The Control condition gives us, essentially, the reactions of *S*s to the tasks and their opinions about the experiment as falsely explained to them, without the experimental introduction of dissonance. The data from the other conditions may be viewed, in a sense, as changes from this baseline.

How Enjoyable the Tasks Were

The average ratings on this question, presented in the first row of figures in Table 1, are the results most important to the experiment. These results are the ones most directly relevant to the specific dissonance which was experimentally created. It will be recalled that the tasks were purposely arranged to be rather boring and monotonous. And, indeed, in the Control condition the average rating was −.45, somewhat on the negative side of the neutral point.

TABLE 1 / Average Ratings on Interview Questions for Each Condition

Question on Interview	Experimental Condition		
	Control (N = 20)	One Dollar (N = 20)	Twenty Dollars (N = 20)
How enjoyable tasks were (rated from −5 to +5)	−.45	+1.35	−.05
How much they learned (rated from 0 to 10)	3.08	2.80	3.15
Scientific importance (rated from 0 to 10)	5.60	6.45	5.18
Participate in similar exp. (rated from −5 to +5)	−.62	+1.20	−.25

In the other two conditions, however, the *S*s told someone that these tasks were interesting and enjoyable. The resulting dissonance could, of course, most directly be reduced by persuading themselves that the tasks were, indeed, interesting and enjoyable. In the One Dollar condition, since the magnitude of dissonance was high, the pressure to reduce this dissonance would also be high. In this condition, the average rating was +1.35, considerably on the positive side and significantly different from the Control condition at the .02 level[1] (*t* = 2.48).

In the Twenty Dollar condition, where less dissonance was created experimentally because of the greater importance of the consonant relations, there is correspondingly less evidence of dissonance reduction. The average rating in this condition is only −.05, slightly and not significantly higher than the Control condition. The difference between the One Dollar and Twenty Dollar conditions is significant at the .03 level (*t* = 2.22). In short, when an *S* was induced, by offer of reward, to say something contrary to his private opinion, this private opinion tended to change so as to correspond more closely with what he had said. The greater the reward offered (beyond what was necessary to elicit the behavior) the smaller was the effect.

Desire to Participate in a Similar Experiment

The results from this question are shown in the last row of Table 1. This question is less directly related to the dissonance that was experimentally created for the Ss. Certainly, the more interesting and enjoyable they felt the tasks were, the greater would be their desire to participate in a similar experiment. But other factors would enter also. Hence, one would expect the results on this question to be very similar to the results on "how enjoyable the tasks were" but weaker. Actually, the results, as may be seen in the table, are in exactly the same direction, and the magnitude of the mean differences is fully as large as on the first question. The variability is greater, however, and the differences do not yield high levels of statistical significance. The difference between the One Dollar condition (+1.20) and the Control condition (−.62) is significant at the .08 level (t = 1.78). The difference between the One Dollar condition and the Twenty Dollar condition (−.25) reaches only the .15 level of significance (t = 1.46).

The Scientific Importance of the Experiment

This question was included because there was a chance that differences might emerge. There are, after all, other ways in which the experimentally created dissonance could be reduced. For example, one way would be for the S to magnify for himself the value of the reward he obtained. This, however, was unlikely in this experiment because money was used for the reward and it is undoubtedly difficult to convince oneself that one dollar is more than it really is. There is another possible way, however. The Ss were given a very good reason, in addition to being paid, for saying what they did to the waiting girl. The Ss were told it was necessary for the experiment. The dissonance could, consequently, be reduced by magnifying the importance of this cognition. The more scientifically important they considered the experiment to be, the less was the total magnitude of dissonance. It is possible, then, that the results on this question, shown in the third row of figures in Table 1, might reflect dissonance reduction.

The results are weakly in line with what one would expect if the dissonance were somewhat reduced in this manner. The One Dollar condition is higher than the other two. The difference between the One and Twenty Dollar conditions reaches the .08 level of significance on a two-tailed test (t = 1.79). The difference between the One Dollar and Control conditions is not impressive at all (t = 1.21). The result that the Twenty Dollar condition is actually lower than the Control condition is undoubtedly a matter of chance (t = 0.58).

How Much They Learned from the Experiment

The results on this question are shown in the second row of figures in Table 1. The question was included because, as far as we could see, it had nothing to do with the dissonance that was experimentally created and could not be used for dissonance reduction. One would then expect no differences at all among the three conditions. We felt it was important to show that the effect was not a completely general one but was specific to the content of the dissonance which was created. As can be readily seen in Table 1, there are only negligible differences among conditions. The highest t value for any of these differences is only 0.48.

DISCUSSION OF A POSSIBLE ALTERNATIVE EXPLANATION

We mentioned in the introduction that Janis and King (1954; 1956) in explaining their findings, proposed an explanation in terms of the self-convincing effect of mental rehearsal and thinking up new arguments by the person who had to improvise a speech. Kelman (1953), in the previously mentioned study, in attempting to explain the unexpected finding that the persons who complied in the moderate reward condition changed their opinion more than in the high reward condition, also proposed the same kind of explanation. If the results of our experiment are to be taken as strong corroboration of the theory of cognitive dissonance, this possible alternative explanation must be dealt with.

Specifically, as applied to our results, this alternative explanation would maintain that perhaps, for some reason, the *S*s in the One Dollar condition worked harder at telling the waiting girl that the tasks were fun and enjoyable. That is, in the One Dollar condition they may have rehearsed it more mentally, thought up more ways of saying it, may have said it more convincingly, and so on. Why this might have been the case is, of course, not immediately apparent. One might expect that, in the Twenty Dollar condition, having been paid more, they would try to do a better job of it than in the One Dollar condition. But nevertheless, the possibility exists that the *S*s in the One Dollar condition may have improvised more.

Because of the desirability of investigating this possible alternative explanation, we recorded on a tape recorder the conversation between each *S* and the girl. These recordings were transcribed and then rated, by two independent raters, on five dimensions. The ratings were, of course done in ignorance of which condition each *S* was in. The reliabilities of these ratings, that is, the correlations between the two independent raters, ranged from .61 to .88, with an average reliability of .71. The five ratings were:

1. The content of what the *S* said *before* the girl made the remark that her friend told her it was boring. The stronger the *S*'s positive statements about the tasks, and the more ways in which he said they were interesting and enjoyable, the higher the rating.
2. The content of what the *S* said *after* the girl made the above-mentioned remark. This was rated in the same way as for the content before the remark.
3. A similar rating of the overall content of what the *S* said.
4. A rating of how persuasive and convincing the *S* was in what he said and the way in which he said it.
5. A rating of the amount of time in the discussion that the *S* spent discussing the tasks as opposed to going off into irrelevant things.

The mean ratings for the One Dollar and Twenty Dollar conditions, averaging the ratings of the two independent raters, are presented in Table 2. It is clear from examining the table that, in all cases, the Twenty Dollar condition is slightly higher. The differences are

small, however, and only on the rating of "amount of time" does the difference between the two conditions even approach significance. We are certainly justified in concluding that the *S*s in the One Dollar condition did not improvise more nor act more convincingly. Hence, the alternative explanation discussed above cannot account for the findings.

SUMMARY

Recently, Festinger (1957) has proposed a theory concerning cognitive dissonance. Two derivations from this theory are tested here. These are:

1. If a person is induced to do or say something which is contrary to his private opinion, there will be a tendency for him to change his opinion so as to bring it into correspondence with what he has done or said.
2. The larger the pressure used to elicit the overt behavior (beyond the minimum needed to elicit it) the weaker will be the above-mentioned tendency.

A laboratory experiment was designed to test these derivations. Subjects were subjected to a boring experience and then paid to tell someone that the experience had been interesting and enjoyable. The amount of money paid the subject was varied. The private

TABLE 2 / Average Ratings of Discussion between Subject and Girl

Dimensions Rated	Condition		
	One Dollar	Twenty Dollars	Value of *t*
Content before remark by girl (rated from 0 to 5)	2.26	2.62	1.08
Content after remark by girl (rated from 0 to 5)	1.63	1.75	0.11
Over-all content (rated from 0 to 5)	1.89	2.19	1.08
Persuasiveness and conviction (rated from 0 to 10)	4.79	5.50	0.99
Time spent on topic (rated from 0 to 10)	6.74	8.19	1.80

opinions of Ae subjects concerning the experiences were then determined.

The results strongly corroborate the theory that was tested.

REFERENCES

Festinger, L. *A theory of cognitive dissonance.* Evanston, Ill.: Row Peterson, 1957.

Janis, I. L., & King, B. T. The influence of role-playing on opinion change. *Journal of Abnormal and Social Psychology,* 1954, *49,* 211–218.

Kelman, H. Attitude change as a function of response restriction. *Human Relations,* 1953, *6,* 185–214.

King, B. T., & Janis, I. L. Comparison of the effectiveness of improvised versus non-improvised role-playing in producing opinion changes. *Human Relations,* 1956, *9,* 177–186.

ENDNOTE

1. All statistical tests referred to in this paper are two-tailed.

CRITICAL THINKING QUESTIONS

1. Using the concept of dissonance theory, select an attitude or belief that you might want to change and design a procedure that could be effective in producing change in the desired direction.
2. This study was cited in Article 2 as an example of some of the ethical issues in social psychological research. What do you see as the ethical issues present in this experiment? Do you see any alternative to deception in this type of study? Why or why not?
3. Based on personal experience, have you ever suspected that cognitive dissonance was operating in some change that came about in your own attitudes? Elaborate on how that may have occurred.
4. Festinger and Carlsmith discuss a possible alternative explanation for the obtained results. What is your position on this alternative explanation? Discuss any other possible explanations for the findings of the study.
5. Might cognitive dissonance be operating in many real-life situations? For example, consider the initiation process (known as *hazing*) used in some social groups, such as fraternities, or the procedures used in the military as part of basic training. How might cognitive dissonance be operating in these or other situations to account for the outcomes of the experience?

ADDITIONAL RELATED READINGS

Norton, M. I., Monin, B., Cooper, J., & Hogg, M. A. (2003). Vicarious dissonance: Attitude change from the inconsistency of others. *Journal of Personality and Social Psychology, 85*(1), 47–62.

Thogersen, J. (2004). A cognitive dissonance interpretation of consistencies and inconsistencies in environmentally responsible behavior. *Journal of Environmental Psychology, 24*(1), 93–103.

ARTICLE 12 _____

In the years since publication of Festinger and Carlsmith's classic study (Article 11), many experiments have been done to test dissonance theory and to elaborate on the conditions necessary for its operation. As it turns out, there are many different causes of dissonance. For example, dissonance may be aroused when an individual puts a great deal of effort into a given activity, as though he or she needs to justify expending so much effort to obtain a certain goal. This is sort of a "suffering leads to liking" effect. Dissonance will also likely be aroused when an individual has the freedom to choose whether to do (or not do) something. There is little reason to experience dissonance when you are forced to do something. You know why you did it: Someone *made* you do it. Finally, issues such as self-esteem may influence the arousal (and subsequent reduction) of cognitive dissonance. People with high levels of self-esteem may actually be *more* likely to engage in dissonance reduction than those with low levels of self-esteem when they see their behavior as inconsistent with their beliefs.

The central premise of cognitive dissonance theory is that people are motivated to avoid or reduce any tension produced by a perceived inconsistency between two attitudes or between an attitude and a behavior. So, what would happen when someone encounters a persuasive argument that is contrary to his or her own privately held beliefs? Dissonance theory suggests that this person will be motivated to reduce the internal tension generated by that perceived inconsistency, which can be accomplished in several ways. For example, he or she simply might not pay attention to the opposing viewpoint, distort the message to make it more consistent with his or her own beliefs, or avoid the message altogether.

The following article by Blake M. McKimmie, Deborah J. Terry, Michael A. Hogg, Antony S. R. Manstead, Russell Spears, and Bertjan Doosje examines the role of social support in dissonance arousal. This article is an excellent example of the contemporary exploration of dissonance theory and a good illustration of the elaboration of research concepts over time. Specifically, when we look at the findings described in the original demonstration of cognitive dissonance, as found in Article 11, the conclusions seem fairly straightforward. (For instance, freely engaging in a behavior that runs counter to a privately held belief will result in changing the belief to bring it more in line with the expressed behavior.) The present article effectively demonstrates the ongoing quest to explore the underlying mechanisms of dissonance and the conditions under which it does and does not occur.

I'm a Hypocrite, but So Is Everyone Else
Group Support and the Reduction of Cognitive Dissonance

■ Blake M. McKimmie, Deborah J. Terry, Michael A. Hogg,
Antony S. R. Manstead, Russell Spears, and Bertjan Doosje

The impact of social support on dissonance arousal was investigated from a social identity view of dissonance theory. This perspective is seen as augmenting current conceptualizations of dissonance theory by predicting when normative information will impact on dissonance arousal and by indicating the availability of identity-related strategies of dissonance reduction. An experiment was conducted to induce feelings of hypocrisy under conditions of behavioral support or nonsupport. Group salience was either high or low, or individual identity was emphasized. As predicted, participants with no support from the salient in-group exhibited the greatest need to reduce dissonance through attitude change and reduced levels of group identification. Results were interpreted in terms of self being central to the arousal and reduction of dissonance.

Festinger's (1957) dissonance theory is enjoying a resurgence of interest (e.g., Harmon-Jones & Mills, 1999; Stone & Cooper, 2001) that pivots around the role of self in dissonance arousal (see also Aronson, Fried, & Stone, 1991; Cooper 1999a, 1999b; Dickerson, Thibodeau, Aronson, & Miller, 1992; Fried & Aronson, 1995; Robertson & Reicher, 1997; Stone, 1999). In this article, we examine the role of social support in the arousal and reduction of cognitive dissonance. In doing so, we propose a perspective based on social identity (Hogg & Abrams, 1988; Tajfel, 1978; Tajfel & Turner, 1979) and self-categorization theories (Turner, Hogg, Oakes, Reicher, & Wetherell, 1987) that takes into account the role of self in determining the extent of dissonance elicited. We regard this conceptualization as augmenting rather than opposing current understandings of dissonance phenomena.

According to Festinger (1957), the relationship between a person's attitudes and behavior is driven by the goal of reducing an aversive psychological state, called dissonance, which arises when two cognitions are inconsistent. Festinger's original monograph foreshadowed the role of group processes in dissonance arousal and reduction. Indeed, his initial research on dissonance phenomena investigated how members of a fringe religious sect aided each other's dissonance reduction (Festinger, Riecken, & Schachter, 1956). However, subsequent dissonance research has tended to overlook the importance of group-derived cognitions in the arousal and reduction of dissonance. One notable exception to this trend is research on the role that social support plays in relation to dissonance phenomena. Early research failed to reach agreement on the role of social support. Lepper, Zanna, and Abelson (1970) found support for the notion that knowing that others have behaved in the same manner (i.e., counterattitudinally) acts as a consonant cognition, thereby reducing dissonance. Cooper, Jones, and Tuller (1972), however, did not find this effect after informing participants that a majority of previous participants had also agreed to write the counterattitudinal essay.

In subsequent research, Stroebe and Diehl (1981) conducted four studies using the induced compliance paradigm to resolve this discrepancy and to determine how social support operates to reduce cognitive dissonance. In their key study (Study 3), freedom of choice in engaging in the counterattitudinal behavior and behavioral support for a counterattitudinal behavior were manipulated. In the high-choice condition (where dissonance should be aroused), there was greatest attitude change when there was no behavioral support from a confederate for the counterattitudinal behavior. Stroebe and Diehl argued that the presence of support acted as a consonant cognition for one's own attitude-discrepant behavior, thereby reducing the need for dissonance reduction through attitude change.

Reprinted from *Group Dynamics: Theory, Research, and Practice*, 2003, *7*(3), 214–224. Copyright © 2003 by the American Psychological Association. Reprinted with permission.

Stroebe and Diehl's (1981) studies offer some support for the notion that social support acts as a consonant cognition. However, from a social identity perspective it would be expected that another's behavior would have implications for the self only when that other is a relevant referent.[1] Stroebe and Diehl's results could be explained if we were to assume that participants in their studies felt that they shared an implicit in-group with the confederate. Such an assumption could be reasonable, given that past research into affiliation under conditions of stress (e.g., Schachter, 1959) has demonstrated that participants prefer to wait with another person prior to an anxiety-provoking experiment—possibly for social comparison reasons. Alternatively, if no implicit in-group was assumed, participants may have changed their attitudes in an attempt to differentiate themselves from the other participant rather than to reduce any feelings of cognitive dissonance. Stroebe and Diehl's results indicated that participants who were given no behavioral support thought that the confederate had a more negative attitude toward the topic (fundamental attribution error; Jones & Nisbett, 1972; Ross, 1977); thus, they may have changed their attitudes to be more positive in an attempt to reflect the difference between their behavior and that of the confederate. Without a manipulation of identity salience, it is difficult to determine whether the effect of social support on dissonance arousal is truly a phenomenon dependent on group processes or whether some mechanism (other than identity management strategies) could explain the effects of social support on dissonance arousal.

A more general limitation of the dissonance literature examining the impact of social support is that it has tended to address the role of social information at the level of the individual. We argue that self-definition is context dependent (see Turner et al., 1987), and as such, social support should be from a salient and common in-group for it to be effective. It is under these conditions that group memberships (and the cognitions associated with them) become an important basis for self-definition. Thus, the extent to which social information acts as a consonant or dissonant cognition should be determined by the relationship between the self and the source of the cognitions. As a theoretical basis for this argument, our analysis is

guided by two theories of social influence—namely, social identity theory and self-categorization theory—and research derived from these theories that has illustrated the importance of norms in the attitude–behavior relationship (e.g., Terry & Hogg, 1996; Terry, Hogg, & Duck, 1999; Terry, Hogg, & McKimmie, 2000; Wellen, Hogg, & Terry, 1998).

SOCIAL IDENTITY AND SELF-CATEGORIZATION THEORIES

Social identity theory (e.g., Hogg & Abrams, 1988; Tajfel, 1978; Tajfel & Turner, 1979; see also Hogg, 1996) proposes that people's self-concept is derived in part from their identifications with social groups when the group context is relevant. Social identification is a result of self-categorization as a group member, a process elaborated on by self-categorization theory. Self-categorization theory (Turner et al., 1987) proposes that individuals categorize others to regulate and structure the social environment in meaningful ways and, in doing so, categorize themselves into groups. Subsequently, group members are seen to share some qualities that are qualitatively different from other groups. When a particular social identity (group membership) is salient, people categorize themselves as group members, and they become aware of the stereotypic in-group norms from the behaviors and attitudes of other group members. Through a process of referent informational influence, these are then in turn cognitively represented and assigned to self—a process referred to as self-stereotyping—and behaviors and attitudes are, as a consequence, guided by the shared normative standards.

According to these theories, social context plays a central role in the definition of the self. Thus, both aspects of the self-concept (personal and social) should be taken into account when explaining dissonance arousal and reduction. The behaviors of other group members may lead to an increase or decrease in cognitive dissonance depending on the consistency between an actor's behavior and the group norm derived from the behavior of other group members. It is also expected that when dissonant cognitions are associated with group membership, social-identity-based dissonance reduction strategies should be accessible to participants. For example, participants may attempt to reduce cognitive dissonance under conditions of behavioral nonsupport by reducing the importance of the lack of support through reduced levels of identification with the group.

ROLE OF THE SELF IN DISSONANCE AROUSAL AND REDUCTION

Since 1957, there has been substantial debate over the role of the self in the arousal of dissonance and the mechanism underlying cognitive dissonance. Cooper and Fazio's (1984) "new look" at dissonance theory argued that it is the taking of responsibility for behavior resulting in a foreseeable aversive consequence that causes the internal aversive state of dissonance. Given the manner in which consequences are defined as aversive—as a conditioned emotional response learned in childhood—this approach suggests a shared or normative underpinning to the arousal of dissonance. Such a position leaves little scope for individual differences to impact on dissonance arousal (see Cooper, 1999a). In contrast, Aronson and colleagues (Aronson, 1968; Aronson & Carlsmith, 1962; Aronson, Chase, Helmreich, & Ruhnke, 1974; Thibodeau & Aronson, 1992) argued that the self is integral to the arousal of dissonance and that it is any violation of an important element of the self-concept that leads to dissonance and attitude change. In a reconciliation of the different approaches to the role of the self-concept in dissonance arousal embodied in the new look and the self-concept approaches, Stone and Cooper's (2001) self-standards model focuses on how dissonance is aroused and reduced when specific types of cognitions are made accessible by taking into account the standards against which behavior is compared. Stone and Cooper argued that there are two standards—self-knowledge and normative information—and that dissonance is aroused when there is a difference between one's behavior and the relevant comparative standard.

Although this model marks an important step in the development of the dissonance literature in the sense that it offers an integration of the theoretical developments to date, the way in which the model predicts which standard behavior is compared against in different types of social settings needs some elaboration. Given the similarities between the self-

standards model's conception of self and the view of self held by social identity and self-categorization theories, adopting a framework based on social identity constructs might be a useful way in which to examine dissonance effects and offer new predictions about when dissonance will be aroused and how it might be reduced. Such a perspective would have the benefit of being able to predict not only when specific types of cognitions are accessible in a given situation but also what types of situations give rise to comparisons with normative or self-standards.

THE PRESENT STUDY

The present study was designed to invoke dissonance arousal through an adaptation of the hypocrisy paradigm (see Aronson, Fried, & Stone, 1991; Dickerson, Thibodeau, Aronson, & Miller, 1992; Fried & Aronson, 1995). In the hypocrisy paradigm, the researcher makes participants aware of an inconsistency between previous behavior and a current attitude. Typically, attitudes studied have been high in social desirability—for example, support for water conservation (Dickerson et al., 1992). According to the self-concept interpretation of dissonance theory (Aronson, 1968), most people have a self-concept that is positive and therefore inconsistent with feelings of hypocrisy. These feelings of hypocrisy are associated with an increase in cognitive dissonance. Previous research using this paradigm has investigated the role of social information. Stone, Weigand, Cooper, and Aronson (1997) found that when participants were asked to focus on the attitude–behavior inconsistency of important others, their own motivation to reduce dissonance was relatively diminished compared with when they focused on their own attitude–behavior inconsistency. The present study extends this research by investigating the extent to which group salience is important in moderating the impact of social information on the need to reduce dissonance.

In the present study, participants were made aware of the discrepancy between their attitude toward generosity and the actual frequency of their generosity. Behavioral support was manipulated through the provision of information detailing whether other in-group members (fellow students) acted generously, and group salience was manipulated through a self-description task (high group salience, low group salience, and individual identity). The current study differed from previous hypocrisy-based research by making dissonance predictions in terms of attitude change rather than behavioral change. Typically, participants are given no opportunity to change their attitudes in hypocrisy studies, as the goal is to bring participants' behaviors in line with their already existing prosocial attitudes. Theoretically, participants' dissonance could be reduced by shifting their attitudes toward their past behaviors if they are given the opportunity to express attitudes following the induction of hypocrisy. Making predictions in this manner diminishes the methodological costs of assessing actual behavior and reduces the possible impact of social desirability on participants' behaviors.

We expected that the level of cognitive dissonance experienced by participants would be dependent on whether they had behavioral support for failing to act in accordance with their beliefs, but only when that support emanated from a salient in-group. Specifically, we expected behavioral support to be more effective at reducing levels of dissonance for those individuals who share a salient common in-group identity with the source of that information (Hypothesis 1).

Further, individuals who share a salient group membership but who are offered no support have access to group-based modes of dissonance reduction. It was expected that such participants would distance themselves from a nonsupportive in-group in an attempt to reduce the importance of the dissonant cognitions and, as a consequence, the magnitude of dissonance (Hypothesis 2).

METHOD

Participants and Design

Participants were 18 male and 81 female undergraduate psychology students with an average age of 20.68 years ($SD = 3.07$), enrolled in a large university in the Netherlands. Participants were randomly assigned to one of six conditions (with between 14 and 19 participants in each) resulting from the manipulation of behavioral support (support or nonsupport) and group salience (individual identity, low group salience, or high group salience).

Manipulations and Measures

All instructions and questions for this study were presented in the form of a questionnaire. After being asked for basic demographic information, participants were told by the female experimenter that the study was about how people perceive different personality qualities, and specifically the quality of generosity.

Manipulation of Group Salience   Participants in the high-salience condition were informed that the research concerned how psychology students from their university ("University A") responded as a whole and that these responses would be compared with an equal status university in the same city ("University B"; the actual university names were used in the questionnaire). Following this, participants were requested to complete a self-description task (Hogg & Hains, 1996) that aimed to make a group identity salient by asking participants to focus on "the three most important positive things that you have in common with other psychology students from University A *and* that differentiate University A psychology students from University B psychology students." Participants in the low-salience condition were told that the research concerned the views of psychology students from "this university" but that reference to the university as a whole was merely for the purpose of simplifying data analysis, as other groups of people were also being surveyed. These participants were requested to complete a self-description, this time focusing on three positive things that they had in common with other psychology students at "this university." Finally, in the individual condition, participants were informed that the researcher was particularly interested in how individuals view generosity and that "we are interested in your thoughts as an individual." These participants completed a self-description task in which they described the three most positive things that make them different from other people.

Hypocrisy Manipulation   Next, participants were subjected to a modified hypocrisy manipulation (adapted from Dickerson et al., 1992) in which they first had their attitudes toward generosity made salient and then were asked to recognize past behaviors that were inconsistent with this attitude. To elicit participants' attitudes toward generosity, we asked how favorable they thought generosity was as a personality quality (1 = *very unfavorable* to 9 = *very favorable*). To make participants aware of previously ungenerous behavior, we asked them to complete a Generosity Checklist. Participants were asked to indicate how often they donated money to charities, paid for the full drinks tab when out with friends, and gave money to homeless people (*every day, once a week, once a year,* or *never*). Pilot work (*N* = 60) indicated that such a shortened procedure was effective at reducing perceptions of attitude–behavior consistency—from an average of 6.82 in the control condition (in which participants indicated their attitudes toward generosity but not their previous behaviors) to 5.85 in the hypocrisy condition (in which participants indicated their attitudes toward generosity and the frequency of their previous generous behaviors), $F(1, 58) = 6.17$, $p < .05$. As a measure of psychological discomfort, participants were also asked to indicate how comfortable, relaxed, calm, and nervous they were feeling after these questions, from 1 (*not at all*) to 9 (*extremely*) ($\alpha = .85$). Additional analyses indicated that the less participants felt their attitudes and behaviors were consistent, the greater was their reported psychological discomfort ($r = -.55$, $p < .01$) and the greater were their feelings of hypocrisy ($r = -.51$, $p < .01$). The hypocrisy manipulation was tested independently of the main study to avoid the possibility that some participants would seek to reinterpret the discrepancy between their attitudes and behavior by claiming to be nonhypocritical and thereby reducing the effect of the hypocrisy procedure on attitude change.

Manipulation of Behavioral Support For the manipulation of behavioral support, participants were given bogus information about a previous study that had been conducted at University A involving 247 psychology students. They were presented with a graph representing the percentage of psychology students from University A who had reported often performing the behaviors in the generosity checklist. In the nonsupport condition, the graph indicated that 87% of the previous participants from University A reported donating money to charities often, 92% reported paying for the full drinks tab, and 82% reported giving money to homeless people. In the support condition, the percentages of previous partic-

ipants who reported each behavior were 17%, 22%, and 12%, respectively. After studying the graph, participants were requested to summarize the information presented by indicating the extent to which psychology students from University A were generous.

Manipulation Checks As a check on the efficacy of the manipulation of behavioral support, participants were asked whether the previous research (bogus information) had shown that in-group members were 1 (*not at all generous*) or 9 (*very generous*). Further, perceptions of attitudinal support were assessed in a similar way, with participants being asked how favorably they thought in-group members would evaluate acting generously, from 1 (*very unfavorably*) to 9 (*very favorably*). Finally, a measure of in-group favoritism was administered. In-group favoritism is an appropriate check on the manipulation of group salience, in that for favoritism to occur, participants must self-categorize as a group member; mere categorization is not sufficient (Grieve & Hogg, 1999). To assess in-group favoritism, we asked participants to give their impression of psychology students from both University B (out-group) and University A (in-group) on six 9-point semantic differential scales. For example, participants were asked to indicate how *unpleasant–pleasant, not likable–likable, unintelligent–intelligent,* and *foolish–wise* students from both universities were. Items assessing out-group evaluation loaded on a single factor (accounting for 74.9% of the variance) and formed a reliable scale ($\alpha = .93$). Similarly, the in-group evaluation items loaded on one factor, which accounted for 73.2% of the variance and constituted a reliable scale ($\alpha = .93$).

Dependent Measures Following the manipulation of behavioral support, the main dependent measures of attitude change and identification were assessed. To allow the assessment of attitude change, we reassessed participants' attitudes toward generosity. Four items assessed participants' identification with the group "psychology students from University A." For example, participants were asked how strongly they identified with the group, how much they felt they belonged to the group, how important the group was to how they saw themselves, and how similar they felt to other in-group members (1 = *not at all* to 9 = *very much;* see Doosje, Ellemers, & Spears, 1995; Hogg, Turner, & Davidson, 1990). These items loaded on a single factor (accounting for 71.6% of the variance; $\alpha = .87$). On completion of the study, participants were debriefed.

RESULTS

Manipulation Checks

Behavioral Support   To check whether participants understood the manipulation of behavioral support, we analyzed participants' perceptions of behavioral support with a 2 (behavioral support) by 3 (group salience) analysis of variance (ANOVA), revealing only a significant effect for behavioral support, $F(1, 93) = 512.66, p < .01, \eta^2 = .85$. As expected, participants in the behavior support condition perceived greater behavioral support ($M = 7.92$) compared with participants in the behavior nonsupport condition ($M = 3.41$).

A 2 (behavioral support) by 3 (group salience) ANOVA was conducted on the measure of perceived attitudinal support, given that behavioral support may impact on dissonance through attitudinal inferences. For example, in the behavior support condition, participants may have inferred that other group members did not act generously because they held a negative attitude toward generosity (the opposite inference could be made in the nonsupport condition). The ANOVA revealed that this was in fact the case. Consistent with the fundamental attribution error, participants in the behavior support condition believed other group members to have significantly less favorable attitudes toward generosity ($M = 5.46$) when compared with the perceptions of participants in the behavior nonsupport condition ($M = 7.51$), $F(1, 93) = 81.91, p < .01, \eta^2 = .47$. In light of this finding, subsequent analyses were conducted using perceptions of attitudinal support as a covariate. Thus, all effects reported subsequently are independent of any effects due to perceived attitude support.[2]

Group Salience   To compute a measure of in-group favoritism, we subtracted participants' evaluation of the out-group from their evaluation of the in-group. A 2 (behavioral support) by 3 (group salience) analysis of covariance (ANCOVA) with perceived attitudinal

support as a covariate revealed only a significant effect for group salience, $F(1, 91) = 3.09, p < .05, \eta^2 = .06$. Planned comparisons (Bonferroni $p < .05$) provided support for the effectiveness of the manipulation of group salience, in that participants in the high-salience condition ($M = 0.63$) favored the in-group to a greater degree than did participants in the individual identity ($M = 0.10$) or low-salience conditions ($M = 0.29$). The extent of in-group favoritism in the low group salience and individual identity conditions was not significantly different. These results provide support for the manipulation of group salience.

Effects of Behavioral Support and Salience

To examine the extent to which dissonance arousal was dependent on behavioral support and group salience, we analyzed attitude change and identification with the in-group with 2 (behavioral support) by 3 (group salience) ANCOVAs with perceived attitude support as the covariate.

Attitude Change   A measure of attitude change was calculated by subtracting participants' attitude toward generosity following completion of the generosity checklist from their prior attitude. Positive scores indicated that participants' attitudes toward generosity were less favorable (bringing their attitudes into line with their behavior). Analyses revealed that there was a significant effect of the covariate, $F(1, 92) = 4.06, p < .05, \eta^2 = .04, \beta = -0.21$, and that there was a significant interaction between salience and behavioral support, $F(2, 92) = 6.74, p < .01, \eta^2 = .13$ (see Figure 1). Analyses of simple effects offered support for Hypothesis 1. As expected, there was no difference in attitude change as a function of behavioral support within the individual identity, $F(1, 92) = 0.42, ns,$ and low-salience, $F(1, 92) = 0.74, ns,$ conditions; however, in the high group salience condition, there was significantly greater attitude change in the opposite direction of participants' original attitudes in the behavioral nonsupport condition ($M = 1.61$) compared with the behavioral support condition ($M = -0.68$), $F(1, 92) = 9.93, p < .01, \eta^2 = .10$.

Additional analyses (one-sample *t*-tests) were conducted to determine whether the attitude change exhibited was significantly different from zero, given that under no-hypocrisy conditions, it would be

FIGURE 1 / Adjusted Means for the Group Salience × Behavior Support Interaction for the Measure of Attitude Change

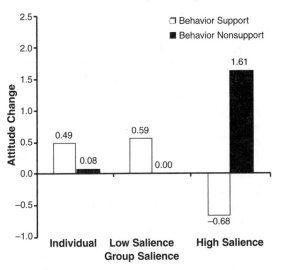

FIGURE 2 / Adjusted Means for the Group Salience × Behavior Support Interaction for the Measure of Identification

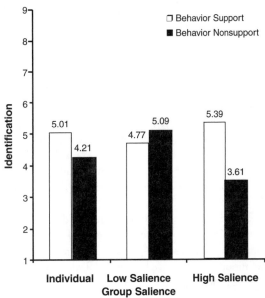

expected that there would be no attitude change. Only those participants in the high-salience nonsupport condition displayed attitude change significantly different from that which would be expected in the absence of dissonance arousal, $t(15) = 2.24$, $p < .05$. Given the lack of significant differences in the individual identity condition, there was no support for the notion that the results of previous research (e.g., Stroebe & Diehl, 1981) investigating the role of social support can be explained purely in terms of identity processes. From these analyses, it can be seen that there is some support for Hypothesis 1 in that the level of dissonance (assessed in terms of attitude change) was greatest for those participants given no support, but only when a shared group membership was made salient.

Identification To examine whether participants engaged in group-based dissonance reduction strategies when the source of nonsupport came from a salient in-group, we analyzed participants' identification with the in-group. A 2 (behavioral support) by 3 (group salience) ANCOVA with perceived attitude support as the covariate revealed a significant interaction between salience and support, $F(2, 92) = 3.68$, $p < .05$, $\eta^2 = .07$ (see Figure 2). Perceived attitude

support was again a significant covariate, $F(1, 92) = 4.81$, $p < .05$, $\eta^2 = .05$, $\beta = .22$. Simple effects revealed some support for the prediction that group members would attempt to reduce the importance of dissonant cognitions through a reduction in levels of group identification (Hypothesis 2). For participants in the high group salience condition, behavioral support was associated with higher levels of identification ($M = 5.39$) than was nonsupport ($M = 3.61$), $F(1, 92) = 7.73$, $p < .01$, $\eta^2 = .08$. For participants in the individual identity, $F(1, 92) = 2.21$, *ns*, and low-salience conditions, $F(1, 92) = 0.41$, *ns*, there were no significant differences as a function of behavioral support.

DISCUSSION

It was predicted that a lack of behavioral support for counterattitudinal behavior would be associated with greater levels of dissonance only for those participants who shared a salient group membership with the source of the normative information. Further, on the basis of the argument that self is at the center of dissonance arousal, it was expected that when dissonant cognitions were tied to group membership, dissonance reduction strategies based on group membership would be accessible to participants. The results for both attitude change and identification with the group provided support for these predictions, to the extent that a lack of behavioral support from a salient in-group was associated with greater attitude change and reduced levels of group identification. In support of the view that social support functions to reduce cognitive dissonance, there was little evidence for an explanation of the results of previous studies (e.g., Stroebe & Diehl, 1981) based solely on the operation of differentiation. Preliminary analyses indicated that the manipulation of group salience and behavioral support were successful, and the pilot study provided support for success of the adapted hypocrisy procedure that was used.

The findings for attitude change and identification offer some support for the proposed view of dissonance theory based on a complex context-sensitive definition of self derived from social identity theory and self-categorization theory. Analyses of participants' attitude change scores indicated that the lack of behavioral support for hypocrisy did not exacerbate the need to resolve inconsistency through attitude change except when that information came from a salient in-group. In other words, a lack of support did not function as a dissonant cognition unless that cognition was tied to the participants' self-definition through a salient common in-group shared with the source of behavioral information. This finding supports Stroebe and Diehl's (1981) argument that social information can act as a consonant or dissonant cognition. Failure to show increased attitude change in the individual identity nonsupport condition is problematic for the alternative interpretation based solely on identity processes such as differentiation. The interaction between group salience and behavioral support suggests that the self-standards model's implication that normative information is relevant for the avoidance of generalized social sanctions does not fully capture the role that group memberships play in the arousal and reduction of dissonance. Specifically, the present findings suggest that for normative standards to impact on dissonance arousal, these standards need to be associated with the self via a salient in-group.

The findings for identification with the in-group offer further support for a social identity view of dissonance theory. Consistent with Hypothesis 2, it was the participants subjected to the highest levels of dissonance (high-salience, nonsupport condition) who distanced themselves from the in-group, as evidenced by the lower levels of identification. In effect, participants faced with a lack of support from a relevant group weakened their relationship with the source of the dissonant cognitions. Such a strategy was presumably not available to participants for whom group membership was not a particularly relevant basis for self-definition. Without reference to the identity mechanisms involved in a context-sensitive notion of self, it is not clear how dissonance theory could account for such a finding. It is possible that this effect merely represents the fact that participants rejected the in-group because it failed to offer support, rather than being a reflection of their desire to reduce the importance of the dissonant cognitions. However, the results for the measure of in-group favoritism (which was assessed following the manipulation of support) go some way to ruling out such an alternative explanation, given that participants in the high-salience condition favored the in-group irrespective of whether they received behavioral support.

In light of the present findings, there is preliminary support for the notion that a social-identity-based view of dissonance theory can augment current approaches to the study of dissonance. For example, the present approach augments Stone and Cooper's (2001) self-standards model by helping to identify which self-standard a person's behavior will be compared with in a given context by considering the salience of their group memberships. Further, the inclusion of a context-sensitive self provides a mechanism by which norms can impact on dissonance arousal within Aronson's (Aronson, 1968; Aronson & Carlsmith, 1962) self-concept approach.

One limitation of the present study is that the presence of dissonance was inferred from the measure of attitude change but was not directly measured in the main study. Future research should attempt to obtain more direct evidence of dissonance, as measured by psychological discomfort, in order to provide stronger support for the effects seen in this study.

Adopting such a measure would help to minimize any impact of social influence on the measure of dissonance. In the present study, it could be expected that the measure of attitude change would be susceptible to social influence. Interestingly, the observed pattern of attitude change is in the opposite direction to what would be expected from social influence (participants had more negative attitudes about generosity when they thought the group was more favorable about generosity, i.e., in the high-salience nonsupport condition).

In conclusion, there was some support for the present approach to dissonance theory based on social identity and self-categorization theories, and for the view that how the self is defined is important for the extent of dissonance arousal and the way in which it is reduced. Alternative views of dissonance theory and an approach based solely on identity concerns could not explain the constellation of effects dependent on social support and group membership. As such, the present findings should provide a starting point from which to explore in greater depth the way in which dissonance phenomena operate within the social context.

REFERENCES

Aronson, E. (1968). Dissonance theory: Progress and problems. In R. P. Abelson, E. Aronson, W. J. McGuire, T. M. Newcomb, M. J. Rosenberg, & P. H. Tannenbaum (Eds.), *Theories of cognitive consistency: A sourcebook* (pp. 5–27). Chicago: Rand McNally.

Aronson, E., & Carlsmith, J. M. (1962). Performance expectancy as a determinant of actual performance. *Journal of Abnormal and Social Psychology, 65,* 178–182.

Aronson, E., Chase, T., Helmreich, R., & Ruhnke, R. (1974). A two-factor theory of dissonance reduction: The effect of feeling stupid or feeling awful on opinion change. *International Journal for Research and Communication, 3,* 59–74.

Aronson, E., Fried, C., & Stone, J. (1991). Overcoming denial and increasing the intention to use condoms through the induction of hypocrisy. *American Journal of Public Health, 81,* 1636–1638.

Cooper, J. (1999a, April). *Understanding dissonance motivation: The self-standards model of cognitive dissonance.* Paper presented at the Second Sydney Symposium of Social Psychology, Sydney, Australia.

Cooper, J. (1999b). Unwanted consequences and the self: In search of the motivation for dissonance reduction. In E. Harmon-Jones & J. Mills (Eds.), *Cognitive dissonance: Progress on a pivotal theory in social psychology* (pp. 149–174). Washington, DC: American Psychological Association.

Cooper, J., & Fazio, R. H. (1984). A new look at dissonance theory. In L. Berkowitz (Ed.), *Advances in experimental social psychology* (Vol. 17, pp. 229–266). San Diego, CA: Academic Press.

Cooper, J., Jones, E. E., & Tuller, S. M. (1972). Attribution, dissonance and the illusion of uniqueness. *Journal of Experimental Social Psychology, 8,* 45–57.

Dickerson, C., Thibodeau, R., Aronson, E., & Miller, D. (1992). Using cognitive dissonance to encourage water conservation. *Journal of Applied Social Psychology, 22,* 841–854.

Doosje, B., Ellemers, N., & Spears, R. (1995). Perceived intragroup variability as a function of group status and identification. *Journal of Experimental Social Psychology, 31,* 410–436.

Festinger, L. (1957). *A theory of cognitive dissonance.* Stanford, CA: Stanford University Press.

Festinger, L., Riecken, H., & Schachter, S. (1956). *When prophecy fails.* Minneapolis: University of Minnesota Press.

Fried, C., & Aronson, E. (1995). Hypocrisy, misattribution, and dissonance reduction: A demonstration of dissonance in the absence of aversive consequences. *Personality and Social Psychology Bulletin, 21,* 925–933.

Grieve, P. G., & Hogg, M. A. (1999). Subjective uncertainty and intergroup discrimination in the minimal group situation. *Personality and Social Psychology Bulletin, 25,* 926–940.

Harmon-Jones, E., & Mills, J. (Eds.). (1999). *Cognitive dissonance: Progress on a pivotal theory in social psychology.* Washington, DC: American Psychological Association.

Hogg, M. A. (1996). Intragroup processes, group structure and social identity. In W. P. Robinson (Ed.), *Social group and identities: Developing the legacy of Henri Tajfel* (pp. 65–93). Oxford, UK: Butterworth-Heinemann.

Hogg, M. A., & Abrams, D. (1988). *Social identifications: A social psychology of intergroup relations and group processes.* London: Routledge.

Hogg, M. A., & Hains, S. C. (1996). Intergroup relations and group solidarity: Effects of group identification and social beliefs on depersonalized attraction. *Journal of Personality and Social Psychology, 70,* 295–309.

Hogg, M. A., Turner, J. C., & Davidson, B. (1990). Polarized norms and social frames of reference: A test of the self-categorization theory of group polarization. *Basic and Applied Social Psychology, 11*, 77–100.

Jones, E. E., & Nisbett, R. E. (1972). The actor and the observer: Divergent perceptions of the causes of behavior. In E. E. Jones, D. E. Kanouse, H. H. Kelly, R. E. Nisbett, S. Valins, & B. Weiner (Eds.), *Attribution: Perceiving the causes of behavior* (pp. 79–94). Morristown, NJ: General Learning Press.

Kelley, H. H. (1973). The process of causal attribution. *American Psychologist, 28*, 107–128.

Lepper, M. R., Zanna, M. P., & Abelson, R. P. (1970). Cognitive irreversibility in a dissonance-reduction situation. *Journal of Personality and Social Psychology, 16*, 191–198.

Robertson, T., & Reicher, S. (1997). Threats to self and the multiple inconsistencies of forced compliance: Some preliminary investigations into the relationship between contradictions and claims to identity. *Social Psychological Review, 1*, 1–15.

Ross, L. (1977). The intuitive psychologist and his shortcomings: Distortions in the attribution process. In L. Berkowitz (Ed.), *Advances in experimental social psychology* (Vol. 10, pp. 173–220). San Diego, CA: Academic Press.

Schachter, S. (1959). *The psychology of affiliation.* Stanford, CA: Stanford University Press.

Stone, J. (1999). What exactly have I done? The role of self-attribute accessibility in dissonance. In E. Harmon-Jones & J. Mills (Eds.), *Cognitive dissonance: Progress on a pivotal theory in social psychology* (pp. 175–200). Washington, DC: American Psychological Association.

Stone, J., & Cooper, J. (2001). A self-standards model of cognitive dissonance. *Journal of Experimental Social Psychology, 37*, 228–243.

Stone, J., Wiegand, A. W., Cooper, J., & Aronson, E. (1997). When exemplification fails: Hypocrisy and the motive for self-integrity. *Journal of Personality and Social Psychology, 72*, 54–65.

Stroebe, W., & Diehl, M. (1981). Conformity and counterattitudinal behavior: The effect of social support on attitude change. *Journal of Personality and Social Psychology, 41*, 876–889.

Tajfel, H. (Ed.). (1978). *Differentiation between social groups.* London: Academic Press.

Tajfel, H., & Turner, J. C. (1979). An integrative theory of intergroup conflict. In W. G. Austin & S. Worchel (Eds.), *The social psychology of intergroup relations* (pp. 33–47). Monterey, CA: Brooks-Cole.

Terry, D. J., & Hogg, M. A. (1996). Group norms and the attitude-behavior relationship: A role for group identification. *Personality and Social Psychology Bulletin, 22*, 776–793.

Terry, D. J., Hogg, M. A., & Duck, J. M. (1999). Group membership, social identity, and attitudes. In D. Abrams & M. A. Hogg (Eds.), *Social identity and social cognition* (pp. 280–314). Oxford, UK: Blackwell Publishers.

Terry, D. J., Hogg, M. A., & McKimmie, B. M. (2000). Attitude-behavior relations: The role of ingroup norms and mode of behavioral decision-making. *British Journal of Social Psychology, 39*, 337–361.

Thibodeau, R., & Aronson, E. (1992). Taking a closer look: Reasserting the role of the self-concept in dissonance theory. *Personality and Social Psychology Bulletin, 18*, 591–602.

Turner, J. C., Hogg, M. A., Oakes, P. J., Reicher, S. D., & Wetherell, M. (1987). *Rediscovering the social group: A self-categorization theory.* Oxford, UK: Blackwell Publishers.

Wellen, J. M., Hogg, M. A., & Terry, D. J. (1998). Group norms and attitude-behavior consistency: The role of group salience and mood. *Group Dynamics, 2*, 48–56.

ENDNOTES

1. From other perspectives, such as Kelley's (1973) covariation model of attribution, the other does not have to be assumed to be a relevant referent, as his or her behavior provides consensus information. From such a perspective, it is the number of these others that is important, not their shared in-group membership. In the present study, the number of others that behavioral information is provided about is held constant, so any observed effect for social support that varies as a function of group salience suggests that the other being a relevant referent is important. Such a conclusion does not discount any possible effects due to changes in consensus information.

2. Group salience had no effect on perceptions of attitude support, nor did it influence perceptions of behavior support.

We thank Jolanda Jetten for her assistance with the translation of the questionnaire from English into Dutch, Boukje Keijzer for her assistance with the administration of the questionnaires, and Jeff Stone for helpful comments on the manuscript.

CRITICAL THINKING QUESTIONS

1. Can the results of the present study be used to produce dissonance and hence change in some real-world applications? For example, suppose that you want to reduce smoking by inducing dissonance in the participants. Design a treatment program that would do so.

2. In what other areas can induced hypocrisy be used to produce behavior and/or attitude change? Be specific.

3. This study notes that one of its limitations is that it used attitude change measures to *infer* the presence of dissonance. Design a study that will more directly *measure* evidence of dissonance arousal, such as by noting levels of psychological discomfort.

4. Question 3 in Article 11 asked, "Based on personal experience, have you ever suspected that cognitive dissonance was operating in some change that came about in your own attitudes?" Elaborate on your answer by including information from the present article on the role of social support in moderating dissonance reduction.

CHAPTER INTEGRATION QUESTIONS

1. Articles 11 and 12 both dealt with aspects of cognitive dissonance. How does this concept also relate to the content of Article 10?

2. Integrate the findings of all three articles into one or two themes. Discuss the practical application of your theme or themes.

3. "Only the most intelligent and most stupid do not change," according to Confucius, a Chinese philosopher. In light of the information presented in this chapter on attitudes and attitude change, do you agree or disagree with this quotation? Be sure to defend your position.

Chapter Five

SOCIAL IDENTITY

THE MAJORITY OF readings that you will encounter in this book focus on what might be called *situational variables:* particular circumstances that elicit predictable patterns of behavior in people. But do all people respond the same way in identical situations? Of course not. We each bring to every situation a set of experiences and characteristics that may influence how we act. Certainly, each of us has had unique life experiences that may be influential; biological dispositions, perhaps present from birth, may also play a role in determining behavior. Another influential factor is the personality of the individual.

But what is *personality?* Many theories have been developed to try to explain what this concept means. Some are *global theories* of personality, which attempt a total comprehensive portrait of an individual (e.g., Freud's), while others are *microtheories,* focusing on narrower, more particular dimensions of personality. Certainly, one major part of personality is *social identity*—the part of personality that is our internalized representation of how we view ourselves as being part of our social world. Two major parts of social identity—the *self* and *gender identity*—are addressed in the readings in this chapter.

Article 13, "The Many Me's of the Self-Monitor," looks at the sense of self that each of us has and asks whether that is comprised of a single sense of self or perhaps a number of selves, depending on the situation.

Article 14, "The Measurement of Psychological Androgyny," is a classic article that challenges the common-sense wisdom that the most appropriate gender-typed behavior is for a male to be masculine and a female, feminine. Perhaps masculinity and femininity are not mutually exclusive ends of a continuum after all.

The contemporary reading found in Article 15, "Understanding Sexual Aggression in Male College Students: The Role of Self-Monitoring and Pluralistic Ignorance," revisits the concept of self-monitoring introduced in Article 13 and considers the role it may play in the sexual aggression of young males. Article 15 also examines how certain other variables, such as pluralistic ignorance, may play a role in that behavior. Given the seriousness of this behavior, the implications of this research are of particular interest.

ARTICLE 13 _____

Think about who you are. Do you have a stable sense of self, of knowing what you feel, believe, and want? Or do you have many selves, depending on when and in what situation you try to answer this question?

Now think about your behavior. Do you act consistently across many different situations? Or does your behavior depend on the specific situation in which you find yourself?

These questions are indeed intriguing. At one extreme may be individuals who consistently act the same way in every situation, even when doing so might not be appropriate. At the other extreme are people who modify their behavior to fit each situation, showing little consistency across contexts. These are the two extremes on a continuum of what is known as *self-monitoring*.

Self-monitoring refers to the extent to which an individual is aware of and able to control the impressions that he or she conveys to others. A high self-monitoring individual is very attuned to the situation and modifies his or her behavior according to the demands of the context. A low self-monitoring individual tends to behave more in accordance with internal dispositions than with the demands of the situation.

What are the consequences of these two styles of behaving? Does a high self-monitoring person actually have many different selves, while a low self-monitoring person has but a single self? The relationship between self-monitoring and the sense of self is but one of the issues addressed in the following article by Mark Snyder.

The Many Me's of the Self-Monitor

■ Mark Snyder

The image of myself which I try to create in my own mind in order that I may love myself is very different from the image which I try to create in the minds of others in order that they may love me.   —W. H. Auden

The concept of the self is one of the oldest and most enduring in psychological considerations of human nature. We generally assume that people are fairly consistent and stable beings: that a person who is generous in one situation is also likely to be generous in other situations, that one who is honest is honest most of the time, that a person who takes a liberal stance today will favor the liberal viewpoint tomorrow.

It's not always so: each of us, it appears, may have not one but many selves. Moreover, much as we might like to believe that the self is an integral feature of personal identity, it appears that, to a greater extent, the self is a product of the individual's relationships with other people. Conventional wisdom to the contrary, there may be striking gaps and contradictions—as Auden suggests—between the public appearances and private realities of the self.

Psychologists refer to the strategies and techniques that people use to control the impressions they convey to others as "impression management." One of my own research interests has been to understand why some individuals are better at impression management than others. For it is clear that some people are particularly sensitive to the ways they express and present themselves in social situations—at parties, job interviews, professional meetings, in confrontations of all kinds where one might choose to create and maintain an appearance, with or without a specific purpose in mind. Indeed, I have found that such people have developed the ability to carefully monitor their own performances and to skillfully adjust their perform-

Reprinted from *Psychology Today,* 1980, *13,* 33–40. Copyright 1980. Reprinted with permission of Mark Snyder.

ances when signals from others tell them that they are not having the desired effect. I call such persons "high self-monitoring individuals," and I have developed a 25-item measure—the Self-Monitoring Scale—that has proved its ability to distinguish high self-monitoring individuals from low self-monitoring individuals (see box [p. 139]). Unlike the high self-monitoring individuals, low self-monitoring individuals are not so concerned about taking in such information; instead, they tend to express what they feel, rather than mold and tailor their behavior to fit the situation.

My work on self-monitoring and impression management grew out of a long-standing fascination with explorations of reality and illusion in literature and in the theater. I was struck by the contrast between the way things often appear to be and the reality that lurks beneath the surface—on the stage, in novels, and in people's actual lives. I wanted to know how this world of appearances in social relationships was built and maintained, as well as what its effects were on the individual personality. But I was also interested in exploring the older, more philosophical question of whether, beneath the various images of self that people project to others, there is a "real me." If we are all actors in many social situations, do we then retain in any sense an essential self, or are we really a variety of selves?

SKILLED IMPRESSION MANAGERS

There are striking and important differences in the extent to which people can and do control their self-presentation in social situations: some people engage in impression management more often—and with greater skill—than others. Professional actors, as well as many trial lawyers, are among the best at it. So are successful salespeople, confidence artists, and politicians. The onetime mayor of New York, Fiorello LaGuardia, was particularly skilled at adopting the expressive mannerisms of a variety of ethnic groups. In fact, he was so good at it that in watching silent films of his campaign speeches, it is easy to guess whose vote he was soliciting.

Of course, such highly skilled performances are the exception rather than the rule. And people differ in the extent to which they can and do exercise control over their self-presentations. It is high self-monitoring individuals among us who are particularly talented in this regard. When asked to describe high self-monitoring individuals, their friends say that they are good at learning which behavior is appropriate in social situations, have good self-control of their emotional expression, and can effectively use this ability to create the impression they want. They are particularly skilled at intentionally expressing and accurately communicating a wide variety of emotions both vocally and facially. As studies by Richard Lippa of California State University at Fullerton have shown, they are usually such polished actors that they can effectively adopt the mannerisms of a reserved, withdrawn, and introverted individual and then do an abrupt about-face and portray, just as convincingly, a friendly, outgoing, and extroverted personality.

High self-monitoring individuals are also quite likely to seek out information about appropriate patterns of self-presentation. They invest considerable effort in attempting to "read" and understand others. In an experiment I conducted with Tom Monson (then one of my graduate students), various cues were given to students involved in group discussions as to what was socially appropriate behavior in the situation. For example, some of them thought that their taped discussions would be played back to fellow students; in those circumstances, I assumed they would want their opinions to appear as autonomous as possible. Others believed that their discussions were completely private; there, I assumed they would be most concerned with maintaining harmony and agreement in the group. High self-monitoring individuals were keenly attentive to these differences; they conformed with the group when conformity was the most appropriate behavior and did not conform when they knew that the norms of the larger student audience would favor autonomy in the face of social pressure. Low self-monitoring individuals were virtually unaffected by the differences in social setting: presumably, their self-presentations were more accurate reflections of their personal attitudes and dispositions. Thus, as we might have guessed, people who are most skilled in the arts of impression management are also most likely to practice it.

Although high self-monitoring individuals are well skilled in the arts of impression management, we

Monitor Your Self

On the scale I have developed to measure self-monitoring, actors are usually high scorers, as are many obese people, who tend to be very sensitive about the way they appear to others. For much the same reason, politicians and trial lawyers would almost certainly be high scorers. Recent immigrants eager to assimilate, black freshmen in a predominantly white college, and military personnel stationed abroad are also likely to score high on the scale.

The Self-Monitoring Scale measures how concerned people are with the impression they are making on others, as well as their ability to control and modify their behavior to fit the situation. I believe that it defines a distinct domain of personality that is quite different from the traits probed by other standard scales.

Several studies show that skill at self-monitoring is not associated with exceptional intelligence or with a particular social class. Nor is it related, among other things, to being highly anxious or extremely self-conscious, to being an extrovert, or to having a strong need for approval. They may be somewhat power-oriented or Machiavellian, but high self-monitoring individuals do not necessarily have high scores on the "Mach" scale, a measure of Machiavellianism developed by Richard Christie of Columbia University. (Two items from the scale: "The best way to handle people is to tell them what they want" and "Anyone who completely trusts anyone else is asking for trouble.") The steely-eyes Machiavellians are more manipulative, detached, and amoral than high self-monitoring individuals.

The Self-Monitoring Scale describes a unique trait and has proved to be both statistically valid and reliable, in tests on various samples.

[Below] is a 10-item abbreviated version of the Self-Monitoring Scale that will give readers some idea of whether they are low or high self-monitoring individuals. If you would like to test your self-monitoring tendencies, follow the instructions and then consult the scoring key.

—M. S.

These statements concern personal reactions to a number of different situations. No two statements are exactly alike, so consider each statement carefully before answering. If a statement is true, or mostly true, as applied to you, circle the T. If a statement is false, or not usually true, as applied to you, circle the F.

1.	I find it hard to imitate the behavior of other people.	T	F
2.	I guess I put on a show to impress or entertain people.	T	F
3.	I would probably make a good actor.	T	F
4.	I sometimes appear to others to be experiencing deeper emotions than I actually am.	T	F
5.	In a group of people I am rarely the center of attention.	T	F
6.	In different situations and with different people, I often act like very different persons.	T	F
7.	I can only argue for ideas I already believe.	T	F
8.	In order to get along and be liked, I tend to be what people expect me to be rather than anything else.	T	F
9.	I may deceive people by being friendly when I really dislike them.	T	F
10.	I'm not always the person I appear to be.	T	F

SCORING: Give yourself one point for each of questions 1, 5 and 7 that you answered F. Give yourself one point for each of the remaining questions that you answered T. Add up your points. If you are a good judge of yourself and scored 7 or above, you are probably a high self-monitoring individual; 3 or below, you are probably a low self-monitoring individual.

should not automatically assume that they necessarily use these skills for deceptive or manipulative purposes. Indeed, in their relationships with friends and acquaintances, high self-monitoring individuals are eager to use their self-monitoring abilities to promote smooth social interactions.

We can find some clues to this motive in the way high self-monitoring individuals tend to react to, and cope with, unfamiliar and unstructured social settings. In a study done at the University of Wisconsin, psychologists William Ickes and Richard Barnes arranged for pairs of strangers to spend time together in a waiting room, ostensibly to wait for an experiment to begin. The researchers then recorded the verbal and nonverbal behavior of each pair over a five-minute period, using video and audio tapes. All possible pairings of same-sex undergraduates at high, moderate, and low levels of self-monitoring were represented. Researchers scrutinized the tapes for evidence of the impact of self-monitoring on spontaneous encounters between strangers.

In these meetings, as in so many other aspects of their lives, high self-monitoring individuals suffered little or no shyness. Soon after meeting the other person, they took an active and controlling role in the conversation. They were inclined to talk first and to initiate subsequent conversational sequences. They also felt, and were seen by their partners to have, a greater need to talk. Their partners also viewed them as having been the more directive member of the pair.

It was as if high self-monitoring individuals were particularly concerned about managing their behavior in order to create, encourage, and maintain a smooth flow of conversation. Perhaps this quality may help self-monitoring people to emerge as leaders in groups, organizations, and institutions.

DETECTING IMPRESSION MANAGEMENT IN OTHERS

High self-monitoring individuals are also adept at detecting impression management in others. To demonstrate this finely tuned ability, three communications researchers at the University of Minnesota made use of videotaped excerpts from the television program "To Tell the Truth." On this program, one of the three guest contestants (all male in the excerpts chosen for the study) is the "real Mr. X." The other two who claim to be the real Mr. X are, of course, lying. Participants in the study watched each excerpt and then tried to identify the real Mr. X. High self-monitoring individuals were much more accurate than their low self-monitoring counterparts in correctly identifying the real Mr. X and in seeing through the deception of the other two contestants.

Not only are high self-monitoring individuals able to see beyond the masks of deception successfully but they are also keenly attentive to the actions of other people as clues to their underlying intentions. E. E.

William James on the Roles We Play

A man has as many social selves as there are individuals who recognize him and carry an image of him in their mind. . . . But as the individuals who carry the images form naturally into classes, we may practically say that he has as many different social selves as there are distinct *groups* of persons about whose opinions he cares. He generally shows a different side of himself to each of these different groups. Many a youth who is demure enough before his parents and teachers swears and swaggers like a pirate among his "tough" young friends. We do not show ourselves to our children as to our club companions, to our masters and employers as to our intimate friends. From this there results what practically is a division of the man into several selves; and this may be a discordant splitting, as where one is afraid to let one set of his acquaintances know him as he is elsewhere; or it may be a perfectly harmonious division of labor, as where one tender to his children is stern to the soldiers or prisoners under his command.

—William James
The Principles of Psychology, 1890

Jones and Roy Baumeister of Princeton University had college students watch a videotaped discussion between two men who either agreed or disagreed with each other. The observers were aware that one man (the target person) had been instructed either to gain the affection or to win the respect of the other. Low self-monitoring observers tended to accept behavior at face value. They found themselves attracted to the agreeable person, whether or not he was attempting to ingratiate himself with his discussion partner. In contrast, high self-monitoring observers were acutely sensitive to the motivational context within which the target person operated. They liked the target better if he was disagreeable when trying to ingratiate himself. But when he sought respect, they were more attracted to him if he chose to be agreeable. Jones and Baumeister suggest that high self-monitoring observers regarded agreeableness as too blatant a ploy in gaining affection and autonomy as an equally obvious route to respect. Perhaps the high self-monitoring individuals felt that they themselves would have acted with greater subtlety and finesse.

Even more intriguing is Jones's and Baumeister's speculation—and I share their view—that high self-monitoring individuals prefer to live in a stable, predictable social environment populated by people whose actions consistently and accurately reflect their true attitudes and feelings. In such a world, the consistency and predictability of the actions of others would be of great benefit to those who tailor and manage their own self-presentation in social situations. From this perspective, it becomes quite understandable that high self-monitoring individuals may be especially fond of those who avoid strategic posturing. Furthermore, they actually may prefer as friends those comparatively low in self-monitoring.

How can we know when strangers and casual acquaintances are engaged in self-monitoring? Are there some channels of expression and communication that are more revealing than others about a person's true, inner "self," even when he or she is practicing impression management?

Both scientific and everyday observers of human behavior have suggested that nonverbal behavior—facial expressions, tone of voice, and body movements—reveals meaningful information about a person's attitudes, feelings, and motives. Often, people who engage in self-monitoring for deceptive purposes are less skilled at controlling their body's expressive movements. Accordingly, the body may be a more revealing source of information than the face for detecting those who engage in self-monitoring and impression management.

More than one experiment shows how nonverbal behavior can betray the true attitude of those attempting impression management. Shirley Weitz of the New School for Social Research reasoned that on college campuses where there are strong normative pressures supporting a tolerant and liberal value system, all students would avoid saying anything that would indicate racial prejudice—whether or not their private attitudes supported such behavior. In fact, she found that among "liberal" white males at Harvard University, the most prejudiced students (as determined by behavioral measures of actual attempts to avoid interaction with blacks) bent over backwards to *verbally* express liking and friendship for a black in a simulated interracial encounter. However, their *nonverbal* behaviors gave them away. Although the prejudiced students made every effort to say kind and favorable things, they continued to do so in a cool and distant tone of voice. It was as if they knew the words but not the music: they knew *what* to say, but not *how* to say it.

Another way that prejudice can be revealed is in the physical distance people maintain between themselves and the target of their prejudice. To demonstrate this phenomenon, psychologist Stephen Morin arranged for college students to be interviewed about their attitudes toward homosexuality. Half the interviewers wore "Gay and Proud" buttons and mentioned their association with the Association of Gay Psychologists. The rest wore no buttons and simply mentioned that they were graduate students working on theses. Without the students' knowledge, the distance they placed their chairs from the interviewer was measured while the interviews were going on. The measure of social distance proved to be highly revealing. When the student and the interviewer were of the same sex, students tended to establish almost a foot more distance between themselves and the apparently gay interviewers. They placed their chairs an average of 32 inches away from apparently gay interviewers, but only 22 inches away from apparently nongay interviewers. Interestingly, most of the students expressed tolerant, and at times favorable, attitudes toward gay people in general. However, the distances they chose to put between themselves and the interviewers they thought gay betrayed underlying negative attitudes.

IMPRESSION MANAGERS' DILEMMAS

The well-developed skills of high self-monitoring individuals ought to give them the flexibility to cope quickly and effectively with a diversity of social roles. They can choose with skill and grace the self-presentation appropriate to each of a wide variety of social situations. But what happens when the impression manager must effectively present a true and honest image to other people?

Consider the case of a woman on trial for a crime that she did not commit. Her task on the witness stand is to carefully present herself so that everything she does and says communicates to the jurors clearly and unambiguously her true innocence, so that they will vote for her acquittal. Chances are good, however, that members of the jury are somewhat skeptical of the defendant's claims of innocence. After all, they might reason to themselves, the district attorney would not have brought this case to trial were the state's case against her not a convincing one.

The defendant must carefully manage her verbal and nonverbal behaviors so as to ensure that even a skeptical jury forms a true impression of her innocence. In particular, she must avoid the pitfalls of an image that suggests that "she doth protest her innocence too much and therefore must be guilty." To the extent that our defendant skillfully practices the art of impression management, she will succeed in presenting herself to the jurors as the honest person that she truly is.

It often can take as much work to present a truthful image as to present a deceptive one. In fact, in this case, just being honest may not be enough when facing skeptical jurors who may bend over backwards to interpret any and all of the defendant's behavior— nervousness, for example—as a sign of guilt.

The message from research on impression management is a clear one. Some people are quite flexible in their self-presentation. What effects do these shifts in public appearance have on the more private realities of self-concept? In some circumstances, we are persuaded by our own appearances: we become the persons we appear to be. This phenomenon is particularly likely to occur when the image we present wins the approval and favor of those around us.

In an experiment conducted at Duke University by psychologists E. E. Jones, Kenneth Gergen, and Keith Davis, participants who had been instructed to win the approval of an interviewer presented very flattering images of themselves. Half the participants (chosen at random) then received favorable reactions from their interviewers; the rest did not. All the participants later were asked to estimate how accurately and honestly their self-descriptions had mirrored their true personalities.

Those who had won the favor of their interviewers considered their self-presentations to have been the most honest of all. One interpretation of this finding is that those people were operating with rather pragmatic definitions of self-concept: that which produced the most positive results was considered to be an accurate reflection of the inner self.

The reactions of other people can make it all the more likely that we become what we claim to be. Other people may accept our self-presentations at face value; they may then treat us as if we really were the way we pretend to be. For example, if I act as if I like Chris, chances are Chris will like me. Chris will probably treat me in a variety of friendly ways. As a result of Chris's friendliness, I may come to like Chris, even though I did not in the first place. The result, in this case, may be beneficial to both parties. In other circumstances, however, the skilled impression manager may pay an emotional price.

High self-monitoring orientation may be purchased at the cost of having one's actions reflect and communicate very little about one's private attitudes, feelings, and dispositions. In fact, as I have seen time and again in my research with my former graduate students Beth Tanke and Bill Swann, correspondence between private attitudes and public behavior is often minimal for high self-monitoring individuals. Evidently, the words and deeds of high self-monitoring individuals may reveal precious little information about their true inner feelings and attitudes.

Yet, it is almost a canon of modern psychology that a person's ability to reveal a "true self" to intimates is essential to emotional health. Sidney Jourard, one of the first psychologists to hold that view, believed that only through self-disclosure could we achieve self-discovery and self-knowledge: "Through my self-disclosure, I let others know my soul. They can know it, really know it, only as I make it known. In fact, I am beginning to suspect that I can't even know *my own soul* except as I disclose it. I suspect that I will know myself 'for real' at the exact moment that I have succeeded in making it known through my disclosure to another person."

Only low self-monitoring individuals may be willing or able to live their lives according to Jourard's prescriptions. By contrast, high self-monitoring individuals seem to embody Erving Goffman's view of human nature. For him, the world of appearances appears to be all, and the "soul" is illusory. Goffman defines social interactions as a theatrical performance in which each individual acts out a "line." A line is a set of carefully chosen verbal and nonverbal acts that express one's self. Each of us, in Goffman's view, seems to be merely the sum of our various performances.

What does this imply for the sense of self and identity associated with low and high self-monitoring individuals?

I believe that high self-monitoring individuals and low self-monitoring individuals have very different ideas about what constitutes a self and that their notions are quite well-suited to how they live. High self-monitoring individuals regard themselves as rather flexible and adaptive people who tailor their social behavior shrewdly and pragmatically to fit appropriate conditions. They believe that a person is whoever he appears to be in any particular situation: "I am me, the me I am right now." This self-image fits well with the way high self-monitoring individuals present themselves to the world. It allows them to act in ways that are consistent with how they believe they should act.

By contrast, low self-monitoring individuals have a firmer, more single-minded idea of what a self should be. They value and strive for congruence between "who they are" and "what they do" and regard their actions as faithful reflections of how they feel and think. For them, a self is a single identity that must not be compromised for other people or in certain situations. Indeed, this view of the self parallels the low self-monitoring individual's consistent and stable self-presentation.

What is important in understanding oneself and others, then, is not the elusive question of whether there is a quintessential self, but rather, understanding how different people define those attributes of their behavior and experience that they regard as "me." Theory and research on self-monitoring have attempted to chart the processes by which beliefs about the self are actively translated into patterns of social behavior that reflect self-conceptions. From this perspective, the processes of self-monitoring are the processes of self—a system of operating rules that translate self-knowledge into social behavior.

CRITICAL THINKING QUESTIONS

1. Self-monitoring can be measured along a continuum. What are the advantages and disadvantages for someone who scores very high on this dimension (i.e., a high self-monitoring individual)? Very low (i.e., a low self-monitoring individual)?

2. How might high versus low self-monitoring individuals act differently in an intimate situation such as dating? Give examples to support your answer.

3. How do you think differences in self-monitoring develop? In other words, why might some people be attuned to external factors while others are not? In your opinion, what level of self-monitoring might be best overall for healthy functioning? Explain your answers.

4. Articles 11 and 12 dealt with the concept of cognitive dissonance. Based on your understanding of the concept, do you think that dissonance arousal in a given situation may be influenced by the level of self-monitoring used by the person? How so?

ARTICLE 14 _____

Let's do a quick exercise. Make a list of words or adjectives that you would use to describe someone that you think of as being feminine. Make another list of masculine descriptors. Next, compare the lists. Does one set of characteristics seem better than the other or just different? Could it be that the different stereotypical characteristics associated with masculinity and femininity might each be important, depending on the situation?

Masculine characteristics are generally considered *instrumental,* meaning that they are useful in task- or goal-oriented situations. Feminine characteristics tend to be more *expressive,* meaning that they focus more on the affective concern of the welfare of others. Typically, American society socializes its members to believe that males should act masculine and females, feminine and that each gender should suppress the characteristics of its opposite.

The following classic article by Sandra L. Bem postulates that when males are only allowed to act masculine and females are only allowed to act feminine, each gender is, in a sense, limited in what it can do. Masculine males are thus good in situations that call for instrumental, get-the-job-done traits, whereas feminine females are good in settings where concern for the feelings of others is important. But what about the person of either gender who has both masculine *and* feminine characteristics? Might he or she not be more adaptive and flexible to a greater variety of human experiences? In short, might not this person be better adjusted than the more rigidly defined masculine males and feminine females? Besides attempting to answer these questions, Bem's article is also a good example of how an instrument designed to measure a dimension of behavior characteristics is developed.

The Measurement of Psychological Androgyny[1]

■ Sandra L. Bem

This article describes the development of a new sex-role inventory that treats masculinity and femininity as two independent dimensions, thereby making it possible to characterize a person as masculine, feminine, or "androgynous" as a function of the difference between his or her endorsement of masculine and feminine personality characteristics. Normative data are presented, as well as the results of various psychometric analyses. The major findings of conceptual interest are: (a) the dimensions of masculinity and femininity are empirically as well as logically independent; (b) the concept of psychological androgyny is a reliable one; and (c) highly sex-typed scores do not reflect a general tendency to respond in a socially desirable direction, but rather a specific tendency to describe oneself in accordance with sex-typed standards of desirable behavior for men and women.

Both in psychology and in society at large, masculinity and femininity have long been conceptualized as bipolar ends of a single continuum; accordingly, a person has had to be either masculine or feminine, but not both. This sex-role dichotomy has served to obscure two very plausible hypotheses: first, that many individuals might be "androgynous"; that is,

Reprinted from *Journal of Consulting and Clinical Psychology,* 1974, *42,* 155–162. Copyright © 1974 by the American Psychological Association. Reprinted by permission.

they might be *both* masculine and feminine, *both* assertive and yielding, *both* instrumental and expressive—depending on the situational appropriateness of these various behaviors; and conversely, that strongly sex-typed individuals might be seriously limited in the range of behaviors available to them as they move from situation to situation. According to both Kagan (1964) and Kohlberg (1966), the highly sex-typed individual is motivated to keep his behavior consistent with an internalized sex-role standard, a goal that he presumably accomplishes by suppressing any behavior that might be considered undesirable or inappropriate for his sex. Thus, whereas a narrowly masculine self-concept might inhibit behaviors that are stereotyped as feminine, and a narrowly feminine self-concept might inhibit behaviors that are stereotyped as masculine, a mixed, or androgynous, self-concept might allow an individual to freely engage in both "masculine" and "feminine" behaviors.

The current research program is seeking to explore these various hypotheses, as well as to provide construct validation for the concept of androgyny (Bem, 1974). Before the research could be initiated, however, it was first necessary to develop a new type of sex-role inventory, one that would not automatically build in an inverse relationship between masculinity and femininity. This article describes that inventory.

The Bem Sex-Role Inventory (BSRI) contains a number of features that distinguish it from other, commonly used, masculinity-femininity scales, for example, the Masculinity-Femininity scale of the California Psychological Inventory (Gough, 1957). First, it includes both a Masculinity scale and a Femininity scale, each of which contains 20 personality characteristics. These characteristics are listed in the first and second columns of Table 1, respectively. Second, because the BSRI was founded on a conception of the sex-typed person as someone who has internalized society's sex-typed standards of desirable behavior for men and women, these personality characteristics were selected as masculine or feminine on the basis of sex-typed social desirability and not on the basis of differential endorsement by males and females as most other inventories have done. That is, a characteristic qualified as masculine if it was judged to be more desirable in American society for a man than for a woman, and it qualified as feminine if it was judged to be more desirable for a woman than for a man. Third, the BSRI characterizes a person as masculine, feminine, or androgynous as a function of the difference between his or her endorsement of masculine and feminine personality characteristics. A person is thus sex typed, whether masculine or feminine, to the extent that this difference score is high, the androgynous, to the extent that this difference score is low. Finally, the BSRI also includes a Social Desirability scale that is completely neutral with respect to sex. This scale now serves primarily to provide a neutral context for the Masculinity and Femininity scales, but it was utilized during the development of the BSRI to insure that the inventory would not simply be tapping a general tendency to endorse socially desirable traits.

TABLE 1 / Sample of Items on the Masculinity, Femininity, and Social Desirability Scales of the BSRI

Masculine Items	Feminine Items	Neutral Items
Aggressive	Tender	Friendly
Competitive	Affectionate	Conscientious

Note: This table includes only a few samples of the items found in the BSRI. For the full list of items in each category, see the original source.

Source: Reproduced by special permission of the Publisher, MIND GARDEN, Inc., 1690 Woodside Road #202, Redwood City, CA 94061 USA www.mindgarden.com from the **Bem Sex Role Inventory** by Sandra Bem. Copyright 1978 by Consulting Psychologists Press, Inc. All rights reserved. Further reproduction is prohibited without the Publisher's written consent.

The 20 characteristics that make up this scale are listed in the third column of Table 1.

ITEM SELECTION

Both historically and cross-culturally, masculinity and femininity seem to have represented two complementary domains of *positive* traits and behaviors (Barry, Bacon, & Child, 1957; Erikson, 1964; Parsons & Bales, 1955). In general, masculinity has been associated with an instrumental orientation, a cognitive focus on "getting the job done"; and femininity has been associated with an expressive orientation, an affective concern for the welfare of others.

Accordingly, as a preliminary to item selection for the Masculinity and Femininity scales, a list was compiled of approximately 200 personality characteristics that seemed to the author and several students to be both positive in value and either masculine or feminine in tone. This list served as the pool from which the masculine and feminine characteristics were ultimately chosen. As a preliminary to item selection for the Social Desirability scale, an additional list was compiled of 200 characteristics that seemed to be neither masculine nor feminine in tone. Of these "neutral" characteristics, half were positive in value and half were negative.

Because the BSRI was designed to measure the extent to which a person divorces himself from those characteristics that might be considered more "appropriate" for the opposite sex, the final items were selected for the Masculinity and Femininity scales if they were judged to be more desirable in American society for one sex than for the other. Specifically, judges were asked to utilize a 7-point scale, ranging from 1 ("Not at all desirable") to 7 ("Extremely desirable"), in order to rate the desirability in American society of each of the approximately 400 personality characteristics mentioned above. (E.g., "In American society, how desirable is it for a man to be truthful?" "In American society, how desirable is it for a woman to be sincere?") Each individual judge was asked to rate the desirability of all 400 personality characteristics either "for a man" or "for a woman." No judge was asked to rate both. The judges consisted of 40 Stanford undergraduates who filled out the questionnaire

during the winter of 1972 and an additional 60 who did so the following summer. In both samples, half of the judges were male and half were female.

A personality characteristic qualified as masculine if it was independently judged by both males and females in both samples to be significantly more desirable for a man than for a woman ($p < .05$).[2] Similarly, a personality characteristic qualified as feminine if it was independently judged by both males and females in both samples to be significantly more desirable for a woman than for a man ($p < .05$). Of those characteristics that satisfied these criteria, 20 were selected for the Masculinity scale and 20 were selected for the Femininity scale (see the first and second columns of Table 1, respectively).

A personality characteristic qualified as neutral with respect to sex and hence eligible for the Social Desirability scale (a) if it was independently judged by both males and females to be no more desirable for one sex than for the other ($t < 1.2$, $p > .2$) and (b) if male and female judges did not differ significantly in their overall desirability judgments of that trait ($t < 1.2$, $p > .2$). Of those items that satisfied these several criteria, 10 positive and 10 negative personality characteristics were selected for the BSRI Social Desirability scale in accordance with Edwards' (1964) finding that an item must be quite positive or quite negative in tone if it is to evoke a social desirability response set. (The 20 neutral characteristics are shown in the third column of Table 1.)

After all of the individual items had been selected, mean desirability scores were computed for the masculine, feminine, and neutral items for each of the 100 judges. As shown in Table 2, for both males and females, the mean desirability of the masculine and feminine items was significantly higher for the "appropriate" sex than for the "inappropriate" sex, whereas the mean desirability of the neutral items was no higher for one sex than for the other. These results are, of course, a direct consequence of the criteria used for item selection.

Table 3 separates out the desirability ratings of the masculine and feminine items for male and female judges rating their *own* sex. These own-sex ratings seem to best represent the desirability of these various items as perceived by men and women when they are asked

TABLE 2 / Mean Social Desirability Ratings of the Masculine, Feminine, and Neutral Items

Item	Male Judges			Female Judges		
	Masculine Item	Feminine Item	Neutral Item	Masculine Item	Feminine Item	Neutral Item
For a man	5.59	3.63	4.00	5.83	3.74	3.94
For a woman	2.90	5.61	4.08	3.46	5.55	3.98
Difference	2.69	1.98	.08	2.37	1.81	.04
t	14.41*	12.13*	.17	10.22*	8.28*	.09

*$p < .001$.

to describe *themselves* on the inventory. That is, the left-hand column of Table 3 represents the phenomenology of male subjects taking the test and the right-hand column represents the phenomenology of female subjects taking the test. As can be seen in Table 3, not only are "sex-appropriate" characteristics more desirable for both males and females than "sex-inappropriate" characteristics, but the phenomenologies of male and female subjects are almost perfectly symmetric: that is, men and women are nearly equal in their perceptions of the desirability of sex-appropriate characteristics, sex-inappropriate characteristics, and the difference between them ($t < 1$ in all three comparisons).

SCORING

The BSRI asks a person to indicate on a 7-point scale how well each of the 60 masculine, feminine, and neutral personality characteristics describes himself. The scale ranges from 1 ("Never or almost never true") to 7 ("Always or almost always true") and is labeled at each point. On the basis of his responses,

TABLE 3 / Mean Social Desirability Ratings of the Masculine and Feminine Items for One's Own Sex

Item	Male Judges for a Man	Female Judges for a Woman
Masculine	5.59	3.46
Feminine	3.63	5.55
Difference	1.96	2.09
t	11.94*	8.88*

*$p < .001$.

each person receives three major scores: a Masculinity score, a Femininity score and, most important, an Androgyny score. In addition, a Social Desirability score can also be computed.

The Masculinity and Femininity scores indicate the extent to which a person endorses masculine and feminine personality characteristics as self-descriptive. Masculinity equals the mean self-rating for all endorsed masculine items, and Femininity equals the mean self-rating for all endorsed feminine items. Both can range from 1 to 7. It will be recalled that these two scores are logically independent. That is, the structure of the test does not constrain them in any way, and they are free to vary independently.

The Androgyny score reflects the relative amounts of masculinity and femininity that the person includes in his or her self-description, and, as such, it best characterizes the nature of the person's total sex role. Specifically, the Androgyny score is defined as Student's *t* ratio for the difference between a person's masculine and feminine self-endorsement; that is, the Androgyny score is the difference between an individual's masculinity and femininity normalized with respect to the standard deviations of his or her masculinity and femininity scores. The use of a *t* ratio as the index of androgyny—rather than a simple difference score—has two conceptual advantages: first, it allows us to ask whether a person's endorsement of masculine attributes differs significantly from his or her endorsement of feminine attributes and, if it does ($|t| \geq 2.025$, $df = 38$, $p < .05$), to classify that person as significantly sex typed; and second, it allows us to compare different populations in terms of the percentage of significantly sex-typed individuals present within each.[3]

It should be noted that the greater the absolute value of the Androgyny score, the more the person is sex typed or sex reversed, with high positive scores indicating femininity and high negative scores indicating masculinity. A "masculine" sex role thus represents not only the endorsement of masculine attributes but the simultaneous rejection of feminine attributes. Similarly, a "feminine" sex role represents not only the endorsement of feminine attributes but the simultaneous rejection of masculine attributes. In contrast, the closer the Androgyny score is to zero, the more the person is androgynous. An "androgynous" sex role thus represents the equal endorsement of both masculine and feminine attributes.

The Social Desirability score indicates the extent to which a person describes himself in a socially desirable direction on items that are neutral with respect to sex. It is scored by reversing the self-endorsement ratings for the 10 undesirable items and then calculating the subject's mean endorsement score across all 20 neutral personality characteristics. The Social Desirability score can thus range from 1 to 7, with 1 indicating a strong tendency to describe oneself in a socially undesirable direction and 7 indicating a strong tendency to describe oneself in a socially desirable direction.

PSYCHOMETRIC ANALYSES

Subjects

During the winter and spring of 1973, the BSRI was administered to 444 male and 279 female students in introductory psychology at Stanford University. It was also administered to an additional 117 male and 77 female paid volunteers at Foothill Junior College. The data that these students provided represent the normative data for the BSRI, and, unless explicitly noted, they serve as the basis for all of the analyses that follow.

Internal Consistency

In order to estimate the internal consistency of the BSRI, coefficient alpha was computed separately for the Masculinity, Femininity and Social Desirability scores of the subjects in each of the two normative samples. (Nunnally, 1967). The results showed all

three scores to be highly reliable, both in the Stanford sample (Masculinity a = .86; Femininity a = .80; Social Desirability a = .75) and in the Foothill sample (Masculinity a = .86; Femininity a = .82; Social Desirability a = .70). Because the reliability of the Androgyny t ratio could not be calculated directly, coefficient alpha was computed for the highly correlated Androgyny difference score, Femininity-Masculinity, using the formula provided by Nunnally (1967) for linear combinations. The reliability of the Androgyny difference score was .85 for the Stanford sample and .86 for the Foothill sample.

Relationship between Masculinity and Femininity

As indicated earlier, the Masculinity and Femininity scores of the BSRI are logically independent. That is, the structure of the test does not constrain them in any way, and they are free to vary independently. The results from the two normative samples reveal them to be empirically independent as well (Stanford male r = .11, female r = −.14; Foothill male r = −.02, female r = −.07). This finding vindicates the decision to design an inventory that would not artifactually force a negative correlation between masculinity and femininity.

Social Desirability Response Set

It will be recalled that a person is sex typed on the BSRI to the extent that his or her Androgyny score reflects the greater endorsement of "sex-appropriate" characteristics than of "sex-inappropriate" characteristics. However, because of the fact that the masculine and feminine items are all relatively desirable, even for the "inappropriate" sex, it is important to verify that the Androgyny score is not simply tapping a social desirability response set.

Accordingly, product-moment correlations were computed between the Social Desirability score and the Masculinity, Femininity, and Androgyny scores for the Stanford and Foothill samples separately. They were also computed between the Social Desirability score and the absolute value of the Androgyny score. These correlations are displayed in Table 4. As expected, both Masculinity and Femininity were correlated with Social Desirability. In contrast, the

TABLE 4 / Correlation of Masculinity, Femininity, and Androgyny with Social Desirability

Sample	Masculinity with Social Desirability		Femininity with Social Desirability		Androgyny with Social Desirability		|Androgyny| with Social Desirability	
	Males	Females	Males	Females	Males	Females	Males	Females
Stanford	.42	.19	.28	.26	.12	.03	.08	−.10
Foothill	.23	.19	.15	.15	−.07	.06	−.12	−.09
Stanford and Foothill combined	.38	.19	.28	.22	.08	.04	.03	−.10

near-zero correlations between Androgyny and Social Desirability confirm that the Androgyny score is not measuring a general tendency to respond in a socially desirable direction. Rather, it is measuring a very specific tendency to describe oneself in accordance with sex-typed standards of desirable behavior for men and women.

Test-Retest Reliability

The BSRI was administered for a second time to 28 males and 28 females from the Stanford normative sample. The second administration took place approximately four weeks after the first. During this second administration, subjects were told that we were interested in how their responses on the test might vary over time, and they were explicitly instructed not to try to remember how they had responded previously. Product-moment correlations were computed between the first and second administrations for the Masculinity, Femininity, Androgyny, and Social Desirability scores. All four scores proved to be highly reliable over the four-week interval (Masculinity $r = .90$; Femininity $r = .90$; Androgyny $r = .93$; Social Desirability $r = .89$).

Correlations with Other Measures of Masculinity-Femininity

During the second administration of the BSRI, subjects were also asked to fill out the Masculinity-Femininity scales of the California Psychological Inventory and the Guilford-Zimmerman Temperament Survey, both of which have been utilized rather frequently in previous research on sex roles. Table 5

presents the correlations between these two scales and the Masculinity, Femininity, and Androgyny scales of the BSRI. As can be seen in the table, the Guilford-Zimmerman scale is not at all correlated with any of the three scales of the BSRI, whereas the California Psychological Inventory is moderately correlated with all three. It is not clear why the BSRI should be more highly correlated with the CPI than with the Guilford-Zimmerman scale, but the fact that none of the correlations is particularly high indicates that the BSRI is measuring an aspect of sex roles which is not directly tapped by either of these two scales.

NORMS

Table 6 presents the mean Masculinity, Femininity, and Social Desirability scores separately by sex for

TABLE 5 / Correlation of the Masculinity-Femininity Scales of the California Psychological Inventory (CPI) and Guilford-Zimmerman Scale with the Masculinity, Femininity, and Androgyny Scales of the BSRI

Scale	CPI		Guilford-Zimmerman	
	Males	Females	Males	Females
BSRI Masculinity	−.42	−.25	.11	.15
BSRI Femininity	.27	.25	.04	−.06
BSRI Androgyny	.50	.30	−.04	−.06

Note: The CPI scale is keyed in the feminine direction, whereas the Guilford-Zimmerman scale is keyed in the masculine direction.

TABLE 6 / Sex Differences on the BSRI

Scale Score	Stanford University			Foothill Junior College		
	Males (*n* = 444)	Females (*n* = 279)	*t*	Males (*n* = 117)	Females (*n* = 77)	*t*
Masculinity						
M	4.97	4.57		4.96	4.55	
SD	.67	.69	7.62*	.71	.75	3.86*
Femininity						
M	4.44	5.01		4.62	5.08	
SD	.55	.52	13.88*	.64	.58	5.02*
Social Desirability						
M	4.91	5.08		4.88	4.89	
SD	.50	.50	4.40*	.50	.53	ns
Androgyny t Ratio						
M	−1.28	1.10		−.80	1.23	
SD	1.99	2.29	14.33*	2.23	2.42	5.98*
Androgyny Difference Score						
M	−0.53	.43		−.34	.53	
SD	.82	.93	14.28*	.97	.97	6.08*

*$p < .001$.

both the Stanford and the Foothill normative samples. It also presents means for both the Androgyny *t* ratio and the Androgyny difference score. As can be seen in the table, males scored significantly higher than females on the Masculinity scale, and females scored significantly higher than males on the Femininity scale in both samples. On the two measures of androgyny, males scored on the masculine side of zero and females scored on the feminine side of zero. This difference is significant in both samples and for both measures. On the Social Desirability scale, females scored significantly higher than males at Stanford but not at Foothill. It should be noted that the size of this sex difference is quite small, however, even in the Stanford sample.

Table 7 presents the percentage of subjects within each of the two normative samples who qualified as masculine, feminine, or androgynous as a function of the Androgyny *t* ratio. Subjects are classified as sex typed, whether masculine or feminine, if the androgyny *t* ratio reaches statistical significance ($|t| \geq 2.025$,

df = 38, *p* < .05), and they are classified as androgynous if the absolute value of the *t* ratio is less than or equal to one. Table 7 also indicates the percentage of subjects who fall between these various cutoff points. It should be noted that these cut-off points are somewhat arbitrary and that other investigators should feel free to adjust them in accordance with the characteristics of their particular subject populations.

CONCLUDING COMMENT

It is hoped that the development of the BSRI will encourage investigators in the areas of sex differences and sex roles to question the traditional assumption that it is the sex-typed individual who typifies mental health and to begin focusing on the behavioral and societal consequences of more flexible sex-role self-concepts. In a society where rigid sex-role differentiation has already outlived its utility, perhaps the androgynous person will come to define a more human standard of psychological health.

TABLE 7 / Percentage of Subjects in the Normative Samples Classified as Masculine, Feminine, or Androgynous

Item	Stanford University		Foothill Junior College	
	Males ($n = 444$)	Females ($n = 279$)	Males ($n = 117$)	Females ($n = 77$)
% feminine ($t \geq 2.025$)	6	34	9	40
% near feminine ($1 < t < 2.025$)	5	20	9	8
% androgynous ($-1 \leq t \leq +1$)	34	27	44	38
% near masculine ($-2.025 < t < -1$)	19	12	17	7
% masculine ($t \leq -2.025$)	36	8	22	8

REFERENCES

Barry, H., Bacon, M. K., & Child, I. L. A cross-cultural survey of some sex differences in socialization. *Journal of Abnormal and Social Psychology,* 1957, *55,* 327–332.

Bem, S. L. Sex-role adaptability: One consequence of psychological androgyny. *Journal of Personality and Social Psychology,* 1974, in press.

Edwards, A. L. The measurement of human motives by means of personality scales. In D. Levine (Ed.), *Nebraska symposium on motivation: 1964.* Lincoln: University of Nebraska Press, 1964.

Erikson, E. H. Inner and outer space: Reflections on womanhood. In R. J. Lifton (Ed.), *The woman in America.* Boston: Houghton Mifflin, 1964.

Gough, H. G. *Manual for the California Psychological Inventory.* Palo Alto, Calif.: Consulting Psychologists Press, 1957.

Kagan, J. Acquisition and significance of sex-typing and sex-role identity. In M. L. Hoffman & L. W. Hoffman (Eds.), *Review of child development research.* Vol. 1. New York: Russell Sage Foundation, 1964.

Kohlberg, L. A cognitive-developmental analysis of children's sex-role concepts and attitudes. In E. E. Maccoby (Ed.), *The development of sex differences.* Stanford, Calif.: Stanford University Press, 1966.

Nunnally, J. C. *Psychometric theory.* New York: McGraw-Hill, 1967.

Parsons, T., & Bales, R. F. *Family, socialization, and interaction process.* New York: Free Press of Glencoe, 1955.

ENDNOTES

1. This research was supported by IROIMH 21735 from the National Institute of Mental Health. The author is grateful to Carol Korula, Karen Rook, Jenny Jacobs, and Odile van Embden for their help in analyzing the data.

2. All significance levels in this article are based on two-tailed *t* tests.

3. A Statistical Package for the Social Sciences (SPSS) computer program for calculating individual *t* ratios is available on request from the author. In the absence of computer facilities, one can utilize the simple Androgyny difference score, Femininity-Masculinity, as the index of androgyny. Empirically, the two indices are virtually identical ($r = .98$), and one can approximate the *t*-ratio value by multiplying the Androgyny difference score by 2.322. This conversion factor was derived empirically from our combined normative sample of 917 students at two different colleges.

CRITICAL THINKING QUESTIONS

1. Examine the sample items in Table 1 that are categorized as masculine, feminine, or neutral. Since this article was written in 1974, these items were selected over three decades ago. Do you think that these items are still applicable today, or are some of them dated and perhaps even controversial? Have notions of masculinity and femininity changed over time? Explain.

2. The BSRI (Bem Self-Role Inventory) is a self-report instrument. Do you think the way someone describes his or her characteristics on paper is necessarily an accurate portrayal of the way he or she really acts? In what way? How could you test this possibility?

3. What do you think of the concept of *androgyny?* Would society be better off if more people were androgynous rather than being either masculine *or* feminine? Why or why not?

4. Based on the information in the article, describe specific situations where an androgynous individual might be better suited than either a masculine or feminine individual. In what, if any, situations would someone only capable of masculine behaviors be more appropriate? What about someone only capable of feminine behaviors? Explain your answers.

5. After reading the article, you should have a good grasp of the concept of androgyny. If you explained this concept to others, do you think that most people would agree that they would be better off if they were androgynous rather than either masculine or feminine? Why or why not?

ADDITIONAL RELATED READINGS

Woodhill, B. M., & Samuels, C. A. (2004). Desirable and undesirable androgyny: A prescription for the twenty-first century. *Journal of Gender Studies, 13*(1), 15–28.

Woodhill, B. M., & Samuels, C. A. (2003). Positive and negative androgyny and their relationship with psychological health and well-being. *Sex Roles, 48*(11–12), 555–565.

ARTICLE 15 _____

In recent years, increased attention has been directed toward the frequency and nature of date rape. What differentiates date rape from other forms of rape is that its motivation often is sex per se, while other forms of rape often involve issues of power and control. Additionally, date rape occurs between people who generally know each other, which means the possibility of consensual sex exists. The concern over the prevalence of date rape is so great that most college freshman orientation programs now address it, both to increase awareness of and to prevent its occurrence.

Why would a man force his partner into having sex with him? Of course, there are many reasons for this behavior, but those reasons can be broadly classified as either *situational* or *dispositional*. *Situational factors* pertain to the circumstances surrounding the event—for instance, becoming highly intoxicated and having clouded judgment. But situational factors also may include the particular beliefs that a person has in a particular situation. For example, if a male thinks that "everyone else is doing it," he may be more likely to feel that sex is something to which he is entitled in a certain situation. That belief, in turn, might make him more coercive regarding sex than would otherwise be the case. The fact is, not everyone else is doing it, but to the extent that he thinks they are, his behavior may be influenced. *Pluralistic ignorance* is the term used to describe people's tendency to believe that others are acting in a way that they are, in fact, not. So, believing that all of your friends expect and get sex in certain situations, when in reality they do not, is an example of pluralistic ignorance.

Dispositional factors include all of the personality factors that predispose us to act in certain ways. Unlike situational factors, which change with the specific situation, dispositional factors are relatively enduring. There are many dispositional factors that may predispose someone toward coercive sexual behavior, including self-monitoring, which was discussed in Article 13. Briefly, *self-monitoring* refers to the tendency to be aware of and control the impressions that we convey to others. At one end of the continuum are high self-monitors, who tend to be very attuned to situational expectations and modify their behavior accordingly. Low self-monitors, on the other hand, tend to act consistently across situations and are less influenced by others in that regard. Thus, a high self-monitor on a date may be more likely to respond to how he thinks he should act in that situation, rather than how he actually feels like acting.

The following article by Janice D. Flezzani and James M. Benshoff explores how these two variables—pluralist ignorance and self-monitoring—may act alone and together in influencing the coercive sexual behavior of male college students. How these factors relate to date rape may, in turn, suggest intervention strategies for reducing the occurrence of that behavior.

Understanding Sexual Aggression in Male College Students
The Role of Self-Monitoring and Pluralistic Ignorance

■ Janice D. Flezzani and James M. Benshoff

The authors examined the relationship between self-monitoring and pluralistic ignorance and self-reported sexually aggressive behaviors by freshman and sophomore male college students. Results indicated that self-monitoring style and level of pluralistic ignorance were correlated positively with sexual aggression. The authors review relevant literature, present research findings, and discuss implications of the findings for college counselors.

Nonstranger sexual assault, commonly referred to as *date rape*, has been documented as a serious problem on college campuses for at least three decades (Kanin, 1967). Date rape can be defined as rape that occurs when two persons are involved in a dating or casual relationship (Rapaport & Posey, 1991). Research indicates that date rape is characterized by unique theoretical explanations, motivations for perpetration, and causal factors that distinguish it from the larger category of rape. For example, in date rape, the perpetrator and victim know each other, and when the rape occurs, they are interacting within a context in which consensual sex is a possibility and social peer support may be linked to perpetration. In addition, in date rape, the man's motivation is sex, not rape, as it is in stranger rape, in which the man's motivation is to degrade and humiliate the victim (Cowling, 1998).

Research has indicated that date rape is an underreported crime. Koss (1988) found a large disparity between the number of women who reported having been victimized (54%) and the number of men who acknowledged having engaged in sexually assaultive behavior (25%). These numbers suggest that men probably do not admit to enough sexual aggression to account for the number of victimizations reported by women. Koss posited that men may have underestimated the amount of force and coerciveness they used or were unable to correctly interpret women's consent

or resistance. Bondurant (1995) noted that women may not report being raped for several reasons, including shame, fear of not being believed, or self-blame for the event. Thus, disparities between perception of date rape by women and men may be even greater than those found by Koss.

Although date rape is considered the most extreme form of nonstranger sexual aggression, attempted rape and sexual coercion are relatively common on college campuses (Koss, 1988). College men reported using verbal coercion, physical force of varying degrees, and efforts to intoxicate women in order to engage in sexual activity (Koss, Gidycz, & Wisniewski, 1987). Men who engage in these behaviors may risk escalating to more severe forms of coercion. Moreover, these coercive behaviors adversely affected women's physical and psychological well-being (Koss, 1988).

Many variables have been examined as contributing factors to date rape and sexual aggression. These include acceptance of rape myths (Burt, 1980, 1991), hedonism (Crossman, 1994), misperception of cues from women (Abbey, 1991), traditional attitudes toward women (Briere, Malamuth, & Check, 1985), differences in conflict resolution tactics (Briere & Malamuth, 1983), previous exposure to violence in the home (McKinney, 1986), and contextual and situational factors (Abbey, 1991; Harney & Muchlenhard, 1991). A particularly important set of variables that has been linked to date rape and other aggressive behaviors is social world influence, specifically peer influence (Crossman, 1994; Kanin, 1985; Schwartz & DeKeseredy, 1997). Two social psychological constructs that are influenced by social and peer influences in shaping men's sexual and coercive behaviors are self-monitoring and *pluralistic ignorance*. There has been an increase in the amount of attention these variables have received in the literature, but little research

Reprinted from *Journal of College Counseling*, 2003, 6(1), 69–79. © ACA. Reprinted with permission. No further reproduction authorized without written permission of the American Counseling Association.

has been conducted to identify their relationship to sexually coercive behaviors. This study, therefore, investigated these two constructs to increase understanding of how sexually aggressive behaviors can be prevented among male college students.

Self-monitoring (Snyder, 1974), the first of the two variables that we investigated, describes the extent to which individuals manage expressive behavior and self-presentation. Snyder hypothesized that individuals may monitor and control their self-presentation and expressive behaviors in order to (a) express a true emotional state, (b) conceal an inappropriate emotional state and appear to be experiencing an appropriate one, or (c) feign some emotion when they are actually experiencing a nonresponse. For example, because high self-monitors (HSMs) are concerned with social appropriateness, they regulate their behavior according to environmental cues (Snyder, 1974). HSMs usually are well liked and considered more socially adept than low self-monitors (LSMs; Snyder, Gangestad, & Simpson, 1983). Snyder, Simpson, and Gangestad (1986) also found that HSMs had more sex partners, were younger at the time of their first sexual experience, and reported that they did not require psychological closeness or intimacy with their sexual partners. In contrast, LSMs typically relied more on internal cues to guide their behavior. Their self-presentation behaviors were more likely to reflect their personal attitudes and values, and their affective states were influenced less by their environment. For example, LSMs often chose friends whom they perceived as having similar interests, rather than seeking out those persons who were considered attractive or popular.

The second variable of interest, pluralistic ignorance, is the result of a misperception of the social norm (Allport, 1924; D. T. Miller & Prentice, 1994; Prentice & Miller, 1993). O'Gorman (1986) described pluralistic ignorance as the "state of believing that one's private attitudes, and judgments are different from those of others, even though one's public behavior is identical" (p. 333). Pluralistic ignorance refers to assumptions about others' attitudes or beliefs that are mistakenly considered to be correct. For example, if an individual votes against letting an African American person join a fraternity, not because

of his own prejudice but because he believes that fellow members are prejudiced, he is engaging in pluralistically ignorant behavior. In adolescence, the interplay between pluralistic ignorance and social influence may be particularly noticeable because of the documented influence of peers at this developmental stage.

Peer influence has been found to significantly affect an individual's attitudes, emotions, perceptions, and behaviors (Allport, 1968). Peer influence has also been identified as a potent factor in decisions related to adolescent smoking, drug use, and sexual activity (Newman & Newman, 1986). During adolescence, peer group affiliation assumes heightened importance. Individual needs related to social approval, status, power, and reputation reflect the type of groups chosen for identification (Kimmel & Weiner, 1984). On one hand, group membership may teach social skills, such as how to manage behaviors to fit in because a certain amount of conforming behavior is a necessary requirement for maintaining inclusion and acceptance by the group. On the other hand, involvement with a peer group opens individuals up to peer pressure and social influence from members of the larger group.

Date rape and other nonstranger sexually aggressive behaviors occur among an adolescent population that, from a developmental perspective, is particularly vulnerable to social, environmental, and peer influences. This vulnerability may be exacerbated when students first go to college and establish new social networks. The immediate tasks of fitting in with peers and adjusting to life away from the security of home may result in increased susceptibility to peer influence. This kind of social world influence may be particularly salient when explaining the phenomenon of date rape and other nonstranger sexually aggressive behaviors.

Self-monitoring, pluralistic ignorance, and social influence may be linked together on the basis of similarities that define the constructs. These similarities include the need for conformity, the need for social acceptance, and awareness of socially desirable behaviors. Although self-monitoring and pluralistic ignorance have not been studied within the domain of sexual aggression, a paper presented by Yescavage and White (1989) suggested that there is a correlation between high self-monitoring and sexual aggression. Traits common to both HSMs and sexually aggressive men include an increased likelihood of engaging in promiscuous sex, having multiple sexual partners, having one's first sexual experience at a younger age as compared with the norm, and not requiring psychological closeness or intimacy for sex (Snyder et al., 1986).

Our study was a preliminary investigation of the proposed theoretical relationship between self-monitoring and pluralistic ignorance as factors that may be related to sexually aggressive behaviors in college men. The study is based on the hypothesis that these two constructs are conceptually related and may help to explain nonstranger sexual aggression and coercion. Specifically, we investigated the following hypotheses: (a) HSMs would self-report engaging in higher levels of sexually aggressive and coercive behaviors as compared with LSMs, and (b) college men who scored higher on pluralistic ignorance would self-report higher levels of aggression and coercion than did college men who scored lower on pluralistic ignorance.

METHOD

Participants

The sample of research participants was drawn from freshman and sophomore men ($N = 120$) attending a midsized public university in the southeastern United States. Traditional-aged (18–20 years) freshman and sophomore students were chosen based on the speculation that a developmental component may influence pluralistically ignorant thinking among students, with younger students being more vulnerable to norm misperception (Schwartz & DeKeseredy, 1997). Because O'Gorman (1986) suggested that pluralistic ignorance is more likely to occur in an environment that is conducive to the misrepresentation of private beliefs, the sample in this study was drawn from male students who were living in residence halls on campus. The rationale for this was that men who live together in the close quarters of a residence hall would be more strongly and consistently

influenced by their peer groups than would college men who lived off campus and, thus, spent typically less time together as a group. Sixty-two percent of the participants were Caucasian, 33% were African American, 3% were Hispanic, and 2% were Asian American.

Instruments

Three instruments, the Self-Monitoring Scale (Snyder, 1974), the Perceptions of College Student Behaviors Scale (PCSBS; created for this study), and the Sexual Experiences Questionnaire (SEQ; White & Hoecker, 1995) were used in this study, in addition to a demographic questionnaire.

The Self-Monitoring Scale (Snyder, 1974) is a popular personality measure that examines individual differences in self-control of expressive behaviors. This instrument consists of 25 items determined to be internally consistent with the self-monitoring construct (Snyder, 1974). The Self-Monitoring Scale has a Kuder-Richardson 20 reliability of .70 and a test–retest reliability of .83 ($df = 51$, $p < .001$, 1-month time interval; Snyder, 1974). Correlations between self-monitoring and related, but conceptually distinct, individual differences measures such as the Marlowe-Crowne Social Desirability Scale (Crowne & Marlowe, 1964) provide evidence for its discriminant validity (Snyder, 1974). Despite criticisms of self-monitoring as a construct (e.g., Briggs & Cheek, 1988; Lenox, 1988), the Self-Monitoring Scale continues to be used widely in social psychology research.

The PCSBS (Flezzani, 2001) was designed to measure level of pluralistic ignorance related to men's beliefs about the likelihood of peers engaging in several negative behaviors thought to be common on college campuses. Although pluralistic ignorance has been recognized widely as a social psychological phenomenon, there has been little empirical research on the construct. Before the development of the PCSBS, no specific scale had been constructed to measure pluralistic ignorance. This may be due, in part, to the fact that pluralistic ignorance has been shown to be associated with behaviors across several domains, thus necessitating the creation of an instrument for each situation.

The SEQ (White & Hoecker, 1995) was used in this study to measure sexual aggression and coercion. The SEQ is a modified version of the Sexual Experiences Survey (SES; Koss & Oros, 1982), the instrument most commonly used to measure sexual perpetration on college campuses. In the modified SEQ, respondents are asked to label the frequency with which they engage in each of the behaviors listed in the SES (e.g., flattery, verbal pressure, use of alcohol and/or drugs, threats, and physical force). In addition, respondents are asked to identify some behaviors that could be considered as less severe forms of coercion (e.g., threatening to break up with a woman if she did not engage in intercourse, telling a woman he loved her just to engage in intercourse). The modified scale also distinguishes between such behaviors as purposefully giving a woman drugs/alcohol to obtain sex and trying to obtain sex with a woman who was already intoxicated. The method used in the modified scale has yielded continuous measures of sexual aggression and coercion that correlate highly with scores obtained on the SES (White, Donat, & Humphrey, 1996).

Through consultation with experts who have written about pluralistic ignorance or have used the construct in their own research, 11 behaviors were identified as being present on college campuses and having psychological reality for college students. The PCSBS assesses pluralistic ignorance, using a format similar to that used by other researchers in the field (e.g., Cohen & Shotland, 1996; D. T. Miller & Prentice, 1994). Historically, validity for this construct has been established by clearly stating the definition of pluralistic ignorance and then stating how it will be measured (Prentice & Miller, 1993). Construct validity for the PCSBS was determined using a process of expert review and recommendations. An acceptable level of internal consistency reliability was also established with the 11 PCSBS items (Cronbach's alpha = .85).

The PCSBS consists of two subscales. The Others subscale asks the respondent to rate the likelihood of peers engaging in certain behaviors, and the Self subscale asks the respondent to rate his own likelihood of engaging in the same behaviors, thus setting a "perceived" and "actual" norm. Participants in the present study were asked to rate their beliefs about behaviors

of the typical college man. Each man was then asked to assess the likelihood that he would engage in these behaviors. Questions regarding the likelihood of their peers engaging in sexual aggression and their own likelihood of engaging in these behaviors were embedded in the instrument to disguise intent. The PCSBS total score was calculated by averaging the 7-point Likert-type scale items on both subscales.

Procedure

A table was set up in the lobby of residence halls, and volunteer participants were asked to complete three instruments: the PCSBS (Flezzani, 2001), the Self-Monitoring Scale (Snyder, 1974), and the SEQ (White & Hoecker, 1995). The Self-Monitoring Scale and the PCSBS were presented in counterbalanced order, with the SEQ always being presented last. Respondents who agreed to participate were informed that this study would investigate dating behaviors, were told that their answers would be completely confidential and that data would be aggregated for data analysis, and were thanked for their participation. After completing the three instruments, participants were given a debriefing statement that explained the purpose of the study.

RESULTS

Analyses of variance (ANOVAs), Tukey's post hoc comparisons, and Pearson product–moment correlations were used to explore the proposed theoretical relationships between self-monitoring style, pluralistic ignorance, and self-reported nonstranger sexual aggression and coercion. Preliminary analyses of the distribution of scores indicated nonnormal distributions, suggesting that analyzing the data in groups would be better than using continuous scores and performing regression analyses. Dividing self-monitoring scores trimodally has been done previously in an analysis by M. L. Miller and Thayer (1988). Distribution of scores on the Self-Monitoring Scale and the Self and Others subscales of the PCSBS was divided into more or less homogeneous high, medium, and low groups.

The first hypothesis that HSMs would self-report higher levels of sexual aggression when compared with low and medium self-monitors was supported, with HSMs engaging in significantly more sexually aggressive behaviors ($n = 32$; $M = 44.38$, $SD = 15.34$) than their low ($n = 30$; $M = 30.70$, $SD = 5.01$) and medium ($n = 38$; $M = 36.44$, $SD = 10.28$) counterparts ($F = 11.93$, $p < .0001$). Post hoc analysis revealed a statistically significant difference between LSMs and HSMs (mean difference = 13.68, $p < .0001$). The difference between LSMs and medium self-monitors was not statistically significant (mean difference = 6.81, $p = .122$). Examination of the Pearson product–moment correlation between the Self-Monitoring Scale and the SEQ ($r = .43$, $p < .001$) revealed that approximately 18% of the variance in self-reported sexual coercion and aggression could be accounted for by self-monitoring style.

Results also indicated that men who scored higher on pluralistic ignorance reported higher levels of sexual aggression and coercion than did men who had lower pluralistic ignorance scores, a finding that supports our second hypothesis in this study. The correlation between pluralistic ignorance and self-reported sexual coercion and aggression was $r = 0.31$ ($p < .01$). Participants were divided into high, medium, and low groups based on their responses on the Others subscale of the PCSBS, with the resulting ANOVA across groups on the SEQ revealing significant differences ($F = 5.20$, $p < .007$). Post hoc comparisons indicated that men who reported a high level of pluralistic ignorance differed significantly (mean difference = 8.93, $p < .005$) in their tendency to engage in sexually coercive and aggressive behaviors as compared with men who displayed relatively lower levels of pluralistic ignorance. The post hoc mean differences between men who displayed high versus medium levels of pluralistic ignorance were not significant (mean difference = 5.02, $p = .20$).

Finally, the interaction effect of high self-monitoring with high pluralistic ignorance on sexually aggressive behaviors was found to be statistically significant ($F = 5.79$, $p = .004$). Post hoc comparisons showed that the group with the combination of high self-monitoring and high pluralistic ignorance reported significantly more sexually aggressive behaviors when compared with all other groups in this study. This powerful interaction effect supports the two primary hypotheses.

DISCUSSION

The purpose of this study was to examine the theoretical relationship between self-monitoring, pluralistic ignorance, and sexually coercive and aggressive behaviors in the nonstranger relationships of college men. Results indicated that self-monitoring style and pluralistic ignorance may be significant social world factors in nonstranger sexual aggression. On the basis of a review of the literature on sexual aggression among acquaintances, self-monitoring, and pluralistic ignorance, we predicted that male college students with high self-monitoring styles would tend to self-report higher levels of coercive and aggressive behaviors. We also predicted that men who displayed higher levels of pluralistic ignorance would tend to self-report more aggressive and coercive behaviors. Findings tended to support both hypotheses. In addition, a strong interaction effect was found between high self-monitoring, high pluralistic ignorance, and sexually aggressive behaviors.

Past research has not specifically linked self-monitoring style to sexually aggressive behavior. However, researchers have found that HSMs tended to date more, have more sexual partners, have more uncommitted sex, and engage in sexual activity at an earlier age as compared with LSMs. Yescavage and White (1989) noted that these factors were common to both HSMs and convicted sexual offenders. Our results support their findings that HSMs tended to report higher levels of nonstranger sexually aggressive and coercive behaviors than did LSMs.

Although the concept of pluralistic ignorance has been observed and discussed by social psychologists and sociologists (e.g., Katz & Allport, 1931; O'Gorman, 1986; Prentice & Miller, 1993), pluralistic ignorance as a distinct phenomenon has not been researched extensively. Although pluralistic ignorance has not been linked specifically to sexual aggression before this study, the construct has been discussed as being a factor in peer-supported sexual aggression (Schwartz & DeKeseredy, 1997) and examined as a factor influencing expectations for sexual intercourse in dating relationships (Cohen & Shotland, 1996).

There were several limitations in this study, including instrumentation requiring self-report, retrospective recall, lack of nonrandom sampling, and the small number of sexually aggressive and coercive college men included in the study. This investigation required the researcher (the first author) to develop an instrument to measure pluralistic ignorance because no psychometric scale had been developed to measure the construct before this study was conducted. The fact that participants in this study did not report a high level of sexually aggressive and coercive behaviors may be due to several factors. For example, men may be more reluctant to admit to engaging in these behaviors because the media attention that has focused on the problem of sexual aggression on college campuses in the last few years may have increased their awareness of society's negative view of these behaviors. It is also possible that men in this study actually were engaging in less sexually aggressive behaviors than men on other campuses. Because of the low number of sexually aggressive men, analyses included all nonconsensual sexual behaviors, even if they reflected a relatively low level of negative behavior. For example, the act of lying to a woman to obtain sex was considered to be coercive behavior for purposes of the analyses in this study. The lack of variance in the sample, however, presents a significant limitation and suggests the need to replicate this study with a larger and more diverse sample.

IMPLICATIONS FOR PRACTICE

Results of this study support the idea that social world influence, specifically peer pressure and faulty beliefs about peers' behaviors and attitudes, may lead to coercive sexual behaviors. These results may have implications for prevention strategies. Presently, many prevention programs focus on increasing empathy for victims, because lack of empathy has been associated with self-reported likelihood of engaging in sexually aggressive behavior (Dietz, Blackwell, Daley, & Bentley, 1982; Edidio & Robertson, 1981). Although some success in using empathy induction techniques in prevention has been demonstrated (e.g., Foubert, 2000), the overall success of this approach to rape prevention remains unclear. Hanson and Gidycz (1993) suggested that men find it difficult to feel empathy for women because contemporary culture supports the idea of blaming women; thus, if society supports women's culpability, it may be difficult for some men

to be sympathetic toward women and the issues that concern them. Furthermore, results of this study suggest that for some men (e.g., HSMs), it may be necessary to help them develop a more realistic understanding of the norms and expectations for behavior on campus, in addition to any empathy-induction efforts.

Prevention strategies that address the possible negative effects of peer pressure and highlight the existence of faulty beliefs about peers' behaviors and attitudes may be useful in deterring perpetrators. Because HSMs seem to be concerned with social appropriateness, programs in which peers express negative attitudes toward aggression may prove to be somewhat compelling for these individuals. College counselors could effectively use psychoeducational and other group experiences, including outreach interventions with groups, to help male students discuss and demystify attitudes toward sexual aggression and women, in general.

The overwhelming presence of pluralistic ignorance found in this study, combined with the fact that social attitudes and beliefs are more changeable than personality traits, suggests prevention strategies that are worth exploring. For example, presentations that highlight the fact that individuals often misperceive the sexual norm and that sexually aggressive behavior is not the norm on campus or in society could be useful. In addition, the overwhelming presence of pluralistic ignorance suggests that prevention efforts should focus on confronting peers who express adherence to rape-supportive beliefs. These kinds of interventions may be particularly needed with college men who are involved with athletics and fraternities, because these all-male activities may create an insular culture in which myths about women and sexual activity can flourish.

The topic of prevention is especially relevant for counselors because the field historically has supported the prevention of psychological distress (Ivey, 1976). Unfortunately, research on the prevention of sexual aggression has not been included as part of the core counseling literature (Betz & Fitzgerald, 1993). Appropriately trained counselors could have much to offer college men in terms of prevention programs. For example, college counselors could present prevention programs during freshman orientation that addressed the presence and possible negative effects of pluralistic ignorance. Such programs could empower freshmen, at the beginning of their college experience, to question assumptions that they may hold about what is happening on campus and help orient them to desirable, socially acceptable standards of behavior at their school. This would be prevention at its best, helping to prepare male students from the beginning of their college careers to deal realistically with critical issues of social acceptance and behavioral norms.

REFERENCES

Abbey, A. (1991). Acquaintance rape and alcohol consumption on college campuses: How are they linked? *Journal of American College Health, 39,* 165–169.

Allport, F. H. (1924). *Social psychology.* Boston: Houghton Mifflin.

Allport, F. H. (1968). The historical background of modern social psychology. In G. Linzey & E. Aronson (Eds.), *The handbook of social psychology. Vol. 1* (2nd ed., pp. 1–80). Reading, MA: Addison-Wesley.

Betz, N. E., & Fitzgerald, L. F. (1993). Individuality and diversity: Theory and research in counseling psychology. *Annual Review of Psychology, 44,* 343–381.

Bondurant, A. B. (1995). *University women's acknowledgment of rape: Individual, interpersonal and social factors.* Unpublished doctoral dissertation, University of North Carolina at Greensboro.

Briere, J., & Malamuth, N. (1983). Self-reported likelihood of sexually aggressive behavior: Attitudinal vs. sexual explanations. *Journal of Research in Personality, 17,* 315–323.

Briere, J., Malamuth, N., & Check, J. V. (1985). Sexuality and rape-supportive beliefs. *International Journal of Women's Studies, 8,* 398–403.

Briggs, S. R., & Check, J. M. (1988). On the nature of self-monitoring: Problems with assessment, problems with validity. *Journal of Personality and Social Psychology, 54,* 663–678.

Burt, M. R. (1980). Cultural myths and supports for rape. *Journal of Personality and Social Psychology, 38,* 217–230.

Burt, M. R. (1991). Rape myths and acquaintance rape. In A. Parrot & L. Bechoffer (Eds.), *Acquaintance rape: The hidden crime* (pp. 26–40). New York: Wiley.

Cohen, L., & Shotland, I. R. (1996). Timing of first sexual intercourse in a relationship: Expectations, experiences and perceptions of others. *The Journal of Sex Research, 33,* 291–299.

Cowling, M. (1998). *Date rape and consent.* Brookfield, CA: Ashgate.

Crossman, L. L. (1994, January). *Date rape and sexual aggression in college males: Incidence and the involvement of impulsivity, anger, hostility, psychopathology, peer influence and pornography use.* Paper presented at the annual meeting of the Southwest Educational Research Association, San Antonio, TX.

Crowne, D. P., & Marlowe, D. (1964). *The approval motive: Studies in evaluative dependence.* New York: Wiley.

Dietz, S. R., Blackwell, K., Daley, P., & Bentley, B. (1982). Measurement of empathy toward rape victims and rapists. *Journal of Personality and Social Psychology, 43,* 372–384.

Edidio, R. K., & Robertson, D. E. (1981). Rape awareness for men. *Journal of College Student Development, 22,* 455–456.

Flezzani, J. D. (2001). *The role of self-monitoring and pluralistic ignorance in understanding sexual aggression and coercion in college males.* Unpublished doctoral dissertation, University of North Carolina at Greensboro.

Foubert, J. D. (2000). The longitudinal effects of a rape prevention program on fraternity men's attitudes, behavioral intent, and behavior. *Journal of American College Health, 48,* 158–163.

Hanson, K. A., & Gidycz, C. A. (1993). Evaluation of a sexual assault prevention program. *Journal of Consulting and Clinical Psychology, 61,* 1046–1052.

Harney, P. A., & Muehlenhard, C. L. (1991). Factors that increase the likelihood of victimization. In A. Parrot & L. Bechhofer (Eds.), *Acquaintance rape: The hidden crime* (pp. 150–175). New York: Wiley.

Ivey, A. (1976). Invited response: The counselor as teacher. *Personnel and Guidance Journal, 54,* 431–434.

Kanin, E. J. (1967). Reference groups and sex conduct norm violations. *The Sociological Quarterly, 8,* 495–504.

Kanin, E. J. (1985). Date rapists: Differential sexual socialization and relative deprivation. *Archives of Sexual Behavior, 14,* 219–231.

Katz, D., & Allport, F. H. (1931). *Student attitudes.* Syracuse, NY: Craftsman.

Kimmel, D. C., & Weiner, I. B. (1984). *Adolescence: A developmental transition.* Hillsdale, NJ: Erlbaum.

Koss, M. P. (1988). Hidden rape: Sexual aggression and victimization in a national sample of higher education. In M. E. Odem & J. Clay-Warner (Eds.), *Confronting rape and sexual aggression: Worlds of women* (pp. 51–69). Wilmington, DE: SR Books/Scholarly Resources.

Koss, M. P., Gidycz, C. A., & Wisniewski, N. (1987). The scope of rape: Incidence and prevalence of sexual aggression and victimization in a national sample of higher education students. *Journal of Counseling and Clinical Psychology, 55,* 162–170.

Koss, M. P., & Oros, C. (1982). Sexual experiences survey: A research instrument investigating sexual aggression and victimization. *Journal of Consulting and Clinical Psychology, 50,* 455–457.

Lenox, R. (1988). The problem with self-monitoring: A two-sided scale and a one-sided theory. *Journal of Personality Assessment, 52,* 58–73.

McKinney, K. (1986). Measures of verbal, physical, and sexual dating violence by gender. *Free Inquiry in Creative Sociology, 14,* 55–60.

Miller, D. T., & Prentice, D. A. (1994). The self and the collective. *Personality and Social Psychology Bulletin, 20,* 451–453.

Miller, M. L., & Thayer, J. F. (1988). On the nature of self-monitoring: Relationships with adjustment and identity. *Personality and Social Psychology Bulletin, 14,* 544–553.

Newman, B. M., & Newman, P. R. (1986). *Adolescent development.* Columbus, OH: Merrill.

O'Gorman, H. J. (1986). The discovery of pluralistic ignorance: An ironic lesson. *Journal of the History of the Behavioral Science, 22,* 333–347.

Prentice, D. A., & Miller, D. T. (1993). Pluralistic ignorance and alcohol use on campus: Some consequences of misperceiving the social norm. *Journal of Personality and Social Psychology, 6,* 243–256.

Rapaport, L. R., & Posey, C. D. (1991). Sexually coercive college males. In A. Parrot & L. Bechhofer (Eds.), *Acquaintance rape: The hidden crime* (pp. 186–195). New York: Wiley.

Schwartz, M. D., & DeKeseredy, W. S. (1997). *Sexual assault on the college campus: The role of peer support.* Thousand Oaks, CA: Sage.

Snyder, M. (1974). Self-monitoring of expressive behavior. *Journal of Personality and Social Psychology, 30,* 526–537.

Snyder, M., Gangestad, S., & Simpson, J. A. (1983). Choosing friends as activity partners: The role of self-monitoring. *Journal of Personality and Social Psychology and Human Sexuality, 45,* 1061–1072.

Snyder, M., Simpson, J. A., & Gangestad, S. (1986). Personality and sexual relations. *Journal of Personality and Social Psychology, 51,* 181–190.

White, J. W., Donat, P. L., & Humphrey, J. A. (1996). An examination of attitudes underlying sexual assault among acquaintances. *The Journal of Psychology and Human Sexuality, 8,* 27–48.

White, J. W., & Hoecker, K. (1995). [Reliability and validity data for a revised Sexual Experiences Survey]. Unpublished raw data. Greensboro, NC: University of North Carolina at Greensboro.

Yescavage, L. M., & White, J. W. (1989, March). *Relating self-monitoring and sexual aggression.* Paper presented at the annual meeting of the Southeastern Psychological Association, Washington, DC.

CRITICAL THINKING QUESTIONS

1. The authors of the article suggest some ways in which the findings can be used in intervention programs designed to prevent date rape. Based on the information in the article, design such an intervention program for college freshmen at your school. Be specific.

2. Subjects in the study were individuals who stopped by a desk in the lobby and agreed to fill out the questionnaire. Furthermore, only freshmen and sophomores living on campus in dormitories participated in the study. Does either or both of these factors limit the generalizability of the findings? Explain the reasoning behind your answer.

3. Victims of date rape often do not report the incident to others. Do self-monitoring and/or pluralistic ignorance play a role in not reporting such offenses? Why or why not? Explain your answer.

4. How might the concepts of self-monitoring and pluralistic ignorance be involved in behaviors other than date rape, such as excessive drinking in college? Design a study to determine if either or both of these factors play a role in drinking behavior. Using the conclusions from this article, what interventions might be successful in reducing excessive drinking on campus? Explain.

CHAPTER INTEGRATION QUESTIONS _____

1. Articles 13 and 15 both dealt with the concept of self-monitoring—an aspect of the self—whereas Article 14 dealt with a different aspect of the self—namely, gender. How might the concept of self-monitoring be related to the concept of androgyny?

2. Might different styles of self-monitoring be related to masculine, feminine, and androgynous orientations? Explain your reasoning.

3. Psychologist Nathaniel Branden said, "Of all of the judgments that we pass in life, none is as important as the one we pass on ourselves." Do you agree or disagree with this quotation? Explain your reasoning. How does this quotation relate to an overall theme in this chapter?

Chapter Six

PREJUDICE
AND DISCRIMINATION

PREJUDICE. THINK OF the implications of that word. It is so negative that even people who are highly prejudiced often are reluctant to use that term to describe themselves. Instead, prejudiced people may say that their opinions about members of certain groups are accurate and well founded, perhaps even that these groups deserve disdain.

Although the words *prejudice* and *discrimination* are often used interchangeably, they actually refer to two different things. *Prejudice* is an attitude, a set of beliefs about a member of a group based just on membership in that group. *Discrimination,* on the other hand, is a behavior, the differential treatment of a person based on membership in a particular group. You do not need to look far for the results of prejudiced attitudes and discriminatory behaviors: History is full of suffering that has been inflicted on people due solely to their membership in particular groups.

During the last several decades of the twentieth century, many great strides were made in the area of social justice. Overt discrimination against various groups was outlawed and, in many cases, was reduced significantly. Consider the overtly stated opinions of people that you hear from day to day. The amount of racism, for example, is less noticeable than it would have been only 20 or 30 years ago.

So, does this mean that the level of prejudiced thinking has, indeed, decreased over time? Not necessarily. It may be that people just *express* these prejudices more subtlety than they did in the past. In fact, prejudiced thinking may be rooted in how our minds process information. Article 16, "Why We Hate," examines how we acquire prejudices and how prejudices manifest themselves. It turns out that prejudice may be expressed in more subtle ways than most of us realize.

Article 17, "Attitudes vs. Actions," deals with the consistency between people's attitudes and behaviors, or, more specifically, the consistency between prejudice and discrimination. Do we always act in accordance with our prejudiced attitudes? Or do we sometimes contradict what we say we believe? This classic article was one of the first to address the issue of whether prejudice and discrimination necessarily occur together.

Finally, Article 18, "Christian Orthodoxy, Religious Fundamentalism, and Right-Wing Authoritarianism as Predictors of Implicit Racial Prejudice," addresses a consideration raised in Article 16: specifically, that prejudice exists but in a more subtle form (i.e., implicit racism) than the overtly expressed racism of the past. This article explores how implicit forms of racism may be related to some dimensions of religiosity.

ARTICLE 16 _____

Just about anyone, by virtue of membership in a particular group, can be a target of prejudice and discrimination. The standard scenario is that a person is prejudged and reacted to not as an individual but as a member of some group, such that the presumed general characteristics of the group are automatically attributed to the individual. This process is known as *stereotyping*.

Stereotyping is an everyday fact of life. Although we may hope that we judge every person as an individual, the cognitive strategies we use to make sense of our would, as discussed in Chapter 3, suggest otherwise. In particular, when confronted with a member of an identifiable group, we may rely on a stereotype as a sort of decision-making shortcut, rather than consider the person on his or her own merits. How we feel about the person and how we treat him or her will be based on the stereotype, not the individual. As such, stereotypes frequently underlie prejudiced attitudes and discriminatory behaviors.

Are people less prejudiced today than in the past? In attempting to answer this question, it may be useful to distinguish between the various ways in which prejudice can be expressed. At one extreme are legalized forms of discrimination, such as the so-called Jim Crow laws of the past, which institutionalized discrimination against African Americans, and current laws that restrict women from combat roles in the U.S. military. At the other extreme are subtle types of differential treatment, such as how people are addressed and even how much eye contact they receive. While subtle, these types of behaviors may have a huge impact on the people against whom they are directed. Furthermore, while it is relatively easy to control what we say (e.g., not making racist remarks), it is much more difficult to control the nonverbal cues that may betray our underlying feelings (e.g., moving away from someone).

The following article by Margo Monteith and Jeffrey Winters examines research that indicates that prejudices are not only easily acquired but also may operate in a very subtle fashion. Perhaps part of the reason we acquire prejudices so readily is that we may be "wired" to make distinctions between *us* and *them*. Once acquired, these prejudices may operate in a very subtle manner, even when we are consciously *not* expressing any overt forms of bias. There is some good news, however: Even these subtle forms of prejudice can be reduced, given the right set of circumstances.

Why We Hate
■ Margo Monteith and Jeffrey Winters

Balbir Singh Sodhi was shot to death on September 15 in Mesa, Arizona. His killer claimed to be exacting revenge for the terrorist attacks of September 11. Upon his arrest, the murderer shouted, "I stand for America all the way." Though Sodhi wore a turban and could trace his ancestry to South Asia, he shared neither ethnicity nor religion with the suicide hijackers. Sodhi—who was killed at the gas station where he worked—died just for being different in a nation gripped with fear.

Reprinted from *Psychology Today,* 2002 (May/June), *35,* 44–50, 87. Reprinted with permission from *Psychology Today* magazine. Copyright © 2002 (Sussex Publishers, Inc.).

For Arab and Muslim Americans, the months after the terrorist attacks have been trying. They have been harassed at work and their property has been vandalized. An Arab San Francisco shop owner recalled with anger that his five-year-old daughter was taunted by name-callers. Classmates would yell "terrorist" as she walked by.

Public leaders from President George W. Bush on down have called for tolerance. But the Center for American-Islamic Relations in Washington, D.C., has tallied some 1,700 incidents of abuse against Muslims in the five months following September 11. Despite our better nature, it seems, fear of foreigners or other strange-seeming people comes out when we are under stress. That fear, known as xenophobia, seems almost hardwired into the human psyche.

Researchers are discovering the extent to which xenophobia can be easily—even arbitrarily—turned on. In just hours, we can be conditioned to fear or discriminate against those who differ from ourselves by characteristics as superficial as eye color. Even ideas we believe are just common sense can have deep xenophobic underpinnings. Research conducted this winter at Harvard reveals that even among people who claim to have no bias, the more strongly one supports the ethnic profiling of Arabs at airport-security checkpoints, the more hidden prejudice one has against Muslims.

But other research shows that when it comes to whom we fear and how we react, we do have a choice. We can, it seems, choose not to give in to our xenophobic tendencies.

THE MELTING POT

America prides itself on being a melting pot of cultures, but how we react to newcomers is often at odds with that self-image. A few years ago, psychologist Markus Kemmelmeier, Ph.D., now at the University of Nevada at Reno, stuck stamped letters under the windshield wipers of parked cars in a suburb of Detroit. Half were addressed to a fictitious Christian organization, half to a made-up Muslim group. Of all the letters, half had little stickers of the American flag.

Would the addresses and stickers affect the rate at which the letters would be mailed? Kemmelmeier wondered. Without the flag stickers, both sets of letters were mailed at the same rate, about 75 percent of the time. With the stickers, however, the rates changed: Almost all the Christian letters were forwarded but only half of the Muslim letters were mailed. "The flag is seen as a sacred object," Kemmelmeier says. "And it made people think about what it means to be a good American."

In short, the Muslims didn't make the cut.

Not mailing a letter seems like a small slight. Yet in the last century, there have been shocking examples of xenophobia in our own back yard. Perhaps the most famous in American history was the fear of the Japanese during World War II. This particular wave of hysteria lead to the rise of slurs and bigoted depictions in the media, and more alarmingly, the mass internment of 120,000 people of Japanese ancestry beginning in 1942. The internments have become a national embarrassment: Most of the Japanese held were American citizens, and there is little evidence that the imprisonments had any real strategic impact.

Today the targets of xenophobia—derived from the Greek word for *stranger*—aren't the Japanese. Instead, they are Muslim immigrants. Or Mexicans. Or Chinese. Or whichever group we have come to fear.

Just how arbitrary are these xenophobic feelings? Two famous public-school experiments show how easy it is to turn one "group" against another. In the late 1960s, California high school history teacher Ron Jones recruited students to participate in an exclusive new cultural program called "the Wave." Within weeks, these students were separating themselves from others and aggressively intimidating critics. Eventually, Jones confronted the students with the reality that they were unwitting participants in an experiment demonstrating the power of nationalist movements.

A few years later, a teacher in Iowa discovered how quickly group distinctions are made. The teacher, Jane Elliott, divided her class into two groups—those with blue eyes and those with brown or green eyes. The brown-eyed group received privileges and treats, while the blue-eyed students were denied rewards and told they were inferior. Within hours, the once-harmonious classroom became two camps, full of mutual fear and resentment. Yet, what is especially shocking is that the students were only in the third grade.

SOCIAL IDENTITY

The drive to completely and quickly divide the world into "us" and "them" is so powerful that it must surely come from some deep-seated need. The exact identity of that need, however, has been subject to debate. In the 1970s, the late Henri Tajfel, Ph.D., of the University of Bristol in England, and John Turner, Ph.D., now of the Australian National University, devised a theory to explain the psychology behind a range of prejudices and biases, not just xenophobia. Their theory was based, in part, on the desire to think highly of oneself. One way to lift your self-esteem is to be part of a distinctive group, like a winning team; another is to play up the qualities of your own group and denigrate the attributes of others so that you feel your group is better.

Tajfel and Turner called their insight "social identity theory," which has proved valuable for understanding how prejudices develop. Given even the slenderest of criteria, we naturally split people into two groups—an "in-group" and an "out-group." The categories can be of geopolitical importance—nationality, religion, race, language—or they can be as seemingly inconsequential as handedness, hair color or even height.

Once the division is made, the inferences and projections begin to occur. For one, we tend to think more highly of people in the in-group than those in the out-group, a belief based only on group identity. Also, a person tends to feel that others in the in-group are similar to one's self in ways that—although stereotypical—may have little to do with the original criteria used to split the groups. Someone with glasses may believe that other people who wear glasses are more voracious readers—even more intelligent—than those who don't, in spite of the fact that all he really knows is that they don't see very well. On the other hand, people in the out-group are believed to be less distinct and less complex than are cohorts in the in-group.

Although Tajfel and Turner found that identity and categorization were the root cause of social bias, other researchers have tried to find evolutionary explanations for discrimination. After all, in the distant past, people who shared cultural similarities were found to be more genetically related than those who did not. Therefore, favoring the in-group was a way of helping perpetuate one's genes. Evolutionary explanations seems appealing, since they rely on the simplest biological urges to drive complicated behavior. But this fact also makes them hard to prove. Ironically, there is ample evidence backing up the "softer" science behind social identity theory.

HIDDEN BIAS

Not many of us will admit to having strong racist or xenophobic biases. Even in cases where bias becomes public debate—such as the profiling of Arab Muslims at airport-security screenings—proponents of prejudice claim that they are merely promoting common sense. That reluctance to admit to bias makes the issue tricky to study.

To get around this problem, psychologists Anthony Greenwald, Ph.D., of the University of Washington in Seattle, and Mahzarin Banaji, Ph.D., of Harvard, developed the Implicit Association Test. The IAT is a simple test that measures reaction time: The subject sees various words or images projected on a screen, then classifies the images into one of two groups by pressing buttons. The words and images need not be racial or ethnic in nature—one group of researchers tested attitudes toward presidential candidates. The string of images is interspersed with words having either pleasant or unpleasant connotations, then the participant must group the words and images in various ways—Democrats are placed with unpleasant words, for instance.

The differences in reaction time are small but telling. Again and again, researchers found that subjects readily tie in-group images with pleasant words and out-group images with unpleasant words. One study compares such groups as whites and blacks, Jews and Christians, and young people and old people. And researchers found that if you identify yourself in one group, it's easier to pair images of that group with pleasant words—and easier to pair the opposite group with unpleasant imagery. This reveals the underlying biases and enables us to study how quickly they can form.

Really though, we need to know very little about a person to discriminate against him. One of the authors of this story, psychologist Margo Monteith, Ph.D., performed an IAT experiment comparing attitudes toward two sets of made-up names; one set was supposedly

"American," the other from the fictitious country of Marisat. Even though the subjects knew nothing about Marisat, they showed a consistent bias against it.

While this type of research may seem out in left field, other work may have more "real-world" applications. The Southern Poverty Law Center runs a Web version of the IAT that measures biases based on race, age and gender. Its survey has, for instance, found that respondents are far more likely to associate European faces, rather than Asian faces, with so-called American images. The implication being that Asians are seen as less "American" than Caucasians.

Similarly, Harvard's Banaji has studied the attitudes of people who favor the racial profiling of Arab Muslims to deter terrorism, and her results run contrary to the belief that such profiling is not driven by xenophobic fears. "We show that those who endorse racial profiling also score high on both explicit and implicit measures of prejudice toward Arab Muslims," Banaji says. "Endorsement of profiling is an indicator of level of prejudice."

BEYOND XENOPHOBIA

If categorization and bias come so easily, are people doomed to xenophobia and racism? It's pretty clear that we are susceptible to prejudice and that there is an unconscious desire to divide the world into "us" and "them." Fortunately, however, new research also shows that prejudices are fluid and that when we become conscious of our biases we can take active— and successful—steps to combat them.

Researchers have long known that when observing racially mixed groups, people are more likely to confuse the identity of two black individuals or two white ones, rather than a white with a black. But Leda Cosmides, Ph.D., and John Tooby, Ph.D., of the Center for Evolutionary Psychology at the University of California at Santa Barbara, and anthropologist Robert Kurzban, Ph.D., of the University of California at Los Angeles, wanted to test whether this was innate or whether it was just an artifact of how society groups individuals by race.

To do this, Cosmides and her colleagues made a video of two racially integrated basketball teams locked in conversation, then they showed it to study participants. As reported in the *Proceedings of the National Academy of Sciences,* the researchers discovered that subjects were more likely to confuse two players on the same team, regardless of race, rather than two players of the same race on opposite teams.

Cosmides says that this points to one way of attacking racism and xenophobia: changing the way society imposes group labels. American society divides people by race and by ethnicity; that's how lines of prejudice form. But simple steps, such as integrating the basketball teams, can reset mental divisions, rendering race and ethnicity less important.

This finding supports earlier research by psychologists Samuel Gaertner, Ph.D., of the University of Delaware in Newark, and John Dovidio, Ph.D., of Colgate University in Hamilton, New York. Gaertner and Dovidio have studied how bias changes when members of racially mixed groups must cooperate to accomplish shared goals. In situations where team members had to work together, bias could be reduced by significant amounts.

Monteith has also found that people who are concerned about their prejudices have the power to correct them. In experiments, she told subjects that they had performed poorly on tests that measured belief in stereotypes. She discovered that the worse a subject felt about her performance, the better she scored on subsequent tests. The guilt behind learning about their own prejudices made the subjects try harder not to be biased.

This suggests that the guilt of mistaking individuals for their group stereotype—such as falsely believing an Arab is a terrorist—can lead to the breakdown of the belief in that stereotype. Unfortunately, such stereotypes are reinforced so often that they can become ingrained. It is difficult to escape conventional wisdom and treat all people as individuals, rather than members of a group. But that seems to be the best way to avoid the trap of dividing the world in two—and discriminating against one part of humanity.

READ MORE ABOUT IT

Nobody Left to Hate: Teaching Compassion After Columbine, Elliot Aronson (W. H. Freeman and Company, 2000)
The Racist Mind: Portraits of American Neo-Nazis and Klansmen, Madonna Kolbenschlag (Penguin Books, 1996)

CRITICAL THINKING QUESTIONS

1. "Endorsement of profiling is an indicator of level of prejudice." React to this quote from the article. Be specific in your response.

2. Based on the information in this article, how would you answer someone who claims that he or she is not in the least bit prejudiced?

3. After reading this article, how optimistic or pessimistic are you that prejudice can be eliminated from society? Specifically, can people overcome prejudiced thinking? Give examples to support your position.

4. If you were a parent and wanted to minimize the formation of prejudiced thinking in your children, what would you do? Despite your good intentions, what might limit your ability to accomplish this? Explain your answers.

5. Many studies on prejudice involve asking subjects about their attitudes toward particular groups. What do the findings of this article suggest about the validity of such self-reporting techniques? What may be a more accurate way of assessing prejudiced attitudes? Explain your answer.

6. What role does the media play in reinforcing, creating, or changing prejudices? Give specific examples to bolster your premise.

ARTICLE 17 _____

As mentioned in the introduction to this chapter, the terms *prejudice* and *discrimination* often are used interchangeably, but, in fact, they refer to two different concepts. Prejudice is an *attitude,* whereby a particular person is judged based solely on his or her membership in a particular group. Discrimination refers to the *behavior* of treating people differently based upon their membership in a group.

While the two terms do, indeed, refer to different things, do they occur together in the real world? It stands to reason that if you have negative beliefs about a particular group of people, then you would act in a negative fashion toward them. Or does it? Are we always consistent in our attitudes and behaviors?

Sometimes there is a strong consistency between what people say about their beliefs and how they act. For example, surveys are usually accurate in predicting outcomes of elections based upon asking people about their attitudes toward the candidates. In other cases, such consistency simply does not exist.

"Attitudes vs. Actions" is a classic work in the field that addresses the issue of attitude-behavior consistency. Before LaPiere's publication of this study in 1934, attitude research on prejudice involved asking respondents to give hypothetical responses to hypothetical situations (e.g., Would you serve a person of a given race at your restaurant?). LaPiere measured the number of times that a Chinese couple was actually refused lodging or food and then followed up with a questionnaire to the same establishments six months later, asking if they would serve Chinese persons. In doing so, LaPiere claimed to demonstrate the lack of consistency between what people say and what they actually do. Even though the study does have some methodological flaws, it is a good example of pioneering research in the field. It also provides an interesting microcosm of prejudice and discrimination issues that existed in the United States over a half-century ago.

Attitudes vs. Actions

■ Richard T. LaPiere

By definition, a social attitude is a behaviour pattern, anticipatory set or tendency, predisposition to specific adjustment to designated social situations, or, more simply, a conditioned response to social stimuli.[1] Terminological usage differs, but students who have concerned themselves with attitudes apparently agree that they are acquired out of social experience and provide the individual organism with some degree of preparation to adjust, in a well-defined way, to certain types of social situations if and when these situations arise. It would seem, therefore, that the totality of the social attitudes of a single individual would include all his socially acquired personality which is involved in the making of adjustments to other human beings.

But by derivation social attitudes are seldom more than a verbal response to a symbolic situation. For the conventional method of measuring social attitudes is to ask questions (usually in writing) which demand a verbal adjustment to an entirely symbolic situation. Because it is easy, cheap, and mechanical, the attitudinal questionnaire is rapidly becoming a major method of sociological and socio-psychological investigation.

Reprinted from *Social Forces,* Vol. 13, 1934. "Attitudes vs. Actions" by Richard T. LaPiere. Copyright © The University of North Carolina Press.

Note: Some of the language used and views presented are indicative of the time in which the article was written. The reader should consider the article in that context.

The technique is simple. Thus from a hundred or a thousand responses to the question "Would you get up to give an Armenian woman your seat in a street-car?" the investigator derives the "attitude" of non-Armenian males toward Armenian females. Now the question may be constructed with elaborate skill and hidden with consumate cunning in a maze of supplementary or even irrelevant questions yet all that has been obtained is a symbolic response to a symbolic situation. The words "Armenian woman" do not constitute an Armenian woman of flesh and blood, who might be tall or squat, fat or thin, old or young, well or poorly dressed—who might, in fact, be a goddess or just another old and dirty hag. And the questionnaire response, whether it be "yes" or "no," is but a verbal reaction and this does not involve rising from the seat or stolidly avoiding the hurt eyes of the hypothetical woman and the derogatory stares of other street-car occupants. Yet, ignoring these limitations, the diligent investigator will jump briskly from his factual evidence to the unwarranted conclusion that he has measured the "anticipatory behavior patterns" of non-Armenian males toward Armenian females encountered on street cars. Usually he does not stop here, but proceeds to deduce certain general conclusions regarding the social relationships between Armenians and non-Armenians. Most of us have applied the questionnaire technique with greater caution, but not I fear with any greater certainty of success.

Some years ago I endeavored to obtain comparative data on the degree of French and English antipathy towards dark-skinned peoples.[2] The informal questionnaire technique was used, but, although the responses so obtained were exceedingly consistent, I supplemented them with what I then considered an index to overt behavior. The hypothesis as then stated *seemed* entirely logical. "Whatever our attitude on the validity of 'verbalization' may be, it must be recognized that any study of attitudes through direct questioning is open to serious objection, both because of the limitations of the sampling method and because in classifying attitudes the inaccuracy of human judgment is an inevitable variable. In this study, however, there is corroborating evidence on these attitudes in the policies adopted by hotel proprietors. Nothing could be used as a more accurate index of color prejudice than the admission or non-admission of colored

people to hotels. For the proprietor must reflect the group attitude in his policy regardless of his own feelings in the matter. Since he determines what the group attitude is towards Negroes through the expression of that attitude in overt behavior and over a long period of actual experience, the results will be exceptionally free from those disturbing factors which inevitably affect the effort to study attitudes by direct questioning."

But at that time I overlooked the fact that what I was obtaining from the hotel proprietors was still a "verbalized" reaction to a symbolic situation. The response to a Negro's request for lodgings might have been an excellent index of the attitude of hotel patrons towards living in the same hotel as a Negro. Yet to ask the proprietor "Do you permit members of the Negro race to stay here?" does not, it appears, measure his potential response to an actual Negro.

All measurement of attitudes by the questionnaire technique proceeds on the assumption that there is a mechanical relationship between symbolic and non-symbolic behavior. It is simple enough to prove that there is no *necessary* correlation between speech and action, between response to words and to the realities they symbolize. A parrot can be taught to swear, a child to sing "Frankie and Johnny" in the Mae West manner. The words will have no meaning to either child or parrot. But to prove that there is no *necessary* relationship does not prove that such a relationship may not exist. There need be no relationship between what the hotel proprietor says he will do and what he actually does when confronted with a colored patron. Yet there may be. Certainly we are justified in assuming that the verbal response of the hotel proprietor would be more likely to indicate what he would actually do than would the verbal response of people whose personal feelings are less subordinated to economic expediency. However, the following study indicates that the reliability of even such responses is very small indeed.

Beginning in 1930 and continuing for two years thereafter, I had the good fortune to travel rather extensively with a young Chinese student and his wife.[3] Both were personable, charming, and quick to win the admiration and respect of those they had the opportunity to become intimate with. But they were foreign-born Chinese, a fact that could not be disguised. Knowing the general "attitude" of Americans towards the Chinese as indicated by the "social distance" studies which have been made, it was with considerable trepidation that I first approached a hotel clerk in their company. Perhaps the clerk's eyebrows lifted slightly, but he accommodated us without a show of hesitation. And this in the "best" hotel in a small town noted for its narrow and bigoted "attitude" towards Orientals. Two months later I passed that way again, phoned the hotel and asked if they would accommodate "an important Chinese gentleman." The reply was an unequivocal "No." That aroused my curiosity and led to this study.

In something like ten thousand miles of motor travel, twice across the United States, up and down the Pacific Coast, we met definite rejection from those asked to serve us just once. We were received at 66 hotels, auto camps, and "Tourist Homes," refused at one. We were served in 184 restaurants and cafes scattered throughout the country and treated with what I judged to be more than ordinary consideration in 72 of them. Accurate and detailed records were kept of all these instances. An effort, necessarily subjective, was made to evaluate the overt response of hotel clerks, bell boys, elevator operators, and waitresses to the presence of my Chinese friends. The factors entering into the situations were varied as far and as often as possible. Control was not, of course, as exacting as that required by laboratory experimentation. But it was as rigid as is humanly possible in human situations. For example, I did not take the "test" subjects into my confidence fearing that their behavior might become self-conscious and thus abnormally affect the response of others towards them. Whenever possible I let my Chinese friend negotiate for accommodations (while I concerned myself with the car or luggage) or sent them into a restaurant ahead of me. In this way I attempted to "factor" myself out. We sometimes patronized high-class establishments after a hard and dusty day on the road and stopped at inferior auto camps when in our most presentable condition.

In the end I was forced to conclude that those factors which most influenced the behavior of others towards the Chinese had nothing at all to do with race. Quality and condition of clothing, appearance of baggage (by which, it seems, hotel clerks are prone to base their quick evaluations), cleanliness and neatness were far more significant for person to person reaction in the situations I was studying than skin pigmentation, straight black hair, slanting eyes, and flat noses. And yet an air of self-confidence might entirely offset the "unfavorable" impression made by dusty clothes and the usual disorder to appearance consequent upon some hundred miles of motor travel. A supercilious desk clerk in a hotel of noble aspirations could not refuse his master's hospitality to people who appeared to take their request as a perfectly normal and conventional thing, though they might look like tin-can tourists and two of them belong to the racial category "Oriental." On the other hand, I became rather adept at approaching hotel clerks with that peculiar crabwise manner which is so effective in provoking a somewhat scornful disregard. And then a bland smile would serve to reverse the entire situation. Indeed, it appeared that a genial smile was the most effective password to acceptance. My Chinese friends were skillful smilers, which may account, in part, for the fact that we received but one rebuff in all our experience. Finally, I was impressed with the fact that even where some tension developed due to the strangeness for the Chinese it would evaporate immediately when they spoke in unaccented English.

The one instance in which we were refused accommodations is worth recording here. The place was a small California town, a rather inferior auto-camp into which we drove in a very dilapidated car plied with camp equipment. It was early evening, the light so dim that the proprietor found it somewhat difficult to decide the genus *voyageur* to which we belonged. I left the car and spoke to him. He hesitated, wavered, said he was not sure that he had two cabins, meanwhile edging towards our car. The realization that the two occupants were Orientals turned the balance or, more likely, gave him the excuse he was looking for. "No," he said, "I don't take Japs!" In a more pretentious establishment we secured accommodations, and with an extra flourish of hospitality.

To offset this one flat refusal were the many instances in which the physical peculiarities of the Chinese served to heighten curiosity. With few exceptions this curiosity was considerably hidden behind an exceptional interest in serving us. Of course, outside of the Pacific Coast region, New York, and Chicago, the Chinese physiognomy attracts attention.

It is different, hence noticeable. But the principal effect this curiosity has upon the behavior of those who cater to the traveler's needs is to make them more attentive, more responsive, more reliable. A Chinese companion is to be recommended to the white traveling in his native land. Strange features when combined with "human" speech and action seems, at times, to heighten sympathetic response, perhaps on the same principle that makes us uncommonly sympathetic toward the dog that has a "human" expression in his face.

What I am trying to say is that in only one out of 251 instances in which we purchased goods or services necessitating intimate human relationships did the fact that my companions were Chinese adversely affect us. Factors entirely unassociated with race were, in the main, the determinant of significant variations in our reception. It would appear reasonable to conclude that the "attitude" of the American people, as reflected in the behavior of those who are for pecuniary reasons presumably most sensitive to the antipathies of their white clientele, is anything but negative towards the Chinese. In terms of "social distance" we might conclude that native Caucasians are not averse to residing in the same hotels, auto-camps, and "Tourist Homes" as Chinese and will with complacency accept the presence of Chinese at an adjoining table in restaurant or cafe. It does not follow that there is revealed a distinctly "positive" attitude towards the Chinese, that whites prefer the Chinese to other whites. But the facts as gathered certainly preclude the conclusion that there is an intense prejudice towards the Chinese.

Yet the existence of this prejudice, very intense, is proven by a conventional "attitude" study. To provide a comparison of symbolic reaction to symbolic social situations with actual reaction to real social situations, I "questionnaired" the establishments which we patronized during the two year period. Six months were permitted to lapse between the time I obtained the overt reaction and the symbolic. It was hoped that the effects of the actual experience with Chinese guests, adverse or otherwise, would have faded during the intervening time. To the hotel or restaurant a questionnaire was mailed with an accompanying letter purporting to be a special and personal plea for response. The questionnaires all asked the same question, "Will you accept members of the Chinese race as guests in your establishment?" Two types of questionnaire were used. In one this question was inserted among similar queries concerning Germans, French, Japanese, Russians, Armenians, Jews, Negroes, Italians, and Indians. In the other the pertinent question was unencumbered. With persistence, completed replies were obtained from 128 of the establishments we had visited; 81 restaurants and cafes and 47 hotels, auto-camps, and "Tourist Homes." In response to the relevant question 92 per cent of the former and 91 per cent of the latter replied "No." The remainder replied "Uncertain; depend upon circumstances." From the woman proprietor of a small auto-camp I received the only "Yes," accompanied by a chatty letter describing the nice visit she had had with a Chinese gentleman and his sweet wife during the previous summer.

A rather unflattering interpretation might be put upon the fact that those establishments who had provided for our needs so graciously were, some months later, verbally antagonistic towards hypothetical Chinese. To factor this experience out responses were secured from 32 hotels and 96 restaurants located in approximately the same regions, but uninfluenced by this particular experience with Oriental clients. In this, as in the former case, both types of questionnaires were used. The results indicate that neither the type of questionnaire nor the fact of previous experience had important bearing upon the symbolic response to symbolic social situations.

It is impossible to make direct comparison between the reactions secured through questionnaires and from actual experience. On the basis of the above data it would appear foolhardy for a Chinese to attempt to travel in the United States. And yet, as I have shown, actual experience indicates that the American people, as represented by the personnel of hotels, restaurants, etc., are not at all averse to fraternizing with Chinese within the limitations which apply to social relationships between Americans themselves. The evaluations which follow are undoubtedly subject to the criticism which any human judgment must withstand. But the fact is that, although they began their travels in this country with considerable trepidations, my Chinese friends soon lost all fear that they might receive a rebuff. At first somewhat timid and considerably dependent upon me for guidance and support, they

TABLE 1 / Distribution of Results from Questionnaire Study of Establishment "Policy" Regarding Acceptance of Chinese as Guests

Replies are to the question: "Will you accept members of the Chinese race as guests in your establishment?"

	Hotels, Etc. Visited		Hotels, Etc. Not Visited		Restaurants, Etc. Visited		Restaurants, Etc. Not Visited	
Total	*47*		*32*		*81*		*96*	
	1*	2*	1	2	1	2	1	2
Number replying	22	25	20	12	43	38	51	45
No	20	23	19	11	40	35	37	41
Undecided: depend upon circumstances	1	2	1	1	3	3	4	3
Yes	1	0	0	0	0	0	0	1

*Column (1) indicates in each case those responses to questionnaires which concerned Chinese only. The figures in column (2) are from the questionnaires in which the above was inserted among questions regarding Germans, French, Japanese, etc.

came in time to feel fully self-reliant and would approach new social situations without the slightest hesitation.

The conventional questionnaire undoubtedly has significant value for the measurement of "political attitudes." The presidential polls conducted by the *Literary Digest* have proven that. But a "political attitude" is exactly what the questionnaire can be justly held to measure; a verbal response to a symbolic situation. Few citizens are ever faced with the necessity of adjusting themselves to the presence of the political leaders whom, periodically, they must vote for—or against. Especially is this true with regard to the president, and it is in relation to political attitudes towards presidential candidates that we have our best evidence. But while the questionnaire may indicate what the voter will do when he goes to vote, it does not and cannot reveal what he will do when he meets Candidate Jones on the street, in his office, at his club, on the golf course, or wherever two men may meet and adjust in some way one to the other.

The questionnaire is probably our only means of determining "religious attitudes." An honest answer to the question "Do you believe in God?" reveals all there is to be measured. "God" is a symbol; "belief" a verbal expression. So here, too, the questionnaire is effica-

cious. But if we would know the emotional responsiveness of a person to the spoken or written word "God" some other method of investigation must be used. And if we would know the extent to which that responsiveness restrains his behavior it is to his behavior that we must look, not to his questionnaire response. Ethical precepts are, I judge, something more than verbal professions. There would seem little to be gained from asking a man if his religious faith prevents him from committing sin. Of course it does—on paper. But "moral attitudes" must have a significance in the adjustment to actual situations or they are not worth the studying. Sitting at my desk in California I can predict with a high degree of certainty what an "average" business man in an average Mid-Western city will reply to the question "Would you engage in sexual intercourse with a prostitute in a Paris brothel?" Yet no one, least of all the man himself, can predict what he would actually do should he by some misfortune find himself face to face with the situation in question. His moral "attitudes" are no doubt already stamped into his personality. But just what those habits are which will be invoked to provide him with some sort of adjustment to this situation is quite indeterminate.

It is highly probable that when the "Southern Gentleman" says he will not permit Negroes to reside

TABLE 2 / Distribution of Results Obtained from Actual Experience in the Situation Symbolized in the Questionnaire Study

Conditions	Hotels, Etc.		Restaurants, Etc.	
	Accompanied by investigator	Chinese not so accompanied at inception of situation*	Accompanied by by investigator	Chinese not so accompanied at inception of situation
Total	*55*	*12*	*165*	*19*
Reception very much better than investigator would expect to have received had he been alone, but under otherwise similar circumstances	6	19	63	9
Reception different only to extent of heightened curiosity, such as investigator might have incurred were he alone but dressed in manner unconventional to region yet not incongruous	3	22	76	6
Reception "normal"	2	9	21	3
Reception perceptibly hesitant and not to be explained on other than "racial" grounds	1	3	4	1
Reception definitely, though temporarily, embarrassing	0	1	1	0
Not accepted	0	1	0	0

*When the investigator was not present at the inception of the situation the judgments were based upon what transpired after he joined the Chinese. Since intimately acquainted with them it is probable that errors in judgment were no more frequent under these conditions than when he was able to witness the inception as well as results of the situation.

in his neighborhood we have a verbal response to a symbolic situation which reflects the "attitudes" which would become operative in an actual situation. But there is no need to ask such a question of the true "Southern Gentleman." We knew it all the time. I am inclined to think that in most instances where the questionnaire does reveal non-symbolic attitudes the case is much the same. It is only when we cannot easily observe what people do in certain types of situations that the questionnaire is resorted to. But it is just here that the danger in the questionnaire technique arises. If Mr. A adjusts himself to Mr. B in a specified way we can deduce from his behavior that he has a certain "attitude" towards Mr. B and, perhaps, all of

Mr. B's class. But if no such overt adjustment is made it is impossible to discover what A's adjustment would be should the situation arise. A questionnaire will reveal what Mr. A writes or says when confronted with a certain combination of words. But not what he will do when he meets Mr. B. Mr. B is a great deal more than a series of words. He is a man and he acts. His action is not necessarily what Mr. A "imagines" it will be when he reacts verbally to the symbol "Mr. B."

No doubt a considerable part of the data which the social scientist deals with can be obtained by the questionnaire method. The census reports are based upon verbal questionnaires and I do not doubt their basic integrity. If we wish to know how many children a man has, his income, the size of his home, his age, and the condition of his parents, we can reasonably ask him. These things he has frequently and conventionally converted into verbal responses. He is competent to report upon them, and will do so accurately, unless indeed he wishes to do otherwise. A careful investigator could no doubt even find out by verbal means whether the man fights with his wife (frequently, infrequently, or not at all), though the neighbors would be a more reliable source. But we should not expect to obtain by the questionnaire method his "anticipatory set or tendency" to action should his wife pack up and go home to Mother, should Elder Son get into trouble with the neighbor's daughter, the President assume the status of a dictator, the Japanese take over the rest of China, or a Chinese gentleman come to pay a social call.

Only a verbal reaction to an entirely symbolic situation can be secured by the questionnaire. It may indicate what the responder would actually do when confronted with the situation symbolized in the question, but there is no assurance that it will. And so to call the response a reflection of a "social attitude" is to entirely disregard the definition commonly given for the phrase "attitude." If social attitudes are to be conceptualized as partially integrated habit sets which will become operative under specific circumstances and lead to a particular pattern of adjustment they must, in the main, be derived from a study of humans behaving in actual social situations. They must not be imputed on the basis of questionnaire data.

The questionnaire is cheap, easy, and mechanical. The study of human behavior is time consuming, intellectually fatiguing, and depends for its success upon the ability of the investigator. The former method gives quantitative results, the latter mainly qualitative. Quantitative measurements arc quantitatively accurate; qualitative evaluations are always subject to the errors of human judgment. Yet it would seem far more worth while to make a shrewd guess regarding that which is essential than to accurately measure that which is likely to prove quite irrelevant.

NOTES

1. See Daniel D. Droba, "Topical Summaries of Current Literature," *The American Journal of Sociology,* 1934, p. 513.
2. "Race Prejudice: France and England," *Social Forces,* September 1928, pp. 102–111.
3. The results of this study have been withheld until the present time out of consideration for their feelings.

CRITICAL THINKING QUESTIONS

1. A central thesis of the LaPiere article was that the method of directly asking people about their attitudes has certain limitations in terms of accuracy and consistency. What are these limitations? How could they be overcome, other than in the ways suggested by the author?
2. LaPiere maintained that there is little consistency between responses to attitude surveys and actual behavior. If that is the case, then what is the value (if any) of the multitude of attitude surveys that are regularly administered in the United States? Support your position.
3. Did the study involve any ethical issues? For example, what do you think about the fact that the author did not tell his Chinese friends that they were part of a study he was conducting? Are there any other ethical considerations? Explain your answers.
4. The article ended by making a distinction between *quantitative results,* such as those obtained by questionnaires, and *qualitative results,* such as those obtained by the author in his visits to the establishments. LaPiere obviously favors qualitative methods, arguing that although they are prone to errors of human judgment, such methods are preferred because it is better to "make a shrewd guess regarding what is essential than to accurately measure that which is likely quite irrelevant." Are the results of attitude questionnaires "likely quite irrelevant"? Why or why not?

5. If you were to conduct the study, what methodological improvements would you make to reduce the subjectivity of the measures?
6. A major conclusion of the study was that responses to hypothetical questions do not necessarily predict actual behavior. Is this evidence for a lack of consistency between attitudes and behavior? In answering this, think of the specific methodology that was employed. Was there anything wrong with it, given the conclusions that were drawn? What methodology could be used to more directly assess the consistency between attitudes and behavior? Explain your answers.
7. LaPiere made the observation that factors such as clothing, cleanliness, and smiles were more important in determining whether the couple was served than was skin color. Design a study that would experimentally test this observation.

ADDITIONAL RELATED READINGS

Argyrides, M., Downey, J. L., & Downey, J. L. (2004). September 11: Immediate and long term effects on measures of aggression, prejudice, and person perception. *North American Journal of Psychology, 6*(1), 175–188.

DeSteno, D., Dasgupta, N., Bartlett, M. Y., & Cajdric, A. Prejudice from thin air: The effect of emotion on automatic intergroup attitudes. *Psychological Science, 15*(5), 319–324.

ARTICLE 18 _____

Why are people prejudiced? Any social psychology text will list a number of reasons that account for prejudiced attitudes and discriminatory behaviors. For example, social learning approaches will focus on the attitudes a person learns in his or her environment, particularly at home, to account for prejudice. The realistic group conflict approach will focus on the competition between groups for scarce resources as a cause of prejudice. Yet other approaches will try to identify a personality type that might be related to prejudice—for instance, the authoritarian personality.

Over the past several decades, the amount of overtly discriminatory behavior based on race has decreased significantly in the United States. This may be due to changes in laws that make certain previously accepted forms of discrimination illegal. It also may be due to changes in attitudes and beliefs regarding prejudice. Regardless, one thing that is certain is that in most quarters today, the expression of overt racism is not nearly as common as it might have been a half-century ago. But does that mean that racial prejudice has indeed decreased? Or has it perhaps just become more subtle?

In answering these questions, it may be useful to distinguish between *explicit* and *implicit* racial prejudice. *Explicit* racial prejudice refers to overt expressions of prejudice, of which we are consciously aware. Saying that you would never live next door to a person of a certain race is an example of explicit racial prejudice. *Implicit* racial prejudice, on the other hand, comprises more subtle forms of prejudice, which typically operate out of conscious awareness. Taking longer to respond to a member of another race and unconsciously associating a certain race with undesirable characteristics are both examples of implicit racial prejudice. A crucial distinction between explicit and implicit racial prejudice is that the former can be consciously controlled (and hence is subject to social desirability), whereas the latter is very difficult to control.

The following article by Wade C. Rowatt and Lewis M. Franklin examines how implicit racial prejudice may be related to some dimensions of religiosity. The study also is of interest for the implications that it makes for reducing prejudice.

Christian Orthodoxy, Religious Fundamentalism, and Right-Wing Authoritarianism as Predictors of Implicit Racial Prejudice

■ Wade C. Rowatt and Lewis M. Franklin

This study examined associations between some dimensions of religiosity and implicit racial prejudice. Implicit racial prejudice was measured with S. D. Farnham's (1998) Implicit Association Test (IAT), a software program that records reaction time as participants categorize names (of Blacks and Whites) and adjectives (pleasant or unpleasant). Participants also completed self-report measures of religious fundamentalism, Christian orthodoxy,

From "Christian Orthodoxy, Religious Fundamentalism, and Right-Wing Authoritarianism as Predictors of Implicit Racial Prejudice," by W. C. Rowatt and L. M. Franklin, 2003, *The International Journal for the Psychology of Religion, 14*(2), pp. 125–138. Copyright 2003 by Lawrence Erlbaum Associates, Inc. Reprinted with permission.

religious orientations (i.e., intrinsic, extrinsic, quest), right-wing authoritarianism, and social desirability. White college students took significantly longer to categorize names and adjectives in one IAT condition (White–unpleasant, Black–pleasant) than in a second IAT condition (White–pleasant, Black–unpleasant), the race-IAT effect. A multiple regression analysis revealed that right-wing authoritarianism was positively associated with the race-IAT effect ($\beta = .31$), Christian orthodoxy was negatively related ($\beta = -.26$), and religious fundamentalism ($\beta = .02$) and social desirability ($\beta = .08$) were less related to this measure of implicit racial prejudice. Intrinsic, extrinsic, and quest religious orientations did not account for unique variation in implicit racial prejudice. Implications of these findings for reducing prejudice are discussed.

Overt acts of racial prejudice and discrimination in the United States appear to have declined over the past 50 years. However, some subtle, covert, implicit forms of racial prejudice still remain (Jones, 2002). The primary purpose of the current study was to determine the amount of variation in implicit racial attitudes attributable to religious dimensions of the self after controlling for some variables known to account for variation in explicit racial attitudes (e.g., right-wing authoritarianism, social desirability).

DISTINCTIONS BETWEEN EXPLICIT AND IMPLICIT ATTITUDES

Before we review some of the literature on religion and prejudice, it is important to emphasize the difference between explicit and implicit psychological attitudes (Dovidio, Kawakami, & Beach, 2001). *Explicit attitudes* are evaluative reactions that operate on a conscious level, similar to explicit memories (Tulving, 1985), and are traditionally measured with self-report scales (Dovidio et al., 2001; Himmelfarb, 1993). *Implicit attitudes,* on the other hand, operate largely outside of conscious awareness (see Banaji, Lemm, & Carpenter, 2001), like implicit memories (Roediger, 1990), and are typically measured using response latency (Greenwald, McGhee, & Schwartz, 1998); evaluative priming (Wittenbrink, Judd, & Park, 1997); or unobtrusive measures of helping behavior,

aggression, or nonverbal communication (see Crosby, Bromley, & Saxe, 1980). We emphasize these two levels of psychological attitudes because the associations between dimensions of religiosity and explicit, self-reported racial attitudes are very well-documented (e.g., Allport & Ross, 1967; Batson, Schoenrade, & Ventis, 1993; Duck & Hunsberger, 1999; Laythe, Finkel, & Kirkpatrick, 2001). To our knowledge, however, this is one of the first experiments to investigate possible associations between dimensions of religiosity and implicit racial attitudes.

RELIGION AND RACIAL ATTITUDES

Most faith traditions teach unconditional acceptance of and compassion toward others (e.g., love your neighbor as yourself), not prejudice and discrimination. Theoretically, as incorporation of religious teachings into everyday life increases, prejudicial attitudes and discriminatory behaviors should decrease. However, the relationship between a person's religion and racial prejudice is not this simple. In fact, early research on religion and prejudice found that church members were more racially prejudiced than nonmembers (for narrative reviews, see Batson et al., 1993, Table 9.2; Gorsuch & Aleshire, 1974, Table 1). Complicating matters somewhat is the fact that there is some evidence that the association between frequency of religious involvement and self-reported racial prejudice is more curvilinear than linear (with moderately involved persons being more racially prejudiced than religiously noninvolved or highly involved persons; see Struening, 1963, Figure 4; Gorsuch & Aleshire, 1974, Table 4).

Whereas people have various motives for attending religious services, church membership and frequency of religious involvement are not the most reliable indicators of religious motivation. Some people who appear to internalize Christian teachings, for example, have other personal or social motives for appearing to be religiously devout. According to Donahue's (1985) meta-analysis of data from 1,891 participants, extrinsic religious orientation correlated positively with various measures of explicit racial prejudice ($r = .34$), but intrinsic religious orientation did not ($r = -.05$). The quest orientation toward religion correlated negatively with self-report and behavioral measures of prejudice

(Batson, Flink, Schoenrade, Fultz, & Pych, 1986; Batson, Naifeh, & Pate, 1978).

However, because racial attitudes are socially sensitive and propensity to respond desirably varies, a person's explicit self-report could be considerably different from his or her implicit thoughts or feelings. As such, dimensions of religiosity might correlate differently with measures of explicit racial prejudice (that are self-reported) than with measures of implicit racial prejudice that are less vulnerable to desirable responding. When racial prejudice was measured indirectly as the discrepancy between preference to be interviewed by a White or Black interviewer, for example, intrinsic religious orientation was not significantly correlated with racial prejudice (Batson et al., 1978). An experiment that used an indirect measure of prejudice—selecting a Black or White person to sit next to—revealed similar patterns (Batson et al., 1986). This led Batson et al. (1986) to conclude that the intrinsic component of religiosity was more directly related to the need to appear unprejudiced than to a true reduction in prejudice (see Gorsuch, 1988, pp. 214–215, for an alternative interpretation).

RIGHT-WING AUTHORITARIANISM (RWA), RELIGIOUS FUNDAMENTALISM (RF), AND CHRISTIAN ORTHODOXY (CO)

Associations between RWA, RF, CO, and explicit self-reported racial prejudice have also been examined. Across studies, right-wing authoritarianism was a strong, positive correlate of self-reported racial prejudice (Altemeyer & Hunsberger, 1992; Hunsberger, 1995; Laythe, Finkel, Bringle, & Kirkpatrick, 2002; Laythe et al., 2001; Wylie & Forest, 1992). Religious fundamentalism has also been found to correlate positively with self-reported racial prejudice (Altemeyer & Hunsberger, 1992; Laythe et al., 2002; Wylie & Forest, 1992) and other discriminatory attitudes toward Blacks (Kirkpatrick, 1993). However, RWA, RF, and CO were strongly and positively intercorrelated in these studies and thus confounded. For example, some of the variance in racial prejudice attributed to RF could have been due to RWA or CO. When RWA and CO were simultaneously controlled using multiple regression analyses, RF was unrelated to self-

reported racial prejudice; however, RWA remained positively related to self-reported racial prejudice and CO was negatively related to self-reported racial prejudice (Laythe et al., 2002). We expected to find a similar pattern when using RWA, CO, and RF to predict a response-latency measure of implicit racial attitude that is more resistant to desirable responding than self-report prejudice scales. For reasons discussed later, we selected the Implicit Association Test (IAT) to operationalize implicit racial prejudice.

MEASURING IMPLICIT PREJUDICE: THE IAT

The IAT (Greenwald et al., 1998) is a relatively new measure of implicit social cognition that, to date, has not been used in religiosity–prejudice research. In general, IATs indirectly measure strengths of associations between different concepts as participants sort words (and sometimes pictures) into categories representing those concepts. Several IATs have been developed to measure self-esteem and implicit prejudices based on a variety of personal characteristics (e.g., age, gender, sexual orientation, race, etc.). One assumption underlying race IATs is that categorization tasks are easier for Whites when two concepts that share a response are positively associated (e.g., White and good) than when the concepts are negatively associated (e.g., White and bad) or weakly associated (see Greenwald et al., 2002, for a review of IAT theory).

We used IAT software developed by Farnham (1998) to measure implicit racial prejudice (see the Method section). In the critical trials of this test, participants sorted terms representing four concepts (White names, Black names, unpleasant words, and pleasant words) into just two response categories (e.g., White–unpleasant, Black–pleasant; see the Method section). Reaction times to categorize the names and adjectives were recorded. Implicitly prejudiced White participants, who might not self-report being racially prejudiced, usually find the IAT to be more difficult, and thus have increased response latencies, when the two sorting categories are more incongruent with respect to their implicit prejudices (i.e., White–unpleasant, Black–pleasant) than when the two sorting categories are more congruent (i.e., White–pleasant, Black–unpleasant). We expected to replicate the *race-IAT effect:* the behavioral tendency for people to more quickly categorize names and adjectives into congruent categories than incongruent categories (Greenwald et al.,1998).

Several psychometric properties of the IAT make it a useful measure for religion–prejudice research. IATs are internally consistent, temporally reliable, and valid (Cunningham, Preacher, & Banaji, 2001; Devine, 2001; Dovidio et al., 2001; Gawronski, 2002). The magnitude of the race-IAT effect (i.e., implicit racial prejudice correlates with discriminatory behavior (McConnell & Leibold, 2001). For example, increases in White college students' implicit racial prejudice (measured with an IAT) were associated with more negative behavioral interactions (e.g., less speaking time, less smiling, more speech errors, more speech hesitation) with a Black research assistant than with a White research assistant (McConnell & Leibold, 2001). Fairly high "immunity" to desirable responding is another advantage of the IAT, compared with explicit self-report measures and some behavioral indexes of racial prejudice. That is, some people who underestimate their racial prejudice on self-report scales or who fake pleasant social interactions cannot easily manipulate the time it takes to categorize pleasant and unpleasant terms and names of Whites or Blacks during an IAT. Even if a few participants do categorize terms in the IAT too quickly (indicating being in a hurry to finish) or too slowly (indicating inattentiveness or not understanding the instructions), the participants with outlying reaction times can be identified and removed.

THEORY AND PREDICTIONS

Our general theory is that authentic internalization of Christian beliefs is associated with reduced implicit racial prejudice. That is, as people internalize Christian beliefs (e.g., love your neighbor as yourself; do unto others as you would have them do unto you), their implicit discriminatory attitudes should decrease. However, CO could be confounded with restrictive religious ideology (e.g., RF) or beliefs that others should submit to authority (e.g., RWA). As such, a measure of RF is important to include to control for the possibility that fundamental religious ideology (regardless of creed) mediates the association

between Christian orthodoxy and implicit racial prejudice. A measure of RWA is important to include so that covariation between CO and implicit racial prejudice due to unquestioning obedience to authority can also be statistically removed. In addition, self-report measures (of religiosity, RWA, and racial prejudice) are susceptible to desirable responding or faking. As such, a measure of socially desirable responding is important to include so that the variation due to this propensity can be statistically controlled.

On the basis of the pattern of associations between measures of religiousness and explicit self-reported racial prejudice described above (e.g., Laythe et al., 2002), we predicted that when regressed on implicit racial prejudice, RWA would be positively associated with the IAT effect, CO would be negatively associated with the IAT effect, and RF would be unassociated with the IAT effect. In other words, CO should correlate negatively with implicit racial prejudice and RWA should correlate positively with implicit racial prejudice when we control for RF and social desirability.

METHOD

Participants

Undergraduates (N = 158; mean age = 19.5 years) in introductory psychology classes at Baylor University participated in this study for extra credit.[1] This sample was somewhat diverse (111 Caucasians, 16 Hispanics, 13 African Americans, 15 Asian American/Pacific Islanders, and 3 participants who specified another ethnicity). As we sought to estimate White persons' implicit prejudice toward Black persons, only data from Caucasians (74 women, 35 men, 2 participants who did not specify a sex) were analyzed and are presented. Of the White participants, 70% were Protestant, 8% were Catholic, and 22% identified "other" as their religious affiliation. The White participants were moderately religious (7% not religious, 18% slightly religious, 41% moderately religious, and 34% very religious).

Procedure

A Microsoft Windows-based software program, Farnham's (1998) IAT (Version 2.3), was used to measure implicit racial prejudice. To complete Farnham's IAT, each participant sat at a computer terminal and read instructions on the monitor. Participants were instructed to press the *a* key (on the left of a standard keyboard), if the name or adjective that appeared on the screen represented the category on the left of the screen and the *5* key on the right number pad if the name or adjective represented the category shown on the right of the screen. After reading the instructions, each participant practiced categorizing the names and adjectives that appeared in a white rectangle in the middle of a light gray box on the screen.[2] A total of seven blocks of trials were conducted with each participant. Blocks 1, 2, 3, 5, and 6 were practice blocks with 20 trials per block. Reaction times were not recorded during practice blocks. Two data-collection blocks, with 40 trials per block, were conducted with each participant (Blocks 4 and 7). For each IAT data-collection block we counterbalanced whether the congruent condition (left: White–pleasant; right: Black–unpleasant) or incongruent condition (left: Black–pleasant; right: White–unpleasant) was encountered first. During practice and data-collection blocks, items from each category pair were selected randomly and without replacement so that all items were used only once before any items were reused. Each stimulus item was displayed until a correct response was made. The next stimulus item followed after a 150-ms intertrial interval. During data-collection blocks, the computer recorded elapsed time between the presentation of each stimulus word and the occurrence of the correct keyboard response.

IAT data for analyses were obtained from data-collection blocks 4 and 7 (i.e., the congruent and incongruent conditions). Consistent with procedures described by Greenwald et al. (1998), (a) the first two trials of each data-collection block were dropped because of their typically lengthened latencies, (b) data from participants with greater than 25% error rates for trials 4 and 7 ($n = 8$) were omitted, (c) latencies less than 300 ms were recoded to 300 ms and latencies greater than 3,000 ms were recoded to 3,000 ms, and (d) a logarithmic transformation was used to normalize the distribution of latencies. The race-IAT effect was computed by subtracting the mean log-latency to categorize terms in the congruent condition from the mean log-latency to categorize terms in the incongru-

ent condition. Positive values of the race-IAT effect were interpreted to be evidence of implicit racial prejudice.

Self-Report Measures of Religiosity, RWA, and Social Desirability

Each participant completed the following self-report measures:

1. The Religious Fundamentalism Scale (Altemeyer & Hunsberger, 1992) measures

the belief that there is one set of religious teachings that clearly contains the fundamental, basic, intrinsic, essential, inerrant truth about human and deity; that this essential truth is fundamentally opposed by forces of evil which must be vigorously fought; that this truth must be followed today according to the fundamental, unchangeable practices of the past; and that those who believe and follow these teachings have a special relationship with the deity. (Altemeyer & Hunsberger, 1992, p. 118)

(1 = *very strongly disagree,* 9 = *very strongly agree;* example reverse-keyed item: "There is no body of teachings, or set of scriptures, which is completely without error.").

2. The Right-Wing Authoritarianism Scale (see Altemeyer & Hunsberger, 1992) taps self-reported authoritarian submission, authoritarian aggression, and conventionalism (1 = *very strongly disagree,* 9 = *very strongly agree;* example item: "Our country will be destroyed someday if we do not smash the perversions eating away at our moral fibers and traditional beliefs").

3. The Christian Orthodoxy Scale—Short Form (Hunsberger, 1989) includes six items that assess the degree to which a person accepts Christian beliefs (1 = *strongly disagree,* 7 = *strongly agree;* example item: "Jesus was crucified, died, and was buried, but on the third day He arose from the dead").

4. Measures of intrinsic, extrinsic, and quest religious orientations (Allport & Ross, 1967; Batson et al., 1993) were administered to assess religion as an end in and of itself (intrinsic; 1 = *strongly disagree,* 5 = *strongly agree*); religion as a means to other personal or social ends (extrinsic; 1 = *strongly disagree,* 5 = *strongly agree*); and religious doubting, openness to religious

change, and existential questioning (quest; 1 = *very strongly disagree*, 9 = *very strongly agree*).

5. The Modern Racism Scale (McConahay, Hardee, & Batts, 1981) taps self-reported covert racial attitudes (1 = *strongly disagree*, 7 = *strongly agree;* example item: "Blacks have more influence upon school desegregation plans than they ought to have").

6. The Balanced Inventory of Desirable Responding (BIDR; Paulhus & Reid, 1991) measures Impression Management (1 = *strongly disagree*, 7 = *strongly agree;* example reverse-keyed item: "I have some pretty awful habits") and Self-Deceptive Enhancement (example item: "I am a completely rational person").

After completing the self-report scales, participants answered some demographic questions, returned their survey, and were given credit for participation.

RESULTS

The Race-IAT Effect Replicated

A 2 × 2 repeated measures multivariate analysis of variance was computed on the log-latencies to catego-

rize terms. The first independent variable was the congruency of the concepts (i.e., congruent: White–pleasant, Black–unpleasant; or incongruent: Black–pleasant, White–unpleasant). The second independent variable was the order in which the participants encountered the conditions (i.e., incongruent first–congruent second or congruent first–incongruent second). White participants had significantly longer log-latencies when categorizing names and adjectives in the incongruent condition (*M* = 6.94, *SD* = 0.20) than in the congruent condition (*M* = 6.58, *SD* = 0.16), $F(1, 109) = 329.73, p < .0001$, which replicated the race-IAT effect (Greenwald et al., 1998). No differences in the log-latencies were found between participants who completed the congruent condition first (*M* = 6.56) or second (*M* = 6.62) or the incongruent condition first (*M* = 6.94) or second (*M* = 6.94), $F(1, 109) < 1$, *ns.* Likewise, no interaction was found between order and the nature of the congruency, $F(2, 109) = 2.54, p = .11$.

The self-report measures had satisfactory internal consistency (see the Cronbach's alphas in Table 1), with the exception of the BIDR self-deception sub-

TABLE 1 / Descriptive Statistics and Zero-Order Intercorrelations between Measures of Religiosity, Right-Wing Authoritarianism, Socially Desirable Responding, and Implicit Racial Prejudice among White College Students

Variable	1	2	3	4	5	6	7	8	9	10	11	12	*M*	*SD*	α
1. Religious fundamentalism	—												5.42	1.42	.89
2. Christian orthodoxy	.58												6.39	0.98	.89
3. Intrinsic religious orientation	.70	.55											3.88	0.77	.87
4. Extrinsic religious orientation	−.56	−.46	−.68										2.09	0.59	.79
5. Extrinsic-personal religious orientation	−.35	−.30	−.42	.81									2.49	0.80	.58
6. Extrinsic-social religious orientation	−.18	−.21	−.24	.67	.44								2.00	0.72	.59
7. Quest religious orientation	−.39	−.24	−.21	.24	.15	.12							4.85	1.12	.73
8. Right-wing authoritarianism	.71	.50	.53	−.37	−.27	.03	−.31						5.41	0.92	.87
9. BIDR–impression management	.15	.29	.35	−.39	−.22	−.21	−.03	.07					0.22	0.17	.76
10. BIDR–self-deceptive enhancement	.01	.11	.15	−.16	−.08	−.11	.04	.06	.58				0.26	0.14	.62
11. Modern racism	.13	.04	.05	.20	.09	.37	−.05	.31	−.13	.00			3.12	1.03	.48
12. Race-IAT effect (log-latency)	.10	−.08	.06	.04	.06	.07	−.15	.20	.03	−.02	.15	—	0.36	0.17	—

Notes: BIDR = Balanced Inventory of Desirable Responding; IAT = Implicit Association Test; *n* = 111.
For *r* > .19, *p* < .05; for *r* > .24, *p* < .01; for *r* > .35, *p* < .001.

scale (α = .62) and the modern racism subscale (α = .48). Because the BIDR self-deception subscale was less internally consistent, we used the BIDR–Impression Management subscale (α = .76) to control for desirable responding in later analyses. We did not have an alternate measure of explicit racial prejudice with adequate internal consistency. As such, we recommend caution when interpreting the few results that involve the modern racism subscale in this study.

Predictors of Implicit Racial Prejudice

The race-IAT effect was not correlated with impression management propensity or self-reported modern racism (see Table 1). When additional zero-order correlations were examined, self-report measures of RF and CO appeared to account for minimal variation in the race-IAT effect (see Table 1). However, CO was positively correlated with impression management propensity (r = .29, p < .01). RF (r = .71, p < .001) and CO (r = .58, p < .001) were strongly correlated with RWA.

A multiple regression analysis was conducted to simultaneously control for the influence of RWA, RF, CO, and social desirability on the race-IAT effect (see Table 2). When entered in the regression analysis as simultaneous predictors, RWA was positively associated with the race-IAT effect (β = .31, p < .05), CO was negatively correlated with the race-IAT effect (β = −.26, p < .05). and RF (β = .02) and social desirability (β = .08) were uncorrelated with the race-IAT effect (R = .29). In other words, even though RWA and CO were positively correlated (r = .50, p < .001), RWA was positively correlated with implicit racial prejudice and CO was negatively correlated with implicit racial prejudice when we controlled for the other variables in the regression equation.

Religious orientations were not correlated with the race-IAT effect (r = .06; $r_{\text{extrinsic-social}}$ = .07; $r_{\text{extrinsic-personal}}$ = .06; r_{quest} = −.15). When simultaneously regressed on the race-IAT effect, intrinsic (β = .07), extrinsic–social (β = .07), extrinsic–personal (β = .09), and quest (β = −.16) did not account for unique variation when we controlled for the other orientations and impression management (β = .03, R = .20). Because of low internal consistency, we did not use the modern racism subscale as a dependent variable in regression analyses.

TABLE 2 / Multiple Regression of the Race–Implicit Association Test Effect on Measures of Religiosity, Right-Wing Authoritarianism, and Impression Management

Independent Variables	β	t	p
Christian orthodoxy	−.26	−2.15	.03
Right-wing authoritarianism	.31	2.22	.03
Religious fundamentalism	.02	0.13	.90
BIDR-impression management	.08	0.76	.45

Note: BIDR = Balanced Inventory of Desirable Responding.

DISCUSSION

Although there are several existing investigations of religion and prejudice, this is the first to our knowledge that examines associations between dimensions of religiosity and the race-IAT effect, a reliable estimate of implicit racial prejudice. At first glance, RF, CO, and RWA did not appear to correlate with this measure of implicit racial prejudice. However, measures of RF, CO, and RWA are positively correlated and thus confounded. In the current study, when we simultaneously controlled for each variable using a multiple regression analysis, RWA correlated positively with implicit racial prejudice, CO correlated negatively with implicit racial prejudice, and RF and social desirability were not significantly associated with implicit racial prejudice. This pattern is most consistent with Laythe et al.'s (2002) findings using a self-report measure of racial prejudice but is also consistent with several studies showing that RWA positively correlates with self-reported racial prejudice (e.g., Altemeyer & Hunsberger, 1992; Hunsberger, 1995). The pattern is also consistent with research showing that people who internalize Christian teachings are generally less racially prejudiced than people who do not internalize Christian teachings (Batson et al., 1993). Our findings are somewhat unique, however, because the IAT is probably more resistant to desirable responding than are explicit self-report measures and more direct than covert behavioral measures, (e.g., choosing not to sit next to a person with a different skin color).

The correspondence between implicit and explicit prejudice in this study was low. That is, response latency on the race-IAT and modern racism scores correlate weakly (r = .15), which is consistent with two other published studies (Dasgupta, McGhee, Greenwald, & Banaji, 2000, $r = -.05$; Greenwald et al., 1998, $r = .07$). Dovidio et al. (2001), in contrast, reported a modest meta-analytic effect size between implicit and explicit racial prejudice ($r = .24$) when additional measures of both constructs were included. The small correlation between the race-IAT effect and self-reported modern racism in our study should be interpreted with caution, however, as the modern racism subscale had low internal consistency ($\alpha = .48$).

The most important finding of this study, in our estimation, is that as agreement with orthodox Christian beliefs increases, implicit racial prejudice decreases when we control for the moderate positive influence of RWA on implicit racial prejudice and other important constructs (i.e., RF and social desirability). This finding has some potential implications for prejudice reduction. Learning more about Christian beliefs that engender tolerance and acceptance of others (e.g., love your neighbor as yourself; do unto others as you would have them do unto you) could reduce some implicit prejudices and engender more positive attitudes between diverse groups. Implicit prejudice might also be reduced by de-emphasizing or discouraging RWA patterns of thinking and behaving.

People with internal motives for being less racially biased are also more able to regulate their explicit and implicit race biases (Devine, Plant, Amodio, Harmon-Jones, & Vance, 2002). As such, another potential step toward reducing prejudice and discrimination is to encourage people to develop their own autonomous reasons for being less biased. Given the patterns of association between variables in this study, it also seems logical to include some religious-belief and religious-experience variables in models examining the development of implicit prejudices and techniques for reducing the formation of negative attitudes toward others (see Dovidio & Gaertner. 1999). Because some implicit prejudices are learned through direct or vicarious experience, more implicit tolerance or acceptance of others could be produced by vicariously observing models who display genuine universal grace or compassion toward others.

As with most other religion–prejudice and IAT research, however, this study contains some inherent limitations (i.e., self-reported religiosity, use of a con-

venience sample of college students, examination of White–Black attitudes only). As such, replication and extension of the current study are needed. Future research could explore whether other dimensions of religiosity account for unique variation in the race-IAT effect (or other forms of implicit racial prejudice; Cunningham et al., 2001) above and beyond the variance accounted for by RWA and CO. In addition, although the current study focused on racial prejudice, it seems logical to investigate whether RWA, RF, CO, and other dimensions of religiosity account for variation in implicit prejudices toward women or homosexuals (cf. Batson, Eidelman, Higley, & Russell, 2001; Herek, 1987, 2000; Hunsberger, Owusu, & Duck, 1999). Future research could also explore whether religious maturation, learning, or change influence implicit racial attitudes, or other implicit attitudes, in other samples (cf. Hunsberger, 1996). Our hope is that as people learn and mature spiritually they also strive to become more open and inclusive.

We began this article by noting that overt acts of prejudice and discrimination appear to have declined in recent years but that subtle implicit prejudices are alive and well. As the etiology of implicit prejudices become better known and understood, models for implicit-prejudice reduction should be developed and implemented. One step in this process could be simply to make people more aware of the implicit prejudices they hold. Another integral step will likely involve allowing people to develop their own autonomous reasons for being less biased (Devine et al., 2002). Given the patterns in this study, it is possible that implicit prejudices could be reduced by autonomously internalizing inclusive Christian teachings and minimizing authoritarian processes.

REFERENCES

Allport, G. W., & Ross, J. M. (1967). Personal religious orientation and prejudice. *Journal of Personality and Social Psychology, 5,* 432–443.

Altemeyer, B., & Hunsberger, B. (1992). Authoritarianism, religious fundamentalism, quest, and prejudice. *The International Journal for the Psychology of Religion, 2,* 113–133.

Banaji, M. R., Lemm, K. M., & Carpenter, S. J. (2001). The social unconscious. In A. Tesser & N. Schwarz (Eds.), *Blackwell handbook of social psychology: Intraindividual processes* (pp. 134–158). Malden, MA: Blackwell.

Batson, C. D., Eidelman, S. H., Higley, S. L., & Russell, S. A. (2001). "And who is thy neighbor?" II. Quest religion as a source of universal compassion. *Journal for the Scientific Study of Religion, 40,* 39–50.

Batson, C. D., Flink, C. H., Schoenrade, P., Fultz, J., & Pych, V. (1986). Religious orientation and overt versus covert racial prejudice. *Journal of Personality and Social Psychology, 50,* 175–181.

Batson, C. D., Naifch, S. J., & Pate, S. (1978). Social desirability, religious orientation, and racial prejudice. *Journal for the Scientific Study of Religion, 17,* 31–41.

Batson, C. D., Schoenrade, P., & Ventis, W. L. (1993). *Religion and the individual: A social-psychological perspective.* New York: Oxford University Press.

Crosby, F., Bromley, S., & Saxe, L. (1980). Recent unobtrusive studies of Black and White discrimination and prejudice: A literature review. *Journal of Personality and Social Psychology, 87,* 546–563.

Cunningham, W. A., Preacher, K. J., & Banaji, M. R. (2001). Implicit attitude measures: Consistency, stability, and convergent validity. *Psychological Science, 12,* 163–170.

Dasgupta, N., McGhee, D. E., Greenwald, A. G., & Banaji, M. R. (2000). Automatic preference for White Americans: Eliminating the familiarity explanation. *Journal of Experimental Social Psychology, 36,* 316–328.

Devine, P. G. (2001). Implicit prejudice and stereotyping: How automatic are they?: Introduction to the special section. *Journal of Personality and Social Psychology, 81,* 757–759.

Devine, P. G., Plant, E. A., Amodio, D. M., Harmon-Jones, E., & Vance, S. L. (2002). The regulation of explicit and implicit race bias. The role of motivations to respond without prejudice. *Journal of Personality and Social Psychology, 82,* 835–848.

Donahue, M. J. (1985). Intrinsic and extrinsic religiousness: Review and meta analysis. *Journal of Personality and Social Psychology, 48,* 400–419.

Dovidio, J. F., & Gaertner, S. L. (1999). Reducing prejudice: Combating intergroup biases. *Current Directions in Psychological Science, 8,* 101–105.

Dovidio, J. F., Kawakami, K., & Beach, K. R. (2001). Implicit and explicit attitudes: Examination between measures of intergroup bias. In R. Brown & S. Gaertner (Eds.), *Blackwell handbook of social psychology: Intergroup processes* (pp. 175–197). Malden, MA: Blackwell.

Duck, R. J., & Hunsberger, B. (1999). Religious orientation and prejudice: The role of religious proscription, right-wing authoritarianism, and social desirability. *The International Journal for the Psychology of Religion, 9,* 157–179.

Farnham, S. D. (1998). FIAT for Windows (Version 2.3) [Computer software]. Seattle, WA.

Gawronski, B. (2002). What does the Implicit Association Test measure? A test of the convergent and discriminant validity of prejudice-related IATs. *Experimental Psychology, 49,* 171–180.

Gorsuch, R. L. (1988). Psychology of religion. *Annual Review of Psychology, 39,* 201–221.

Gorsuch, R. L., & Aleshire, D. (1974). Christian faith and ethnic prejudice: A review and interpretation of research. *Journal for the Scientific Study of Religion, 13,* 281–307.

Greenwald, A. G., Banaji, M. R., Rudman, L. A., Farnham, S. D., Nosek, B. A., & Mellott, D. S. (2002). A unified theory of implicit attitudes, stereotypes, self-esteem, and self-concept. *Psychological Review, 109,* 3–25.

Greenwald, A. G., McGhee, D. E., & Schwartz, J. L. K. (1998). Measuring individual differences in implicit cognition: The Implicit Association Test. *Journal of Personality and Social Psychology, 74,* 1464–1480.

Herek, G. M. (1987). Religious orientation and prejudice: A comparison of racial and sexual attitudes. *Personality and Social Psychology Bulletin, 13,* 34–44.

Herek, G. M. (2000). The psychology of sexual prejudice. *Current Directions in Psychological Science, 9,* 19–22.

Himmelfarb, S. (1993). The measurement of attitudes. In A. Eagly & S. Chaiken (Eds.), *The psychology of attitudes* (pp. 23–87). Fort Worth, TX: Harcourt Brace Jovanovich.

Hunsberger, B. (1989). A short version of the Christian orthodoxy scale. *Journal for the Scientific Study of Religion, 28,* 360–365.

Hunsberger, B. (1995). Religion and prejudice: The role of religious fundamentalism, quest, and right-wing authoritariansim. *Journal of Social Issues, 51,* 113–129.

Hunsberger, B. (1996). Religious fundamentalism, right-wing authoritarianism, and hostility toward homosexuals in non-Christian religious groups. *The International Journal for the Psychology of Religion, 6,* 39–49.

Hunsberger, B., Owusu, V., & Duck, R. (1999). Religion and prejudice in Ghana and Canada: Religious fundamentalism, right-wing authoritarianism, and attitudes toward homosexuals and women. *The International Journal for the Psychology of Religion, 9,* 181–194.

Jones, M. (2002). *The social psychology of prejudice.* Upper Saddle River, NJ: Prentice Hall.

Kirkpatrick, L. A. (1993). Fundamentalism, Christian orthodoxy, and intrinsic religious orientation as predictors of discriminatory attitudes. *Journal for the Scientific Study of Religion, 32,* 256–268.

Laythe, B., Finkel, D. G., Bringle, R. G., & Kirkpatrick, L. A. (2002). Religious fundamentalism as a predictor of prejudice: A two-component model. *Journal for the Scientific Study of Religion, 41,* 623–635.

Laythe, B., Finkel, D. G., & Kirkpatrick, L. A. (2001). Predicting prejudice from religious fundamentalism and right-wing authoritarianism. *Journal for the Scientific Study of Religion, 40,* 1–10.

McConahay, J. B., Hardee, B. B., & Batts, V. (1981). Has racism declined in America? It depends on who is asking and what is asked. *Journal of Conflict Resolution, 25,* 563–579.

McConnell, A. R., & Leibold, J. M. (2001). Relations among the Implicit Association Test, discriminatory behavior, and explicit measures of racial prejudice. *Journal of Experimental Social Psychology, 37,* 435–442.

Paulhus, D., & Reid, D. (1991). Enhancement and denial in socially desirable responding. *Journal of Personality and Social Psychology, 60,* 307–317.

Roediger, H. L. (1990). Implicit memory: Retention without remembering. *American Psychologist, 45,* 1043–1056.

Struening, E. L. (1963). Anti-democratic attitudes in Midwest University. In H. H. Remmers (Ed.), *Antidemocratic attitudes in American schools* (pp. 210–258). Evanston, IL: Northwestern University Press.

Tulving, E. (1985). How many memory systems are there? *American Psychologist, 40,* 385–398.

Wittenbrink, B., Judd, C. M., & Park, B. (1997). Evidence for racial prejudice at the implicit level and its relationship with qustionnaire measures. *Journal of Personality and Social Psychology, 72,* 262–274.

Wylie, L., & Forest, J. (1992). Religious fundamentalism, right-wing authoritarianism, and prejudice. *Psychological Reports, 71,* 1291–1298.

ENDNOTES

1. The authors thank Casey Adrian, Kim Harms, Lloyd Lin, Jennifer Ochs, and Tammy Rowatt for their assistance with data collection and entry.

2. The following names and adjectives were used as stimuli in the IAT. White persons' names: *Meredith, Heather, Judy, Katie, Betsy, Peggy, Kristen, Courtney, Stephanie, Sue-Ellen, Megan, Lauren;* Black persons' names: *Latonya, Shavonin, Tashika, Ebony, Jasmine, Temeka, Shereen, Tia, Sharise, Nichelle, LaTisha, Shanise;* pleasant terms: *pleasure, love, smart, joy, happy, wonderful, laughter, peace, luck, honor, gift, healthy, miracle, kind, hope, cheerful, fortune, moral;* unpleasant terms: *horrible, awful, failure, nasty, agony, evil, war, terrible, poison, grief, disaster, hatred, bomb, filth, accident, sorrow, miser.*

CRITICAL THINKING QUESTIONS

1. This article gives a few examples of how implicit prejudices can be expressed and measured (e.g., how you decide whom you will sit next to). In what other ways can implicit prejudices be manifested? Be specific.

2. The present study measured the implicit prejudice of white college students toward blacks. Would a similar or a different pattern of results be obtained if whites of different ages were employed? What if black subjects' implicit prejudice toward whites was assessed? Explain your reasoning.

3. Using the information in this article and your own reasoning, describe how people can be made more aware of the implicit prejudices that they have? How can these implicit prejudices be reduced?

4. This study only looked at Christian beliefs as they pertain to prejudice and of whites' implicit prejudice toward blacks. How might the teachings of other religions be related to prejudice? How might the methodology of this study be applied to targets of prejudice based on something other than race? Explain your answers.

CHAPTER INTEGRATION QUESTIONS ⎯⎯⎯⎯⎯⎯⎯⎯⎯

1. Søren Kirkegaard, existential philosopher, said, "When you label me, you negate me." What does this quote mean to you? Explain.

2. How would you relate the Kirkegaard quote to each of the articles in this chapter?

3. Is there a common theme among the articles to which this quotation also applies? Discuss.

4. Have you ever felt that you were being judged based on having been assigned some label? Explain how this quotation may be applicable to experiences from your life.

Chapter Seven

INTERPERSONAL ATTRACTION

Do "BIRDS OF A FEATHER flock together," or do "Opposites attract"? Both of these folk wisdoms, as contradictory as they are, attempt to answer an age-old question: To whom are we attracted and why?

The research on *interpersonal attraction* has gone in various directions in an attempt to answer this question. *Attraction* here is defined not in the narrow sense of romantic attraction but as attraction to anyone with whom we may associate—a friend, a co-worker, or even a child. Many factors have been identified as important determinants of interpersonal attraction, but perhaps the most widely investigated factor (and the one with the most distressing findings) is that of *physical attractiveness.* Study after study seems to demonstrate that how someone looks is a major determinant of how he or she is viewed and treated by other people.

"Why I Hate Beauty," Article 19, examines how our perceptions of beauty have been markedly influenced by our almost constant exposure to media images of attractiveness. We are all aware of how we are confronted with very attractive people just about any time we look at television, watch a movie, or pick up a magazine. But what is the cumulative impact of our exposure to attractive people? This article explores the possibility that such exposure may not only have an impact on our satisfaction with our current partners but even on the possibility of our divorcing them later on.

Our judgment of physical attractiveness is not just limited to selecting potential partners, however. It may also influence what other characteristics we ascribe to people based solely on their looks. Article 20, "What Is Beautiful Is Good," is a classic demonstration of how positive stereotypes are associated with physical attractiveness. Given the pervasiveness of this physical attractiveness effect, it has real implications for how we deal with and judge others in our daily lives.

Article 21, "'If Only I Were Thin Like Her, Maybe I Could Be Happy Like Her': The Self-Implications of Associating a Thin Female Ideal with Life Success," examines the possible effects of our constant exposure to thin models in American culture. However, the article suggests that the dissatisfaction that arises from such exposure to thin ideals may not be from a desire to be thin as much as a desire to share in the happiness and well-being supposedly associated with being thin.

ARTICLE 19 _____

Imagine that you are living a thousand years ago in just about any part of the world. If you were like the vast majority of people who lived then, you would be living in a small village and your exposure to other people would be pretty much limited to those living nearby. Without a means of rapid transportation, you most likely would not have ventured beyond a few miles of your birthplace during the course of your lifetime. Even if you were among the more adventurous of your group, you only may have traveled a few hundred miles, and even then, you mostly would have encountered people of similar background to your own. Given this situation, in deciding on a mate, to whom are you going to be most attracted? Will the looks of the other person matter? Research suggests that it will. But what will influence what you consider to be *beautiful?*

Our perceptions of what is beautiful are partly innate and partly learned. For example, research indicates that young infants, well before they have been exposed to media or cultural stereotypes of beauty, spend more time gazing at more attractive faces than less attractive faces. *Sociobiology,* the field that examines the biological or evolutionary underpinnings of our social behaviors, suggests that there is a biological reason we are drawn to attractive people. For example, in evolutionary terms, young, attractive women may suggest health and thus fertility to men seeking to carry on their genes. Sociobiological research even indicates that there are some universal factors associated with beauty, such as facial and body symmetry, which transcend specific cultural ideals of attractiveness. So, there may indeed be at least a partial biological reason as to why we have such a strong preference for beautiful people.

But what is considered physically attractive? While there may be some underlying biological reasons we prefer the more attractive to the less attractive, the specifics of what we may be attracted to are based on what we see around us. Take the opening scenario in the first paragraph. Living long ago, you most likely would have been exposed to a very small number of people in your lifetime. Given the diversity of human appearance, only a very small number of the people you may have encountered in your lifetime might be described as very physically attractive. So, what you as an individual might consider to be attractive would be based on the relative ratings of the people you saw around you. In other words, if you only very rarely (if ever) encountered a highly attractive person, you might consider the normal people surrounding you as more attractive than if you were constantly exposed to many highly attractive people.

Fast forward to the present time: The mass media has done many things to us and the world around us. One thing that it certainly has done, however, is to expose us to a large number of highly attractive people in ways that previously were simply not possible. On a daily basis, we are bombarded with images of young, highly attractive people, be it in advertising, the movies, or television shows. Moreover, people around the world get these same images of highly attractive people, over and over again.

Does this constant exposure to images of highly attractive people affect our perceptions of the real people around us? The following article by Michael Levine and Hara Estroff Marano suggests that it does. As the research described by the authors suggests, such constant exposure to mass media images of beauty actually may impact not only our choices of mates but also our satisfaction with our current mates and even the possibility of our divorcing them.

Why I Hate Beauty

■ Michael Levine with Hara Estroff Marano

Poets rave about beauty. Brave men have started wars over beauty. Women the world over strive for it. Scholars devote their lives to deconstructing our impulse to obtain it. Ordinary mortals erect temples to beauty. In just about every way imaginable, the world honors physical beauty. But I hate beauty.

I live in what is likely the beauty capital of the world and have the enviable fortune to work with some of the most beautiful women in it. With their smooth bodies and supple waists, these women are the very picture of youth and attractiveness. Not only are they exemplars of nature's design for detonating desire in men, but they stir yearnings for companionship that date back to ancestral mating dances. Still, beauty is driving me nuts, and although I'm a successful red-blooded American male, divorced and available, it is beauty alone that is keeping me single and lonely.

It is scant solace that science is on my side. I seem to have a confirmed case of the contrast effect. It doesn't make me any happier knowing it's afflicting lots of others too.

As an author of books on marketing, I have long known about the contrast effect. It is a principle of perception whereby the differences between two things are exaggerated depending on the order in which those things ore presented. If you lift a light object and then a heavy object, you will judge the second object heavier than if you had lifted it first or solo.

Psychologists Sara Gutierres, Ph.D., and Douglas Kenrick, Ph.D., both of Arizona State University, demonstrated that the contrast effect operates powerfully in the sphere of person-to-person attraction as well. In a series of studies over the past two decades, they have shown that, more than any of us might suspect, judgments of attractiveness (of ourselves and of others) depend on the situation in which we find ourselves. For example, a woman of average attractiveness seems a lot less attractive than she actually is if a viewer has first seen a highly attractive woman. If a man is talking to a beautiful female at a cocktail party and is then joined by a less attractive one, the second woman will seem relatively unattractive.

The contrast principle also works in reverse. A woman of average attractiveness will seem more attractive than she is if she enters a room of unattractive women. In other words, context counts.

In their very first set of studies, which have been expanded and refined over the years to determine the exact circumstances under which the findings apply and their effects on both men and women, Gutierres and Kenrick asked male college dormitory residents to rate the photo of a potential blind date. (The photos had been previously rated by other males to be of average attractiveness.) If the men were watching an episode of *Charlie's Angels* when shown the photo, the blind date was rated less desirable than she was by males watching a different show. The initial impressions of romantic partners—women who were actually available to them and likely to be interested in them—were so adversely affected that the men didn't even want to bother.

Since these studies, the researchers have found that the contrast effect influences not only our evaluations of strangers but also our views of our own mates. And it sways self-assessments of attractiveness too.

Most recently, Kenrick and Gutierres discovered that women who are surrounded by other attractive women, whether in the flesh, in films or in photographs, rate themselves as less satisfied with their attractiveness—and less desirable as a marriage partner. "If there are a large number of desirable members of one's own sex available, one may regard one's own market value as lower," the researchers reported in the *Personality and Social Psychology Bulletin.*

If you had to pick ground zero for the contrast effect, it would be Hollywood. To feed the film indus-

Reprinted from *Psychology Today,* 2001 (July/August), *34,* 38–44. Reprinted with permission from *Psychology Today* magazine. Copyright © 2001 (Sussex Publishers, Inc.).

try's voracious appetite for attractive faces, it lures especially beautiful women from around the world. And for those who don't arrive already at the pinnacle of perfection, whole industries exist here to render it attainable, to reshape faces and bodies to the prevailing standard of attractiveness.

There's an extraordinarily high concentration of gorgeous females in Los Angeles, and courtesy of the usually balmy weather and lifestyle, they tend to be highly visible—and not just locally. The film and television industries project their images all over the world, not to mention all the supporting media dealing with celebrities and gossip that help keep them professionally viable.

As the head of a public relations agency, I work with these women day and night. You might expect that to make me feel good, as we normally like being around attractive people. But my exposure to extreme beauty is ruining my capacity to love the ordinarily beautiful women of the real world, women who are more likely to meet my needs for deep connection and partnership of the soul.

The contrast effect doesn't apply just to strangers men have yet to meet who might be most suitable for them. In ongoing studies, Gutierres and Kenrick have found that it also affects men's feelings about their current partner. Viewing pictures of attractive women weakens their commitment to their mates. Men rate themselves as being less in love with their partner after looking at *Playboy* centerfolds than they did before seeing the pictures of beautiful women.

This finding is all the more surprising because getting someone aroused normally boosts their attraction to their partner. But seeing beautiful models wiped out whatever effect the men might have experienced from being sexually aroused.

The strange thing is, being bombarded with visions of beautiful women (or for women, socially powerful men) doesn't make us think our partners are less physically attractive. It doesn't change our perception of our partner. Instead, by some sleight of mind, it distorts our idea of the pool of possibilities.

These images make us think there's a huge field of alternatives. It changes our estimate of the number of people who are available to us as potential mates. In changing our sense of the possibilities, it prods us to

believe we could always do better, keeping us continually unsatisfied.

"The perception of the comparison pool is changed," says Gutierres. "In this context our partner doesn't look so great." Adds Kenrick: "You think, 'Yes, my partner's fine—but why do I have to settle for fine when there are just so many great people out there?'" All you have to do is turn on the TV or look at the covers of magazines in the supermarket checkout line to be convinced there are any number of incredibly beautiful women available.

Kenrick puts it in evolutionary perspective. Like us, he says, our ancestors were probably designed to make some estimation of the possible pool of alternatives and some estimation of their own worth relative to the possibilities.

The catch is they just didn't see that many people, and certainly not many beautiful people. They lived in a little village of maybe 30. Even if you counted distant third cousins, our ancestors might have been exposed to a grand total of 500 people in their lifetime. And among those 500, some were old, some were young, but very few were very attractive.

Today anyone who turns on the TV or looks at a magazine can easily see 500 beautiful people in an hour, certainly in an evening. "My pool includes the people I see in my everyday life," explains Kenrick. "I don't consciously think that the people I see through movies, TV and magazines are artificial. Still, seeing Juliette Binoche all the time registers in my brain."

Our minds have not caught up. They haven't evolved to correct for MTV. "Our research suggests that our brains don't discount the women on the cover of *Cosmo* even when subjects know these women are models. Subjects judge an average attractive woman as less desirable as a date after just having seen models," Kenrick says.

Part of the problem is we're built to selectively remember the really beautiful. They stand out. "That's what you're drawn to," says Kenrick. "It feels good on the brain." And any stimulus that's vivid becomes readily available to memory, encouraging you to overestimate the true frequency of beautiful women out there.

So the women men count as possibilities are not real possibilities for most of them. That leads to a lot of guys sitting at home alone with their fantasies of unobtainable supermodels, stuck in a secret, sorry state that makes them unable to access real love for real women. Or, as Kenrick finds, a lot of guys on college campuses whining, "There are no attractive women to date." Under a constant barrage of media images of beautiful women, these guys have an expectation of attractiveness that is unusually high—and that makes the real people around them, in whom they might really be interested, seem lackluster, even if they are quite good-looking.

The idea that beauty could make so many men so miserable has acquired hard-nosed mathematical proof. In the world of abstract logic, marriage is looked on as a basic matching problem with statistical underpinnings in game theory. Logic says that everybody wants to do as well as they possibly can in selecting a life partner. And when people apply varied criteria for choosing a mate, everybody ends up with a partner with whom they are more or less satisfied. Not everybody gets his or her No. 1 choice, but everybody winds up reasonably content.

But the world has changed since mathematicians first tackled the matching of people with mates in the early 1960s. Films, television and magazines have not only given beauty a commanding presence in our lives but have also helped standardize our vision of attractiveness. Enter Guido Caldarelli, Ph.D., of the University of Rome, and Andrea Capocci, Ph.D., of the University of Fribourg in Switzerland. Once they introduced into their mating equations what they call the "*Vogue* factor"—a measure of the influence of beauty—they found that people become dissatisfied with their sexual partners.

"When the concept of 'most beautiful' people in the world tends to be the same for everyone, it becomes more and more difficult to make more people happy," say the researchers. The same few beautiful people top everyone's list of desired partners—clearly an impossibility—and no one comes close to being matched with any of their choices. So people become unhappy with their partner possibilities.

Alas, it's not simply a theoretical issue. Sociologist Satoshi Kanazawa, Ph.D., finds that real-life consequences of the contrast effect exist, such as divorce. The contrast effect not only undermines marriages; it then keeps men single—and miserable.

Kanazawa, assistant professor of sociology at Indiana University of Pennsylvania, wondered: "If men found themselves being less attracted to their mates after being exposed to eight or 16 pictures in a half-hour experiment, what would be the effect if that happened day in, day out, for 20 years?" It immediately occurred to him that high school and college teachers would be prime candidates for a study; they are constantly surrounded by young women in their reproductive prime. The only other occupation he could think of where the overwhelming majority of people men come in contact with are young women, was Hollywood movie directors, as well as producers and actors—a group not known for their stable marriages. But there was not an available body of data on them like there was on teachers, from a general population survey.

What Kanazawa found was summed up in the title of his report published last year in *Evolution and Human Behavior*: "Teaching May Be Hazardous to Your Marriage." Men are generally less likely to be currently divorced or separated than women, and overall teachers are particularly unlikely to be divorced or separated. But being a male teacher or professor wiped out that advantage. And not just any male teacher is at risk. Male kindergarten and grade school teachers were contentedly monogamous. "There appears to be something about male teachers who come in daily contact with teenage women that increases the likelihood of being currently divorced or separated," Kanazawa says. He adds that these men remain unmarried because any adult women they might meet and date after their divorce would pale in comparison to the pretty young things constantly around them.

"Most real-life divorces happen because one or the other spouse is dissatisfied with their mate," says Kanazawa. "The contrast effect can explain why men might unconsciously become dissatisfied. They don't know why they suddenly find their middle-aged wives not appealing anymore; their exposure to young women might be a reason."

It would be blissfully easy to point a finger and claim that such infatuation with the young and the beautiful is the fault of the media and its barrage of nubile bodies. But it would also be incorrect. They're just giving us what we are naturally interested in.

All the evidence indicates that we are wired to respond to beauty. It's more than a matter of mere aesthetics; beauty is nature's shorthand for healthy and fertile, for reproductive capacity, a visible cue that a woman has the kind of prime partner potential that will bestow good genes on future generations. One of the prime elements of beauty, for example, is symmetry of body features. Research suggests that symmetrical people are physically and psychologically healthier than their less symmetrical counterparts.

If we're now all reeling from a surfeit of images of attractiveness, well, it's a lot like our dietary love affair with sugar. "We want it. We need it. And our ancestors didn't have enough of it," observes Kenrick. "They were more concerned with starving. As a result, we have very hypersensitive detectors for it. And modern technology packages it and sends us doses that are way too large for our health."

There are, of course, beautiful women in other parts of the country. But L.A. is a mecca, attracting the most beautiful. Women don't look like this anywhere else in the country, and certainly not in the quantity they do here.

L.A. is an adopted city for me, as it is for many. Born in New York, I wonder from time to time what shape my life would have taken if I hadn't moved here in the 1970s. Whatever else, I would not have been saturated with the sight of so many beautiful women on a daily basis. But then I remember; these are the women whose images are broadcast all over the globe. While most people do not live in L.A., they visit it every day when they turn on the TV or go to the movies. It is safe to say that, to one degree or another, we all live in the shadow of the Hollywood sign.

CRITICAL THINKING QUESTIONS

1. This article suggests that we are exposed to very attractive people almost constantly in the media. What specific images of attractiveness are presented today in the media? Find media images of physical attractiveness from the 1950s and 1960s. What is the difference, if any, between the images presented then and the images presented now? Would the contrast effect work the same, regardless of the specific images of beauty being portrayed in the media? Explain.

2. Obesity among Americans recently has been described as a major health problem, second only to smoking as being preventable. At the same time, people have complained about the images of the very thin models and media figures that appear all around us. How do you reconcile this modeling of thinness as the ideal of beauty with the fact that Americans are increasingly overweight? In other words, why hasn't the media image of thinness resulted in people losing weight, when the opposite actually seems to have occurred? Explain.

3. This article deals with the issue of the contrast effect and how constant exposure to images of very attractive people may leave us less satisfied with our real-life peers. Besides beauty, what other images conveyed by the media may produce contrast effects, resulting in us being less happy with what we actually have and desirous of what we constantly see in the media?

4. Mass media images of beauty are disseminated worldwide via mechanisms such as movies and magazines. Many, but not all, of these images originate in the United States. Do you think the same contrast effect occurs in cultures that are very dissimilar to that of the United States? For that matter, would the same contrast effect occur even within the various subgroups that comprise the United States? Explain.

5. A common stereotype is that men rate the physical attractiveness of women as more important than women rate the physical attractiveness of men. In fact, much of the research on physical attractiveness focuses on the effects of female beauty on males. Design a study to determine how the contrast effect impacts females who are exposed to male media stereotypes of physical attractiveness.

ARTICLE 20 _____

It may seem obvious that looks matter when it comes to dating and mate selection. While many people would argue that physical attractiveness is not the only thing that they look for in a potential partner, few would argue that they are oblivious to appearance. Furthermore, according to Article 19—which considered how people's beauty preferences might have biological roots—there is fairly strong agreement as to what features people find attractive.

So, what is life like for people who happen to have the features that others find attractive? Are their lives significantly different from those of individuals who do not possess such good looks? Furthermore, do looks have any impact on people's lives outside the areas of dating and mating popularity? For example, compared to a less attractive counterpart, will an attractive person more likely be successful in the work world? Be a better parent? Be a happier person overall? The following classic article by Karen Dion, Ellen Berscheid, and Elaine Walster was one of the first studies to investigate the "What is beautiful is good" effect. As indicated in the article, attractiveness may convey a great many benefits to those people who possess it.

What Is Beautiful Is Good[1]
■ Karen Dion, Ellen Berscheid, and Elaine Walster

A person's physical appearance, along with his sexual identity, is the personal characteristic that is most obvious and accessible to others in social interaction. The present experiment was designed to determine whether physically attractive stimulus persons, both male and female, are (a) assumed to possess more socially desirable personality traits than physically unattractive stimulus persons and (b) expected to lead better lives (e.g., be more competent husbands and wives, be more successful occupationally, etc.) than unattractive stimulus persons. Sex of Subject × Sex of Stimulus Person interactions along these dimensions also were investigated. The present results indicate a "what is beautiful is good" stereotype along the physical attractiveness dimension with no Sex of Judge × Sex of Stimulus interaction. The implications of such a stereotype on self-concept development and the course of social interaction are discussed.

A person's physical appearance, along with his sexual identity, is the personal characteristic most obvious and accessible to others in social interaction. It is perhaps for this reason that folk psychology has always contained a multitude of theorems which ostensibly permit the forecast of a person's character and personality simply from knowledge of his outward appearance. The line of deduction advanced by most physiognomic theories is simply that "What is beautiful is good . . . [Sappho, Fragments, No. 101].," and that "Physical beauty is the sign of an interior beauty, a spiritual and moral beauty . . . [Schiller, 1882]."

Several processes may operate to make the soothsayers' prophecies more logical and accurate than would appear at first glance. First, it is possible that a correlation between inward character and appearance exists because certain personality traits influence one's appearance. For example, a calm, relaxed person may develop fewer lines and wrinkles than a tense, irritable person. Second, cultural stereotypes about the kinds of personalities appropriate for beautiful or ugly people may mold the personalities of these individuals. If

Reprinted from *Journal of Personality and Social Psychology,* 1972, *24,* 285–290. Copyright © 1972 by the American Psychological Association. Reprinted with permission.

casual acquaintances invariably assume that attractive individuals are more sincere, noble, and honest than unattractive persons, then attractive individuals should be habitually regarded with more respect than unattractive persons. Many have noted that one's self-concept develops from observing what others think about oneself. Thus, if the physically attractive person is consistently treated as a virtuous person, he may become one.

The above considerations pose several questions: (*a*) Do individuals in fact have stereotyped notions of the personality traits possessed by individuals of varying attractiveness? (*b*) To what extent are these stereotypes accurate? (*c*) What is the cause of the correlation between beauty and personality if, in fact, such a correlation exists?

Some observers, of course, deny that such stereotyping exists, and thus render Questions *b* and *c* irrelevant. Chief among these are rehabilitation workers (cf. Wright, 1960) whose clients possess facial and other physical disabilities. These researchers, however, may have a vested interest in believing that physical beauty is a relatively unimportant determinant of the opportunities an individual has available to him.

Perhaps more interestingly, it has been asserted that other researchers also have had a vested interest in retaining the belief that beauty is a peripheral characteristic. Aronson (1969), for example, has suggested that the fear that investigation might prove this assumption wrong has generally caused this to be a taboo area for social psychologists:

As an aside, I might mention that physical attractiveness is rarely investigated as an antecedent of liking—even though a casual observation (even by us experimental social psychologists) would indicate that we seem to react differently to beautiful women than to homely women. It is difficult to be certain why the effects of physical beauty have not been studied more systematically. It may be that, at some levels, we would hate to find evidence indicating that beautiful women are better liked than homely women—somehow this seems undemocratic. In a democracy we like to feel that with hard work and a good deal of motivation, a person can accomplish almost anything. But, alas (most of us believe), hard work cannot make an ugly woman beautiful. Because of this suspicion perhaps most social psychologists implicitly prefer to believe that beauty is indeed only skin deep—and avoid the investigation of its social impact for fear they might learn otherwise [p. 160].

The present study was an attempt to determine if a physical attractiveness stereotype exists and, if so, to investigate the content of the stereotype along several dimensions. Specifically, it was designed to investigate (*a*) whether physically attractive stimulus persons, both male and female, are assumed to possess more *socially desirable personality traits* than unattractive persons and (*b*) whether they are expected to *lead better lives* than unattractive individuals. With respect to the latter, we wished to determine if physically attractive persons are generally expected to be better husbands and wives, better parents, and more successful socially and occupationally than less attractive persons.

Because it seemed possible that jealousy might attenuate these effects (if one is jealous of another, he may be reluctant to accord the other the status that he feels the other deserves), and since subjects might be expected to be more jealous of attractive stimulus persons of the same sex than of the opposite sex, we examined the Sex of Subject × Sex of Stimulus Person interactions along the dimensions described above.

METHOD

Subjects

Sixty students, 30 males and 30 females, who were enrolled in an introductory course in psychology at the University of Minnesota participated in this experiment. Each had agreed to participate in return for experimental points to be added to their final exam grade.

Procedure

When the subjects arrived at the designated rooms, they were introduced to the experiment as a study of accuracy in person perception. The experimenter stated that while psychological studies have shown that people do form detailed impressions of others on the basis of a very few cues, the variables determining the extent to which these early impressions are generally accurate have not yet been completely identified.

The subjects were told that the purpose of the present study was to compare person perception accuracy of untrained college students with two other groups who had been trained in various interpersonal perception techniques, specifically graduate students in clinical psychology and clinical psychologists. The experimenter noted his belief that person perception accuracy is a general ability varying among people. Therefore, according to the experimenter, college students who are high on this ability may be as accurate as some professional clinicians when making first-impression judgments based on noninterview material.

The subjects were told that standard sets of photographs would be used as the basis for personality inferences. The individuals depicted in the photographs were said to be part of a group of college students currently enrolled at other universities who were participating in a longitudinal study of personality development scheduled to continue into adulthood. It would be possible, therefore, to assess the accuracy of each subject's judgments against information currently available on the stimulus persons and also against forthcoming information.

Stimulus materials. Following the introduction, each subject was given three envelopes. Each envelope contained one photo of a stimulus person of approximately the subject's own age. One of the three envelopes that the subject received contained a photograph of a physically attractive stimulus person; another contained a photograph of a person of average attractiveness; and the final envelope contained a photograph of a relatively unattractive stimulus person.[2] Half of our subjects received three pictures of girls; the remainder received pictures of boys.

To increase the generalizability of our findings and to insure that the general dimension of attractiveness was the characteristic responded to (rather than unique characteristics such as hair color, etc.), 12 different sets of three pictures each were prepared. Each subject received and rated only 1 set. Which 1 of the 12 sets of pictures the subject received, the order in which each of the three envelopes in the set were presented, and the ratings made of the person depicted, were all randomly determined.

Dependent variables. The subjects were requested to record their judgments of the three stimulus persons in several booklets.[3] The first page of each booklet cautioned the subjects that this study was an investigation of accuracy of person perception and that we were not interested in the subjects' tact, politeness, or other factors usually important in social situations. It was stressed that it was important for the subject to rate the stimulus persons frankly.

The booklets tapped impressions of the stimulus person along several dimensions. First, the subjects were asked to open the first envelope and then to rate the person depicted on 27 different *personality traits* (which were arranged in random order).[4] The subjects' ratings were made on 6-point scales, the ends of which were labeled by polar opposites (i.e., exciting–dull). When these ratings had been computed, the subject was asked to open the second envelope, make ratings, and then open the third envelope.

In a subsequent booklet, the subjects were asked to assess the stimulus persons on five additional personality traits.[5] These ratings were made on a slightly different scale. The subjects were asked to indicate which stimulus person possessed the "most" and "least" of a given trait. The stimulus person thought to best represent a positive trait was assigned a score of 3; the stimulus person thought to possess an intermediate amount of the trait was assigned a score of 2; and the stimulus person thought to least represent the trait was assigned a score of 1.

In a previous experiment (see Endnote 3), a subset of items was selected to comprise an index of the *social desirability* of the personality traits assigned to the stimulus person. The subjects' ratings of each stimulus person on the appropriate items were simply summed to determine the extent to which the subject perceived each stimulus person as socially desirable.

In order to assess whether or not attractive persons are expected to lead happier and more successful lives than unattractive persons, the subjects were asked to estimate which of the stimulus persons would be most likely, and which least likely, to have a number of different life experiences. The subjects were reminded again that their estimates would eventually be checked for accuracy as the lives of the various stimulus persons evolved. The subjects' estimates of the stimulus person's probable life experiences formed indexes of the stimulus person's future happiness in four areas: (*a*) marital happiness (Which stimulus person is most likely to ever be divorced?); (*b*) parental happiness

(Which stimulus person is most likely to be a good parent?); (*c*) social and professional happiness (Which stimulus person is most likely to experience deep personal fulfillment?); and (*d*) total happiness (sum of Indexes *a, b,* and *c*).

A fifth index, an occupational success index, was also obtained for each stimulus person. The subjects were asked to indicate which of the three stimulus persons would be most likely to engage in 30 different occupations. (The order in which the occupations were presented and the estimates made was randomized.) The 30 occupations had been chosen such that three status levels of 10 different general occupations were represented, three examples of which follow: Army sergeant (low status); Army captain (average status); Army colonel (high status). Each time a high-status occupation was foreseen for a stimulus person, the stimulus person was assigned a score of 3; when a moderate status occupation was foreseen, the stimulus person was assigned a score of 2; when a low-status occupation was foreseen, a score of 1 was assigned. The average status of occupations that a subject ascribed to a stimulus person constituted the score for that stimulus person in the occupational status index.

RESULTS AND DISCUSSION

Manipulation Check

It is clear that our manipulation of the relative attractiveness of the stimulus persons depicted was effective. The six unattractive stimulus persons were seen as less attractive than the average stimulus persons, who, in turn, were seen as less attractive than the six attractive stimulus persons. The stimulus persons' mean rankings on the attractiveness dimension were 1.12, 2.02, and 2.87, respectively. These differences were statistically significant ($F = 939.32$).[6]

Test of Hypotheses

It will be recalled that it was predicted that the subjects would attribute more socially desirable personality traits to attractive individuals than to average or unattractive individuals. It also was anticipated that jealousy might attenuate these effects. Since the subjects might be expected to be more jealous of stimulus persons of the same sex than of the opposite sex, we blocked both on sex of subject and sex of stimulus person. If jealousy attenuated the predicted main effect, a significant Sex of Subject × Sex of Stimulus Person interaction should be secured in addition to the main effect.

All tests for detection of linear trend and interaction were conducted via a multivariate analysis of variance. (This procedure is outlined in Hays, 1963.)

The means relevant to the hypothesis that attractive individuals will be perceived to possess more socially desirable personalities than others are reported in Table 1. Analyses reveal that attractive individuals were indeed judged to be more socially desirable than are unattractive ($F = 29.61$) persons. The Sex of Subject × Sex of Stimulus Person interaction was insignificant (interaction $F = .00$). Whether the rater was of the same or the opposite sex as the stimulus person, attractive stimulus persons were judged as more socially desirable.[7]

Furthermore, it was also hypothesized that the subjects would assume that attractive stimulus persons are likely to secure more prestigious jobs than those of lesser attractiveness, as well as experiencing happier marriages, being better parents, and enjoying more fulfilling social and occupational lives.

The means relevant to these predictions concerning the estimated future life experiences of individuals of varying degrees of physical attractiveness are also depicted in Table 1. As shown in the table, there was strong support for all of the preceding hypotheses save one. Attractive men and women were expected to attain more prestigious occupations than were those of lesser attractiveness ($F = 42.30$), and this expectation was expressed equally by raters of the same or the opposite sex as the stimulus person (interaction $F = .25$).

The subjects also assumed that attractive individuals would be more competent spouses and have happier marriages than those of lesser attractiveness ($F = 62.54$). (It might be noted that there is some evidence that this may be a correct perception. Kirkpatrick and Cotton (1951), reported that "well-adjusted" wives were more physically attractive than "badly adjusted" wives. "Adjustment," however, was assessed by friends' perceptions, which may have been affected by the stereotype evident here.)

TABLE 1 / Traits Attributed to Various Stimulus Others

Trait Ascription[a]	Unattractive Stimulus Person	Average Stimulus Person	Attractive Stimulus Person
Social desirability of the stimulus person's personality	56.31	62.42	65.39
Occupational status of the stimulus person	1.70	2.02	2.25
Marital competence of the stimulus person	.37	.71	1.70
Parental competence of the stimulus person	3.91	4.55	3.54
Social and professional happiness of the stimulus person	5.28	6.34	6.37
Total happiness of the stimulus person	8.83	11.60	11.60
Likelihood of marriage	1.52	1.82	2.17

[a]The higher the number, the more socially desirable, the more prestigious an occupation, etc., the stimulus person is expected to possess.

According to the means reported in Table 1, it is clear that attractive individuals were not expected to be better parents ($F = 1.47$). In fact, attractive persons were rated somewhat lower than any other group of stimulus persons as potential parents, although no statistically significant differences were apparent.

As predicted, attractive stimulus persons were assumed to have better prospects for happy social and professional lives ($F = 21.97$). All in all, the attractive stimulus persons were expected to have more total happiness in their lives than those of lesser attractiveness ($F = 24.20$).

The preceding results did not appear to be attenuated by a jealousy effect (Sex of Subject × Stimulus Person interaction Fs = .01, .07, .21, and .05, respectively).

The subjects were also asked to estimate the likelihood that the various stimulus persons would marry early or marry at all. Responses were combined into a single index. It is evident that the subjects assumed that the attractive stimulus persons were more likely to find an acceptable partner than those of lesser attractiveness ($F = 35.84$). Attractive individuals were expected to marry earlier and to be less likely to remain single. Once again, these conclusions were reached by all subjects, regardless of whether they were of the same or opposite sex of the stimulus person (interaction $F = .01$).

The results suggest that a physical attractiveness stereotype exists and that its content is perfectly compatible with the "What is beautiful is good" thesis. Not only are physically attractive persons assumed to possess more socially desirable personalities than those of lesser attractiveness, but it is presumed that their lives will be happier and more successful.

The results also suggest that the physical attractiveness variable may have a number of implications for a variety of aspects of social interaction and influence. For example, it is clear that physically attractive individuals may have even more advantages in the dating market than has previously been assumed. In addition to an aesthetic advantage in marrying a beautiful spouse (cf. Josselin de Jong, 1952), potential marriage partners may also assume that the beautiful attract all of the world's material benefits and happiness. Thus, the lure of an attractive marriage partner should be strong indeed.

We do not know, of course, how well this stereotype stands up against contradictory information. Nor do we know the extent to which it determines the pattern of social interaction that develops with a person of a particular attractiveness level. Nevertheless, it would be odd if people did not behave toward others in accordance with this stereotype. Such behavior has been previously noted anecdotally. Monahan (1941) has observed that

Even social workers accustomed to dealing with all types often find it difficult to think of a normal, pretty girl as being guilty of a crime. Most people, for some

inexplicable reason, think of crime in terms of abnormality in appearance, and I must say that beautiful women are not often convicted [p. 103].

A host of other familiar social psychological dependent variables also should be affected in predictable ways.

In the above connection, it might be noted that if standards of physical attractiveness vary widely, knowledge of the content of the physical attractiveness stereotype would be of limited usefulness in predicting its effect on social interaction and the development of the self-concept. The present study was not designed to investigate the degree of variance in perceived beauty. (The physical attractiveness ratings of the stimulus materials were made by college students of a similar background to those who participated in this study.) Preliminary evidence (Cross & Cross, 1971) suggests that such differences in perceived beauty may not be as severe as some observers have suggested.

REFERENCES

Aronson, E. Some antecedents of interpersonal attraction. In W. J. Arnold & D. Levine (Eds.), *Nebraska Symposium on Motivation,* 1969, *17,* 143–177.

Cross, J. F., & Cross, J. Age, sex, race, and the perception of facial beauty. *Developmental Psychology,* 1971, *5,* 433–439.

Hays, W. L. *Statistics for psychologists.* New York: Holt, Rinehart & Winston, 1963.

Josselin de Jong, J. P. B. *Lévi-Strauss' theory on kinship and marriage.* Leiden, Holland: Brill, 1952.

Kirkpatrick, C., & Cotton, J. Physical attractiveness, age, and marital adjustment. *American Sociological Review,* 1951, *16,* 81–86.

Monahan, F. *Women in crime.* New York: Ives Washburn, 1941.

Schiller, J. C. F. *Essays, esthetical and philosophical, including the dissertation on the "Connexions between the animal and the spiritual in man."* London: Bell, 1882.

Wright, B. A. *Physical disability—A psychological approach.* New York: Harper & Row, 1960.

ENDNOTES

1. This research was financed in part by National Institute of Mental Health Grants MH 16729 to Berscheid and MH 16661 to Walster.

2. The physical attractiveness rating of each of the pictures was determined in a preliminary study. One hundred Minnesota undergraduates rated 50 yearbook pictures of persons of the opposite sex with respect to physical attractiveness. The criteria for choosing the 12 pictures to be used experimentally were (*a*) high-interrater agreement as to the physical attractiveness of the stimulus (the average interrater correlation for all of the pictures was .70); and (*b*) pictures chosen to represent the very attractive category and very unattractive category were not at the extreme ends of attractiveness.

3. A detailed report of the items included in these booklets is available. Order Document No. 01972 from the National Auxiliary Publication Service of the American Society for Information Science, c/o CCM Information Services, Inc., 909 3rd Avenue, New York, New York 10022. Remit in advance $5.00 for photocopies or $2.00 for microfiche and make checks payable to: Research and Microfilm Publications, Inc.

4. The subjects were asked how altruistic, conventional, self-assertive, exciting, stable, emotional, dependent, safe, interesting, genuine, sensitive, outgoing, sexually permissive, sincere, warm, sociable, competitive, obvious, kind, modest, strong, serious, sexually warm, simple, poised, bold, and sophisticated each stimulus person was.

5. The subjects rated stimulus persons on the following traits: friendliness, enthusiasm, physical attractiveness, social poise, and trustworthiness.

6. Throughout this report, *df* = 1/55.

7. Before running the preliminary experiment to determine the identity of traits usually associated with a socially desirable person (see Endnote 3), we had assumed that an exciting date, a nurturant person, and a person of good character would be perceived as quite different personality types. Conceptually, for example, we expected that an exciting date would be seen to require a person who was unpredictable, challenging, etc., while a nurturant person would be seen to be predictable and unthreatening. It became clear, however, that these distinctions were not ones which made sense to the subjects. There was almost total overlap between the traits chosen as representative of an exciting date, of a nurturant person, and a person of good or ethical character. All were strongly correlated with social desirability. Thus, attractive stimulus persons are assumed to be more exciting dates (*F* = 39.97), more nurturant individuals (*F* = 13.96), and to have better character (*F* = 19.57) than persons of lesser attractiveness.

CRITICAL THINKING QUESTIONS

1. The study used college students, presumably most of them ages 18 to 22. Do you think that the age of the subjects might influence the results? Why or why not?
2. The study used photographs as stimulus materials. Do you think that the "What is beautiful is good" effect also would occur in face-to-face encounters? Or might the judgments made in person somehow be different than those made by looking at photographs? How could you test this possibility?
3. The study indicated that physically attractive people are perceived as having more socially desirable traits and are expected to be more successful in life than their less attractive counterparts. Do you think that attractive people *actually* are more desirable and more successful in life? Why or why not?
4. This article suggests that ample positive attributions are made for attractive people. In what ways might being attractive actually be a liability, instead of an asset? Explain your reasoning.

ADDITIONAL RELATED READINGS

Shannon, M. L., & Stark, C. P. (2003). The influence of physical appearance on personnel selection. *Social Behavior and Personality, 31*(6), 613–624.

Wade, T. J., Irvine, K., & Cooper, M. (2004). Racial characteristics and individual differences in women's evaluations of men's facial attractiveness and personality. *Personality and Individual Differences, 36*(5), 1083–1092.

ARTICLE 21 _____

Both of the preceding articles looked at the important role that physical attractiveness plays in interpersonal attraction. Article 19 focused on the effects of constant media exposure to highly attractive people and the subsequent impact of such exposure on our perceptions of the people surrounding us. Article 20 demonstrated that we place great importance on physical attractiveness in deciding whom we want to date and that we associate all sorts of positive and desirable characteristics with people we find attractive. This "what is beautiful is good" effect may bestow significant benefits on people deemed physically attractive in a given society.

Over the years, the media has portrayed increasingly thin female models as the ideal form of attractiveness. By contemporary portrayals of female attractiveness, a former beauty icon of just a few years ago, such as Marilyn Monroe, probably would be considered too heavy. Yet at the same time that media images of female beauty have become increasingly thin, the average body size and weight of American women has increased. *Social comparison* is the name of the concept that defines how we naturally look at others to determine how we feel about ourselves—that is, how we compare ourselves to others to see how our lives and our bodies stack up. It stands to reason that in determining how happy we are with our physical attributes, we will be influenced by the media portrayals of attractiveness to which we are constantly exposed. According to this reasoning, which is supported by research, women who are exposed to thin, attractive models may have more dissatisfaction with their own bodies than women who are not exposed to such models.

But is this dissatisfaction with one's own body after being exposed to thin models simply a desire to be like them, or is there some other underlying reason for this dissatisfaction? The following article by Peggy Chin Evans examines the possibility that it is not the desire for thinness per se that causes dissatisfaction but rather the desire for the greater happiness and well-being that is associated with being thin.

"If Only I Were Thin Like Her, Maybe I Could Be Happy Like Her"

The Self-Implications of Associating a Thin Female Ideal with Life Success

■ Peggy Chin Evans

Women often feel dissatisfied with their appearance after comparing themselves to other females who epitomize the thin-ideal standard of beauty. The current study posits that women associate a thin-ideal female body type with positive life-success, and that it may be this psychological link that drives feelings of negativity toward the self after such upward social comparisons. The results revealed that women reported more self-dissatisfaction and less optimism about their possible future life outcomes after exposure to a thin-ideal female target that ostensibly had a successful life than when the target ostensibly had an unsuccessful life.

Reprinted from *Psychology of Women Quarterly*, 2003, *27*, 209–214. Copyright © 2003 by Blackwell Publishers. Reprinted with permission.

Research indicates that while the ideal standard of beauty for females commonly portrayed in the media has become thinner than it had been in the past (Silverstein, Perdue, Peterson, & Kelly, 1986), the average body size of adult North American females has increased (Spitzer, Henderson, & Zivian, 1999). Not surprisingly, North American women often report being dissatisfied with their bodies and with their weight in particular, especially after exposure to Western media images that display a thin-ideal standard of beauty (e.g., Cattarin, Thompson, Thomas, & Williams, 2000; Thornton & Moore, 1993). These studies suggest that many North American women make upward social comparisons to ideal beauty standards in the media to assess their level of attractiveness and to evaluate their own appearance. However, a number of studies have shown that upward social comparisons to ideal standards of beauty can make women feel negatively about themselves (Thornton & Maurice, 1997, 1999).

A recent meta-analysis which examined the effects of the mass media on female body image revealed that women reported feeling significantly worse after exposure to thin-ideal media images than after viewing average-sized or plus-sized media images (Groesz, Levine, & Murnen, 2002). Similarly, a study on social comparison, body image, and the media showed that women who engaged in social comparisons with thin-ideal female media images in appearance-related commercials reported substantially more anger, anxiety, and depression than women who saw a non-appearance related commercial (Cattarin et al., 2000). Taken together, these studies suggest that women are encouraged by the media to compare themselves to unrealistic thin-ideal standards of bodily attractiveness (Silverstein et al., 1986), which may then lead to their body dissatisfaction (see Myers & Biocca, 1992, for an alternative interpretation). Although conventional wisdom would suggest that women compare themselves to and want to emulate the physiques of thin-ideal standards, which, in turn, affects their perceptions of their own bodies, this assumption may not be entirely correct.

It is possible that women strive for the thin-ideal body type by associating thinness with positive life success, and it may be this life success that women strive to achieve via having a thin-ideal body. A study by Harrison (1997) demonstrated a positive relationship between women's attraction to thin female television characters (operationalized as liking, feeling similar to, and wanting to be like the character) and a personal desire for thinness. This study suggests that thinness alone may not be sufficient to explain why women are motivated to emulate the physiques of female television personalities. Rather, women's desire to become more like the thin image in terms of the character's projected lifestyle and personality may prompt them to strive for these thin-ideal standards.

Women may feel dissatisfied with themselves after engaging in comparisons with thin media ideals because such standards induce women to imagine an alternative world where they could lead very different lives if their physical appearance were altered. Thus, the possible selves that women generate for themselves may influence feelings about the current self. The concept of possible selves is defined as the elements of one's self-concept that represent a sense of what one might become, what one would like to become, and what one is afraid of becoming (Markus & Nurius, 1986). Previous studies indicate that people's possible selves are susceptible to change depending on the current environment and may be sensitive to information that conveys new or inconsistent "data" about the self (Markus & Nurius, 1986). For example, a woman who is exposed to a photograph of a thin, attractive female may feel less attractive and expect her future possible selves to be more negative than before seeing the photograph. Hence, how an individual feels about her possible life-outcomes may depend on the stimulus to which she is exposed.

The purpose of the current study is to examine how life success stereotypes about thin-ideal females can influence women's self-perceptions after a social comparison to an ideal figure. It is hypothesized that when life success stereotypes about a thin-ideal female target are explicitly challenged or negated, women should report more positive self-perceptions than when these life success stereotypes are explicitly or implicitly confirmed. The affirmation of this hypothesis would suggest that it is more than just body dissatisfaction that women experience after exposure to thin-media ideals. Rather, it is also the belief that women with ideal bodies also have ideal lives, and it may be the ideal life that women strive to attain via having a more perfect body.

METHOD

Participants

Participants were 126 women recruited from introductory-level psychology classes at a large Midwestern university in exchange for course-related credit. Of the participants, 83.3% were European American, 11.1% were African American, 3.2% were Asian American, and the remaining 2.4% were from other ethnic backgrounds. Participants' ages ranged from 17 to 42 ($M = 19.5$, $SD = 2.6$) and their body mass index (BMI) ranged from 16.1 to 60.0 ($M = 24.3$, $SD = 5.9$; Healthy BMI scores fall between 18 to 25; Korbonits et al., 1997).

Design and Procedure

Participants were told that this study was about the impact of the media on health. Upon arriving at the laboratory, participants were greeted by a female experimenter who had them complete a consent form and fill out a questionnaire asking them about their dietary habits, including how frequently they skipped meals, ate "junk food," and exercised. They were also asked whether they considered themselves to be in "good shape." In actuality, participants completed this measure in order to activate their thoughts about their weight and lifestyle. Following this, the experimenter weighed the participants in front of a mirror and measured their height in order to make their own physical appearance more highly salient to them. Thoughts about their weight and physical appearance were activated in order to increase the likelihood that participants would attend to the physical appearance of the thin-ideal targets and the lifestyle information, thereby increasing the probability that participants would engage in social comparisons with the thin-ideal target model on those two dimensions.

All participants viewed one of two photographs of a thin, attractive, European American female target (pretested for attractiveness by a separate sample). Participants were then randomly assigned to one of four conditions. In Condition 1, participants read a *positive-success* passage about the target, which stated that, a nationwide survey of 1,000 thin, average-weight, and heavier women showed that "by far, the group with the most life-satisfaction was thin women."

Additionally, the passage stated that the target in the photograph was contacted, and she confirmed that she enjoyed a happy life. In Condition 2, participants read an *unsuccessful* passage, which was identical to the first passage but stated, "by far, the group with the least amount of life-satisfaction was thin women." The target further confirmed that she had an unhappy life. In Condition 3, participants read a *positive-negated* passage, which stated that thin women "do not enjoy more happiness than others, are not more successful than others, and do not benefit from any special advantages over others." Once again, participants were told that the target confirmed that she had an average life with normal "ups and downs" just like everybody else. Participants in Condition 4 were given no information about the target's lifestyle. However, considerable research has shown that thin-ideal females are typically perceived by others to enjoy positive life success (e.g., Hebl & Heatherton, 1998).

After participants were exposed to the photographs and lifestyle passages, they completed the life-outcomes questionnaire. Participants then indicated how they felt at the moment by completing the mood measure and the state self-esteem measure (Heatherton & Polivy, 1991). Participants were fully debriefed about the study at the end of the lab session. They were told that all of the lifestyle information that they received was fabricated and that "in general, most people experience some good things in their lives and some bad things. There is no group that has a particularly happy life based on their physical appearance."

Measures

Life Outcomes Based on a modified version of the possible selves questionnaire (Markus & Nurius, 1986), the life-outcomes measure asked participants to indicate on a scale ranging from 1 (*very unlikely to be true of me*) to 9 (*very likely to be true of me*) the likelihood that they would experience 32 positive (e.g., "I may be admired by others," "I may lead an exciting life") and negative life circumstances (e.g., "I may be pitied by others," "I may be unhealthy"). These items were pilot-tested in an earlier unrelated study measuring the likelihood that a variety of situations could be true of thin and fat women. Participants' scores on the items that measured positive life-outcomes were averaged to constitute the positive life-outcomes variable (alpha = .85) and participants' scores on the items that measured negative life outcomes were averaged to constitute the negative life-outcomes variable (alpha = .86).

Mood General mood after exposure to stimulus materials was measured by asking participants to describe how "thinking about the target in the photograph makes you feel about yourself right now." Participants were asked to make ten bipolar ratings based on 9-point scales ranging from –4 to +4 on the following adjectives: *depressed-elated, stressed-relaxed, dissatisfied-satisfied, unhappy-happy, disappointed-relieved, insecure-secure, self-conscious-self-confident, guilty-innocent, ashamed-proud,* and *negative-positive.* The scores from these ten adjectives were then averaged to create the mood variable (alpha = .96).

State Self-Esteem Possible momentary changes in self-esteem after exposure to stimulus materials were measured using the state self-esteem scale (SSES; Heatherton & Polivy, 1991). This scale is a 20-item questionnaire with three components: (a) appearance (6 items, alpha = .85); (b) social (7 items, alpha = .83); and (c) performance (7 items, alpha = .80). The scale asks participants to reflect on how they feel about themselves "right now" on items such as, "I am pleased with my appearance right now" (appearance), "I feel self-conscious" (social), and "I feel confident about my abilities" (performance). State self-esteem is measured by asking participants to rate themselves on a scale ranging from 1 (*not at all*) to 5 (*extremely*) with some items reverse scored (Heatherton & Polivy, 1991).

RESULTS

Comparability of Stimulus Materials

Because this study used two different photographs of female models, a multivariate analysis of variance (MANOVA) was conducted to show that the two models did not elicit different responses on the dependent variables, $F(6, 119) = .62$, *ns.* Because the two figures in the photographs showed no significant differences across the dependent variables, the data for

the two photographs depicting the female figures were collapsed throughout the rest of the analyses.

Body Mass Index

Participants' actual BMI may influence the degree to which they feel self-dissatisfied after comparing themselves to a thin-ideal female image. Thus, all analyses were conducted with participants' BMI scores covaried out.

Differences Between Conditions (Stereotype Consistent vs. Stereotype Inconsistent)

Two conditions (Condition 1 and Condition 4) composed the stereotype-consistent category, in which Condition 1 explicitly supported the positive life-stereotypes of thin females and Condition 4 implicitly supported the stereotype. The other two conditions (Condition 2 and Condition 3) composed the stereotype-inconsistent category, in which Condition 2 explicitly challenged the positive life-stereotypes of thin females and Condition 3 negated the stereotype. To explore whether the strength of manipulation varied within lifestyle information categories, univariate analyses of covariance (ANCOVA) were conducted to explore the possibility of differences between Conditions 1 and 4, as well as Conditions 2 and 3, on the dependent variables. There were no differences between Conditions 1 and 4 or between Conditions 2 and 3. Of particular interest to this study, the strength of manipulation for both the stereotype-consistent conditions and stereotype-inconsistent conditions did not differ on either the positive or negative life-outcomes variables. As such, all further analyses were conducted weighing Conditions 1 and 4 equivalently (known hereafter as the stereotype-consistent conditions), and Conditions 2 and 3 equivalently (known hereafter as the stereotype-inconsistent conditions).

Before examining the effects of stereotype condition on the individual dependent variables, a multivariate analysis of covariance (MANCOVA) was performed to measure the impact of stereotype condition on all of the key dependent variables. The results revealed a marginally significant effect of condition, $F(6, 118) = 2.06$, $p = .06$, which was sufficient to warrant univariate tests. Hence, orthogonal planned comparisons, weighing the stereotype-consistent conditions against the stereotype-inconsistent conditions (+1 −1 −1 +1), were performed on each of the dependent variables.

Life Outcomes

A planned comparison was conducted to determine whether the average ratings of positive life outcomes differed across stereotype conditions. As hypothesized, this comparison yielded significant results, $t(121) = 1.98$, $p < .05$ with an effect size of $\eta^2 = .03$, indicating that participants in the stereotype-inconsistent conditions predicted more positive life outcomes for themselves than those in the stereotype-consistent conditions (see Table 1 for means and standard deviations of all dependent variables). However, a similar comparison revealed that the negative life outcomes ratings did not differ across stereotype conditions, $t(121) = .79$, *ns*.

Mood

Consistent with the hypothesis, a planned comparison contrasting the average mood scores in the stereotype-consistent conditions against the average mood scores in the stereotype-inconsistent conditions revealed a significant finding, $t(121) = 3.17$, $p < .01$ with an effect size of $\eta^2 = .08$. Thus, participants who received stereotype-consistent information about the thin-ideal target were more likely to report being in a negative mood than participants who received stereotype-inconsistent information about the target.

State Self-Esteem

As expected, those who were exposed to stereotype-consistent information experienced lower levels of state self-esteem relative to those who were exposed to stereotype-inconsistent information. A planned comparison testing whether participants would report different levels of appearance SSES as a function of condition was significant, $t(121) = 2.16$, $p < .05$ with an effect size of $\eta^2 = .04$, as was a similar comparison testing for differences in social SSES as a function of condition, $t(121) = 2.01$, $p < .05$, with an effect size of $\eta^2 = .03$. However, the effect of condition on performance SSES was not significant, $t(121) = .13$, *ns*.

DISCUSSION

It is generally accepted in the body image literature that viewing images of thin, attractive females leads women to feel more negatively about their own bodies. However, the findings from the current study suggest that body image, in and of itself, may not hold all of the answers to understanding why women feel self-dissatisfied after exposure to a thin model. Rather, the social context within which these comparisons take place may be an important component of the self-dissatisfaction, such as the beliefs that women hold

TABLE 1 / Means and Standard Deviations for Dependent Variables by Condition

	Information Given about Target Model/Condition							
	Positive (*n* = 32)		Negative (*n* = 36)		Negated (*n* = 30)		No Info. (*n* = 28)	
Variable	*M*	*SD*	*M*	*SD*	*M*	*SD*	*M*	*SD*
Positive Life Outcomes	6.36	1.10	6.56	.91	6.74	1.07	6.21	.97
Negative Life Outcomes	3.07	1.10	2.87	.95	3.22	1.09	3.31	1.06
Mood	−.98	1.50	−.10	2.02	−.47	1.61	−1.46	1.72
Appearance SSES	3.04	.84	3.21	.85	3.21	.66	2.80	.77
Social SSES	3.68	.84	3.96	.71	3.81	.67	3.54	.90
Performance SSES	3.92	.61	3.90	.74	3.86	.67	3.78	.68

about the lifestyles or personality characteristics of thin-ideal females.

Consistent with the predictions, confirming or disconfirming life stereotypes about thin-ideal females significantly impacted the self-satisfaction of the respondents. Women who received stereotype-disconfirming information about the thin target reported more optimistic future life outcomes for themselves, more positive moods, and higher appearance and social state self-esteem in comparison to women who received stereotype-confirming information about the thin target. Yet, women did not report significant differences on negative life outcomes or performance state self-esteem. These results seem reasonable because respondents typically report low probabilities of negative life outcomes (Markus & Nurius, 1986), and performance self-esteem (e.g., levels of ability) may be more remote from lifestyle and body image concerns.

An alternative explanation for the findings is that women responded only to the life outcome scripts rather than the association between life outcomes and thinness. Under this rationale, however, women should have responded more negatively in Condition 1, when they read the positive stereotype-confirming information than in Condition 4, when they read no lifestyle information. The fact that women responded similarly in these two conditions suggests that women attribute positive life circumstances to thin-ideal females even in the absence of additional cueing and may experience some self-dissatisfaction as a result of this association.

In addition, because thinness and attractiveness were confounded in the images, it is unclear whether thinness or attractiveness affected women's self-perceptions. It is likely, however, that both thinness and attractiveness contributed to women's self-evaluation. Because media figures tend to be facially attractive as well as thin in physique, the dimensions of thin and attractive may be associated in women's minds. Nonetheless, future studies that are interested in exploring the relative effects of weight and attractiveness may want to add images of fat and average-weight women to provide further insights on this topic. Including fat and average-weight images may also enhance our understanding of the stereotypes that

women hold about physical appearance and weight, such as beliefs that not being thin may indeed lead to negative consequences (e.g., Quinn & Crocker, 1998).

Although there appears to be a relationship between stereotype belief and self-satisfaction, several limitations suggest that some caution should be taken in interpreting the results. First, the life outcomes scale is a newly developed measure that has not yet been well validated. Moreover, the effect size of the positive life outcomes finding was rather small, as were the effect sizes of the other significant findings. The lack of validation for the life outcomes measure and the small effect sizes suggest that more research on stereotype beliefs and self-satisfaction is needed before more unequivocal conclusions can be made.

Second, studies have shown that whereas African American women tend to experience more weight-related body satisfaction than European American women (Cash & Henry, 1995), Asian American and Hispanic American women resemble European American women in their rates of body-dissatisfaction (Cash & Henry, 1995; Evans & McConnell, in press). Because racial differences seem to influence women's body satisfaction, it is plausible that race may have affected the results of the current study. Unfortunately, because this study lacks an adequate number of women of color to examine their responses separately from the responses of European American women, these analyses were not performed. Future studies may gain valuable insights into women's body image dissatisfaction by including more participants of color.

Third, because the dependent variables were not assessed prior to stimulus exposure, it is possible that participants differed on negative feelings prior to the experimental manipulations. However, random assignment to the different conditions should have minimized this possibility. Also, because manipulation checks were not performed, it cannot be stated with certainty that participants accepted the lifestyle information that they were given or if participants compared themselves to the target. Finally, the presentation of life information about a thin-ideal female image who is ostensibly "real" may be somewhat removed from typical exposure to such images in decontextualized settings (e.g., fashion magazines, commercials). Future research on this topic should consider adapting the current experimental paradigm using a variety of media outlets.

Limitations aside, the findings from this study are valuable because they bring to light another facet of body image dissatisfaction. Specifically, this study extends past research on body image by demonstrating that women's motivation to attain a thin-ideal physical appearance may not stem merely from their body dissatisfaction, but also from their motivation to attain general life satisfaction. In order to fully understand the psychology of body image dissatisfaction, we should move beyond focusing solely on body-dissatisfaction and move toward a more comprehensive understanding of physical appearance, including how body-dissatisfaction takes place within a social and cultural context.

REFERENCES

Cash, T. F., & Henry, P. E., (1995). Women's body images. The results of a national survey in the U.S.A. *Sex Roles, 33,* 19–28.

Cattarin, J. A., Thompson, J. K., Thomas, C., & Williams, R. (2000). Body image, mood, and televised images of attractiveness: The role of social comparison. *Journal of Social and Clinical Psychology, 19,* 220–239.

Evans, P. C., & McConnell, A. R. (in press). Do racial minorities respond in the same way to mainstream beauty standards? Social comparison processes in Asian, Black, and White women. *Self and Identity.*

Groesz, L. M., Levine, M. P., & Murnen, S. K. (2002). The effect of experimental presentation of thin media images on body satisfaction: A meta-analytic review. *International Journal of Eating Disorders, 31,* 1–16.

Harrison, K. (1997). Does interpersonal attraction to thin media personalities promote eating disorders? *Journal of Broadcasting and Electronic Media, 41,* 478–500.

Heatherton, T. F., & Polivy, J. (1991). Development and validation of a scale for measuring state self-esteem. *Journal of Personality and Social Psychology, 60,* 895–910.

Hebl, M. R., & Heatherton, T. F. (1998). The stigma of obesity in women: The difference is black and white. *Personality and Social Psychology Bulletin, 24,* 417–426.

Korbonits, M., Trainer, P. J., Little, J. A., Edwards, R., Kopelman, P. G., Besser, G. M., Svec, F., & Grossman, A. B. (1997). Leptin levels do not change acutely with food administration in normal or obese subjects, but are negatively correlated with pituitary-adrenal activity. *Clinical Endocrinology, 46,* 751–757.

Markus, H., & Nurius, P. (1986). Possible selves. *American Psychologist, 41,* 954–969.

Myers, P. N., & Biocca, F. A. (1992). The elastic body image: The effect of television advertising and programming on body image distortions in young women. *Journal of Communication, 42,* 108–133.

Quinn, D. M., & Crocker, J. (1998). Vulnerability to the affective consequences of the stigma of overweight. In J. K. Swim & C. Stangor (Eds.), *Prejudice: The targets perspective* (pp. 125–143). San Diego, CA: Academic Press.

Silverstein, B., Perdue, L., Peterson, B., & Kelly, E. (1986). The role of the mass media in promoting a thin standard of bodily attractiveness for women. *Sex Roles, 14,* 519–523.

Spitzer, B. L., Henderson, K. A., & Zivian, M. T. (1999). Gender differences in population versus media body sizes: A comparison over four decades. *Sex Roles, 40,* 545–565.

Thornton, B., & Maurice, J. (1997). Physique contrast effect: Adverse impact of idealized body images for women. *Sex Roles, 37,* 433–439.

Thornton, B., & Maurice, J. (1999). Physical attractiveness contrast effect and the moderating influence of self-consciousness. *Sex Roles, 40,* 379–392.

Thornton, B., & Moore, S. (1993). Physical attractiveness contrast effect: Implications for self-esteem and evaluations of the social self. *Personality and Social Psychology Bulletin, 19,* 474–480.

This research was conducted in partial fulfillment of the requirements for the author's doctoral degree at Michigan State University. The author thanks the three anonymous reviewers who provided helpful comments on previous drafts of this manuscript.

CRITICAL THINKING QUESTIONS

1. This study examined how images of thinness affect women. Are men equally affected by how male models are portrayed in the media? Why or why not? If thinness is one of the norms for female models, what are the norms for male models? Have the norms of male model attractiveness changed over time? If so, how so?

2. This article indicates that the variables of thinness and attractiveness may have been confounded. That is, the female image used was both facially attractive and thin. Would the same effect occur if the female image used was thin but facially not as attractive? What about the reverse case? Discuss your answers.

3. Design and conduct a small study to replicate the findings of this article using real media images of thin models as your stimuli. Relate your findings to those reported in this article.

4. Given the emphasis that U.S. society (and thus the mass media) places on female physical attractiveness, what can be done to help women from developing personal dissatisfaction upon exposure to thin portrayals of female attractiveness? What interventions might be made on these women's behalf to reduce the impact of such exposure?

CHAPTER INTEGRATION QUESTIONS —————————

1. All three articles in this chapter are concerned with the importance placed on physical attractiveness. Taken together, what implications do these articles have for how attractiveness affects us? Do the articles suggest how the impact of attractiveness can be minimized? If so, how?

2. What factors besides physical beauty may affect our attraction to other people? Might these factors, in turn, affect how physically attractive we find others? Explain.

3. "Beauty is in the eye of the beholder," according to an old proverb. In light of the information presented in the articles in this chapter, discuss whether this proverb is true or false or both.

Chapter Eight

CLOSE RELATIONSHIPS

OF ALL THE interactions that occur between human beings, perhaps none is more capable of producing such intense feelings as love. If we look at how often love is portrayed in the popular media, we get the definite impression that it is a major concern, almost a preoccupation, of most people. However, if we look at the literature in social psychology, we might get a very different impression. Until recently, the topic of love was largely ignored in the research literature.

A specific subject of interest to many people is the failure of love and the dissolution of relationships. Anyone who has been through a divorce or has witnessed its effects on someone close to them knows that the ending of a marriage is usually an extremely painful ordeal. Yet in spite of the pain involved in splitting up, nearly half of all marriages end up in divorce. What goes wrong? More importantly, what can be done earlier in a relationship to decrease the likelihood of divorce later on? Article 22, "Great Expectations," examines the types of unrealistic expectations that people today have for marriage as well as the origins of such beliefs. Perhaps having more realistic expectations for marriage is a key component to having a successful relationship.

After meeting someone who catches your attention, and then deciding that you would like to get to know him or her better, comes a big step: asking the person out. So you take the chance and ask for a date. Which response to your request would increase your liking of the recipient of your request the most: The person enthusiastically accepts your offer, or the person first plays "hard to get" and then later accepts your invitation? Much folk wisdom would suggest the value of not appearing too eager. But does that hard-to-get strategy actually work? Article 23, "Playing Hard to Get," is an amusing classic article that addresses this dating dilemma.

Finally, Article 24, "Romantic Behaviors of University Students: A Cross-Cultural and Gender Analysis in Puerto Rico and the United States," is a contemporary article that looks at what behaviors males and females consider to be romantic as well as whether such beliefs are culture and gender specific or transcend gender and cultural lines. In other words, are men and women the world over the same or different when it comes to ideas of romance?

ARTICLE 22 _____

The high divorce rate in the United States is of social concern to a large number of Americans. Current statistics indicate that nearly half of all marriages will end in divorce. And while the number of divorces has decreased slightly in the last few years, it still remains around the 50% mark. Whether the high rates of divorce seen over the last few decades will remain the same, increase, or decrease remains to be seen. Nonetheless, the prevalence of divorce is certainly characteristic of contemporary U.S. society.

In spite of the 50/50 odds that a marriage will not last, nearly 95% of the adult U.S. population will marry at least once in their lifetimes. Marriage obviously holds a strong attraction for most people. Even among those who divorce, many will remarry, further pointing to the importance that most people place on the institution of marriage. It probably is a rare couple who marry with the thought that they will divorce. Indeed, most people take to heart the wedding vows of "For better or worse, in sickness and in health, until death do us part," believing that the dire divorce statistics apply to other couples, not them.

So, why has the divorce rate risen and continued to hover around the 50% mark? And for those married people today who have not divorced, are they less satisfied with their marriages than were their counterparts in the past? The answers to both of these questions are quite complex. However, one common denominator may lie in the reasons that people now have for getting married. If you are not married, take a moment and ask yourself (or someone else who is not married) why you want to get married. If you are married, why did you choose to do so? Chances are, the most common answer is for love, with the implication being that marriage provides people with unique happiness and satisfaction. Yet surveys of young adults a century ago found that the majority wanted to get married for much more pragmatic reasons, such as to have children and to own a home.

What does getting married for love (or happiness) have to do with the higher divorce rate? The problem is not marrying for love per se but rather entering a marriage with certain expectations. If a person marries for love and the love he or she experiences after marriage does not conform to his or her expectations, then the logical conclusion may be that he or she made a mistake. That is the thinking of many people today. We live in a culture that highly promotes individual happiness and fulfillment. Such an attitude suggests that individual happiness and fulfillment are paramount and should take precedence over all else. Thus, divorce is seen as an acceptable way to pursue individual happiness and fulfillment.

As mentioned earlier, a major part of the problem may be the unrealistic expectations that people today bring with them to marriage. These expectations may be impossible to meet and thus undoubtedly result in unhappiness in the relationship. The following article by Polly Shulman examines the types of unrealistic expectations that people today have for marriage as well as the sources of such expectations. Perhaps having more realistic views of courtship and marriage can provide a major antidote to the high rate of divorce.

Great Expectations

■ Polly Shulman

Marriage is dead! The twin vises of church and law have relaxed their grip on matrimony. We've been liberated from the grim obligation to stay in a poisonous or abusive marriage for the sake of the kids or for appearances. The divorce rate has stayed constant at nearly 50 percent for the last two decades. The ease with which we enter and dissolve unions makes marriage seem like a prime-time spectator sport, whether it's Britney Spears in Vegas or bimbos chasing after the Bachelor.

Long live the new marriage! We once prized the institution for the practical pairing of a cash-producing father and a home-building mother. Now we want it all—a partner who reflects our taste and status, who sees us for who we are, who loves us for all the "right" reasons, who helps us become the person we want to be. We've done away with a rigid social order, adopting instead an even more onerous obligation: the mandate to find a perfect match. Anything short of this ideal prompts us to ask: Is this all there is? Am I as happy as I should be? Could there be somebody out there who's better for me? As often as not, we answer yes to that last question and fall victim to our own great expectations.

That somebody is, of course, our soul mate, the man or woman who will counter our weaknesses, amplify our strengths and provide the unflagging support and respect that is the essence of a contemporary relationship. The reality is that few marriages or partnerships consistently live up to this ideal. The result is a commitment limbo, in which we care deeply for our partner but keep one stealthy foot out the door of our hearts. In so doing, we subject the relationship to constant review: Would I be happier, smarter, a *better person* with someone else? It's a painful modern quandary. "Nothing has produced more unhappiness than the concept of the soul mate," says Atlanta psychiatrist Frank Pittman.

Consider Jeremy, a social worker who married a businesswoman in his early twenties. He met another woman, a psychologist, at age 29, and after two agonizing years, left his wife for her. But it didn't work out—after four years of cohabitation, and her escalating pleas to marry, he walked out on her, as well. Jeremy now realizes that the relationship with his wife was solid and workable but thinks he couldn't have seen that 10 years ago, when he left her. "There was always someone better around the corner—and the safety and security of marriage morphed into boredom and stasis. The allure of willing and exciting females was too hard to resist," he admits. Now 42 and still single, Jeremy acknowledges, "I hurt others, and I hurt myself."

Like Jeremy, many of us either dodge the decision to commit or commit without fully relinquishing the right to keep looking—opting for an arrangement psychotherapist Terrence Real terms "stable ambiguity."

"You park on the border of the relationship, so you're in it but not of it," he says. There are a million ways to do that: You can be in a relationship but not be sure it's really the right one, have an eye open for a better deal or something on the side, choose someone impossible or far away.

Yet commitment and marriage offer real physical and financial rewards. Touting the benefits of marriage may sound like conservative policy rhetoric, but nonpartisan sociological research backs it up: Committed partners have it all over singles, at least on average. Married people are more financially stable, according to Linda Waite, a sociologist at the University of Chicago and a coauthor of *The Case for Marriage: Why Married People Are Happier, Healthier and Better Off*. Both married men and married women have more assets on average than singles; for women, the differential is huge.

The benefits go beyond the piggy bank. Married people, particularly men, tend to live longer than people who aren't married. Couples also live better: When people expect to stay together, says Waite, they pool their resources, increasing their individual stan-

Reprinted from *Psychology Today,* 2004 (March/April), *37,* 32–42. Reprinted with permission from *Psychology Today* magazine. Copyright © 2004 (Sussex Publishers, Inc.).

dard of living. They also pool their expertise—in cooking say, or financial management. In general, women improve men's health by putting a stop to stupid bachelor tricks and bugging their husbands to exercise and eat their vegetables. Plus, people who aren't comparing their partners to someone else in bed have less trouble performing and are more emotionally satisfied with sex. The relationship doesn't have to be wonderful for life to get better, says Waite: The statistics hold true for mediocre marriages as well as for passionate ones.

The pragmatic benefits of partnership used to be foremost in our minds. The idea of marriage as a vehicle for self-fulfillment and happiness is relatively new, says Paul Amato, professor of sociology, demography and family studies at Penn State University. Surveys of high school and college students 50 or 60 years ago found that most wanted to get married in order to have children or own a home. Now, most report that they plan to get married for love. This increased emphasis on emotional fulfillment within marriage leaves couples ill-prepared for the realities they will probably face.

Because the early phase of a relationship is marked by excitement and idealization, "many romantic, passionate couples expect to have that excitement forever," says Barry McCarthy, a clinical psychologist and coauthor—with his wife, Emily McCarthy—of *Getting It Right the First Time: How to Build a Healthy Marriage.* Longing for the charged energy of the early days, people look elsewhere or split up.

Flagging passion is often interpreted as the death knell of a relationship. You begin to wonder whether you're really right for each other after all. You're comfortable together, but you don't really connect the way you used to. Wouldn't it be more honest—and braver—to just admit that it's not working and call it off? "People are made to feel that remaining in a marriage that doesn't make you blissfully happy is an act of existential cowardice," says Joshua Coleman, a San Francisco psychologist.

Coleman says that the constant cultural pressure to have it all—a great sex life, a wonderful family—has made people ashamed of their less-than-perfect relationships and question whether such unions are worth hanging on to. Feelings of dissatisfaction or disap-

pointment are natural, but they can seem intolerable when standards are sky-high. "It's a recent historical event that people expect to get so much from individual partners," says Coleman, author of *Imperfect Harmony,* in which he advises couples in lackluster marriages to stick it out—especially if they have kids. "There's an enormous amount of pressure on marriages to live up to an unrealistic ideal."

Michaela, 28, was drawn to Bernardo, 30, in part because of their differences: She'd grown up in European boarding schools, he fought his way out of a New York City ghetto. "Our backgrounds made us more interesting to each other," says Michaela. "I was a spoiled brat and he'd been supporting himself from the age of 14, which I admired." Their first two years of marriage were rewarding, but their fights took a toll. "I felt that because he hadn't grown up in a normal family, he didn't grasp basic issues of courtesy and accountability," says Michaela. They were temperamental opposites: He was a screamer, and she was a sulker. She recalls, "After we fought, I needed to be drawn out of my corner, but he took that to mean that I was a cold bitch." Michaela reluctantly concluded that the two were incompatible.

In fact, argue psychologists and marital advocates, there's no such thing as true compatibility.

"Marriage is a disagreement machine," says Diane Sollee, founder of the Coalition for Marriage, Family and Couples Education. "All couples disagree about all the same things. We have a highly romanticized notion that if we were with the right person, we wouldn't fight." Discord springs eternal over money, kids, sex and leisure time, but psychologist John Gottman has shown that long-term, happily married couples disagree about these things just as much as couples who divorce.

"There is a mythology of 'the wrong person,'" agrees Pittman. "All marriages are incompatible. All marriages are between people from different families, people who have a different view of things. The magic is to develop binocular vision, to see life through your partner's eyes as well as through your own."

The realization that we're not going to get everything we want from a partner is not just sobering, it's downright miserable. But it is also a necessary step in building a mature relationship, according to Real, who has written about the subject in *How Can I Get Through to You: Closing the Intimacy Gap Between Men and Women.* "The paradox of intimacy is that our ability to stay close rests on our ability to tolerate solitude inside a relationship," he says. "A central aspect of grown-up love is grief. All of us long for—and think we deserve—perfection."

We can hardly be blamed for striving for bliss and self-fulfillment in our romantic lives—our inalienable right to the pursuit of happiness is guaranteed in the first blueprint of American society.

This same respect for our own needs spurred the divorce-law reforms of the 1960s and 1970s. During that era, "The culture shifted to emphasize individual satisfaction, and marriage was part of that," explains Paul Amato, who has followed more than 2,000 families for 20 years in a long-term study of marriage and divorce. Amato says that this shift did some good by freeing people from abusive and intolerable marriages. But it had an unintended side effect: encouraging people to abandon relationships that may be worth salvaging.

In a society hell-bent on achievement and autonomy, working on a difficult relationship may get short shrift, says psychiatrist Peter Kramer, author of *Should You Leave?*

"So much of what we learn has to do with the self, the ego, rather than giving over the self to things like a relationship," Kramer says. In our competitive world, we're rewarded for our individual achievements rather than for how we help others. We value independence over cooperation, and sacrifices for values like loyalty and continuity seem foolish. "I think we get the divorce rate that we deserve as a culture."

The steadfast focus on our *own* potential may turn a partner into an accessory in the quest for self-actualization, says Maggie Robbins, a therapist in New York City. "We think that this person should reflect the beauty and perfection that is the inner me—or, more often, that this person should compensate for the yuckiness and mess that is the inner me," says Robbins. "This is what makes you tell your wife, 'Lose some weight—you're making me look bad,' not 'Lose some weight, you're at risk for diabetes.'"

Michaela was consistently embarrassed by Bernardo's behavior when they were among friends.

"He'd become sullen and withdrawn—he had a shifty way of looking off to the side when he didn't want to talk. I felt like it reflected badly on me," she admits. Michaela left him and is now dating a wealthy entrepreneur. "I just thought there had to be someone else out there for me."

The urge to find a soul mate is not fueled just by notions of romantic manifest destiny. Trends in the workforce and in the media create a sense of limitless romantic possibility. According to Scott South, a demographer at SUNY-Albany, proximity to potential partners has a powerful effect on relationships. South and his colleagues found higher divorce rates among people living in communities or working in professions where they encounter lots of potential partners—people who match them in age, race and education level. "These results hold true not just for unhappy marriages but also for happy ones," says South.

The temptations aren't always living, breathing people. According to research by psychologists Sara Gutierres and Douglas Kenrick, both of Arizona State University, we find reasonably attractive people less appealing when we've just seen a hunk or a hottie—and we're bombarded daily by images of gorgeous models and actors. When we watch *Lord of the Rings,* Viggo Mortensen's kingly mien and Liv Tyler's elfin charm can make our husbands and wives look all too schlumpy.

Kramer sees a similar pull in the narratives that surround us. "The number of stories that tell us about other lives we could lead—in magazine articles, television shows, books—has increased enormously. We have an enormous reservoir of possibilities," says Kramer.

And these possibilities can drive us to despair. Too many choices have been shown to stymie consumers . . . and an array of alternative mates is no exception. In an era when marriages were difficult to dissolve, couples rated their marriages as more satisfying than do today's couples, for whom divorce is a clear option, according to the National Opinion Research Center at the University of Chicago.

While we expect marriage to be "happily ever after," the truth is that for most people, neither marriage nor divorce seem to have a decisive impact on happiness. Although Waite's research shows that married people are happier than their single counterparts, other studies have found that after a couple years of marriage, people are just about as happy (or unhappy) as they were before settling down. And assuming that marriage will automatically provide contentment is itself a surefire recipe for misery.

"Marriage is not supposed to make you happy. It is supposed to make you married," says Pittman. "When you are all the way in your marriage, you are free to do useful things, become a better person." A committed relationship allows you to drop pretenses and seductions, expose your weaknesses, be yourself—and know that you will be loved, warts and all. "A real relationship is the collision of my humanity and yours, in all its joy and limitations," says Real.

"How partners handle that collision is what determines the quality of their relationship."

Such a down-to-earth view of marriage is hardly romantic, but that doesn't mean it's not profound: An authentic relationship with another person, says Pittman, is "one of the first steps toward connecting with the human condition—which is necessary if you're going to become fulfilled as a human being." If we accept these humble terms, the quest for a soul mate might just be a noble pursuit after all.

LEARN MORE ABOUT IT

101 Things I Wish I Knew When I Got Married   Linda and Charlie Bloom (New World Library, 2004)

CRITICAL THINKING QUESTIONS

1. "Nothing has produced more unhappiness than the concept of the soul mate." Discuss this quote from the article, giving specific examples to support why you do or do not agree with it.

2. Do an informal survey of people to find out what they think is the most important factor in a successful marriage. Chances are, "good communication" will most often be cited. How does this factor (or whatever factor your survey finds most important) relate to the information contained in the article? Discuss.

3. List five things that you learned from this article that may decrease your chance of getting divorced. Which of these factors would be the easiest to change or control? Which would be the most difficult? Explain your answers.

4. How are love and marriage portrayed in the movies? Identify specific films, and discuss each in terms of whether it portrays a realistic or unrealistic view of love and marriage. What, if any, problems are associated with the general media portrayals of love and marriage?

5. Article 19 discussed the concept of the contrast effect and how being exposed to very attractive people might make us less attracted to our actual partners. Beyond physical attractiveness, how else might the contrast effect be working to the detriment of successful marriages?

ARTICLE 23 _____

Wanting to love and be loved is perhaps the most profound and universal human longing. As personal experience teaches us, love is not only a highly desired and sought after state but it also may actually be necessary for our very well-being. Yet exactly what love means and how it is expressed and felt may be something that differs in each of us.

Let's back up a step. Before talking about a deep and profound love for another person, what about the initial stages that may precede it? In other words, what factors are involved in the initial attraction to another potential romantic partner? People vary considerably in what they find attractive and desirable in another person, but there are common dimensions that seem to be fairly universal—the importance of physical attractiveness and certain personality traits such as intelligence, for instance.

Suppose that you have just met someone who has caught your attention. You are interested enough that you want to ask the person out on a date. Whether you are the iniator or the recipient of the request, a date often creates a set of mixed feelings. On one hand, the potential pleasure that one can have in a successful relationship is highly desirable. On the other hand, most people do not like rejection, and any such beginning also carries with it the possibility of an end.

All right, so he finally asks her out. (Although females certainly initiate dates, research still shows that males typically take this first step in U.S. culture.) How does she respond to his request? Obviously, she can say no. If she says yes, however, there are many ways that it can be said. Which do you think would be most favorably received by the man—someone who enthusiastically and without hesitation says "Yes. I thought you'd never ask" or someone who plays hard to get, ultimately accepting the invitation but only after some hesitation or convincing?

Folk advice going back thousands of years states that playing hard to get might be the way to proceed. As this classic article by Elaine Hatfield, G. William Walster, Jane Piliavin, and Lynn Schmidt indicates, however, that might not be the best advice to follow.

"Playing Hard to Get"
Understanding an Elusive Phenomenon
■ Elaine Hatfield, G. William Walster, Jane Piliavin, and Lynn Schmidt

According to folklore, the woman who is hard to get is a more desirable catch than the woman who is too eager for an alliance. Five experiments were conducted to demonstrate that individuals value hard-to-get dates more than easy-to-get ones. All five experiments failed. In Experiment VI, we finally gained an understanding of this elusive phenomenon. We proposed that two components contribute to a woman's desirability: (a) how hard the woman is for the subject to get and (b) how hard she is for other men to get. We predicted that the selectively hard-to-get woman (i.e., a woman who is easy for the subject to get but hard for all other men to get) would be preferred to either a uniformly hard-to-get woman, a uniformly easy-to-get woman, or a woman about which the subject has no information. This hypothesis received strong support. The reason for the popularity of the selec-

Reprinted from *Journal of Personality and Social Psychology,* 1973, *26,* 113–121. Copyright © 1973 by the American Psychological Association. Reprinted by permission.

tive woman was evident. Men ascribe to her all of the assets of uniformly hard-to-get and the uniformly easy-to-get women and none of their liabilities.

According to folklore, the woman who is hard to get is a more desirable catch than is the woman who is overly eager for alliance. Socrates, Ovid, Terence, the *Kama Sutra,* and Dear Abby all agree that the person whose affection is easily won is unlikely to inspire passion in another. Ovid, for example, argued:

> *Fool, if you feel no need to guard your girl for her own sake, see that you guard her for mine, so I may want her the more. Easy things nobody wants, but what is forbidden is tempting. . . . Anyone who can love the wife of an indolent cuckold, I should suppose, would steal buckets of sand from the shore. (pp. 65–66)*

When we first began our investigation, we accepted cultural lore. We assumed that men would prefer a hard-to-get woman. Thus, we began our research by interviewing college men as to why they preferred hard-to-get women. Predictably, the men responded to experimenter demands. They explained that they preferred hard-to-get women because the elusive woman is almost inevitably a valuable woman. They pointed out that a woman can only afford to be "choosy" if she is popular—and a woman is popular for some reason. When a woman is hard to get, it is usually a tip-off that she is especially pretty, has a good personality, is sexy, etc. Men also were intrigued by the challenge that the elusive woman offered. One can spend a great deal of time fantasizing about what it would be like to date such a woman. Since the hard-to-get woman's desirability is well recognized, a man can gain prestige if he is seen with her.

An easy-to-get woman, on the other hand, spells trouble. She is probably desperate for a date. She is probably the kind of woman who will make too many demands on a person; she might want to get serious right away. Even worse, she might have a "disease."

In brief, nearly all interviewees agreed with our hypothesis that a hard-to-get woman is a valuable woman, and they could supply abundant justification for their prejudice. A few isolated men refused to cooperate. These dissenters noted that an elusive woman is not always more desirable than an available woman. Sometimes the hard-to-get woman is not

only hard to get—she is *impossible* to get, because she is misanthropic and cold. Sometimes a woman is easy to get because she is a friendly, outgoing woman who boosts one's ego and insures that dates are "no hassle." We ignored the testimony of these deviant types.

We then conducted five experiments designed to demonstrate that an individual values a hard-to-get date more highly than an easy-to-get date. All five experiments failed.

THEORETICAL RATIONALE

Let us first review the theoretical rationale underlying these experiments.

In Walster, Walster, and Berscheid (1971) we argued that if playing hard to get does increase one's desirability, several psychological theories could account for this phenomenon:

1. Dissonance theory predicts that if a person must expend great energy to attain a goal, one is unusually appreciative of the goal (see Aronson and Mills, 1959; Gerard and Mathewson, 1966; Zimbardo, 1965). The hard-to-get date requires a suitor to expend more effort in her pursuit than he would normally expend. One way for the suitor to justify such unusual effort is by aggrandizing her.

2. According to learning theory, an elusive person should have two distinct advantages: (*a*) Frustration may increase drive—by waiting until the suitor has achieved a high sexual drive state, heightening his drive level by introducing momentary frustration, and then finally rewarding him, the hard-to-get woman can maximize the impact of the sexual reward she provides (see Kimball, 1961, for evidence that frustration does energize behavior and does increase the impact of appropriate rewards). (*b*) Elusiveness and value may be associated—individuals may have discovered through frequent experience that there is more competition for socially desirable dates than for undesirable partners. Thus, being "hard to get" comes to be associated with "value." As a consequence, the conditional stimulus (CS) of being hard to get generates a fractional antedating goal response and a fractional goal response, which leads to the conditioned response of liking.

3. In an extension of Schachterian theory, Walster (1971) argued that two components are necessary

before an individual can experience passionate love; (*a*) He must be physiologically aroused; and (*b*) the setting must make it appropriate for him to conclude that his aroused feelings are due to love. On both counts, the person who plays hard to get might be expected to generate unusual passion. Frustration should increase the suitor's physiological arousal, and the association of "elusiveness" with "value" should increase the probability that the suitor will label his reaction to the other as "love."

From the preceding discussion, it is evident that several conceptually distinct variables may account for the hard-to-get phenomenon. In spite of the fact that we can suggest a plethora of reasons as to why the playing hard-to-get strategy might be an effective strategy, all five studies failed to provide any support for the contention that an elusive woman is a desirable woman. Two experiments failed to demonstrate that outside observers perceive a hard-to-get individual as especially "valuable." Three experiments failed to demonstrate that a suitor perceives a hard-to-get date as especially valuable.

Walster, Walster, and Berscheid (1971) conducted two experiments to test the hypothesis that teenagers would deduce that a hard-to-get boy or girl was more socially desirable than was a teenager whose affection could be easily obtained. In these experiments high school juniors and seniors were told that we were interested in finding out what kind of first impression various teenagers made on others. They were shown pictures and biographies of a couple. They were told how romantically interested the stimulus person (a boy or girl) was in his partner after they had met only four times. The stimulus person was said to have liked the partner "extremely much," to have provided no information to us, or to have liked the partner "not particularly much." The teenagers were then asked how socially desirable both teenagers seemed (i.e., how likable, how physically attractive, etc.). Walster, Walster, and Berscheid, of course, predicted that the more romantic interest the stimulus person expressed in a slight acquaintance, the less socially desirable that stimulus person would appear to an outside observer. The results were diametrically opposed to those predicted. The more romantic interest the stimulus person expressed in an acquaintance, the *more* socially desirable teenagers judged him to be. Restraint does

not appear to buy respect. Instead, it appears that "All the world *does* love a lover."

Lyons, Walster, and Walster (1971) conducted a field study and a laboratory experiment in an attempt to demonstrate that men prefer a date who plays hard to get. Both experiments were conducted in the context of a computer matching service. Experiment III was a field experiment. Women who signed up for the computer matching program were contacted and hired as experimenters. They were then given precise instructions as to how to respond when their computer match called them for a date. Half of the time they were told to pause and think for 3 seconds before accepting the date. (These women were labeled "hard to get.") Half of the time they were told to accept the date immediately. (These women are labeled "easy to get.") The data indicated that elusiveness had no impact on the man's liking for his computer date.

Experiment IV was a laboratory experiment. In this experiment, Lyons et al. hypothesized that the knowledge that a woman is elusive gives one indirect evidence that she is socially desirable. Such indirect evidence should have the biggest impact when a man has no way of acquiring *direct* evidence about a coed's value or when he has little confidence in his own ability to assess value. When direct evidence is available, and the man possesses supreme confidence in his ability to make correct judgments, information about a woman's elusiveness should have little impact on a man's reaction to her. Lyons et al. thus predicted that when men lacked direct evidence as to a woman's desirability, a man's self-esteem and the woman's elusiveness should interact in determining his respect and liking for her. Lyons et al. measured males' self-esteem via Rosenberg's (1965) measure of self-esteem, Rosenfeld's (1964) measure of fear of rejection, and Berger's (1952) measure of self-acceptance.

The dating counselor then told subjects that the computer had assigned them a date. They were asked to telephone her from the office phone, invite her out, and then report their first impression of her. Presumably the pair would then go out on a date and eventually give us further information about how successful our computer matching techniques had been. Actually, all men were assigned a confederate as a date. Half of the time the woman played hard to get. When the man asked her out she replied:

Mmm [slight pause] No, I've got a date then. It seems like I signed up for that Date Match thing a long time ago and I've met more people since then—I'm really pretty busy all this week.

She paused again. If the subject suggested another time, the confederate hesitated only slightly, then accepted. If he did not suggest another time, the confederate would take the initiative of suggesting: "How about some time next week—or just meeting for coffee in the Union some afternoon?" And again, she accepted the next invitation. Half of the time, in the easy-to-get condition, the confederate eagerly accepted the man's offer of a date.

Lyons et al. predicted that since men in this blind date setting lacked direct evidence as to a woman's desirability, low-self-esteem men should be more receptive to the hard-to-get woman than were high-self-esteem men. Although Lyons et al.'s manipulation checks indicate that their manipulations were successful and their self-esteem measure was reliable, their hypothesis was not confirmed. Elusiveness had no impact on liking, regardless of subject's self-esteem level.

Did we give up our hypothesis? Heavens no. After all, it had only been disconfirmed four times.

By Experiment V, we had decided that perhaps the hard-to-get hypothesis must be tested in a sexual setting. After all, the first theorist who advised a woman to play hard to get was Socrates; his pupil was Theodota, a prostitute. He advised:

They will appreciate your favors most highly if you wait till they ask for them. The sweetest meats, you see, if served before they are wanted seem sour, and to those who had enough they are positively nauseating; but even poor fare is very welcome when offered to a hungry man. [Theodota inquired] And how can I make them hungry for my fare? [Socrates' reply] Why, in the first place, you must not offer it to them when they have had enough—but prompt them by behaving as a model of Propriety, by a show of reluctance to yield, and by holding back until they are as keen as can be; and then the same gifts are much more to the recipient than when they're offered before they are desired. (see Xenophon, p. 48)

Walster, Walster, and Lambert (1971) thus proposed that a prostitute who states that she is selective in her choice of customers will be held in higher regard than will be the prostitute who admits that she is completely unselective in her choice of partners.

In this experiment, a prostitute served as the experimenter. When the customer arrived, she mixed a drink for him; then she delivered the experimental manipulation. Half of the time, in the hard-to-get condition, she stated, "Just because I see you this time it doesn't mean that you can have my phone number or see me again. I'm going to start school soon, so I won't have much time, so I'll only be able to see the people that I like the best." Half of the time, in the easy-to-get condition, she did not communicate this information. From this point on, the prostitute and the customer interacted in conventional ways.

The client's liking for the prostitute was determined in two ways: First, the prostitute estimated how much the client had seemed to like her. (Questions asked were, for example, How much did he seem to like you? Did he make arrangements to return? How much did he pay you?) Second, the experimenter recorded how many times within the next 30 days the client arranged to have sexual relations with her.

Once again we failed to confirm the hard-to-get hypothesis. If anything, those clients who were told that the prostitute did not take just anyone were *less* likely to call back and liked the prostitute less than did other clients.

At this point, we ruefully decided that we had been on the wrong track. We decided that perhaps all those practitioners who advise women to play hard to get are wrong. Or perhaps it is only under very special circumstances that it will benefit one to play hard to get.

Thus, we began again. We reinterviewed students—this time with an open mind. This time we asked men to tell us about the advantages *and* disadvantages of hard-to-get and easy-to-get women. This time replies were more informative. According to reports, choosing between a hard-to-get woman and an easy-to-get woman was like choosing between Scylla and Charybdis—each woman was uniquely desirable and uniquely frightening.

Although the elusive woman was likely to be a popular prestige date, she presented certain problems.

Since she was not particularly enthusiastic about you, she might stand you up or humiliate you in front of your friends. She was likely to be unfriendly, cold, and to possess inflexible standards.

The easy-to-get woman was certain to boost one's ego and to make a date a relaxing, enjoyable experience, but . . . Unfortunately, dating an easy woman was a risky business. Such a woman might be easy to get, but hard to get rid of. She might "get serious." Perhaps she would be so oversexed or overaffectionate in public that she would embarrass you. Your buddies might snicker when they saw you together. After all, they would know perfectly well why you were dating *her.*

The interlocking assets and difficulties envisioned when they attempted to decide which was better—a hard-to-get or an easy-to-get woman—gave us a clue as to why our previous experiments had not worked out. The assets and liabilities of the elusive and the easy dates had evidently generally balanced out. On the average, then, both types of women tended to be equally well liked. When a slight difference in liking did appear, it favored the easy-to-get woman.

It finally impinged on us that there are *two* components that are important determinants of how much a man likes a woman: (*a*) How hard or easy she is for him to get, and (*b*) how hard or easy she is for *other men* to get. So long as we were examining the desirability of women who were hard or easy for everyone to get, things balanced out. The minute we examined other possible configurations, it became evident that there is one type of woman who can transcend the limitations of the uniformly hard-to-get or the uniformly easy-to-get woman. If a woman has a reputation for being hard to get, but for some reason she is easy for the subject to get, she should be maximally appealing. Dating such a woman should insure one of great prestige; she is, after all, hard to get. Yet, since she is exceedingly available to the subject, the dating situation should be a relaxed, rewarding experience. Such a *selectively* hard-to-get woman possesses the assets of both the easy-to-get and the hard-to-get women, while avoiding all of their liabilities.

Thus, in Experiment VI, we hypothesized that a selectively hard-to-get woman (i.e., a woman who is easy for the subject to get but very hard for any other

man to get) will be especially liked by her date. Women who are hard for everyone—including the subject—to get, or who are easy for everyone to get— or control women, about whom the subject had no information—will be liked a lesser amount.

METHOD

Subjects were 71 male summer students at the University of Wisconsin. They were recruited for a dating research project. This project was ostensibly designed to determine whether computer matching techniques are in fact more effective than is random matching. All participants were invited to come into the dating center in order to choose a date from a set of five potential dates.

When the subject arrived at the computer match office, he was handed folders containing background information on five women. Some of these women had supposedly been "randomly" matched with him; others had been "computer matched" with him. (He was not told which women were which.)

In reality, all five folders contained information about fictitious women. The first item in the folder was a "background questionnaire" on which the woman had presumably described herself. This questionnaire was similar to one the subject had completed when signing up for the match program. We attempted to make the five women's descriptions different enough to be believable, yet similar enough to minimize variance. Therefore, the way the five women described themselves was systematically varied. They claimed to be 18 or 19 years old; freshmen or sophomores; from a Wisconsin city, ranging in size from over 500,000 to under 50,000; 5 feet 2 inches to 5 feet 4 inches tall; Protestant, Catholic, Jewish or had no preference; graduated in the upper 10 to 50 percent of their high school class; and Caucasians who did not object to being matched with a person of another race. The women claimed to vary on a political spectrum from "left of center" through "moderate" to "near right of center"; to place little or no importance on politics and religion; and to like recent popular movies. Each woman listed four or five activities she liked to do on a first date (i.e., go to a movie, talk in a quiet place, etc.).

In addition to the background questionnaire, three of the five folders contained five "date selection forms." The experimenter explained that some of the women had already been able to come in, examine the background information of their matches, and indicate their first impression of them. Two of the subject's matches had not yet come in. Three of the women had already come in and evaluated the subject along with her four other matches. These women would have five date selection forms in their folders. The subject was shown the forms, which consisted of a scale ranging from "definitely do *not* want to date" (–10) to "definitely want to date" (+10). A check appeared on each scale. Presumably the check indicated how much the woman had liked a given date. (At this point, the subject was told his identification number. Since all dates were identified by numbers on the forms, this identification number enabled him to ascertain how each date had evaluated both him and her four other matches.)

The date selection forms allowed us to manipulate the elusiveness of the woman. One woman appeared to be uniformly hard to get. She indicated that though she was willing to date any of the men assigned to her, she was not enthusiastic about any of them. She rated all five of her date choices from +1 to +2, including the subject (who was rated 1.75).

One woman appeared to be uniformly easy to get. She indicated that she was enthusiastic about dating all five of the men assigned to her. She rated her desire to date all five of her date choices +7 to +9. This included the subject, who was rated 8.

One woman appeared to be easy for the subject to get but hard for anyone else to get (i.e., the selectively hard-to-get woman). She indicated minimal enthusiasm for four of her date choices, rating them from +2 to +3, and extreme enthusiasm (+8) for the subject.

Two women had no date selection forms in their folders (i.e., no information women).

Naturally, each woman appeared in each of the five conditions.

The experimenter asked the man to consider the folders, complete a "first impression questionnaire" for each woman, and then decide which *one* of the women he wished to date. (The subject's rating of the dates constitute our verbal measure of liking; his choice in a date constitutes our behavioral measure of liking.)

The experimenter explained that she was conducting a study of first impressions in conjunction with the dating research project. The study, she continued, was designed to learn more about how good people are at forming first impressions of others on the basis of rather limited information. She explained that filling out the forms would probably make it easier for the man to decide which one of the five women he wished to date.

The first impression questionnaire consisted of three sections:

Liking for Various Dates   Two questions assessed subjects' liking for each woman: "If you went out with this girl, how well do you think you would get along?"—with possible responses ranging from "get along extremely well" (5) to "not get along at all" (1)—and "What was your overall impression of the girl?"—with possible responses ranging from "extremely favorable" (7) to "extremely unfavorable" (1). Scores on these two questions were summed to form an index of expressed liking. This index enables us to compare subjects' liking for each of the women.

Assets and Liabilities Ascribed to Various Dates   We predicted that subjects would prefer the selective woman, because they would expect her to possess the good qualities of both the uniformly hard-to-get and the uniformly easy-to-get woman, while avoiding the bad qualities of both her rivals. Thus, the second section was designed to determine the extent to which subjects imputed good and bad qualities to the various dates.

This section was comprised of 10 pairs of polar opposites. Subjects were asked to rate how friendly–unfriendly, cold–warm, attractive–unattractive, easygoing–rigid, exciting–boring, shy–outgoing, fun-loving–dull, popular–unpopular, aggressive–passive, selective–nonselective each woman was. Ratings were made on a 7-point scale. The more desirable the trait ascribed to a woman, the higher the score she was given.

Liabilities Attributed to Easy-to-Get Women   The third scale was designed to assess the extent to which subjects attributed selected negative attributes to each woman. The third scale consisted of six statements:

She would more than likely do something to embarrass me in public.

She probably would demand too much attention and affection from me.

She seems like the type who would be too dependent on me.

She might turn out to be too sexually promiscuous.

She probably would make me feel uneasy when I'm with her in a group.

She seems like the type who doesn't distinguish between the boys she dates. I probably would be "just another date."

Subjects were asked whether they anticipated any of the above difficulties in their relationship with each woman. They indicated their misgivings on a scale ranging from "certainly true of her" (1) to "certainly not true of her" (7).

The experimenter suggested that the subject carefully examine both the background questionnaires and the date selection forms of all potential dates in order to decide whom he wanted to date. Then she left the subject. (The experimenter was, of course, unaware of what date was in what folder.)

The experimenter did not return until the subject had completed the first impression questionnaires. Then she asked him which woman he had decided to date.

After his choice had been made, the experimenter questioned him as to what factors influenced his choice. Frequently men who chose the selectively easy-to-get woman said that "She chose me, and that made me feel really good" or "She seemed more selective than the others." The uniformly easy-to-get woman was often rejected by subjects who complained "She must be awfully hard up for a date—she really would take anyone." The uniformly hard-to-get woman was once described as a "challenge" but more often rejected as being "snotty" or "too picky."

At the end of the session, the experimenter debriefed the subject and then gave him the names of five actual dates who had been matched with him.

RESULTS

We predicted that the selectively hard-to-get woman (easy for me but hard for everyone else to get) would be liked more than women who were uniformly hard to get, uniformly easy to get, or neutral (the no information women). We had no prediction as to whether or not her three rivals would differ in attractiveness. The results strongly support our hypothesis.

Dating Choices

When we examine the men's choices in dates, we see that the selective woman is far more popular than any of her rivals. (See Table 1.) We conducted a chi-square test to determine whether or not men's choices in dates were randomly distributed. They were not (χ^2 = 69.5, df = 4, p < .001). Nearly all subjects preferred to date the selective woman. When we compare the frequency with which her four rivals (combined) are chosen, we see that the selective woman does get far more than her share of dates (χ^2 = 68.03, df = 1, p < .001).

We also conducted an analysis to determine whether or not the women who are uniformly hard to get, uniformly easy to get, or whose popularity is unknown, differed in popularity. We see that they did not (χ^2 = 2.86, df = 3).

Liking for the Various Dates

Two questions tapped the men's romantic liking for the various dates: (*a*) "If you went out with this woman,

TABLE 1 / Men's Choices in a Date

Item	Selectively Hard to Get	Uniformly Hard to Get	Uniformly Easy to Get	No Information for No. 1	No Information for No. 2
Number of men choosing to date each woman	42	6	5	11	7

how well do you think you'd get along?"; and (*b*) "What was your overall impression of the woman?" Scores on these two indexes were summed to form an index of liking. Possible scores ranged from 2 to 12.

A contrast was then set up to test our hypothesis that the selective woman will be preferred to her rivals. The contrast that tests this hypothesis is of the form $\Gamma_1 = 4\mu$ (selectively hard to get) – 1 (uniformly hard to get) – 2μ (neutral). We tested the hypothesis $\Gamma_1 = 0$ against the alternative hypothesis $\Gamma_1 \neq 0$. An explanation of this basically simple procedure may be found in Hays (1963). If our hypothesis is true, the preceding contrast should be large. If our hypothesis is false, the resulting contrast should not differ significantly from 0. The data again provide strong support for the hypothesis that the selective woman is better liked than her rivals ($F = 23.92$, $df = 1/70$, $p < .001$).

Additional Data Snooping

We also conducted a second set of contrasts to determine whether the rivals (i.e., the uniformly hard-to-get woman, the uniformly easy-to-get woman, and the control woman) were differentially liked. Using the procedure presented by Morrison (1967) in chapter 4, the data indicate that the rivals are differentially liked ($F = 4.43$, $df = 2/69$). As Table 2 indicates, the uniformly hard-to-get woman seems to be liked slightly less than the easy-to-get or control woman.

In any attempt to explore data, one must account for the fact that observing the data permits the researcher to capitalize on chance. Thus, one must use simultaneous testing methods so as not to spuriously inflate the probability of attaining statistical significance. In the present situation, we are interested in comparing the means of a number of dependent measures, namely the liking for the different women in the dating situation. To perform post hoc multiple comparisons in this situation, one can use a transformation of Hotelling's t^2 statistic, which is distributed as F. The procedure is directly analogous to Scheffé's multiple-comparison procedure for independent groups, except where one compares means of a number of dependent measures.

To make it abundantly clear that the main result is that the discriminating woman is better liked than each of the other rivals, we performed an additional post hoc analysis, pitting each of the rivals separately against the discriminating woman. In these analyses, we see that the selective woman is better liked than the woman who is uniformly easy to get ($F = 3.99$, $df = 3/68$), than the woman who is uniformly hard to get ($F = 9.47$, $df = 3/68$), and finally, than the control women ($F = 4.93$, $df = 3/68$).

TABLE 2 / Men's Reactions to Various Dates

Item	Type of Date			
	Selectively Hard to Get	Uniformly Hard to Get	Uniformly Easy to Get	No Information
Men's liking for dates	9.41[a]	7.90	8.53	8.58
Evaluation of women's assets and liabilities				
Selective[b]	5.23	4.39	2.85	4.30
Popular[b]	4.83	4.58	4.65	4.83
Friendly[c]	5.58	5.07	5.52	5.37
Warm[c]	5.15	4.51	4.99	4.79
Easy Going[c]	4.83	4.42	4.82	4.61
Problems expected in dating	5.23[d]	4.86	4.77	4.99

[a]The higher the number, the more liking the man is expressing for the date.
[b]Traits we expected to be ascribed to the selectively hard-to-get and the uniformly hard-to-get dates.
[c]Traits we expected to be ascribed to the selectively hard-to-get and the uniformly easy-to-get dates.
[d]The higher the number the *fewer* the problems the subject anticipates in dating.

Thus, it is clear that although there are slight differences in the way rivals are liked, these differences are small, relative to the overwhelming attractiveness of the selective woman.

Assets and Liabilities Attributed to Dates

We can now attempt to ascertain *why* the selective woman is more popular than her rivals. Earlier, we argued that the selectively hard-to-get woman should occupy a unique position; she should be assumed to possess all of the virtues of her rivals, but none of their flaws.

The virtues and flaws that the subject ascribed to each woman were tapped by the polar–opposite scale. Subjects evaluated each woman on 10 characteristics.

We expected that subjects would associate two assets with a uniformly hard-to-get woman: Such a woman should be perceived to be both "selective" and "popular." Unfortunately, such a woman should also be assumed to possess three liabilities—she should be perceived to be "unfriendly," "cold," and "rigid." Subjects should ascribe exactly the opposite virtues and liabilities to the easy-to-get woman: Such a woman should possess the assets of "friendliness," "warmth," and "flexibility," and the liabilities of "unpopularity" and "lack of selectivity." The selective woman was expected to possess only assets: She should be perceived to be as "selective" and "popular" as the uniformly elusive woman, and as "friendly," "warm," and "easy-going" as the uniformly easy woman. A contrast was set up to test this specific hypothesis. (Once again, see Hays for the procedure.) This contrast indicates that our hypothesis is confirmed ($F = 62.43$, $df = 1/70$). The selective woman is rated most like the uniformly hard-to-get woman on the first two positive characteristics and most like the uniformly easy-to-get woman on the last three characteristics.

For the reader's interest, the subjects' ratings of all five women's assets and liabilities are presented in Table 2.

Comparing the Selective and the Easy Women

Scale 3 was designed to assess whether or not subjects anticipated fewer problems when they envisioned dating the selective woman than when they envisioned dating the uniformly easy-to-get woman. On the basis of pretest interviews, we compiled a list of many of the concerns men had about easy women (e.g., "She would more than likely do something to embarrass me in public.").

We, of course, predicted that subjects would experience more problems when contemplating dating the uniformly easy woman than when contemplating dating a woman who was easy for *them* to get, but hard for anyone else to get (i.e., the selective woman).

Men were asked to say whether or not they envisioned each of the difficulties were they to date each of the women. Possible replies varied from 1 (certainly true of her) to 7 (certainly not true of her). The subjects' evaluations of each woman were summed to form an index of anticipated difficulties. Possible scores ranged from 6 to 42.

A contrast was set up to determine whether the selective woman engendered less concern than the uniformly easy-to-get woman. The data indicate that she does ($F = 17.50$, $df = 1/70$). If the reader is interested in comparing concern engendered by each woman, these data are available in Table 2.

The data provide clear support for our hypotheses: The selective woman is strongly preferred to any of her rivals. The reason for her popularity is evident. Men ascribe to her all of the assets of the uniformly hard-to-get and the uniformly easy-to-get women, and none of their liabilities.

Thus, after five futile attempts to understand the "hard-to-get" phenomenon, it appears that we have finally gained an understanding of this process. It appears that a woman can intensify her desirability if she acquires a reputation for being hard-to-get and then, by her behavior, makes it clear to a selected romantic partner that she is attracted to him.

In retrospect, especially in view of the strongly supportive data, the logic underlying our predictions sounds compelling. In fact, after examining our data, a colleague who had helped design the five ill-fated experiments noted that, "That is exactly what I would have predicted" (given his economic view of man). Unfortunately, we are all better at postdiction than prediction.

REFERENCES

Aronson, E., and Mills, J. The effect of severity of initiation on liking for a group. *Journal of Abnormal and Social Psychology,* 1959, 67, 31–36.

Berger, E. M. The relation between expressed acceptance of self and expressed acceptance of others. *Journal of Abnormal and Social Psychology,* 1952, 47, 778–782.

Gerard, H. B. and Mathewson, G. C. The effects of severity of initiation and liking for a group: A replication. *Journal of Experimental Social Psychology,* 1966, 2, 278–287.

Hays, W. L. *Statistics for psychologists.* New York: Holt, Rinehart, 1963.

Kimball, G. A. *Hilgard and Marquis' conditioning and learning.* New York: Appleton-Century-Crofts, 1961.

Lyons, J., Walster, and Walster, G. W. Playing hard-to-get: An elusive phenomenon University of Wisconsin, Madison: Author, 1971. (Mimeo)

Morrison, D. F. *Multivariate statistical methods.* New York: McGraw-Hill, 1967.

Ovid. *The art of love.* Bloomington: University of Indiana Press, 1963.

Rosenberg, M. *Society and the adolescent self image.* Princeton, N.J.: Princeton University Press, 1965.

Rosenfeld, H. M. Social choice conceived as a level of aspiration. *Journal of Abnormal and Social Psychology,* 1964, 68, 491–499.

Walster, E. Passionate love. In B. I. Murstein (Ed.), *Theories of attraction and love.* New York: Springer, 1971.

Walster, E., Walster, G. W., and Berscheid, E. The efficacy of playing hard-to-get. *Journal of Experimental Education,* 1971, 39, 73–77.

Walster, G. W., and Lambert, P. Playing hard-to-get: A field study. University of Wisconsin, Madison: Author, 1971. (Mimeo)

Xenophon. *Memorabilia.* London: Heinemann, 1923.

Zimbardo, P. G. The effect of effort and improvisation on self persuasion produced by role-playing. *Journal of Experimental Social Psychology,* 1965, 1, 103–120.

This research was supported in part by National Science Foundation Grants GS 2932 and GS 30822X and in part by National Institute for Mental Health Grant MH 16661.

CRITICAL THINKING QUESTIONS

1. Nonsignificant results are difficult to interpret in research. For example, if a woman playing hard to get is not viewed differently from one playing "easy," is there really no difference? Why or why not? Or is it possible that the experimental manipulation (how playing hard to get or easy were varied in the study) was not strong enough to produce an effect? Discuss this possibility by examining how playing hard to get was manipulated in the first five experiments reported in this article.

2. Are ethical issues involved in any of the studies? In particular, what are your views of Study 5, which involved the services of a prostitute?

3. This study ultimately determined that selectively hard-to-get women were most preferred by the men. Do you think the reverse is true—that women most prefer selectively hard-to-get men? Why or why not?

4. Do you think that the results of this study could be generalized to the sexual arena (i.e., when it comes to sex, a selectively hard-to-get woman would be preferred over either a hard-to-get or easy-to-get woman)? Explain.

ADDITIONAL RELATED READINGS

Meston, C. M., & Frohlich, P. F. (2003). Love at first fright: Partner salience moderates roller-coaster-induced excitation transfer. *Archives of Sexual Behavior, 32*(6), 537–544.

Richards, J. M., Butler, E. A., & Gross, J. J. (2003). Emotion regulation in romantic relationships: The cognitive consequences of concealed feelings. *Journal of Social and Personal Relationships, 20*(5), 599–620.

ARTICLE 24 _____

What is *love?* The topic certainly has been and continues to be a popular one in the realm of philosophy, theology, and the arts. Yet in spite of the high value that people place on this experience, social scientists did not begin to investigate it until recently, for a variety of reasons. First and foremost is the subject matter itself. What, exactly, is *love?* How can we begin to define it, let alone measure it? Other reasons explain why the question was not addressed, as well. Many people think that the very importance of this feeling is why it should not be addressed. Perhaps love is supposed to be entirely private and best left alone.

But back to the question of what is *love.* You may know that you love someone based on the thoughts and feelings you have about him or her. But how does that person know that you love him or her? That person cannot tap directly into the private thoughts and feelings that you have for him or her. He or she can only infer that information from the ways that you act, whether in making certain gestures that are considered loving or by saying certain words. Just as the word *love* may have different meanings for different people, perhaps how people show their love also differs.

While this individuality of expressing love certainly exists, there also may be some common behaviors that most people would view as loving acts. Think for a second about the multitude of movies and novels that deal with romance. Do any common themes emerge for how people express their loving feelings?

The following article by José A. Quiles looks at what males and females consider to be romantic behaviors. Furthermore, the article attempts to answer the question of whether such romantic behaviors are culture specific or the same across cultures. It may be that men and women are at the same time similar yet different in what they consider romantic.

Romantic Behaviors of University Students

A Cross-Cultural and Gender Analysis in Puerto Rico and the United States

■ José A. Quiles

This study examined cultural and gender differences in romantic behaviors among university students in Puerto Rico and the United States. The data were collected from a total of N = 395 students using a field-based, self-ranking fifteen-item scale. Descriptive statistics were used to obtain the means and standard deviations, and t-tests calculated to determine the differences between the groups. It was found that Puerto Rico respondents showed less discrepancy among their rankings of romantic behaviors, whereas the United States respondents exhibited more discrepancy among their rankings. Same gender cross-cultural data analyses indicated higher disagreement between the female than between the male rankings. The results provide support for the theoretical utility of the 15-item romantic scripts construct across cultures.

The ways in which human beings behave in romantic relationships or romantic love situations have been the focus of extensive research studies through the cen-

Reprinted from *College Student Journal*, 2003, *37*(2), 354–366. Copyright © 2003 by Project Innovation. Reprinted with permission.

turies. The contemporary popular culture literature continues to provide a rich source of different perspectives that have been used to understand the nature of romantic relationships as one of the most important areas of our human experience. The professional scientific literature also offers a broad range of approaches and modes of inquiry focusing on the themes of romantic relationships (Hendrick & Hendrick, 1989; Hendrick, Hendrick & Adler, 1988) and on romantic love's distinctive qualities as a source of passionate or compassionate behaviors between human beings (Hatfield & Rapson, 1987; Walster & Walster, 1978).

Historically, the studies of romantic relationships have used diverse methods that can roughly be grouped into various research emphases. Some studies treat romantic love or romance as a fleeting feeling (Stearns & Knapp, 1993) and its emotional pitfalls among people are highlighted (Sternberg, 1987). Others have been studies about more formal relationships such as engaged couples (Rusbult, Onizuka, & Lipkus, 1993), ideal versus real romantic expectations (Lester, 1985), and hopes for a lasting relationship (Hong, Evans, & Hall, 1994; Sternberg & Barnes, 1988). A strong scholarly effort has emphasized the development of measures or instruments for assessing sub-components of romantic love (Forgas & Dobosz, 1980) or for self-reporting of personal romantic profiles (Bessell, 1984; Rubin, 1970). The focus on psycho-history, social scripts (Rechtein & Fiedler, 1988) and on cultural aspects for identifying the potential underlying social rules for romantic behaviors (Koenigsberg, 1967), have been other approaches to the study of romantic relationships. Yet another emphasis concerns the study of changing aspects of romantic behaviors (Hazan & Shaver, 1987), short term attachments and attraction (Feingold, 1990), and passion cycles in romantic relationships (Peele, 1988; Sprecher & Duck, 1994). A parallel research emphasis has been on the physiological and body chemistry of romantic love which attempts to isolate the physical and hormonal aspects involved in the romantic behaviors of people (Crenshaw, 1997; Walsh, 1996).

While the number of studies focusing on these different emphases continue to grow, there has been until recently a scarcity of research attention to an important aspect of romantic love such as, individual romantic behaviors or acts of romantic courtship. The research efforts to develop a conceptual definition of romantic behaviors in courtship seem to be in their early stages (Tucker, 1992). Several studies have been undertaken by Tucker, Vivian, and Marvin (1992) and Tucker, Marvin, and Vivian (1991) with the purpose of developing an operational definition for romantic acts and for identifying specific courtship's scripts, people use while engaged in romantic relationships. The current operational definition for courtship behaviors proposed by Tucker (1992) consists of a romantic acts construct composed of thirteen items originally isolated through informal conversations with hundreds of people in a learning seminar context.

Tucker et al. (1992) found considerable agreement among their respondents on the items the participants considered to be a romantic act or a courtship's script. The list of 13 romantic acts Tucker et al. (1992) identified empirically are the following (listed alphabetically): "Candlelight dinner," "Cuddling," "Giving and receiving flowers," "Giving and receiving surprise gifts," Hearing/saying "I love you," "Kissing," "Holding hands," "Making love," "Sending/receiving love cards/love letters," "Sitting by the fireplace," "Slow dancing," "Taking walks."

Need and Purpose

No study was found in the literature which had used the romantic acts construct developed by Tucker (1992) to examine these behaviors cross-culturally. Given the results obtained by this line of research, the investigator in this study assumed that the romantic acts construct would be appropriate for studying romantic scripts among university students across two different cultures. Considering that the United States and the Island of Puerto Rico differ in normative cultural values and other formative historical events, it was expected that significant cross-cultural differences in romantic behaviors may be found between university students in each country.

The purpose of the present study was to extend the application of the romantic acts construct and to focus on the following aims: First, to test the utility of the romantic acts construct between two relatively distinct cultures and to get empirical support for the theoretical construct of the courtship's scripts. Second, to identify and interpret the cross-cultural gender differences that may be found regarding romantic acts preferences between university students. And third, to identify other romantic acts participants may suggest as common courtship's scripts that were not included in the current instrument, which should be considered as additional items for the operational definition of romantic behaviors.

METHOD

Sample and Procedures

Each institution represented in the study was initially contacted by the investigator by mail to request their participation in the study of romantic behaviors. After permission was received and a contact person identified at each institution, follow up phone calls were made to those individuals to arrange for data gathering visits on site. A sample total of $N = 395$ participants provided usable data for the study. One hundred and sixty men between the ages of 17 to 53 years and 235 women between the ages 17 to 44 years were represented in the sample from universities in Puerto Rico and the United States Mainland. The mean age for the Puerto Rico sample was 22.4 years ($SD = .86$), while the mean age for the United States sample was 19.6 years ($SD = 1.05$). Seventy-nine percent of the participants were single and all the respondents were involved in some form of university undergraduate educational training at the time of their participation in the study.

The Puerto Rico sample consisted of $N = 235$ participants from two universities identified for the purpose of anonymity as University-A, geographically located on the southwest of the Island, and University-B, located on the northeast. Data collection in Puerto Rico were completed during a three-half-day time periods. A total of $n = 143$ participants came from University-A, an urban-private, religiously affiliated 4-year comprehensive institution; $n = 92$ participants came from University-B, an urban-secular 4-year comprehensive institution in Puerto Rico. The United States sample consisted of $n = 160$ participants and data collection were conducted also during a

three-half-day time periods in an urban-public 4-year comprehensive university located in New Jersey. The university participants in both Puerto Rico and the United States Mainland volunteered to participate in the study and no academic credit or monetary fee was offered to the students for their participation.

The Instrument

The instrument used in this study was divided into two parts presented on a single page. *Part One* requested demographic information for gender, age, and marital status, and *Part Two* listed 15 romantic acts under the following question and instructions:

> *What do you consider to be romantic behaviors or acts of romantic courtship?*
>
> *This survey seeks to collect views from university students about romantic behaviors. More to the point, we would like to know what* you *consider to be romantic behaviors or acts of romantic courtship. Your task is to rank the 15 items below using the blank space from highly romantic (using #1) to least romantic (using #15). Please do not repeat a number, but you must rank all items. There are no right or wrong answers!*

The instrument was comprised of the complete set of 13 items tested by Tucker, Vivian and Marvin (1992), and two additional items used for a pilot test: "Going out (to dinner or movies)" and "Talking on the phone." The respondents were advised that if after ranking the 15-items they felt other romantic scripts should have been included, please to write them at the bottom of the page. A Spanish translation of the instrument was copied onto the back page of the English version. The Spanish version of the instrument was prepared using a three people translation-reverse-translation method for establishing parallel correspondence between the English and Spanish versions of the instrument. Both in Puerto Rico and the United States Mainland participants were asked to answer the instrument in the language version they felt most comfortable. About 8% of respondents in Puerto Rico opted to use the English version, while about 2% of the United States respondents opted for the Spanish version. In every setting, the instrument was administered using a pre-arranged time period of twenty minutes at the beginning of each research session. Only two instruments from Puerto Rico and one instrument from the United States respondents were unusable and eliminated from the data treatment.

Treatment of the Data

Summary statistics including data frequencies to determine the demographic characteristics of the samples and descriptive statistics to review the mean rankings, standard deviations, and the variance between the variables for the 15 romantic acts from the data of the Puerto Rico and the United States samples were calculated using the *Statistical Package for the Social Sciences* (Foster, 1998). Separate t-tests at the *alpha* .05 level of confidence (two-tailed test), were conducted with the 15 romantic acts for male and female respondents for the purpose of identifying the statistically significant differences between the genders within each country and between the same gender across the two national groups (i.e., Puerto Rico and United States).

RESULTS

The mean ranks, standard deviations, and significant gender differences for romantic behaviors among university students in Puerto Rico are presented in Table 1. According to the ranking scale used, a rank of #1 = most romantic, while a rank of #15 = least romantic; it is important to remember when interpreting these results that *low mean* scores represent "most romantic" scripts, and *high mean* scores represent "least romantic" scripts.

Puerto Rico Sample

A noticeable feature of the rankings by male (n = 80) and female (n = 155) respondents from Puerto Rico is the high degree of agreement between the genders. Only the ranking differences between the genders for the item "Making love" was statistically significant (t-test = −2.32, p = .01) in the Puerto Rico sample, with males ranking this item as more romantic (M = 5.30) than did the females (M = 6.94). The ranking differ-

TABLE 1 / Ranks and Significant Gender Differences for Romantic Behaviors among University Students in Puerto Rico

Puerto Rico Sample (N = 235)	Males			Females			
Romantic Behaviors	Rk	Mean	SD	Rk	Mean	SD	T-Test
Kissing	1	4.54	3.26	1	5.25	3.79	−1.42
Making-love	2	5.30	4.84	5	6.94	5.26	−2.32**
Flowers (receive/send)	3	5.74	4.33	2	5.37	4.35	0.62
Saying "I love you"	4	5.90	3.63	4	6.19	3.76	−0.56
Hugging	5	5.96	3.32	5	5.78	3.24	0.40
Candlelight dinner	6	7.71	3.94	6	7.36	4.26	0.61
Slow dancing	7	8.00	3.70	7	7.59	7.59	0.77
Cuddling	8	8.46	3.50	8	8.23	3.53	0.49
Love cards/letters	9	8.70	3.81	9	8.47	3.65	0.44
Holding hands	10	8.79	4.03	11	8.75	3.74	0.07
Going-out (movies)	11	8.89	3.60	12	9.10	3.82	−0.42
Taking walks	12	9.25	4.12	10	8.54	3.14	1.26
Sitting by fireplace	13	9.45	3.71	14	9.81	3.69	−0.71
Surprise gifts	14	10.05	3.58	13	9.61	3.54	0.91
Phone calls	15	13.15	2.68	15	12.90	2.95	0.65

Note: The romantic behaviors as ranked by the males have been used as a reference in this table (ranking scale: #1 = most romantic, #15 = least romantic). *Rk* = Rank, *SD* = Standard deviations. Males: (*n* = 80), Females: (*n* = 155).
**p < .01 significant at (Two-tailed test).

ences between the genders for the other 14 romantic items on the scale were all not-significant, which accounts for a total of 93% of the items on the instrument.

A note of caution is necessary here regarding the "most romantic" ranking (#1) given to the item "Kissing" by both males (M = 4.54) and females (M = 5.25). It is possible that the rankings for the item "Kissing" may have been biased by the use of this particular item as an example while the investigator was explaining the instructions for responding to the survey. Quite surprising, however, were the fairly low and not significant rankings reported by the Puerto Rico sample for the two pilot-test items: "Going out (dinner/movies)," ranked #11 by males (M = 8.89), and #12 by females (M = 9.10), and "Talking on the phone," ranked #15 by both males (M = 13.15) and females (M = 12.90). The low rankings given by the respondents to these pilot-test items were not expected and the results appear to be somewhat counterintuitive, considering the frequent use and common practice of these behaviors among men and women involved in romantic relationships. In the discussion section of this paper, some explanations will be offered for interpreting these results.

United States Sample

The mean ranks, standard deviations, and significant gender differences for romantic behaviors among university students in the United States Mainland are presented in Table 2. In contrast to the items ranking pattern of high agreement found in the Puerto Rico sample, the item rankings by the United States males (n = 80) and females (n = 80) exhibited greater degrees of disparity between the genders. Statistically significant differences were reported for eight out of the fifteen items on the scale between males and females by the United States sample, while seven items (or 47% of the total scale) were not significant. Five of the eight statistically significant items were ranked by males as more romantic than as reported by females.

TABLE 2 / Ranks and Significant Gender Differences for Romantic Behaviors among University Students in the United States Mainland

United States Sample (N = 160)	Males			Females			
Romantic Behaviors	Rk	Mean	SD	Rk	Mean	SD	T-Test
Kissing	1	3.40	2.52	6	6.71	3.79	−6.52***
Making-love	2	5.74	4.71	9	7.90	5.24	−2.74**
Holding hands	3	6.30	2.94	8	6.96	3.53	−1.29
Cuddling	4	6.43	4.11	1	5.50	3.21	1.59
Hugging	5	6.80	3.82	3	5.76	3.49	1.79
Candlelight dinner	6	6.95	4.29	7	6.78	4.05	0.27
Slow dancing	7	7.65	3.27	10	9.05	4.01	−2.42**
Saying "I love you"	8	8.58	3.70	2	5.74	3.62	4.90***
Love cards/letters	9	8.59	4.48	4	5.96	3.73	4.02***
Flowers (receive/send)	10	8.95	4.03	5	6.30	3.32	4.54***
Sitting by fireplace	11	8.98	4.16	13	10.31	3.54	−2.19*
Taking walks	12	9.01	3.81	14	10.59	3.96	−2.56**
Going-out (movies)	13	9.61	3.63	11	9.21	3.70	0.69
Surprise gifts	14	10.28	3.88	12	10.09	3.46	0.32
Phone calls	15	12.68	2.72	15	13.01	3.22	−0.72

Note: The romantic behaviors as ranked by the males have been used as a reference in this table (ranking scale: #1 = most romantic, #15 = least romantic). *Rk* = Rank, *SD* = Standard deviations. Males: (n = 80), Females: (n = 80). Significant at *p < .05, **p < .01, ***p < .001 (Two-tailed test).

Three of the eight significant items were ranked by females as more romantic than as reported by males. The data show that males ranked as most highly romantic (M = 3.40) and significant the item "Kissing," (*t-test* = –6.52, *p* = .001), while females ranked as most highly romantic (M = 5.50) but not significant the item "Cuddling." The second most romantic (M = 5.74) and significant item for females was "Saying 'I love you'" (*t-test* = 4.90, *p* = .001), while males ranked this item #8 (M = 8.58), which was not significant.

The significant rankings for several other items are worthy of closer review (see Table 2). Similar to the males from Puerto Rico, males from the United States ranked "Making-love" (#2, M = 5.74) as significantly (*t-test* = –2.74, *p* = .01) more romantic than did females (#9, M = 7.90), while females ranked "Flowers (receiving/sending)" (#5, M = 6.30) as significantly (*t-test* = 4.54, *p* = .001) more romantic than males (#10, M = 8.95). Females ranked the item "Love cards/letters" (#4, M = 5.96) as significantly (*t-test* = 4.02, *p* = .001) more romantic than males (#9, M = 8.59), while males ranked the item "Slow dancing" (#7, M = 7.65) as significantly (*t-test* = –2.42, *p* = .01) more romantic than females (#10, M = 9.05). Males ranked the item "Sitting by fireplace" (#11, M = 8.98) as significantly (*t-test* = –2.19, *p* = .05) more romantic than did the females (#13, M = 10.31), and males also

ranked the item "Taking walks" (#12, M = 9.01) as significantly (*t-test* = –2.56, *p* = .01) more romantic than the females (#14, M = 10.59).

Similar to the gender rankings in Puerto Rico, both males (M = 12.68) and females (M = 13.01) in the United States ranked the pilot-test item "Talking on the phone" (#15) as the least romantic behavior and not significant. The pilot-test item "Going out (dinner/movies)" was also not significant and ranked less romantic by both the males (#13, M = 9.61) and the females (#11, M = 9.21) in the United States.

Same Gender Differences between Puerto Rico and the United States

The cross-cultural differences in romantic behaviors which were found to be statistically significant between the same gender university students in Puerto Rico and the United States are presented in Table 3. Significant differences between the males from Puerto Rico (n = 80) and the United States (n = 80) were found in the rankings for three romantic behaviors: "Kissing," "Holding hands," and "Saying I love you." United States males reported the items "Kissing" (M = 3.40, *t-test* = 2.53, *p* = .01) and "Holding hands" (M = 6.30, *t-test* = 4.47, *p* =.001) as significantly more romantic than the Puerto Rico males (M = 4.54 and

TABLE 3 / Significant Same Gender Differences for Romantic Behaviors between University Students in the Puerto Rico and the United States

Romantic Behaviors	Puerto Rico		United States		N = 395
Males (*n* = 160)	Mean	SD	Mean	SD	T-Test
Kissing	4.54	3.26	3.40	2.52	2.53**
Holding hands	8.79	4.03	6.30	2.94	4.47***
Saying "I love you"	5.90	3.63	8.58	3.70	–4.36***
Females (*n* = 235)	Mean	SD	Mean	SD	T-Test
Love cards/letters	8.47	3.65	5.96	3.73	2.60*
Flowers (receive/send)	5.37	4.35	6.30	3.32	–2.63*
Kissing	5.25	3.79	6.71	3.79	–2.82*
Holding hands	8.75	3.74	6.96	3.53	2.60*
Sitting by fireplace	9.81	3.69	10.31	3.54	–3.44***
Taking walks	8.54	3.14	10.59	3.96	–2.87*

Note: SD = Standard deviations. Significant at **p* < .05, ***p* < .01, ****p* < .001 (Two-tailed test).

M = 8.79 respectively), while the Puerto Rico males reported the item "Saying I love you" (M = 5.90, *t-test* = −4.36, p = .001) as significantly more romantic than the United States males (M = 8.58). The cross-cultural mean ranking differences between the Puerto Rico and the United States males were not significant for the other twelve items (or 80% of the scale) on the instrument.

Cross-cultural statistically significant differences were reported between females from Puerto Rico (n = 155) and the United States (n = 80) for six romantic behaviors. United States females ranked the item "Love cards/letters (M = 5.96) as significantly (*t-test* = 2.60, p = .05) more romantic than did the females from Puerto Rico (M = 8.47), while the Puerto Rico females ranked the item "Kissing" (M = 5.25) as significantly (*t-test* = −2.82, p = .05) more romantic than United States females (M = 6.71). The item "Holding hands" was ranked (M = 6.96) by the United States females as significantly (*t-test* = 2.60, p = .05) more romantic than the females from Puerto Rico (M = 8.75), while the Puerto Rico females ranked (M = 5.37) the item "Flowers (receive/send)" as significantly (*t-test* = −2.63, p = .05) more romantic than the United States females (M = 6.30). Puerto Rico females ranked the item "Taking walks" (M = 8.54) as significantly (*t-test* = −2.87, p = .05) more romantic than did United States females (M = 10.59), and Puerto Rico females also ranked the item "Sitting by fireplace" (M = 9.81) as significantly (*t-test* = −3.44, p = .001) more romantic than the United States females (M = 10.31). The cross-cultural mean ranking differences between the Puerto Rico and United States females for the other nine items (or 60% of the scale) on the instrument were not significant.

New Suggested Romantic Acts

Consistent with one of the aims of this study, which was to report other romantic acts participants may identify as common romantic scripts not examined by the current instrument, a total of 19 respondents (n = 12) from Puerto Rico and (n = 7) from the United States Mainland, suggested additional romantic acts, with several of the items overlapping between the lists. The following nine additional items were suggested as romantic acts to consider as possible courtship's behaviors: "Expressions of caring and kindness," "Gazing at the stars/moon," "Leaving loving and caring notes," "Listening and talking intimately," "Playful teasing/flirting," "Taking baths/showers together," "Taking a scenic car drive," "Walking on the beach," and "Watching the sunset/sunrise."

DISCUSSION

As originally stated, the purpose of this study focused on several aims: To test the utility of the romantic acts construct between two relatively distinct cultures (i.e., Puerto Rico and United States); to get empirical support for the theoretical construct of the courtship's scripts; to identify and interpret the gender differences that may be found in the two cultures regarding romantic acts preferences; and to identify other romantic acts participants may suggest as common romantic courtship's scripts, which were not examined by the instrument used in the current study.

The first important conclusion, which is supported by the results of this study is that, the romantic acts construct as defined by Tucker et al. (1992) appear to be sensitive and useful for studying romantic behaviors cross-culturally. A second conclusion, which may be drawn from these results is that, the set of fifteen romantic scripts represent specific theoretically acceptable socio-cultural romantic behaviors, that can be used to discriminate between cultural normative preferences in Puerto Rico and the United States Mainland. A third conclusion, which can be derived from these results is that, the cross-cultural gender differences between the two groups appear to confirm the utility of these romantic scripts to discriminate between degrees of similarity or disparity of preferences within and across different national groups. And a four conclusion that can be offered from these results is that the romantic acts construct as developed by Tucker et al. (1992) can be expanded to a set of at least twenty-four items or more.

Clearly, the ranking pattern of romantic acts found in Puerto Rico between male and female respondents shows considerable similarity (see Table 1). This high degree of gender response similarity may represent culturally-based influences unique to Puerto Rico. In Puerto Rico, only the item "Making love" was found to be significantly different, which was endorsed by male university students as more romantic than reported by female students. Male university students from the United States Mainland also endorsed the item "Making love" as significantly more romantic than reported by the female respondents. These findings are consistent with the results reported by Tucker et al. (1992), who found that only male university students identified the item "Making love" as a romantic script. These results support the notion that males, both in Puerto Rico and the United States, more than females tend to define the behavior of making love as a dominant romantic script. Perhaps, there is a distinct threshold point between males and females that serves as a boundary for defining "making love" as a romantic act versus a sexual act.

In contrast, the ranking pattern of romantic acts that was found in the United States Mainland between male and female respondents indicates greater degrees of disparity (see Table 2). These degrees of gender response disparity may also represent culturally-based influences unique to the United States Mainland. The insights provided by these findings may be used to speculate that, the degrees of similarity or disparity found between Puerto Rico and the United States respondents in specific romantic acts, may be influenced by the cultural norms particular to each national group.

Overall, a very interesting pattern was found when examining the statistically significant romantic acts rankings of the United States males and females. The items endorsed by the males as most romantic (i.e., "Kissing," "Making love," "Holding hands," "Taking walks," "Slow dancing," and "Sitting by the fireplace") are often characterized by actions that involve aspects of physicality, while the items endorsed by the females (i.e., "Saying 'I love you,'" "Flowers (receiving/sending)," and "Love cards/letters") are generally characterized by actions that connote aspects of emotional symbolism. This pattern of gender differentiation is consistent with and provides verification to the conclusions reported by other researchers in the social and behavioral sciences, which have found the romantic behavior of males to project more physicality (Cate & Lloyd, 1992; Duck, 1993; Fletcher & Fitness, 1996; Wink & Helson, 1993), and the romantic behavior of females to indicate more emotionality (Gilligan, 1982; Peplau & Peterson, 1983; Wood, 1994).

Another interesting finding as well is the observed cross-cultural ranking differences between the Puerto Rico and United States males which show considerable congruence among the statistically significant items (see Table 3). The United States males ranked the items "*Holding hands,*" and "*Kissing*" as most romantic. Cultural norms in both Puerto Rico and the United States might have influenced men and women differently about holding hands in public. United States females also ranked this item as most romantic as compared to Puerto Rico females. A possible explanation for this difference could be that in Puerto Rico cultural and religious taboo norms about sexuality (i.e, disapproval of physical contact in courtship) may serve to discourage Puerto Ricans from *holding hands* in public as a display of physical romantic behavior, while in the United States cultural and religious taboo norms about sexuality seems to be more liberal. In contrast, Puerto Rico males ranked the item "Saying 'I love you'" as most romantic as compared to the United States males. This significant ranking may be interpreted as providing some evidence that, perhaps the image of a "Latin lover" may be related to men's willingness to express emotional romantic feelings subjectively, which is different from the more pragmatic "Northern lover" image often attributed by Puerto Ricans to United States males. Although these observations offer interesting insights about the two cultures, more systematic study should explore further the role of other behaviors in relationship to these romantic scripts, with particular attention to defining more empirically the "Latin lover" image for men and women in the United States.

The most unexpected finding from this study was the higher ranking given to "Sitting by the fireplace" by Puerto Rican females (see Table 3). The significant rankings discrepancy found between the two groups of females may signal an important cross-cultural difference of theoretical relevance. Although it should not be surprising that United State females may take the fact of "Sitting by the fireplace" for granted, it is very curious to discover that Puerto Rico females ranked "Sitting by the fireplace" as the most romantic item as compared with the United States females. Considering the fact that real and functional fireplaces are seldom found in Puerto Rico, this high ranking may be explained by the popular influence of Hollywood's movies and television shows in shaping this romantic script in Puerto Rico. The image for Puerto Rico females of "Sitting by the fireplace" seems to connote fantasized emotional behaviors created in part by the absence of the experiences of having access to fireplaces. It is likely that the main reason for the significant endorsement of the romantic script, "Sitting by the fireplace" by Puerto Rican females is related to those idealized romantic images presented constantly in the American mass media, which increasingly dominate popular culture globally.

The significant cross-cultural ranking disparity between the Puerto Rico and United States females for the items "Taking walks," "Kissing," "Flowers (receiving/sending)," and "Love cards/letters," may be preferences influenced by the respective ecological-socio-cultural environment. For example, *taking walks* and *sending or receiving flowers* are appropriate behaviors for a tropical climate where it's warm all year and flowers are inexpensive due to high supply. One possible explanation for why the United States females ranked the item "Love cards/letters" as more romantic than the Puerto Rico females might be based on a different tradition of the commercialization of love or romance in the United States than in Puerto Rico. Culturally at present, Puerto Rico continues to be a society composed of small communities, where gestures of friendship and subjective face-to-face contact are rewarded. Direct interpersonal exchanges may often be expected instead of using other symbolic artifacts or gestures as substitutes for personal contact. Perhaps for Puerto Ricans, sending love cards or letters is seen as a more impersonal behavior concerning a romantic relationship. More qualitative inquiry may be necessary to uncover further the specific cultural meanings behind these romantic behaviors.

SUGGESTIONS FOR FURTHER RESEARCH

Although the set of 15 romantic acts examined in this study appears to represent acceptable behaviors that people feel comfortable using as scripts in their romantic relationships, further research on romantic behaviors should examine additional romantic acts that we often see in our common everyday social life

and which the mass media continuously presents on television, magazines, and the movies.

The list of nine romantic scripts suggested by the respondents in this study may be a good starting point for developing a more comprehensive instrument. Also, the use of a multi-dimensional instrument, which includes other non-romantic items as controls may contribute other valuable data for understanding better these romantic scripts. Specific attention should be paid to the items of "Talking on the phone" and "Going out (dinner/movies)," which as romantic scripts seem to make common sense, but their rankings by both male and female university students in this study were quite paradoxical. The question to answer is: Are these scripts viewed more as means toward romance by those involved in a relationship than as unique romantic behaviors into themselves? Future research should address this question.

Although the scope of this study provides only preliminary information for explaining the patterns of similarity and disparity across cultures, it is possible to speculate that the degree of similarity found in the Puerto Rico sample may represent culturally-based norms which are substantially different from the United States sample. Future research should try to replicate these findings by testing this issue as a potentially valuable hypothesis. The cross-sectional research method using an ordinal scale and the descriptive statistical data analysis design, should be improved by the use of a more complex research design that employs the application of other statistical approaches for explaining in more comprehensively the romantic scripts.

In particular, a promising area of further research is to seek empirical support for the assumption proposed by Tucker et al. (1992, p. 119) that ". . . while there may be potentially an infinite number of romantic acts, the responses suggest people seem to engage in only a few." A more parsimonious operational definition of romantic behaviors may improve the predictive power of the scale and its use in cross-cultural research.

New research efforts should include other ethnic and Hispanic groups to test further the cross-cultural usefulness of the scale. Other assumptions should be used to explore more systematically which romantic acts may influence directly our courtship behaviors, that may help to explain why people act as they do in different romantic situations.

REFERENCES

Bessell, H. (1984). *The lover test.* New York: William Morrow.

Cate, R. M., & Lloyd, S. A. (1992). *Courtship.* Newbury Park, CA: Sage.

Crenshaw, T. (1997). *The alchemy of love and lust.* New York, NY: Academic Press.

Duck, S. (1993). *Individuals in relationships.* Newbury Park, CA: Sage.

Feingold, A. (1990). Gender differences in effects of physical attractiveness on romantic attraction: A comparison across five research paradigms. *Journal of Personality and Social Psychology, 59,* 981–993.

Fletcher, J. O., & Fitness, J. (Eds.). (1996). *Knowledge structure and close relationships.* Hillsdale, NJ: Erlbaum.

Forgas, J. P., & Dobosz, B. (1980). Dimensions of romantic involvement: Toward a taxonomy of heterosexual relationships. *Social Psychology Quarterly, 43,* 290–300.

Foster, J. J. (1998). *Data analysis using SPSS for Windows.* Thousand Oaks, CA: Sage.

Hatfield, E., & Rapson, R. L. (1987). Passionate love: New directions in research. In W. H. Jones & D. Perlman (Eds.), *Advances in personal relationships, vol. 1* (pp. 109–139). Greenwich, CT: JAI Press.

Hazan, C., & Shaver, P. (1987). Romantic love conceptualization as an attachment process. *Journal of Personality and Social Psychology, 52,* 511–524.

Hendrick, C., & Hendrick, S. S. (1989). Research on love: Does it measure up? *Journal of Personality and Social Psychology, 56,* 784–794.

Hendrick, S. S., Hendrick, C., & Adler, N. (1988). Romantic relationships: Love, satisfaction, and staying together. *Journal of Personality and Social Psychology, 54,* 980–988.

Hong, S. M., Evans, M., & Hall, T. (1994). Making love: Australian adults' rating of its importance as a romantic act in a relationship (Part 1). *Psychological Reports, 75,* 47–50.

Koenigsberg, R. A. (1967). Culture and unconscious fantasy observations on courtly love. *Psychoanalytic Review, 54,* 36–50.

Lester, D. (1985). Romantic attitudes toward love in men and women. *Psychological Reports, 56,* 622.

Peele, S. (1988). Fools for love: The romantic ideal, psychological theory, and addictive love. In R. J. Sternberg & M. L. Barnes (Eds.), *The psychology of love* (pp. 159–188). New Haven, CT: Yale University Press.

Peplau, L. A., & Peterson, D. R. (Eds.). (1983). *Close relationships.* New York: W. H. Freeman.

Rechtein, J. G., & Fiedler, E. (1988). Contributions to Psychohistory: Courtly love today: Romance and socialization in interpersonal scripts. *Psychological Reports, 63,* 683–695.

Rubin, Z. (1970). Measurement of romantic love. *Journal of Personality and Social Psychology, 16,* 265–273.

Rusbult, C. E., Onizuka, R. K., & Lipkus, I. (1993). What do we really want? Mental models of ideal romantic involvement explored through multidimensional scaling. *Journal of Experimental Social Psychology, 29,* 493–527.

Sprecher, S., & Duck, S. (1994). Sweet talk: The importance of perceived communication for romantic and friendship attraction experienced through multidimensional scaling. *Journal of Experimental Social Psychology, 29,* 493–527.

Stearns, P. N., & Knapp, M. (1993). Men and romantic love: Pinpointing a 20th Century change. *Journal of Social History, 26,* 769–795.

Sternberg, R. J. (1987). Liking versus loving: A comparative evaulation of theories. *Psychological Bulletin, 102,* 331–345.

Sternberg, R. J., & Barnes, M. L. (1988). *The psychology of love.* New Haven, CT: Yale University Press.

Tucker, R. K. (1992). Men's and women's rankings of thirteen acts of romance. *Psychological Reports, 71,* 640–642.

Tucker, R. K., Vivian, B., & Marvin, M. G. (1992). Operationalizing the romance construct in an adult sample. *Psychological Reports, 71,* 115–120.

Tucker, R. K., Marvin, M. G., & Vivian, B. (1991). What constitutes a romantic act? An empirical study. *Psychological Reports, 69,* 651–654.

Walsh, A. (1998). *The science of love: Understanding love and its effects on mind and body.* Boise, ID: Boise State University Press.

Walster, E., & Walster, G. W. (1978). *A new look at love.* Reading, MA: Addison-Wesley.

Wink, P., & Helson, R. (1993). Personality change in women and their partners. *Journal of Personality and Social Psychology, 65,* 597–605.

Wood, J. T. (1994). *Gendered lives: Communication, gender, and culture.* Belmont, CA: Wadsworth.

CRITICAL THINKING QUESTIONS

1. This article states that men tend to rate as romantic acts that are more physical in nature, while females tend to rate as romantic acts that are more emotional or symbolic in nature. How does this conclusion, as well as the other findings presented in the article, compare to your own views of romantic behavior? How about those of your friends? What, if any, other examples of what you or your friends consider to be romantic behaviors are not listed in the article?

2. Subjects in the experiment were mostly traditional-aged college students. Would the ratings of which behaviors are considered the most romantic likely be different with older populations? Why or why not? Administer the survey instrument in the article to small numbers of people in various age groups and discuss your findings.

3. The United States produces the majority of movies in the world, and they, in turn, are seen around the world. Does exposure to how romance is portrayed in the movies impact viewers? Why or why not? How could you go about testing your hypothesis?

4. Examine the explanations given by the author of the article for the differences (and similarities) between men and women in general and between those in the United States and Puerto Rico specifically on the ranking of romantic behaviors. Do you agree or disagree with the author's conclusions? What else might explain the findings? Defend your answers.

CHAPTER INTEGRATION QUESTIONS _____

1. In a sense, the three articles in this chapter progress through the possible stages of a relationship, from the initial attraction ("playing hard to get") to the behaviors that people consider romantic in relationships to divorce. What similar themes run through these different articles? Specifically, do any of the factors discussed in the articles on initial attraction affect the likelihood of being divorced later on?

2. What factors identified in the article on divorce may be useful in developing more satisfying relationships earlier on? Explain your answers.

3. In *Keeping the Love You Find: A Guide for Singles,* the author, Harville Hendrix, said, "Love is hard—life is hard—but it's the only game in town. It's a high-stakes game, because how well you play determines how you will thrive and grow. You might as well learn to play it as well as possible as soon as possible." What does this quotation mean to you? Do you agree or disagree with it? Explain.

Chapter Nine

SOCIAL INFLUENCE

Social influence is the process of inducing change in other people. Sometimes social change results from direct orders to do something, such as when a military officer gives an order to a subordinate. When this happens, we call it *obedience.* Basic to situations involving obedience is some sort of power, either real or imagined, that the person giving the orders has over the person obeying him or her.

Not all social influence is due to direct orders from people in positions of authority. Instead, we may simply ask that a person do something for us. *Compliance* is when a person does something just because he or she was asked to, not because the requestor had any type of power over him or her.

Finally, social influence also operates in a very subtle way when people follow *norms,* or generally expected ways of behaving in certain situations. For example, when you are in an elevator, what do you do? Most likely, you face forward and stare at the numbers. *Conformity* occurs in many situations where norms exist for proper behavior. In a sense, conformity is the lifeblood of a society, for without conformity to rules, society could not exist.

Article 25, "'Obedience in Retrospect," examines the classic obedience study by Stanley Milgram (presented in its entirety in the next reading, Article 26) from a unique perspective. The author of Article 25 was a research assistant in the original Milgram obedience studies and, as such, is able to provide a unique view of this classic research. Additionally, this article examines some of the reactions to this classic piece of research over the years. (While this article can be read prior to reading the Milgram study, it might be best if you read Article 26 prior to reading Article 25.)

Article 26, a classic work on obedience to authority, is perhaps one of the most widely known studies in the field of social psychology. "Behavioral Study of Obedience" seeks to demonstrate experimentally that the average person could be induced to harm another person simply by being ordered to do so by someone in a position of authority. The large number of people who fully obeyed orders is surprising.

Article 27, "Pluralistic Ignorance and College Student Perceptions of Gender-Specific Alcohol Norms," examines how our beliefs about what other people are doing, even if incorrect, nonetheless may affect our own attitudes and behaviors. With regard to this article, college students' drinking behavior may, in part, be influenced by what they *think* their peers are doing, rather than what they actually *are* doing.

ARTICLE 25 _____

Note: This article discusses the classic study of Stanley Milgram, "Behavioral Study of Obedience," which appears in its entirety in the next article in this chapter, Article 26. You will benefit most if you read Article 26 before reading this article.

When people read about a horrendous act that has been committed, they naturally think that the person who committed it is somehow deranged or inhuman. Sometimes that is indeed the case, as when a psychotic commits an act under orders he or she has supposedly received during hallucinations. Personal pathology and mental illness are certainly involved in many of the hideous acts that people commit. But are personality or psychological factors always the cause of such behavior? Is it possible that an otherwise normal individual may commit an abnormal, sick act not because there is something wrong with him or her but because of the situation he or she might be in?

History is full of examples of normal people who have committed abnormal acts. For example, warfare has often induced otherwise normal, nonviolent people not only to kill but also to commit atrocities. Yet the suggestion that somehow anyone placed in the same situation may act the same way is repugnant. It might be a lot more personally comforting to believe that people who do bad things are somehow different from us. We, after all, are good and certainly incapable of being mass murderers. Only other people who are either sick or are somehow overly conforming could do such things. In other words, we tend to attribute others' acts to their disposition—that is, some personality or other enduring trait causes them to act that way.

The work of Stanley Milgram, which appears in Article 26, is the classic study in the field of social psychology that suggested that perhaps individual characteristics (dispositions) are less responsible for people performing terrible acts than are the situations that produce such behavior. The present article, by Alan C. Elms, provides a unique perspective on Milgram's work. Dr. Elms worked as an assistant to Milgram while this classic study was conducted. Dr. Elms not only provides some first-hand accounts of the study but also addresses some of the reactions to the classic work over the years.

Obedience in Retrospect

■ Alan C. Elms

Milgram's original paradigm for studying obedience to authority is briefly described, and the main results are summarized. Personal observations of the conduct of the initial studies give added context for interpreting the results. Psychologists' reactions to the Milgram experiments are discussed in terms of (1) rejecting the research on ethical grounds, (2) explaining away the results as expressions of trivial phenomena, (3) subsuming obedience to destructive authority under other explanatory rubrics, and (4) endorsing or rejecting the results in terms of their perceived social relevance or irrelevance.

Reprinted from *Journal of Social Issues*, 1995 (Fall), *51*(3), 21–31. Copyright © 1995 by Blackwell Publishers. Reprinted by permission.

Quotations from unpublished correspondence of Stanley Milgram are used by permission of Alexandra Milgram.

The problem of obedience to authority may well be the crucial issue of our time. The experiments you took part in represent the first efforts to understand this phenomenon in an objective, scientific manner. (Stanley Milgram, Report to Memory Project Subjects, *1962b)*

INTRODUCTION

Obedience to destructive authority was indeed a crucial social issue in 1962. The Holocaust had ended less than two decades earlier. Adolf Eichmann recently had been sentenced to death for expediting it, despite his plea than he had just been "following orders." American military advisers were being ordered to Vietnam in increasing numbers to forestall Communist control of Southeast Asia. Whether destructive obedience could reasonably be described as *the* crucial issue of the time is a judgment call; surely other issues offered competition for that status. But there can be little argument that Stanley Milgram's experiments were indeed "the first efforts to understand this phenomenon in an objective, scientific manner."

Milgram was not seeking to develop a grand theory of obedience. His main concern was with the phenomenon itself. He advised his graduate students that as they began their own research, "First decide what questions you want to answer." For him those first questions were typically substantive, not theoretical. He also told his students he sought to collect data that would still be of interest 100 years later, whatever theoretical interpretations might be made of the data. For his data on obedience, we are a third of the way through that 100 years. Those data remain of high interest indeed, offering continual challenges to our theories and to our confidence as psychologists that we really understand important aspects of human social behavior.

Milgram eventually proposed his own theoretical interpretations. But what most people still remember are the data themselves, the sheer numbers of research volunteers who obeyed every order to the very end. Before Milgram, creative writers had incorporated striking incidents of obedience into novels, poems, and screenplays. Historians had written factual accounts of remarkably obedient individuals and groups. Psychologists had developed F- and other scales to measure inclinations toward authoritarian

tyranny and subservience. Milgram instead established a realistic laboratory setting where actual obedience and its circumstances might be closely studied.

THE OBEDIENCE PARADIGM

For those who have forgotten the details, and for the few who have never read them, here is the basic situation that Milgram devised. First, he advertised in the New Haven (Connecticut) daily newspaper and through direct mail for volunteers for a study of memory and learning. Volunteers were promised $4.00 for an hour of their time, plus 50 cents carfare. (At the time, $4 was well above minimum wage for an hour of work; 50 cents would have paid for a round-trip bus ride to and from most areas of New Haven.) Most of those who volunteered were scheduled by telephone to come at a given time to a laboratory on the Yale University campus.

In the basic experiments, two volunteers arrived at the laboratory at about the same time. Both were invited into the lab by the experimenter. The experimenter explained that one volunteer would be assigned the role of teacher and the other would become the learner. The teacher would administer an electric shock to the learner whenever the learner made an error, and each additional shock would be 15 volts higher than the previous one. By drawing slips of paper from a hat, one volunteer became the teacher. His first task was to help strap the arms of the other volunteer to the arms of a chair, so the electrodes from the shock generator would not fall off accidentally. The teacher was given a sample 45 volt electric shock from the shock generator, a level strong enough to be distinctly unpleasant. Then the experimenter asked the teacher to begin teaching the learner a list of word pairs. The learner did fairly well at first, then began to make frequent errors. Soon the teacher found himself administering higher and higher shock levels, according to the experimenter's instructions. (Male pronouns are used here because most volunteers were male; in only one experimental condition out of 24 were female subjects used.)

After a few shocks the learner began to object to the procedure. After more shocks and more objections, he loudly refused to participate further in the learning task, and stopped responding. If the teacher stopped giving him electric shocks at this point, the experimenter ordered the teacher to continue, and to administer stronger and stronger shocks for each failure to respond—all the way to the end of the graded series of levers, whose final labels were "Intense Shock," "Extreme Intensity Shock," "Danger: Severe Shock," and "XXX," along with voltage levels up to 450 volts. In the first experimental condition, the teacher was separated from the learner by a sound-proofed wall; the learner could communicate his distress only by kicking on the wall. In subsequent conditions, teachers could hear the learner's voice through a speaker system, or sat near the learner in the same room while the learning task proceeded, or sat next to the learner and had to force his hand down onto a shock grid if he refused to accept the shocks voluntarily.

Teachers were not told several important pieces of information until their participation in the experiment was finished. Number one, the experiment was a study of obedience to authority, not a study of memory and learning. Number two, the volunteer who assumed the role of learner was actually an experimental confederate. Number three, the only shock that anyone ever got was the 45 volt sample shock given to each teacher; the shock generator was not wired to give any shocks to the learner. Number four, the learner's kicks against the wall, his screams, his refusals to continue, were all carefully scripted and rehearsed, as were the experimenter's orders to the teacher. A number of variables could be (and were) added to the research design in different conditions (see Miller, Collins, & Brief, this issue[1]), but these aspects were constant.

OBSERVATIONS FROM THE INSIDE

The basic series of obedience experiments took place in the summer of 1961. Milgram was at that time a very junior assistant professor, 27 years old, with no professional publications yet in print. I had just finished my first year of graduate school when he hired me to be his research assistant for the summer. Stanley sent me a letter on June 27, a week before I was scheduled to return to New Haven from a brief summer vacation:

Matters have been proceeding apace on the project. The apparatus is almost done and looks thoroughly professional; just a few small but important pieces remain to be built. It may turn out that you will build them, but that depends on factors at present unknown.

The advertisement was placed in the New Haven Register *and yielded a disappointingly low response. There is no immediate crisis, however, since we do have about 300 qualified applicants. But before long, in your role of Solicitor General, you will have to think of ways to deliver more people to the laboratory. This is a very important practical aspect of the research. I will admit it bears some resemblance to Mr. Eichmann's position, but you at least should have no misconceptions of what we do with our daily quota. We give them a chance to resist the commands of malevolent authority and assert their alliance with morality.*

. . . The goal this summer is to run from 250–300 subjects in nine or ten experimental conditions. Only if this is accomplished can the summer be considered a success. Let me know if there is something I have overlooked.

The summer was a success by any reasonable standards, if not fully by Milgram's. He had not overlooked anything procedural; even at that early stage in his career, he was already the most well-organized researcher I have ever encountered. But he had hardly come close to anticipating the degree to which his subjects would yield to the commands of malevolent authority, or how readily they would abrogate their alliance with morality. Milgram knew he would get some obedience; in a pilot study the previous winter, he had found Yale undergraduates disturbingly willing to shock their victims. But he recognized that Yale undergraduates were a special sample in many ways; that the prototype shock generator was rather crude and perhaps not altogether convincing; and that the simulated victim's displays of pain were fairly easy to ignore. For the main experiments, Milgram auditioned and rehearsed a victim whose cries of agony were truly piercing. He recruited a larger and diverse sample of nonstudent adults from the New Haven area, ranging from blue-collar workers to professionals and from 20 to 50 years in age. He constructed a professional-looking shock generator and purchased other high-quality equipment, including a 20-pen Esterline Angus Event Recorder that registered the duration and latency of each "shock" administration to the nearest hundredth of a second. He had decided that his main dependent variable would be the mean shock level at which subjects refused to go further in each experimental condition, but he wanted to be able to examine more subtle differences in their performance as well.

In early August the curtains went up on the first official obedience experiment. (More accurately, the curtains were drawn aside; Yale's new Social Interaction Laboratory, on temporary loan from the Sociology Department, was enclosed by two-way mirrors and heavy soundproofing curtains.) Would subjects be convinced of the reality of the learning-and-memory experiment, the shock generator, the victim's suffering? They were. Would subjects obey the experimenter? They did. How far would they go? On and on up the sequence of shock levels. Would any subjects go all the way to the end of the shock board? Yes indeed.

Behind the two-way mirrors, Stanley Milgram and I (as well as occasional visitors) watched each early subject with fascination and with our own share of tension. Stanley had made broad predictions concerning the relative amounts of obedience in different conditions, but we paid little attention to the gradual confirmation of those predictions. Instead we tried to predict the behavior of each new subject, based on his initial demeanor and the little we knew about his background. We were gratified when any subject resisted authority. Sometimes it was quiet resistance, sometimes noisy, but it was exciting each time it happened. As more and more subjects obeyed every command, we felt at first dismayed, then cynically confirmed in our bleakest views of humanity. We were distressed when some volunteers wept, appalled when others laughed as they administered shock after shock. The experimenter gave each subject a standard debriefing at the end of the hour, to minimize any continuing stress and to show that the "victim" had not been injured by the "shocks." When a subject appeared especially stressed, Milgram often moved out from behind the curtains to do an especially thorough job of reassurance and stress reduction. When a subject did something truly unexpected during the experiment—an especially resolute show of resistance, for instance, or a long laughing jag—Milgram would join the experimenter in giving the subject a detailed cross-examination about why he had displayed such behavior. For us as well as for the subjects, the situation quickly became more than an artificially structured experiment. Instead it presented slice after slice of real life, with moral decisions made and unmade every evening.

THE MOST PROMINENT RESULTS

As matters turned out, Milgram did not need equipment sensitive enough to measure shock intervals in hundredths of a second. By the end of the second run of 40 subjects, if not before, his main dependent variable had become simply the percentage of subjects who obeyed the experimenter's commands all the way to the end of the shock series, contrasted with the percentage who disobeyed by quitting at any point in the whole long sequence of shock levels. In the first condition, a substantial majority of subjects (26 out of 40, or 65%) obeyed completely. That was the condition with minimal feedback from the learner—a few vigorous kicks on the wall. But wouldn't obedience drop substantially if the teacher could actually hear the learner screaming and demanding to be set free? It didn't. Twenty-five out of 40 were fully obedient in this second condition. Even when Milgram tried to encourage disobedience by having the learner claim a preexisting heart condition ("It's bothering me now!"), obedience remained at a high level: 26 of 40 subjects again (Milgram, 1974, pp. 56–57). Putting the victim in the same room and near the teacher reduced obedience somewhat, but 40% still obeyed fully. Indeed, even when teachers were ordered to press the hand of the screaming victim down onto a shock plate to complete the electrical circuit, a majority did so at least twice before quitting, and 30% obeyed in this fashion to the end of the shock board (Milgram, 1974, p. 35).

Milgram ran approximately a thousand subjects through various obedience conditions in less than a year. (The National Science Foundation, which financed the research, got its money's worth from two grants totaling about $60,000.) Each subject was run through the procedure individually, then was subjected to both immediate and follow-up questionnaires of various kinds. Milgram looked at the effects not only of the victim's physical proximity to the subject but of the experimenter's proximity, the amount of group support either for obedience or for defiance, and the learning experiment's apparent institutional backing. He made a variety of interesting findings—enough to fill a book, and more. But the data that carried the greatest impact, on other psychologists and on the general public, came from those first few experimental conditions: two-thirds of a sample of average Americans were willing to shock an innocent victim until the poor man was screaming for his life, and to go on shocking him well after he had lapsed into a perhaps unconscious silence, all at the command of a single experimenter with no apparent means of enforcing his orders.

REACTIONS TO THE RESEARCH

Once these data appeared in professional psychological journals (after initial resistance from editors), they were rather quickly disseminated through newspaper and magazine stories, editorials, sermons, and other popular media. With few exceptions, the nonprofessional citations of the experiments emphasized their social relevance: Milgram had revealed in ordinary Americans the potential for behavior comparable to that of the Nazis during the European Holocaust. (According to a *TV Guide* ad for a docudrama with William Shatner as a fictionalized Milgram, the research revealed "A world of evil so terrifying no one dares penetrate its secret. Until now!" [August 21, 1976, p. A-86.])

Psychologists responded in more diverse ways. Authors eager to enliven their introductory and social psychology textbooks soon made the obedience experiments a staple ingredient (see Miller, this issue[1]). Other psychologists seemed to regard Milgram's results as a challenge of one sort or another: conceptual, ethical, theoretical, political. The obedience studies were related, historically and procedurally, to earlier studies of social influence, but they did not fit readily into current theoretical models or research trends. Because of their rapidly achieved visibility inside and outside the field, they were soon treated as fair game for elucidation or attack by psychologists with a multitude of orientations.

Ethical Concerns

One type of response to the disturbing results of the obedience studies was to shift attention from the amounts of obedience Milgram obtained to the ethics of putting subjects through such a stressful experience. The first substantial published critique of Milgram's studies focused on the presumed psychic damage wreaked on his subjects by their ordeal (Baumrind, 1964). Milgram was not altogether surprised by such criticism; similar concerns had been expressed by several Yale faculty members during or soon after the experiments, and ethical questions had been raised about the research when Milgram first applied for American Psychological Association membership. But he was disappointed that his critics did not recognize the care he had put into responding to his subjects' high stress levels immediately after their participation, as well as into checking on any lingering effects over time (Milgram, 1964). Milgram was a pioneer in the debriefing procedures that are now a matter of course in psychological experiments on human subjects—debriefing in the sense not only of questioning the subject about his or her perception of the experiment, but of providing the subject with information and encouragement that will counteract any reactions to participation that might damage the subject's self-esteem. As Milgram told me later,

> My membership application to APA was held up for one year while they investigated the ethicality of the obedience experiment. In the end, they gave me a clean bill of health and admitted me to membership. Whenever any group has seriously considered the merits and problems of the experiment, they have concluded that it was an ethical experiment. Nonetheless, isolated individuals still feel strongly enough to attack it. (Personal communication, July 3, 1969)

One consequence of those individual attacks was a set of stringent federal regulations that made it virtually impossible ever again to conduct a close replication of the Milgram studies at any U.S. educational or research institution.

Many social scientists who have considered the ethics of the obedience studies in print have taken a neutral position or have come down on the side of Milgram. But outside the field, a similar perception of appropriate research and debriefing procedures is not widespread. When I participated in a conference on social science research ethics at the Kennedy Institute of Ethics 18 years after the obedience research was completed, several philosophers and professional ethicists devoted a large part of their energies to what struck me as rather crude Milgram bashing. The research scientists at the conference were not so inclined, but they had to work hard to communicate the virtues of a set of studies that had raised important issues about both the bad and the good in human nature (Beauchamp, Faden, Wallace, & Walters, 1982).

Questions of Belief

Among other early commentaries on the research, several psychologists argued that the results were not credible because the subjects did not believe they were actually harming the victim (e.g., Orne & Holland, 1968). Milgram's own data, showing that during the experiment a very high percentage of subjects believed the victim was receiving extremely painful shocks (1974, pp. 171–174), were ignored or dismissed as attempts by the subjects to give Milgram the answers he wanted. Researchers' descriptions of many subjects' visible signs of high stress were also ignored, or were assumed to be evidence merely of the subjects' enthusiastic play acting. Even a filmed record of several actual subjects (Milgram, 1965a), displaying either great stress or extraordinary improvisational acting ability, did not convince psychologists who took this dismissive position. Some critics may have assumed that the four subjects shown at length in the film, plus several others who appeared more briefly, were the most convincingly emotional subjects Milgram could find among his thousand participants. In fact, Milgram chose all of them from the 14 subjects who happened to be "selected in the normal manner for recruitment" during the two days he brought movie cameras to the laboratory (Milgram, 1965c, p. 5).

Theoretical Alternatives

Many social psychologists have accepted the ethical appropriateness of Milgram's procedures and the believability of the experimental context. Even they, however, have often redirected attention away from the specific phenomenon of destructive obedience by subsuming it under a broader theoretical approach or alternative hypothetical constructs.

Milgram was slow to offer a comprehensive theoretical account of his own. His definitions of obedience to authority, from his first to his final writings on the subject, drew upon no theoretical assumptions. Rather, they were commonsense or dictionary definitions: "Every power system implies a structure of command and action in response to the command" (Milgram, 1961, p. 2); "If Y follows the command of X we shall say that he has obeyed X; if he fails to carry out the command of X, we shall say that he has disobeyed X" (Milgram, 1965b, p. 58); "[I]t is only the man dwelling in isolation who is not forced to respond, through defiance or submission, to the commands of others" (Milgram, 1974, p. 1). In his grant proposals he referred to "internal restraints" or "internal resistances" that were pitted against the acceptance of authoritative commands, but he did not specify the nature of these internal processes (Milgram, 1961, p. 3; Milgram, 1962a, p. 1). He raised the possibility of predispositional factors and of "highly complex, and possibly, idiosyncratic motive structures" (1962a, p. 17), but in the research itself he directed his efforts mainly toward identifying situational factors that increased or decreased obedience. In his most extensive early discussion of his results (Milgram, 1965b, largely written in 1962), he cited such midlevel hypothetical constructs as "empathic cues," "denial and narrowing of the cognitive field," and a varying "sense of *relatedness* between his [the subject's] own actions and the consequences of those actions for the victim" (pp. 61–63; his italics).

Though it took Milgram less than a year to run all his subjects and not much longer than that to write several papers on the results, he worked on his book about obedience for over five years. He attributed the slowness of the book's writing in part to his becoming engaged in other sorts of research. But much of his struggle with the book appears to have centered on the difficulty of developing a general theory of obedience. The principal theoretical concepts he advanced in the book, including the agentic state (Milgram, 1974, pp. 133–134) and the evolution of a potential for obedience in humans (pp. 123–125), impressed many readers rather less than the results themselves—a reaction that both frustrated and pleased the data-centric Milgram. Though he had collected demographic information on all participants and had supported my collection of personality data from subsamples of obedient and disobedient subjects (Elms & Milgram, 1965), he gave short shrift to such data in his book, concluding that "It is hard to relate performance to personality because we really do not know very much about how to measure personality" (p. 205).

Others have usefully discussed the interaction of personality and situational variables in the obedience situations (e.g., Blass, 1991). A majority of the alternative explanations, however, have stressed cognitive processes, emphasizing ways in which the subject processed information about the situation that might have justified his obedience or strengthened his resistance. Milgram viewed such alternative explanations with interest, but took steps to rule out certain of them experimentally. One of the most obvious of these alternatives was the idea that subjects might be so awed by Yale University and so certain of its virtue that they would do anything they were told within those august halls, regardless of any general proclivity toward destructive obedience. Even before this environment-based explanation of his subjects' obedience was first offered in print, Milgram had largely vitiated it by moving the experiments from the awe-inspiring Interaction Laboratory to a rather less impressive basement facility and then to the intentionally unimpressive office of a fly-by-night company in industrial Bridgeport, Connecticut. He got essentially the same results in all three locations. A number of alternative or additional explanations of Milgram's results remain as operable hypotheses, but none has decisively carried the day. Their very diversity ensures that the larger audience for the research will continue to be concerned primarily about the subjects' disturbing behavior rather than about the internal processes that may have produced it.

The Question of Relevance

Finally among ways in which psychologists have responded to Milgram's findings are arguments concerning the social relevance of the experiments. Many psychologists, at least in their textbooks, have embraced his findings as being highly relevant to important social phenomena, including destructive obedience not only in totalitarian states but among American soldiers, Bosnian combatants, and suicidal religious cults. But others (including some who also argued that the research was unethical or experientially unconvincing) have denied any real social relevance. Even if subjects believed they were really shocking the victim, these psychologists say, they knew the situation must not be as bad as it appeared, because somebody would have stopped them if it was. Or the subjects were in a situation where the experimenter accepted responsibility for the effects of their behavior, so their behavior is not really relevant to real-world situations where blame is less readily transferred to another individual. Or some other rationale is advanced, presumably peculiar to the Milgram obedience situation, that somehow does not translate into real-world social dynamics. Milgram rightly dismissed all such explanations that had been advanced up to the time of his final writings, and very likely would have dismissed all subsequent ones, for two simple reasons: Any effective authority figure in the real world always finds ways to justify imposing his or her will on underlings. The underlings who obey authoritative commands in the real world always find rationales for their obedience. In most prominent real-world cases of destructive obedience that have been compared (or discompared) to the Milgram studies, the authorities were able to call upon a social rationale for their commands that was at least as strong as or stronger than that available to any psychological experimenter. In addition, they were often able to promise their followers much greater rewards for obedience and punishments for disobedience.

Stanley Milgram's research on obedience tapped into psychological processes that ranked as neither new nor extreme in the history of human behavior. A "crucial issue of our time," perhaps the crucial issue, obedience unfortunately remains. Though Milgram was proud that his studies were "the first efforts to understand this phenomenon in an objective, scientific manner," he did not want them to be the last. This issue of the *Journal of Social Issues*[1] gives strong evidence that the efforts of other researchers to expand upon his groundbreaking work will continue unabated.

REFERENCES

Baumrind, D. (1964). Some thoughts on ethics of research: After reading Milgram's "Behavioral Study of Obedience." *American Psychologist, 19,* 421–423.

Beauchamp, T. L., Faden, R. R., Wallace, R. J., Jr., & Walters, L. (Eds.). (1982). *Ethical issues in social science research.* Baltimore, MD: Johns Hopkins University Press.

Blass, T. (1991). Understanding behavior in the Milgram obedience experiment: The role of personality, situations, and their interactions. *Journal of Personality and Social Psychology, 60,* 398–413.

Elms, A. C., & Milgram, S. (1965). Personality characteristics associated with obedience and defiance toward authoritative command. *Journal of Experimental Research in Personality, 1,* 282–289.

Milgram, S. (1961). *Dynamics of obedience: Experiments in social psychology.* Application for National Science Foundation research grant, Yale University.

Milgram, S. (1962a). *Obedience to authority: Experiments in social psychology.* Application for National Science Foundation grant renewal, Yale University.

Milgram, S. (1962b). *Report to Memory Project subjects.* Unpublished manuscript, Yale University.

Milgram, S. (1964). Issues in the study of obedience: A reply to Baumrind. *American Psychologist, 19,* 848–852.

Milgram, S. (1965a). *Obedience* [Film]. (Available from the Pennsylvania State University Audiovisual Services.)

Milgram, S. (1965b). Some conditions of obedience and disobedience to authority. *Human Relations, 18,* 57–76.

Milgram, S. (1965c). Study notes for "Obedience." (Distributed by the New York University Film Library.)

Milgram, S. (1974). *Obedience to authority.* New York: Harper & Row.

Orne, M. T., & Holland, C. C. (1968). On the ecological validity of laboratory deceptions. *International Journal of Psychiatry, 6,* 282–293.

ENDNOTE

1. References to "this issue" are to the *Journal of Social Issues,* Fall 1995, vol. 51, no. 3.

CRITICAL THINKING QUESTIONS

1. Discuss the ethical issues pertaining to the study from both sides of the argument. Defend your positions on this issue.
2. Discuss the issue of the credibility of the study to the subjects involved in it. Based on your understanding of the article, did the subjects believe that what they were doing was real, or did other factors influence their behavior? Defend your position.
3. Discuss the issues of *theoretical alternatives,* as discussed in the article.
4. What is the perceived social relevance or irrelevance of the Milgram experiments? Defend your position.

ARTICLE 26 _____

Stanley Milgram's article "Behavioral Study of Obedience" was one of his first describing a series of studies investigating the conditions that produce obedience to authority. This study, as well as Milgram's subsequent research, is truly classic. In fact, if you asked someone who has had only minimal exposure to the field of social psychology about landmark research, this study would perhaps come to mind.

Part of the widespread interest in Milgram's work is due to the implications it has. Basically, Milgram took a group of male volunteers from various backgrounds and ages and induced them to perform acts that appeared to harm another person. Nearly two-thirds of the subjects were fully obedient, continuing to give shocks even though it was apparent that they were harming the victim. Does that mean that just about anyone could be made to do the same? More importantly, while reading the article, keep in mind the actual situation confronting the subjects: What would have happened to them if they had refused to obey? Would the effect demonstrated by Milgram be greater for real-life situations, where there might be punishments for failing to obey?

Besides the implications of the research, Milgram's work on obedience also has attracted considerable interest over the years because of the ethical issues raised. When reading the article, try to put yourself in the shoes of the subjects: How would you feel if you volunteered for a study on learning and instead walked out of the experiment an hour later with the realization that you were willing to harm someone just because an authority figure told you to do so? Think about the ethical issues involved in the study, including the issue of debriefing subjects following an experiment.

Behavioral Study of Obedience

■ Stanley Milgram

This chapter describes a procedure for the study of destructive obedience in the laboratory. It consists of ordering a naive S to administer increasingly more severe punishment to a victim in the context of a learning experiment. Punishment is administered by means of a shock generator with thirty graded switches ranging from Slight Shock to Danger: Severe Shock. The victim is a confederate of the E. The primary dependent variable is the maximum shock the S is willing to administer before he refuses to continue further. Twenty-six Ss obeyed the experimental commands fully, and administered the highest shock on the generator. Fourteen Ss broke off the experiment at some point after the victim protested and refused to provide further answers. The procedure created extreme levels of nervous tension in some Ss. Profuse sweating, trembling and stuttering were typical expressions of this emotional disturbance. One unexpected sign of tension—yet to be explained—was the regular occurrence of nervous laughter, which in some Ss developed into uncontrollable seizures. The variety of interesting behavioral dynamics observed in the experiment, the reality of the situation for the S, and the possibility of parametric variation within the framework of the procedure, point to the fruitfulness of further study.

Obedience is as basic an element in the structure of social life as one can point to. Some system of authority is a requirement of all communal living, and it is only the man dwelling in isolation who is not forced to respond, through defiance or submission, to the

Reprinted from *Journal of Abnormal and Social Psychology*, 1963, *67,* 371–378. Copyright renewed 1991 by Alexandra Milgram. All rights reserved. Reprinted by permission.

commands of others. Obedience, as a determinant of behavior, is of particular relevance to our time. It has been reliably established that from 1933–1945 millions of innocent persons were systematically slaughtered on command. Gas chambers were built, death camps were guarded, daily quotas of corpses were produced with the same efficiency as the manufacture of appliances. These inhumane policies may have originated in the mind of a single person, but they could only be carried out on a massive scale if a very large number of persons obeyed orders.

Obedience is the psychological mechanism that links individual action to political purpose. It is the dispositional cement that binds men to systems of authority. Facts of recent history and observation in daily life suggest that for many persons obedience may be a deeply ingrained behavior tendency, indeed, a prepotent impulse overriding training in ethics, sympathy, and moral conduct. C. P. Snow (1961) points to its importance when he writes:

> When you think of the long and gloomy history of man, you will find more hideous crimes have been committed in the name of obedience than have ever been committed in the name of rebellion. If you doubt that, read William Shirer's "Rise and Fall of the Third Reich." The German Officer Corps were brought up in the most rigorous code of obedience . . . in the name of obedience they were party to, and assisted in, the most wicked large scale actions in the history of the world. (p. 24)

While the particular form of obedience dealt with in the present study has its antecedents in these episodes, it must not be thought all obedience entails acts of aggression against others. Obedience serves numerous productive functions. Indeed, the very life of society is predicated on its existence. Obedience may be ennobling and educative and refer to acts of charity and kindness, as well as to destruction.

GENERAL PROCEDURE

A procedure was devised which seems useful as a tool for studying obedience (Milgram, 1961). It consists of ordering a naive subject to administer electric shock to a victim. A simulated shock generator is used, with 30 clearly marked voltage levels that range from 15 to 450 volts. The instrument bears verbal designations that range from Slight Shock to Danger: Severe Shock. The responses of the victim, who is a trained confederate of the experimenter, are standardized. The orders to administer shocks are given to the naive subject in the context of a "learning experiment" ostensibly set up to study the effects of punishment on memory. As the experiment proceeds the naive subject is commanded to administer increasingly more intense shocks to the victim, even to the point of reaching the level marked Danger: Severe Shock. Internal resistances become stronger, and at a certain point the subject refuses to go on with the experiment. Behavior prior to this rupture is considered "obedience," in that the subject complies with the commands of the experimenter. The point of rupture is the act of disobedience. A quantitative value is assigned to the subject's performance based on the maximum intensity shock he is willing to administer before he refuses to participate further. Thus for any particular subject and for any particular experimental condition the degree of obedience may be specified with a numerical value. The crux of the study is to systematically vary the factors believed to alter the degree of obedience to the experimental commands.

The technique allows important variables to be manipulated at several points in the experiment. One may vary aspects of the source of command, content and form of command, instrumentalities for its execution, target object, general social setting, etc. The problem, therefore, is not one of designing increasingly more numerous experimental conditions, but of selecting those that best illuminate the process of obedience from the sociopsychological standpoint.

RELATED STUDIES

The inquiry bears an important relation to philosophic analyses of obedience and authority (Arendt, 1958; Friedrich, 1958; Weber, 1947), an early experimental study of obedience by Frank (1944), studies in "authoritarianism" (Adorno, Frenkel-Brunswik, Levinson, and Sanford, 1950; Rokeach, 1961), and a recent series of analytic and empirical studies in social power (Cartwright, 1959). It owes much to the long concern with *suggestion* in social psychology, both in its normal forms (e.g., Binet, 1900) and in its clinical manifestations (Charcot, 1881). But it derives, in the first instance, from direct observation of a social fact; the individual who is commanded by a legitimate authority ordinarily obeys. Obedience comes easily and often. It is a ubiquitous and indispensable feature of social life.

METHOD

Subjects

The subjects were 40 males between the ages of 20 and 50, drawn from New Haven and the surrounding communities. Subjects were obtained by a newspaper advertisement and direct mail solicitation. Those who responded to the appeal believed they were to participate in a study of memory and learning at Yale University. A wide range of occupations is represented in the sample. Typical subjects were postal clerks, high school teachers, salesmen, engineers, and laborers. Subjects ranged in educational level from one who had not finished elementary school, to those who had doctorate and other professional degrees. They were paid $4.50 for their participation in the experiment. However, subjects were told that payment was simply for coming to the laboratory, and that the money was theirs no matter what happened after they arrived. Table 1 shows the proportion of age and occupational types assigned to the experimental condition.

Personnel and Locale

The experiment was conducted on the grounds of Yale University in the elegant interaction laboratory. (This detail is relevant to the perceived legitimacy of the experiment. In further variations, the experiment was dissociated from the university, with consequences for performance.) The role of experimenter was played by a 31-year-old high school teacher of biology. His manner was impassive, and his appearance somewhat stern throughout the experiment. He was dressed in a gray technician's coat. The victim was played by a 47-year-old accountant, trained for the role; he was of Irish-American stock, whom most observers found mild-mannered and likable.

Procedure

One naive subject and one victim (an accomplice) performed in each experiment. A pretext had to be devised that would justify the administration of electric shock by the naive subject. This was effectively accomplished by the cover story. After a general introduction on the presumed relation between punishment and learning, subjects were told:

> But actually, we know very little *about the effect of punishment on learning, because almost no truly scientific studies have been made of it in human beings.*
>
> *For instance, we don't know how* much *punishment is best for learning—and we don't know how much difference it makes as to who is giving the punishment, whether an adult learns best from a younger or an older person than himself—or many things of that sort.*
>
> *So in this study we are bringing together a number of adults of different occupations and ages. And we're asking some of them to be teachers and some of them to be learners.*

TABLE 1 / Distribution of Age and Occupational Types in the Experiment

Occupations	20–29 Years n	30–39 Years n	40–50 Years n	Percentage of Total (Occupations)
Workers, skilled and unskilled	4	5	6	37.5
Sales, business, and white-collar	3	6	7	40.0
Professional	1	5	3	22.5
Percentage of total (age)	20	40	40	

Note: Total *n* = 40.

*We want to find out just what effect different peo-
ple have on each other as teachers and learners, and
also what effect punishment will have on learning in
this situation.*

*Therefore, I'm going to ask one of you to be the
teacher here tonight and the other one to be the
learner.*

Does either of you have a preference?

Subjects then drew slips of paper from a hat to
determine who would be the teacher and who would
be the learner in the experiment. The drawing was
rigged so that the naive subject was always the teacher
and the accomplice always the learner. (Both slips
contained the word "Teacher.") Immediately after the
drawing the teacher and learner were taken to an adja-
cent room and the learner was strapped into an "electric chair" apparatus.

The experimenter explained that the straps were to
prevent excessive movement while the learner was
being shocked. The effect was to make it impossible
for him to escape from the situation. An electrode was
attached to the learner's wrist, and electrode paste was
applied "to avoid blisters and burns." Subjects were
told that the electrode was attached to the shock generator in the adjoining room.

In order to improve credibility the experimenter
declared, in response to a question by the learner:
"Although the shocks can be extremely painful, they
cause no permanent tissue damage."

Learning Task   The lesson administered by the subject was a paired-associate learning task. The subject
read a series of word pairs to the learner, and then read
the first word of the pair along with four terms. The
learner was to indicate which of the four terms had
originally been paired with the first word. He com-
municated his answer by pressing one of four switches
in front of him, which in turn lit up one of four num-
bered quadrants in an answer-box located atop the
shock generator.

Shock Generator   The instrument panel consists of
30 lever switches set in a horizontal line. Each switch
is clearly labeled with a voltage designation that ranges
from 15 to 450 volts. There is a 15-volt increment
from one switch to the next going from left to right.

In addition, the following verbal designations are
clearly indicated for groups of four switches going
from left to right: Slight Shock, Moderate Shock,
Strong Shock, Very Strong Shock, Intense Shock,
Extreme Intensity Shock, Danger: Severe Shock. (Two
switches after this last designation are simply marked
XXX.)

Upon depressing a switch: a pilot light corresponding to each switch is illuminated in bright red; an
electric buzzing is heard; an electric blue light, labeled
"voltage energizer," flashes; the dial on the voltage
meter swings to the right; various relay clicks are
sounded.

The upper left-hand corner of the generator is
labeled Shock Generator, Type ZLB, Dyson Instrument Company, Waltham, Mass. Output 15 Volts–
450 Volts.

Details of the instrument were carefully handled to
insure an appearance of authenticity. The panel was
engraved by precision industrial engravers, and all
components were of high quality. No subject in the
experiment suspected that the instrument was merely
a simulated shock generator.[1]

Sample Shock   Each naive subject is given a sample
shock on the shock generator, prior to beginning his
run as teacher. This shock is always 45 volts, and is
applied by pressing the third switch of the generator.
The shock is applied to the wrist of the naive subject,
and has its source in a 45-volt battery wired into the
generator. This further convinces the subject of the
authenticity of the generator.

Shock Instructions   The subject is told to administer
a shock to the learner each time he gives a wrong
response. Moreover—and this is the key command—
the subject is instructed to "move one lever higher on
the shock generator each time the learner flashes a
wrong answer." He is also instructed to announce the
voltage level before administering a shock. This serves
to continually remind subjects of the increasing intensity of shocks administered to the learner.

Preliminary and Regular Run   Pretests revealed that
the procedure of reading words and administering
shocks requires some practice before it can be handled
smoothly. Therefore, immediately preceding the regu-

lar run, the teacher is given a preliminary series of 10 words to read to the learner. There are 3 neutral words in the practice series (i.e., words that the learner answers correctly), so that shocks are administered for 7 of the words, with the maximum shock at 105 volts (moderate shock). Almost all subjects master the procedure by the time the preliminary run is over.

Subjects are then presented with a second list, and are told that the procedure is the same as for the first list; the experimenter adds, however:

When you get to the bottom of the list, repeat it over again, and continue giving shocks, until the learner has learned all the pairs correctly.

The experimenter instructs the subject to

start from 15 volts and increase the shock level one step each time the learner gives a wrong answer.

Feedback from the Victim In all conditions the learner gives a predetermined set of responses to the word pair test, based on a schedule of approximately three wrong answers to one correct answer. In the present experimental condition no vocal response or other sign of protest is heard from the learner until Shock Level 300 is reached. When the 300-volt shock is administered, the learner pounds on the wall of the room in which he is bound to the electric chair. The pounding can be heard by the subject. From this point on, the learner's answers no longer appear on the four-way panel.

At this juncture, subjects ordinarily turn to the experimenter for guidance. The experimenter instructs the subject to treat the absence of a response as a wrong answer, and to shock the subject according to the usual schedule. He advises the subjects to allow 5–10 seconds before considering no response as a wrong answer, and to increase the shock level one step each time the learner fails to respond correctly. The learner's pounding is repeated after the 315-volt shock is administered; afterwards he is not heard from, nor do his answers reappear on the four-way signal box.

Experimenter Feedback At various points in the experiment the subject may turn to the experimenter

for advice on whether he should continue to administer shocks. Or he may indicate that he does not wish to go on. It was important to standardize the experimenter's responses to these inquiries and reactions.

If the subject indicated his unwillingness to go on, the experimenter responded with a sequence of "prods," using as many as necessary to bring the subject into line.

> *Prod 1: Please continue* or *Please go on.*
> *Prod 2: The experiment requires that you continue.*
> *Prod 3: It is absolutely essential that you continue.*
> *Prod 4: You have no other choice, you* must *go on.*

The prods were always made in sequence: Only if Prod 1 had been unsuccessful, could Prod 2 be used. If the subject refused to obey the experimenter after Prod 4, the experiment was terminated. The experimenter's tone of voice was at all times firm, but not impolite. The sequence was begun anew on each occasion that the subject balked or showed reluctance to follow orders.

Special Prods If the subject asked if the learner was liable to suffer permanent physical injury, the experimenter said:

> *Although the shocks may be painful, there is no permanent tissue damage, so please go on. [Followed by Prods 2, 3, and 4 if necessary.]*

If the subject said that the learner did not want to go on, the experimenter replied:

> *Whether the learner likes it or not, you must go on until he has learned all the word pairs correctly. So please go on. [Followed by Prods 2, 3, and 4 if necessary.]*

Dependent Measures

The primary dependent measure for any subject is the maximum shock he administers before he refuses to go any further. In principle this may vary from 0 (for a subject who refuses to administer even the first shock) to 30 (for a subject who administers the highest shock on the generator). A subject who breaks off the experiment at any point prior to administering the thirtieth shock level is termed a *defiant* subject. One who complies with experimental commands fully, and proceeds to administer all shock levels commanded, is termed an *obedient* subject.

Further Records　With few exceptions, experimental sessions were recorded on magnetic tape. Occasional photographs were taken through one-way mirrors. Notes were kept on any unusual behavior occurring during the course of the experiments. On occasion, additional observers were directed to write objective descriptions of the subjects' behavior. The latency and duration of shocks were measured by accurate timing devices.

Interview and Dehoax　Following the experiment, subjects were interviewed; open-ended questions, projective measures, and attitude scales were employed. After the interview, procedures were undertaken to assure that the subject would leave the laboratory in a state of well being. A friendly reconciliation was arranged between the subject and the victim, and an effort was made to reduce any tensions that arose as a result of the experiment.

RESULTS

Preliminary Notions

Before giving an account of the experimental results, it is instructive to consider how persons predict others will perform when commanded to administer powerful shocks to another person. Fourteen Yale seniors, all psychology majors, were provided with a detailed description of the experimental situation. They were asked to reflect carefully on it, and to predict the behavior of 100 hypothetical subjects. More specifically, they were instructed to plot the distribution of obedience of "100 Americans of diverse occupations, and ranging in age from 20 to 50 years," who were placed in the experimental situation.

There was considerable agreement among the respondents on the expected behavior of hypothetical subjects. All respondents predicted that only an insignificant minority would go through to the end of the shock series. (The estimates ranged from 0 to 3 percent; i.e., the most "pessimistic" member of the class predicted that of 100 persons, 3 would continue through to the most potent shock available on the

shock generator—450 volts.) The class mean was 1.2 percent. The question was also posed informally to colleagues of the author, and the most general feeling was that few if any subjects would go beyond the designation Very Strong Shock.

Result of Experiment 1

Subjects Accept Situation　With few exceptions subjects were convinced of the reality of the experimental situation, that they were administering shocks to another person, and the most potent shocks were extremely painful. In the post-experimental interview subjects were asked: "How painful to the learner were the last few shocks that you administered to him?" Subjects were instructed to indicate their answers on a printed 14-point scale ranging from "Not at all painful" to "Extremely painful." The modal response was 14 (Extremely painful) with the mean at 13.42.

Signs of Extreme Tension　Many subjects showed signs of nervousness in the experimental situation, and especially upon administering the more powerful shocks. In a large number of cases the degree of tension reached extremes that are rarely seen in sociopsychological laboratory studies. Subjects were observed to sweat, tremble, stutter, bite their lips, groan, and dig their fingernails into their flesh. These were characteristic rather than exceptional responses to the experiment.

One sign of tension was the regular occurrence of nervous laughing fits. Fourteen of the 40 subjects showed definite signs of nervous laughter and smiling. The laughter seemed entirely out of place, even bizarre. Full-blown, uncontrollable seizures were observed for 3 subjects. On one occasion we observed a seizure so violently convulsive that it was necessary to call a halt to the experiment. The subject, a 46-year-old encyclopedia salesman, was seriously embarrassed by his untoward and uncontrollable behavior. In the post-experimental interviews subjects took pains to point out that they were not sadistic types, and that the laughter did not mean they enjoyed shocking the victim.

Distribution of Scores　It had been conjectured that persons would not, in general, agree to administer shocks beyond the level designated as Very Strong Shock. The distribution of maximum shocks for this experiment is shown in Table 2. The obtained distribution of scores deviates radically from the prediction.

Upon command of the experimenter, each of the 40 subjects went beyond the expected breakoff point. No subject stopped prior to administering Shock Level 20. (At this level—300 volts—the victim kicks on the wall and no longer provides answers to the teacher's multiple-choice questions.)

Of the 40 subjects, 5 refused to obey the experimental commands beyond the 300-volt level. Four more subjects administered one further shock, and then refused to go on. Two broke off at the 330-volt level, and 1 each at 345, 360, and 375 volts. Thus a total of 14 subjects defied the experimenter. It is instructive to reprint their remarks at the point of defiance, as transcribed from the tape recordings:

> *[0124] I think he's trying to communicate, he's knocking . . . Well it's not fair to shock the guy . . . these are terrific volts. I don't think this is very humane . . . Oh, I can't go on with this; no, this isn't right. It's a hell of an experiment. The guy is suffering in there. No, I don't want to go on. This is crazy. [Subject refused to administer more shocks.]*
>
> *[0123] He's hanging in there. I'm gonna chicken out. I'd like to continue, but I can't do that to a man . . . I'm sorry I can't do that to a man. I'll hurt his heart. You take your check . . . No really, I couldn't do it.*

These subjects were frequently in a highly agitated and even angered state. Sometimes, verbal protest was at a minimum, and the subject simply got up from his chair in front of the shock generator, and indicated that he wished to leave the laboratory.

Of the 40 subjects, 26 obeyed the orders of the experimenter to the end, proceeding to punish the victim until they reached the most potent shock available on the shock generator. At that point, the experimenter called a halt to the session. (The maximum shock is labeled 450 volts, and is two steps beyond the designation: Danger: Severe Shock.) Although obedient subjects continued to administer shocks, they often did so under extreme stress. Some expressed reluctance to administer shocks beyond the 300-volt level, and displayed fears similar to those who defied the experimenter; yet they obeyed.

TABLE 2 / Distribution of Breakoff Points

Verbal Designation and Voltage Indication	Number of Subjects for Whom This Was Maximum Shock
Slight Shock	
15	
30	0
45	0
60	0
Moderate Shock	
75	0
90	0
105	0
120	0
Strong Shock	
135	0
150	0
165	0
180	0
Very Strong Shock	
195	0
210	0
225	0
240	0
Intense Shock	
255	0
270	0
285	0
300	5
Extreme Intensity Shock	
315	4
330	2
345	1
360	1
Danger: Severe Shock	
375	1
390	0
405	0
420	0
XXX	
435	0
450	26

After the maximum shocks had been delivered, and the experimenter called a halt to the proceedings, many obedient subjects heaved sighs of relief, mopped their brows, rubbed their fingers over their eyes, or nervously fumbled cigarettes. Some shook their heads, apparently in regret. Some subjects had remained calm throughout the experiment, and displayed only minimal signs of tension from beginning to end.

DISCUSSION

The experiment yielded two findings that were surprising. The first finding concerns the sheer strength of obedient tendencies manifested in this situation. Subjects have learned from childhood that it is a fundamental breach of moral conduct to hurt another person against his will. Yet, 26 subjects abandon this tenet in following the instructions of an authority who has no special powers to enforce his commands. To disobey would bring no material loss to the subject; no punishment would ensue. It is clear from the remarks and outward behavior of many participants that in punishing the victim they are often acting against their own values. Subjects often expressed deep disapproval of shocking a man in the face of his objections, and others denounced it as stupid and senseless. Yet the majority complied with the experimental commands. This outcome was surprising from two perspectives: first, from the standpoint of predictions made in the questionnaire described earlier. (Here, however, it is possible that the remoteness of the respondents from the actual situation, and the difficulty of conveying to them the concrete details of the experiment, could account for the serious underestimation of obedience.)

But the results were also unexpected to persons who observed the experiment in progress, through one-way mirrors. Observers often uttered expressions of disbelief upon seeing a subject administer more powerful shocks to the victim. These persons had a full acquaintance with the details of the situation, and yet systematically underestimated the amount of obedience that subjects would display.

The second unanticipated effect was the extraordinary tension generated by the procedures. One might suppose that a subject would simply break off or continue as his conscience dictated. Yet, this is very far from what happened. There were striking reactions of tension and emotional strain. One observer related:

I observed a mature and initially poised businessman enter the laboratory smiling and confident. Within 20 minutes he was reduced to a twitching, stuttering wreck, who was rapidly approaching a point of nervous collapse. He constantly pulled on his earlobe, and twisted his hands. At one point he pushed his fist into his forehead and muttered: "Oh God, let's stop it." And yet he continued to respond to every word of the experimenter and obeyed to the end.

Any understanding of the phenomenon of obedience must rest on an analysis of the particular conditions in which it occurs. The following features of the experiment go some distance in explaining the high amount of obedience observed in the situation.

1. The experiment is sponsored by and takes place on the grounds of an institution of unimpeachable reputation, Yale University. It may be reasonably presumed that the personnel are competent and reputable. The importance of this background authority is now being studied by conducting a series of experiments outside of New Haven, and without any visible ties to the university.

2. The experiment is, on the face of it, designed to attain a worthy purpose—advancement of knowledge about learning and memory. Obedience occurs not as an end in itself, but as an instrumental element in a situation that the subject construes as significant, and meaningful. He may not be able to see its full significance, but he may properly assume that the experimenter does.

3. The subject perceives that the victim has voluntarily submitted to the authority system of the experimenter. He is not (at first) an unwilling captive impressed for involuntary service. He has taken the trouble to come to the laboratory presumably to aid the experimental research. That he later becomes an involuntary subject does not alter the fact that, initially, he consented to participate without qualification. Thus he has in some degree incurred an obligation toward the experimenter.

4. The subject, too, has entered the experiment voluntarily, and perceives himself under obligation to aid the experimenter. He has made a commitment, and to disrupt the experiment is a repudiation of this initial promise of aid.

5. Certain features of the procedure strengthen the subject's sense of obligation to the experimenter. For

one, he has been paid for coming to the laboratory. In part this is canceled out by the experimenter's statement that:

> Of course, as in all experiments, the money is yours simply for coming to the laboratory. From this point on, no matter what happens, the money is yours.[2]

6. From the subject's standpoint, the fact that he is the teacher and the other man the learner is purely a chance consequence (it is determined by drawing lots) and he, the subject, ran the same risk as the other man in being assigned the role of learner. Since the assignment of positions in the experiment was achieved by fair means, the learner is deprived of any basis of complaint on this count. (A similar situation obtains in Army units, in which—in the absence of volunteers—a particularly dangerous mission may be assigned by drawing lots, and the unlucky soldier is expected to bear his misfortune with sportsmanship.)

7. There is, at best, ambiguity with regard to the prerogatives of a psychologist and the corresponding rights of his subject. There is a vagueness of expectation concerning what a psychologist may require of his subject, and when he is overstepping acceptable limits. Moreover, the experiment occurs in a closed setting, and thus provides no opportunity for the subject to remove these ambiguities by discussion with others. There are few standards that seem directly applicable to the situation, which is a novel one for most subjects.

8. The subjects are assured that the shocks administered to the subject are "painful but not dangerous." Thus they assume that the discomfort caused the victim is momentary, while the scientific gains resulting from the experiment are enduring.

9. Through Shock Level 20 the victim continues to provide answers on the signal box. The subject may construe this as a sign that the victim is still willing to "play the game." It is only after Shock Level 20 that the victim repudiates the rules completely, refusing to answer further.

These features help to explain the high amount of obedience obtained in this experiment. Many of the arguments raised need not remain matters of speculation, but can be reduced to testable propositions to be confirmed or disproved by further experiments.[3]

The following features of the experiment concern the nature of the conflict which the subject faces.

10. The subject is placed in a position in which he must respond to the competing demands of two persons: the experimenter and the victim. The conflict must be resolved by meeting the demands of one or the other; satisfaction of the victim and the experimenter are mutually exclusive. Moreover, the resolution must take the form of a highly visible action, that of continuing to shock the victim or breaking off the experiment. Thus the subject is forced into a public conflict that does not permit any completely satisfactory solution.

11. While the demands of the experimenter carry the weight of scientific authority, the demands of the victim spring from his personal experience of pain and suffering. The two claims need not be regarded as equally pressing and legitimate. The experimenter seeks an abstract scientific datum; the victim cries out for relief from physical suffering caused by the subject's actions.

12. The experiment gives the subject little time for reflection. The conflict comes on rapidly. It is only minutes after the subject has been seated before the shock generator that the victim begins his protests. Moreover, the subject perceives that he has gone through but two-thirds of the shock levels at the time the subject's first protests are heard. Thus he understands that the conflict will have a persistent aspect to it, and may well become more intense as increasingly more powerful shocks are required. The rapidity with which the conflict descends on the subject, and his realization that it is predictably recurrent may well be sources of tension to him.

13. At a more general level, the conflict stems from the opposition of two deeply ingrained behavior dispositions: first, the disposition not to harm other people, and second, the tendency to obey those whom we perceive to be legitimate authorities.

REFERENCES

Adorno, T., Frenkel-Brunswik, Else, Levinson, D. J., and Sanford, R. N. *The authoritarian personality.* New York: Harper, 1950.

Arendt, H. What was authority? In C. J Friedrich (ed.), *Authority.* Cambridge: Harvard Univer. Press, 1958. Pp. 81–112.

Binet, A. *La suggestibilité.* Paris: Schleicher, 1900.

Buss, A. H. *The psychology of aggression.* New York: Wiley, 1961.

Cartwright, S. (ed.) *Studies in social power.* Ann Arbor: University of Michigan Institute for Social Research, 1959.

Charcot, J. M. *Oeuvres complètes.* Paris: Bureaux du Progrès Médical, 1881.

Frank, J. D. Experimental studies of personal pressure and resistance. *J. Gen. Psychol.* 1944, *30,* 23–64.

Freidrich, C. J. (ed.) *Authority.* Cambridge: Harvard Univer. Press, 1958.

Milgram, S. Dynamics of obedience. Washington: National Science Foundation, 25 January 1961. (Mimeo).

Milgram, S. Some conditions of obedience and disobedience to authority. *Hum. Relat.,* 1965, *18,* 57–76.

Rokeach, M. Authority, authoritarianism, and conformity. In I. A. Berg and B. M. Bass (eds.), *Conformity and deviation.* New York: Harper, 1961. Pp. 230–257.

Snow, C. P. Either-or. *Progressive,* 1961 (Feb.) 24.

Weber, M. *The theory of social and economic organization.* Oxford: Oxford Univer. Press, 1947.

ENDNOTES

1. A related technique, making use of a shock generator, was reported by Buss (1961) for the study of aggression in the laboratory. Despite the considerable similarity of technical detail in the experimental procedures, each investigator proceeded in ignorance of the other's work. Milgram provided plans and photographs of his shock generator, experimental procedure, and first results in a report to the National Science Foundation in January 1961. This report received only limited circulation. Buss reported his procedure six months later, but to a wider audience. Subsequently, technical information and reports were exchanged. The present article was first received in the editor's office on December 27, 1961; it was resubmitted with deletions on July 27, 1962.

2. Forty-three subjects, undergraduates at Yale University, were run in the experiment without payment. The results are very similar to those obtained with paid subjects.

3. A series of recently completed experiments employing the obedience paradigm is reported in Milgram (1965).

This research was supported by a grant (NSF G-17916) from the National Science Foundation. Exploratory studies conducted in 1960 were supported by a grant from the Higgins Fund at Yale University. The research assistance of Alan E. Elms and Jon Wayland is gratefully acknowledged.

CRITICAL THINKING QUESTIONS

1. What are the ethical implications of this study? In particular, are you satisfied that no lasting harm was done to the participants? Would the debriefing at the end of the experiment be sufficient to eliminate any long-term problems from participation in the study? What about short-term effects? Many of the subjects obviously suffered during the experiment. Was the infliction of this distress on the subjects justified? Support your answers. (*Note:* For a good discussion of the ethics of the study, see the Baumrind and Milgram articles cited below.)

2. What are the implications of this study for people accused of committing atrocities? Suppose that the results of this study had been known when the Nazi war criminals were put on trial in Nuremberg. Could the information have been used in their defense? Do the results remove some of the personal responsibility that people have for their actions? Explain your answers.

3. Subjects were paid a nominal amount for participation in the study. They were told that the money was theirs to keep simply because they showed up, regardless of what happened after they arrived. Do you think that this payment was partly responsible for the findings? Why or why not? Do you think that paying someone, no matter how small the amount, somehow changes the dynamics of the situation? Explain.

ADDITIONAL RELATED READINGS

Baumrind, D. (1964). Some thoughts on ethics of research after reading Milgram's "Behavioral study of obedience." *American Psychologist, 19,* 421–423.

Mastroianni, G. E. (2002). Milgram and the Holocaust: A reexamination. *Theoretical and Philosophical Psychology, 22*(2), 158–173.

Milgram, S. (1964). Issues in the study of obedience: A reply to Baumrind. *American Psychologist, 19,* 848–852.

ARTICLE 27 _____

Conformity is a fact of life yet a behavior toward which we have decidedly ambivalent feelings. On the one hand, none of us like to think of ourselves as *conformist*. For most people, this word has a fairly negative connotation, suggesting people who mindlessly go along with the group rather than thinking for themselves. Even people who see themselves as nonconformist (such as in how they dress) often are just conforming to an alternative set of norms. Perhaps the best example of this is the teenager who dyes his hair blue because he wants to be "different in a conforming sort of way."

On the other hand, conformity is the very background of culture. How could we drive our cars, engage in social interactions, or do just about anything involving other people if we did not conform to what was expected of us in those situations? Without some level of conformity, total chaos would result. Even when we feel independent in the decisions we make, in fact, our choice is not *whether* to conform but rather which norms to conform to.

So, why is conformity such a vital part of the human experience? At a very basic level, it helps to promote survival of the group. After all, people are fundamentally social creatures, and without conformity, the daily interactions that make life possible would be impossible. But people conform for other reasons, as well. One such reason may be to obtain information about an otherwise ambiguous situation. For example, if you wanted to know the distance between Washington, DC, and New York City, you could look it up in a book. That information is a *fact:* an agreed upon, accepted piece of knowledge. As such, you need only to consult the proper source to find it.

But how much of social life is about readily determinable facts? Not much. Most of the situations and questions we face are not factual but rather matters of belief, custom, or opinion. Whom should I vote for? What is the right thing to do? What is the best way to live my life? The answers to questions such as these often come from other people. Thus, another reason we conform is because other people often are able to provide us with clues for how to behave, especially when the situation is otherwise ambiguous and we are unsure of what is expected of us.

People also conform to be accepted. If you have ever deviated from the norms or beliefs of a group to which you belong, you already know the intensely uncomfortable experience of being rejected or pressured by others in the group. To be accepted by the group, we must go along with them. Thus, we sometimes conform just to be accepted and to fit into a particular group.

Of course, we sometimes conform to the actual behaviors of those around us. We see people acting in a certain way, and we do likewise. But very often, we base our behaviors not on what we actually *see* others doing but on what we *think* they are doing. Thus, we may be tempted to do something because "everyone else is doing it," even if in reality, they are not. This is known as *pluralistic ignorance,* or the erroneous belief that our own privately held beliefs are somehow different than those held by others. The following article by Jerry Suls and Peter Green examines how factors such as pluralistic ignorance may play a role in college students' attitudes about drinking. The article also has some serious implications for efforts to moderate or reduce drinking on campuses.

Pluralistic Ignorance and College Student Perceptions of Gender-Specific Alcohol Norms

■ Jerry Suls and Peter Green

Students' perceived norms and personal concern about alcohol use were examined in 4 (N = 971) experiments. Men reported that same-sex peers were less concerned about campus alcohol practices than themselves or female students; women believed that they were more concerned about campus alcohol practices than both same- and opposite-sex peers (Experiments 1 and 2). Additional evidence suggested that students were not merely engaging in impression management. Men reported more social pressure to drink and greater embarrassment about expressing drinking-related concerns; women expected more severe consequences if they drank excessively (Experiment 3). A male student (vs. female student) expressing concerns about alcohol was believed to experience greater difficulties fitting in (Experiment 4). Implications for peer influence and drug use intervention are discussed.

Key Words   college student, alcohol use, pluralistic ignorance, social influence, substance abuse

Recent surveys indicate that almost half of college students frequently consume alcohol in excessive amounts (e.g., Wechsler, Davenport, Dowdall, Moeykens, & Castillo, 1994; cf. Weingardt et al., 1998). This problem pertains to both genders, although men tend to consume more alcohol and experience more adverse consequences than do women (O'Hare, 1990; Wechsler, Dowdall, Davenport, & Castillo, 1995). Excessive alcohol consumption on college campuses, because of its role in motor vehicle fatalities, unsafe sex, unintentional injuries, and poor academic performance (Perkins & Berkowitz, 1986; P. Wood, Sher, Erickson, & DeBord, 1997), has received widespread attention and concern from public health officials, university administrators, parents, and the media (e.g., Wechsler et al., 1995). Virtually all theories consider active social pressure to try alcohol, social modeling (Collins, Parks, & Marlatt, 1985), stress (Wills, 1986), risk prototypes (Gibbons & Gerrard,

1997), and the misperception of peer substance use behavior to be important for adoption of risky health-related behaviors (Borsari & Carey, 2001; Graham, Marks, & Hansen, 1991; Kandel, 1980; Perkins, 2002; Sher, Bartholow, & Nanda, 2001). The last route, the construal of social norms concerning campus alcohol practices, is the focus of the present research.

One form of norm construal concerns estimates of how much and how frequently others use alcohol; Borsari and Carey (2001) referred to these as "descriptive norms" (see also Cialdini, Reno, & Kallgren, 1990). Survey evidence indicates that young adults tend to overestimate the level of alcohol consumption and illicit drug use among their peers (Baer, Stacy, & Larimer, 1991; Sherman, Presson, Chassin, Corty, & Olshavsky, 1983; Suls, Wan, & Sanders, 1988). Overestimation of campus drinking may result from the vividness and availability of flagrant abuses (Kahneman & Tversky, 1973) and/or the desire to see one's own behavior in a more favorable light (Suls & Wan, 1987). The overestimation bias is important because numerous studies also show that one of the most consistent predictors of adolescent alcohol use is perceived alcohol use by peers (e.g., Marks, Graham, & Hansen, 1992; Sher et al., 2001; Stein, Newcomb, & Bender, 1987).

Perceptions of prevalence should be distinguished, however, from estimates of personal support for campus alcohol norms. Perceptions of others' approval of drinking may be considered "injunctive norms" (Borsari & Carey, 2001). Public behavior among college students appears to support alcohol use, but students privately may have misgivings about excessive drinking because of exposure to its negative consequences (e.g., sick roommates). Because excessive drinking at bars and parties on campus is highly visible, but individuals might be inhibited about sharing their private concerns, erroneous perceptions about other people's

Reprinted from *Health Psychology,* 2003, *22*(5), 479–486. Copyright © 2003 by the American Psychological Association. Reprinted with permission.

private feelings about alcohol may result. Everyone may conclude (erroneously) that their peers have no serious qualms about alcohol. This represents a case of *pluralistic ignorance,* in which students "assume that their own privately held attitudes are more conservative than those of other students" (Schroeder & Prentice, 1998, p. 2152).[1] Consistent with this reasoning, in a study conducted at Princeton University, college students rated themselves as less comfortable with drinking on campus than the average student and their friends (Prentice & Miller, 1993). Perkins and Berkowitz (1986) reported similar findings: Students thought they personally were less permissive about alcohol than were other college students.

The present experiments were conducted to assess how personally concerned college men and women attending a large midwestern public university were about alcohol practices relative to same- and opposite-sex peers. Although Prentice and Miller (1993, Study 1) found that both genders estimated that their comfort levels were lower than those of the average student, the gap was larger for women than for men. Also, in a prospective study (Prentice & Miller, 1993, Study 3), women were less apt to change their attitudes or their drinking in the direction of what they perceived to be the campus norm. These results are suggestive of a gender difference in the perception and role of pluralistic ignorance in campus drinking. However, only opinions about "the average student" and "friends" have been assessed in prior studies, so whether men and women hold gender-specific norms for personal concern about alcohol on campus remains unknown.

We predicted that both genders would perceive men to be less concerned about campus alcohol practices because college men consume more alcohol than do women (O'Hare, 1990; Wechsler et al., 1995). Also, because any discomfort that men privately experience about excessive drinking may seem blatantly contradicted by the dominant role that alcohol plays in men's campus social life (Prentice & Miller, 1993; M. Wood, Nasgoshi, & Dennis, 1992), they may be especially reluctant to communicate their concerns (and violate a masculine image), resulting in a greater disjunction between their privately held beliefs and publicly observable behavior. Thus, men may feel more deviant from same-sex peers than do women. We conducted three survey experiments and an impression formation experiment to assess gender-specific norms about campus alcohol practices.

EXPERIMENT 1

Method

Participants   College students (*n* = 344) enrolled in a large midwestern university participated as part of a large group testing session that counted as research credit for the students' Elementary Psychology requirement. Of the participants, 145 (42%) were men and 199 (58%) were women. Elementary Psychology fulfills a general education requirement and draws a broad spectrum of first- and second-year students at the university. No identifying information was written on the questionnaire, and participants' anonymity was assured. The surveys were administered along with several unrelated inventories included by other researchers.

Procedure and Materials   Five questions assessed pluralistic ignorance regarding concern about alcohol consumption on campus. The item assessing personal concern was "How do you feel about the level of alcohol consumption by students at the university?" Level of concern was indicated by circling a number on an 11-point Likert-type scale ranging from 0 (*It doesn't bother me at all*) to 10 (*It bothers me very much*). Other items inquired about concern of other reference groups, such as "How do you think the average male student at this university feels about the level of alcohol consumption on this campus?," with responses made on an 11-point scale ranging from 0 (*It doesn't bother them to all*) to 10 (*It bothers them very much*). This was followed by questions using the same format about the concern of "the average female student," "male friends," and "female friends."

To assess perceptions about frequency of excessive alcohol consumption, we asked participants how often they got drunk, followed by questions about how often they thought the average male student, the average female student, male friends, and female friends drank excessively. The item for frequency of intoxication, "How often do you drink enough alcohol to become drunk?" was answered on a 6-point scale, with 1 (*I never drink or I never drink enough to get drunk*), 2 (*I get drunk 1–3 times a year*), 3 (*I get* drunk 1–2 times a month), 4 (*I get drunk 1–2 times a week*), 5 (*I get drunk 3–4 times a week*), and 6 (*I get drunk almost every day*) as possible response alternatives. The alternatives for the average students and friends items were the same as above except for changes in pronouns.

Items about concern and frequency of driving under the influence of alcohol also were included. Personal concern was assessed in response to the question, "How do you feel about the amount of drunk driving occurring in [name of the small midwestern city where the university was located]?" with responses rated on an 11-point scale ranging from 0 (*It doesn't bother me at all*) to 10 (*It bothers me very much*). Participants also used similar scales to rate their impressions of the views of other reference groups—average male student, average female student, male friends, and female friends—concerning drunk driving. Frequency of driving under the influence was assessed with the question, "How often do you drive after having more than 2 alcoholic drinks?" Responses were made on a 6-point scale, with 1 (*I never drive after drinking alcoholic beverages*), 2 (*I've driven a couple of times after drinking alcohol*), 3 (*Once or twice in the past year*), 4 (*Once or twice in the past month*), 5 (*Once or twice in the past week*), and 6 (*I always drive no matter how much I've had to drink*) as alternatives. (Data from participants who reported not having a driver's license, not having access to an automobile, and/or rarely having the opportunity to drive were excluded.) Participants also were asked to rate frequency of driving under the influence of the average male student, the average female student, male friends, and female friends on campus.

A fixed order was used, with the frequency questions preceding the concern questions, because Prentice and Miller (1993) found that self-comfort was rated lower than estimates of others, regardless of order. Driving under the influence items and excessive alcohol consumption items were counterbalanced across participants.

Results

Intoxication   Ratings of concern about campus alcohol practices were examined with a 2 (gender) × 5 (target: self, average male student, male friends, average female student, or female friends) analysis of variance (ANOVA), with repeated measures on the second factor. Gender, $F(1, 342) = 4.06$, $p < .05$, and target, $F(4, 1368) = 87.30$, $p < .001$, main effects were significant, as was the Gender × Target interaction, $F(4, 1368) = 4.63$, $p < .001$ (see Figure 1). Simple effects analyses, $F(4, 1368) = 32.79$, $p < .001$, indicated that men reported having as much personal concern about excessive alcohol consumption as their best female friend and the average female student, and they reported having more concern than that predicted for the average male student ($d = 1.04$) and best male friend ($d = 1.01$). In contrast, female students reported being more concerned than all reference groups (although closer to other women than to men), $F(4, 1368) = 64.11$, $p < .001$ (ds ranged from 0.65 to 1.50).

A 2 × 5 ANOVA of the frequency of intoxication estimates for self- and other targets indicated a significant main effect of target, $F(4, 1368) = 107.91$, $p < .001$, with participants reporting that they drank to intoxication less frequently than did peers or friends. However, female friends were perceived to be closer to self than were the other groups. The main effect of gender was not significant ($F < 1$), but there was a Gender × Target interaction, $F(4, 1368) = 10.93$, $p < .001$. The form of the interaction indicated that male students' own estimates of excessive drinking ($M = 3.07$, $SD = 1.18$) were lower than their estimates for all groups (average male student, $M = 3.77$, $SD = 0.85$; male friend, $M = 3.48$, $SD = 1.56$; average female student, $M = 3.33$, $SD = 0.86$; ds ranged from 0.24 to 0.85) except female friends ($M = 3.11$, $SD = 1.09$), $F(4, 1368) = 26.47$, $p < .001$. Female students ($M = 2.64$, $SD = 1.14$) reported that they drank to intoxication less frequently than all others (average male student, $M = 3.92$, $SD = 0.83$; male friend, $M = 3.43$, $SD = 1.13$; average female student, $M = 3.51$, $SD = 0.78$; female friend, $M = 2.99$, $SD = 1.09$; ds ranged from 0.84 to 1.40), $F(4, 1368) = 104.20$, $p < .001$.

Driving under the Influence   The number of participants ($n = 311$) included in the analyses of the driving drunk items was smaller than that for the intoxication items because respondents for whom driving was not applicable were excluded. In comparison with general concern about level of excessive drinking, driving

FIGURE 1 / Mean Self- and Perceived Other Concern Ratings (with Standard Errors Bars) by Male and Female Participants for Level of Alcohol Consumption on Campus (A) and for Drunk Driving (B)

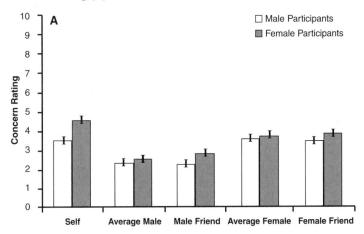

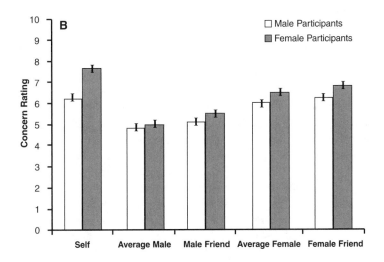

under the influence items showed a higher absolute level of concern. Ratings ranged from 4.82 to 7.64 on the 0–10-point scale (compared with 2.30–4.54 for campus alcohol practices). Although students believed there were greater risks associated with driving under the influence of alcohol, the pattern for self versus others was similar to that found for campus alcohol practices. The gender main effect, $F(1, 309) = 6.17$, $p < .02$ ($d = 0.28$), indicated that men reported less concern about driving drunk. A significant target main effect, $F(4, 1236) = 126.40$, $p < .001$, and Gen-

der × Target interaction, $F(4, 1236) = 9.27$, $p < .001$, also were indicated (see Figure 1). Post hoc tests of the simple effect, $F(2, 1236) = 34.18$, $p < .001$, showed that male students reported having as much concern about drunk driving as the average female student and female friend but more concern than the average male student ($d = 1.10$) and male friend ($d = 0.52$). Female students thought they were more concerned than all reference groups (ds ranged from 0.80 to 1.60), although somewhat closer in sentiment to other women, $F(4, 1236) = 114.13$, $p < .001$.

For frequency estimates, the results for driving drunk were similar to those found for intoxication. (The degrees of freedom differ from those reported earlier because 7 participants provided incomplete data regarding frequency.) There was a main effect of target, $F(4, 1208) = 89.42$, $p < .001$, and a significant Gender $\times$ Target interaction, $F(4, 1208) = 5.21$, $p < .001$. Men reported that they drove drunk as frequently ($M = 2.63$, $SD = 1.29$) as their female friends ($M = 2.58$, $SD = 1.32$) but less than all other groups (male friend, $M = 3.14$, $SD = 1.36$; average male student, $M = 3.50$, $SD = 1.21$; average female student, $M = 2.85$, $SD = 1.18$), $F(4, 1208) = 27.44$, $p < .001$ (ds ranged from 0.30 to 0.82). Women ($M = 2.08$, $SD = 1.03$) reported engaging in drunk driving less frequently than all groups ($ps < .05$), although they thought their rate was closest to that of female friends (average male student, $M = 3.44$, $SD = 1.28$; male friend, $M = 3.03$, $SD = 1.38$; average female student, $M = 2.86$, $SD = 1.07$; female friend, $M = 2.34$, $SD = 1.16$; ds ranged from 0.20 to 0.91).

Discussion

College students at a large public midwestern university believed that large segments of the campus were not as concerned about alcohol practices as they personally were; however, there were noteworthy gender differences. Male students reported being more concerned about excessive alcohol consumption on campus than other male students and believed their personal feelings were closer in sentiment to those of their female friends. Also, male students reported engaging in excessive drinking less frequently than their same-sex peers and at the lower rate estimated for female peers. The pattern of men's concern ratings implies that they felt deviant from their same-sex peers; that is, personal concern about excessive drinking was inconsistent with the stereotype of the campus male student. Female students, however, believed that they think and behave more responsibly than both same- and opposite-sex reference groups. Although the absolute level of concern about excessive consumption was low (not surprising in light of the amount of drinking reported), misgivings about drunk driving were greater. Gender differences in norm perceptions, however, were seen with respect to both excessive consumption and driving under the influence.

EXPERIMENT 2

Although college students reported being more concerned than their peers, one might ask whether they were reporting their true feelings or merely trying to make a more socially responsible impression. A reason to doubt the impression management account is that all surveys were collected under conditions of anonymity; however, even under such conditions, people may try to present a more positive image. An impression management explanation for the previous results, therefore, cannot be completely discounted.

Experiment 2 directly assessed whether impression management posed an interpretational problem for previous findings. Participants were led to believe their survey responses would be shared with groups that should have been perceived to differ in friendliness about expressing concerns or reporting excessive drinking (i.e., university administrators, fraternity and sorority groups, or researchers). If impression management is operating, even when responding anonymously students should present themselves as least concerned when they complete surveys that are expected to be seen by fraternal groups and most concerned when the surveys are expected to be seen by university administrators, who in public meetings and in the college newspaper were considering making alcohol policies on campus more restrictive.

In Experiment 1, students were asked how "bothered" they were about the level of drinking on campus. Prentice and Miller (1993), however, asked participants to rate how "comfortable" they felt about alcohol drinking habits. To ensure that the phrasing of the questions was not responsible for the obtained gender differences, in Experiment 2 we had students complete items comparable with those used by Prentice and Miller (1993). Also, instead of asking about frequency of intoxication, we asked questions about the typical number of alcoholic drinks consumed, adapted from Wechsler et al. (1994). Students could have varied in their definitions of being drunk, creating ambiguity about the estimates made for self and others. Asking about the number of alcoholic drinks consumed seemed less susceptible to idiosyncratic interpretation.

Method

Participants College students (n = 190) enrolled in a large Elementary Psychology course took part in a group testing session involving the completion of a series of unrelated surveys under anonymous conditions. Of the participants, 74 (39%) were men and 116 (61%) were women.

Procedure and Materials One third of the survey booklets contained instructions stating that "the data may be shared with University Administrators. As you know, the University administration is concerned about the role of alcohol on campus." Another third contained instructions stating that "the data may be shared with fraternity and sorority organizations. As you know, fraternities and sororities are concerned about possible changes in campus alcohol policies." The final third of the surveys contained instructions stating that "the data are being obtained exclusively for research purposes." Surveys for the three conditions were randomly assigned.

Concern about campus drinking was assessed with the question, "'How comfortable do you feel with alcohol drinking habits of students at this university?' Participants also answered similar questions with respect to "your male friends" and "your female friends." Responses were made on 11-point scales ranging from 1 (*Not at all*) to 11 (*Very comfortable*). Unlike in Experiment 1, participants were asked only about male friends and female friends because they should be more important sources of influence than the average student (the latter also might have had a negative connotation).

Three items concerning quantity of alcohol consumed on a typical occasion were adapted from Wechsler et al. (1994). Participants were asked to answer the question for self, "When you drink, how much do you drink? (Circle your best estimate.)," with 1 (*1 drink*), 2 (*2 drinks*), 3 (*3–4 drinks*), 4 (*5–6 drinks*), and 5 (*7 or more drinks*) as alternatives. They also made their best estimates for a male friend and a

female friend using the same response categories. Instructions indicated that "one drink = a 12 oz can or bottle of beer, a 4 oz glass of wine, or a shot of liquor in a mixed drink." After completion of the questionnaire booklets, participants were debriefed about the deception.

Results

Manipulation Check After completing the alcohol surveys, participants were asked to check whether survey results would be shared with administrators, would be shared with fraternal and sorority organizations, or were collected only for research purposes. A total of 183 participants (96%) checked the correct recipient mentioned in the survey instructions, with no difference across conditions. Thus, the vast majority of participants paid attention to and remembered the cover story.

Comfort A 2 (gender) × 3 (recipients: administrators, fraternal organizations, or researchers) × 3 (target: self, male friends, or female friends) ANOVA was conducted with repeated measures on the last factor. The main effect for participant gender was nonsignificant, but there was a referent main effect, $F(2, 368) = 69.55$, $p < .0001$, and a Gender × Referent interaction, $F(2, 368) = 7.38$, $p < .01$. Estimates differed depending on the gender of the participant. As in Experiment 1, men reported discomfort levels ($M = 7.81$, $SD = 2.75$) comparable with their estimate of those for women ($M = 8.04$, $SD = 2.47$) but significantly higher than their estimate for male friends ($M = 8.91$, $SD = 2.37$; $d = 0.51$), $F(2, 368) = 13.50$, $p < .001$. Women described themselves as significantly less comfortable ($M = 7.20$, $SD = 2.34$) than their female friends ($M = 8.16$, $SD = 1.86$; $d = 0.59$), who were perceived as more uncomfortable than their male friends ($M = 9.22$, $SD = 1.81$; $d = 0.70$), $F(2, 368) = 84.48$, $p < .001$. Women also saw themselves as less comfortable than male friends ($d = 1.09$). Most important, there was no effect of the survey recipient manipulation, and there were no interactions involving this factor ($Fs < 1$). No trends in the means as a function of manipulated recipients were evident. Therefore, impression management seems unlikely as an alternative explanation for the concern or discomfort reported by the students.

Quantity A similar analysis was conducted on the number of drinks measure. (The degrees of freedom differ from the preceding analyses because some participants did not complete all quantity items.) There was no significant effect or interaction involving instructional condition ($Fs < 1$). Men did make higher estimates overall ($M = 4.15$, $SD = 1.17$) than did women ($M = 3.80$, $SD = 1.24$), $F(1, 169) = 10.15$, $p < .002$ ($d = 0.21$). Estimates significantly differed across self, male friends, and female friends, $F(2, 338) = 15.73$, $p < .001$. Most notable, the Participant Gender × Target interaction was significant, $F(2, 338) = 13.39$, $p < .001$. Simple effects analyses and Newman–Keuls post hoc tests indicated that men perceived themselves as drinking less ($M = 4.34$, $SD = 0.86$) than their same-sex friends ($M = 4.60$, SD 0.67; $d = 0.45$), but more than their female friends ($M = 3.56$, $SD = 0.78$; $d = 0.95$), $F(2, 338) = 59.91$, $p < .001$. (This pattern differs somewhat from Experiment 1 in which men estimated they got intoxicated as frequently as women.) Men's estimates for same-sex friends were also significantly greater than their estimates for female friends ($d = 1.34$). Women estimated that they drank less ($M = 3.29$, $SD = 1.04$) than other women ($M = 3.53$, $SD = 0.78$; $d = 0.27$) and much less than male students ($M = 4.56$, $SD = 0.72$; $d = 1.28$), $F(2, 338) = 137.46$, $p < .001$. The women's estimate for male friends was also significantly greater than that for their same-sex friends ($d = 1.28$).

Discussion

Students' reports of personal concern were similar to those in the prior experiment even when we manipulated the recipients of the surveys from unfriendly (i.e., university administrators) to friendly (i.e., fraternal organizations) concerning campus drinking. These data lend no support to the idea that students reported being more personally concerned merely because they were trying to make a socially desirable impression. Also, as in Experiment 1, men reported personal discomfort levels that were more comparable with their impressions about women than about other men. Women reported being more uncomfortable

than male and female friends. These patterns were found with the question format originally used by Prentice and Miller (1993), showing the gender effects were not a function of the way the questions were asked in Experiment 1.

EXPERIMENT 3

We hypothesized that believing that others do not share one's misgivings about alcohol stems from individuals' embarrassment about disclosing their concerns (Prentice & Miller, 1993). This should be especially problematic for men because drinking is integral to masculine social identity on most campuses. To the extent the illusion of belief uniformity is not dispelled, campus men should feel more social pressure to drink. College women also should find themselves in an awkward position because they apparently see themselves as deviant from both same- and opposite-sex peers. (At least men find some similarity with their female friends.) One reason women may accommodate to this situation is that alcohol plays a lesser role in campus life for women. There also is evidence that female alcohol use is condoned less (Huselid & Cooper, 1992). In addition, women may anticipate experiencing more severe negative consequences (e.g., unintended sex, rape, or pregnancy) if they drink excessively, which places a check on their drinking. To examine these possibilities, we surveyed college students about feelings concerning social pressure, embarrassment, and consequences concerning alcohol.

Method

Participants College students ($N = 223$; 111 men, 50%; 112 women, 50%) were recruited for a large group testing session involving administration of a large series of psychological measures completed anonymously. They received credit toward their Elementary Psychology research exposure requirement.

Materials and Procedure Three questions were embedded in a larger packet. To assess perceptions of social pressure, we asked, "Do college men or women tend to experience more social pressures from their friends and others to drink more than they may be inclined to do on social occasions?" To assess potential embarrassment about disclosure, we asked, "Would college women or men tend to be more embarrassed if they expressed concerns about drinking too much or too frequently?" We used the question, "Do college men or women tend to experience more severe negative consequences if they engage in excessive drinking?" to assess consequences. Responses were made on 7-point scales with 1 (*women experience more*), 4 (*about the same*), and 7 (*men experience more*) as scale anchors.

Results and Discussion

Social Pressure   Both men and women perceived that men experienced more social pressure to drink; men's mean responses differed from the midpoint, $t(110) = 53.26$, $p < .001$, as did women's, $t(111) = 38.89$, $p < .001$. In addition, the men's ratings were more extreme ($M = 5.23$, $SD = 1.04$) than the women's ($M = 4.83$, $SD = 1.31$), $F(1, 221) = 6.49$, $p < .01$ ($d = 0.24$).

Embarrassment   Both genders also perceived that men would be more embarrassed about expressing concerns about drinking; men's mean responses differed significantly from the midpoint, $t(110) = 33.50$, $p < .001$, as did women's, $t(111) = 32.43$, $p < .001$. Men did not differ in their perceptions ($M = 5.03$, $SD = 1.58$) from women ($M = 4.91$, $SD = 1.60$; $F < 1$).

Negative Consequences   Men and women thought that women would suffer more aversive consequences as a result of excessive drinking; men's mean responses differed significantly from the midpoint, $t(110) = 25.50$, $p < .001$, as did women's, $t(111) = 24.19$, $p < .001$. Women's ratings ($M = 3.04$, $SD = 1.39$) also were more extreme than men's ($M = 3.45$, $SD = 1.33$), $F(1, 221) = 5.05$, $p < .03$ ($d = 0.21$).

Consistent with predictions, college men were believed to experience more social pressure and more embarrassment if they disclosed concerns about drinking to friends. Women, on the other hand, were perceived to incur more serious consequences if they drank excessively. Such perceptions may explain why

men may have greater difficulty resisting the practice of excessive drinking whereas women may be able to resist, despite seeing themselves as deviant.

EXPERIMENT 4

The perceived drinking norm for college men is higher than that for college women, but expressing reservations about alcohol appears to be viewed as being more embarrassing for men. In contrast, women are aware that their drinking norm is lower and believe that the dangers associated with excessive drinking may be more severe for them. An impression formation experiment was conducted to test the hypothesis that men (vs. women) perceive same-sex peers who voice misgivings about alcohol consumption as suffering more serious social consequences.

Method

Participants   College undergraduates ($N = 216$; 86 men, 40%; 130 women, 60%) were recruited from the same large midwestern university used in prior studies and received credit toward their Elementary Psychology research requirement.

Materials and Procedure   Materials for this experiment were completed as part of a larger packet of unrelated questionnaires. Each participant received a 1-page sheet with the title "Impression Formation Study." The sheet explained that "sometimes people form impressions on the basis of limited information." Participants were asked to assume that an undergraduate at the university had responded to the questionnaire item written below. The item was "'How do you feel about the level of alcohol consumption by students at this university?" An 11-point scale with endpoints of 0 (*doesn't bother me at all*) and 11 (*bothers me very much*) was also printed below the question, and one of two response alternatives was circled: either 3 or 7. Male participants read that the questionnaire had been completed by another male undergraduate attending the university. Female participants read similar instructions, except the undergraduate was described as female. Participants were exposed only to a same-sex target because our aim was to assess whether men or women would perceive negative social consequences for someone of their own gender who voiced strong concerns about alcohol. Participants were randomly assigned to the 3 or 7 Likert-type response conditions.

Participants were asked to judge, "Compared to other undergraduate [males/females] at the University, how typical is this undergraduate?" Ratings were made on a 7-point Likert-type scale ranging from 1 (*very atypical*) to 7 (*very typical*). This was followed by "How well do you think this undergraduate would 'fit in' with other [male/female] undergraduates at the university?" Responses were made on a 7-point Likert-type scale ranging from 1 (*Not at all*) to 7 (*Very much*).

Results and Discussion

The ratings of typicality were analyzed with a 2 × 2 between-subjects ANOVA with participant gender and manipulated concern rating (3 vs. 7) as independent factors. The main effects for gender, $F(1, 212) = 28.12$, $p < .0001$, and concern, $F(1, 212) = 8.12$, $p < .001$, were significant, as was the interaction, $F(1, 212) = 8.13$, $p < .001$. Men's ratings of typicality ($M = 4.29$, $SD = 2.01$) were lower than women's ($M = 4.86$, $SD = 1.40$; $d = 0.23$). Post hoc tests indicated that men and women evaluated a same-sex peer who was relatively unconcerned comparably ($M = 5.20$, $SD = 1.80$, vs. $M = 5.18$, $SD = 1.29$). Men, however, perceived a concerned male student as less typical ($M = 3.38$, $SD = 1.58$) than women perceived a female student who expressed a comparable level of concern ($M = 4.55$, $SD = 1.52$; $p < .05$; $d = 0.24$).

Ratings of how well the target was perceived to 'fit in' with his or her same-sex peers showed similar effects. The main effects of gender, $F(1, 212) = 3.83$, $p < .05$, concern, $F(1, 212) = 45.19$, $p < .0001$, and the Gender × Concern interaction, $F(1, 212) = 5.88$, $p < .01$, were significant. Both male and female students' assessments of how well a target with few misgivings would fit in were comparable ($Ms = 5.55$, $SD = 1.21$, vs. $M = 5.45$, $SD = 0.93$; ns). However, male students thought that a male target who expressed concern would 'fit in' less with peers ($M = 3.96$, $SD = 1.40$) than did the female students about a female target who expressed a similar level of concern ($M = 4.67$, $SD = 1.28$; $p < .05$; $d = 0.35$).

Both men and women thought a same-sex undergraduate who voiced misgivings about campus alcohol practices was less typical and would have more difficulty fitting in on campus. More critical, extreme impressions were formed about a male student with strong misgivings about alcohol, suggesting that men who do not accede to social pressure encounter more social problems.

GENERAL DISCUSSION

In two survey experiments, several hundred college students at a large Midwestern university reported that their personal misgivings about alcohol practices were not shared with large segments of the campus. Confidence in the authenticity of these reports is bolstered by finding (in Experiment 2) that manipulating the friendliness of recipients (fraternal organization vs. university administration) of the survey responses did not modify students' responses. College men perceived their personal concerns about general campus alcohol practices and drunk driving and their frequency of drinking were closer to what they estimated for women than for other men. Women, in contrast, believed that their concerns and drinking frequency were not shared with same- or opposite-sex friends and peers. College men may be reluctant to publicly admit their concerns about excessive alcohol consumption because it figures more prominently in their campus social lives (Capraro, 2000; Huselid & Cooper, 1992; M. Wood et al., 1992). Furthermore, publicly admitting discomfort about alcohol may signal a lack of 'machismo' that is socially damaging. Consistent with this idea, men were perceived to be subject to more social pressure to drink and to experience more embarrassment if they expressed concerns about drinking (in Experiment 3). Male students were also rated as incurring more negative social consequences if they voiced strong concerns about alcohol (Experiment 4).

If men believe that their personal sentiments are closer to those of the opposite sex but do not wish to be ostracized and want to 'fit-in' with same-sex peers, men may feel increasing pressure to "learn to be comfortable with alcohol" (Prentice & Miller, 1993, p. 249). Theories of small-group social influence emphasize the strength of in-group norms (Crandall, 1988; Schachter, 1951). Same-sex norms should be considered more appropriate and influential than opposite-sex norms (e.g., Deaux, 1998). Of no surprise, Prentice and Miller (1993) found increased consistency of attitudes, norms, and behavior concerning alcohol for men over time on campus, although not for women. Because men tended to think that they share more with college women than with other college men (as we found in Experiments 1 and 2), men's identification with the opposite-sex reference group may operate much like a negative reference group and intensify perceived pressure to comply publicly with the same-sex norm (e.g., Carver & Humphries, 1981; Suls, Martin, & Wheeler, 2000). Although women also appear to think they feel and behave differently from their peers, they may be better able to resist the public norm because excessive drinking does not carry as positive a connotation for women; in fact, they perceive less social pressure to drink and are more concerned about (nonsocial) consequences, such as unprotected sex, pregnancy, and so forth (Experiment 3).

Identification of gender differences in alcohol norms may provide useful information for the development of educational interventions to reduce pluralistic ignorance. Particularly relevant is a recent study by Schroeder and Prentice (1998; see also Donaldson, Graham, Piccinin, & Hansen, 1995) who exposed freshman college students to an intervention involving peer-oriented discussion focusing on pluralistic ignorance versus an individually oriented discussion. Evidence of less drinking was found among students in the peer-oriented condition 4–6 months later, especially among participants who were very concerned about negative social evaluations. The study also reported that over time men perceived more agreement with their peers but that women's beliefs remained stable. Men apparently felt the need to resolve the apparent discrepancy between themselves and their peer group whereas women did not. This differential shift in men versus women is congruent with the idea that men should feel more pressure to align themselves with their same-sex peers. In light of

the present results, peer-oriented discussions to dispel pluralistic ignorance (Perkins, 2002) should recognize and address the different meanings that alcohol has for men versus women in college life.

Exclusive reliance on self-report measures is a limitation of the experiments, although comparable measures have shown adequate reliability and validity (Wechsler et al., 1994). Reliance on cross-sectional data also restricts discussion about causal mechanisms. It seems likely that perceptions of other's concerns and consumption are reciprocally related to self-concern and self-use. Furthermore, alcohol consumption is multiply determined; our focus was exclusively on construal of social norms, but personality variables, family history, alcohol expectancies, and so forth, also contribute. It remains for future research to ascertain whether the degree of pluralistic ignorance varies as a function of these other factors. We also should acknowledge that we could not distinguish periodic heavy drinkers from those with the riskiest or worst abuse problems. The latter may not be basing their drinking patterns on the drinking of others and are thus less influenced by normative interventions, a consideration needing further study.

One interesting paradox should be noted. Experiment 4 showed that male students recognize that there are considerable situational pressures on their fellow male students not to express concerns for fear of being socially excluded, but this did not lead male students in Experiments 1 and 2 to appreciate the implication that other male students' level of concern may be higher than they convey publicly. This failure to take into account situational pressures, however, is entirely consistent with the classic fundamental attribution error (Ross, 1977).

In conclusion, men saw their concerns about alcohol and sometimes their drinking behavior as more consistent with those of female students than with those of other male students. Women perceived themselves to be deviant in attitude and behavior from both same- and opposite-sex peers. The present identification of gender-specific alcohol norms and perceptions suggests the need for the development of special normative interventions to address the different meanings that alcohol has in the social lives of college men and women.

REFERENCES

Baer, J., Stacy, A., & Larimer, M. (1991). Biases in the perception of drinking norms among college students. *Journal of Studies in Alcohol, 52,* 580–586.

Borsari, B. G., & Carey, K. (2001). Peer influences on college drinking: A review of the research. *Journal of Substance Abuse, 13,* 391–424.

Capraro, R. L. (2000). Why college men drink: Alcohol, adventure and the paradox of masculinity. *Journal of American College Health, 48,* 307–315.

Carver, C. S., & Humphries, C. (1981). Havana daydreaming: A study of self-consciousness and the negative reference group among Cuban Americans. *Journal of Personality and Social Psychology, 40,* 545–552.

Cialdini, R., Reno, R., & Kallgren, C. (1990). A focus theory of normative conduct: Recycling the concept of norms to reduce littering in public places. *Journal of Personality and Social Psychology, 58,* 1015–1026.

Collins, R., Parks, G., & Marlatt, G. A. (1985). Social determinants of alcohol consumption: The effects of social interaction and model status on self-administration of alcohol. *Journal of Consulting and Clinical Psychology, 53,* 189–201.

Crandall, C. (1988). Social contagion of binge eating. *Journal of Personality and Social Psychology, 55,* 588–598.

Deaux, K. (1998). Gender. In D. Gilbert, S. Fiske, & G. Lindzey (Eds.), *Handbook of social psychology* (Vol. 1, pp. 788–827). Boston: McGraw-Hill.

Donaldson, S., Graham, J., Piccinin, A., & Hansen, W. (1995). Resistance skills training and onset of alcohol use: Evidence for beneficial and potentially harmful effects in public schools and private Catholic schools. *Health Psychology, 14,* 291–300.

Gibbons, F. X., & Gerrard, M. (1997). Health images and their effects on health behavior. In B. Buunk & F. X. Gibbons (Eds.), *Health, coping and well-being: Perspectives from social comparison theory* (pp. 63–94). Mahwah, NJ: Erlbaum.

Graham, J., Marks, G., & Hansen, W. (1991). Social influence processes affecting adolescent substance use. *Journal of Applied Psychology, 76,* 291–298.

Huselid, R., & Cooper, M. L. (1992). Gender roles as mediators of sex differences in adolescent alcohol use and abuse. *Journal of Health and Social Behavior, 33,* 348–362.

Kahneman, D., & Tversky, A. (1973). On the psychology of prediction. *Psychological Review, 80,* 237–251.

Kandel, D. B. (1980). Drug and drinking behavior among youth. *Annual Review of Sociology, 6,* 235–285.

Marks, G., Graham, J., & Hansen, W. (1992). Social projection and social conformity in adolescent alcohol use: A longitudinal analysis. *Personality and Social Psychology Bulletin, 18,* 96–101.

Miller, D. T., & Nelson, L. (2002). Seeing approach motivation in the avoidance behavior of others: Implications for an understanding of pluralistic ignorance. *Journal of Personality and Social Psychology, 83,* 1066–1075.

O'Hare, T. (1990). Drinking in college: Consumption patterns, problems, sex differences and legal drinking age. *Journal of Studies on Alcohol, 51,* 536–541.

Perkins, H. W. (2002). Social norms and the prevention of alcohol misuse in collegiate contexts. *Journal of Studies in Alcohol, 14,* 164–172.

Perkins, H. W., & Berkowitz, A. (1986). Perceiving the community norms of alcohol use among students: Some research implications for campus alcohol education programming. *International Journal of the Addictions, 21,* 961–976.

Prentice, D. A., & Miller, D. T. (1993). Pluralistic ignorance and alcohol use on campus: Some consequences of misperceiving the norm. *Journal of Personality and Social Psychology, 64,* 243–256.

Ross, L. (1977). The intuitive psychologist and his shortcomings: Distortions in the attribution process. In L. Berkowitz (Ed.), *Advances in experimental social psychology* (Vol. 10, pp. 173–220). New York: Academic Press.

Schachter, S. (1951). Deviation, rejection, and communication. *Journal of Abnormal and Social Psychology, 40,* 190–207.

Schroeder, C. M., & Prentice, D. A. (1998). Exposing pluralistic ignorance to reduce alcohol use among college students. *Journal of Applied Social Psychology, 28,* 2150–2180.

Sher, K. J., Bartholow, B., & Nanda, S. (2001). Short- and long-term effects of fraternity and sorority membership on heavy drinking: A social norms perspective. *Psychology of Addictive Behaviors, 15,* 42–51.

Sherman, S., Presson, C., Chassin, L., Corty, E., & Olshavsky, R. (1983). The false consensus effect in estimates of smoking prevalence: Underlying mechanisms. *Personality and Social Psychology Bulletin, 9,* 197–207.

Stein, J., Newcomb, M., & Bender, P. (1987). An 8-year study of multiple influences on drug use and drug use consequences. *Journal of Personality and Social Psychology, 53,* 1094–1105.

Suls, J., Martin, R., & Wheeler, L. (2000). Three kinds of opinion comparison: The triadic model. *Personality and Social Psychology Review, 4,* 219–237.

Suls, J., & Wan, C. K. (1987). In search of the false uniqueness phenomenon: Fear and estimates of social consensus. *Journal of Personality and Social Psychology, 52,* 211–217.

Suls, J., Wan, C. K., & Sanders, G. (1988). False consensus and false uniqueness in estimating the prevalence of health-protective behaviors. *Journal of Applied Social Psychology, 18,* 66–79.

Wechsler, H., Davenport, A., Dowdall, G., Moeykens, B., & Castillo, S. (1994). Health and behavioral consequences of binge drinking in college: A national survey of students at 140 campuses. *Journal of the American Medical Association, 272,* 1672–1677.

Wechsler, H., Dowdall, G., Davenport, A., & Castillo, S. (1995). Correlates of college student binge drinking. *American Journal of Public Health, 85,* 921–925.

Weingardt, K. R., Baer, J. S., Kivlahan, D. R., Roberts, L. J., Miller, E. T., & Marlatt, G. A. (1998). Episodic heavy drinking among college students: Methodological issues and longitudinal perspectives. *Psychology of Addictive Behaviors, 12,* 155–167.

Wills, T. A. (1986). Stress and coping in early adolescence: Relationships to substance use in urban school samples. *Health Psychology, 5,* 503–529.

Wood, M., Nasgoshi, C., & Dennis, D. (1992). Alcohol norms and expectations as predictors of alcohol use and problems in a college student sample. *American Journal of Alcohol Abuse, 18,* 461–476.

Wood, P., Sher, K., Erickson, D., & DeBord, K. (1997). Predicting academic problems in college from freshman alcohol involvement. *Journal of Studies on Alcohol, 58,* 200–210.

ENDNOTE

1. Miller and Nelson (2002) have recently proposed another general explanation for pluralistic ignorance—mainly that there is a strong tendency to assume others' choices are approach rather than avoidance motivated. In other words, students may recognize that they drink more than they are personally inclined to do to avoid being socially excluded but assume their peers must drink because they enjoy it. This explanation is not mutually exclusive of the embarrassment idea; both may be operating.

The research was supported in part by National Science Foundation Grant BCS 99-10592. We thank René Martin and Peter Nathan for their comments on a previous version of this article.

CRITICAL THINKING QUESTIONS

1. This article found that alcohol norms and perceptions are gender specific, suggesting that different intervention strategies are needed for men and for women. What may account for these differences in alcohol norms and perceptions? What differences in intervention strategies do these gender differences suggest? Explain.

2. Do the issues and processes presented in this article apply to areas other than alcohol, such as engaging in sexual activity? Explain your answer.

3. The subjects in this study were all college students. Given this, are the findings limited to college students, or do they apply to 18- to 22-year-old noncollege students, as well? Why or why not? How would you go about answering this question with data?

4. The purpose of advertising is to sell a product. Examine television and print ads for alcohol advertising. What images and messages do they convey, and how might these concepts contribute to a sense of pluralistic ignorance regarding alcohol norms?

5. What personality factors, family background, or prior history with alcohol could influence someone's perception of alcohol consumption? Examine literature on the topic in developing your answer.

CHAPTER INTEGRATION QUESTIONS

1. President John F. Kennedy said, "Conformity is the jailer of freedom and the enemy of growth," and social manners writer Emily Post said, "To do exactly as your neighbors do is the only sensible rule." These two apparently contradictory quotations pertain to *conformity,* a type of social influence process. All of the articles in this chapter concern social influence processes. How do these quotes support or contradict these articles?

2. Develop an argument as to how *both* of the preceding quotes can be applied to the articles collectively. In other words, what theme from this chapter can you use to address this question?

3. The first two articles in this chapter were about Milgram's study on obedience. How might the concept of *pluralistic ignorance,* discussed in the last article in this chapter, be applied to explain the results described in the first two articles?

4. Many of the chapters in this book have direct relevance in understanding a very dark period of human history: the Holocaust. Perhaps no topic is more germane in helping us understand how such a horror came to pass than that of social influence processes. How can some of the concepts on social influence be applied to how and why the Holocaust occurred? (You can find some useful information on this topic by visiting the website of the United States Holocaust Memorial Museum at www.ushmm.org. Click on "Online Exhibitions," some of which are permanent and some of which change, to address this topic.)

Chapter Ten

PROSOCIAL BEHAVIOR

HELP. IT IS something that we all need at some time in our lives, and hopefully, it is something that we all give to others. Dramatic examples of helping or failing to help are not hard to find in the mass media. Consider the various published accounts of people needing help yet receiving none versus those of people who risk their own lives to help strangers.

Why do people help or not help? Is helpfulness a personality trait, so that some people are simply helpful individuals who give assistance in a variety of settings? Or does it have more to do with the specific situation, so that a person who helps in one situation is not necessarily more likely to help in another? Or perhaps these two factors somehow interact with one another, so that people with a certain type of personality in a certain type of situation are more likely to help than others.

Article 28, "Why Don't Moral People Act Morally? Motivational Considerations," examines the question of moral motivation in explaining why people act the way they do. The article not only attributes the failure to act morally to not having been properly socialized or to the situational forces operating at the moment; it also explores the underlying motivations people may have for acting morally in the first place.

Article 29, "From Jerusalem to Jericho," is a classic example of a study that examines both situational and personality factors as influences on helping behavior. It turns out that both factors may be operating, with situational factors determining whether people will offer help in the first place and dispositional factors determining the character of the helping response.

Finally, Article 30, "The Effect of Smiling on Helping Behavior: Smiling and Good Samaritan Behavior," looks at how one situational factor—having someone smile at you—may have an impact on your subsequent helping behavior. Does just being exposed to a smile, even if it isn't from the person you may be helping, increase your likelihood of helping?

ARTICLE 28 _____

If asked whether they consider themselves moral and decent individuals, most people would likely say yes. With the exception of those individuals who blatantly consider only their own self-interests, most people seem to want to do the right thing. Even those individuals who are blatantly selfish often justify their behavior in moral terms. Thus, the person who kills does so for a higher cause, and the person who steals has needs that are more important than those of the victim.

Reflect for a moment on your own life. Do you always act consistently with your moral principles, or have you done things that you knew were not the right things to do? If you are like most people, you do not always act with total moral integrity. The fact is, most of us violate our own moral codes. But why?

Two general theoretical explanations may help account for this tendency. First, perhaps we did not know or were not sure of what was the right thing to do at the moment. This is a *developmental* perspective, one that explains moral failings as the result of not having learned the correct moral principles—or at least not having learned them well enough to make them salient at the proper time. The other explanation is a *situational* perspective, whereby moral lapses are attributed to external influences that constrain our otherwise tendency to act morally. Thus, external pressures—such as being in a hurry or wanting to fit in with a certain group—may result in people not acting in accord with their moral principles.

The following article by C. Daniel Batson and Elizabeth R. Thompson addresses the very important question of why moral people do not always act morally. The authors begin with the developmental and situational perspectives just described and then expand on other explanations of this fairly common moral dilemma.

Why Don't Moral People Act Morally?
Motivational Considerations
■ C. Daniel Batson and Elizabeth R. Thompson

Abstract

Failure of moral people to act morally is usually attributed to either learning deficits or situational pressures. We believe that it is also important to consider the nature of moral motivation. Is the goal actually to be moral (moral integrity) or only to appear moral while, if possible, avoiding the cost of being moral (moral hypocrisy)? Do people initially intend to be moral, only to surrender this goal when the costs of being moral become clear (overpowered integrity)? We have found evidence of both moral hypocrisy and overpowered integrity. Each can lead ostensibly moral people to act immorally. These findings raise important questions for future research on the role of moral principles as guides to behavior.

Moral people often fail to act morally. One of the most important lessons to be learned from the tragically common atrocities of the past century—the endless procession of religious wars, mass killings, ethnic cleansings, terrorist bombings, and corporate coverups of product dangers—is that horrendous deeds are not done only by monsters. People who sincerely value morality can act in ways that seem to show a blatant

Reprinted from *Current Directions in Psychological Science*, 2001, *10*(2), 54–57. Copyright © 2001 by American Psychological Society. Reprinted with permission of Blackwell Publishers.

disregard for the moral principles held dear. How is this possible?

Answers by psychologists tend to be of two types. Those who approach the problem from a developmental perspective are likely to blame a learning deficit: The moral principles must not have been learned well enough or in the right way. Those who approach the problem from a social-influence perspective are likely to blame situational pressures: Orders from a higher authority (Milgram, 1974) and pressure to conform (Asch, 1956) can lead one to set aside or disengage moral standards (Bandura, 1999).

There is truth in each of these explanations of moral failure. Yet neither, nor the two combined, is the whole truth. Even people who have well-internalized moral principles, and who are in relatively low-pressure situations, can fail to act morally. To understand how, one needs to consider the nature of moral motivation.

MORAL HYPOCRISY

It is often assumed that moral individuals want to be moral, to display *moral integrity*. But our research suggests that at least some individuals want to appear moral while, if possible, avoiding the cost of actually being moral. We call this motive *moral hypocrisy*.

To examine the nature of moral motivation, we have used a simple—but real—moral dilemma. The dilemma involves having research participants assign themselves and another participant (actually fictitious) to different tasks. One task is clearly more desirable; it has positive consequences (the chance to earn raffle tickets). The other task has neutral consequences (no chance to earn raffle tickets) and is described as rather dull and boring. Participants are told that the other participant will not know that they were allowed to assign the tasks; the other participant will think the assignment was made by chance.

Most research participants faced with this simple situation assign themselves the positive-consequences task (70% to 80%, depending on the specific study), even though in retrospect very few (less than 10%) say that this was the moral thing to do. Their actions fail to fit their moral principles (Batson, Kobrynowicz, Dinnerstein, Kampf, & Wilson, 1997).

Adding a Salient Moral Standard . . . and a Coin

Other participants have been confronted with a slightly more complex situation. The written instructions that inform them of the opportunity to assign the tasks include a sentence designed to make the moral standard of fairness salient: "Most participants feel that giving both people an equal chance—by, for example, flipping a coin—is the fairest way to assign themselves and the other participant to the tasks." A coin is provided for participants to flip if they wish. Under these conditions, virtually all participants say in retrospect that either assigning the other participant the positive-consequences task or using a fair method such as the coin flip is the most moral thing to do. Yet only about half choose to flip the coin.

Of those who choose not to flip, most (80% to 90%, depending on the specific study) assign themselves to the positive-consequences task. More interesting and revealing, the same is true of those who flip the coin; most (85% to 90%) assign themselves the positive consequences. In study after study, the proportion who assign themselves the positive-consequences task after flipping the coin has been significantly greater than the 50% that would be expected by chance. This was true even in a study in which the coin was labeled "SELF to POS" on one side and "OTHER to POS" on the other side. Clearly, some participants who flip the coin do not abide by the outcome. To appear fair by flipping the coin, yet still serve self-interest by ignoring the coin and assigning oneself the positive-consequences task, seems to be evidence of moral hypocrisy. Ironically, this hypocrisy pattern was especially strong among persons scoring high on a self-report measure of moral responsibility (Batson et al., 1997; Batson, Thompson, Seuferling, Whitney, & Strongman, 1999).

. . . And a Mirror

Other participants face an even more complex situation. After being provided the fairness standard and coin to flip, they assign the tasks while sitting in front of a mirror. The mirror is used to increase self-awareness and, thereby, pressure to reduce discrepancy between the moral standard of fairness and the task assignment (Wicklund 1975). In a study that presented participants with this situation, exactly half of those who chose to flip the coin assigned themselves to the positive-consequences task. Apparently, having to face head-on the discrepancy between their avowed moral standard (be fair) and their standard-violating behavior (unfairly ignoring the result of the coin flip) was too much. In front of the mirror, those who wish to appear moral must be moral (Batson et al., 1999).

Taken together, the results of these studies seem to provide considerable evidence of moral hypocrisy. They conform precisely to the pattern we would expect if the goal of at least some research participants is to appear moral yet, if possible, avoid the cost of being moral. To the extent that moral hypocrisy is their motive, it is hardly surprising that ostensibly moral people fail to act morally. Any situational ambiguity that allows them to feign morality yet still serve self-interest—such as we provide by allowing participants to flip the coin—will undermine moral action if their motive is moral hypocrisy.

OVERPOWERED INTEGRITY

Before concluding that the world is full of moral hypocrites, it is important to consider a quite different motivational explanation for the failure of participants in our studies to act morally. Perhaps at least some of those who flip the coin do so with a genuine intent to assign the tasks fairly. Their initial motive is to be moral (moral integrity). But when they discover that the flip has gone against them and their intent to be moral will cost them the positive-consequences task, conflict arises. Self-interest overpowers integrity, with the result that they appear moral by flipping the coin, yet still serve self-interest. The general idea of overpowered integrity is, then, that a person's motivation to be truly moral may be overpowered by stronger self-interested motives when being moral entails personal cost (as it often does). In the words of the oft-quoted biblical phrase, "The spirit is willing, but the flesh is weak" (Matthew 26: 41).

Empirically Differentiating Moral Hypocrisy and Overpowered Integrity

How might one know which motivational process is operating, moral hypocrisy or overpowered integrity?

The key difference between the two is the actor's intent when initially faced with a moral dilemma. In the former process, the initial motive is to appear moral yet avoid the cost of being moral; in the latter, the initial motive is to be moral. One factor that should clarify which of these motives is operating when people initially face a moral dilemma is whether they want to maintain control over the outcome of an apparently moral way to resolve the dilemma.

In our task-assignment paradigm, research participants motivated by moral hypocrisy, who intend to give themselves the positive consequences yet also appear moral, should be reluctant to let someone else flip the coin. If a coin is to be flipped, it is important that they be the ones to do so because only then can they rig the outcome. In contrast, participants initially motivated to be moral, who genuinely want to assign the tasks fairly, should have no need to maintain control of the flip. It should make no difference who flips the coin; any fair-minded person will do.

Following this logic, we gave participants an additional decision option: They could allow the task assignment to be determined by the experimenter flipping a coin. Of participants who were faced with this situation (no mirror present) and used a coin flip, 80% chose to have the assignment determined by the experimenter's flip rather than their own. This pattern suggested that many participants' initial motive was moral integrity, not moral hypocrisy (Batson, Tsang, & Thompson, 2000).

Two further studies provided evidence that this integrity could be overpowered. In these studies, we increased the cost of being moral. Instead of being neutral, consequences of the less desirable task were negative. Participants were told that every incorrect response on the negative-consequences task would be punished with a mild but uncomfortable electric shock. Faced with the prospect of receiving shocks, only one fourth of the participants were willing to let the experimenter's flip determine the task assignment. Another fourth flipped the coin themselves; of these, 91% assigned themselves the positive consequences task, indicating once again a biased coin flip. Almost all of the remaining one half showed clear signs of overpowered integrity. They gave up any pretense of morality and assigned themselves the positive-consequences task without even feigning fairness.

They were also quite ready, in retrospect, to admit that the way they assigned the tasks was not morally right.

Cost-Based Justification for Setting Morality Aside

How did these last participants deal with the clear discrepancy between their moral standards and their action? Comments made during debriefing suggest that many considered the relatively high personal cost introduced by the prospect of receiving electric shocks to be sufficient justification for not acting on their principles.

A cost-based justification for setting aside moral principles may seem quite understandable. After all, it is no surprise that participants do not want to receive electric shocks. But a cost-based justification carries ironic and chilling implications. Just think: If personal cost is sufficient to justify setting aside moral principles, then one can set aside morality when deciding whether to stand by or intervene as the perpetrators of hate crimes pursue their victims. One can set aside morality when considering one's own position of wealth while others are in poverty. One can set aside morality when considering whether to recycle newspaper or plastic containers or whether to contribute one's fair share to public television. Yet is it not in precisely such situations that moral principles are supposed to do their most important work as guides to behavior?

If, as is often assumed, the social role of morality is to keep individuals from placing their own interests ahead of the parallel interests of others, then cost-based justification poses a serious problem. A principle that says, "Do not give your own interests priority . . . unless there is personal cost," is tantamount to having no real principle at all. It turns morality into a luxury item—something one might love to have but, given the cost, is content to do without.

CONCLUSION

We have considered the interplay of three different motives: First is self-interest. If the self has no clear stake in a situation, then moral principles are not needed to restrain partiality. Second is moral integrity, motivation to be moral as an end in itself. Third is

moral hypocrisy, motivation to appear moral while, if possible, avoiding the cost of actually being moral. We have suggested two motivational explanations for the failure of ostensibly moral people to act morally: moral hypocrisy and overpowered integrity. The latter is the product of a conflict between self-interest and moral integrity: A person sincerely intends to act morally, but once the costs of being moral become clear, this initial intent is overpowered by self-interest. Our research indicates that both moral hypocrisy and overpowered integrity exist, and that each can lead moral people to act immorally. Moreover, our research indicates that the problem is not simply one of inconsistency between attitude and behavior—between saying and doing—produced by failure to think about relevant behavioral standards. Making relevant moral standards salient (e.g., by suggesting that a coin toss would be the fairest way to assign tasks) did little to increase moral behavior. The moral lapses we have observed are, we believe, best understood motivationally.

We have only begun to understand the nature of moral motivation. There are persistent and perplexing questions still to be answered. For example, what socialization experiences stimulate moral integrity and hypocrisy, respectively? To what degree do parents preach the former but teach the latter? How might one structure social environments so that even those individuals motivated by moral hypocrisy or vulnerable to overpowered integrity might be led to act morally? Answers to such intriguing—and challenging—questions may help society avoid the atrocities of the past century in the next.

RECOMMENDED READING

Bandura, A. (1999). (See References)

Batson, C.D., Kobrynowicz, D., Dinnerstein, J.L., Kampf, H.C., & Wilson, A.D. (1997). (See References)

Batson, C.D., Thompson, E.R., Seuferling, G., Whitney, H., & Strongman, J. (1999). (See References)

Bersoff, D.M. (1999). Why good people sometimes do bad things: Motivated reasoning and unethical behavior. *Personality and Social Psychology Bulletin, 25,* 28–39.

Todorov, T. (1996). *Facing the extreme: Moral life in the concentration camps* (A. Denner & A. Pollak, Trans.). New York: Henry Holt.

REFERENCES

Asch, S. (1956). Studies of independence and conformity: A minority of one against a unanimous majority. *Psychological Monographs, 70*(Whole No. 416).

Bandura, A. (1999). Moral disengagement in the perpetration of inhumanities. *Personality and Social Psychology Review, 3,* 193–209.

Batson, C.D., Kobrynowicz, D., Dinnerstein, J.L, Kampf, H.C., & Wilson, A.D. (1997). In a very different voice: Unmasking moral hypocrisy. *Journal of Personality and Social Psychology, 72,* 1335–1348.

Batson, C.D., Thompson, E.R., Seuferling, G., Whitney, H., & Strongman, J. (1999). Moral hypocrisy: Appearing moral to oneself without being so. *Journal of Personality and Social Psychology, 77,* 525–537.

Batson, C.D., Tsang, J., & Thompson, E.R. (2000). *Weakness of will: Counting the cost of being moral.* Unpublished manuscript, University of Kansas, Lawrence.

Milgram, S. (1974). *Obedience to authority: An experimental view.* New York: Harper & Row.

Wicklund, R.A. (1975). Objective self-awareness., In L. Berkowitz (Ed.), *Advances in experimental and social psychology* (Vol. 8, pp. 233–275). New York: Academic Press.

CRITICAL THINKING QUESTIONS

1. On a personal level, reflect on when you have engaged in *moral hypocrisy.* Have you ever experienced *overpowered integrity?* In retrospect, why did you not act in accord with your moral values? Did you learn anything from that experience that would make you less likely to act the same way in a similar situation in the future? Explain your answers.

2. Based on the concepts discussed in the article, what could a parent do to help develop a strong sense of moral integrity in his or her children? Explain your suggestions.

3. Find examples of moral hypocrisy in the public domain—that is, situations in which a public figure, such as a politician or member of the clergy, has espoused certain moral values yet acted inconsistently with them. Do these public moral lapses affect the moral behavior of other people? Discuss.

4. Respond to the question from the article: "How might one structure social environments so that even those individuals motivated by moral hypocrisy might be led to act morally?"

ARTICLE 29 _____

Many variables can potentially influence whether an individual will help someone in need. One such factor, moral motivation, was discussed in the previous article. But what other factors may influence prosocial behavior?

Broadly speaking, two types of determinants can be considered. The first concerns *situational* factors: What circumstances surrounding the specific situation may affect helping behavior? The second variable concerns *dispositions:* To what extent are decisions to help due to relatively permanent personality factors? In other words, are some people more likely to help than others because of their unique personality makeup? Or does the situation, rather than personality, influence helping?

In "From Jerusalem to Jericho," John M. Darley and C. Daniel Batson examine both situational and dispositional variables in an experiment modeled after a biblical parable. Specifically, the study looks at helping as influenced by situational variables—whether the subjects were in a hurry and what they were thinking at the time—and dispositional variables—the religious orientations of the subjects. This classic article is interesting not only because of the methodology used but also because of the important implications of the results.

"From Jerusalem to Jericho"
A Study of Situational and Dispositional Variables in Helping Behavior
■ John M. Darley and C. Daniel Batson

The influence of several situational and personality variables on helping behavior was examined in an emergency situation suggested by the parable of the Good Samaritan. People going between two buildings encountered a shabbily dressed person slumped by the side of the road. Subjects in a hurry to reach their destination were more likely to pass by without stopping. Some subjects were going to give a short talk on the parable of the Good Samaritan, others on a nonhelping relevant topic; this made no significant difference in the likelihood of their giving the victim help. Religious personality variables did not predict whether an individual would help the victim or not. However, if a subject did stop to offer help, the character of the helping response was related to his type of religiosity.

Helping other people in distress is, among other things, an ethical act. That is, it is in act governed by ethical norms and precepts taught to children at home, in school, and in church. From Freudian and other personality theories, one would expect individual differences in internalization of these standards that would lead to differences between individuals in the likelihood with which they would help others. But recent research on bystander intervention in emergency situations (Bickman, 1969; Darley & Latané, 1968; Korte, 1969; but see also Schwartz & Clausen, 1970) has had bad luck in finding personality determinants of helping behavior. Although personality variables that one might expect to correlate with helping behavior have been measured (Machiavellianism, authoritarianism, social desirability, alienation, and social responsibility), these were not predictive of helping. Nor was this due to a generalized lack of predictability in the helping situation examined, since

Reprinted from *Journal of Personality and Social Psychology*, 1973, *27*, 100–108. Copyright © 1973 by the American Psychological Association. Reprinted by permission.

variations in the experimental situation, such as the availability of other people who might also help, produced marked changes in rates of helping behavior. These findings are reminiscent of Hartshorne and May's (1928) discovery that resistance to temptation, another ethically relevant act, did not seem to be a fixed characteristic of an individual. That is, a person who was likely to be honest in one situation was not particularly likely to be honest in the next (but see also Burton, 1963).

The rather disappointing correlation between the social psychologist's traditional set of personality variables and helping behavior in emergency situations suggests the need for a fresh perspective on possible predictors of helping and possible situations in which to test them. Therefore, for inspiration, we turned to the Bible, to what is perhaps the classical helping story in the Judeo-Christian tradition, the parable of the Good Samaritan. The parable proved of value in suggesting both personality and situational variables relevant to helping.

"And who is my neighbor?" Jesus replied, "A man was going down from Jerusalem to Jericho, and he fell among robbers, who stopped him and beat him, and departed, leaving him half dead. Now by chance a priest was going down the road; and when he saw him he passed by on the other side. So likewise a Levite, when he came to the place and saw him, passed by on the other side. But a Samaritan, as he journeyed, came to where he was; and when he saw him, he had compassion, and went to him and bound his wounds, pouring on oil and wine; then he set him on his own beast and brought him to an inn, and took care of him. And the next day he took out two dennarii and gave them to the innkeeper, saying, "Take care of him; and whatever more you spend, I will repay you when I come back." Which of these three, do you think, proved neighbor to him who fell among the robbers? He said, "The one who showed mercy on him." And Jesus said to him, "Go and do likewise." (Luke 10: 29–37 RSV)

To psychologists who reflect on the parable, it seems to suggest situational and personality differences between the nonhelpful priest and Levite and the helpful Samaritan. What might each have been thinking and doing when he came upon the robbery victim on that desolate road? What sort of persons were they?

One can speculate on differences in thought. Both the priest and the Levite were religious functionaries who could be expected to have their minds occupied with religious matters. The priest's role in religious activities is obvious. The Levite's role, although less obvious, is equally important: The Levites were necessary participants in temple ceremonies. Much less can be said with any confidence about what the Samaritan might have been thinking, but, in contrast to the others, it was most likely not of a religious nature, for Samaritans were religious outcasts.

Not only was the Samaritan most likely thinking about more mundane matters than the priest and Levite, but, because he was socially less important, it seems likely that he was operating on a quite different time schedule. One can imagine the priest and Levite, prominent public figures, hurrying along with little black books full of meetings and appointments, glancing furtively at their sundials. In contrast, the Samaritan would likely have far fewer and less important people counting on him to be at a particular place at a particular time, and therefore might be expected to be in less of a hurry than the prominent priest or Levite.

In addition to these situational variables, one finds personality factors suggested as well. Central among these, and apparently basic to the point that Jesus was trying to make, is a distinction between types of religiosity. Both the priest and Levite are extremely "religious." But it seems to be precisely their type of religiosity that the parable challenges. At issue is the motivation for one's religion and ethical behavior. Jesus seems to feel that the religious leaders of his time, though certainly respected and upstanding citizens, may be "virtuous" for what it will get them, both in terms of the admiration of their fellowmen and in the eyes of God. New Testament scholar R. W. Funk (1966) noted that the Samaritan is at the other end of the spectrum:

The Samaritan does not love with side glances at God. The need of neighbor alone is made self-evident, and the Samaritan responds without other motivation. (pp. 218–219)

That is, the Samaritan is interpreted as responding spontaneously to the situation, not as being preoccupied with the abstract ethical or organizational do's and don'ts of religion as the priest and Levite would seem to be. This is not to say that the Samaritan is portrayed as irreligious. A major intent of the parable would seem to be to present the Samaritan as a religious and ethical example, but at the same time to contrast his type of religiosity with the more common conception of religiosity that the priest and Levite represent.

To summarize the variables suggested as affecting helping behavior by the parable, the situational variables include the content of one's thinking and the amount of hurry in one's journey. The major dispositional variable seems to be differing types of religiosity. Certainly these variables do not exhaust the list that could be elicited from the parable, but they do suggest several research hypotheses.

Hypothesis 1   The parable implies that people who encounter a situation possibly calling for a helping response while thinking religious and ethical thoughts will be no more likely to offer aid than persons thinking about something else. Such a hypothesis seems to run counter to a theory that focuses on norms as determining helping behavior because a normative account would predict that the increased salience of helping norms produced by thinking about religious and ethical examples would increase helping behavior.

Hypothesis 2   Persons encountering a possible helping situation when they are in a hurry will be less likely to offer aid than persons not in a hurry.

Hypothesis 3   Concerning types of religiosity, persons who are religious in a Samaritan-like fashion will help more frequently than those religious in a priest or Levite fashion.

Obviously, this last hypothesis is hardly operationalized as stated. Prior research by one of the investigators on types of religiosity (Batson, 1971), however, led us to differentiate three distinct ways of being religious: (a) for what it will gain one (cf. Freud, 1927, and perhaps the priest and Levite), (b) for its own intrinsic value (cf. Allport & Ross, 1967), and (c) as a response to and quest for meaning in one's everyday life (cf. Batson, 1971). Both of the latter conceptions would be proposed by their exponents as

related to the more Samaritanlike "true" religiosity. Therefore, depending on the theorist one follows, the third hypothesis may be stated like this: People (a) who are religious for intrinsic reasons (Allport & Ross, 1967) or (b) whose religion emerges out of questioning the meaning of their everyday lives (Batson, 1971) will be more likely to stop to offer help to the victim.

The parable of the Good Samaritan also suggested how we would measure people's helping behavior— their response to a stranger slumped by the side of one's path. The victim should appear somewhat ambiguous—dressed, possibly in need of help, but also possibly drunk or even potentially dangerous.

Further, the parable suggests a means by which the incident could be perceived as a real one rather than part of a psychological experiment in which one's behavior was under surveillance and might be shaped by demand characteristics (Orne, 1962), evaluation apprehension (Rosenberg, 1965), or other potentially artifactual determinants of helping behavior. The victim should be encountered not in the experimental context but on the road between various tasks.

METHOD

In order to examine the influence of these variables on helping behavior, seminary students were asked to participate in a study on religious education and vocations. In the first testing session, personality questionnaires concerning types of religiosity were administered. In a second individual session, the subject began experimental procedures in one building and was asked to report to another building for later procedures. While in transit, the subject passed a slumped "victim" planted in an alleyway. The dependent variable was whether and how the subject helped the victim. The independent variables were the degree to which the subject was told to hurry in reaching the other building and the talk he was to give when he arrived there. Some subjects were to give a talk on the jobs in which seminary students would be most effective, others, on the parable of the Good Samaritan.

Subjects

The subjects for the questionnaire administration were 67 students at Princeton Theological Seminary.

Forty-seven of them, those who could be reached by telephone, were scheduled for the experiment. Of the 47, 7 subjects' data were not included in the analyses—3 because of contamination of the experimental procedures during their testing and 4 due to suspicion of the experimental situation. Each subject was paid $1 for the questionnaire session and $1.50 for the experimental session.

Personality Measures

Detailed discussion of the personality scales used may be found elsewhere (Batson, 1971), so the present discussion will be brief. The general personality construct under examination was religiosity. Various conceptions of religiosity have been offered in recent years based on different psychometric scales. The conception seeming to generate the most interest is the Allport and Ross (1967) distinction between "intrinsic" versus "extrinsic" religiosity (cf. also Allen & Spilka, 1967, on "committed" versus "consensual" religion). This bipolar conception of religiosity has been questioned by Brown (1964) and Batson (1971), who suggested three-dimensional analyses instead. Therefore, in the present research, types of religiosity were measured with three instruments which together provided six separate scales; (a) a *doctrinal orthodoxy* (D-O) scale patterned after that used by Glock and Stark (1966), scaling agreement with classic doctrines of Protestant theology; (b) the Allport-Ross *extrinsic* (AR-E) scale, measuring the use of religion as a means to an end rather than as an end in itself; (c) the Allport-Ross *intrinsic* (AR-I) scale, measuring the use of religion as an end in itself; (d) the *extrinsic external* scale of Batson's Religious Life Inventory (RELI-EE), designed to measure the influence of significant others and situations in generating one's religiosity; (e) the *extrinsic internal* scale of the Religious Life Inventory (RELI-EI), designed to measure the degree of "driveness" in one's religiosity; and (f) the *intrinsic* scale of the Religious Life Inventory (RELI-I), designed to measure the degree to which one's religiosity involves a questioning of the meaning of life arising out of one's interactions with his social environment. The order of presentation of the scales in the questionnaire was RELI, AR, D-O.

Consistent with prior research (Batson, 1971), a principal-component analysis of the total scale scores

and individual items for the 67 seminarians produced a theoretically meaningful, orthogonally rotated three-component structure with the following loadings:

Religion as means received a single very high loading from AR-E (.903) and therefore was defined by Allport and Ross's (1967) conception of this scale as measuring religiosity as a means to other ends. This component also received moderate negative loadings from D-O (−.400) and AR-I (−.372) and a moderate positive loading from RELI-EE (.301).

Religion as an end received high loadings from RELI-EI (.874), RELI-EE (.725), AR-I (.768), and D-O (.704). Given this configuration, and again following Allport and Ross's conceptualization, this component seemed to involve religiosity as an end in itself with some intrinsic value.

Religion as quest received a single very high loading from RELI-I (.945) and a moderate loading from RELI-EE (.75). Following Batson, this component was conceived to involve religiosity emerging out of an individual's search for meaning in his personal and social world.

The three religious personality scales examined in the experimental research were constructed through the use of complete-estimation factor score coefficients from these three components.

Scheduling of Experimental Study

Since the incident requiring a helping response was staged outdoors, the entire experimental study was run in 3 days, December 14–16, 1970, between 10 A.M. and 4 P.M. A tight schedule was used in an attempt to maintain reasonably consistent weather and light conditions. Temperature fluctuation according to the *New York Times* for the 3 days during these hours was not more than 5 degrees Fahrenheit. No rain or snow fell, although the third day was cloudy, whereas the first two were sunny. Within days the subjects were randomly assigned to experimental conditions.[1]

Procedure

When a subject appeared for the experiment, an assistant (who was blind with respect to the personality scores) asked him to read a brief statement which explained that he was participating in a study of the vocational careers of seminary students. After developing the rationale for the study, the statement read:

What we have called you in for today is to provide us with some additional material which will give us a clearer picture of how you think than does the questionnaire material we have gathered thus far. Questionnaires are helpful, but tend to be somewhat oversimplified. Therefore, we would like to record a 3–5 minute talk you give based on the following passage. . . .

Variable 1: Message In the task-relevant condition the passage read,

With increasing frequency the question is being asked: What jobs or professions do seminary students subsequently enjoy most, and in what jobs are they most effective? The answer to this question used to be so obvious that the question was not even asked. Seminary students were being trained for the ministry, and since both society at large and the seminary student himself had a relatively clear understanding of what made a "good" minister, there was no need even to raise the question of for what other jobs seminary experience seems to be an asset. Today, however, neither society nor many seminaries have a very clearly defined conception of what a "good" minister is or of what sorts of jobs and professions are the best context in which to minister. Many seminary students, apparently genuinely concerned with "ministering," seem to feel that it is impossible to minister in the professional clergy. Other students, no less concerned, find the clergy the most viable profession for ministry. But are there other jobs and/or professions for which seminary experience is an asset? And, indeed, how much of an asset is it for the professional ministry? Or, even more broadly, can one minister through an "establishment" job at all?

In the helping-relevant condition, the subject was given the parable of the Good Samaritan exactly as printed earlier in this article. Next, regardless of condition, all subjects were told,

You can say whatever you wish based on the passage. Because we are interested in how you think on your feet, you will not be allowed to use notes in giving the

talk. Do you understand what you are to do? If not, the assistant will be glad to answer questions.

After a few minutes the assistant returned, asked if there were any questions, and then said:

Since they're rather tight on space in this building, we're using a free office in the building next door for recording the talks. Let me show you how to get there [draws and explains map on 3 × 5 card]. This is where Professor Steiner's laboratory is. If you go in this door [points at map], there's a secretary right here, and she'll direct you to the office we're using for recording. Another of Professor Steiner's assistants will set you up for recording your talk. Is the map clear?

Variable 2: Hurry In the high-hurry condition the assistant then looked at his watch and said, "Oh, you're late. They were expecting you a few minutes ago. We'd better get moving. The assistant should be waiting for you so you'd better hurry. It shouldn't take but just a minute." In the intermediate-hurry condition he said, "The assistant is ready for you, so please go right over." In the low-hurry condition, he said, "It'll be a few minutes before they're ready for you, but you might as well head on over. If you have to wait over there, it shouldn't be long."

The Incident When the subject passed through the alley, the victim was sitting slumped in a doorway, head down, eyes closed, not moving. As the subject went by, the victim coughed twice and groaned, keeping his head down. If the subject stopped and asked if something was wrong or offered to help, the victim, startled and somewhat groggy, said, "Oh, thank you [cough]. . . . No, it's all right. [Pause] I've got this respiratory condition [cough]. . . . The doctor's given me these pills to take, and I just took one. . . . If I just sit and rest for a few minutes I'll be O.K. . . . Thanks very much for stopping though [smiles weakly]." If the subject persisted, insisting on taking the victim inside the building, the victim allowed him to do so and thanked him.

Helping Ratings The victim rated each subject on a scale of helping behavior as follows:

0 = failed to notice the victim as possibly in need at all; 1 = perceived the victim as possibly in need but did not offer aid; 2 = did not stop but helped indi-

rectly (e.g., by telling Steiner's assistant about the victim); 3 = stopped and asked if victim needed help; 4 = after stopping, insisted on taking the victim inside and then left him.

The victim was blind to the personality scale scores and experimental conditions of all subjects. At the suggestion of the victim, another category was added to the rating scales, based on his observations of the pilot subjects' behavior:

5 = after stopping, refused to leave the victim (after 3–5 minutes) and/or insisted on taking him somewhere outside experimental context (e.g., for coffee or to the infirmary).

(In some cases it was necessary to distinguish Category 0 from Category 1 by the postexperimental questionnaire and Category 2 from Category 1 on the report of the experimental assistant.)

This 6-point scale of helping behavior and a description of the victim were given to a panel of 10 judges (unacquainted with the research) who were asked to rank order the (unnumbered) categories in terms of "the amount of helping behavior displayed toward the person in the doorway." Of the 10, 1 judge reversed the order of Categories 0 and 1. Otherwise there was complete agreement with the ranking implied in the presentation of the scale above.

The Speech   After passing through the alley and entering the door marked on the map, the subject entered a secretary's office. She introduced him to the assistant who gave the subject time to prepare and privately record his talk.

Helping Behavior Questionnaire   After recording the talk, the subject was sent to another experimenter, who administered "an exploratory questionnaire on personal and social ethics." The questionnaire contained several initial questions about the interrelationship between social and personal ethics, and then asked three key questions: (a) "When was the last time you saw a person who seemed to be in need of help?" (b) "When was the last time you stopped to help someone in need?" (c) "Have you had experience helping persons in need? If so, outline briefly." These data were collected as a check on the victim's ratings of whether subjects who did not stop perceived the situation in the alley as one possibly involving need or not.

When he returned, the experimenter reviewed the subject's questionnaire, and, if no mention was made of the situation in the alley, probed for reactions to it and then phased into an elaborate debriefing and discussion session.

Debriefing

In the debriefing, the subject was told the exact nature of the study, including the deception involved, and the reasons for the deception were explained. The subject's reactions to the victim and to the study in general were discussed. The role of situational determinants of helping behavior was explained in relation to this particular incident and to other experiences of the subject. All subjects seemed readily to understand the necessity for the deception, and none indicated any resentment of it. After debriefing, the subject was thanked for his time and paid, then he left.

RESULTS AND DISCUSSION

Overall Helping Behavior

The average amount of help that a subject offered the victim, by condition, is shown in Table 1. The unequal-N analysis of variance indicates that while the hurry variable was significantly ($F = 3.56$, $df = 2.34$, $p < .05$) related to helping behavior, the message variable was not. Subjects in a hurry were likely to offer less help than were subjects not in a hurry. Whether the subject was going to give a speech on the parable of the Good Samaritan or not did not significantly affect his helping behavior on this analysis.

Other studies have focused on the question of whether a person initiates helping action or not, rather than on scaled kinds of helping. The data from the present study can also be analyzed on the following terms: Of the 40 subjects, 16 (40%) offered some form of direct or indirect aid to the victim (Coding Categories 2–5), 24 (60%) did not (Coding Categories 0 and 1). The percentages of subjects who offered aid by situational variable were, for low hurry, 63% offered help, intermediate hurry 45%, and high hurry 10%, for helping-relevant message 53%, task-relevant message 29%. With regard to this more general question of whether help was offered or not, an unequal-N analysis of variance (arc sine transformation of percentages of helpers, with low- and intermediate-hurry conditions pooled) indicated that again only the hurry main effect was significantly ($F = 5.22$, $p < .05$) related to helping behavior; the subjects in a hurry were more likely to pass by the victim than were those in less of a hurry.

Reviewing the predictions in the light of these results, the second hypothesis, that the degree of hurry a person is in determines his helping behavior, was supported. The prediction involved in the first hypothesis concerning the message content was based on the parable. The parable itself seemed to suggest that thinking pious thoughts would not increase helping. Another and conflicting prediction might be produced by a norm salience theory. Thinking about the parable should make norms for helping salient and

therefore produce more helping. The data, as hypothesized, are more congruent with the prediction drawn from the parable. A person going to speak on the parable of the Good Samaritan is not significantly more likely to stop to help a person by the side of the road than is a person going to talk about possible occupations for seminary graduates.

Since both situational hypotheses are confirmed, it is tempting to stop the analysis of these variables at this point. However, multiple regression analysis procedures were also used to analyze the relationship of all of the independent variables of the study and the helping behavior. In addition to often being more statistically powerful due to the use of more data information, multiple regression analysis has an advantage over analysis of variance in that it allows for a comparison of the relative effect of the various independent variables in accounting for variance in the dependent variable. Also, multiple regression analysis can compare the effects of continuous as well as nominal independent variables on both continuous and nominal dependent variables (through the use of point biserial correlations, rpb) and shows considerable robustness to violation of normality assumptions (Cohen, 1965, 1968). Table 2 reports the results of the multiple regression analysis using both help versus no help and the graded helping scale as dependent measures. In this table the overall equation Fs show the F value of the entire regression equation as a particular row variable enters the equation. Individual variable Fs were computed with all five independent variables in the equation. Although the two situational variables, hurry and message condition, correlated more highly with the dependent measure than any of the religious dispositional variables, only hurry was a significant predictor of whether one will help or not (column 1) or of the overall amount of help given (column 2). These results corroborate the findings of the analysis of variance.[2]

Notice also that neither form of the third hypothesis, that types of religiosity will predict helping, received support from these data. No correlation between the various measures of religiosity and any form of the dependent measure ever came near statistical significance, even though the multiple regression analysis procedure is a powerful and not particularly conservative statistical test.

TABLE 1 / Means and Analysis of Variance of Graded Helping Responses

Message	M			Summary
	Hurry			
	Low	Medium	High	
Helping relevant	3.800	2.000	1.000	2.263
Task relevant	1.667	1.667	.500	1.333
Summary	3.000	1.818	.700	

Analysis of Variance				
Source	SS	df	MS	F
Message (A)	7.766	1	7.766	2.65
Hurry (B)	20.884	2	10.442	3.50*
A x B	5.237	2	2.619	.89
Error	99.633	34	2.930	

Note: $N = 40$.
*$p < .05$.

TABLE 2 / Stepwise Multiple Regression Analysis

	Help vs. No Help					Graded Helping			
	Individual Variable		Overall Equation			Individual Variable		Variable Equation	
Step	r^a	F	R	F	Step	r	F	R	F
1. Hurry[b]	−.37	4.537*	.37	5.884*	1. Hurry	−.42	6.665*	.42	8.196**
2. Message[c]	.25	1.495	.41	3.834*	2. Message	.25	1.719	.46	5.083*
3. Religion as quest	−.03	.081	.42	2.521	3. Religion as quest	−.16	1.297	.50	3.897*
4. Religion as means	−.03	.003	.42	1.838*	4. Religion as means	−.08	.018	.50	2.848*
5. Religion as end	.06	.000	.42	1.430	5. Religion as end	−.07	.001	.50	2.213

Note: $N = 40$. Helping is the dependent variable. $df = 1/34$.
[a]Individual variable correlation coefficient is a point biserial where appropriate.
[b]Variables are listed in order of entry into stepwise regression equations.
[c]Helping-relevant message is positive.
*$p < .05$.
**$p < .01$.

Personality Difference among Subjects Who Helped

To further investigate the possible influence of personality variables, analyses were carried out using only the data from subjects who offered some kind of help to the victim. Surprisingly (since the number of these subjects was small, only 16) when this was done, one religiosity variable seemed to be significantly related to the kind of helping behavior offered. (The situational variables had no significant effect.) Subjects high on the religion as quest dimension appear likely, when they stop for the victim, to offer help of a more tentative or incomplete nature than are subjects scoring low on this dimension ($r = -.53$, $p < .05$).

This result seemed unsettling for the thinking behind either form of Hypothesis 3. Not only do the data suggest that the Allport-Ross-based conception of religion as *end* does not predict the degree of helping, but the religion as quest component is a significant predictor of offering less help. This latter result seems counterintuitive and out of keeping with previous research (Batson, 1971), which found that this type of religiosity correlated positively with other socially valued characteristics. Further data analysis, however, seemed to suggest a different interpretation of this result.

It will be remembered that one helping coding category was added at the suggestion of the victim after his observation of pilot subjects. The correlation of religious personality variables with helping behavior dichotomized between the added category (1) and all of the others (0) was examined. The correlation between religion as quest and this dichotomous helping scale was essentially unchanged ($rpb = -.54$, $p < .05$). Thus, the previously found correlation between the helping scale and religion as quest seems to reflect the tendency of those who score low on the quest dimension to offer help in the added helping category.

What does help in this added category represent? Within the context of the experiment, it represented an embarrassment. The victim's response to persistent offers of help was to assure the helper he was all right, had taken his medicine, just needed to rest for a minute or so, and, if ultimately necessary, to request the helper to leave. But the *super* helpers in this added category often would not leave until the final appeal was repeated several times by the victim (who was growing increasingly panicky at the possibility of the arrival of the next subject). Since it usually involved the subject's attempting to carry through a preset plan (e.g., taking the subject for a cup of coffee or revealing to him the strength to be found in Christ), and did not allow information from the victim to change that plan, we originally labeled this kind of helping as rigid—an interpretation supported by its increased likelihood among highly doctrinal orthodox subjects

($r = .63$, $p < .01$). It also seemed to have an inappropriate character. If this more extreme form of helping behavior is indeed effectively less helpful, then the second form of Hypothesis 3 does seem to gain support.

But perhaps it is the experimenters rather than the super helpers who are doing the inappropriate thing; perhaps the best characterization of this kind of helping is as different rather than as inappropriate. This kind of helper seems quickly to place a particular interpretation on the situation, and the helping response seems to follow naturally from this interpretation. All that can safely be said is that one style of helping that emerged in this experiment was directed toward the presumed underlying needs of the victim and was little modified by the victim's comments about his own needs. In contrast, another style was more tentative and seemed more responsive to the victim's statements of his need.

The former kind of helping was likely to be displayed by subjects who expressed strong doctrinal orthodoxy. Conversely, this fixed kind of helping was unlikely among subjects high on the religion as quest dimension. These latter subjects, who conceived their religion as involving an ongoing search for meaning in their personal and social world, seemed more responsive to the victim's immediate needs and more open to the victim's definitions of his own needs.

CONCLUSION AND IMPLICATIONS

A person not in a hurry may stop and offer help to a person in distress. A person in a hurry is likely to keep going. Ironically, he is likely to keep going even if he is hurrying to speak on the parable of the Good Samaritan, thus inadvertently confirming the point of the parable. (Indeed, on several occasions, a seminary student going to give his talk on the parable of the Good Samaritan literally stepped over the victim as he hurried on his way!)

Although the degree to which a person was in a hurry had a clearly significant effect on his likelihood of offering the victim help, whether he was going to give a sermon on the parable or on possible vocational roles of ministers did not. This lack of effect of sermon topic raises certain difficulties for an explanation of helping behavior involving helping norms and their salience. It is hard to think of a context in which

norms concerning helping those in distress are more salient than for a person thinking about the Good Samaritan, and yet it did not significantly increase helping behavior. The results were in the direction suggested by the norm salience hypothesis, but they were not significant. The most accurate conclusion seems to be that salience of helping norms is a less strong determinant of helping behavior in the present situation than many, including the present authors, would expect.

Thinking about the Good Samaritan did not increase helping behavior, but being in a hurry decreased it. It is difficult not to conclude from this that the frequently cited explanation that ethics becomes a luxury as the speed of our daily lives increases is at least an accurate description. The picture that this explanation conveys is of a person seeing another, consciously noting his distress, and consciously choosing to leave him in distress. But perhaps this is not entirely accurate, for, when a person is in a hurry, something seems to happen that is akin to Tolman's (1948) concept of the "narrowing of the cognitive map." Our seminarians in a hurry noticed the victim in that in the postexperiment interview almost all mentioned him as, on reflection, possibly in need of help. But it seems that they often had not worked this out when they were near the victim. Either the interpretation of their visual picture as a person in distress or the empathic reactions usually associated with that interpretation had been deferred because they were hurrying. According to the reflections of some of the subjects, it would be inaccurate to say that they realized the victim's possible distress, then chose to ignore it; instead, because of the time pressures, they did not perceive the scene in the alley as an occasion for an ethical decision.

For other subjects it seems more accurate to conclude that they decided not to stop. They appeared aroused and anxious after the encounter in the alley. For these subjects, what were the elements of the choice that they were making? Why were the seminarians hurrying? Because the experimenter, *whom the subject was helping* was depending on him to get to a particular place quickly. In other words, he was in conflict between stopping to help the victim and continuing on his way to help the experimenter. And this is often true of people in a hurry; they hurry because somebody depends on their being somewhere. Conflict, rather than callousness, can explain their failure to stop.

Finally, as in other studies, personality variables were not useful in predicting whether a person helped or not. But in this study, unlike many previous ones, considerable variations were possible in the kinds of help given, and these variations did relate to personality measures—specifically to religiosity of the quest sort. The clear light of hindsight suggests that the dimension of kinds of helping would have been the appropriate place to look for personality differences all along; *whether* a person helps or not is an instant decision likely to be situationally controlled. How a person helps involves a more complex and considered number of decisions, including the time and scope to permit personality characteristics to shape them.

REFERENCES

Allen, R. O., & Spilka, B. Committed and consensual religion. A specification of religion-prejudice relationships. *Journal for the Scientific Study of Religion,* 1967, *6,* 191–206.

Allport, G. W., & Ross, J. M. Personal religious orientation and prejudice. *Journal of Personality and Social Psychology,* 1967, *5,* 432–443.

Batson, C. D. Creativity and religious development: Toward a structural-functional psychology of religion Unpublished doctoral dissertation, Princeton Theological Seminary, 1971.

Bickman, L. B. The effect of the presence of others on bystander intervention in an emergency. Unpublished doctoral dissertation, City College of the City University of New York, 1969.

Brown, L. B. Classifications of religious orientation. *Journal for the Scientific Study of Religion,* 1964, *4,* 91–99.

Burton, R. V. The generality of honesty reconsidered. *Psychological Review,* 1963, *70,* 481–499.

Cohen, J. Multiple regression as a general data-analytic system. *Psychological Bulletin,* 1968, *70,* 426–443.

Cohen, J. Some statistical issues in psychological research. In B. B. Wolman (Ed.), *Handbook of clinical psychology.* New York: McGraw-Hill, 1965.

Darley, J. M., & Latané, B. Bystander intervention in emergencies: Diffusion of responsibility. *Journal of Personality and Social Psychology,* 1968, *8,* 377–383.

Freud, S. *The future of an illusion.* New York: Liveright, 1953.

Funk, R. W. *Language, hermeneutic, and word of God.* New York: Harper & Row, 1966.

Glock, C. Y., & Stark, R. *Christian beliefs and anti-Semitism.* New York: Harper & Row, 1966.

Hartshorne, H., & May, M. A. *Studies in the nature of character.* Vol. 1. *Studies in deceit.* New York: Macmillan, 1928.

Korte, C. Group effects on help-giving in an emergency. *Proceedings of the 77th Annual Convention of the American Psychological Association,* 1969, *4,* 383–384. (Summary)

Orne, M. T. On the social psychology of the psychological experiment: With particular reference to demand characteristics and their implications. *American Psychologist,* 1962, *17,* 776–783.

Rosenberg, M. J. When dissonance fails: On eliminating evaluation apprehension from attitude measurement. *Journal of Personality and Social Psychology,* 1965, *1,* 28–42.

Schwartz, S. H., & Clausen, G. T. Responsibility, norms, and helping in an emergency. *Journal of Personality and Social Psychology,* 1970, *16,* 299–310.

Tolman, E. C. Cognitive maps in rats and men. *Psychological Review,* 1948, *55,* 189–208.

ENDNOTES

1. An error was made in randomizing that increased the number of subjects in the intermediate-hurry conditions. This worked against the prediction that was most highly confirmed (the hurry prediction) and made no difference to the message variable tests.

2. To check the legitimacy of the use of both analysis of variance and multiple regression analysis, parametric analyses, on this ordinal data, Kendall rank correlation coefficients were calculated between the helping scale and the five independent variables. As expected t approximated the correlation quite closely in each case and was significant for hurry only (hurry $\tau -.38, p < .001$).

For assistance in conducting this research thanks are due Robert Wells, Beverly Fisher, Mike Shafto, Peter Sheras, Richard Detweiler, and Karen Glasser. The research was funded by National Science Foundation Grant GS-2293.

CRITICAL THINKING QUESTIONS

1. Being prompted to think of the parable of the Good Samaritan did not increase the subjects' helping behavior in this study, but being in a hurry actually decreased it. Suppose that you are in the business of soliciting money for a worthy purpose. What strategies could you use to maximize the money you receive, based on the implications of this study? Explain.

2. *Rush hour,* as the name implies, describes a time of day when people are in a hurry to get to or from work. Do you think that people would be less likely to help someone in need during rush hour than at other times of the day? What about on weekends? Design a study to test this possibility, being sure to address any ethical issues that may be involved.

3. Reading about the Good Samaritan had no impact on subsequent helping behavior. Do you think that reading an article such as this one would change people's helping behavior? Why or why not? Specifically, now that you know that being in a hurry will decrease the likelihood of your giving help, do you think that this awareness will make you more likely to give help in the future, even if you are in a hurry? Why or why not? If simply telling someone about the Good Samaritan was not enough to improve people's helping behavior, what might be more effective?

ADDITIONAL RELATED READINGS

Batson, C .D., Lishner, D. A., Carpenter, A., Dulin, L., Harjusola-Webb, S., Stocks, E. L., Gale, S., Hassan, O., & Sampat, B. (2003). ". . . As you would have them do unto you": Does imagining yourself in the others' place stimulate moral action? *Personality and Social Psychology Bulletin, 29*(9), 1190–1201.

Greitemeyer, T., Rudolph, U., & Weiner, B. (2003). Whom would you rather help: An acquaintance not responsible for her plight or a responsible sibling? *Journal of Social Psychology, 143*(3), 331–340.

ARTICLE 30 _____

The literature on helping behavior indicates that quite a few situational factors can influence our tendency to help someone in need. For example, the previous article noted that being in a hurry significantly reduces the amount of helping we offer. Other factors—such as being exposed to enjoyable music and pleasant aromas and even being out on a beautiful, sunny day—all may increase the likelihood of helping behavior.

But what do many of these factors have in common? It could be that each of them puts us in a better mood, and in turn, we are more likely to help someone if we are in a good, rather than a neutral or bad, mood. Indeed, many previous studies have indicated that being in a good mood is more likely to lead to increased helping.

If you want to increase the likelihood that someone will offer you assistance, you can do many things to enhance his or her mood and hence helping. One such behavior, which is fairly easy to control, is smiling at the person. Research (and common sense) indicates that we respond more positively to a smiling person than to a person with a more neutral expression. We tend to view a smiling person as more attractive, more interesting, more intelligent, and, in general, as having more of a variety of positive traits. We also tend to behave more positively toward people who smile at us—for instance, by helping them more.

What is unique about the following article by Nicolas Gueguen and Marie-Agnes De Gail is that they look at the effect of smiling on helping behavior when the person smiling is *not* the one receiving help. In other words, they consider whether merely being exposed to someone smiling makes us more likely to help someone else later on. Perhaps the old adage "Smile and the world smiles with you" has important practical implications after all.

The Effect of Smiling on Helping Behavior
Smiling and Good Samaritan Behavior

■ Nicolas Gueguen and Marie-Agnes De Gail

Research has shown that a person receives more help when smiling. Nevertheless, this effect of smiling was only tested when the smiler was requesting help. An experiment was completed in which 8 confederates (4 young men and 4 young women) tested 800 passersby. In half of the cases, the confederate smiled at the passerby. A few seconds after this interaction, the passersby had the opportunity to help another confederate who dropped his/her computer diskettes on the ground. This research found that the previous smile of a stranger enhanced later help-ing behavior. A positive mood induced by the smile of the first confederate could help to explain this result.

The positive effect of smiling on interpersonal attraction and perception is well established in the psychosocial literature. Adding a smile to the photograph of a face leads to more favorable perception of the target, and this effect was found on multiple personality dimensions. Lau (1982) reports finding that when smiling, a target was perceived to be more intelligent

Reprinted from N. Guegnen and M.-A. De Gail, "The Effect of Smiling on Helping Behavior: Smiling and Good Samaritan Behavior," *Communication Reports*, 2003, *16*(2), 133–140. Copyright © 2003 by Western States Communication Association. Reprinted with permission.

than the same, nonsmiling, target. Otta, Pereira, Delavati, Pimentel and Pires (1993) report that they found that a smiling person receives more positive scores on the dimensions of leadership, optimism, sincerity, and kindness. A smile also enhances helping behavior toward the smiling person. Tidd and Lockard (1978) report that patrons in a bar give significantly larger tips to a waitress who approached them with a broad smile than to one with a minimal smile. In a similar vein, Solomon et al. (1981) report that a smiling confederate in a large department store receives more help than a nonsmiling one.

The effect of smiling on helping behavior is well established, but the factors that explain this effect still remain in question. One possible explanation is that a positive perception of the solicitor, mediated by his/her smile, could predispose the subject to comply with his/her request. Research connecting perception of the solicitor with helping behavior has found that positive perceptions of the solicitor increases helping behavior (Takemura, 1993). For Tidd and Lockard (1978), who have found that a smile by a waitress enhanced her tips, the result was explained in terms of reciprocal altruism. Patrons gave the waitress larger tips to reciprocate the better service of the waitress. For Solomon et al. (1981), the effect of smiling is explained in terms of anonymity. When a stranger smiles at the subject, he/she becomes identifiable and thus is more likely to receive help than is a control subject who did not smile and thus is more anonymous.

Even though these explanations of the effect of smiling on helping behavior are of interest, they have not been tested empirically. They also presuppose that smiling has an effect only in the interaction between the smiler and the recipient of the smile. Another possible explanation is that smiling enhances a positive mood that, in return, enhances helping behavior (Deutsch & Lamberti, 1986).

Many experimental studies report finding that positive mood activation when compared to neutral mood activation, increases helping behavior (Bizman, Yinin, Ronco & Schachar, 1980; Forgas, 1997, 1998; Harris & Smith, 1975; Job, 1987; Levin & Isen, 1975; Rind, 1997; Weyant, 1978). This positive mood can be activated in many different ways and, most of the time, does not require

elaborate means. A false attribution of success or failure in a task leads to activation of a positive/negative mood that, in turn, affects helping behavior in a way that is congruent with the mood (Clark & Waddell, 1986). Finding a coin in a phone box or on the ground is sufficient to induce a positive mood that in return enhances altruism (Batson, Coke, Chard, Smith & Talaferro, 1979; Blevins & Murphy, 1974; Isen & Levin, 1972; Isen & Simmonds, 1978; Levin & Isen, 1975). To be offered a candy or a cookie brings about the same effect (Harris & Smith, 1975; Isen & Levin, 1972).

Some empirical studies also find that familiar environmental factors activate a positive mood and helping behavior. For instance, the amount of tips given by customers increases on sunny days (Cunningham, 1979). Further, Rind (1996) reports finding that even information about the weather, given by a waiter to customers who had not yet seen the color of the sky, is sufficient to make the waiter's tip vary, depending on whether he told them it was sunny or rainy. Even pleasant smells can enhance helping behavior. Pleasant ambient smells (e.g., baking, cooking, roasting coffee) in a shopping mall lead passersby to provide change for a dollar to a same-sex confederate more readily than in the absence of such odors (Baron, 1997). A heavy perfume worn by a female-confederate led the passersby to help her in a more substantial way. Pleasant ambient music also has an important effect on helping behavior (Galizio & Hendricks, 1972).

Another way of inducing moods in participants consists of exposing them to pleasant versus unpleasant pictures or texts (Forgas, 1997, 1998). In this respect, it has been shown that a drawing may activate a positive mood and, as a consequence, helping behavior. Drawing a smiling face on the bill increases the rate of tips granted to a waitress (Rind & Bordia, 1996). In the same way, a mere hand-made drawing of the sun, added at the bottom of the bill of customers having a drink outside a cafe, led them to up the waiter or waitress more frequently and in a much more substantial way (Gueguen & LeGoherel, 2000). Attaching a small card with a joke printed on it to the bill produced the same effects (Gueguen, 2002).

These studies seem to show that the effect of a positive mood on helping behavior is robust and is very easily obtained. It thus appears possible that the effect of smiling on helping is mediated by a positive mood. Kleinke and Walton (1982) have found that in an interaction with a confederate who was instructed to smile, participants reported significantly more positive feelings than in a control situation where the confederate was instructed to show a neutral expression. So, if the effect of smiling on helping behavior is mediated by a positive mood and not just by a positive perception of the smiler, then it might be expected that smiling would enhance helping behavior even when the solicitor is not the smiler. To test this hypothesis, an experiment was carried out in which subjects had the opportunity to help a confederate a few seconds after another confederate had smiled/not smiled to them.

METHOD

Participants

Eight hundred passersby (400 men and 400 women), aged approximately between 20 and 50, served as participants in this experiment. They were randomly selected from passersby who were walking in a supermarket of a medium-size city (more than 100,000 inhabitants) in a very attractive spot. This provincial town was Vannes, located in the west of France on the Breton Atlantic Coast.

Procedure

Eight individuals, 4 men and 4 women, aged 19–21 years old, served as confederates in this experiment. All of them were first-year students from the Department of Marketing at the University of Bretagne-Sud in Vannes and volunteered to participate as confederates in this experiment. Both the female and male confederates were selected by two other male and two other female evaluators who were asked to select confederates on their physical attractiveness. These evaluators were instructed to evaluate the attractiveness of student-photographs and to select people, males and females, with neutral attractiveness. After this, those selected were solicited to participate in the experiment, which they all agreed to do. The confederates were dressed casually and similarly to young people of their age (t-shirts, jeans and light colored tennis shoes). Each confederate was instructed to set off down the stairs and look for the first participant, man

or woman, aged between 20 to 50, who took the stairs. The confederate was instructed to look the participant in the eyes. If the participant returned the gaze, then he/she was instructed to smile (or not) at the subject and then to look in another direction. The smiling/not smiling condition was assigned randomly. Following this manipulation, a second confederate, who was blind to the smiling condition, appeared in front of the participant. This second confederate held a portfolio and a package of computer diskettes in one hand and two bags of food in the other. The confederate was instructed not to look the participant in the eyes because some studies have shown that gaze had an effect on compliance to a request (Brockner, Pressman, Cabitt, & Mora, 1982; Gueguen & Jacob, 2002). When the participant was two meters (6/7 feet) in front of the confederate, the confederate simulated a difficulty with his/her two grocery bags and accidentally dropped the diskettes on the ground. Still avoiding eye contact, the confederate bent down to collect the diskettes that had scattered all around him/her. An observer located not far away evaluated if the participant helped the confederate. Afterwards, the observer asked the first confederate to say if he/she had or had not smiled to the participant. The scene was then repeated until each confederate of each sex had tested 100 subjects (50 males and 50 females) in the two conditions (50 in the smile condition and 50 in the no-smile condition).

RESULTS

As no differences were found between the confederates [X.sup.2] (7, 800) = 11.24, $p > .10$, the data were aggregated for the men and for the women confederates. The number of passersby who helped, according to their gender, the two confederates' genders and the experimental conditions, is presented in Table 1.

A log-linear statistical method was used to analyze our data. A significant effect for smiling was found, [X.sup.2] (1, 799) = 9.16, $p < .005$. When the first confederate smiled, 29.5% of the passersby helped the second confederate whereas only 20.3% helped the second confederate in the nonsmiling condition. No significant effect of the first or of the second confederate's gender was found ($p > .20$ for both). Similarly, no significant effect of participant gender was found

($p > .20$). A 2 (smile/no smile) $\times$ 2 (1st male/female confederate) $\times$ 2 (2nd male/female confederate) $\times$ 2 (male/female participant) log-linear analysis revealed a significant interaction between the 2nd confederate's gender and the participant's gender, $[X.sup.2]$ (4, 796) = 17.81, $p < .001$. Results showed that male participants were more helpful toward female (30.0%) than male confederates (17.0%) whereas female participants were more helpful toward male (30.0%) than female confederates (23.0%). This was the only statistically significant interaction in this factorial analysis.

DISCUSSION

In the current experiment, female participants helped male confederates more readily than the female confederates, whereas male participants helped female confederates more often than male confederates. This pattern of results is congruent with previous studies (Bickman, 1974). This effect could be explained by traditional roles of self-presentation in opposite-sex behavior (Gruder & Cook, 1971; Harris & Bays, 1973). For these authors, a member of the opposite-sex would be helped more because the helper wanted to look good in his/her eyes. Seduction motivation could explain why men helped women and why women helped men more favorably than solicitors of the same-sex as the requester.

Our results show that being smiled at by a stranger enhances subsequent helping behavior towards another person. These findings are congruent with the results found in the literature connecting smiling and helping behavior (Solomon et al., 1981; Tidd & Lockard, 1978) and confirm the influence of smiling on helping behavior in a new situation. Furthermore, these findings show that smiling enhances helping behavior toward a person who is not the smiler. These findings are congruent with other results concerning the effect of nonverbal behavior on helping behavior. Deutsch and Lamberti (1986) found that people were more likely to help a confederate who had dropped books if they had been socially rewarded by an experimenter a few minutes beforehand. In Deutsch and Lamberti's experiment, the social reward was manipulated by various nonverbal behaviors such as smiling and eye contact versus cold and distant facial expressions and no eye contact, and by different verbal behaviors such as

pleasant conversation versus abrupt conversation. However, Deutsch and Lamberti's study amalgamated various nonverbal behaviors and the effect of simply smiling was not tested. Moreover, Deutsch and Lamberti tested the effects of positive and negative nonverbal behavior on subsequent helping behavior. In our experiment, smiling was the only nonverbal behavior manipulated and the effect of positive social behavior was compared to neutral social behavior. Our findings seem to support the hypothesis that smiling is sufficient to enhance subsequent helping behavior toward a confederate who was not the smiler.

Such an effect seems to support the idea that neither positive perceptions of the smiling confederate (Lau, 1982) nor reciprocal altruism (Tidd & Lockard, 1978) nor identification theory (Solomon et al., 1981) are complete theoretical explanations of the effect found in the present research. These explanations supposed that smiling had an effect only between the smiler and the participant, whereas our results show that smiling has an effect beyond this relationship. In the present experiment, the participant had no reason to reciprocate altruism towards the second confederate, no additional variable had affected his/her perception of the second confederate and the participant was clearly anonymous for the second confederate.

It therefore seems that another explanation must be evoked to explain these results. Kleinke and Walton (1982) have found that a smile by confederates enhanced positive perceptions but also induced a good feeling in the participant. Various studies have shown that nonverbal behavioral cues enhance positive mood in the target. Fisher, Rytting and Heslin (1976) have found that touch led the person who was touched to feel more positively. The same effect is found with gaze (Jourard & Friedman, 1970). These findings are congruent with the results found by Kleinke and Walton and confirm that nonverbal behavior affects mood. A host of previous studies have shown that positive mood is associated with altruism (Bizman, Yinin, Ronco & Schachar, 1980; Forgas, 1997, 1998; Harris & Smith, 1975; Job, 1987; Levin & Isen, 1975; Rind, 1997; Weyant, 1978). In the current experiment, then, it is possible that the effect of smiling by the first confederate on the participant's helping behavior towards the second confederate is

TABLE 1 / Rate of Subjects (in %) Who Stopped and Helped According to the Smile Condition (Smile/No Smile) and Gender of the Confederates and the Participants[1]

	No Smile				Smile				
	First Confederate Male		First Confederate Female		First Confederate Male		First Confederate Female		Average 2nd Confederate
	Males	Females	Males	Females	Males	Females	Males	Females	
Second confederate male	16.0	20.0	12.0	22.0	12.0	40.0	28.0	36.0	23.3
Second confederate female	24.0	24.0	24.0	20.0	28.0	24.0	44.0	24.0	26.5
Average (1st confederate)	21.0		19.5		26.0		33.0		
Average (smile/no smile)		20.3				29.5			

[1]There are 50 subjects per case.

mediated by a positive mood activated by this nonverbal behavior. Of course, this mood activation hypothesis needs to be further studied to substantiate its theoretical validity, and in order to produce clear understanding of the link between affective states and smiling. An evaluation of the participants' moods by numerical scales should be introduced in these studies.

REFERENCES

Baron, R. (1997). The sweet smell of . . . helping: Effects of pleasant ambient fragrance on prosocial behavior in shopping malls. *Personality and Social Psychology Bulletin, 23,* 498–503.

Batson, D., Coke, J., Chard, F., Smith, D., & Talaferro, A. (1979). Generality of the "glow of goodwill": Effects of mood on helping and information acquisition. *Social Psychology Quarterly, 42,* 176–179.

Bickman, L. (1974). Sex and helping behavior. *The Journal of Social Psychology, 92,* 43–53.

Bizman, A., Yinin, Y., Ronco, B., & Schachar, T. (1980). Regaining self-esteem through helping behavior. *The Journal of Psychology, 105,* 203–209.

Blevins, G., & Murphy, T. (1974). Feeling good and helping: Further phonebooth findings. *Psychological Reports, 34,* 326.

Brockner, J., Pressman, B., Cabitt, J., & Moran, P. (1982). Nonverbal intimacy, sex, and compliance: A field study. *Journal of Nonverbal Behavior, 6,* 253–258.

Clark, M., & Waddell, B. (1986). Effects of mood on thoughts about helping, attraction and information acquisition. *Social Psychology Quarterly, 56,* 31–35.

Cunningham, M. R. (1979). Weather, mood and helping behavior: Quasi experiments with the sunshine Samaritan. *Journal of Personality and Social Psychology, 37,* 1947–1956.

Deutsch, F., & Lamberti, D. (1986). Does social approval increase helping? *Personality and Social Psychology Bulletin, 12,* 149–157.

Fisher, J., Rytting, M., & Heslin, R. (1976). Hands touching hands: Affective and evaluative effects of an interpersonal touch. *Sociometry, 39,* 416–421.

Forgas, J. P. (1997). Affect and strategic communication: The effects of mood on the production and interpretation of verbal requests. *Polish Psychological Bulletin, 28,* 145–173.

Forgas, J. P. (1998). Asking nicely? The effects of mood on responding to more or less polite requests. *Personality and Social Psychology Bulletin, 24,* 173–185.

Galizio, M., & Hendrick, C. (1972). Effect of musical accompaniment on attitude: The guitar as a prop for persuasion. *Journal of Applied Social Psychology, 2,* 350–359.

Gruder, C. L., & Cook, T. D. (1971). Sex, dependency, and helping. *Journal of Personality and Social Psychology, 19,* 290–294.

Gueguen, N. (2002). The effects of a joke on tipping when it is delivered at the same time as the bill. *Journal of Applied Social Psychology, 32,* 1955–1963.

Gueguen, N., & Jacob, C. (2002). Direct look versus evasive glance and compliance with a request. *The Journal of Social Psychology, 142,* 393–396.

Gueguen, N., & LeGoherel, P. (2000). Effect on barmen's tipping of drawing a sun on the bottom of customers' checks. *Psychological Reports, 87,* 223–226.

Harris, M., & Bays, G. (1973). Altruism and sex roles. *Psychological Reports, 32,* 1002.

Harris, M. B., & Smith, R. J. (1975). Mood and helping. *The Journal of Social Psychology, 91,* 215–221.

Isen, A., & Levin, P. (1972). Effect of feeling good on helping. *Journal of Personality and Social Psychology, 21,* 384–388.

Isen, A., & Simmonds, S. (1978). The effect of feeling good on a helping task that is incompatible with good mood. *Social Psychology Quarterly, 41,* 346–349.

Job, S. (1987). The effect of mood on helping behavior. *The Journal of Social Psychology, 127,* 323–328.

Jourard, S., & Friedman, R. (1970). Experimenter-subject "distance" and self-disclosure. *Journal of Personality and Social Psychology, 15,* 278–282.

Kleinke, C., & Walton J. (1982). Influence of reinforced smiling on affective responses in an interview. *Journal of Personality and Social Psychology, 42,* 557–565.

Lau, S. (1982). The effect of smiling on person perception. *The Journal of Social Psychology, 117,* 63–67.

Levin, P., & Isen, A. (1975). Further studies on the effect of feeling good on helping. *Sociometry, 38,* 141–147.

Otta, E., Pereira, B., Delavati, N., Pimentel, O., & Pires, C. (1993). The effects of smiling and of head tilting on person perception. *The Journal of Psychology, 128,* 323–331.

Rind, B. (1996). Effect of beliefs about weather conditions on tipping. *Journal of Applied Social Psychology, 26,* 137–147.

Rind, B. (1997). Effect of interest arousal on compliance with a request for help. *Basic and Applied Social Psychology, 19,* 49–59.

Rind, B., & Bordia, P. (1996). Effect on restaurant tipping of male and female servers drawing a happy, smiling face on backs of customers' checks. *Journal of Applied Social Psychology, 26,* 218–225.

Solomon, H., Zener-Solomon, L., Arnone, M., Maur, B., Reda, R., & Roth, E. (1981). Anonymity and helping. *The Journal of Social Psychology, 113,* 37–43.

Takemura, K. (1993). The effect of interpersonal sentiments on behavioral intention of helping behavior among Japanese students. *The Journal of Social Psychology, 133,* 675–681.

Tidd, K., & Lockard, J. (1978). Monetary significance of the affiliative smile: A case of reciprocal altruism. *Bulletin of the Psychonomic Society, 11,* 344–346.

Weyant, J. (1978). Effects of mood states, costs, and benefits of helping. *Journal of Personality and Social Psychology, 36,* 1169–1176.

CRITICAL THINKING QUESTIONS

1. The results reported in this article indicate that people were more likely to help someone else in need immediately after being exposed to someone else who smiled at them. How long do you think the effect of being exposed to a smile on subsequent helping behavior lasts? Just a few moments or much longer? Why? Design a study to determine how long the effects of smiling persist.

2. The present study demonstrated that being exposed to a smile resulted in a higher rate of helping another person in need. The study did not determine, however, if the mediating variable that results in increased helping is that the person being smiled at is in a better mood. What other possibilities might explain the results (i.e., other than that the subject was in a better mood)? Design a study to determine if being in a better mood, as opposed to some other reason, is responsible for increased helping behavior.

3. The confederates in this study all were college-aged students of average attractiveness and appearance. Could the age or appearance of who is doing the smiling affect the subsequent helping behavior? Explain your reasoning.

4. Besides the variables described in this article, what other factors may impact people's helping behavior? Explain why you think each may influence helping behavior.

CHAPTER INTEGRATION QUESTIONS

1. "The only thing that is necessary for the triumph of evil is for good men to do nothing," according to eighteenth-century political writer Edmund Burke. Discuss why you either agree or disagree with this statement.

2. Integrate the content of the three articles in this chapter to identify one or more themes regarding helping behavior. Can Burke's quote be used to help understand the theme or themes? Explain.

3. Besides the factors covered in the articles, what else might have an impact on helping behavior? Discuss.

Chapter Eleven

AGGRESSION

PICK UP A COPY of today's newspaper. How much of it concerns acts of violence, whether from war, terrorism, homicide, or domestic violence? Aggression seems to be a fairly common part of modern life.

Now think about your own experiences. Chances are, you have not directly experienced a murder or assault. But what other types of aggressive behavior have you witnessed? Have you seen verbal aggression, where the intention was to hurt another person's feelings? Have you experienced cruelty in one form or another, where pain was experienced, even though no blood was shed?

Must aggression be part of life? Is it simply human nature and consequently something that cannot be changed? Or is it possible that the amount of aggression in the world could be reduced, if not actually eliminated?

Article 31, "Bad Girls," reports on an alarming trend in the last few years in which rates of female aggression are increasing dramatically—in some cases, nearly equaling those of males. This article suggests that it may no longer be warranted to think of aggression as a male tendency.

In contrast, Article 32, "Transmission of Aggression through Imitation of Aggressive Models," represents one of the earliest studies demonstrating that aggression is learned and in particular that the violence portrayed on television may contribute to aggressiveness in children. Since many behavioral patterns, such as aggression, may be learned in childhood, knowledge about what contributes to aggression can be used to help reduce those very behaviors.

Finally, Article 33 provides a contemporary examination of children's attitudes toward media violence. "Types of Media Violence and Degree of Acceptance in Under-18s" looks at how different types of media violence may have different impacts on viewers and how gender also may play a role in the process. This article also illustrates how the pioneering work discussed in Article 32 has been expanded over the years.

ARTICLE 31 _____

What causes aggression? Psychologists have asked that question for nearly a century now. In their search for an answer, several theoretical perspectives have emerged.

One such perspective holds that aggression is an innate tendency, something toward which people are biologically predisposed. This view, espoused by theorists such as Sigmund Freud, maintains that people periodically need to discharge a natural buildup of aggressive energy. Thus, human aggressiveness may be a normal and perhaps unavoidable fact of life.

A second view suggests that aggression is a drive to harm someone elicited by some external stimulus. In other words, certain external conditions, such as frustration, produce a tendency for people to want to harm or injure others.

Other theories of aggression maintain that aggressive behavior is purely the product of social learning. People are aggressive because they have *learned* how to be aggressive, perhaps by watching other people act in such a fashion.

If aggressive behavior is somehow a biological predisposition, we might expect a universal manifestation of its occurrence. For example, if males are naturally more aggressive than females, then this pattern should be relatively constant in varying cultures around the world. Furthermore, we might expect that the rates of aggression for males and females in a given culture would likewise be fairly constant, with males consistently acting more aggressively than females across different points in time.

Common-sense observations, as well as attention to media reports, certainly confirm the fact that men are more aggressive than women. Or are they? Perhaps male aggression is more likely to be noticed and reported than female aggression. Or maybe males are more likely to be punished than females who commit the same acts. The following article by Barry Yeoman presents strong evidence that the rates of female violence may be much higher than most people think. Moreover, the incidence of female aggression may be increasing at rates far exceeding those of males.

Bad Girls

■ Barry Yeoman

Sante Kimes doesn't exactly match the popular image of the career outlaw. A low-rent Elizabeth Taylor look-alike, the 64-year-old widow is partial to gaudy jewelry, thick perfume and towering black wigs, and to rid herself of her wattles, she got lipo-sculpture at a California clinic.

But beneath the big hair is a criminal whose rap sheet dates back almost four decades. In the mid-'80s, Kimes went to prison for enslaving a platoon of teenage maids from Mexico City. The women were forced to work 18-hour days without weekend breaks, and Kimes kept them in line by beating them with coat hangers and throwing them into searing showers. When one young woman declined to strip for an inspection, according to court records and news reports, Kimes attacked her with a hot iron.

Then came the apparent murders, for which Kimes is a principal suspect. A banker vanished after a dinner

Reprinted from *Psychology Today,* 1999 (November/December), *32*(6), 54–57, 71. Reprinted with permission from *Psychology Today* magazine. Copyright © 2001 (Sussex Publishers, Inc.).

appointment with her. A family friend was pulled out of a dumpster, a bullet in his head, after expressing his reservations about a real-estate scam involving Kimes and her husband. And last summer, New Yorkers were shocked by the disappearance of 82-year-old Irene Silverman, a diminutive former ballerina who was the landlady of Kimes' son. The Kimeses were allegedly trying to defraud Silverman out of her $4 million mansion—and then the retired dancer turned up missing. Kimes claims she's innocent.

What makes this gruesome crime spree hard to grasp is that Kimes, a former pinup model, doesn't fit any of our ruffian archetypes: the L.A. gang member, the Mafia hit man, the young street punk. She's now at an age when many women are described as grandmotherly. Most significantly, she's a woman. "Woman is the creator and fosterer of life; man has been the mechanizer and destroyer of life," anthropologist Ashley Montagu once said. "Women love the human race; men are on the whole hostile to it."

But our cultural assumptions may be off the mark. Witness the proliferation of female perpetrators like Kimes making headlines. The tabloids had a field day with Lorena Bobbitt, who amputated the penis of her sleeping husband. She in turn was eclipsed by Susan Smith, who drowned her two sons in a South Carolina lake. More recently came the murder last May of former Saturday Night Live actor Phil Hartman by his wife Brynn, who then turned around and shot herself.

The increase in female violence over the past century has been dramatic. When Auburn University sociologist Penelope Hanke, Ph.D., reviewed records from an Alabama prison from 1929 to 1985, she discovered that 95% of the cases where women murdered strangers occurred after 1970, along with 60% of slayings of friends and relatives. In another study of 460 female murderers, Illinois State University's Ralph Weisheit, Ph.D., Distinguished Professor of criminal justice, found that women were becoming more stereotypically male in their reasons for murdering. He revealed that robbery-murders accounted for 42% of the cases in 1983, compared to 18% in 1940. And even though males commit the vast majority of street violence, females seem to be catching up. "In 10 or 20 years, those statistics should be equal," predicts Coramae Ritchey Mann, Ph.D., professor emerita of criminal justice at Indiana University.

The recent surge in crime among women illustrates that in spite of their stereotype as gentle nurturers, women have the natural capacity to be as violent as men, according to a growing number of experts. The difference, behavioral studies suggest, is that women need greater incentives to express that violence. Social changes over the years—especially the movement toward gender equality—have provided several.

Freda Adler, Ph.D., Distinguished Professor of criminal justice at Rutgers University, calls this the "liberation hypothesis." As the tightly constructed sex roles of previous years start to weaken, she says, women simply have more and more opportunities to break the law. "Women are more involved in what's going on in the world than they were a generation ago," she says. "You can't embezzle if you're not near funds. You can't get involved in a fight at the bar if you're not allowed in the bar."

VIOLENCE AT HOME

The most revolutionary discoveries about women and aggression involve violence toward loved ones. A preponderance of evidence shows that women can be just as ferocious as men. The most famous of these studies comes from Murray Straus, Ph.D., the founder and co-director of the University of New Hampshire's Family Research Laboratory. His National Family Violence Surveys, conducted in 1975 and 1985 with a total of 8,145 married and cohabiting couples, showed that 12.4% of women have assaulted their spouses, compared to 12.2% of men. When it comes to severe assaults, the numbers were 4.6% for women and 5% for men.

A 1999 study by the British Home Office, a government agency in the United Kingdom, found that 4.2% of men—the exact same figure as for women—had been assaulted by a partner in the previous year.

The patterns go back before marriage. Irene Frieze, Ph.D., remembers seeing studies that showed women to be more prone to violence in dating situations. "I didn't believe it," recalls Frieze, a professor of psychology and women's studies at the University of Pittsburgh. "I said, 'This can't be true. I'm going to do my

---

Really Bad Girls:
The violence that made headlines

For Love or Money

From 1896 to 1908, Belle Gunness killed between 16 and 49 people, including her stepdaughter, hired hands, lovers and husbands. When her homestead mysteriously burned in 1908, officials unearthed the bodies of 10 men and two women. Gunness escaped.

Sinister Sisters

"Sister Amy" Gilligan charged new patients $1,000 upon entry into the Archer Home for Elderly and Indigent Persons in Windsor, Connecticut, and then promptly dispatched them with arsenic, often tricking them into leaving her their insurance money. Arrested in 1916, Gilligan may have killed as many as 40 people in her care.

Angel Makers

Between 1911 and 1929, the Hungarian towns of Nagyrev and Tiszakurt saw the deaths of more than 100 people at the hands of women, led by village midwife Susanna Fazekas. She would boil flypaper and distribute the resulting poison to the women. Thirty-four women were put on trial; 18 went to prison; eight were executed. Fazekas killed herself with poison.

Brutal Brothel

For 10 years, sisters Delfine and Maria Gonzales ran a brothel on a ranch in central Mexico, torturing girls who resisted and killing those who fell ill, tried to run away or lost their looks. When police raided the ranch in 1964, the bodies of some 80 women were found buried, along with countless babies and 11 male migrant workers.

Smother Love

Over 13 years, Marybeth Tining killed nine of her own children while authorities held that the deaths were natural. "I smothered them each with a pillow," she said later, "because I'm not a good mother." In 1987, she was sentenced to 20 years to life, her husband still believing she was innocent.

Angel of Death

Waltraud Wagner used lethal injections, strangulation or drowning to kill between 49 and 300 elderly patients in an Austrian hospital in the mid-1980s. Wagner's motive, as one of her three conspirators put it: "The ones who got on my nerves were dispatched directly to a free bed with the good Lord." All four were sent to prison.

—*Sarah Blustain*

---

own study.'" Sure enough, of the college students she surveyed, 58% of women had assaulted their dates, compared to 55% of men.

When Frieze brought up her findings in her classes, the students weren't surprised. "One woman said, 'Well, it makes me feel strong and powerful when I hit my boyfriend.' They feel safe—that they can get away with this behavior—because the men have this moral code and they'll never strike back." The men, Frieze adds, don't take the violence seriously, because little of it causes serious injuries.

Straus admits that when it comes to the most brutal domestic assaults, the domain is still men's—they commit six times the number women do. "If by violence, you mean 'who's injured?,' then it's an overwhelmingly male crime," he says. That's why there's no great demand for battered men's shelters, and why a disproportionate number of wife beatings get reported to the police.

"You can't just equate numbers," says Ruth Brandwein, Ph.D., a social policy professor at the State University of New York at Stony Brook. "Women who engage in violence are often already in violent relationships. They are living under such unbearable tension that it gives them some control over when they're going to be abused."

VIOLENCE ON THE STREET

Except for high profile lawbreakers like Aileen Wuornos, the Florida prostitute who robbed and killed at least seven of her johns, most of the crime news involves male perpetrators. If a woman is involved, she's generally considered an accomplice to a man. When Bonnie and Clyde were killed in the 1930s, the *New York Times* headline read, "Barrow and woman slain in Louisiana trap!" Even Karla Faye Tucker, executed in Texas last year for a pickax slaying, was working in concert with her boyfriend.

According to the FBI's Uniform Crime Report, women made up only 15% of all those arrested for violent crimes in 1996, but the gap is closing. The statistics show that arrests of women for violent crimes increased 90% between 1985 and 1994, compared to 43% for men. The numbers hold up across many specific crimes: aggravated assault, other assault, and sex offenses other than rape and prostitution. Only in the case of murder did men widen their lead: a 13% rise for men compared to a 4% drop for women.

Indiana University's Mann believes that crime statistics are only now starting to catch up with reality. "Women are just as violent as men, and were often just getting away with the violence," she says.

"Now, with equal rights, the justice system is looking at females differently," explains Mann. "Whereas before they were excused or overlooked, now they are being apprehended."

A criminal defense lawyer admitted, "If she hasn't committed murder and she has children at home, she walks." A judge confided, "It's difficult to send a mature woman to prison. I keep thinking, 'Hey! She is somebody's mother!'"

Frank Julian, J.D., a professor of legal studies at Murray State University in Kentucky, cites a Florida-based study showing that men were 23% more likely to be imprisoned than women who committed the same crime, partly because of the sentencing recommendations of the probation officers. "Women offenders were often viewed as suffering from psychological or emotional problems, or as victims of family problems, bad marriages or dependent relationships," Julian writes. "Men were more likely to have their cases judged in view of the seriousness of the offense committed, employment history and prior record."

IS VIOLENCE IN THE GENES?

In the 1960s, famed psychologist Albert Bandura conducted a series of experiments in which children watched adult models hitting inflatable Bobo dolls. The children were then offered the opportunity to imitate the behavior. Under normal circumstances, the boys knocked down the dolls far more often than the girls did. But when the models got rewarded for knocking down the Bobos, the children's behavior, changed—the boys and girls became almost equally aggressive.

That seems to suggest that males are innately more violent than females—but that women will resort to aggression when given an incentive. Which makes sense to Brenda Shook, Ph.D., a biological psychologist at Union Institute in Sacramento. "Females of all species will go to great lengths, including violence, to protect the young," says Shook. But among humans, the primary responsibility for defending the family—and thus preserving the family genes—went to the male.

But both biological and cultural theories of women's innate capacity for violence hinge on one major trigger. Says Freda Adler: "We're talking about socialization." And for time immemorial, males have been conditioned to be aggressive. Boys got G.I. Joes; girls got Barbies. Men were sent off to war; women bandaged their wounds.

But American girls have always gotten mixed messages. Our culture rewards a certain type of violence in women. "It is the height of femininity to slap a man's face," says Murray Straus. "It's drilled into them."

The groundwork for female violence, it seems, has been there all along. But what may have been a subtler message in a more genteel society has become a clearer directive. The media increasingly promote female violence: Weapon-wielding women are becoming commonplace in everything from Hollywood movies to Saturday morning cartoons.

Women also absorb the cultural norms aimed at everyone, and "this is a violent country," says Cora-mae Ritchey Mann. "There's no reason this wouldn't have rubbed off on them."

READ MORE ABOUT IT

When She Was Bad: Violent Women and the Myth of Innocence, Patricia Pearson (Viking, 1997).

Abused Men: The Hidden Side of Domestic Violence, Philip W. Cook (Praeger, 1997).

CRITICAL THINKING QUESTIONS

1. Interview someone who has worked or volunteered in a women's shelter. How does his or her report of the role of female aggression in domestic relationships confirm or differ from the information presented in the article?

2. Are "role models" of violent females more prevalent in the media today than they were 20 years ago? To test your hypothesis, sample four or five contemporary films as well as some released two decades ago.

3. Discuss the so-called liberation hypothesis discussed in the article. Develop your own list of reasons that may account for the increase in female aggression in recent years.

4. The article notes that women who commit the same aggressive acts as men may be less likely to be sentenced. What factors other than the actual crime may influence sentencing decisions? Explain your answers.

5. Survey your friends or fellow students regarding the use of aggression by males and females in dating relationships. Do you find results similar to those reported in the article? Explain.

ARTICLE 32 _____

Think of the amount of time that a typical child spends in front of the television. Do you think that what that child sees on "the tube" influences his or her behavior to a great extent? Or is television more neutral—just entertainment with no lasting effects?

A major concern of parents and social psychologists alike is the impact of one particular aspect of television on children's subsequent behavior: aggression. If you have not done so in a long time, sit down and watch the Saturday morning cartoons or other programs shown after school or in the early evening, when children are most likely to be watching. How many of these programs involve some sort of violence? What are these shows teaching children, not only in terms of behaviors but also in terms of values?

The following article by Albert Bandura, Dorothea Ross, and Sheila A. Ross was one of the earliest studies to examine the impact of televised aggression on the behavior of children. In the more than 40 years since its publication, numerous other experiments have been conducted on the same topic. These studies strongly suggest that viewing televised aggression has a direct impact on the aggressive behavior of its viewers. The research by Bandura and his colleagues helped initiate this important line of research.

Transmission of Aggression through Imitation of Aggressive Models[1]

■ Albert Bandura, Dorothea Ross, and Sheila A. Ross[2]

A previous study, designed to account for the phenomenon of identification in terms of incidental learning, demonstrated that children readily imitated behavior exhibited by an adult model in the presence of the model (Bandura & Huston, 1961). A series of experiments by Blake (1958) and others (Grosser, Polansky, & Lippitt, 1951; Rosenblith, 1959; Schachter & Hall, 1952) have likewise shown that mere observation of responses of a model has a facilitating effect on subjects' reactions in the immediate social influence setting.

While these studies provide convincing evidence for the influence and control exerted on others by the behavior of a model, a more crucial test of imitative learning involves the generalization of imitative response patterns to new settings in which the model is absent.

In the experiment reported in this paper, children were exposed to aggressive and nonaggressive adult models and were then tested for amount of imitative learning in a new situation in the absence of the model. According to the prediction, subjects exposed to aggressive models would reproduce aggressive acts resembling those of their models and would differ in this respect both from subjects who observed nonaggressive models and from who had no prior exposure to any models. This hypothesis assumed that subjects had learned imitative habits as a result of prior reinforcement, and these tendencies would generalize to some extent to adult experimenters (Miller & Dollard, 1941).

It was further predicted that observation of subdued nonaggressive models would have a generalized inhibiting effect on the subjects' subsequent behavior, and this effect would be reflected in a difference between the nonaggressive and the control groups, with subjects in the latter group displaying significantly more aggression.

Hypotheses were also advanced concerning the influence of the sex of model and sex of subjects on

Reprinted from *Journal of Abnormal and Social Psychology,* 1961, *63,* 575–582.

imitation. Fauls and Smith (1956) have shown that preschool children perceive their parents as having distinct preferences regarding sex appropriate modes of behavior for their children. Their findings, as well as informal observation, suggest that parents reward imitation of sex appropriate behavior and discourage or punish sex inappropriate imitative responses, e.g., a male child is unlikely to receive much reward for performing female appropriate activities, such as cooking, or for adopting other aspects of the maternal role, but these same behaviors are typically welcomed if performed by females. As a result of differing reinforcement histories, tendencies to imitate male and female models thus acquire differential habit strength. One would expect, on this basis, subjects to imitate the behavior of a same-sex model to a greater degree than a model of the opposite sex.

Since aggression, however, is a highly masculine-typed behavior, boys should be more predisposed than girls toward imitating aggression, the difference being most marked for subjects exposed to the male aggressive model.

METHOD

Subjects

The subjects were 36 boys and 36 girls enrolled in the Stanford University Nursery School. They ranged in age from 37 to 69 months, with a mean age of 52 months.

Two adults, a male and a female, served in the role of model, and one female experimenter conducted the study for all 72 children.

Experimental Design

Subjects were divided into eight experimental groups of six subjects each and a control group consisting of 24 subjects. Half the experimental subjects were exposed to aggressive models and half were exposed to models that were subdued and nonaggressive in their behavior. These groups were further subdivided into male and female subjects. Half the subjects in the aggressive and nonaggressive conditions observed same-sex models, while the remaining subjects in each group viewed models of the opposite sex. The control

group had no prior exposure to the adult models and was tested only in the generalization situation.

It seemed reasonable to expect that the subjects' level of aggressiveness would be positively related to the readiness with which they imitated aggressive modes of behavior. Therefore, in order to increase the precision of treatment comparisons, subjects in the experimental and control groups were matched individually on the basis of ratings of their aggressive behavior in social interactions in the nursery school.

The subjects were rated on four five-point rating scales by the experimenter and a nursery school teacher, both of whom were well acquainted with the children. These scales measured the extent to which subjects displayed physical aggression, verbal aggression, aggression toward inanimate objects, and aggressive inhibition. The latter scale, which dealt with the subjects' tendency to inhibit aggressive reactions in the face of high instigation, provided a measure of aggression anxiety.

Fifty-one subjects were rated independently by both judges so as to permit an assessment of interrater agreement. The reliability of the composite aggression score, estimated by means of the Pearson product-moment correlation, was .89.

The composite score was obtained by summing the ratings on the four aggression scales; on the basis of these scores, subjects were arranged in triplets and assigned at random to one of two treatment conditions or to the control group.

Experimental Conditions

In the first step in the procedure subjects were brought individually by the experimenter to the experimental room and the model who was in the hallway outside the room was invited by the experimenter to come and join in the game. The experimenter then escorted the subject to one corner of the room, which was structured as the subject's play area. After seating the child at a small table, the experimenter demonstrated how the subject could design pictures with potato prints and picture stickers provided. The potato prints included a variety of geometrical forms; the stickers were attractive multicolor pictures of animals, flowers, and western figures to be pasted on a pastoral scene. These activities were selected since they had been established, by previous studies in the nursery school, as having high interest value for the children.

After having settled the subject in his corner, the experimenter escorted the model to the opposite corner of the room which contained a small table and chair, a tinker toy set, a mallet, and a 5-foot inflated Bobo doll. The experimenter explained that these were the materials provided for the model to play with and, after the model was seated, the experimenter left the experimental room.

With subjects in the *nonaggressive condition,* the model assembled the tinker toys in a quiet subdued manner totally ignoring the Bobo doll.

In contrast, with subjects in the *aggressive condition,* the model began by assembling the tinker toys but after approximately a minute had elapsed, the model turned to the Bobo doll and spent the remainder of the period aggressing toward it.

Imitative learning can be clearly demonstrated if a model performs sufficiently novel patterns of responses which are unlikely to occur independently of the observation of the behavior of a model and if a subject reproduces these behaviors in substantially identical form. For this reason, in addition to punching the Bobo doll, a response that is likely to be performed by children independently of a demonstration, the model exhibited distinctive aggressive acts which were to be scored as imitative responses. The model laid Bobo on its side, sat on it and punched it repeatedly in the nose. The model then raised the Bobo doll, picked up the mallet and struck the doll on the head. Following the mallet aggression, the model tossed the doll up in the air aggressively and kicked it about the room. This sequence of physically aggressive acts was repeated approximately three times, interspersed with verbally aggressive responses such as "Sock him in the nose . . . ," "Hit him down . . . ," "Throw him in the air . . . ," "Kick him . . . ," "Pow . . . ," and two nonaggressive comments, "He keeps coming back for more" and "He sure is a tough fella."

Thus in the exposure situation, subjects were provided with a diverting task which occupied their attention while at the same time insured observation of the model's behavior in the absence of any instructions to observe or to learn the responses in question.

Since subjects could not perform the model's aggressive behavior, any learning that occurred was purely on an observational or covert basis.

At the end of 10 minutes, the experimenter entered the room, informed the subject that he would now go to another game room, and bid the model goodbye.

AGGRESSION AROUSAL

Subjects were tested for the amount of imitative learning in a different experimental room that was set off from the main nursery school building. The two experimental situations were thus clearly differentiated; in fact, many subjects were under the impression that they were no longer on the nursery school grounds.

Prior to the test for imitation, however, all subjects, experimental and control, were subjected to mild aggression arousal to insure that they were under some degree of instigation to aggression. The arousal experience was included for two main reasons. In the first place, observation of aggressive behavior exhibited by others tends to reduce the probability of aggression on the part of the observer (Rosenbaum & deCharms, 1960). Consequently, subjects in the aggressive condition, in relation both to the nonaggressive and control groups, would be under weaker instigation following exposure to the models. Second, if subjects in the nonaggressive condition expressed little aggression in the face of appropriate instigation, the presence of an inhibitory process would seem to be indicated.

Following the exposure experience, therefore, the experimenter brought the subject to an anteroom that contained these relatively attractive toys: a fire engine, a locomotive, a jet fighter plane, a cable car, a colorful spinning top, and a doll set complete with wardrobe, doll carriage, and baby crib. The experimenter explained that the toys were for the subject to play with but, as soon as the subject became sufficiently involved with the play material (usually in about 2 minutes), the experimenter remarked that these were her very best toys, that she did not let just anyone play with them, and that she had decided to reserve these toys for the other children. However, the subject could play with any of the toys that were in the next room. The experimenter and the subject then entered the adjoining experimental room.

It was necessary for the experimenter to remain in the room during the experimental session; otherwise a number of the children would either refuse to remain alone or would leave before the termination of the session. However, in order to minimize any influence her presence might have on the subject's behavior, the experimenter remained as inconspicuous as possible by busying herself with paper work at a desk in the far corner of the room and avoiding any interaction with the child.

Test for Delayed Imitation

The experimental room contained a variety of toys including some that could be used in imitative or nonimitative aggression, and others that tended to elicit predominantly nonaggressive forms of behavior. The aggressive toys included a 3-foot Bobo doll, a mallet and peg board, two dart guns, and a tether ball with a face painted on it which hung from the ceiling. The nonaggressive toys, on the other hand, included a tea set, crayons and coloring paper, a ball, two dolls, three bears, cars and trucks, and plastic farm animals.

In order to eliminate any variation in behavior due to mere placement of the toys in the room, the play material was arranged in a fixed order for each of the sessions.

The subject spent 20 minutes in this experimental room during which time his behavior was rated in terms of predetermined response categories by judges who observed the session through a one-way mirror in an adjoining observation room. The 20-minute session was divided into 5-second intervals by means of an electric interval timer, thus yielding a total number of 240 response units for each subject.

The male model scored the experimental sessions for all 72 children. Except for the cases in which he served as model, he did not have knowledge of the subjects' group assignments. In order to provide an estimate of interscorer agreement, the performances of half the subjects were also scored independently by a second observer. Thus one or the other of the two observers usually had no knowledge of the conditions to which the subjects were assigned. Since, however, all but two of the subjects in the aggressive condition performed the models' novel aggressive responses while subjects in the other conditions only rarely exhibited such reactions, subjects who were exposed to the aggressive models could be readily identified through their distinctive behavior.

The responses scored involved highly specific concrete classes of behavior and yielded high interscorer reliabilities, the product-moment coefficients being in the .90s.

Response Measures

Three measures of imitation were obtained:

> *Imitation of physical aggression:* This category included acts of striking the Bobo doll with the mallet, sitting on the doll and punching it in the nose, kicking the doll, and tossing it in the air.
>
> *Imitative verbal aggression:* Subject repeats the phrases, "Sock him," "Hit him down," "Kick him," "Throw him in the air," or "Pow."
>
> *Imitative nonaggressive verbal responses:* Subject repeats, "He keeps coming back for more," or "He sure is a tough fella."

During the pretest, a number of the subjects imitated the essential components of the model's behavior but did not perform the complete act, or they directed the imitative aggressive response to some object other than the Bobo doll. Two responses of this type were therefore scored and were interpreted as partially imitative behavior.

> *Mallet aggression:* Subject strikes objects other than the Bobo doll aggressively with the mallet.
>
> *Sits on the Bobo doll:* Subject lays the Bobo doll on its side and sits on it, but does not aggress toward it.

The following additional nonimitative aggressive responses were scored:

> *Punched Bobo doll:* Subject strikes, slaps, or pushes the doll aggressively.
>
> *Nonimitative physical and verbal aggression:* This category included physically aggressive acts directed toward objects other than the Bobo doll and any hostile remarks except for those in the verbal imitation category; e.g., "Shoot the Bobo," "Cut him," "Stupid ball," "Knock over people," "Horses fighting, biting."

Aggressive gun play: Subject shoots darts or aims the guns and fires imaginary shots at objects in the room.

Ratings were also made of the number of behavior units in which subjects played nonaggressively or sat quietly and did not play with any of the material at all.

RESULT

Complete Imitation of Models' Behavior

Subjects in the aggression condition reproduced a good deal of physical and verbal aggressive behavior resembling that of the models, and their mean scores differed markedly from those of subjects in the nonaggressive and control groups who exhibited virtually no imitative aggression (see Table 1).

Since there were only a few scores for subjects in the nonaggressive and control conditions (approximately 70% of the subjects had zero scores), and the

assumption of homogeneity of variance could not be made, the Friedman two-way analysis of variance by ranks was employed to test the significance of the obtained differences.

The prediction that exposure of subjects to aggressive models increases the probability of aggressive behavior is clearly confirmed (see Table 2). The main effect of treatment conditions is highly significant both for physical and verbal imitative aggression. Comparison of pairs of scores by the sign test shows that the obtained over-all differences were due almost entirely to the aggression displayed by subjects who had been exposed to the aggressive models. Their scores were significantly higher than those of either the nonaggressive or control groups, which did not differ from each other (Table 2).

Imitation was not confined to the model's aggressive responses. Approximately one-third of the subjects in the aggressive condition also repeated the model's nonaggressive verbal responses while none of

TABLE 1 / Mean Aggression Scores for Experimental and Control Subjects

| | Experimental Groups | | | | |
| | Aggressive | | Nonaggressive | | |
Response Category	F Model	M Model	F Model	M Model	Control Groups
Imitative physical aggression					
Female subjects	5.5	7.2	2.5	0.0	1.2
Male subjects	12.4	25.8	0.2	1.5	2.0
Imitative verbal aggression					
Female subjects	13.7	2.0	0.3	0.0	0.7
Male subjects	4.3	12.7	1.1	0.0	1.7
Mallet aggression					
Female subjects	17.2	18.7	0.5	0.5	13.1
Male subjects	15.5	28.8	18.7	6.7	13.5
Punches Bobo doll					
Female subjects	6.3	16.5	5.8	4.3	11.7
Male subjects	18.9	11.9	15.6	14.8	15.7
Nonimitative aggression					
Female subjects	21.3	8.4	7.2	1.4	6.1
Male subjects	16.2	36.7	26.1	22.3	24.6
Aggressive gun play					
Female subjects	1.8	4.5	2.6	2.5	3.7
Male subjects	7.3	15.9	8.9	16.7	14.3

TABLE 2 / Significance of the Differences between Experimental and Control Groups in the Expression of Aggressive

Response Category	χ^2_r	Q	P	Comparison of Pairs of Treatment Conditions		
				Aggressive vs. Nonaggressive *p*	Aggressive vs. Control *p*	Nonaggressive vs. Control *p*
Imitative responses						
Physical aggression	27.17		< .001	< .001	< .001	.09
Verbal aggression	9.17		< .02	.004	.048	.09
Nonaggressive verbal responses		17.50	< .001	.004	.004	*ns*
Partial imitation						
Mallet aggression	11.06		< .01	.026	*ns*	.005
Sits on Bobo		13.44	< .01	.018	.059	*ns*
Nonimitative aggression						
Punches Bobo doll	2.87		*ns*			
Physical and verbal	8.96		< .02	.026	*ns*	*ns*
Aggressive gun play	2.75		*ns*			

Note: ns = nonsignificant.

the subjects in either the nonaggressive or control groups made such remarks. This difference, tested by means of the Cochran *Q* test, was significant well beyond the .001 level (Table 2).

Partial Imitation of Models' Behavior

Differences in the predicted direction were also obtained on the two measures of partial imitation.

Analysis of variance of scores based on the subjects' use of the mallet aggressively toward objects other than the Bobo doll reveals that treatment conditions are a statistically significant course of variation (Table 2). In addition, individual sign tests show that both the aggressive and the control groups, relative to subjects in the nonaggressive condition, produced significantly more mallet aggression, the difference being particularly marked with regard to female subjects. Girls who observed nonaggressive models performed a mean number of 0.5 mallet aggression responses as compared to mean values of 18.0 and 13.1 for girls in the aggressive and control groups, respectively.

Although subjects who observed aggressive models performed more mallet aggression (*M* = 20.0) than

their controls (*M* = 13. 3), the difference was not statistically significant.

With respect to the partially imitative response of sitting on the Bobo doll, the over-all group differences were significant beyond the .01 level (Table 2). Comparison of pairs of scores by the sign test procedure reveals that subjects in the aggressive group reproduced this aspect of the models' behavior to a greater extent than did the nonaggressive (*p* = .018) or the control (*p* = .059) subjects. The latter two groups, on the other hand, did not differ from each other.

Nonimitative Aggression

Analyses of variance of the remaining aggression measures (Table 2) show that treatment conditions did not influence the extent to which subjects engaged in aggressive gun play or punched the Bobo doll. The effect of conditions is highly significant (χ^2_r = 8.96, *p* < .02), however, in the case of the subjects' expression of nominative physical and verbal aggression. Further comparison of treatment pairs reveals that the main source of the over-all difference was the aggressive and nonaggressive groups which differed significantly from each other (Table 2), with subjects exposed to the aggressive models displaying the greater amount of aggression.

Influence of Sex of Model and Sex of Subjects on Imitation

The hypothesis that boys are more prone than girls to imitate aggression exhibited by a model was only partially confirmed. *t* tests computed for subjects in the aggressive condition reveal that boys reproduced more imitative physical aggression than girls (*t* = 2.50, *p* < .01). The groups do not differ, however, in their imitation of verbal aggression.

The use of nonparametric tests, necessitated by the extremely skewed distributions of scores for subjects in the nonaggressive and control conditions, preclude an over-all test of the influence of sex of model per se, and of the various interactions between the main effects. Inspection of the means presented in Table 1 for subjects in the aggression condition, however, clearly suggests the possibility of a Sex × Model interaction. This interaction effect is much more consistent and pronounced for the male model than for the female model. Male subjects, for example, exhibited more physical (*t* = 2.07, *p* < .05) and verbal imitative aggression (*t* = 2.51, *p* < .05), more nonimitative aggression (*t* = 3.15, *p* < .025), and engaged in significantly more aggressive gun play (*t* = 2.12, *p* < .05) following exposure to the aggressive male model than the female subjects. In contrast, girls exposed to the female model performed considerably more imitative verbal aggression and more nonimitative aggression than did the boys (Table 1). The variances, however, were equally large and with only a small *N* in each cell the mean differences did not reach statistical significance.

Data for the nonaggressive and control subjects provide additional suggestive evidence that the behavior of the male model exerted a greater influence than the female model on the subjects' behavior in the generalization situation.

It will be recalled that, except for the greater amount of mallet aggression exhibited by the control subjects, no significant differences were obtained between the nonaggressive and control groups. The data indicate, however, that the absence of significant differences between these two groups was due primarily to the fact that subjects exposed to the nonaggressive female model did not differ from the controls on any of the measures of aggression. With respect to the male model, on the other hand, the differences between the groups are striking. Comparison of the sets of scores by means of the sign test reveals that, in relation to the control group, subjects exposed to the nonaggressive male model performed significantly less imitative physical aggression (*p* = .06), less imitative verbal aggression (*p* = .002), less mallet aggression (*p* = .003), less nonimitative physical and verbal aggression (*p* = .03) and they were less inclined to punch the Bobo doll (*p* = .07).

While the comparison of subgroups, when some of the over-all tests do not reach statistical significance, is likely to capitalize on chance differences, nevertheless the consistency of the findings adds support to the interpretation in terms of influence by the model.

Nonaggressive Behavior

With the exception of expected sex differences, Lindquist (1956) Type III analyses of variance of the nonaggressive response scores yielded few significant differences.

Female subjects spent more time than boys playing with dolls (*p* < .001), with the tea set (*p* < .001), and coloring (*p* < .05). The boys, on the other hand, devoted significantly more time than the girls to exploratory play with the guns (*p* < .01). No sex differences were found in respect to the subjects' use of the other stimulus objects, i.e., farm animals, cars, or tether ball.

Treatment conditions did produce significant differences on two measures of nonaggressive behavior that are worth mentioning. Subjects in the nonaggressive condition engaged in significantly more nonaggressive play with dolls than either subjects in the aggressive group (*t* = 2.67, *p* < .02), or in the control group (*t* = 2.57, *p* < .02).

Even more noteworthy is the finding that subjects who observed nonaggressive models spent more than twice as much time as subjects in aggressive condition (*t* = 3.07, *p* < .01) in simply sitting quietly without handling any of the play material.

DISCUSSION

Much current research on social learning is focused on the shaping of new behavior through rewarding and punishing consequences. Unless responses are emitted, however, they cannot be influenced. The results of this study provide strong evidence that observation of cues produced by the behavior of others is one effective means of eliciting certain forms of responses for which the original probability is very low or zero. Indeed, social imitation may hasten or short-cut the acquisition of new behaviors without the necessity of reinforcing successive approximations as suggested by Skinner (1953).

Thus subjects given an opportunity to observe aggressive models later reproduced a good deal of physical and verbal aggression (as well as nonaggressive responses) substantially identical with that of the model. In contrast, subjects who were exposed to nonaggressive models and those who had no previous exposure to any models only rarely performed such responses.

To the extent that observation of adult models displaying aggression communicates permissiveness for aggressive behavior, such exposure may serve to weaken inhibitory responses and thereby to increase the probability of aggressive reactions to subsequent frustrations. The fact, however, that subjects expressed their aggression in ways that clearly resembled the novel patterns exhibited by the models provides striking evidence for the occurrence of learning by imitation.

In the procedure employed by Miller and Dollard (1941) for establishing imitative behavior, adult or peer models performed discrimination responses following which they were consistently rewarded, and the subjects were similarly reinforced whenever they matched the leaders' choice responses. While these experiments have been widely accepted as demonstrations of learning by means of imitation, in fact, they simply involve special case of discrimination learning in which the behavior of others serves as discriminative stimuli for responses that are already part of the subject's repertoire. Auditory or visual environmental cues could easily have been substituted for the social stimuli to facilitate the discrimination learning. In contrast, the process of imitation studied in the present experiment differed in several important respects from the one investigated by Miller and Dollard in that subjects learned to combine fractional responses into relatively complex novel patterns solely by observing the performance of social models without any opportunity to perform the models' behavior in the exposure setting, and without any reinforcers delivered either to the models or to the observers.

An adequate theory of the mechanisms underlying imitative learning is lacking. The explanations that have been offered (Logan, Olmsted, Rosner, Schwartz, & Stevens, 1955; Maccoby, 1959) assume that the imitator performs the model's responses covertly. If it can be assumed additionally that rewards and punishments are self-administered in conjunction with the covert responses, the process of imitative learning could be accounted for in terms of the same principles that govern instrumental trial-and-error learning. In the early stages of the developmental process, however, the range of component responses in the organism's repertoire is probably increased through a process of classical conditioning (Bandura & Huston, 1961; Mowrer, 1950).

The data provide some evidence that the male model influenced the subjects' behavior outside the exposure setting to a greater extent than was true for the female model. In the analyses of the Sex × Model interactions, for example, only the comparisons involving the male model yielded significant differences. Similarly, subjects exposed to the nonaggressive male model performed less aggressive behavior than the controls, whereas comparisons involving the female model were consistently nonsignificant.

In a study of learning by imitation, Rosenblith (1959) has likewise found male experimenters more effective than females in influencing children's behavior. Rosenblith advanced the tentative explanation that the school setting may involve some social deprivation in respect to adult males which, in turn, enhances the male's reward value.

The trends in the data yielded by the present study suggest an alternative explanation. In the case of a highly masculine-typed behavior such as physical aggression, there is a tendency for both male and female subjects to imitate the male model to a greater degree than the female model. On the other hand, in the case of verbal aggression, which is less clearly sex linked, the greatest amount of imitation occurs in relation to the same-sex model. These trends together with the finding that boys in relation to girls are in general more imitative of physical aggression but do not differ in imitation of verbal aggression, suggest that subjects may be differentially affected by the sex of the model but that predictions must take into account the degree to which the behavior in question is sex-typed.

The preceding discussion has assumed that maleness-femaleness rather than some other personal characteristics of the particular models involved, is the significant variable—an assumption that cannot be tested directly with the data at hand. It was clearly evident, however, particularly from boys' spontaneous remarks about the display of aggression by the female model, that some subjects at least were responding in terms of a sex discrimination and their prior learning about what is sex appropriate behavior (e.g., "Who is that lady? That's not the way for a lady to behave. Ladies are supposed to act like ladies. . . ." "You should have seen what that girl did in there. She was just acting like a man. I never saw a girl act like that before. She was punching and fighting but not swearing."). Aggression by the male model, on the other hand, was more likely to be seen as appropriate and approved by both the boys ("Al's a good socker, he beat up Bobo. I want to sock like Al.") and the girls ("That man is a strong fighter, he punched and punched and he could hit Bobo right down to the floor and if Bobo got up he said, 'Punch your nose.' He's a good fighter like Daddy.").

The finding that subjects exposed to the quiet models were more inhibited and unresponsive than subjects in the aggressive condition, together with the obtained difference on the aggression measures, suggests that exposure to inhibited models not only decreases the probability of occurrence of aggressive behavior but also generally restricts the range of behavior emitted by the subjects.

"Identification with aggressor" (Freud, 1946) or "defensive identification" (Mowrer, 1950), whereby a person presumably transforms himself from object to agent of aggression by adopting the attributes of an aggressive threatening model so as to allay anxiety, is widely accepted as an explanation of the imitative learning of aggression.

The development of aggressive modes of response by children of aggressively punitive adults, however, may simply reflect object displacement without involving any such mechanism of defensive identification. In studies of child training antecedents of aggressively antisocial adolescents (Bandura & Walters, 1959) and of young hyperaggressive boys (Bandura, 1960), the parents were found to be nonpermissive and punitive of aggression directed toward themselves. On the other hand, they actively encouraged and reinforced their sons' aggression toward persons outside the home. This pattern of differential reinforcement of aggressive behavior served to inhibit the boys' aggression toward the original instigators and fostered the displacement of aggression toward objects and situations eliciting much weaker inhibitory responses.

Moreover, the findings from an earlier study (Bandura & Huston, 1961), in which children imitated to an equal degree aggression exhibited by a nurturant and a nonnurturant model, together with the results of the present experiment in which subjects readily imitated aggressive models who were more or less neutral figures suggest that mere observation of aggression, regardless of the quality of the model-subject relationship, is a sufficient condition for producing imitative aggression in children. A comparative study of the subjects' imitation of aggressive models who are feared, who are liked and esteemed, or who are essentially neutral figures would throw some light on whether or not a more parsimonious theory than the one involved in "identification with the aggressor" can explain the modeling process.

SUMMARY

Twenty-four preschool children were assigned to each of three conditions. One experimental group observed aggressive adult models; a second observed inhibited nonaggressive models; while subjects in a control group had no prior exposure to the models. Half the subjects in the experimental conditions observed same-sex models and half viewed models of the opposite sex. Subjects were then tested for the amount of imitative as well as nonimitative aggression performed in a new situation in the absence of the models.

Comparison of the subjects' behavior in the generalization situation revealed that subjects exposed to aggressive models reproduced a good deal of aggression resembling that of the models, and that their mean scores differed markedly from those of subjects in the nonaggressive and control groups. Subjects in the aggressive condition also exhibited significantly more partially imitative and nonimitative aggressive behavior and were generally less inhibited in their behavior than subjects in the nonaggressive condition.

Imitation was found to be differentially influenced by the sex of the model with boys showing more aggression than girls following exposure to the male model, the difference being particularly marked on highly masculine-typed behavior.

Subjects who observed the nonaggressive models, especially the subdued male model, were generally less aggressive than their controls.

The implications of the findings based on this experiment and related studies for the psychoanalytic theory of identification with the aggressor were discussed.

REFERENCES

Bandura, A. Relationship of family patterns to child behavior disorders. Progress Report, 1960, Stanford University, Project No. M-1734, United States Public Health Service.

Bandura, A., & Huston, Aletha C. Identification as a process of incidental learning. *J. abnorm. soc. Psychol.,* 1961, *63,* 311–318.

Bandura, A., & Walters, R. H. *Adolescent aggression.* New York: Ronald, 1959.

Blake, R. R. The other person in the situation. In R. Tagiuri & L. Petrullo (Eds.), *Person perception and interpersonal behavior.* Stanford, Calif.: Stanford Univer. Press, 1958. Pp. 229–242.

Fauls, Lydia B., & Smith, W. D. Sex-role learning of five-year olds. *J. genet. Psychol.,* 1956, *89,* 105–117.

Freud, Anna. *The ego and the mechanisms of defense.* New York: International Univer. Press, 1946.

Grosser, D., Polansky, N., & Lippitt, R. A laboratory study of behavior contagion. *Hum. Relat.,* 1951, *4,* 115–142.

Lindquist, E. F. *Design and analysis of experiments.* Boston: Houghton Mifflin, 1956.

Logan, F., Olmsted, O. L., Rosner, B. S., Schwartz, R. D., & Stevens, C. M. *Behavior theory and social science.* New Haven: Yale Univer. Press, 1955.

Maccoby, Eleanor E. Role-taking in childhood and its consequences for social learning. *Child Develpm.,* 1959, *30,* 239–252.

Miller, N. E., & Dollard, J. *Social learning and imitation.* New Haven: Yale Univer. Press, 1941.

Mowrer, O. H. (Ed.) Identification: A link between learning theory and psychotherapy In, *Learning theory and personality dynamics.* New York: Ronald, 1950. Pp. 69–94.

Rosenbaum, M. E., & deCharms, R. Direct and vicarious reduction of hostility. *J. abnorm. soc. Psychol.,* 1960, *60,* 105–111.

Rosenblith, Judy F. Learning by imitation in kindergarten children. *Child Develpm.,* 1959, *30,* 69–80.

Schachter, S., & Hall, R. Group-derived restraints and audience persuasion. *Hum. Relat.,* 1952, *5,* 397–406.

Skinner, B. F. *Science and human behavior.* New York: Macmillan, 1953.

ENDNOTES

1. This investigation was supported by Research Grant M-4398 from the National Institute of Health, United States Public Health Service.

2. The authors wish to express their appreciation to Edith Dowley, Director, and Patricia Rowe, Head Teacher, Stanford University Nursery School for their assistance throughout this study.

CRITICAL THINKING QUESTIONS

1. Notice that the children's anger was aroused prior to their being placed in the situation where their aggression would be measured. Why was this done? What might have resulted had their anger not been aroused beforehand? Were there different effects, depending on whether the children experienced prior anger arousal? If so, then what are the implications for generalizing the results of this study to how violent television affects its young viewers? Explain your answers.

2. This study reported that the gender of the actor made a difference in how much physical aggression was imitated. It also mentioned that some of the children simply found it inappropriate for a female actor to act aggressively. Over 40 years have passed since pub-

lication of this study. Do you think children today would still see physical aggression by a female as inappropriate? Support your answer.

3. Analyze the content of television shows directed toward children (including cartoons) for aggression, examining the type of aggression (physical versus verbal) and the gender of the aggressive character. Relate the findings to Question 2, above.

4. Examine research conducted over the last three decades that documents the impact of televised aggression on children's behavior. Given these findings, what should be done? Should laws be passed to regulate the amount of violence shown on television? Or should this form of censorship be avoided? Explain. What other alternatives might exist to reverse or prevent the potential harm of observing violence on television?

ADDITIONAL RELATED READINGS

Haridakis, P. M., & Rubin, A. M. (2003). Motivation for watching television violence and viewer aggression. *Mass Communication and Society, 6*(1), 29–56.

Huesmann, L. R., Moise-Titus, J., Podolski, C., & Eron, L. D. (2003). Longitudinal relations between children's exposure to TV violence and their aggressive and violent behavior in young adulthood. *Developmental Psychology, 39*(2), 201–221.

ARTICLE 33 _____

An important area of research on aggression concerns its causes. Three general classes of theories have emerged: The first class, which can be called *instinct theories,* explains aggression as somehow rooted in biology. Thus, aggression stems from internally generated forces and is something that human beings are genetically programmed to do. A second type of theory, called *drive reduction,* essentially explains aggression as arising from forces outside the individual; for instance, experiencing frustration may produce readiness to engage in aggressive behavior. *Social learning* is the third theoretical explanation of aggression. Basically, this approach maintains that aggression, like many other complex social behaviors, is learned. It is not instinctive nor is it simply a reaction to a specific external event.

Each of these theoretical views attributes aggression to a different cause. It follows, then, that whichever theoretical explanation you adopt will influence how optimistic you are about the possible control of aggression. For example, if you believe that aggression is innate, a biological predisposition of sorts, then there is not much that can be done about it. It is simply human nature to be aggressive. However, if you believe that aggression is learned, then it is not inevitable that people be aggressive. After all, if aggressive behaviors can be learned, then nonaggressive behaviors can be learned, as well. And if aggression arises from forces outside the individual, then aggression can be reduced to the extent that one can control those outside forces.

The following contemporary article by Miguel Ángel Vidal, Miguel Clemente, and Pablo Espinosa examines the effects that viewing television violence may have on children. This line of research is an extension of the pioneering studies done by Albert Bandura and others (Article 32) and attempts to answer more specifically how accepting children are of media violence as a function of the type of violence and the gender of the children. This study also is of interest in that the children being studied live in Spain, furthering the generalizability of studies on aggression in children.

Types of Media Violence and Degree of Acceptance in Under-18s

■ Miguel Ángel Vidal, Miguel Clemente, and Pablo Espinosa

It is an established fact that almost every TV channel offers a high level of violent content. The object of this study is to check the degree of acceptance of this media violence in under-18s. We will also check what cognitive and emotional effects the viewing of different types of violence has. A sample of 203 subjects aged 13 years from Madrid, Spain, viewed a clip from different films. Before and after the film, data were collected about their opinion on violence. Three viewing conditions were established according to the degree and type of violence shown and based an Berkowitz [(1996): Desclée De Brouwer]: action without violence, socially justified violence, and socially unjustified violence. Several ANOVAs were carried out revealing that violence is better valued and more

Reprinted from M. A. Vidal, M. Clemente, & P. Espinosa, "Types of Media Violence and Degree of Acceptance in Under-18s," *Aggressive Behavior,* 2003, *29,* 381–392. Copyright © 2003 John Wiley & Sons. This material is used by permission of Wiley-Liss, Inc., a subsidiary of John Wiley & Sons, Inc.

attractive after watching the film sequences than before the showing.

Key Words media; violence; youth

INTRODUCTION

There has always been great concern about the effects of the media on aggressiveness. For the past decades, extensive research has been carried out to try to highlight the link between broadcast violence and the influence on the viewers. For instance, in the Spanish context, there is a great amount of research and compilation studies on this topic [see Clemente and Vidal, 1994, 1995, 1997; Garcia Galera, 2000; Vilchez, 1999]. This research has mainly dealt with determining the effects of media violence on the viewers, in our case, under-18s. Empirical research has conceptualized TV violence as an important risk factor for aggressive behavior. In this sense, the Causal Effect Theory has been proposed to explain this link [Drewer et al., 1995]. According to this model, the psychological mechanism through which aggressive behavior can be introduced in the behavioral repertoire of the young person is social learning.

Many factors influence violence learning, and a fair amount of research deals with this issue. Peña et al. [1999] quote the most important related variables: justified or unjustified nature of TV aggression [Berkowitz and Powers, 1979]; self-identification with aggression and its consequences [Rowe and Herstand, 1986]; attitudes and normative beliefs toward interpersonal aggression and the viewing of violence on TV [Huesmann et al., 1996; Walker and Morley, 1991]; self identification with aggressive characters [Huesmann et al., 1984]; moral attributions and evaluations of violence perpetrators [Rule and Ferguson, 1986]; and the salience of the observed aggression [Mustonen and Pulkkinen, 1993], which becomes relevant if we define a boundary between acceptable and censored aggression.

Gunter [1996] classifies the effects caused by the previously mentioned variables into three categories: behavioural, cognitive, and emotional. Among behavioral effects, Gunter mentions several processes, such as Catharsis, Arousal, Lack of Inhibition, Imitation, and Desensitisation. Clemente and Vidal [1996] and

Urra et al. [2000] reviewed the following:

Aggressive attitude and behavior learning. As Social Cognitive Theory [Bandura, 1996] predicts, it is plain to see that through observational learning, children internalize aggressive behaviors and attitudes viewed on TV. In addition, aggression is more easily learned if it is performed by an attractive character and for morally adequate reasons [León et al., 1997]. Learning is also facilitated if the character is involved in realistic violent acts, is rewarded for his behavior, uses conventional weapons, her/his violent actions lack visible consequences, and the story has a humorous approach. In any case, the more violence on TV an individual watches, the more likely he/she will get involved in real violence.

Desensitisation or insensitivity toward violence. Cognitive desensitization makes our own aggressiveness more acceptable. Moreover, the continual appearance of violence in the media hampers our emotional response toward aggressive behaviors to the point that it could make us unable to answer properly.

Fear of being a victim of violence. The constant displays of violence on TV may lead us to think that the city is a dangerous wilderness. In some individuals, this image may increase the fear or anxiety of living in an urban environment. In some cases, this situation may lead these individuals to respond with violence to the actions of other people.

Cognitive justification processes. Under this heading we include the assumption that violent people enjoy violent television because by watching violent programs they can easily justify their own behavior.

Cognitive association. Through the priming effect [Berkowitz, 1996; Jo and Berkowitz, 1996], acquired aggressive habits can be reinforced by watching violent scenes in the media.

Arousal transference. Violent images increase our arousal. This general increase in arousal augments the probability of aggressive behavior when it ceases to be motivated by a fictional event (such as a movie) and translates into actual behavior.

These are the main effects caused in children by watching violence on TV, but, obviously, the link between excessive viewing and aggressive responses is not straightforward. There are many other variables related to violent behavior. The matter is that we have verified, the same as other authors [Comstock and

Paik, 1991; Gunter, 1996; Gunter and McAleer, 1997; Mustonen, 1997; Potter, 1999], that children watch every kind of television program, including those intended for mature audiences. Data collected in Sweden by Von Feilitzen [1990] show that almost 75% of the children aged 3 to 8 years watch programs that are not specifically intended for them. In addition, this percentage has even decreased in the past 20 years, thanks to higher parental awareness. Our data [Clemente et al., 1999; Urra et al., 2000] indicate that viewing habits are similar in the whole Spanish population, irrespective of age, cultural level, or social class. This is even more significant given that only 1 of every 10 Spaniards does not watch television. The rest are regular television consumers, and most watch the same programs. It is also untrue that television products are differentiated according to age groups, and this undermines the concept of specific programming for each age sector [see Clemente, 1998; Vidal and Clemente, 1998]. In this sense, programmers usually schedule programs that satisfy every taste equally (e.g., grandparents, sons and grandchildren, men and women). Regarding daily amount of television viewing, it must be pointed out that more than 16% of children aged 4 to 12 years watch television from Monday to Thursday after 22:00. Also, we have data showing that, at the present time, more than 30% of the children evaluated by us in Spain watch TV in their own rooms. This duplicates the ratio obtained in a previous measure 3 years ago [Clemente et al., 2000]. So, it is evinced that television is viewed for long periods of time. An average of 4 hours a day is being surpassed, especially by children; some studies even indicate that they remain an average of 5 hours a day in front of the television. So, as Gerbner et al. [1996] point out, the cultivation process begins early in the child's life.

Another question is, "What draws the child's attention most?" We agree with Goldstein [1998] that the answer is complex. The child's attention is more easily drawn by pragmatic features that provide short-term benefits and that display a lack of effort, egocentrism, or immediate rewards. Collective moral values, long-term benefits, subordinating personal interests to the common good, and all that the child needs to learn to live in society and that allows community survival is not so attractive.

It must be remembered that children alone, without watching television, are already egocentric and that the younger they are, the more competitively they behave [for a full explanation of this assertion, see Vidal, 1999]. So, from this perspective television is contrary to a proper education, as it encourages individualism, immediate rewards, and egocentrism. Also, while a child is watching television, he or she does not have to make any effort to evolve from his egocentrism and start to understand the moral and ethical concepts of adult society.

We tried to take a further step in the research about youths and the media. So, we have raised the question of whether violence is attractive for under-18s. Hence, the aim of this research is checking if there is any prior tendency to being desensitized toward violence viewed on television. For this reason, attraction toward violence will be analyzed in both excessive and moderate young viewers. In a previous study by Clemente et al. [1999], we examined the specific effects on children that media violence displayed in broadcast bullfights. We will try to confirm as well whether the results found in this study are applicable to less specific settings. We also wanted to check out the emotional and cognitive effects that cause watching violence. This could provide relevant information to answer why we enjoy violence.

Our research hypothesis is, in the first place, that attraction toward violence is related to the amount of TV usage. The more a youth remains in front of the television, the more positive will be the attraction toward violence, via a desensitization effect. On the other hand, we will try to demonstrate that there is a positive relationship among cognitive and emotional measures of violence.

A third hypothesis is that a more negative perception of violence will be displayed in the pre-viewing than in the post-viewing measures. This effect will be caused by social desirability, as children are usually told at home that violence is negative.

We also expect to find that as girls and boys experience a distinct socialization, there will be wider gender differences in the pre-viewing than in the post-viewing measure. Girls are usually more encouraged to reject violence, but this tendency will be attenuated after the viewing. A sub-hypothesis related to gender differences is that when the symbolic model is female, girls will find violence more appealing. When this happens, they will reach levels of attraction toward violence comparable to boys.

Our last hypothesis is that the evaluation of violence will be different for each clip, in the sense that if the violence displayed is not socially justified, subjects will perceive it more negatively.

METHOD

Sample

The sample was composed of 203 subjects aged 13 years from schools in Madrid, Spain. Of the 203 participants, 66.5% were male (therefore, 33.5% were female). We chose our subjects from an upper and middle social class because they are not usually high television consumers, and for this reason, we resorted to three mixed independent schools. Having a sample with an overall high amount of television viewing was a contaminating variable detected in other studies.

Measures

Three video films were selected. From each film we selected a 15-min clip, which was shown to each group. All of the clips were appropriate for 13-year-old viewers in the industry rating system. We used the appropriate audiovisual means so the subjects could watch the pertinent clip: a VHS video player and a monitor connected to the video. Of the three clips that were presented to the subjects, two displayed different types of violence and the other did not show any violence at all and was used as a control clip, as we describe in the following lines:

Action without Violence   This clip was used as a control and to detect the number of false memories. We chose a fragment from the film *Indiana Jones and the Temple of Doom*. It completely lacked violence but contained a great deal of action. It was quite possible that children attributed that it displayed violence, but it did not exist.

Socially Justified Violence   We chose a clip, also 15 min of duration, from the film *Matilda*. In particular, this clip contained aggressions with deadly intent. This kind of aggressions dealt with justified violence

in the sense that the aggressive behavior displayed by the main character happened within a playful and socially acceptable context. Both the main character (Matilda) and the headmistress of her school attack each other. The difference among them is that the headmistress is portrayed as the bad character, and Matilda tries to escape from her attacks, although she also makes plans to do away with her.

Socially Unjustified Violence   A sequence from the film *Perfect Weapon* was chosen. In this clip, aggressions were not justified since there were not apparent reasons to justify the characters' violent behavior (for instance, the film displayed deliberate destruction of private property, physical cruelty, and a variety of fights and shoot-outs).

Unlike other studies [see Peña et al., 1999], where the main character is the same across every experimental condition, we chose to use clips with different characters. The reason was to check the extent to which identification with the protagonist was related to a higher acceptance of violence. Details on this are fully covered in another article [Vidal et al., unpublished data].

An ad hoc sociodemographic questionnaire was also built. Additionally, before and after the viewing of the clips, the subjects answered to a questionnaire evaluating their perceptions of violence. This questionnaire was a semantic differential with 13 questions broken down into two groups. The first group had 10 pairs of adjectives and dealt with the question "You think violent films are . . ." while the second group, which included the 3 remaining pairs, was provided to answer the question "Violent films cause you. . . ." Once they had seen the clip, these two questions were modified in the post-viewing questionnaire replacing the words "violent films" with "what you saw in the clip." Specifically, the adjectives used in the semantic differential for the first question were good-bad, nice-awful, violent-peaceful, smart-stupid, necessary-unnecessary, false-real, adequate-inadequate, pleasant-unpleasant, positive-negative, and funny-boring. When asked for the emotions they felt when watching violent media content, the adjectives used were to be at peace-to be nervous, aggressiveness-to be calmed down, and attraction-rejection. This distinction among cognitive and emotional perceptions was based on Berkowitz [1996] and Rule and Ferguson [1986].

This questionnaire had a 5-point rating system: the lowest values were for positive features and the highest values were for negative features.

We still must pay attention to two main questions regarding the film sequences shown. The first one is that both the film that portrays socially justified violence and the film that portrays socially unjustified violence contain many scenes with a great dose of aggressiveness and violence (in the first film the characters intend to kill each other, in the second one characters try to kill each other and this is achieved in several occasions). The second question is that the three films that are recommended for children younger than 13 years in their age ratings (in particular, the film displaying action without violence was intended for general audiences; the film showing socially justified violence is recommended for 7-year-old or older audiences; and the socially unjustified violence film is recommended for audiences aged 13 years or older).

The measures were administered in seminar classrooms in each of the selected schools, making sure that each subject could comfortably answer the questionnaire previous to the film, watch the clip, and answer the post-film questionnaire.

Procedure

Once contact was made with the schools, we explained to its headmasters the nature of the study we intended to carry out, asking for their collaboration and inquiring whether we needed permission from the Association of Pupil Parents (APA in Spanish, this association exists in every school in Spain) to proceed with the study. Once permission was given, we asked the headmaster for a class of children aged 13 years and arranged an appointment with the pupils' tutor/s. We again explained to the tutor/s the purpose of the study, asking them not to reveal this information to the pupils.

Just before implementing the measures and displaying the clips, we presented our research to the children, telling them that it was an experiment about their ability to recall events and that for that reason they should try to remember as much of the clip that was about to be displayed as they could. They were told that participation was not compulsory and that if they did not wish to complete the experiment they were free to leave the classroom and to enjoy a break. The pupils who stayed in the classroom were asked to complete the previous questionnaire, then they watched one of the three clips and in the end answered the post-viewing questionnaire. They were thanked for their participation.

The three schools in the study were the only ones we made contact with. In other words, no school declined to participate. Also, no pupil refused to participate in the study. Most of them made comments regarding that the fragment of the film viewed was too short. (In fact, we chose a 15-min clip because in previous studies, using clips that lasted 5 or 10 min, the subjects had the same complaint.)

RESULTS

First of all, we present the results regarding desensitization effects of media violence and its general valuing. Our sample was divided into two groups (low and high consumers) according to the number of hours they reported in the socio-demographic questionnaire that they watched television daily. Low television viewers watched it up to 1 hr a day, whereas high television viewers were those who watched television for 3 hr or more a day. We compared the answers of these two groups regarding enjoying violence or not with the pre-viewing stage semantic differential.

The overall results show that there are significant differences for low and high television consumers in the 13 pairs of adjectives. The average for high television consumers was 3.03, and that for low consumers was 3.71. That is, perceptions of violence from low television viewers were more negative, $t(64) = 3.99$, $P < .01$.

Breaking down the semantic differential into its cognitive and emotional components, we found that only the first ones show a significant difference. Its average for high television consumers is 3.04, as opposed to the average of 3.86 that low consumers get, $t(64) = 4.62$, $P < .01$.

It is worth noting that after watching the clips, although both high and low television consumers perceive violence more positively, the greater change is for youths that watch less television. In this case, we did not obtain significant differences between low and high television consumers and the post-viewing questionnaire. It seems that the mere watching of a short sequence containing violence produces a desensitization effect, although we cannot say whether it is lasting or not.

In the second place, we analyzed the semantic differential dealing with children's general assessment of violent films. The average global score of the pre-viewing measure was 3.44, whereas for the post-viewing measure the average was 2.83. For the cognitive scales, the previous measurement had an average score of 3.53 and the post-viewing cognitive average was 2.90. Regarding the emotional valuing, the average goes from 3.16 to 2.65. Consequently, there is a better valuing of post-viewing violence. These results also indicate a positive relationship among emotional and cognitive valuing.

Regarding the cognitive influence of the viewing of violence, the type of violence, and gender, an ANOVA was carried out. The ANOVA thus had three factors: A*B*C (2*3*2). The first factor, the viewing of violent films, is the only repeated measure factor and has two levels: pre- and post-viewing. The second factor includes three levels: action without violence (*Indiana Jones and the Temple of Doom*), justified violence (*Matilda*), and unjustified violence (*Perfect Weapon*). Finally, the third factor is gender and comprises two levels: male and female.

The ANOVA was performed after verifying previous requirements (normality of variables and homogeneity of variances), and always using the most appropriate statistical techniques. The results show that the first of the independent variables, the viewing of violence, is highly significant, that is, the cognitive valuing of violence changes substantially from the previous to the post-viewing measure, $F(1) = 104.77$, $P < .01$. The gender factor also has high significance, that is, males and females cognitively value violence in a different way, $F(1) = 19.90$, $P < .01$. So, the three factors are significant irrespective of each other. Finally, the factor of the type of violence is also highly significant; in other words, the cognitive valuing is quite different depending on the type of violence viewed, $F(2) = 8.09$, $P < .01$. In this case, as the factor has three levels, we can perform post-hoc tests,

and they confirm the existence of significant differences between *Indiana Jones and the Temple of Doom* and *Perfect Weapon* and between *Matilda* and *Perfect Weapon* ($P < .01$ in both cases).

On the other hand, the analysis of the interactions between variables, as summarized below, shows that every interaction but the interaction among the three factors, is significant to the $P < .01$ level. The results are the following: viewing or violence by type of film, $F(2) = 30.05$ (significant differences among viewing of violence and both violent clips but not with the control clip); viewing of violence by gender, $F(1) = 16.80$ (significant differences for gender before viewing the clips but not afterward); and type of film by gender, $F(2) = 8.18$. In this last interaction, results show that there are differences between each type of film for female subjects but not for males. Females value the better violence from the *Matilda* clip. These results are displayed in Figures 1–3.

A second ANOVA, with the same independent variables, but using emotional valuing as a dependent variable, was performed. It indicates, as in the previous analysis, that viewing violence causes changes that are statistically significant over the dependent variable (in this case, emotional impact), $F(1) = 65.95$, $P < .01$. It happens the same with the type of violence watched by minors, $F(2) = 6.63$, $P < .01$. As this variable has three levels, we could perform post-hoc tests. The results are similar to those obtained in the previous ANOVA, that is, there are significant differences

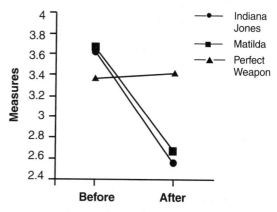

FIGURE 1 / Viewing and Film (Cognitive)

FIGURE 2 / Viewing and Sex (Cognitive)

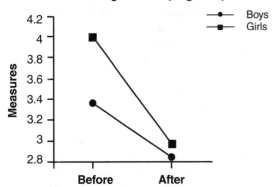

FIGURE 3 / Sex and Film (Cognitive)

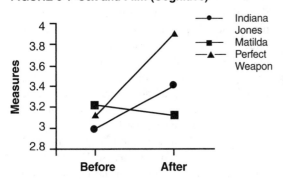

FIGURE 4 / Viewing and Film (Emotional)

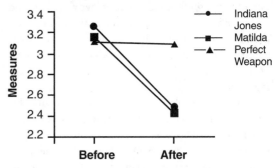

FIGURE 5 / Viewing and Sex (Emotional)

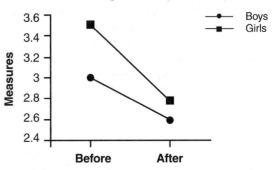

FIGURE 6 / Viewing and Sex (*Indiana Jones*)

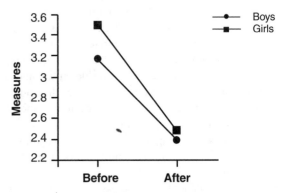

between *Perfect Weapon* and both *Indiana Jones* and *Matilda* (in both cases, $P < .01$). Regarding the main effects, the factor gender also displays significant differences, $F(1) = 12.87$, $P < .01$.

In the analysis of interactions, only the type of film by gender showed no significance. Every other interaction, profusely detailed in Figures 4 to 8, was significant. For the viewing variable (pre or post) by type of film we get an $F(2) = 15.23$, $P < .05$. The interaction of viewing by sex gets an $F(1) = 5.49$, $P < .05$. Last, the triple interaction obtains an $F(2) = 3.24$, $P < .05$.

DISCUSSION

Our data confirm the first hypothesis of this study, since under-18s who spend more hours watching TV value violence more positively. These results are congruent with previous studies from Bandura [1996] and Urra et al. [2000].

So, it may well be that there is not a predisposition toward watching violent films in people with violent impulses but rather an early learning that generates a selective attentional or observational process when ex-

FIGURE 7 / Viewing and Sex (*Matilda*)

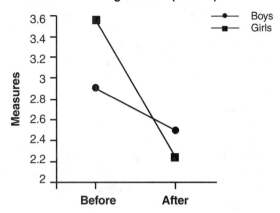

FIGURE 8 / Viewing and Sex (*Perfect Weapon*)

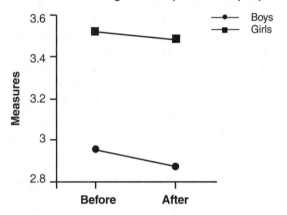

posed to rewarded violent behaviors. This is coherent with the idea that young people perceive violence more positively as they watch more and more violence.

As regarding our second hypothesis, we notice a positive relationship among the emotional and cognitive components of our analysis. Changes in the emotional and cognitive perceptions of subjects follow the same direction, although it is the cognitive component that experiences the greatest changes. In this sense, Berkowitz [1996] points out that cognitions probably emerge once basic emotional feelings have already taken place.

As we have just stated, the results of the variables that explain the valuing of violence show that violence valuing shares similar characteristics both cognitively and emotionally, so we will discuss these results

together. So, regarding our third hypothesis, data indicate that the initial valuing of violence is neutral, that is, youths do not like or dislike violence, and they are supposedly indifferent to it. Of course, this might be mediated by a social desirability factor, since the same subjects tell that most of their friends enjoy violence. This explanation in terms of social desirability is congruent with the fact that very few subjects admit that their parents like violence. However, most parents do not enforce any limit on the violent content children watch on television, so it is quite possible that we are faced with a social desirability phenomenon. Children understand that it is socially unacceptable to show a taste for violence, but this does not prevent them from telling that others do. We may conclude, accordingly, that there is no rejection to violence and that there is strong evidence that violence is pleasing. Results from a previous study by the authors support this statement [Clemente et al., 1999].

Going deeply into this idea, violence gets a negative general valuing both cognitively and emotionally. From the emotional perspective, violent films result in nervousness, aggressiveness, and some rejection. Perhaps we should take into account the general affective aggression model proposed by Anderson [1997] and assume that emotion is essential to cause attraction, as Clemente and Vidal [2000] and Vidal and Clemente [2000] also point out. Fortunately, the negative youths' perception of violent content might reveal a mechanism that allows youths to reject rather than assimilate or imitate violent behavior. Also, according to Anderson's model [1997], media violence effects on emotion may well be strong enough to color self-judgments of another person's intent in ambiguously aggressive situations, thus increasing the likelihood of an aggressive response. So, the worst evaluations for violent films correspond to emotional effects, being much more negative than those for cognitive effects. From the cognitive point of view, they are considered even a bit funny.

This point of view varies substantially after the showing of the clips, as in the post-test we find much more positive scores. So, it is made clear that violence is regarded as more negative before being displayed on the clip than afterward. Not only that, it becomes something positively valued after the pertinent showings. We could conclude, in accordance with Vidal and Clemente [2000], that the more violence we watch, the more positively we perceive it. Although in this case we are talking about a short-term effect, we have just seen that it also happens in the long term, as under-18s with higher TV usage end up valuing violence more positively.

With respect to the gender variable (fourth hypothesis), we notice a considerable difference between males and females. The valuing of violence is far more negative for females than for males. Nevertheless, after viewing violence, children change their opinion about it. Females show a higher increase in their positive evaluation, nearly equaling males in the posttest. This means that males reject violence much less than females before viewing the clip, but the scores from both genders become almost the same in the end. So, the change of mind is far more notable in females, especially in the *Matilda* film clip.

Our results follow the line of those previously found by Huesmann and Eron [1986] using a cohort design. These results seem to be corroborated by our current study in the sense that females initially value violence much more negatively but later on show as high an interest for violence as males do. This evinces that the change in females is much greater than in males. Huesmann and Eron also added that criminality in females over time reached higher levels than in males. All these findings seem to point out that females are more socialized than males in the social desirable values fostered early in childhood, but this varnish is nothing more than a thin layer that disappears as soon as they discover their liking for violence. For this reason, we are inclined to think that there may be a greater degree of realism or sincerity in the responses of males, although this explanation is not valid for the changes in the pre- and post-viewing measures. In any case, we understand that subjects are as sincere before the viewing as they are afterward.

Finally, regarding our fifth hypothesis, we find that both action without violence and socially justified violence are not considered violent, although unjustified violence is. For this last type of violence, its evaluation is somewhat negative and it is maintained after the repeated measure (in any case, it is not decreased). It may be that violence is not considered negative in itself and that it is only regarded as negative if it lacks social sanction, probably as a result of the socialization process. This is congruent with a number of studies, such as those of Clemente and Vidal [2000], Clemente et al. [1999], Peña et al. [1999], Vidal and Clemente [2000], and Mustonen [1997].

Summarizing, the more youths watch violence, the more they enjoy it. So, arguments saying that it is positive to watch violence to be "immunized" against it and to learn what is not to be valued as positive do not seem supportable [Vidal, 2001]. The same as every behavior an individual watches repeatedly, we get used to repeated violence and learn to value it positively.

As Kremar and Valkenburg [1999] state, children who watch a lot of fantasy violence consider justified violence to be less wrong, and, in addition, they use less advanced moral reasoning strategies in explaining their judgments. This finding opens a new research line that can be very useful in understanding the influence of the media in under-18s and the attraction toward violence in relation to the media. Our research in the line of Kremar and Valkenburg of the link between moral judgment and behaviors shows that certain kinds of antisocial behavior are related to moral development in youths [Espinosa et al., 2002]. We have grouped these behaviors into a factor we named *Lack of Civic and Ecological Consciousness* that correlates positively with high television consumption [Vidal et al., unpublished data]. Perhaps this findings will provide us with new insight on why people enjoy violence.

REFERENCES

Anderson CA. 1997. Effects of violent movies and trait hostility on hostile feelings and aggressive thoughts. Aggr Behav 23:161–178.

Bandura A. 1996. Teoria social cognitiva de la comunicación de masas. In: Bryant J, Zillmann D, comps. Los efectos de los medios de comunicaion: investigaciones y teorias. Barcelona: Paidós, p 89–126.

Bandura A, Walters RH. 1974. Aprendizaje Social y desarrollo de la personalidad. Madrid: Alianza.

Berkowitz L. 1996. Agresión: causas, consecuencias y control. Bilbao: Desclée De Brouwer.

Berkowitz L, Powers PC. 1979. Effects of timing and justification of witnessed aggression on the observers punitiveness. J Res Pers 13:71–80.

Clemente M. 1998. Violencia, medios de comunicación y niños y jóvenes. In: Sanmartín J, Grisolia JS, Grisolia S, editors. Violencia, televisión y cine. Barcelona: Ariel. p 67–85.

Clemente M, Vidal MA. 1994. La violencia simbólica: la televisión como medio generador de delincuencia en los niños. Apuntes de Psicologia 41–42:47–60.

Clemente M, Vidal MA. 1995. La violencia simbólica: la television como socializadora del menor. In: Centro de estudios juridicos: justicia con menores y jóvenes. Madrid: Ministerio de Justicia c Interior. p 63–93.

Clemente M, Vidal MA. 1996. Violencia y televisión. Madrid: Noesis.

Clemente M, Vidal MA. 1997. La televisión como ente socializador del menor: los problemas de la violencia simbólica. In Urra J, Clemente M, cords. Psicologia juridica del menor. Madrid: Fundación Universidad-Empresa. p 367–400.

Clemente M, Vidal MA. 2000. La socialización de la violencia culturalmente aceptada. In: Fariña F, Arce R, cords. Psicologia juridica al servicio del menor. Madrid: Cedecs. p 75–91.

Clemente M, Vidal MA, Espinosa P. 1999. Repercusiones psiquicas en los menores del visionado mediátrico de espectáculos taurinos. Madrid: Defensor del Menor en la Comunidad de Madrid.

Clemente M, Vidal MA, Espinosa P. 2000. Desarrollo sociomoral en los niños a través del juego. Santiago de Compostela: Xunta de Galicia.

Comstock G, Palk H. 1991. Television and the American child. San Diego, CA: Academic Press.

Drewer D, Hawkins JD, Catalano R, Neckerman H. 1993. Preventing serious, violent, and chronic juvenile offending: a review of evaluations of selected strategies in childhood, adolescence and the community. In: Hawkins JD, Wilson JJ, editors. Serious, violent and chronic juvenile offenders. Thousand Oaks: Sage. p 61–141.

Espinosa P, Clemente M, Vidal MA. 2002. Conducta antisocial y desarrollo moral en el menor: la falta de conciencia, cívica y ecológica como factor conductual vinculado al razonamiento moral. Psicothema 14:26–36.

Garcia Galera MC. 2000. Televisión, violencia e infancia: el impacto de los medios. Barcelona: Gedisa.

Gerbner G, Gross L, Morgan M, Signorielli N. 1996. Crecer con la televisión: la perspectiva de aculturación. In:

Bryant J, Zillmann D, comps. Los efectos de los medios de comunicación: investigaciones y teorías. Barcelona: Paidós. p 35–66.

Goldstein JH, ed. 1998. Why we watch? the attraction of violent entertainment. New York: Oxford University Press.

Gunter B. 1996. Acerca de la violencia de los media. In: Bryant J, Zillmann D, comps. Los efectos de los medios de comunicación: investigaciones y teorias. Barcelona: Paidós. p 223–286.

Gunter B, McAleer J. 1991. Children and television. 2nd ed. London: Routledge.

Huesmann LR, Eron LD. 1986. The development of aggression in American children as a consequence of television viewing. In: Huesmann LR, Eron LD, editors. Television and the aggressive child: a cross-national comparison. Hillsdale, NJ: Lawrence Erlbaum Associates. p 45–80.

Huesmann LR, Lagerspetz K, Eron LD. 1984. Intervening variables in the TV-violence-aggression relation: evidence from two countries. Dev Psychol 20: 746–745.

Huesmann LR, Moise J, Podolski CL, Eron LD. 1996. The roles of normative beliefs and fantasy rehearsal in mediating the observational learning of aggression. Abstract presented at: the International ISRA Meeting, August 25–30, Strasbourg, France.

Jo E, Berkowitz L. 1996. Análisis del efecto priming sobre la influencia de los media: una puesta al día. In: Bryant J, Zillmann D, comps. Los efectos de los medios de comunicación: investigaciones y teorias. Barcelona: Paidós. p 67–88.

Kremar M, Valkenburg PM. 1999. A scale to assess children's moral interpretations of justified and unjustified violence and its relationship to television viewing. Comunication Res 26:608–634.

León JM, Cantero FJ, Gómez T. 1997. Efectos de la clasifiación del comportamiento del modelo simbólico televisado sobre la agresividad infantil. Rev Psicologia Soc 12:31–42.

Mustonen A. 1997. Nature of screen violence and its relation to program popularity. Aggr Behav 23:281–292.

Mustonen A, Pulkkinen L. 1993. Aggression in television programs in Finland. Aggr Behav 19:175–183.

Peña ME, Andreu JM, Muñoz MJ. 1999. Efectos de la visión de escenas violentas en la conducta agresiva infantil. Psicothema 11:27–36.

Potter WJ. 1999. On media violence. Thousand Oaks, CA: Sage.

Rowe DC, Herstand SE. 1986. Familiar influences on television viewing and aggression: a sibling study. Aggr Behav 12:111–120.

Rule BG, Ferguson TJ. 1986. The effects of media violence on attitudes, emotions and cognitions. J Soc Issues 42:29–50.

Urra J, Clemente M, Vidal MA. 2000. Televisión: impacto en la infancia. Madríd: Siglo XXI.

Vidal MA. 1999. La transmisión intergeneracional de los valores. Sociedad y Utopia: 275–283.

Vidal MA. 2001. Delito y medios de comunición social. In: Clemente M, Espinosa P, coords. La mente criminal: teorías explicativas del delito desde la Psicologia Juridica. Madrid: Dikinson. p 193–207.

Vidal MA, Clemente M. 1998. El pensamiento social único en la aldea global. Sociedad y Utopia 12:231–243.

Vidal MA, Clemente M. 2000. A atraçao pela violencia mediática. Psico 31:49–80.

Vilchez LF. 1999. Televisión y familia: un reto educativo. Madrid: PPC.

Von Feilitzen C. 1990. Tres tesis sobre los niños y los medios de comunicación. Infancia y Sociedad 3:31–47.

Walker KB, Morley DD. 1991. Attitudes and parental factors as intervening variables in the television violence-aggression relation. Communication Res Rep 8:41–47.

The preparation of this article was partly supported by Caixa Galicia studies grant 2002, awarded to the third author.

CRITICAL THINKING QUESTIONS

1. This study used three different classifications of violent media behavior: action without violence, socially justified violence, and socially unjustified violence. Can you think of any other types of violence, besides these three? Explain each type of violence and give an example from the media.

2. Give specific examples from the movies and television of each of the three types of media violence used in this study.

3. This study used 13-year-old children. Would the same findings likely apply to older adolescents (e.g., 18-year-olds)? Adults? Explain your reasoning. Then design a study to test your hypotheses.

4. Examine your own assumptions about aggression. Do you believe that it is part of human nature (i.e., genetically or biologically determined), due to forces outside the individual (e.g., heat), or due to learning and experience (e.g., family or cultural background)? How do your personally held assumptions influence your view of the purpose of punishing criminals, in general, and the issue of capital punishment, in particular? Explain your answers.

CHAPTER INTEGRATION QUESTIONS _____

1. Revisit the introduction to Article 31, which outlines three theoretical perspectives on aggression. Considering the three articles in this chapter together, which theoretical perspective do you feel is most supported by the data? Why?

2. Based on the information from the three articles, can you recommend one or more ways to reduce the occurrence of aggression? Explain your answer.

3. One major concern facing the world today is *terrorism*. What insights, if any, can you draw from the articles in this chapter regarding the causes of and potential control of terrorism? What factors other than those discussed in the articles are important in understanding the causes and control of terrorism? Explain your answers.

Chapter Twelve

GROUP BEHAVIOR

How MUCH OF your life is spent interacting with people in some sort of group? If we use the simple definition of a *group* as "two or more individuals that have some unifying relationship," then most likely a significant amount of your time is spent in groups, whether informal (such as two friends trying to decide what to do on a Saturday night) or formal (a work group deciding on a course of action).

Research on group behavior has gone in many directions. The three articles selected for this chapter focus on some of the most commonly investigated topics. Article 34, "Groupthink," examines a set of circumstances found in certain types of groups that may lead them to make very poor decisions, even when they may be composed of very competent individuals. Since the conditions that may contribute to groupthink are not uncommon, the implications of the article for developing more effective groups are clearly important.

Article 35, "The Effect of Threat upon Interpersonal Bargaining," is a classic work. Think of these two possible situations: In the first situation, Party 1 has the potential to inflict harm on Party 2, but Party 2 cannot reciprocate. In the second situation, both parties have equal threat potential; that is, if Party 1 inflicts harm, Party 2 can reciprocate. Which situation would yield the best outcomes for *both* parties? As the article demonstrates, the answer is not what you might think.

Article 36 returns to the concept of groupthink by examining how it may have contributed to a decision that resulted in a well-known tragedy. "Group Decision Fiascoes Continue: Space Shuttle *Challenger* and a Revised Groupthink Framework" applies the groupthink concept to the *Challenger* disaster, which occurred in 1986. This article also suggests how the concept should be revised to account for other variables that may be involved. While the publication date of this article is not as recent as the other contemporary articles in this book (it was published in 1991), it is one of the best examples of the applications of groupthink to a fairly recent real-world event.

ARTICLE 34 _____

Let us suppose that you are in a position of authority. As such, you are called on to make some very important decisions. You want to make the best possible decisions, so you turn to other people for input. You assemble the best possible set of advisors—people distinguished by their abilities and knowledge. Before making a final decision, you meet with them to discuss the options.

Following such a procedure would seem to ensure that the decision you make will be a good one. After all, with your expert resources, how can you go wrong?

Actually, it is not very hard to imagine that the above procedure could go wrong. Working in a group, even when that group is composed of very competent individuals, does not guarantee quality decision making. To the contrary, as the following article by Irving L. Janis explains, groups may actually make some very poor decisions. The concept of *groupthink,* a term coined by Janis, explains how and why some groups come to make poor decisions, not only failing to recognize that these are poor decisions but actually convincing themselves more and more that these are good decisions. Considering the number of decisions that are made in groups, the process of groupthink, as well as the suggestions for how it can be minimized, are important indeed.

Groupthink
■ Irving L. Janis

The idea of "groupthink" occurred to me while reading Arthur M. Schlesinger's chapters on the Bay of Pigs in *A Thousand Days.* At first I was puzzled: How could bright men like John F. Kennedy and his advisers be taken in by such a stupid, patchwork plan as the one presented to them by the C.I.A. representatives? I began wondering if some psychological contagion of complacency might have interfered with their mental alertness.

I kept thinking about this notion until one day I found myself talking about it in a seminar I was conducting at Yale on the psychology of small groups. I suggested that the poor decision-making performance of those high officials might be akin to the lapses in judgment of ordinary citizens who become more concerned with retaining the approval of the fellow members of their work group than with coming up with good solutions to the tasks at hand.

When I re-read Schlesinger's account I was struck by many further observations that fit into exactly the pattern of concurrence-seeking that has impressed me in my research on other face-to-face groups when a "we" feeling of solidarity is running high. I concluded that a group process was subtly at work in Kennedy's team which prevented the members from debating the real issues posed by the C.I.A.'s plan and from carefully appraising its serious risks.

By now I was sufficiently fascinated by what I called the "groupthink" hypothesis to start looking into similar historic fiascoes. I selected for intensive analysis three that were made during the administrations of three other American presidents: Franklin D. Roosevelt (failure to be prepared for Pearl Harbor), Harry S. Truman (the invasion of North Korea) and Lyndon B. Johnson (escalation of the Vietnam war). Each decision was a group product, issuing from a series of meetings held by a small and cohesive group of government officials and advisers. In each case I found the same kind of detrimental group process that was at work in the Bay of Pigs decision.

Reprinted with permission from *Yale Alumni Magazine,* January 1973. Copyright 1973 by Yale Alumni Publications, Inc.

In my earlier research with ordinary citizens I had been impressed by the effects—both unfavorable and favorable—of the social pressures that develop in cohesive groups: in infantry platoons, air crews, therapy groups, seminars and self-study or encounter groups. Members tend to evolve informal objectives to preserve friendly intra-group relations, and this becomes part of the hidden agenda at their meetings. When conducting research on groups of heavy smokers, for example, at a clinic established to help people stop smoking, I noticed a seemingly irrational tendency for the members to exert pressure on each other to increase their smoking as the time for the final meeting approached. This appeared to be a collusive effort to display mutual dependence and resistance to the termination of the sessions.

Sometimes, even long before the final separation, pressures toward uniformity subverted the fundamental purpose. At the second meeting of one group of smokers, consisting of 12 middle-class American men and women, two of the most dominant members took the position that heavy smoking was an almost incurable addiction. Most of the others soon agreed that nobody could be expected to cut down drastically. One man took issue with this consensus, arguing that he had stopped smoking since joining the group and that everyone else could do the same. His declaration was followed by an angry discussion. Most of the others ganged up against the man who was deviating from the consensus.

At the next meeting the deviant announced that he had made an important decision. "When I joined," he said, "I agreed to follow the two main rules required by the clinic—to make a conscientious effort to stop smoking, and to attend every meeting. But I have learned that you can only follow one of the rules, not both. I will continue to attend every meeting but I have gone back to smoking two packs a day and I won't make any effort to stop again until after the last meeting." Whereupon the other members applauded, welcoming him back to the fold.

No one mentioned that the whole point of the meetings was to help each person to cut down as rapidly as possible. As a psychological consultant to the group, I tried to call this to the members' attention and so did my collaborator, Dr. Michael Kahn. But the members ignored our comments and reiterated their consensus that heavy smoking was an addiction from which no one would be cured except by cutting down gradually over a long period of time.

This episode—an extreme form of groupthink—was only one manifestation of a general pattern that the group displayed. At every meeting the members were amiable, reasserted their warm feelings of solidarity and sought concurrence on every important topic, with no reappearance of the unpleasant bickering that would spoil the cozy atmosphere. This tendency could be maintained, however, only at the expense of ignoring realistic challenges—like those posed by the psychologists.

The term "groupthink" is of the same order as the words in the "newspeak" vocabulary that George Orwell uses in *1984*—a vocabulary with terms such as "doublethink" and "crimethink." By putting "groupthink" with those Orwellian words, I realize that it takes on an invidious connotation. This is intentional: groupthink refers to a deterioration of mental efficiency, reality testing and moral judgment that results from in-group pressures.

When I investigated the Bay of Pigs invasion and other fiascoes, I found that there were at least six major defects in decision-making which contributed to failures to solve problems adequately.

First, the group's discussions were limited to a few alternatives (often only two) without a survey of the full range of alternatives. Second, the members failed to re-examine their initial decision from the standpoint of non-obvious drawbacks that had not been originally considered. Third, they neglected courses of action initially evaluated as unsatisfactory; they almost never discussed whether they had overlooked any nonobvious gains.

Fourth, members made little or no attempt to obtain information from experts who could supply sound estimates of losses and gains to be expected from alternative courses. Fifth, selective bias was shown in the way the members reacted to information and judgments from experts, the media and outside critics; they were only interested in facts and opinions that supported their preferred policy. Finally, they spent little time deliberating how the policy might be hindered by bureaucratic inertia, sabotaged by political opponents or derailed by the accidents that happen to the best of well-laid plans. Consequently, they failed to work out contingency plans to cope with foreseeable setbacks that could endanger their success.

I was surprised by the extent to which the groups involved in these fiascoes adhered to group norms and pressures toward uniformity, even when their policy was working badly and had unintended consequences that disturbed the conscience of the members. Members consider loyalty to the group the highest form of morality. That loyalty requires each member to avoid raising controversial issues, questioning weak arguments or calling a halt to soft-headed thinking.

Paradoxically, soft-headed groups are likely to be extremely hard-hearted toward out-groups and enemies. In dealing with a rival nation, policy-makers constituting an amiable group find it relatively easy to authorize dehumanizing solutions such as large-scale bombings. An affable group of government officials is unlikely to pursue the difficult issues that arise when alternatives to a harsh military solution come up for discussion. Nor are they inclined to raise ethical issues that imply that this "fine group of ours, with its humanitarianism and its high-minded principles, could adopt a course that is inhumane and immoral."

The greater the threat to the self-esteem of the members of a cohesive group, the greater will be their inclination to resort to concurrence-seeking at the expense of critical thinking. Symptoms of groupthink will therefore be found most often when a decision poses a moral dilemma, especially if the most advantageous course requires the policy-makers to violate their own standards of humanitarian behavior. Each member is likely to become more dependent than ever on the in-group for maintaining his self-image as a decent human being and will therefore be more strongly motivated to maintain group unity by striving for concurrence.

Although it is risky to make huge inferential leaps from theory to practice, we should not be inhibited from drawing tentative inferences from these fiascoes. Perhaps the worst mistakes can be prevented if we take steps to avoid the circumstances in which groupthink is most likely to flourish. But all the prescriptive hypotheses that follow must be validated by systematic research before they can be applied with any confidence.

The leader of a policy-forming group should, for example, assign the role of critical evaluator to each member, encouraging the group to give high priority to airing objections and doubts. He should also be impartial at the outset, instead of stating his own preferences and expectations. He should limit his briefings to unbiased statements about the scope of the problem and the limitations of available resources.

The organization should routinely establish several independent planning and evaluation groups to work on the same policy question, each carrying out its deliberations under a different leader.

One or more qualified colleagues within the organization who are not core members of the policy-making group should be invited to each meeting and encouraged to challenge the views of the core members.

At every meeting, at least one member should be assigned the role of devil's advocate, to function like a good lawyer in challenging the testimony of those who advocate the majority position.

Whenever the policy issue involves relations with a rival nation, a sizable block of time should be spent surveying all warning signals from the rivals and constructing alternative scenarios.

After reaching a preliminary consensus the policy-making group should hold a "second chance" meeting at which all the members are expected to express their residual doubts and to rethink the entire issue. They might take as their model a statement made by Alfred P. Sloan, a former chairman of General Motors, at a meeting of policy-makers:

"Gentlemen, I take it we are all in complete agreement on the decision here. Then I propose we postpone further discussion until our next meeting to give ourselves time to develop disagreement and perhaps gain some understanding of what the decision is all about."

It might not be a bad idea for the second-chance meeting to take place in a relaxed atmosphere far from the executive suite, perhaps over drinks. According to a report by Herodotus dating from about 450 B.C., whenever the ancient Persians made a decision following sober deliberations, they would always reconsider the matter under the influence of wine. Tacitus claimed that during Roman times the Germans also had a custom of arriving at each decision twice—once sober, once drunk.

Some institutionalized form of allowing second thoughts to be freely expressed might be remarkably effective for breaking down a false sense of unanimity and related illusions, without endangering anyone's reputation or liver.

PEARL HARBOR: GENIALITY AND SECURITY

On the night of Dec. 6, 1941—just 12 hours before the Japanese struck—Admiral Husband E. Kimmel (Commander in Chief of the Pacific Fleet) attended a dinner party given by his old crony, Rear Admiral H. Fairfax Leary, and his wife. Other members of the in-group of naval commanders and their wives were also present. Seated next to Admiral Kimmel was Fanny Halsey, wife of Admiral Halsey, who had left Hawaii to take his task force to the Far East. Mrs. Halsey said that she was certain the Japanese were going to attack. "She was a brilliant woman," according to Captain Joel Bunkley, who described the party, "but everybody thought she was crazy."

Admiral Leary, at a naval inquiry in 1944, summarized the complacency at that dinner party and at the daily conferences held by Admiral Kimmel during the preceding weeks. When asked whether any thought had been given to the possibility of a surprise attack by the Japanese, he said, "We all felt that the contingency was remote . . . and the feeling strongly existed that the Fleet would have adequate warning of any chance of an air attack." The same attitude was epitomized in testimony given by Captain J. B. Earle, chief of staff, Fourteenth Naval District. "Somehow or other," he said, "we always felt that 'it couldn't happen here.'"

From the consistent testimony given by Admiral Kimmel's advisers, they all acted on the basis of an "unwarranted feeling of immunity from attack," though they had been given a series of impressive warnings that they should be prepared for war with Japan.

Most illuminating of the norm-setting behavior that contributed to the complacency of Kimmel's in-group is a brief exchange between Admiral Kimmel and Lieutenant Commander Layton. Perturbed by the loss of radio contact with the Japanese aircraft carriers, Admiral Kimmel asked Layton on Dec. 1, 1941, to check with the Far East Command for additional information. The next day, discussing the lost carriers again with Layton, he remarked jokingly: "What, you don't know where the carriers are? Do you mean to say that they could be rounding Diamond Head [at Honolulu] and you wouldn't know it?" Layton said he hoped they would be sighted well before that.

This exchange implies an "atmosphere of geniality and security." Having relegated the Japanese threat to the category of laughing matters, the admiral was making it clear that he would be inclined to laugh derisively at anyone who thought otherwise. "I did not at any time suggest," Layton later acknowledged at a Congressional hearing, "that the Japanese carriers were under radio silence approaching Oahu. I wish I had."

But the admiral's foolish little joke may have induced Layton to remain silent about any vague, lingering doubts he may have had. Either man would risk the scornful laughter of the other—whether expressed to his face or behind his back—if he were to express second thoughts such as, "Seriously, though, shouldn't we do something about the slight possibility that those carriers might *really* be headed this way?" Because this ominous inference was never drawn, not a single reconnaissance plane was sent out to the north of the Hawaiian Islands, allowing the Japanese to win the incredible gamble they were taking in trying to send their aircraft carriers within bombing distance of Pearl Harbor without being detected.

That joking exchange was merely the visible part of a huge iceberg of solid faith in Pearl Harbor's invulnerability. If a few warm advocates of preparedness had been within the Navy group, steamed up by the accumulating warning signals, they might have been able to melt it. But they would certainly have had a cold reception. To urge a full alert would have required presenting unwelcome arguments that countered the myth of Pearl Harbor's impregnability. Anyone who was tempted to do so knew that he would be deviating from the group norm: the others were likely to consider him "crazy," just as the in-group regarded Mrs. Halsey at the dinner party on the eve of the disaster when she announced her deviant opinion that the Japanese would attack.

ESCALATION IN VIETNAM: HOW COULD IT HAPPEN?

A highly revealing episode occurred soon after Robert McNamara told a Senate committee some impressive facts about the ineffectiveness of the bombings. President Johnson made a number of bitter comments about McNamara's statement. "That military genius, McNamara, has gone dovish on me," he complained to one Senator. To someone in his White House staff he spoke even more heatedly, accusing McNamara of playing into the hands of the enemy. He drew the analogy of "a man trying to sell his house while one of his sons went to the prospective buyer to point out that there were leaks in the basement."

This strongly suggests that Johnson regarded his in-group of policy advisers as a family and its leading dissident member as an irresponsible son who was sabotaging the family's interest. Underlying this revealing imagery are two implicit assumptions that epitomize groupthink: We are a good group, so any deceitful acts that we perpetrate are fully justified. Anyone who is unwilling to distort the truth to help us is disloyal.

This is only one of the many examples of how groupthink was manifested in Johnson's inner circle.

A PERFECT FIASCO: THE BAY OF PIGS

Why did President Kennedy's main advisers, whom he had selected as core members of his team, fail to pursue the issues sufficiently to discover the shaky ground on which the faulty assumptions of the Cuban invasion plan rested? Why didn't they pose a barrage of penetrating and embarrassing questions to the representatives of the C.I.A. and the Joint Chiefs of Staff? Why were they taken in by the incomplete and inconsistent answers they were given in response to the relatively few critical questions they raised?

Schlesinger says that "for all the utter irrationality with which retrospect endowed the project, it had a certain queer logic at the time as it emerged from the bowels of government." Why? What was the source of the "queer logic" with which the plan was endowed? If the available accounts describe the deliberations accurately, many typical symptoms of groupthink can be discerned among the members of the Kennedy team: an illusion of invulnerability, a collective effort to rationalize their decision, an unquestioned belief in the group's inherent morality, a stereotyped view of enemy leaders as too evil to warrant genuine attempts to negotiate, and the emergence of self-appointed mind-guards.

Robert Kennedy, for example, who had been constantly informed about the Cuban invasion plan, asked Schlesinger privately why he was opposed. The President's brother listened coldly and then said: "You may be right or you may be wrong, but the President has made his mind up. Don't push it any further. Now is the time for everyone to help him all they can."

Here is a symptom of groupthink, displayed by a highly intelligent man whose ethical code committed him to freedom of dissent.

Robert Kennedy was functioning in a self-appointed role that I call being a "mind-guard." Just as a bodyguard protects the President and other high officials from physical harm, a mindguard protects them from thoughts that might damage their confidence in the soundness of the policies which they are about to launch.

CRITICAL THINKING QUESTIONS

1. How common is groupthink? Do you think that the conditions that give rise to groupthink are relatively rare or relatively common? Explain your answers. Cite additional examples of decisions that may have been influenced by groupthink.

2. Have you ever been involved in a group that experienced some sort of groupthink process? Describe the situation, and discuss the process in terms of groupthink.

3. If groupthink is common, then it would be useful if people were made aware of how it works. Should the conditions of groupthink, as well as how it can be prevented, be taught to leaders and potential leaders? How could this be accomplished?

4. The article gave some suggestions as to how groupthink could be prevented or at least minimized. Would all leaders be equally open to following these suggestions? Or might individual characteristics influence how open various leaders might be? How so?

ARTICLE 35 _____

Whenever two or more individuals act as a group, a central part of the interaction may involve trying to reach some agreement about an issue or activity. When the group consists of individuals or nations, reaching agreement is often a major concern.

Bargaining is one form that such negotiations take. The bargaining may be about something small and be informal in style, such as a couple deciding on which movie to see, or it may be major and formal, such as two nations trying to reach an agreement on nuclear arms control. In either case, central to the bargaining is the belief by both parties that reaching a mutually agreed upon solution will possibly benefit both of them.

Two broad approaches to bargaining are cooperation and competition. In a *competitive* situation, individuals or groups view the situation in "win-lose" terms: I want to win, and it most likely will be at your expense. In a *cooperative* arrangement, the situation is more likely to be viewed as a "win-win" opportunity: We can both get something good out of this; neither one has to lose. Other things being equal, a cooperative strategy is more likely to ensure a good outcome for all concerned. But is that the strategy most likely to be used? Or do individuals and groups tend to use competitive strategies instead, even if it might not ultimately be in their best interest to do so?

The following classic contribution by Morton Deutsch and Robert M. Krauss examines the effect of threat on interpersonal bargaining. One major finding of the study is that the presence of threat, as well as whether only one or both parties are capable of threat, has a major impact on the outcome of the bargaining situation. Common sense might suggest that if my opponent has some threat that he or she can use against me, then I would be better off having the same level of threat to use against him or her, rather than having no threat to retaliate with. The findings of the study do not confirm this expectation, however, and may suggest a rethinking of the use of threat and power in real-world negotiations.

The Effect of Threat
upon Interpersonal Bargaining

■ Morton Deutsch and Robert M. Krauss

A bargain is defined in *Webster's Unabridged Dictionary* as "an agreement between parties settling what each shall give and receive in a transaction between them"; it is further specified that a bargain is "an agreement or compact viewed as advantageous or the reverse." When the term "agreement" is broadened to include tacit, informal agreements as well as explicit agreements, it is evident that bargains and the processes involved in arriving at bargains ("bargaining") are pervasive characteristics of social life.

The definition of bargain fits under sociological definitions of the term "social norm." In this light, the experimental study of the bargaining process and of bargaining outcomes provides a means for the laboratory study of the development of certain types of social norms. But unlike many other types of social situations, bargaining situations have certain distinctive features that make it relevant to consider the conditions that determine whether or not a social norm will develop as well as those that determine the nature

Reprinted from *Journal of Personality and Social Psychology,* 1960, *61,* 181–189.

of the social norm if it develops. Bargaining situations highlight the possibility that, even where cooperation would be mutually advantageous, shared purposes may not develop, agreement may not be reached, and interaction may be regulated antagonistically rather than normatively.

The essential features of a bargaining situation exist when:

1. Both parties perceive that there is the possibility of reaching an agreement in which each party would be better off, or no worse off, than if no agreement were reached.
2. Both parties perceive that there is more than one such agreement that could be reached.
3. Both parties perceive each other to have conflicting preferences or opposed interests with regard to the different agreements that might be reached.

Everyday examples of bargaining include such situations as: the buyer-seller relationship when the price is not fixed, the husband and wife who want to spend an evening out together but have conflicting preferences about where to go, union-management negotiations, drivers who meet at an intersection when there is no clear right of way, disarmament negotiations.

In terms of our prior conceptualization of cooperation and competition (Deutsch, 1949) bargaining is thus a situation in which the participants have mixed motives toward one another: on the one hand, each has interest in cooperating so that they reach an agreement; on the other hand, they have competitive interests concerning the nature of the agreement they reach. In effect, to reach agreement the cooperative interest of the bargainers must be strong enough to overcome their competitive interests. However, agreement is not only contingent upon the *motivational* balances of cooperative to competitive interests but also upon the situational and *cognitive* factors which facilitate or hinder the recognition or invention of a bargaining agreement that reduces the opposition of interest and enhances the mutuality of interest.[1]

These considerations lead to the formulation of two general, closely related propositions about the likelihood that a bargaining agreement will be reached.

1. Bargainers are more likely to reach an agreement, the stronger are their cooperative interests in comparison with their competitive interests.
2. Bargainers are more likely to reach an agreement, the more resources they have available for recognizing or inventing potential bargaining agreements and for communicating to one another once a potential agreement has been recognized or invented.

From these two basic propositions and additional hypotheses concerning conditions that determine the strengths of the cooperative and competitive interests and the amount of available resources, we believe it is possible to explain the ease or difficulty of arriving at a bargaining agreement. We shall not present a full statement of these hypotheses here but turn instead to a description of an experiment that relates to Proposition 1.

The experiment was concerned with the effect of the availability of threat upon bargaining in a two-person experimental bargaining game.[2] Threat is defined as the expression of an intention to do something detrimental to the interests of another. Our experiment was guided by two assumptions about threat:

1. If there is a conflict of interest and one person is able to threaten the other, he will tend to use the threat in an attempt to force the other person to yield. This tendency should be stronger, the more irreconcilable the conflict is perceived to be.
2. If a person uses threat in an attempt to intimidate another, the threatened person (if he considers himself to be of equal or superior status) would feel hostility toward the threatener and tend to respond with counterthreat and/or increased resistance to yielding. We qualify this assumption by stating that the tendency to resist should be greater, the greater the perceived probability and magnitude of detriment to the other and the less the perceived probability and magnitude of detriment to the potential resister from the anticipated resistance to yielding.

The second assumption is based upon the view that when resistance is not seen to be suicidal or useless, to allow oneself to be intimidated, particularly by someone who does not have the right to expect deferential behavior, is to suffer a loss of social face and, hence, of self-esteem: and that the culturally defined way of maintaining self-esteem in the face of attempted intimidation is to engage in a contest for supremacy vis-à-vis the power to intimidate or, minimally, to resist intimidation. Thus, in effect, the use of threat (and if it is available to be used, there will be a tendency to use it) should strengthen the competitive interests of the bargainers in relationship to one another by introducing or enhancing the competitive struggle for self-esteem. Hence, from Proposition 1, it follows that the availability of a means of threat should make it more difficult for the bargainers to reach agreement (providing that the threatened person has some means of resisting the threat). The preceding statement is relevant to the comparison of both of our experimental conditions of threat, bilateral and unilateral (described below), with our experimental condition of nonthreat. We hypothesize that a bargaining agreement is more likely to be achieved when neither party can threaten the other, than when one or both parties can threaten the other.

Consider now the situations of bilateral threat and unilateral threat. For several reasons, a situation of bilateral threat is probably less conducive to agreement than is a condition of unilateral threat. First, the sheer likelihood that a threat will be made is greater when two people rather than one have the means of making the threat. Secondly, once a threat is made in the bilateral case it is likely to evoke counterthreat. Withdrawal of threat in the face of counterthreat probably involves more loss of face (for reasons analogous to those discussed in relation to yielding to intimidation) than does withdrawal of threat in the face of resistance to threat. Finally, in the unilateral case, although the person without the threat potential can resist and not yield to the threat, his position vis-à-vis the other is not so strong as the position of the threatened person in the bilateral case. In the unilateral case, the threatened person may have a worse outcome than the other whether he resists or yields; while in the bilateral case, the threatened person is sure to have a worse outcome if he yields but he may insure that he does not have a worse outcome if he does not yield.

METHOD

Procedure

Subjects (*S*s) were asked to imagine that they were in charge of a trucking company, carrying merchandise over a road to a destination. For each trip completed they made $.60, minus their operating expenses. Operating expenses were calculated at the rate of one cent per second. So, for example, if it took 37 seconds to complete a particular trip, the player's profit would be $.60 – $.37 or a net profit of $.23 for that particular trip.

Each *S* was assigned a name, Acme or Bolt. As the "road map" (see Figure 1) indicates, both players start from separate points and go to separate destinations. At one point their paths cross. This is the section of road labeled "one lane road," which is only one lane wide, so that two trucks, heading in opposite directions, could not pass each other. If one backs up the other can go forward, or both can back up, or both can sit there head-on without moving.

There is another way for each *S* to reach the destination on the map, labeled the "alternate route." The two players' paths do not cross on this route, but the alternative is 56% longer than the main route. *S*s were told that they could expect to lose at least $.10 each time they used the alternate route.

At either end of the one-lane section there is a gate that is under the control of the player to whose starting point it is closest. By closing the gate, one player can prevent the other from traveling over that section of the main route. The use of the gate provides the threat potential in this game. In the bilateral threat potential condition (Two Gates) both players had gates under their control. In a second condition of unilateral threat (One Gate) Acme had control of a gate but Bolt did not. In a third condition (No Gates) neither player controlled a gate.

*S*s played the game seated in separate booths placed so that they could not see each other but could see the experimenter (*E*). Each *S* had a "control panel" mounted on a 12" x 18" x 12" sloping-front cabinet (see Figure 2). The apparatus consisted essentially of a reversible impulse computer that was pulsed by a recycling timer. When the *S* wanted to move her truck forward she threw a key that closed a circuit pulsing the "add" coil of the impulse counter mounted on her

FIGURE 1 / Subject's Road Map

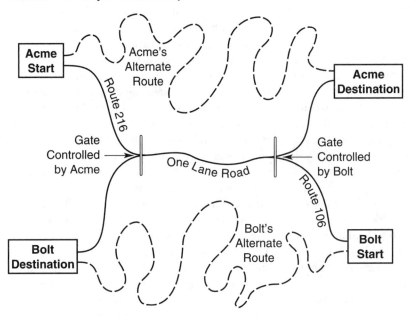

FIGURE 2 / Subject's Control Panel

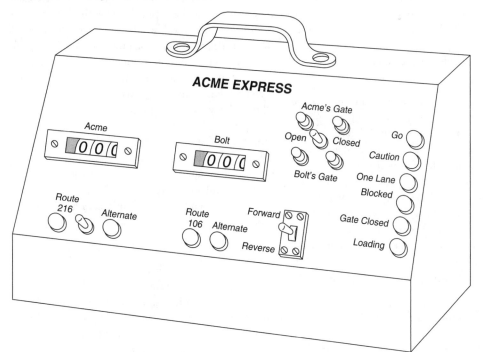

control panel. As the counter cumulated, *S* was able to determine her "position" by relating the number on her counter to reference numbers that had been written in on her road map. Similarly, when she wished to reverse, she would throw a switch that activated the "subtract" coil of her counter, thus subtracting from the total on the counter each time the timer cycled.

S's counter was connected in parallel to counters on the other *S*'s panel and on *E*'s panel. Thus each player had two counters on her panel, one representing her own position and the other representing the other player's. Provision was made in construction of the apparatus to permit cutting the other player's counter out of the circuit, so that each *S* knew only the position of her own truck. This was done in the present experiment. Experiments now in progress are studying the effects of knowledge of the other person's position and other aspects of interpersonal communication upon the bargaining process.

The only time one player definitely knew the other player's position was when they had met head-on on the one-way section of road. This was indicated by a traffic light mounted on the panel. When this light was on, neither player could move forward unless the other moved back. The gates were controlled by toggle switches and panel-mounted indicator lights showed, for both *S*s, whether each gate was open or closed.

The following "rules of the game" were stated to the *S*s:

1. A player who started out on one route and wished to switch to the other route could only do so after first reversing and going back to the start position. Direct transfer from one route to the other was not permitted except at the start position.
2. In the conditions where *S*s had gates, they were permitted to close the gates no matter where they were on the main route, so long as they were on the main route (i.e., they were not permitted to close the gate while on the alternate route or after having reached their destinations). However, *S*s were permitted to open their gates at any point in the game.

*S*s were taken through a number of practice exercises to familiarize them with the game. In the first trial they were made to meet head-on on the one-lane

path; Acme was then told to back up until she was just off the one-lane path and Bolt was told to go forward. After Bolt had gone through the one-lane path, Acme was told to go forward. Each continued going forward until each arrived at her destination. The second practice trial was the same as the first except that Bolt rather than Acme backed up after meeting head-on. In the next practice trial, one of the players was made to wait just before the one-way path while the other traversed it and then was allowed to continue. In the next practice trial, one player was made to take the alternate route and the other was made to take the main route. Finally, in the bilateral and unilateral threat conditions the use of the gate was illustrated (by having the player get on the main route, close the gate, and then go back and take the alternate route). The *S*s were told explicitly, with emphasis, that they did *not* have to use the gate. Before each trial in the game the gate or gates were in the open position.

The instructions stressed an individualistic motivation orientation. *S*s were told to try to earn as much money for themselves as possible and to have no interest in whether the other player made money or lost money. They were given $4.00 in poker chips to represent their working capital and told that after each trial they would be given "money" if they made a profit or that "money" would be taken from them if they lost (i.e., took more than 60 seconds to complete their trip). The profit or loss of each *S* was announced so that both *S*s could hear the announcement after each trial. Each pair of *S*s played a total of 20 trials; on all trials, they started off together. In other words each trial presented a repetition of the same bargaining problem. In cases where *S*s lost their working capital before the 20 trials were completed, additional chips were given them. *S*s were aware that their monetary winnings and losses were to be imaginary and that no money would change hands as a result of the experiment.

Subjects

Sixteen pairs of *S*s were used in each of the three experimental conditions. The *S*s were female clerical and supervisory personnel of the New Jersey Bell Telephone Company who volunteered to participate during their working day.[3] Their ages ranged from 20 to

39, with a mean of 26.2. All were naive to the purpose of the experiment. By staggering the arrival times and choosing girls from different locations, we were able to insure that the *S*s did not know with whom they were playing.

Data Recorded

Several types of data were collected. We obtained a record of the profit or loss of each *S* on each trial. We also obtained a detailed recording of the actions taken by each *S* during the course of a trial. For this purpose, we used an Esterline-Angus model AW Operations Recorder which enabled us to obtain a "log" of each move each *S* made during the game (e.g., whether and when she took the main or alternate route; when she went forward, backward, or remained still; when she closed and opened the gate; when she arrived at her destination).

RESULTS[4]

The best single measure of the difficulty experienced by the bargainers in reaching an agreement is the sum of each pair's profits (or losses) on a given trial. The higher the sum of the payoffs to the two players on a given trial, the less time it took them to arrive at a procedure for sharing the one-lane path of the main route. (It was, of course, possible for one or both of the players to decide to take the alternate route so as to avoid a protracted stalemate during the process of bargaining. This, however, always results in at least a $.20 smaller joint payoff if only one player took the alternate route, than an optimally arrived at agreement concerning the use of the one-way path.) Figure 3 presents the medians of the summed payoffs (i.e., Acme's plus Bolt's) for all pairs in each of the three experimental conditions over the 20 trials.[5] These striking results indicate that agreement was least difficult to arrive at in the no threat condition, was more difficult to arrive at in the unilateral threat condition, and exceedingly difficult or impossible to arrive at in the bilateral threat condition (see also Table 1).

Examination of Figure 3 suggests that learning occurred during the 20 trials: the summed payoffs for pairs of *S*s tend to improve as the number of trials increases. This suggestion is confirmed by an analysis

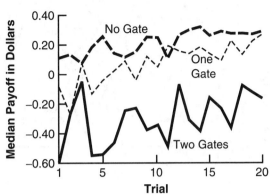

FIGURE 3 / Median Joint Payoff (Acme + Bolt) over Trials

of variance of the slopes for the summed payoffs[6] over the 20 trials for each of the 16 pairs in each of the 3 experimental treatments. The results of this analysis indicate that the slopes are significantly greater than zero for the unilateral threat ($p < .01$) and the no threat ($p < .02$) conditions; for the bilateral threat condition, the slope does not reach statistical significance ($.10 < p < .20$). The data indicate that the pairs in the no threat condition started off at a fairly high level but, even so, showed some improvement over the 20 trials; the pairs in the unilateral threat condition started off low and, having considerable opportunity for improvement, used their opportunity; the pairs in the bilateral threat condition, on the other hand, did not benefit markedly from repeated trials.

Figure 4 compares Acme's median profit in the three experimental conditions over the 20 trials; while Figure 5 compares Bolt's profit in the three conditions. (In the unilateral threat condition, it was Acme who controlled a gate and Bolt who did not.) Bolt's as well as Acme's outcome is somewhat better in the no threat condition than in the unilateral threat condition; Acme's, as well as Bolt's, outcome is clearly worst in the bilateral threat condition (see Table 1 also). However, Figure 6 reveals that Acme does somewhat better than Bolt in the unilateral condition. Thus, if threat-potential exists within a bargaining relationship it is better to possess it oneself than to have the other party possess it. However, it is even better for neither party to possess it. Moreover, Figure 5 shows that Bolt is better off not having than having a gate even when

FIGURE 4 / Acme's Median Payoff

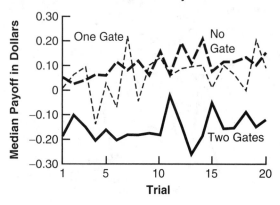

FIGURE 5 / Bolt's Median Payoff

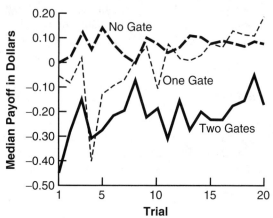

Acme has a gate: Bolt tends to do better in the unilateral threat condition than in the bilateral threat condition.

The size of the absolute discrepancy between the payoffs of the two players in each pair provides a measure of the confusion or difficulty in predicting what the other player was going to do. Thus, a large absolute discrepancy might indicate that after one player had gone through the one-way path and left it open, the other player continued to wait; or it might indicate that one player continued to wait at a closed gate hoping the other player would open it quickly but the other player did not; etc. Figure 7 indicates that the discrepancy between players in the no threat condition is initially small and remains small for the 20 trials. For the players in both the bilateral and unilateral threat conditions, the discrepancy is initially

relatively larger; but it decreases more noticeably in the unilateral threat condition by the tenth trial and, therefore, is consistently smaller than in the bilateral condition.

By way of concrete illustration, we present a synopsis of the game for one pair in each of three experimental treatments.

No Threat Condition

Trial 1 The players met in the center of the one-way section. After some back-and-forth movement Bolt reversed to the end of the one-way section, allowing Acme to pass through, and then proceeded forward herself.

TABLE 1 / Mean Payoffs Summated over the Twenty Trials

	Means			Statistical Comparisons: p values[a]			
Variable	(1) No Threat	(2) Unilateral Threat	(3) Bilateral Threat	Overall	(1) vs. (2)	(1) vs. (3)	(2) vs. (3)
Summed Payoffs (Acme + Bolt)	203.31	−405.88	−875.12	.01	.01	.01	.05
Acme's Payoff	122.44	−118.56	−406.56	.01	.10	.01	.05
Bolt's Payoff	80.88	−287.31	−468.56	.01	.01	.01	.20
Absolute Differences in Payoff (A − B)	125.94	294.75	315.25	.05	.05	.01	*ns*

[a]Evaluation of the significance of overall variation between conditions is based on an *F* test with 2 and 45 *df.*
Comparisons between treatments are based on a two-tailed *t* test.

FIGURE 6 / Acme's and Bolt's Median Payoffs in Unilateral Threat Condition

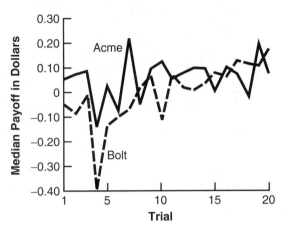

FIGURE 7 / Median Absolute Differences in Payoff

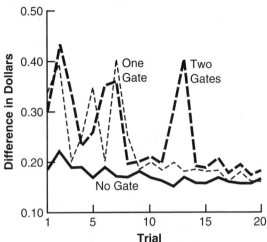

Trial 2   They again met at the center of the one-way path. This time, after moving back and forth dead-locked for some time, Bolt reversed to "start" and took the alternate route to her destination, thus leaving Acme free to go through on the main route.

Trial 3   The players again met at the center of the one-way path. This time, however, Acme reversed to the beginning of the path, allowing Bolt to go through to her destination. Then Acme was able to proceed forward on the main route.

Trial 5   Both players elected to take the alternate route to their destinations.

Trial 7   Both players took the main route and met in the center. They waited, deadlocked, for a consider-able time. Then Acme reversed to the end of the one-way path allowing Bolt to go through, then proceeded through to her destination.

Trials 10–20   Acme and Bolt fall into a pattern of alternating who is to go first on the one-way section. There is no deviation from this pattern.

The only other pattern that emerges in this condi-tion is one in which one player dominates the other. That is, one player consistently goes first on the one-way section and the other player consistently yields.

Unilateral Threat Condition

Trial 1   Both players took the main route and met in the center of it. Acme immediately closed the gate, reversed to "start," and took the alternate route to her destination. Bolt waited for a few seconds, at the closed gate, then reversed and took the alternate route.

Trial 2   Both players took the main route and met in the center. After moving back and forth deadlocked for about 15 seconds, Bolt reversed to the beginning of the one-way path, allowed Acme to pass, and then proceeded forward to her destination.

Trial 3   Both players started out on the main route, meeting in the center. After moving back and forth deadlocked for a while, Acme closed her gate, reversed to "start," and took the alternate route. Bolt, mean-while, waited at the closed gate. When Acme arrived at her destination she opened the gate, and Bolt went through to complete her trip.

Trial 5   Both players took the main route, meeting at the center of the one-way section. Acme immedi-ately closed her gate, reversed, and took the alternate route. Bolt waited at the gate for about 10 seconds, then reversed and took the alternate route to her destination.

Trial 10 Both players took the main route and met in the center. Acme closed her gate, reversed, and took the alternate route. Bolt remained waiting at the closed gate. After Acme arrived at her destination, she opened the gate and Bolt completed her trip.

Trial 15 Acme took the main route to her destination and Bolt took the alternate route.

Trials 17–20 Both players took the main route and met in the center. Bolt waited a few seconds, then reversed to the end of the one-way section allowing Acme to go through. Then Bolt proceeded forward to her destination.

Other typical patterns that developed in this experimental condition included an alternating pattern similar to that described in the no threat condition, a dominating pattern in which Bolt would select the alternate route leaving Acme free to use the main route unobstructed, and a pattern in which Acme would close her gate and then take the alternate route, also forcing Bolt to take the alternate route.

Bilateral Threat Condition

Trial 1 Acme took the main route and Bolt took the alternate route.

Trial 2 Both players took the main route and met head-on. Bolt closed her gate. Acme waited a few seconds, then closed her gate, reversed to "start," then went forward again to the closed gate. Acme reversed and took the alternate route. Bolt again reversed, then started on the alternate route. Acme opened her gate and Bolt reversed to "start" and went to her destination on the main route.

Trial 3 Acme took the alternate route to her destination. Bolt took the main route and closed her gate before entering the one-way section.

Trial 5 Both players took the main route and met head-on. After about 10 seconds spent backing up and going forward, Acme closed her gate, reversed, and took the alternate route. After waiting a few seconds, Bolt did the same.

Trials 8–10 Both players started out on the main route, immediately closed their gates, reversed to "start," and took the alternate route to their destinations.

Trial 15 Both players started out on the main route and met head-on. After some jockeying for position, Acme closed her gate, reversed, and took the alternate route to her destination. After waiting at the gate for a few seconds, Bolt reversed to "start" and took the alternate route to her destination.

Trials 19–20 Both players started out on the main route, immediately closed their gates, reversed to "start," and took the alternate routes to their destinations.

Other patterns that emerged in the bilateral threat condition included alternating first use of the one-way section, one player's dominating the other on first use of the one-way section, and another dominating pattern in which one player consistently took the main route while the other consistently took the alternate route.

DISCUSSION

From our view of bargaining as a situation in which both cooperative and competitive tendencies are present and acting upon the individual, it is relevant to inquire as to the conditions under which a stable agreement of any form develops. However, implicit in most economic models of bargaining (e.g., Stone, 1958; Zeuthen, 1930) is the assumption that the cooperative interests of the bargainers are sufficiently strong to insure that some form of mutually satisfactory agreement will be reached. For this reason, such models have focused upon the form of the agreement reached by the bargainers. Siegel and Fouraker (1960) report a series of bargaining experiments quite different in structure from ours in which only one of many pairs of *S*s were unable to reach agreement. Siegel and Fouraker explain this rather startling result as follows:

> *Apparently the disruptive forces which lead to the rupture of some negotiations were at least partially controlled in our sessions. . . .*

Some negotiations collapse when one party becomes incensed at the other, and henceforth strives to maximize his opponent's displeasure rather than his own satisfaction. . . . Since it is difficult to transmit insults by means of quantitative bids, such disequilibrating behavior was not induced in the present studies. If subjects were allowed more latitude in their communications and interactions, the possibility of an affront offense-punitive behavior sequence might be increased (p. 100).

In our experimental bargaining situation, the availability of threat clearly made it more difficult for bargainers to reach a mutually profitable agreement. These results, we believe, reflect psychological tendencies that are not confined to our bargaining situation: the tendency to use threat (if the means for threatening is available) in an attempt to force the other person to yield, when the other is seen as obstructing one's path; the tendency to respond with counterthreat or increased resistance to attempts at intimidation. How general are these tendencies? What conditions are likely to elicit them? Answers to these questions are necessary before our results can be generalized to other situations.

Dollard, Doob, Miller, Mowrer, and Sears (1939) have cited a variety of evidence to support the view that aggression (i.e., the use of threat) is a common reaction to a person who is seen as the agent of frustration. There seems to be little reason to doubt that the use of threat is a frequent reaction to interpersonal impasses. However, everyday observation indicates that threat does not inevitably occur when there is an interpersonal impasse. We would speculate that it is most likely to occur: when the threatener has no positive interest in the other person's welfare (he is either egocentrically or competitively related to the other); when the threatener believes that the other has no positive interest in his welfare; and when the threatener anticipates either that his threat will be effective or, if ineffective, will not worsen his situation because he expects the worst to happen if he does not use his threat. We suggest that these conditions were operative in our experiment; Ss were either egocentrically or competitively oriented to one another[7] and they felt that they would not be worse off by the use of threat.

Everyday observation suggests that the tendency to respond with counterthreat or increased resistance to attempts at intimidation is also a common occurrence. We believe that introducing threat into a bargaining situation affects the meaning of yielding. Although we have no data to support this interpretation directly, we will attempt to justify it on the basis of some additional assumptions.

Goffman (1955) has pointed out the pervasive significance of "face" in the maintenance of the social order. In this view, self-esteem is a socially validated system that grows out of the acceptance by others of the claim for deference, prestige, and recognition that a person presents in his behavior toward others. Since the rejection of such a claim would be perceived (by the recipient) as directed against his self-esteem, he must react against it rather than accept it in order to maintain the integrity of his self-esteem system.

One may view the behavior of our Ss as an attempt to make claims upon the other, an attempt to develop a set of shared expectations as to what each was entitled to. Why then did the Ss' reactions differ so markedly as a function of the availability of threat? The explanation lies, we believe, in the cultural interpretation of yielding (to a peer or subordinate) under duress, as compared to giving in without duress. The former, we believe, is perceived as a negatively valued form of behavior, with negative implications for the self-image of the person who so behaves. At least partly, this is so because the locus of causality is perceived to be outside the person's voluntary control. No such evaluation, however, need be placed on the behavior of one who "gives in" in a situation where no threat or duress is a factor. Rather, we should expect the culturally defined evaluation of such a person's behavior to be one of "reasonableness" or "maturity," because the source of the individual's behavior is perceived to lie within his own control.

Our discussion so far has suggested that the psychological factors which operate in our experimental bargaining situation are to be found in many real-life bargaining situations. However, it is well to recognize some unique features of our experimental game. First, the bargainers had no opportunity to communicate verbally with one another. Prior research on the role of communication in trust (Deutsch, 1958, 1960; Loomis, 1959) suggests that the opportunity for communication would have made reaching an agreement easier for individualistically-oriented bargainers. This same research (Deutsch, 1960) indicates, however, that communication may not be effective between competitively oriented bargainers. This possibility was expressed spontaneously by a number of our Ss in a post-game interview.

Another characteristic of our bargaining game is that the passage of time, without coming to an agreement, is costly to the players. There are, of course, bargaining situations in which lack of agreement may simply preserve the *status quo* without any worsening of the bargainers' respective situations. This is the case in the typical bilateral monopoly case, where the buyer and seller are unable to agree upon a price (e.g., see Siegel & Fouraker, 1960). In other sorts of bargaining situations, however, (e.g., labor-management negotiations during a strike, international negotiations during an expensive cold war) the passage of time may play an important role. In our experiment, we received the impression that the meaning of time changed as time passed without the bargainers reaching an agreement. Initially, the passage of time seemed to place the players under pressure to come to an agreement before their costs mounted sufficiently to destroy their profit. With the continued passage of time, however, their mounting losses strengthened their resolution not to yield to the other player. They comment: "I've lost so much, I'll be damned if I give in now. At least I'll have the satisfaction of doing better than she does." The mounting losses and continued deadlock seemed to change the game from a mixed motive into a predominantly competitive situation.

It is, of course, hazardous to generalize from a laboratory experiment to the complex problems of the real world. But our experiment and the theoretical ideas underlying it can perhaps serve to emphasize some notions which, otherwise, have an intrinsic plausibility. In brief, these are that there is more safety in cooperative than in competitive coexistence, that it is dangerous for bargainers to have weapons, and that it is possibly even more dangerous for a bargainer to have the capacity to retaliate in kind than not to have this capacity when the other bargainer has a weapon. This last statement assumes that the one who yields has more of his values preserved by accepting the agreement preferred by the other than by extended conflict. Of course, in some bargaining situations in the real world, the loss incurred by yielding may exceed the losses due to extended conflict.

SUMMARY

The nature of bargaining situations was discussed. Two general propositions about the conditions affecting the likelihood of a bargaining agreement were presented. The effects of the availability of threat upon interpersonal bargaining were investigated experimentally in a two-person bargaining game. Three experimental conditions were employed: no threat (neither player could threaten the other), unilateral threat (only one of the players had a means of threat available to her), and bilateral threat (both players could threaten each other). The results indicated that the difficulty in reaching an agreement and the amount of (imaginary) money lost, individually as well as collectively, was greatest in the bilateral and next greatest in the unilateral threat condition. Only in the no threat condition did the players make an overall profit. In the unilateral threat condition, the player with the threat capability did better than the player without the threat capability. However, comparing the bilateral and unilateral threat conditions, the results also indicate that when facing a player who had threat capability one was better off *not* having than having the capacity to retaliate in kind.

REFERENCES

Deutsch, M. A theory of cooperation and competition. *Hum. Relat.,* 1949, *2,* 129–152.

Deutsch, M. Trust and suspicion. *J. conflict Resolut.,* 1958, *2,* 265–279.

Deutsch, M. The effect of motivational orientation upon trust and suspicion. *Hum. Relat.,* 1960, *13,* 123–140.

Dollard, J., Doob, L. W., Miller, N. E., Mowrer, O. H., & Sears, R. H. *Frustration and aggression.* New Haven: Yale Univer. Press, 1939.

Goffman, E. On face-work, *Psychiatry,* 1955, *18,* 213–231.

Loomis, J. L. Communication, the development of trust and cooperative behavior. *Hum. Relat.,* 1959, *12,* 305–315.

Schelling, T. C. Bargaining, communication and limited war. *J. conflict Resolut.,* 1957, *1,* 19–38.

Schelling, T. C. The strategy of conflict: Prospectus for the reorientation of game theory. *J. conflict Resolut.*, 1958, *2*, 203–264.

Siegel, S., & Fouraker, L. E. *Bargaining and group decision making.* New York: McGraw-Hill, 1960.

Stone, J. J. An experiment in bargaining games. *Econometrica*, 1958, *26*, 286–296.

Zeuthen, F. *Problems of monopoly and economic warfare.* London: Routledge, 1930.

NOTES

1. Schelling in a series of stimulating papers on bargaining (1957, 1958) has also stressed the "mixed motive" character of bargaining situations and has analyzed some of the cognitive factors which determine agreements.

2. The game was conceived and originated by M. Deutsch; R. M. Krauss designed and constructed the apparatus employed in the experiment.

3. We are indebted to the New Jersey Bell Telephone Company for their cooperation in providing *S*s and facilities for the experiment.

4. We are indebted to M. J. R. Healy for suggestions concerning the statistical analysis of our data.

5. Medians are used in graphic presentation of our results because the wide variability of means makes inspection cumbersome.

6. A logarithmic transformation of the summed payoffs on each trial for each pair was made before computing the slopes for a given pair.

7. A post-experimental questionnaire indicated that, in all three experimental conditions, the *S*s were most strongly motivated to win money, next most strongly motivated to do better than the other player, next most motivated to "have fun," and were very little or not at all motivated to help the other player.

CRITICAL THINKING QUESTIONS

1. For many years, the mutually assured destruction (MAD) policy defined U.S. nuclear strategy. That is, nuclear war was to be prevented by the threat of assured destruction of the aggressor nation. What might be the implications of this study for the nuclear policies of nations?

2. The best performance in this study was obtained in the no-threat condition; the unilateral threat condition, in turn, produced better results than the bilateral threat condition, which did the worst. To what extent are these findings generalizable to other situations? In some situations, might it be best to have bilateral threat instead of unilateral threat? What variables might be important in determining when each would be preferred? Explain.

3. In an area such as international relations, how can the existence of threat be reduced? What role may communication play in the process?

ADDITIONAL RELATED READINGS

Anderhub, V., Guth, W., & Marchand, N. (2004). Early or late conflict settlement in a variety of games—An experimental study. *Journal of Economic Psychology, 25*(2), 177–194.

Chudhuri, A., Kahn, S. A., Lakshmiratan, A., Py, A., & Shah, L. (2003). Trust and trustworthiness in a sequential bargaining game. *Journal of Behavioral Decision Making, 16*(5), 331–340.

ARTICLE 36 _____

Article 34 in this chapter presented the concept known as *groupthink*. Since Irving L. Janis proposed this hypothesis over 30 years ago, he and others have continued to refine understanding of the antecedent conditions, symptoms, and consequences of groupthink. Since its introduction, groupthink has been widely studied and broadly incorporated into the literature and knowledge base, not only in the field of social psychology but also in areas such as management and organizational behavior.

Since the concept of groupthink provides the information necessary for identifying its causes as well as its symptoms, we would hope that the occurrence of groupthink would diminish. After all, the concept includes recommendations for decreasing the likelihood of its development. Unfortunately, that might not be the case.

The following article by Gregory Moorhead, Richard Ference, and Chris P. Neck applies the groupthink concept to the ill-fated decision to launch the space shuttle *Challenger* in 1986. The implication that the ensuing tragedy could have been prevented had groupthink not prevailed in the decision to launch is indeed sobering.

Group Decision Fiascoes Continue
Space Shuttle *Challenger* and a
Revised Groupthink Framework
■ Gregory Moorhead, Richard Ference, and Chris P. Neck

This paper reviews the decision situation surrounding the decision to launch the space shuttle Challenger in January 1986 in the light of the groupthink hypothesis. A revised framework is presented that proposes time and leadership style as moderators of the manner in which group characteristics lead to groupthink symptoms.

INTRODUCTION

In 1972, a new dimension was added to our understanding of group decision making with the proposal of the groupthink hypothesis by Janis (1972). Janis coined the term "groupthink" to refer to "a mode of thinking that people engage in when they are deeply involved in a cohesive in-group, when the members' striving for unanimity override their motivation to realistically appraise alternative courses of action" (Janis, 1972, p. 8). The hypothesis was supported by his hindsight analysis of several political-military fiascoes and successes that are differentiated by the occurrence or non-occurrence of antecedent conditions, groupthink symptoms, and decision making defects.

In a subsequent volume, Janis further explicates the theory and adds an analysis of the Watergate transcripts and various published memoirs and accounts of principals involved, concluding that the Watergate cover-up decision also was a result of groupthink (Janis, 1983). Both volumes propose prescriptions for preventing the occurrence of groupthink, many of which have appeared in popular press, in books on executive decision making, and in management textbooks. Multiple advocacy decision-making procedures have been adopted at the executive levels in many organizations, including the executive branch of the government. One would think that by 1986, 13 years after the publication of a popular book, that its prescriptions might be well ingrained in our management and decision-making styles. Unfortunately, it has not happened.

Reprinted from G. Moorhead, R. Ference, and C. P. Neck, "Group Decision Fiascoes Continue," *Human Relations*, 1991, 44, 539–549. Copyright © 1991, Tavistock Institute. Reprinted by permission.

On January 28, 1986, the space shuttle Challenger was launched from Kennedy Space Center. The temperature that morning was in the mid-20's, well below the previous low temperatures at which the shuttle engines had been tested. Seventy-three seconds after launch, the Challenger exploded, killing all seven astronauts aboard, and becoming the worst disaster in space flight history. The catastrophe shocked the nation, crippled the American space program, and is destined to be remembered as the most tragic national event since the assassination of John F. Kennedy in 1963.

The Presidential Commission that investigated the accident pointed to a flawed decision-making process as a primary contributory cause. The decision was made the night before the launch in the Level I Flight Readiness Review meeting. Due to the work of the Presidential Commission, information concerning that meeting is available for analysis as a group decision possibly susceptible to groupthink.

In this paper, we report the results of our analysis of the Level I Flight Readiness Review meeting as a decision-making situation that displays evidence of groupthink. We review the antecedent conditions, the groupthink symptoms, and the possible decision-making defects, as suggested by Janis (1983). In addition, we take the next and more important step of going beyond the development of another example of groupthink to make recommendations for renewed inquiry into group decision-making processes.

THEORY AND EVIDENCE

The groupthink hypothesis has been presented in detail in numerous publications other than Janis' books (Flowers, 1977; Courtright, 1978; Leana, 1985; Moorhead, 1982; Moorhead & Montanari, 1986) and will not be repeated here. The major categories will be used as a framework for organizing the evidence from the meeting. Within each category the key elements will be presented along with meeting details that pertain to each.

The meeting(s) took place throughout the day and evening from 12:36 pm (EST), January 27, 1986 following the decision to not launch the Challenger due to high crosswinds at the launch site. Discussions continued through about 12:00 midnight (EST) via tele-

conferencing and Telefax systems connecting the Kennedy Space Center in Florida, Morton Thiokol (MTI) in Utah, Johnson Space Center in Houston, and the Marshall Space Flight Center. The Level I Flight Readiness Review is the highest level of review prior to launch. It comprises the highest level of management at the three space centers and at MTI, the private supplier of the solid rocket booster engines.

To briefly state the situation, the MTI engineers recommended not to launch if temperatures of the O-ring seals on the rocket were below 53 degrees Fahrenheit, which was the lowest temperature of any previous flight. Laurence B. Mulloy, manager of the Solid Rocket Booster Project at Marshall Space Flight Center, states:

> . . . *The bottom line of that, though, initially was that Thiokol engineering, Bob Lund, who is the Vice President and Director of Engineering, who is here today, recommended that 51-L [the Challenger] not be launched if the O-ring temperatures predicted at launch time would be lower than any previous launch, and that was 53 degrees . . .* (Report of the Presidential Commission on the Space Shuttle Accident, *1986, p. 91–92*).

This recommendation was made at 8:45 pm, January 27, 1986 (*Report of the Presidential Commission on the Space Shuttle Accident,* 1986). Through the ensuing discussions the decision to launch was made.

Antecedent Conditions

The three primary antecedent conditions for the development of groupthink are: a highly cohesive group, leader preference for a certain decision, and insulation of the group from qualified outside opinions. These conditions existed in this situation.

Cohesive Group The people who made the decision to launch had worked together for many years. They were familiar with each other and had grown through the ranks of the space program. A high degree of *esprit de corps* existed between the members.

Leader Preference Two top level managers actively promoted their pro-launch opinions in the face of opposition. The commission report states that several managers at space centers and MTI pushed for launch, regardless of the low temperatures.

Insulation from Experts   MTI engineers made their recommendations relatively early in the evening. The top level decision-making group knew of their objections but did not meet with them directly to review their data and concerns. As Roger Boisjoly, a Thiokol engineer, states in his remarks to the Presidential Commission:

> . . . and the bottom line was that the engineering people would not recommend a launch below 53 degrees Fahrenheit . . . From this point on, management formulated the points to base their decision on. There was never one comment in favor, as I have said, of launching by any engineer or other nonmanagement person. . . . I was not even asked to participate in giving any input to the final decision charts (Report of the Presidential Commission on the Space Shuttle Accident, *1986, p. 91–92*).

This testimonial indicates that the top decision-making team was insulated from the engineers who possessed the expertise regarding the functioning of the equipment.

Groupthink Symptoms

Janis identified eight symptoms of groupthink. They are presented here along with evidence from the *Report of the Presidential Commission on the Space Shuttle Accident* (1986).

Invulnerability   When groupthink occurs, most or all of the members of the decision-making group have an illusion of invulnerability that reassures them in the face of obvious dangers. This illusion leads the group to become overly optimistic and willing to take extraordinary risks. It may also cause them to ignore clear warnings of danger.

The solid rocket joint problem that destroyed Challenger was discussed often at flight readiness review meetings prior to flight. However, Commission member Richard Feynman concluded from the testimony that a mentality of overconfidence existed due to the extraordinary record of success of space

flights. Every time we send one up it is successful. Involved members may seem to think that on the next one we can lower our standards or take more risks because it always works (*Time*, 1986).

The invulnerability illusion may have built up over time as a result of NASA's own spectacular history. NASA had not lost an astronaut since 1967 when a flash fire in the capsule of Apollo 1 killed three. Since that time NASA had a string of 55 successful missions. They had put a man on the moon, built and launched Skylab and the shuttle, and retrieved defective satellites from orbit. In the minds of most Americans and apparently their own, they could do no wrong.

Rationalization   Victims of groupthink collectively construct rationalizations that discount warnings and other forms of negative feedback. If these signals were taken seriously when presented, the group members would be forced to reconsider their assumptions each time they re-commit themselves to their past decisions.

In the Level I flight readiness meeting when the Challenger was given final launch approval, MTI engineers presented evidence that the joint would fail. Their argument was based on the fact that in the coldest previous launch (air temperature 30 degrees) the joint in question experienced serious erosion and that no data existed as to how the joint would perform at colder temperatures. Flight center officials put forth numerous technical rationalizations faulting MTI's analysis. One of these rationalizations was that the engineer's data were inconclusive. As Mr. Boisjoly emphasized to the Commission:

> . . . I was asked, yes, at that point in time I was asked to quantify my concerns, and I said I couldn't. I couldn't quantify it. I had no data to quantify it, but I did say I knew that it was away from goodness in the current data base. Someone on the net commented that we had soot blow-by on SRM-22 [Flight 61-A, October, 1985] which was launched at 75 degrees. I don't remember who made the comment but that is where the first comment came in about the disparity between my conclusion and the observed data because SRM-22 [Flight 61-A, October 1985] had blow-by

at essentially a room temperature launch. I then said that SRM-15 [Flight 51-C, January, 1985] had much more blow-by indication and that it was indeed telling us that lower temperature was a factor. I was asked again for data to support my claim, and I said I have none other than what is being presented. (Report of the Presidential Commission on the Space Shuttle Accident, *1986, p. 89*).

Discussions became twisted (compared to previous meetings) and no one detected it. Under normal conditions, MTI would have to prove the shuttle boosters readiness for launch, instead they found themselves being forced to prove that the boosters were unsafe. Boisjoly's testimony supports this description of the discussion:

. . . This was a meeting where the determination was to launch, and it was up to us to prove beyond a shadow of a doubt that it was not safe to do so. This is in total reverse to what the position usually is in a preflight conversation or a flight readiness review. It is usually exactly opposite of that . . . (Report of the Presidential Commission on the Space Shuttle Accident, *1986, p. 93*).

Morality Group members often believe, without question, in the inherent morality of their position. They tend to ignore the ethical or moral consequences of their decision.

In the Challenger case, this point was raised by a very high level MTI manager, Allan J. McDonald, who tried to stop the launch and said that he would not want to have to defend the decision to launch. He stated to the Commission:

. . . I made the statement that if we're wrong and something goes wrong on this flight, I wouldn't want to have to be the person to stand up in front of board in inquiry and say that I went ahead and told them to go ahead and fly this thing outside what the motor was qualified to . . . (Report of the Presidential Commission on the Space Shuttle Accident, *1986, p. 95*).

Some members did not hear this statement because it occurred during a break. Three top officials who did hear it ignored it.

Stereotyped Views of Others Victims of groupthink often have a stereotyped view of the opposition of anyone with a competing opinion. They feel that the opposition is too stupid or too weak to understand or deal effectively with the problem.

Two of the top three NASA officials responsible for the launch displayed this attitude. They felt that they completely understood the nature of the joint problem and never seriously considered the objections raised by the MTI engineers. In fact they denigrated and badgered the opposition and their information and opinions.

Pressure on Dissent Group members often apply direct pressure to anyone who questions the validity of the arguments supporting a decision or position favored by the majority. These same two officials pressured MTI to change its position after MTI originally recommended that the launch not take place. These two officials pressured MTI personnel to prove that it was not safe to launch, rather than to prove the opposite. As mentioned earlier, this was a total reversal of normal preflight procedures. It was this pressure that top MTI management was responding to when they overruled their engineering staff and recommended launch. As the Commission report states:

. . . At approximately 11 p.m. Eastern Standard Time, the Thiokol/NASA teleconference resumed, the Thiokol management stating that they had reassessed the problem, that the temperature effects were a concern, but that the data was admittedly inconclusive . . . (p. 96)

This seems to indicate that NASA's pressure on these Thiokol officials forced them to change their recommendation from delay to execution of the launch.

Self-Censorship Group members tend to censor themselves when they have opinions or ideas that deviate from the apparent group consensus. Janis feels that this reflects each member's inclination to minimize to himself or herself the importance of his or her own doubts and counter-arguments.

The most obvious evidence of self-censorship occurred when a vice president of MTI, who had previously presented information against launch, bowed to pressure from NASA and accepted their rationalizations for launch. He then wrote these up and presented them to NASA as the reasons that MTI had changed its recommendation to launch.

Illusion of Unanimity Group members falling victim to groupthink share an illusion of unanimity concerning judgments made by members speaking in favor of the majority view. This symptom is caused in part by the preceding one and is aided by the false assumption that any participant who remains silent is in agreement with the majority opinion. The group leader and other members support each other by playing up points of convergence in their thinking at the expense of fully exploring points of divergence that might reveal unsettling problems.

No participant from NASA ever openly agreed with or even took sides with MTI in the discussion. The silence from NASA was probably amplified by the fact that the meeting was a teleconference linking the participants at three different locations. Obviously, body language which might have been evidenced by dissenters was not visible to others who might also have held a dissenting opinion. Thus, silence meant agreement.

Mindguarding Certain group members assume the role of guarding the minds of others in the group. They attempt to shield the group from adverse information that might destroy the majority view of the facts regarding the appropriateness of the decision.

The top management at Marshall knew that the rocket casings had been ordered redesigned to correct a flaw 5 months previous to this launch. This information and other technical details concerning the history of the joint problem was withheld at the meeting.

Decision-Making Defects

The result of the antecedent conditions and the symptoms of groupthink is a defective decision-making process. Janis discusses several defects in decision making that can result.

Few Alternatives The group considers only a few alternatives, often only two. No initial survey of all possible alternatives occurs. The Flight Readiness Review team had a launch/no-launch decision to make. These were the only two alternatives considered. Other possible alternatives might have been to delay the launch for further testing, or to delay until the temperatures reached an appropriate level.

No Re-Examination of Alternatives The group fails to re-examine alternatives that may have been initially discarded based on early unfavorable information. Top NASA officials spent time and effort defending and strengthening their position, rather than examining the MTI position.

Rejecting Expert Opinions Members make little or no attempt to seek outside experts opinions. NASA did not seek out other experts who might have some expertise in this area. They assumed that they had all the information.

Rejecting Negative Information Members tend to focus on supportive information and ignore any data or information that might cast a negative light on their preferred alternative. MTI representatives repeatedly tried to point out errors in the rationale the NASA officials were using to justify the launch. Even after the decision was made, the argument continued until a NASA official told the MTI representative that it was no longer his concern.

No Contingency Plans Members spend little time discussing the possible consequences of the decision and, therefore, fail to develop contingency plans. There is no documented evidence in the Rogers Commission Report of any discussion of the possible consequences of an incorrect decision.

Summary of the Evidence

The major categories and key elements of the groupthink hypothesis have been presented (albeit somewhat briefly) along with evidence from the discussions prior to the launching of the Challenger, as reported in the President's Commission to investigate the accident. The antecedent conditions were present in the decision-making group, even though the group was in several physical locations. The leaders had a preferred solution and engaged in behaviors designed to promote it rather than critically appraise alternatives. These behaviors were evidence of most of the symptoms leading to a defective decision-making process.

DISCUSSION

This situation provides another example of decision making in which the group fell victim to the groupthink syndrome, as have so many previous groups. It illustrates the situation characteristics, the symptoms of groupthink, and decision-making defects as described by Janis. This situation, however, also illustrates several other aspects of situations that are critical to the development of groupthink that need to be included in a revised formulation of the groupthink model. First, the element of time in influencing the development of groupthink has not received adequate attention. In the decision to launch the space shuttle Challenger, time was a crucial part of the decision-making process. The launch had been delayed once, and the window for another launch was fast closing. The leaders of the decision team were concerned about public and congressional perceptions of the entire space shuttle program and its continued funding and may have felt that further delays of the launch could seriously impact future funding. With the space window fast closing, the decision team was faced with a launch now or seriously damage the program decision. One top level manager's response to Thiokol's initial recommendation to postpone the launch indicates the presence of time pressure:

> With this LCC (Launch Commit Criteria), i.e., do not launch with a temperature greater [sic] than 53 degrees, we may not be able to launch until next April. We need to consider this carefully before we jump to any conclusions . . . (Report of the Presidential Commission on the Space Shuttle Accident, *1986, p. 96*).

Time pressure could have played a role in the group choosing to agree and to self-censor their comments. Therefore, time is a critical variable that needs to be highlighted in a revised groupthink framework. We propose that time is an important moderator between group characteristics and the development of the groupthink symptoms. That is, in certain situations when there is pressure to make a decision quickly, the

elements may combine to foster the development of groupthink.

The second revision needs to be in the role of the leadership of the decision-making group. In the space shuttle Challenger incident, the leadership of the group varied from a shared type of leadership to a very clear leader in the situation. This may indicate that the leadership role needs to be clearly defined and a style that demands open disclosure of information, points of opposition, complaints, and dissension. Inclusion of leadership in a more powerful role in the groupthink framework needs to be more explicit than in the Janis formulation in which leadership is one of several group characteristics that can lead to the development of the groupthink symptoms. We propose the leadership style is a crucial variable that moderates the relationship between the group characteristics and the development of the symptoms. Janis (1983) is a primary form of evidence to support the inclusion of leadership style in the enhanced model. His account of why the same group succumbed to groupthink in one decision (Bay of Pigs) and not in another (Cuban Missile Crisis) supports the depiction of leadership style as a moderator variable. In these decisions, the only condition that changed was the leadership style of the President. In other words, the element that seemed to distinguish why groupthink occurred in the Bay of Pigs decision and not in the Cuban Missile Crisis situation is the president's change in his behavior.

These two variables, time and leadership style, are proposed as moderators of the impact of the group characteristics on groupthink symptoms. This relationship is portrayed graphically in Fig. 1. In effect, we propose that the groupthink symptoms result from the group characteristics, as proposed by Janis, but only in the presence of the moderator variables of time and certain leadership styles.

Time, as an important element in the model, is relatively straightforward. When a decision must be made within a very short time frame, pressure on members to agree, to avoid time-consuming arguments and reports from outside experts, and to self-censor themselves may increase. These pressures inevitably cause group members to seek agreement. In Janis's original model, time was included indirectly as a function of the antecedent condition, group cohe-

FIGURE 1 / Revised Groupthink Framework

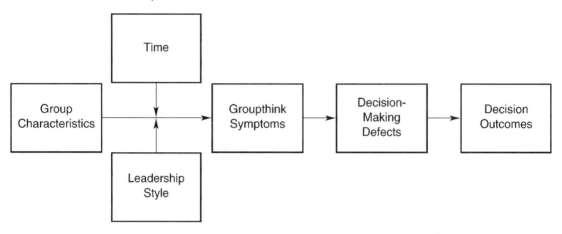

sion. Janis (1983) argued that time pressures can adversely affect decision quality in two ways. First, it affects the decision makers' mental efficiency and judgment, interfering with their ability to concentrate on complicated discussions, to absorb new information, and to use imagination to anticipate the future consequences of alternative courses of action. Second, time pressure is a source of stress that will have the effect of inducing a policy-making group to become more cohesive and more likely to engage in groupthink.

Leadership style is shown to be a moderator because of the importance it plays in either promoting or avoiding the development of the symptoms of the groupthink. The leader, even though she or he may not promote a preferred solution, may allow or even assist the group seeking agreement by not forcing the group to critically appraise all alternative courses of action. The focus of this leadership variable is on the degree to which the leader allows or promotes discussion and evaluation of alternatives. It is not a matter of simply not making known a preferred solution; the issue is one of stimulation of critical thinking among the group.

Impact on Prescriptions for Prevention

The revised model suggests that more specific prescriptions for prevention of groupthink can be made. First, group members need to be aware of the impact that a short decision time frame has on decision processes. When a decision must be made quickly, there will be more pressure to agree, i.e., discouragement of dissent, self-censorship, avoidance of expert opinion, and assumptions about unanimity. The type of leadership suggested here is not one that sits back and simply does not make known her or his preferred solution. This type of leader must be one that requires all members to speak up with concerns, questions, and new information. The leader must know what some of these concerns are and which members are likely to have serious doubts so that the people with concerns can be called upon to voice them. This type of group leadership does not simply assign the role of devil's advocate and step out of the way. This leader actually plays the role or makes sure that others do. A leader with the required style to avoid groupthink is not a laissez faire leader or non-involved participative leader. This leader is active in directing the activities of the group but does not make known a preferred solution. The group still must develop and evaluate alternative courses of action, but under the direct influence of a strong, demanding leader who forces critical appraisal of all alternatives.

Finally, a combination of the two variables suggests that the leader needs to help members to avoid the problems created by the time element. For example, the leader may be able to alter an externally imposed time frame for the decision by negotiating an extension or even paying late fees, if necessary. If an extension is not possible, the leader may need to help the group eliminate the effects of time on the decision processes. This can be done by forcing attention to issues rather than time, encouraging dissension and confrontation, and scheduling special sessions to hear reports from outside experts that challenge prevailing views within the group.

Janis presents, in both editions of his book, several recommendations for preventing the occurrence of groupthink. These recommendations focus on the inclusion of outside experts in the decision-making process, all members taking the role of devil's advocate and critically appraising all alternative courses of action, and the leader not expressing a preferred solution. The revised groupthink framework suggests several new prescriptions that may be helpful in preventing further decision fiascoes similar to the decision to launch the space shuttle Challenger.

Much additional research is necessary to test the revised framework. First, laboratory research is needed to refine details of how time affects the development of groupthink. Second, the impact of various types of leadership style that may be appropriate for group decision-making situations needs to be investigated. Finally, research which tests the revised framework with real decision-making groups will be needed to refine new prescriptions for preventing groupthink.

CONCLUSION

This paper has reviewed the basic tenets of groupthink and examined the decision to launch the space shuttle Challenger in January 1986. The report of the Presidential Commission provided enough evidence of the antecedent conditions, the symptoms, and the decision-making defects to support a conclusion that the decision to launch can be classified as a groupthink situation. We have proposed, in addition, that other conditions may play important roles in the development of groupthink. These two variables, time and leadership style, are proposed as moderators of the relationship between group characteristics and groupthink symptoms. These two moderators lead to new prescriptions for the prevention of groupthink. Much additional research is needed to test the degree to which the revised framework can be used to guide prescriptions for prevention.

REFERENCES

Courtright, J. A. A laboratory investigation of groupthink. *Communications Monographs*, 1978, *45*, 229–246.

Flowers, M. L. A laboratory test of some implications of Janis's groupthink hypothesis. *Journal of Personality and Social Psychology*, 1977, *35*, 888–896.

Janis, I. L. *Victims of groupthink*. Boston: Houghton Mifflin, 1972.

Janis, I. L. *Groupthink* (2nd ed., revised). Boston: Houghton Mifflin, 1983.

Leana, C. R. A partial test of Janis's groupthink model: Effects of group cohesiveness and leader behavior on defective decision making. *Journal of Management*, 1985, *11*, 5–17.

Moorhead, G. Groupthink: Hypothesis in need of testing. *Group and Organization Studies*, 1982, *7*, 429–444.

Moorhead, G., & Montanari, J. R. Empirical analysis of the groupthink phenomenon. *Human Relations*, 1986, *39*, 399–410.

Report of the Presidential Commission on the Space Shuttle Accident. Washington, D.C.: July 1986.

Time. Fixing NASA. June 9, 1986.

CRITICAL THINKING QUESTIONS

1. Why do you think groupthink became a factor in the decision to launch the *Challenger?* In other words, why was no one involved in making the decision able to recognize what was going on and thus do something about it? How commonly understood is the concept of groupthink in the real world? Is it important that leaders in all walks of life know about groupthink? How could the message be spread to them?

2. The article states that one of the two moderating variables that influence whether groupthink symptoms develop is leadership style. To what extent can leadership style be taught to people? On the other hand, to what extent is leadership style a product of individual personality? Describe the personality characteristics of a leader who would not likely try to prevent the development of groupthink.

3. The second moderating variable discussed in the article is time. Design a laboratory study to investigate the impact of time on the development of groupthink.
4. Consult a social psychology textbook and read about different styles of leadership. Which styles might be most relevant to the development of groupthink? Design either a laboratory or a field study to examine the impact of leadership style on the emergence of groupthink.

CHAPTER INTEGRATION QUESTIONS

1. While the three articles in this chapter do not deal primarily with leadership per se, they all have implications for how leaders can affect the outcomes of group decisions. What are those implications?

2. Based on your own experience with working in groups, what factors other than those presented in the articles may influence the functioning and outcomes of groups? Explain why you think these factors are important.

3. Abraham Lincoln said, "Nearly all men can stand adversity, but if you want to test a man's character, give him power." Relate this quotation to a unifying theme or themes in the articles in this chapter.

Chapter Thirteen

BUSINESS PSYCHOLOGY

A MAJOR PART of your waking life will be spent at work. You may already be in a full-time position (or have been), or you may have had experience working at a part-time job. When you think about the work you are doing now or hope to do in the future, you may have many concerns. For instance, you may wonder how much money you will make. But you also may be concerned about whether you will enjoy what you do. If you become a manager and are responsible for other people's behavior, you also may be concerned with how best to utilize the human resources available for the benefit of the organization as well as that of the individual employee.

Social psychology has long been involved in the area of business, or *organizational*, psychology. Early work in the field looked at factors such as leadership style and how it may contribute to worker behavior. While work in that area has continued, the influence of social psychology has expanded into virtually all domains of work-related activities, including productivity, job satisfaction, and employee motivation, to name but a few. The articles in this chapter provide a sampling of the many ways in which social psychology contributes to our understanding of work behavior.

Article 37, "The New-Boy Network: What Do Job Interviews Really Tell Us?" examines the job interview process. Incorporating many of the concepts introduced in Chapters Two and Three (social perception and social cognition, respectively), this article looks at how natural human tendencies and biases may operate in a job interview. Besides the theoretical importance of such research, there are obvious personal applications of the findings, as well.

Article 38, "One More Time: How Do You Motivate Employees?" is a truly classic piece that examines the questions of what motivates people, what factors are involved in job satisfaction, and what conditions influence productivity. Your beliefs about what motivates you and others to work may change after you read this article.

Finally, Article 39, "Relationship between Emotional Intelligence and Transformational Leadership Style: A Gender Comparison," looks at the issue of what makes an effective leader. Specifically, the article looks at the role of *emotional intelligence* in predicting successful styles of leadership. Emotional intelligence, a fairly recent concept, concerns the behaviors that seem to enhance successful social functioning. This article considers whether this factor is important in predicting effective leadership and if it differs for men and for women.

ARTICLE 37 _____

At the heart of any organization—whether a small, family-run business or a large, multinational corporation—are its *people*. Perhaps nothing is more critical to the ultimate success or failure of an organization than the hiring of the best people for the appropriate jobs.

While the hiring process obviously is of great importance, what goes into the decision to hire someone? Many factors do, of course. Some are directly related to a person's specific talents, such as whether he or she has the appropriate training and experience necessary for the position. Often, however, other factors that perhaps should not even be relevant come into play. For example, someone's physical appearance may have an impact on whether he or she is hired. Many of the studies that have been summarized in previous chapters—such as those on interpersonal attraction (Chapter Seven), social perception (Chapter Two), and prejudice (Chapter Six)—have shown how seemingly irrelevant personal characteristics may influence our perception of someone.

Given the critical nature of the hiring process, what exactly do job interviewers look for in applicants? As it turns out, the methods that most job interviewers use are less than scientific and instead based largely on intuition. As Article 4 demonstrated, "gut feelings" are not necessarily bad. In fact, we very often are able to form an impression of someone in a very short period of time. While our intuition may sometimes be very accurate, at other times it may blind us to really seeing what is before us. The following article by Malcolm Gladwell looks at what really goes on in the job interview process and how these all-too-common human biases may be problematic. Since virtually everyone will interview for a job at some point in their lives, the information in this article has real personal relevance.

The New-Boy Network
What Do Job Interviews Really Tell Us?
■ Malcolm Gladwell

Nolan Myers grew up in Houston, the elder of two boys in a middle-class family. He went to Houston's High School for the Performing and Visual Arts and then Harvard, where he intended to major in History and Science. After discovering the joys of writing code, though, he switched to computer science. "Programming is one of those things you get involved in, and you just can't stop until you finish," Myers says. "You get involved in it, and all of a sudden you look at your watch and it's four in the morning! I love the elegance of it." Myers is short and slightly stocky and has pale-blue eyes. He smiles easily, and when he speaks

he moves his hands and torso for emphasis. He plays in a klezmer band called the Charvard Chai Notes. He talks to his parents a lot. He gets B's and B-pluses.

This spring, in the last stretch of his senior year, Myers spent a lot of time interviewing for jobs with technology companies. He talked to a company named Trilogy, down in Texas, but he didn't think he would fit in. "One of Trilogy's subsidiaries put ads out in the paper saying that they were looking for the top tech students, and that they'd give them two hundred thousand dollars and a BMW," Myers said, shaking his head in disbelief. In another of his interviews, a

Reprinted from *The New Yorker,* May 29, 2000, pp. 68–86. © 2000 by Malcolm Gladwell. Reprinted by permission.

recruiter asked him to solve a programming problem, and he made a stupid mistake and the recruiter pushed the answer back across the table to him, saying that his "solution" accomplished nothing. As he remembers the moment, Myers blushes. "I was so nervous. I thought, Hmm, that sucks!" The way he says that, though, makes it hard to believe that he really was nervous, or maybe what Nolan Myers calls nervous the rest of us call a tiny flutter in the stomach. Myers doesn't seem like the sort to get flustered. He's the kind of person you would call the night before the big test in seventh grade, when nothing made sense and you had begun to panic.

I like Nolan Myers. He will, I am convinced, be very good at whatever career he chooses. I say those two things even though I have spent no more than ninety minutes in his presence. We met only once, on a sunny afternoon in April at the Au Bon Pain in Harvard Square. He was wearing sneakers and khakis and a polo shirt, in a dark-green pattern. He had a big backpack, which he plopped on the floor beneath the table. I bought him an orange juice. He fished around in his wallet and came up with a dollar to try and repay me, which I refused. We sat by the window. Previously, we had talked for perhaps three minutes on the phone, setting up the interview. Then I E-mailed him, asking him how I would recognize him at Au Bon Pain. He sent me the following message, with what I'm convinced—again, on the basis of almost no evidence—to be typical Myers panache: "22ish, five foot seven, straight brown hair, very good-looking :)." I have never talked to his father, his mother, or his little brother, or any of his professors. I have never seen him ecstatic or angry or depressed. I know nothing of his personal habits, his tastes, or his quirks. I cannot even tell you why I feel the way I do about him. He's good-looking and smart and articulate and funny, but not so good-looking and smart and articulate and funny that there is some obvious explanation for the conclusions I've drawn about him. I just like him, and I'm impressed by him, and if I were an employer looking for bright young college graduates, I'd hire him in a heartbeat.

I heard about Nolan Myers from Hadi Partovi, an executive with Tellme, a highly touted Silicon Valley startup offering Internet access through the telephone.

If you were a computer-science major at M.I.T., Harvard, Stanford, Caltech, or the University of Waterloo this spring, looking for a job in software, Tellme was probably at the top of your list. Partovi and I talked in the conference room at Tellme's offices, just off the soaring, open floor where all the firm's programmers and marketers and executives sit, some of them with bunk beds built over their desks. (Tellme recently moved into an old printing plant—a low-slung office building with a huge warehouse attached—and, in accordance with new-economy logic, promptly turned the old offices into a warehouse and the old warehouse into offices.) Partovi is a handsome man of twenty-seven, with olive skin and short curly black hair, and throughout our entire interview he sat with his chair tilted precariously at a forty-five-degree angle. At the end of a long riff about how hard it is to find high-quality people, he blurted out one name: Nolan Myers. Then, from memory, he rattled off Myers's telephone number. He very much wanted Myers to come to Tellme.

Partovi had met Myers in January, during a recruiting trip to Harvard. "It was a heinous day," Partovi remembers. "I started at seven and went until nine. I'd walk one person out and walk the other in." The first fifteen minutes of every interview he spent talking about Tellme—its strategy, its goals, and its business. Then he gave everyone a short programming puzzle. For the rest of the hour-long meeting, Partovi asked questions. He remembers that Myers did well on the programming test, and after talking to him for thirty to forty minutes he became convinced that Myers had, as he puts it, "the right stuff." Partovi spent even less time with Myers than I did. He didn't talk to Myers's family, or see him ecstatic or angry or depressed, either. He knew that Myers had spent last summer as an intern at Microsoft and was about to graduate from an Ivy League school. But virtually everyone recruited by a place like Tellme has graduated from an élite university, and the Microsoft summer-internship program has more than six hundred people in it. Partovi didn't even know why he liked Myers so much. He just did. "It was very much a gut call," he says.

This wasn't so very different from the experience Nolan Myers had with Steve Ballmer, the C.E.O. of

Microsoft. Earlier this year, Myers attended a party for former Microsoft interns called Gradbash. Ballmer gave a speech there, and at the end of his remarks Myers raised his hand. "He was talking a lot about aligning the company in certain directions," Myers told me, "and I asked him about how that influences his ability to make bets on other directions. Are they still going to make small bets?" Afterward, a Microsoft recruiter came up to Myers and said, "Steve wants your E-mail address." Myers gave it to him, and soon he and Ballmer were E-mailing. Ballmer, it seems, badly wanted Myers to come to Microsoft. "He did research on me," Myers says. "'He knew which group I was interviewing with, and knew a lot about me personally. He sent me an E-mail saying that he'd love to have me come to Microsoft, and if I had any questions I should contact him. So I sent him a response, saying thank you. After I visited Tellme, I sent him an E-mail saying I was interested in Tellme, here were the reasons, that I wasn't sure yet, and if he had anything to say I said I'd love to talk to him. I gave him my number. So he called, and after playing phone tag we talked—about career trajectory, how Microsoft would influence my career, what he thought of Tellme. I was extremely impressed with him, and he seemed very genuinely interested in me."

What convinced Ballmer he wanted Myers? A glimpse! He caught a little slice of Nolan Myers in action and—just like that—the C.E.O. of a four-hundred-billion-dollar company was calling a college senior in his dorm room. Ballmer somehow knew he liked Myers, the same way Hadi Partovi knew, and the same way I knew after our little chat at Au Bon Pain. But what did we know? What could we know? By any reasonable measure, surely none of us knew Nolan Myers at all.

It is a truism of the new economy that the ultimate success of any enterprise lies with the quality of the people it hires. At many technology companies, employees are asked to all but live at the office, in conditions of intimacy that would have been unthinkable a generation ago. The artifacts of the prototypical Silicon Valley office—the videogames, the espresso bar, the bunk beds, the basketball hoops—are the elements of the rec room, not the workplace. And in the rec room you want to play only with your friends. But how do you find out who your friends are? Today,

recruiters canvas the country for résumés. They analyze employment histories and their competitors' staff listings. They call references, and then do what I did with Nolan Myers: sit down with a perfect stranger for an hour and a half and attempt to draw conclusions about that stranger's intelligence and personality. The job interview has become one of the central conventions of the modem economy. But what, exactly, can you know about a stranger after sitting down and talking with him for an hour?

Some years ago, an experimental psychologist at Harvard University, Nalini Ambady, together with Robert Rosenthal, set out to examine the nonverbal aspects of good teaching. As the basis of her research, she used videotapes of teaching fellows which had been made during a training program at Harvard. Her plan was to have outside observers look at the tapes with the sound off and rate the effectiveness of the teachers by their expressions and physical cues. Ambady wanted to have at least a minute of film to work with. When she looked at the tapes, though, there was really only about ten seconds when the teachers were shown apart from the students.

"I didn't want students in the frame, because obviously it would bias the ratings," Ambady says. "So I went to my adviser, and I said, 'This isn't going to work.'"

But it did. The observers, presented with a ten-second silent video clip, had no difficulty rating the teachers on a fifteen-item checklist of personality traits. In fact, when Ambady cut the clips back to five seconds, the ratings were the same. They were even the same when she showed her raters just two seconds of videotape. That sounds unbelievable unless you actually watch Ambady's teacher clips, as I did, and realize that the eight seconds that distinguish the longest clips from the shortest are superfluous: anything beyond the first flash of insight is unnecessary. When we make a snap judgment, it is made in a snap. It's also, very clearly, a judgment: we get a feeling that we have no difficulty articulating.

Ambady's next step led to an even more remarkable conclusion. She compared those snap judgments of teacher effectiveness with evaluations made, after a full semester of classes, by students of the same teachers. The correlation between the two, she found, was astoundingly high. A person watching a two-second silent video clip of a teacher he has never met will reach conclusions about how good that teacher is that are very similar to those of a student who sits in the teacher's class for an entire semester.

Recently, a comparable experiment was conducted by Frank Bernieri, a psychologist at the University of Toledo. Bernieri, working with one of his graduate students, Neha Gada-Jain, selected two people to act as interviewers, and trained them for six weeks in the proper procedures and techniques of giving an effective job interview. The two then interviewed ninety-eight volunteers, of various ages and backgrounds. The interviews lasted between fifteen and twenty minutes, and afterward each interviewer filled out a six-page, five-part evaluation of the person he'd just talked to. Originally, the intention of the study was to find out whether applicants who had been coached in certain nonverbal behaviors designed to ingratiate themselves with their interviewers—like mimicking the interviewers' physical gestures or posture—would get better ratings than applicants who behaved normally. As it turns out, they didn't. But then another of Bernieri's students, an undergraduate named Tricia Prickett, decided that she wanted to use the interview videotapes and the evaluations that had been collected to test out the adage that "the handshake is everything."

"She took fifteen seconds of videotape showing the applicant as he or she knocks on the door, comes in, shakes the hand of the interviewer, sits down, and the interviewer welcomes the person," Bernieri explained. Then, like Ambady, Prickett got a series of strangers to rate the applicants based on the handshake clip, using the same criteria that the interviewers had used. Once more, against all expectations, the ratings were very similar to those of the interviewers. "On nine out of the eleven traits the applicants were being judged on, the observers significantly predicted the outcome of the interview," Bernieri says. "The strength of the correlations was extraordinary."

This research takes Ambady's conclusions one step further. In the Toledo experiment, the interviewers were trained in the art of interviewing. They weren't dashing off a teacher evaluation on their way out the door. They were filling out a formal, detailed questionnaire, of the sort designed to give the most thor-ough and unbiased account of an interview. And still their ratings weren't all that different from those of people off the street who saw just the greeting.

This is why Hadi Partovi, Steve Ballmer, and I all agreed on Nolan Myers. Apparently, human beings don't need to know someone in order to believe that they know someone. Nor does it make that much difference, apparently, that Partovi reached his conclusion after putting Myers through the wringer for an hour, I reached mine after ninety minutes of amiable conversation at Au Bon Pain, and Ballmer reached his after watching and listening as Myers asked a question.

Bernieri and Ambady believe that the power of first impressions suggests that human beings have a particular kind of prerational ability for making searching judgments about others. In Ambady's teacher experiments, when she asked her observers to perform a potentially distracting cognitive task—like memorizing a set of numbers—while watching the tapes, their judgments of teacher effectiveness were unchanged. But when she instructed her observers to think hard about their ratings before they made them, their accuracy suffered substantially. Thinking only gets in the way. "The brain structures that are involved here are very primitive," Ambady speculates. "All of these affective reactions are probably governed by the lower brain structures." What we are picking up in that first instant would seem to be something quite basic about a person's character, because what we conclude after two seconds is pretty much the same as what we conclude after twenty minutes or, indeed, an entire semester. "Maybe you can tell immediately whether someone is extroverted, or gauge the person's ability to communicate," Bernieri says. "Maybe these clues or cues are immediately accessible and apparent." Bernieri and Ambady are talking about the existence of a powerful form of human intuition. In a way, that's comforting, because it suggests that we can meet a perfect stranger and immediately pick up on something important about him. It means that I shouldn't be concerned that I can't explain why I like Nolan Myers, because, if such judgments are made without thinking, then surely they defy explanation.

But there's a troubling suggestion here as well. I believe that Nolan Myers is an accomplished and likable person. But I have no idea from our brief encounter how honest he is, or whether he is self-centered, or whether he works best by himself or in a group, or any number of other fundamental traits. That people who simply see the handshake arrive at the same conclusions as people who conduct a full interview also implies, perhaps, that those initial impressions matter too much—that they color all the other impressions that we gather over time.

For example, I asked Myers if he felt nervous about the prospect of leaving school for the workplace, which seemed like a reasonable question, since I remember how anxious I was before my first job. Would the hours scare him? Oh no, he replied, he was already working between eighty and a hundred hours a week at school. "Are there things that you think you aren't good at, which make you worry?" I continued.

His reply was sharp: "Are there things that I'm not good at, or things that I can't learn? I think that's the real question. There are a lot of things I don't know anything about, but I feel comfortable that given the right environment and the right encouragement I can do well at." In my notes, next to that reply, I wrote "Great answer!" and I can remember at the time feeling the little thrill you experience as an interviewer when someone's behavior conforms with your expectations. Because I had decided, right off, that I liked him, what I heard in his answer was toughness and confidence. Had I decided early on that I didn't like Nolan Myers, I would have heard in that reply arrogance and bluster. The first impression becomes a self-fulfilling prophecy: we hear what we expect to hear. The interview is hopelessly biased in favor of the nice.

When Ballmer and Partovi and I met Nolan Myers, we made a prediction. We looked at the way he behaved in our presence—at the way he talked and acted and seemed to think—and drew conclusions about how he would behave in other situations. I had decided, remember, that Myers was the kind of person you called the night before the big test in seventh grade. Was I right to make that kind of generalization?

This is a question that social psychologists have looked at closely. In the late nineteen-twenties, in a famous study, the psychologist Theodore Newcomb analyzed extroversion among adolescent boys at a summer camp. He found that how talkative a boy was in one setting—say, lunch—was highly predictive of

how talkative that boy would be in the same setting in the future. A boy who was curious at lunch on Monday was likely to be curious at lunch on Tuesday. But his behavior in one setting told you almost nothing about how he would behave in a different setting: from how someone behaved at lunch, you couldn't predict how he would behave during, say, afternoon playtime. In a more recent study, of conscientiousness among students at Carleton College, the researchers Walter Mischel, Neil Lutsky, and Philip K. Peake showed that how neat a student's assignments were or how punctual he was told you almost nothing about how often he attended class or how neat his room or his personal appearance was. How we behave at any one time, evidently, has less to do with some immutable inner compass than with the particulars of our situation.

This conclusion, obviously, is at odds with our intuition. Most of the time, we assume that people display the same character traits in different situations. We habitually underestimate the large role that context plays in people's behavior. In the Newcomb summer-camp experiment, for example, the results showing how little consistency there was from one setting to another in talkativeness, curiosity, and gregariousness were tabulated from observations made and recorded by camp counsellors on the spot. But when, at the end of the summer, those same counsellors were asked to give their final impressions of the kids, they remembered the children's behavior as being highly consistent.

"The basis of the illusion is that we are somehow confident that we are getting what is there, that we are able to read off a person's disposition," Richard Nisbett, a psychologist at the University of Michigan, says. "When you have an interview with someone and have an hour with them, you don't conceptualize that as taking a sample of a person's behavior, let alone a possibly biased sample, which is what it is. What you think is that you are seeing a hologram, a small and fuzzy image but still the whole person."

Then Nisbett mentioned his frequent collaborator, Lee Ross, who teaches psychology at Stanford. "There was one term when he was teaching statistics and one term he was teaching a course with a lot of humanistic psychology. He gets his teacher evaluations. The first referred to him as cold, rigid, remote, finicky, and uptight. And the second described this wonderful warm-hearted guy who was so deeply concerned with questions of community and getting students to grow. It was Jekyll and Hyde. In both cases, the students thought they were seeing the real Lee Ross."

Psychologists call this tendency—to fixate on supposedly stable character traits and overlook the influence of context—the Fundamental Attribution Error, and if you combine this error with what we know about snap judgments the interview becomes an even more problematic encounter. Not only had I let my first impressions color the information I gathered about Myers, but I had also assumed that the way he behaved with me in an interview setting was indicative of the way he would always behave. It isn't that the interview is useless; what I learned about Myers— that he and I get along well—is something I could never have got from a résumé or by talking to his references. It's just that our conversation turns out to have been less useful, and potentially more misleading, than I had supposed. That most basic of human rituals—the conversation with a stranger—turns out to be a minefield.

Not long after I met with Nolan Myers, I talked with a human-resources consultant from Pasadena named Justin Menkes. Menkes's job is to figure out how to extract meaning from face-to-face encounters, and with that in mind he agreed to spend an hour interviewing me the way he thinks interviewing ought to be done. It felt, going in, not unlike a visit to a shrink, except that instead of having months, if not years, to work things out, Menkes was set upon stripping away my secrets in one session.

Consider, he told me, a commonly asked question like "Describe a few situations in which your work was criticized. How did you handle the criticism?" The problem, Menkes said, is that it's much too obvious what the interviewee is supposed to say. "There was a situation where I was working on a project, and I didn't do as well as I could have," he said, adopting a mock-sincere singsong. "My boss gave me some constructive criticism. And I redid the project. It hurt. Yet we worked it out." The same is true of the question "What would your friends say about you?"—to which the correct answer (preferably preceded by a pause, as

if to suggest that it had never dawned on you that someone would ask such a question) is "My guess is that they would call me a people person—either that or a hard worker."

Myers and I had talked about obvious questions, too. "What is your greatest weakness?" I asked him. He answered, "I tried to work on a project my freshman year, a children's festival. I was trying to start a festival as a benefit here in Boston. And I had a number of guys working with me. I started getting concerned with the scope of the project we were working on—how much responsibility we had, getting things done. I really put the brakes on, but in retrospect I really think we could have done it and done a great job."

Then Myers grinned and said, as an aside, "Do I truly think that is a fault? Honestly, no." And, of course, he's right. All I'd really asked him was whether he could describe a personal strength as if it were a weakness, and, in answering as he did, he had merely demonstrated his knowledge of the unwritten rules of the interview.

But, Menkes said, what if those questions were rephrased so that the answers weren't obvious? For example: "At your weekly team meetings, your boss unexpectedly begins aggressively critiquing your performance on a current project. What do you do?"

I felt a twinge of anxiety. What would I do? I remembered a terrible boss I'd had years ago. "I'd probably be upset," I said. "But I doubt I'd say anything. I'd probably just walk away." Menkes gave no indication whether he was concerned or pleased by that answer. He simply pointed out that another person might well have said something like "I'd go and see my boss later in private, and confront him about why he embarrassed me in front of my team." I was saying that I would probably handle criticism—even inappropriate criticism—from a superior with stoicism; in the second case, the applicant was saying he or she would adopt a more confrontational style. Or, at least, we were telling the interviewer that the workplace demands either stoicism or confrontation—and to Menkes these are revealing and pertinent pieces of information.

Menkes moved on to another area—handling stress. A typical question in this area is something like "Tell me about a time when you had to do several things at once. How did you handle the situation? How did you decide what to do first?" Menkes says this is also too easy. "I just had to be very organized," he began again in his mock-sincere singsong. "I had to multitask. I had to prioritize and delegate appropriately. I checked in frequently with my boss." Here's how Menkes rephrased it: "You're in a situation where you have two very important responsibilities that both have a deadline that is impossible to meet. You cannot accomplish both. How do you handle that situation?"

"Well," I said, "I would look at the two and decide what I was best at, and then go to my boss and say, 'It's better that I do one well than both poorly,' and we'd figure out who else could do the other task."

Menkes, immediately seized on a telling detail in my answer. I was interested in what job I would do best. But isn't the key issue what job the company most needed to have done? With that comment, I had revealed something valuable: that in a time of work-related crisis I start from a self-centered consideration. "Perhaps you are a bit of a solo practitioner," Menkes said diplomatically, "That's an essential bit of information."

Menkes deliberately wasn't drawing any broad conclusions. If we are not people who are shy or talkative or outspoken but people who are shy in some contexts, talkative in other situations, and outspoken in still other areas, then what it means to know someone is to catalogue and appreciate all those variations. Menkes was trying to begin that process of cataloguing. This interviewing technique is known as "structured interviewing," and in studies by industrial psychologists it has been shown to be the only kind of interviewing that has any success at all in predicting performance in the workplace. In the structured interviews, the format is fairly rigid. Each applicant is treated in precisely the same manner. The questions are scripted. The interviewers are carefully trained, and each applicant is rated on a series of predetermined scales.

What is interesting about the structured interview is how narrow its objectives are. When I interviewed Nolan Myers I was groping for some kind of global sense of who he was; Menkes seemed entirely uninterested in arriving at that same general sense of me—he seemed to realize how foolish that expectation was for an hour-long interview. The structured interview works precisely because it isn't really an interview; it isn't about getting to know someone, in a traditional sense. It's as much concerned with rejecting information as it is with collecting it.

Not surprisingly, interview specialists have found it extraordinarily difficult to persuade most employers to adopt the structured interview. It just doesn't feel right. For most of us, hiring someone is essentially a romantic process, in which the job interview functions as a desexualized version of a date. We are looking for someone with whom we have a certain chemistry, even if the coupling that results ends in tears and the pursuer and the pursued turn out to have nothing in common. We want the unlimited promise of a love affair. The structured interview, by contrast, seems to offer only the dry logic and practicality of an arranged marriage.

Nolan Myers agonized over which job to take. He spent half an hour on the phone with Steve Ballmer, and Ballmer was very persuasive. "He gave me very, very good advice," Myers says of his conversations with the Microsoft C.E.O. "He felt that I should go to the place that excited me the most and that I thought would be best for my career. He offered to be my mentor." Myers says he talked to his parents every day about what to do. In February, he flew out to California and spent a Saturday going from one Tellme executive to another, asking and answering questions. "Basically, I had three things I was looking for. One was long-term goals for the company. Where did they see themselves in five years? Second, what position would I be playing in the company?" He stopped and burst out laughing. "And I forget what the third one is." In March, Myers committed to Tellme.

Will Nolan Myers succeed at Tellme? I think so, although I honestly have no idea. It's a harder question to answer now than it would have been thirty or forty years ago. If this were 1965, Nolan Myers would have gone to work at I.B.M. and worn a blue suit and sat in a small office and kept his head down, and the particulars of his personality would not have mattered so much. It was not so important that I.B.M. understood who you were before it hired you, because you understood what I.B.M. was. If you walked through the door at Armonk or at a branch office in Illinois, you knew what you had to be and how you were supposed to act. But to walk through the soaring, open offices of Tellme, with the bunk beds over the desks, is to be struck by how much more demanding the culture of Silicon Valley is. Nolan Myers will not be provided with a social script, that blue suit and organization chart. Tellme, like any technology startup these days, wants its employees to be part of a fluid team, to be flexible and innovative, to work with shifting groups in the absence of hierarchy and bureaucracy, and in that environment, where the workplace doubles as the rec room, the particulars of your personality matter a great deal.

This is part of the new economy's appeal, because Tellme's soaring warehouse is a more productive and enjoyable place to work than the little office boxes of the old I.B.M. But the danger here is that we will be led astray in judging these newly important particulars of character. If we let personality—some indefinable, prerational intuition, magnified by the Fundamental Attribution Error—bias the hiring process today, then all we will have done is replace the old-boy network, where you hired your nephew, with the new-boy network, where you hire whoever impressed you most when you shook his hand. Social progress, unless we're careful, can merely be the means by which we replace the obviously arbitrary with the not so obviously arbitrary.

Myers has spent much of the past year helping to teach Introduction to Computer Science. He realized, he says, that one of the reasons that students were taking the course was that they wanted to get jobs in the software industry. "I decided that, having gone through all this interviewing, I had developed some expertise, and I would like to share that. There is a real skill and art in presenting yourself to potential employers. And so what we did in this class was talk about the kinds of things that employers are looking for—what are they looking for in terms of personality. One of the most important things is that you have to come across as being confident in what you are doing and in who you are. How do you do that? Speak clearly and smile." As he said that, Nolan Myers smiled. "For a lot of people, that's a very hard skill to learn. But for some reason I seem to understand it intuitively."

CRITICAL THINKING QUESTIONS

1. Based on the information in this article, what can you do to enhance your chances of being hired for a job? Be specific.
2. Consider the information in this article along with that from Article 4 on the power of first impressions. Based on this information, what recommendations can you make for improving the accuracy of the job interview process from the standpoint of the *interviewer*? From the standpoint of the *interviewee*? Explain your answers.
3. The concept of *emotional intelligence* has attracted a good deal of interest in recent years. Find out more about this concept, and relate it to the ideas presented in this article.
4. What information or advice have you received from others or from articles about how to make a good impression during a job interview? How consistent or inconsistent is that information with the information contained in this article? Explain.

ARTICLE 38 _____

Why do people work? Is it just to earn a living (or in some cases, to make a lot of money), or are there other reasons, too? If you look at the number of references in American culture to the "Monday morning blues" and "TGIF," you might get the impression that people would rather not work, if given a choice. Many people would consider it distinctly odd if someone expressed joy at the prospect of returning to work after a weekend off. Do most workers really feel that way? Is that the way it *should* be?

The question of what motivates people to work has been of major interest to industrial/ organizational psychologists for quite some time. Ultimately concerned with productivity and profits, business has an obvious interest in trying to discover ways to increase employee motivation, since increased motivation is often viewed as synonymous with increased output. Different theories of motivation have been drawn from areas in the behavioral sciences, ranging from learning theory to humanistic theories of motivation. All seek to identify the factors that motivate people and how to implement these factors to increase motivation levels.

One person who has made significant contributions to the understanding of motivation in the workplace is Frederick Herzberg. In the following classic article, he presents an analysis of commonly used methods of motivation and why they don't work, followed by his own theory and research. Whether you fully accept the tenets and suggestions found in the article, it will most likely get you to reexamine your own assumptions about what motivates people to work.

One More Time
How Do You Motivate Employees?

■ Frederick Herzberg

KITA—the externally imposed attempt by management to "install a generator" in the employee—has been demonstrated to be a total failure, the author says. The absence of such "hygiene" factors as good supervisor-employee relations and liberal fringe benefits can make a worker unhappy, but their presence will not make him want to work harder. Essentially meaningless changes in the tasks that workers are assigned to do have not accomplished the desired objective either. The only way to motivate the employee is to give him challenging work in which he can assume responsibility. Frederick Herzberg, who is Professor and Chairman of the Psychology Department at Case Western Reserve University, has devoted many years to the study of motivation in the United States and abroad. He is the author of Work and Nature of Man *(World Publishing Company, 1966).*

How many articles, books, speeches, and workshops have pleaded plaintively, "How do I get an employee to do what I want him to do?"

The psychology of motivation is tremendously complex, and what has been unraveled with any degree of assurance is small indeed. But the dismal ratio of knowledge to speculation has not dampened the enthusiasm for new forms of snake oil that are constantly coming on the market, many of them with

Reprinted by permission of *Harvard Business Review.* From "One More Time: How Do You Motivate Employees?" by Frederick Herzberg (September/October 1987). Copyright © 1987 by the Harvard Business School Publishing Corporation; all rights reserved.
Note: The above article was first printed in the January/February 1968 *Harvard Business Review.*

academic testimonials. Doubtless this article will have no depressing impact on the market for snake oil, but since the ideas expressed in it have been tested in many corporations and other organizations, it will help—I hope—to redress the imbalance in the afore-mentioned ratio.

"MOTIVATING" WITH KITA

In lectures to industry on the problem, I have found that the audiences are anxious for quick and practical answers, so I will begin with a straightforward, practical formula for moving people.

What is the simplest, surest, and most direct way of getting someone to do something? Ask him? But if he responds that he does not want to do it, then that calls for a psychological consultation to determine the reason for his obstinacy. Tell him? His response shows that he does not understand you, and now an expert in communication methods has to be brought in to show you how to get through to him. Give him a monetary incentive? I do not need to remind the reader of the complexity and difficulty involved in set-ting up and administering an incentive system. Show him? This means a costly training program. We need a simple way.

Every audience contains the "direct action" man-ager who shouts, "Kick him!" And this type of man-ager is right. The surest and least circumlocuted way of getting someone to do something is to kick him in the pants—give him what might be called the KITA.

There are various forms of KITA, and here are some of them:

Negative Physical KITA This is a literal application of the term and was frequently used in the past. It has, however, three major drawbacks: (1) it is inelegant; (2) it contradicts the precious image of benevolence that most organizations cherish; and (3) since it is a physical attack it directly stimulates the autonomic nervous system, and this often results in negative feed-back—the employee may just kick you in return. These factors give rise to certain taboos against nega-tive physical KITA.

The psychologist has come to the rescue of those who are no longer permitted to use negative physical KITA. He has uncovered infinite sources of psycho-logical vulnerabilities and the appropriate methods to play tunes on them. "He took my rug away"; "I won-der what he meant by that"; "The boss is always going around me"—these symptomatic expressions of ego sores that have been rubbed raw are the result of appli-cation of:

Negative Psychological KITA This has several advan-tages over negative physical KITA. First, the cruelty is not visible; the bleeding is internal and comes much later. Second, since it affects the higher cortical centers of the brain with its inhibitory powers, it reduces the possibility of physical backlash. Third, since the num-ber of psychological pains that a person can feel is almost infinite, the direction and site possibilities of the KITA are increased many times. Fourth, the per-son administering the kick can manage to be above it all and let the system accomplish the dirty work. Fifth, those who practice it receive some ego satisfaction (one-upmanship), whereas they would find drawing blood abhorrent. Finally, if the employee does com-plain, he can always be accused of being paranoid since there is no tangible evidence of an actual attack.

Now, what does negative KITA accomplish? If I kick you in the rear (physically or psychologically), who is motivated? I am motivated; you move! Negative KITA does not lead to motivation, but to movement. So:

Positive KITA Let us consider motivation. If I say to you, "Do this for me or the company, and in return I will give you a reward, an incentive, more status, a promotion all the quid pro quos that exist in the industrial organization," am I motivating you? The overwhelming opinion I receive from management people is, "Yes, this is motivation."

I have a year-old Schnauzer. When it was a small puppy and I wanted it to move, I kicked it in the rear and it moved. Now that I have finished its obedience training, I hold up a dog biscuit when I want the Schnauzer to move. In this instance, who is moti-vated—I or the dog? The dog wants the biscuit, but it is I who want it to move. Again, I am the one who is motivated, and the dog is the one who moves. In this instance all I did was apply KITA frontally; I exerted a pull instead of a push. When industry wishes to use such positive KITAs, it has available an incredible number and variety of dog biscuits (jelly beans for humans) to wave in front of the employee to get him to jump.

Why is it that managerial audiences are quick to see that negative KITA is *not* motivation, while they are almost unanimous in their judgment that positive KITA *is* motivation? It is because negative KITA is rape, and positive KITA is seduction. But it is infinitely worse to be seduced than to be raped; the latter is an unfortunate occurrence, while the former signifies that you were a party to your own downfall. This is why positive KITA is so popular: it is a tradition; it is in the American way. The organization does not have to kick you; you kick yourself.

Myths about Motivation

Why is KITA not motivation? If I kick my dog (from the front or the back), he will move. And when I want him to move again, what must I do? I must kick him again. Similarly, I can charge a man's battery, and then recharge it, and recharge it again. But it is only when he has his own generator that we can talk about motivation. He then needs no outside stimulation. He *wants to* do it.

With this in mind, we can review some positive KITA personnel practices that were developed as attempts to instill "motivation":

1. *Reducing time spent at work*—This represents a marvelous way of motivating people to work—getting them off the job! We have reduced (formally and informally) the time spent on the job over the last 50 or 60 years until we are finally on the way to the "6 1/2-day weekend." An interesting variant of this approach is the development of off-hour recreation programs. The philosophy here seems to be that those who play together, work together. The fact is that motivated people seek more hours of work, not fewer.

2. *Spiraling wages*—Have these motivated people? Yes, to seek the next wage increase. Some medievalists still can be heard to say that a good depression will get employees moving. They feel that if rising wages don't or won't do the job, perhaps reducing them will.

3. *Fringe benefits*—Industry has outdone the most welfare-minded of welfare states in dispensing cradle-to-the-grave succor. One company I know of had an informal "fringe benefit of the month club" going for a while. The cost of fringe benefits in this country has reached approximately 25% of the wage dollar, and we still cry for motivation.

People spend less time working for more money and more security than ever before, and the trend cannot be reversed. These benefits are no longer rewards; they are rights. A 6-day week is inhuman, a 10-hour day is exploitation, extended medical coverage is a basic decency, and stock options are the salvation of American initiative. Unless the ante is continuously raised, the psychological reaction of employees is that the company is turning back the clock.

When industry began to realize that both the economic nerve and the lazy nerve of their employees had insatiable appetites, it started to listen to the behavioral scientists who, more out of a humanist tradition than from scientific study, criticized management for not knowing how to deal with people. The next KITA easily followed.

4. *Human relations training*—Over 30 years of teaching and, in many instances, of practicing psychological approaches to handling people have resulted in costly human relations programs and, in the end, the same question: How do you motivate workers? Here, too, escalations have taken place. Thirty years ago it was necessary to request, "Please don't spit on the floor." Today the same admonition requires three "please"s before the employee feels that his superior has demonstrated the psychologically proper attitudes toward him.

The failure of human relations training to produce motivation led to the conclusion that the supervisor or manager himself was not psychologically true to himself in his practice of interpersonal decency. So an advanced form of human relations KITA, sensitivity training, was unfolded.

5. *Sensitivity training*—Do you really, really understand yourself? Do you really, really, really trust the other man? Do you really, really, really, really cooperate? The failure of sensitivity training is now being explained, by those who have become opportunistic exploiters of the technique, as a failure to really (five times) conduct proper sensitivity training courses.

With the realization that there are only temporary gains from comfort and economic and interpersonal

KITA, personnel managers concluded that the fault lay not in what they were doing, but in the employee's failure to appreciate what they were doing. This opened up the field of communications, a whole new area of "scientifically" sanctioned KITA.

6. *Communications*—The professor of communications was invited to join the faculty of management training programs and help in making employees understand what management was doing for them. House organs, briefing sessions, supervisory instruction on the importance of communication, and all sorts of propaganda have proliferated until today there is even an International Council of Industrial Editors. But no motivation resulted, and the obvious thought occurred that perhaps management was not hearing what the employees were saying. That led to the next KITA.

7. *Two-way communication*—Management ordered morale surveys, suggestion plans, and group participation programs. Then both employees and management were communicating and listening to each other more than ever, but without much improvement in motivation.

The behavioral scientists began to take another look at their conceptions and their data, and they took human relations one step further. A glimmer of truth was beginning to show through in the writings of the so-called higher-order-need psychologists. People, so they said, want to actualize themselves. Unfortunately, the "actualizing" psychologists got mixed up with the human relations psychologists, and a new KITA emerged.

8. *Job participation*—Though it may not have been the theoretical intention, job participation often became a "give them the big picture" approach. For example, if a man is tightening 10,000 nuts a day on an assembly line with a torque wrench, tell him he is building a Chevrolet. Another approach had the goal of giving the employee a *feeling* that he is determining, in some measure, what he does on his job. The goal was to provide a *sense* of achievement rather than a substantive achievement in his task. Real achievement, of course, requires a task that makes it possible.

But still there was no motivation. This led to the inevitable conclusion that the employees must be sick, and therefore to the next KITA.

9. *Employee counseling*—The initial use of this form of KITA in a systematic fashion can be credited to the Hawthorne experiment of the Western Electric Company during the early 1930's. At that time, it was found that the employees harbored irrational feelings that were interfering with the rational operation of the factory. Counseling in this instance was a means of letting the employees unburden themselves by talking to someone about their problems. Although the counseling techniques were primitive, the program was large indeed.

The counseling approach suffered as a result of experiences during World War II, when the programs themselves were found to be interfering with the operation of the organizations; the counselors had forgotten their role of benevolent listeners and were attempting to do something about the problems that they heard about. Psychological counseling, however, has managed to survive the negative impact of World War II experiences and today is beginning to flourish with renewed sophistication. But, alas, many of these programs, like all the others, do not seem to have lessened the pressure of demands to find out how to motivate workers.

Since KITA results only in short-term movement it is safe to predict that the cost of these programs will increase steadily and new varieties will be developed as old positive KITAs reach their satiation points.

HYGIENE VS. MOTIVATORS

Let me rephrase the perennial question this way: How do you install a generator in an employee? A brief review of my motivation-hygiene theory of job attitudes is required before theoretical and practical suggestions can be offered. The theory was first drawn from an examination of events in the lives of engineers and accountants. At least 16 other investigations, using a wide variety of populations (including some in the Communist countries), have since been completed, making the original research one of the most replicated studies in the field of job attitudes.

The findings of these studies, along with corroboration from many other investigations using different procedures, suggest that the factors involved in producing job satisfaction (and motivation) are separate and distinct from the factors that lead to job dissatisfaction. Since separate factors need to be considered, depending on whether job satisfaction or job dissatisfaction is being examined, it follows that these two feelings are not opposites of each other. The opposite of job satisfaction is not job dissatisfaction but, rather, *no* job satisfaction; and, similarly, the opposite of job dissatisfaction is not job satisfaction, but *no* job dissatisfaction.

Stating the concept presents a problem in semantics, for we normally think of satisfaction and dissatisfaction as opposites—i.e., what is not satisfying must be dissatisfying, and vice versa. But when it comes to understanding the behavior of people in their jobs, more than a play on words is involved.

Two different needs of man are involved here. One set of needs can be thought of as stemming from his animal nature—the built-in drive to avoid pain from the environment, plus all the learned drives which become conditioned to the basic biological needs. For example, hunger, a basic biological drive, makes it necessary to earn money, and then money becomes a specific drive. The other set of needs relates to that unique human characteristic, the ability to achieve and, through achievement, to experience psychological growth. The stimuli for the growth needs are tasks that induce growth; in the industrial setting, they are the *job content*. Contrariwise, the stimuli inducing pain-avoidance behavior are found in the *job environment*.

The growth or *motivator* factors that are intrinsic to the job are: achievement, recognition for achievement, the work itself, responsibility, and growth or advancement. The dissatisfaction-avoidance of *hygiene* (KITA) factors that are extrinsic to the job include: company policy and administration, supervision, interpersonal relationships, working conditions, salary, status, and security.

A composite of the factors that are involved in causing job satisfaction and job dissatisfaction, drawn from samples of 1,685 employees, is shown in Exhibit I. The results indicate that motivators were the primary cause of satisfaction, and hygiene factors the primary cause of unhappiness on the job. The employees, studied in 12 different investigations, included lower-level supervisors, professional women, agricultural administrators, men about to retire from management positions, hospital maintenance personnel, manufacturing supervisors, nurses, food handlers, military officers, engineers, scientists, housekeepers,

teachers, technicians, female assemblers, accountants, Finnish foremen, and Hungarian engineers.

They were asked what job events had occurred in their work that had led to extreme satisfaction or extreme dissatisfaction on their part. Their responses are broken down in the exhibit into percentages of total "positive" job events and of total "negative" job events. (The figures total more than 100% on both the "hygiene" and "motivators" sides because often at least two factors can be attributed to a single event; advancement, for instance, often accompanies assumption of responsibility.)

To illustrate, a typical response involving achievement that had a negative effect for the employee was, "I was unhappy because I didn't do the job successfully." A typical response in the small number of positive job events in the Company Policy and Administration grouping was, "I was happy because the company reorganized the section so that I didn't report any longer to the guy I didn't get along with."

As the lower right-hand part of the exhibit shows, of all the factors contributing to job satisfaction, 81% were motivators. And of all the factors contributing to the employees' dissatisfaction over their work, 69% involved hygiene elements.

Eternal Triangle

There are three general philosophies of personnel management. The first is based on organizational theory, the second on industrial engineering, and the third on behavioral science.

The organizational theorist believes that human needs are either so irrational or so varied and adjustable to specific situations that the major function of personnel management is to be as pragmatic as the occasion demands. If jobs are organized in a proper manner, he reasons, the result will be the most efficient job structure, and the most favorable job attitudes will follow as a matter of course.

The industrial engineer holds that man is mechanistically oriented and economically motivated and his needs are best met by attuning the individual to the most efficient work process. The goal of personnel management therefore should be to concoct the most appropriate incentive system and to design the specific working conditions in a way that facilitates the most

EXHIBIT I / Factors Affecting Job Attitudes, as Reported in 12 Investigations

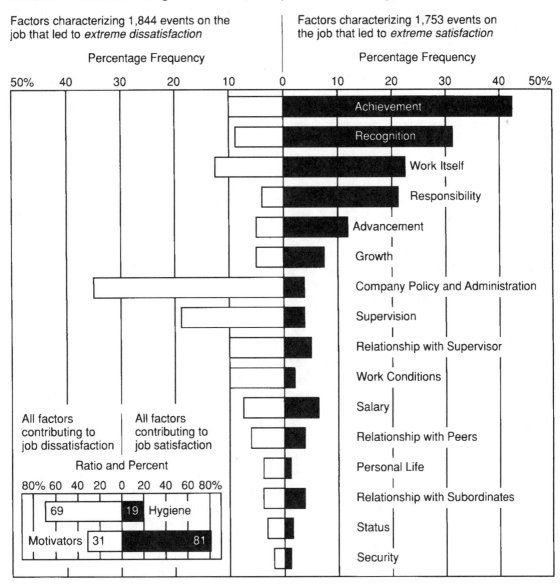

Factors characterizing 1,844 events on the job that led to *extreme dissatisfaction*

Factors characterizing 1,753 events on the job that led to *extreme satisfaction*

Percentage Frequency

Percentage Frequency

50% 40 30 20 10 0 10 20 30 40 50%

Achievement
Recognition
Work Itself
Responsibility
Advancement
Growth
Company Policy and Administration
Supervision
Relationship with Supervisor
Work Conditions
Salary
Relationship with Peers
Personal Life
Relationship with Subordinates
Status
Security

All factors contributing to job dissatisfaction

All factors contributing to job satisfaction

Ratio and Percent

80% 60 40 20 0 20 40 60 80%

69 | 19 Hygiene

Motivators | 31 | 81

efficient use of the human machine. By structuring jobs in a manner that leads to the most efficient operation, the engineer believes that he can obtain the optimal organization of work and the proper work attitudes.

The behavioral scientist focuses on group sentiments, attitudes of individual employees, and the organization's social and psychological climate. According

to his persuasion, he emphasizes one or more of the various hygiene and motivator needs. His approach to personnel management generally emphasizes some form of human relations education, in the hope of instilling healthy employee attitudes and an organizational climate which he considers to be felicitous to human values. He believes that the proper attitudes will lead to efficient job and organizational structure.

There is always a lively debate as to the overall effectiveness of the approaches of the organizational theorist and the industrial engineer. Manifestly they have achieved much. But the nagging question for the behavioral scientist has been: What is the cost in human problems that eventually cause more expense to the organization—for instance, turnover, absenteeism, errors, violation of safety rules, strikes, restriction of output, higher wages, and greater fringe benefits? On the other hand, the behavioral scientist is hard put to document much manifest improvement in personnel management, using his approach.

The three philosophies can be depicted as a triangle as is done in Exhibit II, with each persuasion claiming the apex angle. The motivation-hygiene theory claims the same angle as industrial engineering but for opposite goals. Rather than rationalizing the work to increase efficiency, the theory suggests that work be *enriched* to bring about effective utilization of personnel. Such a systematic attempt to motivate employees by manipulating the motivator factors is just beginning.

The term *job enrichment* describes this embryonic movement. An older term, job enlargement, should be avoided because it is associated with past failures stemming from a misunderstanding of the problem. Job enrichment provides the opportunity for the employee's psychological growth, while job enlargement merely makes a job structurally bigger. Since scientific job enrichment is very new, this article only

suggests the principles and practical steps that have recently emerged from several successful experiments in industry.

Job Loading

In attempting to enrich an employee's job, management often succeeds in reducing the man's personal contribution, rather than giving him an opportunity for growth in his accustomed job. Such an endeavor, which I shall call horizontal job loading (as opposed to vertical loading, or providing motivator factors), has been the problem of earlier job enlargement programs. This activity merely enlarges the meaninglessness of the job. Some examples of this approach, and their effect, are:

■ Challenging the employee by increasing the amount of production expected of him. If he tightens 10,000 bolts a day, see if he can tighten 20,000 bolts a day. The arithmetic involved shows that multiplying zero by zero still equals zero.
■ Adding another meaningless task to the existing one, usually some routine clerical activity. The arithmetic here is adding zero to zero.
■ Rotating the assignments of a number of jobs that need to be enriched. This means washing dishes for a while, then washing silverware. The arithmetic is substituting one zero for another zero.
■ Removing the most difficult parts of the assignment in order to free the worker to accomplish more of the less challenging assignments. This traditional industrial engineering approach amounts to subtraction in the hope of accomplishing addition.

These are common forms of horizontal loading that frequently come up in preliminary brainstorming sessions on job enrichment. The principles of vertical loading have not all been worked out as yet, and they remain rather general, but I have furnished seven useful starting points for consideration in Exhibit III.

A Successful Application

An example from a highly successful job enrichment experiment can illustrate the distinction between horizontal and vertical loading of a job. The subjects of this

EXHIBIT II / "Triangle" of Philosophies of Personnel Management

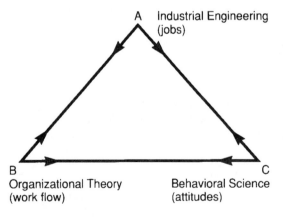

A Industrial Engineering (jobs)

B Organizational Theory (work flow)

C Behavioral Science (attitudes)

EXHIBIT III / Principles of Vertical Job Loading

Principle	Motivators Involved
A. Removing some controls while retaining accountability	Responsibility and personal achievement
B. Increasing the accountability of individuals for own work	Responsibility and recognition
C. Giving a person a complete natural unit of work (module, division, area, and so on)	Responsibility, achievement, and recognition
D. Granting additional authority to an employee in his activity; job freedom	Responsibility, achievement, and recognition
E. Making periodic reports directly available to the worker himself rather than to the supervisor	Internal recognition
F. Introducing new and more difficult tasks not previously handled	Growth and learning
G. Assigning individuals specific or specialized tasks, enabling them to become experts	Responsibility, growth, and advancement

study were the stockholder correspondents employed by a very large corporation. Seemingly, the task required of these carefully selected and highly trained correspondents was quite complex and challenging. But almost all indexes of performance and job attitudes were low, and exit interviewing confirmed that the challenge of the job existed merely as words.

A job enrichment project was initiated in the form of an experiment with one group, designated as an achieving unit, having its job enriched by the principles described in Exhibit III. A control group continued to do its job in the traditional way. (There were also two "uncommitted" groups of correspondents formed to measure the so-called Hawthorne Effect—that is, to gauge whether productivity and attitudes toward the job changed artificially merely because employees sensed that the company was paying more attention to them in doing something different or novel. The results for these groups were substantially the same as for the control group, and for the sake of simplicity I do not deal with them in this summary.) No changes in hygiene were introduced for either group other than those that would have been made anyway, such as normal pay increases.

The changes for the achieving unit were introduced in the first two months, averaging one per week of the seven motivators listed in Exhibit III. At the end of six months the members of the achieving unit were found to be outperforming their counterparts in the control group, and in addition indicated a marked increase in their liking for their jobs. Other results showed that the achieving group had lower absenteeism and, subsequently, a much higher rate of promotion.

Exhibit IV illustrates the changes in performance, measured in February and March, before the study period began, and at the end of each month of the study period. The shareholder service index represents quality of letters, including accuracy of information, and speed of response to stockholders' letters of inquiry. The index of a current month was averaged into the average of the two prior months, which means that improvement was harder to obtain if the indexes of the previous months were low. The "achievers" were performing less well before the six-month period started, and their performance service index continued to decline after the introduction of the motivators, evidently because of uncertainty over their newly granted responsibilities. In the third month, however, performance improved, and soon the members of this group had reached a high level of accomplishment.

Exhibit V shows the two groups' attitudes toward their job, measured at the end of March, just before

EXHIBIT IV / Shareholder Service Index in Company Experiment (Three-Month Cumulative Average)

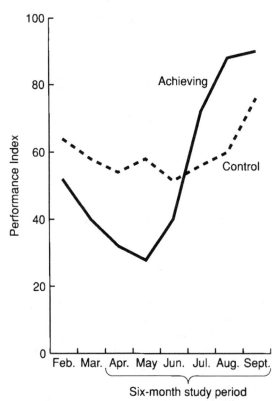

Six-month study period

EXHIBIT V / Changes in Attitudes toward Tasks in Company Experiment (Changes in Mean Scores over Six-Month Period)

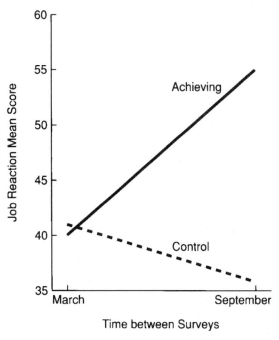

Time between Surveys

closely to the list of common manifestations of the phenomenon in Exhibit III, left column.

STEPS TO JOB ENRICHMENT

the first motivator was introduced, and again at the end of September. The correspondents were asked 16 questions, all involving motivation. A typical one was, "As you see it, how many opportunities do you feel that you have in your job for making worthwhile contributions?" The answers were scaled from 1 to 5, with 80 as the maximum possible score. The achievers became much more positive about their job, while the attitude of the control unit remained about the same (the drop is not statistically significant).

How was the job of these correspondents restructured? Exhibit VI lists the suggestions made that were deemed to be horizontal loading, and the actual vertical loading changes that were incorporated in the job of the achieving unit. The capital letters under "Principle" after "Vertical loading" refer to the corresponding letters in Exhibit III. The reader will note that the rejected forms of horizontal loading correspond

Now that the motivator idea has been described in practice, here are the steps that managers should take in instituting the principle with their employees:

1. Select those jobs in which (a) the investment in industrial engineering does not make changes too costly, (b) attitudes are poor, (c) hygiene is becoming very costly, and (d) motivation will make a difference in performance.

2. Approach these jobs with the conviction that they can be changed. Years of tradition have led managers to believe that the content of the jobs is sacrosanct and the only scope of action that they have is in ways of stimulating people.

3. Brainstorm a list of changes that may enrich the jobs, without concern for their practicality.

4. Screen the list to eliminate suggestions that involve hygiene, rather than actual motivation.

EXHIBIT VI / Enlargement vs. Enrichment of Correspondents'Tasks in Company Experiment

Horizontal loading suggestions (rejected)	Vertical loading suggestions (adopted)	Principle
Firm quotas could be set for letters to be answered each day, using a rate which would be hard to reach.	Subject matter experts were appointed within each unit for other members of the unit to consult with before seeking supervisory help. (The supervisor had been answering all specialized and difficult questions.)	G
The women could type the letters themselves, as well as compose them, or take on any other clerical functions.	Correspondents signed their own names on letters. (The supervisor had been signing all letters.)	B
All difficult or complex inquiries could be channeled to a few women so that the remainder could achieve high rates of output. These jobs could be exchanged from time to time.	The work of the more experienced correspondents was proofread less frequently by supervisors and was done at the correspondents' desks, dropping verification from 100% to 10%. (Previously, all correspondents' letters had been checked by the supervisor.)	A
The women could be rotated through units handling different customers, and then sent back to their own units.	Production was discussed, but only in terms such as "a full day's work is expected." As time went on, this was no longer mentioned. (Before, the group had been constantly reminded of the number of letters that needed to be answered.)	D
	Outgoing mail went directly to the mailroom without going over supervisors' desks. (The letters had always been routed through the supervisors.)	A
	Correspondents were encouraged to answer letters in a more personalized way. (Reliance on the form-letter approach had been standard practice.)	C
	Each correspondent was held personally responsible for the quality and accuracy of letters. (This responsibility had been the province of the supervisor and the verifier.)	B, E

5. Screen the list for generalities, such as "give them more responsibility," that are rarely followed in practice. This might seem obvious, but the motivator words have never left industry; the substance has just been rationalized and organized out. Words like "responsibility," "growth," "achievement," and "challenge," for example, have been elevated to the lyrics of the patriotic anthem for all organizations. It is the old problem typified by the pledge of allegiance to the flag being more important than contributions to the country—of following the form, rather than the substance.

6. Screen the list to eliminate any *horizontal* loading suggestions.

7. Avoid direct participation by the employees whose jobs are to be enriched. Ideas they have expressed previously certainly constitute a valuable source for recommended changes, but their direct involvement contaminates the process with human relations *hygiene* and, more specifically, gives them only a *sense* of making a contribution. The job is to be changed, and it is the content that will produce the motivation, not attitudes about being involved or the challenge inherent in setting up a job. That process will be over shortly, and it is what the employees will be doing from then on that will determine their motivation. A sense of participation will result only in short-term movement.

8. In the initial attempts at job enrichment, set up a controlled experiment. At least two equivalent groups should be chosen, one an experimental unit in which the motivators are systematically introduced over a period of time, and the other one a control group in which no changes are made. For both groups, hygiene should be allowed to follow its natural course for the duration of the experiment. Pre- and post-installation tests of performance and job attitudes are necessary to evaluate the effectiveness of the job enrichment program. The attitude test must be limited to motivator items in order to divorce the employee's view of the job he is given from all the surrounding hygiene feelings that he might have.

9. Be prepared for a drop in performance in the experimental group the first few weeks. The change-over to a new job may lead to a temporary reduction in efficiency.

10. Expect your first-line supervisors to experience some anxiety and hostility over the changes you are making. The anxiety comes from their fear that the changes will result in poorer performance for their unit. Hostility will arise when the employees start assuming what the supervisors regard as their own responsibility for performance. The supervisor without checking duties to perform may then be left with little to do.

After a successful experiment however, the supervisor usually discovers the supervisory and managerial functions he has neglected, or which were never his because all his time was given over to checking the work of his subordinates. For example, in the R&D division of one large chemical company I know of, the supervisors of the laboratory assistants were theoretically responsible for their training and evaluation. These functions, however, had come to be performed in a routine, unsubstantial fashion. After the job enrichment program, during which the supervisors were not merely passive observers of the assistants' performance, the supervisors actually were devoting their time to reviewing performance and administering thorough training.

What has been called an employee-centered style of supervision will come about not through education of supervisors, but by changing the jobs that they do.

CONCLUDING NOTE

Job enrichment will not be a one-time proposition, but a continuous management function. The initial changes, however, should last for a very long period of time. There are a number of reasons for this:

■ The changes should bring the job up to the level of challenge commensurate with the skill that was hired.

■ Those who have still more ability eventually will be able to demonstrate it better and win promotion to higher-level jobs.

■ The very nature of motivators, as opposed to hygiene factors, is that they have a much longer-term effect on employees' attitudes. Perhaps the job will have to be enriched again, but this will not occur as frequently as the need for hygiene.

Not all jobs can be enriched, nor do all jobs need to be enriched. If only a small percentage of the time and money that is now devoted to hygiene, however, were given to job enrichment efforts, the return in human satisfaction and economic gain would be one of the largest dividends that industry and society have ever reaped through their efforts at better personnel management.

The argument for job enrichment can be summed up quite simply: If you have someone on a job, use him. If you can't use him on the job, get rid of him, either via automation or by selecting someone with lesser ability. If you can't use him and you can't get rid of him, you will have a motivation problem.

NOTES

Readers of this article may be interested in "What Job Attitudes Tell About Motivation," by Lyman W. Porter and Edward E. Lawler, III, *Harvard Business Review,* Vol. 46, January/February 1968, pp. 118–126.

Author's note: I should like to acknowledge the contributions that Robert Ford of the American Telephone and Telegraph Company has made to the ideas expressed in this paper, and in particular to the successful application of these ideas in improving work performance and the job satisfaction of employees.

CRITICAL THINKING QUESTIONS

1. Suppose we change the topic of the article from how to motivate *employees* to how to motivate *students.* Can Herzberg's principles of employee motivation be used in the academic environment? How? As part of this question, conduct a survey of students to identify what school factors lead to extreme satisfaction and extreme dissatisfaction. Classify these as hygiene or motivation factors.
2. Would the principles of successful job enrichment outlined by Herzberg apply equally to all employees in all situations? What individual- or work-related factors might mediate whether the principles will work?
3. Conduct an informal survey of people you know who work full time, asking them the same questions about job satisfaction and dissatisfaction outlined in the article. How well do your observations correspond with the information presented by Herzberg?
4. After reading an article such as this, why might some managers still be reluctant to undertake recommended changes? Are any of these concerns legitimate? Why or why not?

ADDITIONAL RELATED READINGS

DeVoe, S. E., & Iyengar, S. S. (2004). Managers' theories of subordination: A cross-cultural examination of manager perceptions of motivation on appraisal of performance. *Organizational Behavior and Human Decision Processes, 93*(1), 47–61.

Steelman, L. A., & Rutkowski, K. A. (2004). Moderators of employee reactions to negative feedback. *Journal of Managerial Psychology, 19*(1), 6–18.

ARTICLE 39 _____

What makes an effective leader? Is it having a unique personality or the particular type of leadership needed in a particular situation? The study of what factors contribute to effective leadership has a long history and both theoretical and practical implications. After all, if we can identify the characteristics of effective leaders, then we can help move people to positions where their leadership abilities can be best utilized.

Broadly speaking, early work on leadership tended to focus on two types of factors: trait and situational. Interestingly, these two factors also parallel what has been found in much social psychological inquiry. *Situational factors* are those that can change depending on the specific context. The classic study presented in Article 38 examined situational factors. By varying their leadership styles in different situations, the leaders were able to elicit very different behaviors in their followers. *Trait factors,* on the other hand, pertain to those relatively enduring characteristics of the individual. Early research on leadership focused on such trait characteristics as intelligence. While being highly intelligent was shown to be important in an effective leader, ongoing research made it apparent that intelligence was not enough by itself. Something more was needed.

Recently, researchers Peter Salovey and John Meyer coined the term *emotional intelligence* to describe the qualities that seem to enhance successful social behavior. For example, factors such as empathy and delay of gratification often characterize people who are particularly socially successful. This concept became wildly popular with the publication of the best-selling book *Emotional Intelligence,* by Daniel Goleman, who also introduced the shortened term *EQ* to refer to these qualities. The basic notion is that just as IQ (i.e., intelligence quotient) may give some indication of the overall level of a person's intellectual ability, EQ may give some insight into the level of social skills that an individual possesses.

The following article by Barbara Mandell and Shilpa Pherwani examines the role of emotional intelligence in leadership style. The article not only examines the possible role of emotional intelligence in predicting successful styles of leadership, but it also seeks to determine if there are any gender differences in leadership style and/or emotional intelligence.

Relationship between Emotional Intelligence and Transformational Leadership Style
A Gender Comparison

■ Barbara Mandell and Shilpa Pherwani

Abstract: *This study examined the predictive relationship between emotional intelligence and transformational leadership style. The researchers also wanted to determine gender differences in the relationship between emotional intelligence and transformational leadership style, as well as the gender differences in the emotional intelligence scores and transformational leadership style of managers. A significant predictive relationship (p < .05) was found between transformational leadership style and emotional intelligence. No significant interaction (p > .05) was*

Reprinted from B. Mandell and S. Pherwani, "Relationship between Emotional Intelligence and Transformational Leadership Style: A Gender Comparison," *Journal of Business and Psychology,* 2003, *17*(3), 387–404. Copyright © 2003 by Kluwer Academic/Plenum Publishers, Inc. Reprinted with permission.

found between gender and emotional intelligence while predicting transformational leadership style. A significant difference (p < .05) was found in the emotional intelligence of scores of male and female managers. Lastly, no significant difference (p > .05) was found in the transformational leadership scores of male and female managers.

Key Words: emotional intelligence; leadership style, gender

During the first half of the 20th century Intelligence Quotient (IQ) tests were considered adequate measures of intelligence. Society linked IQ scores to an individual's potential for success in life (Wechsler, 1958). Reviews of early leadership studies by Bass (1990a) and by Lord, DeVader, and Alliger (1986) found that intelligence did contribute to leadership success. These studies focused on the traditional IQ concept of academic intelligence and consistently correlated positive perceptions of leadership and leaders' IQ scores.

Opponents of the IQ approach claimed an overemphasis on the role of general academic intelligence in predicting leadership success. This early approach has also been criticized because it did not consider situational factors in the assessment of leadership success (Riggio, Murphy & Pirozzolo, 2002).

Current research has moved away from IQ scores as the only measure of intelligence. As early as 1920 Thorndike hypothesized that true intelligence was composed of not only an academic component, but also emotional and social components. In 1967 Guilford presented a view of intelligence as a multifaceted construct composed of one hundred and twenty different types of intelligence.

Shanley, Walker, and Foley (1971) hypothesized that social intelligence was distinct from academic intelligence, but they found little empirical evidence to support social intelligence as a separate construct. Salovey and Mayer (1990) suggested social intelligence had been defined too broadly. They investigated emotional intelligence, as a specific aspect of social intelligence. Salovey and Mayer (1990) defined emotional intelligence as the "ability to monitor one's own and others' feelings and emotions, to discriminate among them and to use this information to

guide one's own thinking and actions" (p. 189). They suggested that emotional intelligence would be easier to distinguish from academic intelligence.

While society has traditionally placed a great deal of weight on academic intelligence, Bar-On (1997) argued that emotional and social intelligences were better predictors of success in life. The more recent writings and research of Gardner (1983, 1993, 1999), Sternberg (1985), Sternberg and Wagner (1986), and Wagner and Sternberg (1985) have added support to the concept of multiple intelligences. Gardner has proposed a model of at least 8 types of intelligence including spatial, musical, intrapersonal, interpersonal, bodily-kinesthetic, naturalistic, and the traditional academic intelligence: linguistic and logical-mathematical. Sternberg's theory (1985) identifies three types of mental abilities: analytical intelligence, creative intelligence and practical intelligence. Riggio, Murphy and Pirozzolo (2002) propose these multiple forms of intelligence are possessed by effective leaders and allow these leaders to respond successfully to a range of situations.

Most recently the interest in leadership and intelligence has been increased by the popular writings of Daniel Goleman (1995, 1998). Other authors (Cooper & Sawaf, 1997; Feldman, 1999; Ryback, 1997; Weisinger, 1998) have contributed to the construct of emotional intelligence and its importance in the workplace. Zaccaro (1996, 1999, 2001) emphasized the important role of social intelligence in organizational leadership by developing a model of organizational leadership that identified the various performance requirements leaders needed to address at ascending levels in the organization. Such skills as flexibility, conflict management, persuasion and social reasoning became more important as leaders advanced in the hierarchy.

Two models of emotional intelligence have emerged. The ability model, defines emotional intelligence as a set of abilities that involves perceiving and reasoning abstractly with information that emerges from feelings. This model has been supported by the research of Mayer, Caruso and Salovey (1999); Mayer, DiPaolo, and Salovey (1990); Mayer and Salovey (1993, 1997); and Salovey and Mayer (1990). The mixed model defines emotional intelligence as an ability with social behaviors, traits and competencies. This model has found support in the writings of Goleman (1995, 1998) and Bar-On (1997).

Davies, Stankov, and Roberts (1998) proposed that emotional intelligence should not be considered a unique human ability until there was an appropriate instrument for the construct's measurement. Mayer, Salovey and Caruso (1997) developed an ability based emotional intelligence test. The early version, the Multifactor Emotional Intelligence Scale MEIS) (1997) and the more recent version, the Mayer-Salovey-Caruso Emotional Intelligence Test (MSCEIT) (1999) both measure four ability areas of emotional intelligence: perception, facilitation of thought, understanding, and management.

Reflecting the mixed model of emotional intelligence, Bar-On (1996) developed an instrument to measure a more comprehensive concept of emotional intelligence, which he labeled emotional quotient (EQ). Bar-On (1997) defined emotional intelligence as "an array of non-cognitive capabilities, competencies, and skills that influence one's ability to succeed in coping with environmental demands and pressures" (p. 14). The Bar-On Emotional Quotient Inventory (EQ-i) divides emotional intelligence into five major components. Bar-On (1996) labeled the components 'intrapersonal,' 'interpersonal,' 'adaptability,' 'stress management' and 'general mood.' As emotional intelligence is a new construct, the MEIS, the MSCEIT and the EQ-i are undergoing considerable validation studies, and early research has been promising (Mayer, Caruso, & Salovy, 1999 & Bar-On, 1997). Bar-On reviews a substantial amount of validation research in the EQ-i manual (1997). Results indicate that the scales have good internal consistency and test-retest reliability. Factor analyses also provide support for the inventory's structure and the convergent and discriminate validity of the EQ-i is generally supported. In a recent study (Dada & Hart, 2000) the reliability and validity of the Bar-On Emotional Quotient Inventory was investigated with a sample of 243 university students. The results also provided support for the reliability and validity of the EQ-i.

Bass (1997) examined the profiles of successful individuals, but within the context of leadership style. In the past, leadership studies focused on trait and situational approaches. Current developments in leadership have focused on transformational and transactional approaches (Hackman, Hills, Furniss, & Peterson, 1992). Burns (1978) proposed that leadership process occurs in one of two ways, either transactional or transformational.

Bass and Avolio (1994) defined transformational leadership as leadership that occurs when the leader stimulates the interest among colleagues and followers to view their work from a new perspective. The transformational leader generates an awareness of the mission or vision of the organization, and develops colleagues and followers to higher levels of ability and potential. In addition, the transformational leader motivates colleagues and followers to look beyond their own interests towards interests that will benefit the group. Bass and Avolio (1994) proposed that transformational leadership comprises four dimensions—the "Four I's." The four dimensions were: Idealized Influence, Inspirational Motivation, Intellectual Stimulation, and Individualized Consideration.

In comparison to transformational leadership, Bass and Avolio (1994) described transactional leadership occurring when the leader rewards or disciplines the follower with regards to performance. Burns (1978) described transactional leaders as leaders that emphasize work standards, assignments, and task-oriented goals. In addition, transactional leaders tend to focus on task completion and employee compliance, and these leaders rely quite heavily on organizational rewards and punishments to influence employee performance (Burns, 1978).

Bass (1997) suggested that transformational leaders (TF) achieved higher levels of success in the workplace than transactional leaders (TA). He noted that TF leaders were promoted more often and produced better financial results that TA leaders (Bass, 1997). Bass (1997) also observed that employees rated TF leaders more satisfying and effective than TA leaders. Bar-On (1997) would attribute transformational leaders' superior work performance to high EQ-i scores.

Several researchers have investigated the effects of transformational and transactional leadership. Hater and Bass (1988) found transformational leadership, when compared to transactional leadership, predicted higher employee ratings of effectiveness and satisfaction. In addition, Keller (1995) found that certain aspects of transformational leadership predicted higher group performance. Also, Seltzer and Bass (1990) found moderate correlations between transformational leadership and leader effectiveness, subordinate extra effort, and satisfaction of the subordinate with the leader. Lastly, top performing managers are seen as more transformational in their leadership style than ordinary managers (Hater & Bass, 1988).

Researchers have focused their efforts on the behaviors and characteristics of effective leaders. According to Goleman (1998c), most effective leaders are alike in they all have a high degree of emotional intelligence. Goleman (1998c) claimed, "emotional intelligence is the sine qua non of leadership. . . . Without it, a person can have the best training in the world, an incisive analytic mind, and an endless supply of smart ideas, but he still won't make a great leader" (p. 93). Emotional intelligence plays an increasingly important role at the highest levels of the company, where differences in technical skills are of negligible importance (Goleman, 1998c).

Bass (1990b) proposes that transformational leaders must possess multiple types of intelligence and that social and emotional intelligence are critical because these are important to the leader's ability to inspire employees and build relationships. Caruso, Mayer and Salovey (2002) support Bass' thesis. According to these authors emotional intelligence underlies a leader's relationship skills. They contend that organizations should consider emotional intelligence in the selection and development of leaders.

A review (Avolio & Bass, 1997) of organizational research studies consistently found that transformational leaders as measured by the Management Leadership Questionnaire (MLQ) were more effective and satisfying leaders than were transactional leaders. Transformational leaders appear to be more behavioral and less emotional when dealing with stress and conflict. They demonstrate internal locus of control, self-confidence and self-acceptance. They appear to be better adjusted than transactional leaders with a strong sense of responsibility and clear goals. Focusing on a multiple model of intelligence, a review of studies (Atwater & Yammarino, 1993; Gibbons, 1986; Howell & Avolio, 1993; Ross & Offerman, 1997; Southwick, 1998) that examined the relationship between leadership style and emotional intelligence found evidence of correlations between transformational leadership and traits of emotional intelligence, less for social intelligence and least for cognitive intelligence.

Researchers in the past have also looked at the gender differences for both transformational leadership style and emotional intelligence. Although past research on leadership style differences between men and women has been inconclusive, a review of research on leadership and gender consistently demonstrates that women leaders are often negatively evaluated in comparison to their male counterparts, especially when they employ an autocratic leadership style (Eagly, Makhijani, & Klonsky, 1992).

Research on gender differences in emotional intelligence has been limited. Although Goleman (1995) considered males and females to have their own personal profiles of strengths and weaknesses for emotional intelligence capacities, studies conducted by Mayer, Caruso and Salovey in 1999 and Mayer and Geher in 1996 indicate that women score higher on measures of emotional intelligence than men.

METHOD

Based on the previous research in the areas of leadership and emotional intelligence, the current investigation was designed to determine the predictive relationship between emotional intelligence and transformational leadership style. The researchers also investigated any gender differences in the relationship between emotional intelligence and transformational leadership style and the gender differences in the emotional intelligence scores and transformational leadership style of male and female managers.

The researchers conducted a hierarchical regression analysis to determine if emotional intelligence is a predictor of transformational leadership style. The analysis was also used to investigate the gender differences in the relationship between emotional intelligence and transformational leadership style. To investigate the gender differences in the relationship, the researchers used the hierarchical regression analysis to determine the interaction between gender and emotional intelligence when predicting transformational leadership style. Independent *t*-tests were performed to determine gender differences in the emotional intelligence scores and transformational leadership style of male and female managers.

Participants

The researchers sent a letter to the human resources representatives of volunteering organizations explaining the design and purpose of the study. A second letter was sent to exempt employees asking for their participation in the research. The volunteer sample consisted of 32 male and female managers or supervisors employed in mid-sized to large organizations in the northeastern section of the United States.

Measurement Instruments

The researchers used the Multi-factor Leadership Questionnaire (MLQ, 5x-Revised; Bass & Avolio, 1996) to determine the leadership style of individuals. The Bar-On Emotional Quotient Inventory (EQ-i; Bar-On, 1996) was used to obtain the emotional intelligence scores of leaders. A demographic questionnaire was also administered to collect participant personal data. The latest version of the MLQ (5x-Revised; Bass & Avolio, 1996) is available in two forms: the self-rating form, where supervisors rate themselves as leaders; and the rater form, where associates rate their leaders. For the current study, the leaders responded to the MLQ (5x-Revised; Bass & Avolio, 1996) self-rating form.

The MLQ (5x-Revised; Bass & Avolio, 1996) contains 45 items and assesses five components of transformational leadership, three components of transactional leadership, one non-transactional leadership component, and three outcome components. The five components of transformational leadership are 'Idealized Influence (Behavior),' 'Idealized Influence (Attributed),' 'Inspirational Motivation,' 'Intellectual Stimulation,' 'Individualized Consideration' (Bass & Avolio, 1996).

The three components of transactional leadership are categorized under constructive transactions or corrective transactions. The first category is based on 'Contingent Reward,' and the second on 'Manage-

ment-by-Exception (Active),' and 'Management-by-Exception (Passive)' (Bass & Avolio, 1996). The non-transactional component is 'Laissez-Faire,' and the three outcome components are 'Satisfaction with the Leader,' 'Individual, Group, and Organizational Effectiveness,' and 'Extra Effort by Associates' (Bass & Avolio, 1996).

The MLQ (5x-Revised; Bass & Avolio, 1996) was scored by adding all factors to get a transformational, transactional, and 'Laissez-Faire' score for each participant. For the purpose of this study, the researchers used the transformational leadership scores only.

Bass and Avolio (1996) reported the alpha reliability coefficients for the MLQ (5x-Revised; Bass & Avolio, 1996) rater form scales for 2080 cases. The Spearman Brown estimated reliabilities ranged from .81 to .96. The alpha reliabilities coefficients for the MLQ (5x-Revised; Bass & Avolio, 1996) self-rating form were slightly lower. The test-retest reliabilities ranged from .44 to .74 for the self-ratings and .53 to .85 for the ratings by others.

A confirmatory factor analysis was conducted to establish the construct validity of the MLQ (5x-Revised; Bass & Avolio, 1996). The analysis was based on data generated by raters who evaluated their leaders within a broad range of organizations and at varying levels within those organizations. Bass and Avolio (1996) also computed reliability coefficients for each leadership factor. The coefficients ranged from .73 to .94 (Bass & Avolio, 1996).

The EQ-i (Bar-On, 1996), originally designed in 1980 by Bar-On, was used to measure emotional intelligence. The instrument has 133 items that are categorized into five main components and 15 factorial components. The five main components are 'Intrapersonal,' 'Interpersonal,' 'Adaptability,' 'Stress Management,' and 'General Mood.' Bar-On (1996) described the first component, Intra-personal, as a scale that assesses the inner self. Individuals who score high on this scale are considered to be in touch with their feelings, they feel good about themselves, and they feel positive about the way things move in their lives (Bar-On, 1996). Bar-On (1996) identified the second component, Inter-personal, to be characteristic of responsible and dependable individuals who have good people skills. Individuals who score high on this scale understand, interact and relate well with others (Bar-On, 1996). The third component, Adaptability, is a sign of how well individuals are able to cope with environmental demands and pressures (Bar-On, 1996). Bar-On (1996), stated that the fourth component, Stress Management, reflects how people handle stress. The fifth and final component, General Mood, is an indicator of an individual's ability to enjoy life (Bar-On, 1996).

For the EQ-i (Bar-On, 1996) high and low scores are identified by how distant they are from the mean score of 100. Scores exceeding the mean or falling below the mean by 1 SD (15 points) are considered to be within the normal range. The average time to complete the test is 20–50 min.

Bar-On (1996) focused on two aspects of reliability, internal consistency and test-retest reliability. The test-retest reliability for the EQ-i (Bar-On, 1996) after 1 month was .85, and .75 after 4 months.

The EQ-i (Bar-On, 1996) has been validated in many ways. As reported by Bar-On (1996) completed validity studies include the following: (a) correlation between the EQ-i (Bar-On, 1996) and various personality measures; (b) comparisons between successful and unsuccessful groups in terms of their EQ-i (Bar-On, 1996) scores; (c) comparison between obtained EQ-i (Bar-On, 1996) scores and what was theoretically expected from particular groups; (d) comparison between EQ-i (Bar-On, 1996) scores and coping styles; (e) comparison between EQ-i (Bar-On, 1996) scores and job performance and job satisfaction; (f) comparison between EQ-i scores and attributional styles; and (g) analysis of the sensitivity of the EQ-i (Bar-On, 1996) to remedial interventions.

Bar-On (1996) reported that the correlation with personality measures was high enough to firmly support that the EQ-i (Bar-On, 1996) subscales are measuring the constructs that they were intended to measure. Discriminant validity was established by Bar-On (1996) by comparing successful and unsuccessful groups in terms of their EQ-i (Bar-On, 1996) scores. The EQ-i (Bar-On, 1996) can differentiate among various groups and can distinguish more successful respondents from less successful ones in various areas.

Bar-On (1996) established criterion-group validity by comparing obtained EQ-i (Bar-On, 1996) scores with what was theoretically expected for particular groups. Bar-On (1996) reported that the criterion validity of the EQ-i (Bar-On, 1996) was supported to the extent that the test produced high scores in the appropriate areas for groups known to be strong in those particular areas. Likewise, unsuccessful groups obtained low scores.

Bar-On (1996) administered the EQ-i (Bar-On, 1996) and the Coping Inventory for Stressful Situations (CISS) (Endler & Parker, 1990) in an attempt to gauge the convergent validity of EQ-i (Bar-On, 1996). Bar-On (1996) reported that a number of EQ-i (Bar-On, 1996) scales and subscales were significantly correlated with a measure of successful and efficient coping with stressful situations.

Bar-On (1996) determined a high correlation between EQ-i (Bar-On, 1996) and satisfaction with work conditions and suggested a relationship between emotional intelligence and job satisfaction. Bar-On (1996) performed another study in South Africa on alcoholics in a substance abuse center, to establish the predictive validity of the instrument. Bar-On (1996) reported significant differences in emotional intelligence between the onset of the treatment and its termination 3 weeks later. Bar-On (1996) concluded that this particular program succeeded in improving emotional skills as measured by the EQ-i (Bar-On, 1996) and thus supported the instrument's sensitivity to picking up changes in emotional intelligence and demonstrated predictive validity. The validity studies for this instrument are still in process.

Procedures

The researchers contacted executives or Human Resources managers of a varied sample of organizations. After receiving permission to test employees within their companies, the researchers sent a request form to Human Resources professionals explaining the design and purpose of the study in greater detail. A letter was sent to the managerial employees soliciting their participation in the study. Before the participants took the tests, the researchers explained the purpose of the study and obtained their informed consent. If the participants wanted to receive a copy of the EQ-i (Bar-On, 1996) results, the researchers asked them to provide their mailing address on the consent form. The researchers then distributed the demographic form, the MLQ and the Bar-On and data were collected.

Statistical Analyses

Hierarchical Regression analysis was conducted to examine the predictive relationship between emotional intelligence and transformational leadership style. The analysis was also used to examine interaction of gender with emotional intelligence when predicting transformational leadership style. The analysis also helped the researchers identify gender differences in the relationship between emotional intelligence and transformational leadership style. Emotional intelligence, gender and interaction of gender and emotional intelligence were the predictor variables and transformational leadership style was the criterion variable in the study. Independent *t*-tests were conducted to determine gender differences in the emotional intelligence scores and leadership styles of male and female managers. The REGRESSION procedure from the SPSS for Windows Statistical Package was used to test the prediction models (SPSS, 1999).

RESULTS

This research was designed to determine the predictive relationship between emotional intelligence and transformational leadership style. The researchers also determined gender differences in the relationship between emotional intelligence and transformational leadership style of male and female managers. Lastly, we determined if gender differences existed in the emotional intelligence scores, and transformational leadership style of male and female leaders.

In the total investigation, 32 managers were tested of which 13 were males and 19 females. The mean age of the participants was 39 years. The leadership or supervisory experience of the participants ranged from 1 year to 40 years. 18 of the 32 participants had Masters level degree, 8 participants had a Bachelor's degree and the rest had either a high school diploma or an associate's degree. The industrial settings of the participants included business, medical, education, financial and high-tech. 7 of the participants were team leaders, 1 was an organization president, 3 were senior executives and the rest of the participants were at different levels of management.

The mean of transformational leadership score for all participants was 64.44, with a standard deviation of ±6.82. The mean of emotional intelligence was 105.00, with a standard deviation of ±11.75. The transformational leadership scores ranged from a low of 49 to a high of 75. The emotional intelligence scores ranged from a low of 78 to a high of 123. The mean transformational leadership score of females was slightly higher than the mean transformational leadership score of males (65.21 and 63.31 respectively). Similarly, the mean emotional intelligence score for females was higher than the mean emotional intelligence score for females (109.58 and 98.31 respectively). A summary of the descriptive statistics for males and females is presented in Table 1.

A hierarchical regression analysis was conducted to test the predictive relationship between emotional intelligence and transformational leadership style. Emotional intelligence was used as the predictor variable and transformational leadership as the criterion variable. A significant ($R = .499$, $R^2 = .249$, $p < .05$) linear relationship was found between emotional intelligence and transformational leadership style. The results of this procedure are presented in Table 2.

The hierarchical regression analysis was also used to examine the interaction of gender with emotional

TABLE 1 / Descriptive Statistics for Emotional Intelligence and Transformational Leadership Scores of Male and Female Managers

Variable	Males			Females		
	M	*SD*	*n*	*M*	*SD*	*n*
Transformational Leadership Style	63.31	7.89	13	65.21	6.08	19
Emotional Intelligence	98.31	8.30	13	109.58	11.72	19

TABLE 2 / Summary of Hierarchical Regression Analysis for Variables Predicting Transformational Leadership Style (N = 32)

Variable	B	SE B	β
Step 1			
Emotional Intelligence	.28	.09	.49
Step 2			
Emotional Intelligence	.32	.10	.56
Gender	−1.76	2.49	−.12
Step 3			
Emotional Intelligence	.37	.18	.64
Gender	.39	7.39	.02
Interaction	−2.29	.07	−.21

Note: R^2 = .249 for Step 1; R^2 = .262 for Step 2 and R^2 = .264 for Step 3.

intelligence while predicting transformational leadership style. To test this, gender was added as a predictor in step 2, the gender and emotional intelligence interaction was added in step 3. The difference in the R^2 values between step 2 and step 3 was −.002. The results suggested that there is no difference in the relationship between emotional intelligence and transformational leadership style of male and female managers. The results of this procedure are presented in Table 2.

Independent groups t-tests were used to compare the mean totals of transformational and emotional intelligence scores of male and female managers. A significant ($p < .05$) difference was found in the emotional intelligence scores of male and female managers. The mean total emotional intelligence score of females was 109.56 and that of males was 98.31. No

significant ($p > .05$) difference was found in the transformational leadership scores of male and female managers. The results of these tests are presented in Table 3.

DISCUSSION

Based on the analyses, a significant relationship between transformational leadership style and emotional intelligence was found. The regression analysis suggested that transformational leadership style of managers could be predicted from their emotional intelligence scores. Past researchers have stressed the importance of emotional intelligence for effective leadership (Goleman, 1998b; Cooper & Sawaf, 1997). Research studies in leadership style have established transformational leadership style as one of the most effective way of leading people (Burns, 1978; Bass & Avolio, 1996; Tichy & Devanna, 1986). Society today is faced with many challenges that require exceptional leadership. Today's and tomorrow's leaders will not only need to possess effective managerial skills but also highly developed social and emotional skills. IQ and technical skills are probably baseline requirements for executive roles, but without emotional intelligence the best-trained manager won't make a great leader (Goleman, 1998b).

Several researchers (Cooper, 1997; Goleman, 1995) have expressed the importance of emotional intelligence for leaders. Cooper (1997) stated that one of the foremost challenges facing leaders and organizations is to learn and lead through emotional intelligence. According to Goleman (1998c), leaders with high levels of emotional intelligence articulate and

TABLE 3 / Independent Groups t-Ratios Comparing Mean Transformational Leadership Scores and Emotional Intelligence Scores for Males and Females

Variable	Means	n	Mean Diff.	SE Diff.	t	p
Transformational Leadership Style						
Males	63.31	13	−1.90	2.19	−.771	>.05
Females	65.21	19				
Emotional Intelligence						
Males	98.31	13	−11.27	2.30	−2.98	<.05
Females	109.58	19				

arouse enthusiasm for a shared vision. Shared vision is also a common characteristic of transformational leaders (Burns, 1978). Goleman (1998b) also stated that the ability to convey emotions convincingly is what separates a charismatic leader from an ordinary leader.

A transformational leader exhibits qualities including empathy, motivation, self-awareness, and self-confidence (Bass, 1985; Burns, 1978; Ross & Offerman, 1997). Goleman (1995) described all the above qualities as subcomponents of emotional intelligence. Transformational leadership style and emotional intelligence have several other characteristics in common. Bass (1990) established trust to be a major component of transformational leadership style. Transformational leaders are able to gain respect and trust of their employees. Cooper (1997) classified trust as the key characteristic of emotional intelligence. Cooper (1997) also stated that trust is mandatory for the optimization of any system.

Another common characteristic between the two constructs is motivation. Goleman (1995) considered motivation as one trait that virtually all effective leaders possess. These leaders are driven to achieve beyond expectations. Motivation is also a characteristic that defines transformational leaders. Bass (1990b) explained that transformational leaders use motivation to communicate high expectation to their employees. Bass (1990a) established that leadership is positively related to self-confidence, conviction, self-control, ability to handle conflict and tolerance for stress. Such characteristics are also an essential component of emotional intelligence.

Previous research studies on transformational leadership and emotional intelligence have shown that individuals that score high on either of these constructs exhibit superior performance (Goleman, 1995; Keller, 1995). Transformational leaders seem to spread their own sense of confidence and competence, and they inspire people to be more imaginative. Goleman (1995) stated that all these characteristics of transformational leaders are also essential characteristics of emotional intelligence.

The researchers found no significant interaction between gender and emotional intelligence while predicting transformational leadership style. As a result it can be suggested that there is no difference in the relationship between transformational leadership style and emotional intelligence for male and female managers. The results of the current investigation imply that the interaction of gender and emotional intelligence would have no effect while predicting transformational leadership from emotional intelligence.

The researchers found a significant difference ($p < .05$) in the emotional intelligence scores of male and female managers. The mean total of emotional intelligence scores of females was higher than that for males. The results suggested that females might be better at managing their emotions and the emotions of others as compared to males. Other researchers (Mayer, Caruso & Salovey, 1999; Mayer & Geher, 1996) have found similar results with females scoring higher on measures of emotional intelligence.

No gender differences were found for transformational leadership scores of male and female managers. The results of the present study imply that as far as leadership style goes males are as transformational in their leadership style as females. Previous research on this subject has revealed ambiguous findings. Some researchers have found females to be more transformational than males (Carless, 1998). While other researchers concluded that there were no differences between men and women on these dimensions (Eagley & Johnson, 1990).

Several conclusions can be drawn from the current investigation. Both of the constructs, transformational leadership style and emotional intelligence are based on relationships and are thus related to one another. By examining the previous research studies, it can be established that individuals who score high on either one of the two constructs have several common attributes. The relationship between the two constructs could have several positive implications for assessing and training people to be effective leaders.

The application of the positive relationship between transformational leadership and emotional intelligence could benefit organizations in several ways. Companies that hire and promote people to leadership positions may find the positive relationship between transformational leadership style and emotional intelligence useful. The results imply that an individual who tested high on emotional intelligence would probably be a transformational leader. Knowledge of this relationship would help organizations identify and train potential leaders. Previous research in this field claims that organizations with transformational leaders are not only better at handling change but are also more effective and profitable (Bass, 1985). If emotional intelligence scores can predict transformational leadership, organizations may find emotional intelligence measures to be valuable tools in the hiring, promotion and development of organizational leaders.

The results of this study also showed that there are gender differences in the emotional intelligence scores of male and female managers. This result was in contradiction to Goleman's (1998c) findings that for the overall emotional intelligence score there are no differences for male and female managers. If women score higher in emotional intelligence than their male counterparts, and if emotional intelligence is considered a most needed ability for effective leadership, especially useful as organizations go through transformations, then women may possess a unique and timely leadership quality. Since recent research (Martell & DeSmet, 2001) indicates that men's and women's leadership abilities are still assessed differently, with the perceived likelihood of a number of key leader behaviors deemed significantly lower for females, the results of the present study may provide a more positive view for the potential of women as leaders. As the construct of effective leadership changes it may become more critical to encourage the mentoring and leadership development of women, as well as interpersonal skills training for future male leaders.

Although the results of the current study suggest that females have higher emotional intelligence scores than males, it is possible that women as compared to men scored high on certain components (for example, empathy and social skills) and low on certain other components (for example, motivation and self-regulation).

Goleman (1998c) stated that for the bell curves of the two groups there is an immense overlap, and an edge where they differ. That is, while on an average women may be better than men at some emotional skills, some men will still be better than most women, despite there being a statistically significant difference between the groups.

The current study may have been confounded by several limitations. The MLQ leadership form (5x-Revised; Bass & Avolio, 1996) did not classify participants as either transformational or transactional. A participant could score high in either transformational or transactional or in both the categories. The instrument gave three different scores for the three leadership styles. The researchers only used the self-report transformational scores to examine the relationship with emotional intelligence. Future investigators may consider a different measure to examine leadership style or the MLQ subordinate report measure may provide additional valuable insights.

Another recommendation for future research is to examine a larger and more similar sample of leaders. The sample for this study included managers from different settings and different levels of the organization. In the future, researchers may want to replicate the study with a larger and more consistent sample.

Future investigators may also want to use a larger sample to examine gender differences. By using a larger sample researchers may be able to examine the different components of emotional intelligence and establish in which components females score higher than males. The researchers believe that in order to expand the current study, future research could also examine the relationship between the components and subcomponents of transformational leadership style and emotional intelligence. The study may also add valuable information if other variables like cultural background, age, length of experience as manager, and type of work setting are taken into account.

In summary, the researchers attempted to look at the relationship between transformational leadership style and emotional intelligence. We also examined if there were any gender differences in the relationship between transformational leadership style and emotional intelligence. Lastly, the researchers examined any gender differences in the transformational leadership style and emotional intelligence of male and female managers. Based on the results of the study, the researchers suggested that there is a significant predictive relationship between transformational leadership style and emotional intelligence. The researchers also suggested that there are gender differences in the emotional intelligence scores of male and female managers. We could not establish any gender differences in the relationship between emotional intelligence and transformational leadership style, as gender did not have a significant interaction with emotional intelligence while predicting transformational leadership style. The results also suggested that there are no gender differences for transformational leadership scores of male and female managers.

REFERENCES

Atwater, L. E., & Yammarino, F. J. (1993). Personal attributes as predictors of superiors' and subordinates' perceptions of military leadership. *Human Relations, 46,* 645–668.

Avolio, B. J., & Bass, B. M. (1997). *The full range of leadership development: Manual.* Redwood City, CA: Mind Garden.

Bar-On, R. (1996). *The Emotional Quotient Inventory: A measure of emotional intelligence.* Toronto, ON: Multi Health Systems.

Bar-On, R. (1997). *Bar-On Emotional Quotient Inventory: Technical manual.* Toronto, ON: Multi Health Systems.

Bar-On, R. (1997, August). *Development of the Bar-On EQ-i: A measurement of emotional and social intelligence.* Paper presented at the 105th annual convention of the American Psychological Association, Chicago, IL.

Bass, B. M. (1985). *Leadership performance beyond expectations.* New York: Free Press.

Bass, B. M. (1990a). *Bass & Stogdill's handbook of leadership: Theory, research, and managerial applications.* (3rd ed.). New York: Free Press.

Bass, B. M. (1990b). From transactional to transformational leadership: Learning to share the vision. *Organizational Dynamics, 18,* 19–31.

Bass, B. M. (1997). Does the transactional-transformational leadership paradigm transcend organizational and national boundaries? *American Psychologist, 52,* 130–139.

Bass, B. M., & Avolio, B. J. (1994). *Improving organizational effectiveness through transformational leadership.* Thousand Oaks, CA: Sage.

Bass, B. M., & Avolio, B. J. (1996). *Transformational leadership development: Manual for the Multifactor Leadership Questionnaire.* Palo Alto, CA: Consulting Psychologists Press.

Bass, B. M., & Avolio, B. J. (1997). *Manual for the Multifactor Leadership Questionnaire.* Palo Alto, CA: Mind Garden.

Burns, J. M. (1978). *Leadership.* New York: Harper and Row.

Carless, S. A. (1998). Gender differences in transformational leadership: An examination of superior, leader, and subordinate perspectives. *Sex Roles: A Journal of Research, 39,* 887–897.

Caruso, D. R., Mayer, J. D., & Salovey, P. (2002). Emotional intelligence and emotional leadership. In R. E. Riggio, S. E. Murphy, & F. J. Pirozzolo (Eds.), *Multiple intelligences and leadership* (pp. 55–74). Mahwah, NJ: Lawrence Erlbaum Associates.

Cooper, R. K. (1997). Applying emotional intelligence in workplace. *Training & Development, 51,* 31–38.

Cooper, R. K., & Sawaf, A. (1997). *Executive EQ: Emotional intelligence in leadership and organizations.* New York: Berkeley.

Dada, D., & Hart, S. D. (2000). Assessing emotional intelligence: Reliability and validity of the Bar-On Emotional Quotient Inventory (EQ-i) in university students. *Personality and Individual Differences, 28,* 797–812.

Davis, M., Stankov, L., & Roberts, R. D. (1998). Emotional intelligence: In search of an elusive construct. *Journal of Personality and Social Psychology, 75,* 989–1015.

Dodge, D., & Wong, L. (Eds.). *Out-of-the-box leadership: Transforming the twenty-first-Century Army and other top-performing organizations.* Stamford, CT: JAI Press.

Eagley, A. H., & Johnson, B. T. (1990). Gender and leadership style: A meta-analysis. *Journal of Personality and Social Psychology, 60,* 685–710.

Eagly, A. H., Makhijani, M. G., & Klonsky, B. G. (1992). Gender and the evaluation of leaders: A meta-analysis. *Psychological Bulletin, 111,* 3–22.

Feldman, D. A. (1999). *The handbook of emotionally intelligent leadership: Inspiring others to achieve results.* New York: Leadership Performance Solutions.

Gardner, H. (1983). *Frames of mind: The theory of multiple intelligences.* New York: Basic Books.

Gardner, H. (1993). Intelligence and intelligences: Universal principles and individual differences. *Archives de Psychologie, 61,* 169–172.

Gardner, H. (1999). Are there additional intelligences? The case for naturalist, spiritual, and existential intelligences. In J. Kane (ed.), *Education, information, and transformation* (pp. 111–131). Upper Saddle River, NJ: Prentice Hall.

Gibbons, T. C. (1986). *Revisiting: The question of born vs. made: Toward a theory of development of transformational leaders.* Doctoral dissertation, Fielding Institute, Santa Barbara, CA.

Goleman, D. (1995). *Emotional intelligence.* New York: Bantam Books.

Goleman, D. (1998a). Success secret: A high emotional IQ. *Fortune,* 293–295.

Goleman, D. (1998b). What makes a leader? *Harvard Business Review, 1,* 93–104.

Goleman, D. (1998c). *Working with emotional intelligence.* New York: Bantam Books.

Guilford, J. P. (1967). Three faces of intellect. *American Psychologist, 14,* 469–479.

Hackman, Z. M., Hills, M. J., Furniss, A. H., & Peterson, T. J. (1992). Perceptions of gender-role characteristics and transformational and transactional leadership behaviors. *Perceptual and Motor Skills, 75,* 311–319.

Hater, J. J., & Bass, B. M. (1988). Superior's evaluations and subordinates' perceptions of transformational and transactional leadership. *Journal of Applied Psychology, 73*(4), 695–702.

Howell, J. M., & Avolio, B. J. (1993). Transformational leadership, transactional leadership, locus of control, and support for innovation: Key predictors of consolidated business-unit performance. *Journal of Applied Psychology, 78,* 891–902.

Keller, R. T. (1995). Transformational leaders make a difference. *Journal of Research & Technology Management, 38,* 41–44.

Lord, R. G., DeVader, C. L., & Alliger, G. M. (1986). A meta-analysis of the relationship between personality traits and leadership perceptions: An application of validity generalization procedures. *Journal of Applied Psychology, 71,* 402–410.

Martell, R. F., & DeSmet, A. L. (2001). A diagnostic-ratio approach to measuring beliefs about leadership abilities of male and female managers. *Journal of Applied Psychology, 86,* 1223–1231.

Mayer, J. D., Caruso, D. R., & Salovey, P. (1999). Emotional intelligence meets standards for traditional intelligence. *Intelligence, 27,* 267–298.

Mayer, J. D., DiPaolo, M. T., & Salovey, P. (1990). Perceiving affective content in ambiguous visual stimuli: A component of emotional intelligence. *Journal of Personality Assessment, 54,* 772–781.

Mayer, J. D., & Geher, G. (1996). Emotional intelligence and the identification of emotion. *Intelligence, 22,* 89–113.

Mayer, J. D., & Salovey, P. (1993). The intelligence of emotional intelligence. *Intelligence, 17*(4), 433–442.

Mayer, J. D. & Salovey, P. (1997). What is emotional intelligence? In P. Salovey & D. Sluyter (Eds.), *Emotional development and emotional intelligence: Implications for educators* (pp. 3–31). New York: Basic Books.

Mayer, J. D., Salovey, P., & Caruso, D. R. (1997). *The Multifactor Emotional Intelligence Scale (MEIS).* Simsbury, CT: www.EmotionalIQ.com.

Norusis, M. J. (1999). *SPSS for Windows: Base system user's guide release 9.0.* Chicago, IL: SPSS.

Riggio, R. E., Murphy, S. E., & Pirozzolo, F. J. (Eds.). (2002). *Multiple intelligences and leadership.* Mahwah, NJ: Lawrence Erlbaum Associates.

Ross, S. M., & Offermann, L. R. (1997). Transformational leaders: Measurement of personality attributes and work group performance. *Personality and Social Psychology Bulletin, 23*(10), 1078–1086.

Ryback, D. (1997). *Putting emotional intelligence to work: Successful leadership is more than IQ.* Oxford: Butterworth-Heinemann.

Salovey, P., & Mayer, J. D. (1990). Emotional intelligence. *Imagination, Cognition & Personality, 9*(3), 185–211.

Seltzer, J., & Bass, B. M. (1990). Transformational leadership: Beyond initiation and consideration. *Journal of Management, 16,* 693–703.

Shanley, L. A., Walker, R. E., & Foley, J. M. (1971). Social intelligence: A concept in search of data. *Psychological Reports, 29,* 1123–1132.

Southwick, R. B. (1998). *Antecedents of transformational, transactional, and laissez-faire leadership.* Doctoral Dissertation, University of Georgia, Athens, GA.

Sternberg, R. J. (1985). *Beyond IQ: A triarchic theory of human intelligence.* Cambridge: University Press.

Sternberg, R. J., & Wagner, R. K. (1986). *Practical intelligence: Nature and origins of competence in the everyday world.* Cambridge: University Press.

Thorndike, E. L. (1920). Intelligence and its uses. *Harper's Magazine, 140,* 227–235.

Tichy, N. M., & Devanna, M. A. (1986). *The transformational leader.* New York: John Wiley & Sons.

Wagner, R. K., & Sternberg, R. J. (1985). Practical intelligence in real world pursuits: The role of tacit knowledge. *Journal of Personality and Social Psychology, 48,* 436–458.

Wechsler, D. (1958). *The measurement and appraisal of adult intelligence* (4th ed.). Baltimore: Williams & Wilkins.

Weisinger, H. (1998). *Emotional intelligence at work.* San Francisco, CA: Jossey-Bass.

Zaccaro, S. J. (1996). *Models and theories of executive leadership: A conceptual/empirical review and integration.* Alexandria, VA: U.S. Army Research Institute for the Behavioral and Social Sciences.

Zaccaro, S. J. (1999). Social complexity and the competencies required for effective military leadership. In J. G. Hunt, G. E. Dodge, & L. Wong (Eds.), *Out-of-the-box leadership: Transforming the twenty-first-Century Army and other top-performing organizations.* Stamford, CT: JAI Press.

Zaccaro, S. J. (2001). *The nature of executive leadership: A conceptual and empirical analysis of success.* Washington, D.C.: American Psychological Association.

CRITICAL THINKING QUESTIONS

1. Think of a person you know whom you consider to be very socially successful. Does he or she seem to possess the qualities associated with emotional intelligence, as discussed in this article? Elaborate on how these (or other) qualities may contribute to this person's social success.

2. Discuss the pros and cons of using an EQ test to screen potential employees for a job.

3. Besides those discussed in the article, what connections may exist between high emotional intelligence and successful leadership? Design a study that would test whether one such connection exists.

4. Should emotional intelligence be taught to children? Why or why not? What issues would need to be considered? For instance, what emotional responses are deemed proper, and by whom would that be determined? Defend your position.

5. Would it be possible to teach a sort of remedial emotional intelligence to adults? Why or why not? Describe a study that would attempt to answer this question empirically.

6. According to this article, women tend to score higher than men on overall levels of emotional intelligence. At the same time, women are less likely than men to be in positions of leadership. Explain this apparent inconsistency using concepts and terminology from other topics in social psychology.

CHAPTER INTEGRATION QUESTIONS

1. The concept of *emotional intelligence* was most fully explained in the last reading, Article 39. Discuss how this concept can be related to the other two articles in this chapter.

2. What other factors besides those discussed in these articles may be important in understanding business psychology? For example, what topics of previous chapters may have particular relevance for the study of business psychology? Discuss why you think these topics/chapters may be relevant.

3. An old proverb tells us, "It is not whether you win or lose but how you play the game." Yet according to Vince Lombardi, a former professional football coach, "Winning isn't everything, it's the only thing." These quotes typically are associated with sports, but can they be applied to how people approach business, as well? How so? What are both the potential short-term and long-term implications for someone who follows either of these quotes in his or her approach to business? Explain.

Chapter Fourteen

FORENSIC PSYCHOLOGY

YOU PROBABLY HAVE had some contact with the legal system, in one form or another. Perhaps you (or someone you know) have been arrested and even tried for some offense. Maybe you have been asked to be a juror. More likely, you have watched televised trials or read about real or fictional trials in the media. Given your experience, does the legal system, as it presently operates, guarantee an objective, unbiased outcome?

Forensic psychology has emerged in recent years as a major discipline that tries to understand the entire judicial process and to make it as fair as possible. Originally an outgrowth of social psychology and other psychological disciplines, forensic psychology has become an area of study in its own right. Nonetheless, it remains strongly rooted in the principles and findings of social psychological research.

Social psychologists working in the field of forensic psychology have examined a number of factors that may influence the outcomes in legal settings. Many of the findings summarized in previous articles in this book can be applied to forensic settings, as well. For example, the findings pertaining to prejudice, discrimination, social influence, and attitude change, to name but a few, can easily be extended to the courtroom. Some of the biases that enter into the judicial process may be byproducts of how we think and process information (i.e., social cognition). Some of these biases may stem from how we naturally deal with the complex world around us, and as such, they may have been present from the first time that someone's guilt or innocence was put in question. However, there also may be some new biases entering the modern courtroom based on technological changes.

Article 40, "Illusory Causation in the Courtroom," examines the crucial role that confessions play in the courtroom. Interestingly, something as simple as the camera angle of a videotaped confession can influence the perceived guilt or innocence of the defendant.

Article 41, "Beautiful but Dangerous," likewise examines jury trials. However, this classic article looks at the relationship between the attractiveness of the offender and the nature of the crime and how it may influence the jury's judgment.

Finally, Article 42, "Effects of Defendant Age on Severity of Punishment for Different Crimes," is a contemporary exploration of variables that may influence the outcomes of jury trials. Like the classic Article 41, which found that physical appearance may have a big impact on perceptions of guilt or innocence, this article looks at how a single factor, such as the age of the defendant, may affect the jury's decision making.

ARTICLE 40 _____

One cornerstone of the U.S. legal system is the right to a jury trial by one's peers. Perhaps you have already served as a juror. If not, you may very well have that opportunity in the future. As a juror, you are expected to make a conscientious effort to determine a defendant's guilt or innocence based on the weight of the evidence presented in the trial. Your personal biases and beliefs should not come into play. Your decision is supposed to be made objectively.

But is that the way the legal system really works? Is it possible for people to somehow disconnect themselves from their own attitudes and biases and really judge a case objectively? A great deal of social psychological research conducted over the years suggests that achieving this objectivity may be easier said than done. For example, irrelevant factors such as a defendant's physical appearance, gender, and race have been found to impact jurors' decisions.

Some of the biases affecting jurors' decision making, such as their response to the defendant's appearance, have existed since the beginning of court proceedings. Yet other new biases may be entering the judicial system with the introduction of technology. For example, one crucial element in a jury trial is the use of a confession given by the defendant. Such confessions have been known to carry a great deal of weight in influencing the jury's decision of guilt or innocence. But people have become increasingly aware that just because someone confesses to a crime does not actually mean that he or she did it. In fact, a confession may result from how the interrogation was conducted.

Because of the possibility of getting a false confession, people in the judicial system increasingly have used videotaped confessions in the courtroom, not only to further demonstrate the guilt of the person on trial but also to show that the confession was not due to improper interrogation techniques. While the use of videotaped confessions is increasingly common, it may be accompanied by some unanticipated biases. The following article by G. Daniel Lassiter exposes these potential biases along with their implications for the criminal justice system.

Illusory Causation in the Courtroom

■ G. Daniel Lassiter

Abstract
A large body of evidence indicates that people attribute unwarranted causality (influence) to a stimulus simply because it is more noticeable or salient than other available stimuli. This article reviews recent research demonstrating that this illusory-causation phenomenon can produce serious prejudicial effects with regard to how people evaluate certain types of legal evidence. Specifically, evaluations of videotaped confessions can be significantly altered by presumably inconsequential changes in the camera perspective taken when the confessions are

initially recorded. Videotaped confessions recorded with the camera focused on the suspect—compared with videotapes from other camera points of view (e.g., focused equally on the suspect and interrogator) or with more traditional presentation formats (i.e., transcripts and audiotapes)—lead mock jurors to judge that the confessions were more voluntary and, most important, that the suspects are more likely to be guilty. Because actual criminal interrogations are customarily videotaped with the camera lens zeroed in on the suspect, these findings are of considerable practical significance.

Reprinted from *Current Directions in Psychological Science*, 2002, *11*(6), 204–208. Copyright © 2002 by the American Psychological Society. Reprinted with permission of Blackwell Publishing.

Keywords illustory causation; videotaped confessions; bias

In 1935, Koffka noted that objects that stand out in our visual field, or are the focus of our attention, are more likely than less conspicuous objects to be judged the originators of a physical event, even when there is no objective basis for such a conclusion. For example, when placed in a darkened room, people judge that a widening gap between two pinpoints of light is caused by the one that they happen to be looking at regardless of whether it is actually the one moving.

This phenomenon, referred to as illusory causation (McArthur, 1980), is not limited to cases involving interactions among simple physical objects. Research indicates that it affects people's causal attributions for more complex social interactions as well. In the first systematic demonstration of illusory causation in the social domain, Taylor and Fiske (1975) had observers view a casual, two-person conversation. The vantage point of the observers was varied by seating them in different locations around the two interactants. After the conversation ended, observers rated each interactant in terms of the amount of causal influence he or she exerted during the exchange. The results revealed that greater causality was attributed to whichever person observers happened to be facing, which, of course, was determined by their seating position—an entirely incidental factor that logically should have had no bearing on their causal judgments.

Misidentifying which of multiple points of light is moving in a darkened room, or even overestimating the causal influence of a particular participant in a "getting acquainted" interaction, I daresay, is not an error in judgment that is likely to keep us awake at night. Is the illusory-causation phenomenon, then, simply an intriguing psychological quirk that has essentially no impact on matters of true substance? I posed this question nearly 20 years ago, and the answer provided by two decades of subsequent research is both surprising and disturbing.

RELEVANCE OF ILLUSORY CAUSATION FOR OUR SYSTEM OF JUSTICE

As of May 2002, the Death Penalty Information Center had documented 101 cases in which death-row inmates (from 24 states) were set free because new evidence (e.g., DNA test results) conclusively established their innocence. In many instances, the cause of such wrongful convictions can be traced back to the interrogation phase of criminal investigations (Dwyer, Neufeld, & Scheck, 2000).[1] There is now incontrovertible proof that false confessions are sometimes extracted from detained crime suspects during this critical stage of the judicial process. Numerous legal scholars, criminal-justice practitioners, political leaders, and social scientists have called for the videotaping of all police interrogations as a solution to the problem of some innocent people being induced to incriminate themselves when confronted by standard police interrogation tactics. Those who advocate videotaping interrogations argue that the presence of the camera will deter the use of coercive methods to induce confessions and will provide complete and objective records of the interrogations so that judges and jurors can evaluate thoroughly and accurately the voluntariness and veracity of any confessions.

Under certain circumstances, I have no doubt that the videotape method, compared with more traditional methods of evidence presentation, can improve assessment of the voluntariness and reliability of confessions. Certainly, if interrogators use obviously assaultive coercion, any reasonable observer will recognize the illegitimacy of the confession. However, such third-degree intimidation has been replaced by nonassaultive psychological manipulation that is not always recognized as coercive but, as research has shown, can nonetheless lead to false admissions of guilt (cf. Kassin & Kiechel, 1996). In this age of psychologically oriented interrogation techniques, videotaping interrogations and confessions may not be a surefire preventive against convicting the truly innocent. In the United States and in many other countries (such as Canada, Australia, and the United Kingdom), videotaped interrogations and confessions are typically recorded with the camera focused on the suspect. Positioning the camera in this manner seems straightforward and logical because trial fact finders presumably need to see directly what the suspect said and did to best assess the voluntariness and veracity of his or her statements.

The illusory-causation phenomenon, however, suggests the alarming possibility that the default camera perspective taken when recording criminal confessions (i.e., focused on the suspect) could have an unintended prejudicial effect on trial participants' subsequent evaluations of the voluntariness of the confessions. More specifically, observers of a videotaped confession recorded with the camera focused on the suspect, compared with the same confession recorded from a different camera perspective, might be more likely to judge the confession as voluntary (i.e., attributable to the suspect). I now describe a systematic program of research that indicates that this is not simply a possibility; it is in fact a reality.

EVIDENCE FOR A BIASING EFFECT OF CAMERA PERSPECTIVE ON EVALUATIONS OF VIDEOTAPED CONFESSIONS

The research (Lassiter, Geers, Handley, Weiland, & Munhall, 2002; Lassiter, Geers, Munhall, Handley, & Beers, 2001; Lassiter, Geers, Munhall, Ploutz-Snyder, & Breitenbecher, 2002) proceeded in three stages. Stage One focused on establishing the existence and robustness of the camera-perspective bias in videotaped confessions. Stage Two examined the extent to which the bias generalized to more real-world contexts. Finally, Stage Three investigated the mechanisms hypothesized to underlie the biasing effect of camera perspective.

Summary of Stage One Experiments

Stage One of the research comprised eight studies that were, for the most part, relatively simple in their design and in the stimulus materials used. The mock confessions that were constructed for five of the experiments were designed to be composites of various elements that have been documented to occur in real interrogations or that police manuals advise should occur. None of the stimulus tapes resulting from these staged interrogations and confessions lasted longer than 5 min. (Leo, 1996, reported that interrogations of this length are not typical, but they do occur.) For the remaining three experiments, the confession stimulus was developed from the transcript of an actual police interrogation and was approximately 30 min in duration.

Seven of the experiments in Stage One employed only continuous (rating scale) measures of participants' judgments because such ratings often exhibit greater sensitivity than dichotomous responses and because they are amenable to more powerful statistical analyses. (In a true courtroom, judgments concerning voluntariness and guilt would ultimately be rendered in a dichotomous fashion. However, at this point the primary concern was to detect the bias, if it actually existed. Issues of external validity could always be addressed later—and were in Stage Two.) Finally, all participants in the Stage One experiments were college students recruited from introductory psychology courses.

Consistent with the largely innocuous instances of illusory causation described earlier, the Stage One experiments revealed that videotaped confessions recorded with the camera focused on the suspect—compared with videotapes from other camera points of view (i.e., focused equally on the suspect and interrogator or focused solely on the interrogator) or with more traditional presentation formats (i.e., transcripts and audiotapes)—resulted in the judgment that the confessions were more voluntary. This biasing effect of camera perspective proved to be quite robust and pervasive. It influenced not only judgments of voluntariness, but also perceived likelihood of guilt and sentencing recommendations—perceived likelihood of guilt was greater and recommended sentences were more severe when the suspect-focus videotape of a confession was viewed. It generalized across confessions dealing with such crimes as shoplifting, burglary, drug trafficking, rape, and manslaughter. It affected the judgments of individuals who were naturally motivated to be effortful and critical thinkers, as well as the judgments of individuals who lacked such motivation. It was not reduced by the opportunity for decision makers to deliberate before rendering their judgments, and it persisted even when they believed they would have to justify their evaluations to a local judge. Finally, urging mock jurors to concentrate on the content of the confession, rather than the manner in which it was presented, did not diminish the prejudicial effect of camera perspective.

Summary of Stage Two Experiments

Diamond (1997) has argued that trial simulations, at Stage One of a research program, that involve relatively "easy" methods (e.g., using college-student participants and brief stimulus materials) should be followed up with Stage Two research that involves more elaborate, representative methods (e.g., using community members as participants and extensive videotaped trials as stimuli). As Bornstein (1999) has noted, courts are more likely to be receptive to psycholegal research findings that are of the Stage Two variety.

The Stage Two portion of this research, then, comprised three experiments that are notable for their, in Bornstein's (1999, p. 88) words, "harder, more representative methods." All three studies involved extensive videotaped trial simulations that required from 3 to 5 hr of participants' time. In two of the experiments, all participants were nonstudent, jury-eligible adults recruited from both rural and urban communities in Ohio. In the other experiment, both nonstudent and student participants were used so that a systematic comparison of their responses could be made. In all Stage Two studies, participants made dichotomous judgments (e.g., guilty or not guilty). In addition to addressing these issues of external validity, the Stage Two experiments continued to explore possible ways of preventing camera perspective from influencing the judgment process of observers.

Even though these studies used realistic, videotaped simulations of actual trials that included the direct testimony and cross-examination of several witnesses, the presentation of physical evidence, prosecution and defense arguments, judicial rulings on points of law, and most of the other trappings associated with such legal proceedings, camera perspective still swayed mock jurors' judgments. The magnitude of the bias under these conditions was remarkable; in one instance, the simple change from an equal-focus confession to a suspect-focus confession doubled the conviction rate! Furthermore, this effect was impervious to various debiasing attempts. Judicial instruction emphasizing the need to be cognizant of reliability and fairness concerns in evaluating the confession and, in some cases, directly alerting mock jurors to the potentially prejudicial effect of camera perspective did not mitigate the bias. This was true whether the judicial instruction preceded or followed the presentation of the confession. Allowing mock jurors to view the videotaped confession a second time also failed to attenuate the biasing effect of camera perspective. Finally, gender was not a significant factor, and jury-

eligible adults in their 40s and 50s fared no better (or worse) than their college-age counterparts.

Summary of Stage Three Experiments

The findings of the first two stages of research clearly demonstrated the practical significance of illusory causation. The final stage of the research was more theoretical in that it focused on identifying the processes mediating this phenomenon.

Early attempts to specify a mediator of illusory causation emphasized memory processes (cf. McArthur, 1980). Generally, it was argued that salient information tends to be more memorable than nonsalient information, and this difference in memory is responsible for the greater causality ascribed to salient information. Later, Newtson (Newtson, Rindner, Miller, & LaCross, 1978) and McArthur (1980) suggested that illusory causation may have more to do with how people initially pick up or register information from an observed interaction than with how they subsequently remember that information. That is, Newtson and McArthur argued that the point of view from which individuals observe an interaction influences the initial registration or perceptual organization of information from the ongoing interaction, which in turn directly influences causal attributions and related judgments.

Stage Three, then, comprised four experiments whose main purpose was to assess the relative tenability of the memory-mediated and perception-mediated explanations of illusory causation. Like the Stage One studies, these experiments used rather simple stimulus materials and participants drawn from college populations. Because the focus of this stage of the research was on pinning down the basic mechanisms underlying the illusory-causation phenomenon, the stimuli used in three of the experiments were similar to those in the original studies conducted by Taylor and Fiske (1975)—that is, 5-min "getting acquainted" conversations between two college students. The remaining experiment, however, demonstrated that the same basic effects found with these stimuli do generalize to the kinds of videotaped confession materials that were used in Stage One.

The results indicated that illusory causation, to paraphrase Gilbert (1995), is less a species of memory and more a species of perception. That is, taken together, the four experiments provided considerable support for the notion that a person's literal point of view (which, in these instances, was determined completely by the camera's perspective) affects how he or she initially registers, or extracts, information from an observed interaction, which in turn affects his or her judgments regarding the causal influence exerted by each interactant.

POLICY IMPLICATIONS

Earlier in this article, I noted that many scientific, legal, and political experts have called for the universal adoption of videotaping as a "quick fix" for the problem of some innocent people being induced to incriminate themselves when confronted by standard police interrogation tactics. The research I have summarized, however, indicates that the indiscriminate application of videotaping to solve the problem of coerced or false confessions slipping through the system could exacerbate the situation.

Am I thus recommending that videotaped interrogation and confession evidence not be used in courts of law? No, because the research does not paint an entirely negative picture with regard to introducing videotaped confessions in the courtroom. It was found that videotaped confessions that focused on the suspect and the interrogator equally generated judgments that were comparable to those based on more traditional presentation formats—that is, audiotapes and transcripts. Thus, it is clear that the videotaping procedure per se is not inherently prejudicial. Rather, it is the manner in which the videotaping procedure is implemented that holds the potential for bias. It appears, then, that the advantages associated with the videotape method—for example, a more detailed record of the interrogation is provided to trial participants—can be maintained without introducing bias if an equal-focus perspective is taken by the video camera.

RESEARCH DIRECTIONS

Videotaping is only one of several technologies that have found their way into the courtroom. Computer simulations, videoconferencing, and even virtual-real-ity technology are currently, or soon will be, used in trial settings. As noted by Federal Judicial Center researcher Meghan Dunn, "to preserve the sanctity of the legal process, we need to know how that technology is affecting trial participants" (quoted in Carpenter, 2001, p. 31). For example, can videoconferencing diminish the perceived legitimacy of court proceedings? Do computer simulations facilitate jurors' comprehension of complex evidence or testimony? Does the degree of familiarity with new technology influence trial participants' receptivity to evidence presented in a high-tech manner? Will the use of virtual reality in trials erode the objectivity that jurors are supposed to maintain as triers of fact? Further research is needed to answer these and related questions concerning the impact of technology on American jurisprudence.

RECOMMENDED READING

Dwyer, J., Neufeld, P., & Scheck, B. (2000). (See References)

Kassin, S.M. (1997). The psychology of confession evidence. *American Psychologist, 52,* 221–233.

Lassiter, G.D., Geers, A.L., Munhall, P.J., Handley, I.M., & Beers, M.J. (2001). (See References)

Lassiter, G.D., Geers, A.L., Munhall, P.J., Ploutz-Snyder, R.J., & Breitenbecher, D.L. (2002). (See References)

Zebrowitz, L.A. (1990). *Social perception.* Pacific Grove, CA: Brooks/Cole.

REFERENCES

Bornstein, B.H. (1999). The ecological validity of jury simulations: Is the jury still out? *Law and Human Behavior, 23,* 75–91.

Carpenter, S. (2001, October). Technology gets its day in court. *Monitor on Psychology, 32,* 30–32.

Diamond, S.S. (1997). Illuminations and shadows from jury simulations. *Law and Human Behavior, 21,* 561–571.

Dwyer, J., Neufeld, P., & Scheck, B. (2000). *Actual innocence.* New York: Doubleday.

Gilbert, D.T. (1995). Attribution and interpersonal perception. In A. Tesser (Ed.), *Advanced social psychology* (pp. 99–147). New York: McGraw-Hill.

Kassin, S.M., & Kiechel, K.L. (1996). The social psychology of false confessions: Compliance, internalization, and confabulation. *Psychological Science, 7,* 125–128.

Koffka, K. (1935). *Principles of gestalt psychology.* New York: Harcourt Brace.

Lassiter, G.D., Geers, A.L., Handley, I.M., Weiland, P.E., & Munhall, P.J. (2002). Videotaped interrogations and confessions: A simple change in camera perspective alters verdicts in simulated trials. *Journal of Applied Psychology, 87,* 867–874.

Lassiter, G.D., Geers, A.L., Munhall, P.J., Handley, I.M., & Beers, M.J. (2001). Videotaped confessions: Is guilt in the eye of the camera? In M.P. Zanna (Ed.), *Advances in experimental social psychology* (Vol. 33, pp. 189–254). New York: Academic Press.

Lassiter, G.D., Geers, A.L., Munhall, P.J., Ploutz-Snyder, R.J., & Breitenbecher, D.L. (2002). Illusory causation: Why it occurs. *Psychological Science, 13,* 299–305.

Leo, R.A. (1996). Inside the interrogation room. *The Journal of Criminal Law and Criminology, 86,* 266–303.

McArthur, L.Z. (1980). Illusory causation and illusory correlation: Two epistemological accounts. *Personality and Social Psychology Bulletin, 6,* 507–519.

Newtson, D., Rindner, R.J., Miller, R., & LaCross, K. (1978). Effects of availability of feature changes on behavior segmentation. *Journal of Experimental Social Psychology, 14,* 379–388.

Taylor, S.E., & Fiske, S.T. (1975). Point of view and perceptions of causality. *Journal of Personality and Social Psychology, 32,* 439–445.

NOTE

1. Additional factors responsible for miscarriages of justice identified by Dwyer et al. (2000) include egregiously incompetent defense lawyers, erroneous eyewitness accounts, scientifically unreliable evidence, and prosecutorial misconduct.

CRITICAL THINKING QUESTIONS

1. The section of the article labeled "Research Directions" contained several possible directions for further studies in this area. Select one of them, and design a study to investigate it.
2. This article primarily dealt with the issue of illusory causation in videotaped confessions. Give examples of where else we might expect to find this effect. Outline a study to investigate one of your examples.
3. Considering the practical implications of this article, what rules should govern the use of videotaped confessions in the courtroom? How might these rules affect the roles of the lawyers for the prosecution and the defense? Defend your position.
4. Based on information that you encountered in reading the articles in Chapters Two and Three (on social perception and social cognition, respectively), what other sources of bias may commonly intrude on courtroom proceedings? Explain your answer.

ARTICLE 41

The previous reading (Article 40) examined some of the biases inherent in jury trials. But what additional factors may have an impact on determining the defendant's guilt or innocence? Jurors are asked to weigh the evidence presented during the trial. Hopefully, they will not permit irrelevant characteristics of the defendant—such as his or her physical appearance, race, or sex—to affect their judgment. But is it really possible to be totally objective in such situations? Or do irrelevant factors play a role in our beliefs about guilt or innocence?

The following article by Harold Sigall and Nancy Ostrove is a classic piece of research that investigated the impact of the defendant's physical attractiveness on the severity of sentences given to her. Earlier studies had indicated that physically attractive individuals often have great advantages over less attractive people in a variety of situations. This study not only examined the role of physical attractiveness in a trial-like setting but also how the nature of the crime and attractiveness interact to influence judgments about the defendant. The article also tests two different models that may explain why this particular effect occurs.

Beautiful but Dangerous

Effects of Offender Attractiveness and Nature of the Crime on Juridic Judgment

■ Harold Sigall and Nancy Ostrove

The physical attractiveness of a criminal defendant (attractive, unattractive, no information) and the nature of the crime (attractiveness-related, attractiveness-unrelated) were varied in a factorial design. After reading one of the case accounts, subjects sentenced the defendant to a term of imprisonment. An interaction was predicted: When the crime was unrelated to attractiveness (burglary), subjects would assign more lenient sentences to the attractive defendant than to the unattractive defendant; when the offense was attractiveness-related (swindle), the attractive defendant would receive harsher treatment. The results confirmed the predictions, thereby supporting a cognitive explanation for the relationship between the physical attractiveness of defendants and the nature of the judgments made against them.

Research investigating the interpersonal consequences of physical attractiveness has demonstrated clearly that good-looking people have tremendous advantages over their unattractive counterparts in many ways. For example, a recent study by Miller (1970) provided evidence for the existence of a physical attractiveness stereotype with a rather favorable content. Dion, Berscheid, and Walster (1972) reported similar findings: Compared to unattractive people, better-looking people were viewed as more likely to possess a variety of socially desirable attributes. In addition, Dion et al.'s subjects predicted rosier futures for the beautiful stimulus persons—attractive people were expected to have happier and more successful lives in store for them. Thus, at least in the eyes of others, good looks imply greater potential.

Since physical attractiveness hardly seems to provide a basis for an *equitable* distribution of rewards, one might hope that the powerful effects of this variable would occur primarily when it is the only source

Reprinted from *Journal of Personality and Social Psychology*, 1975, *31*, 410–414. Copyright © 1975 by the American Psychological Association. Reprinted by permission.

of information available. Unfair or irrational consequences of differences in beauty observed in some situations would cause less uneasiness if, in other situations given other important data, respondents would tend to discount such "superficial" information. Unfortunately, for the vast majority of us who have not been blessed with a stunning appearance, the evidence does not permit such consolation. Consider, for example, a recent study by Dion (1972) in which adult subjects were presented with accounts of transgressions supposedly committed by children of varying physical attractiveness. When the transgression was severe the act was viewed less negatively when committed by a good-looking child, than when the offender was unattractive. Moreover, when the child was unattractive the offense was more likely to be seen as reflecting some enduring dispositional quality: Subjects believed that unattractive children were more likely to be involved in future transgressions. Dion's findings, which indicate that unattractive individuals are penalized when there is no apparent logical relationship between the transgression and the way they look, underscore the importance of appearance because one could reasonably suppose that information describing a severe transgression would "overwhelm the field," and that the physical attractiveness variable would not have any effect.

Can beautiful people get away with murder? Although Dion (1972) found no differences in the punishment recommended for offenders as a function of attractiveness, Monahan (1941) has suggested that beautiful women are convicted less often of crimes they are accused of, and Efran (1974) has recently demonstrated that subjects are much more generous when assigning punishment to good-looking as opposed to unattractive transgressors.

The previous findings which indicate a tendency toward leniency for an attractive offender can be accounted for in a number of ways. For example, one might explain such results with the help of a reinforcement-affect model of attraction (e.g., Byrne & Clore, 1970). Essentially, the argument here would be that beauty, having positive reinforcement value, would lead to relatively more positive affective responses toward a person who has it. Thus we like an attractive person more, and since other investigators have shown that liking for a defendant increases leniency (e.g., Landy & Aronson, 1969), we would

expect good-looking (better liked) defendants to be punished less than unattractive defendants. Implicit in this reasoning is that the nature of the affective response, which influences whether kind or harsh treatment is recommended, is determined by the stimulus features associated with the target person. Therefore, when other things are equal, benefit accrues to the physically attractive. A more cognitive approach might attempt to explain the relationship between physical appearance and reactions to transgressions by assuming that the subject has a "rational" basis for his responses. It is reasonable to deal harshly with a criminal if we think he is likely to commit further violations, and as Dion's (1972) study suggests, unattractive individuals are viewed as more likely to transgress again. In addition, inasmuch as attractive individuals are viewed as possessing desirable qualities and as having relatively great potential, it makes sense to treat them leniently. Presumably they can be successful in socially acceptable ways, and rehabilitation may result in relatively high payoffs for society.

There is at least one implication that follows from the cognitive orientation which would not flow readily from the reinforcement model. Suppose that situations do exist in which, because of his high attractiveness, a defendant is viewed as more likely to transgress in the future. The cognitive approach suggests that in such instances greater punishment would be assigned to the attractive offender. We might add that in addition to being more dangerous, when the crime is attractiveness related, a beautiful criminal may be viewed as taking advantage of a God-given gift. Such misappropriation of a blessing may incur animosity, which might contribute to severe judgments in attractiveness-related situations.

In the present investigation, the attractiveness of a defendant was varied along with the nature of the crime committed. It was reasoned that most offenses do not encourage the notion that a criminal's attractiveness increases the likelihood of similar transgressions in the future. Since attractive offenders are viewed as less prone to recidivism and as having greater potential worth, it was expected that under such circumstances an attractive defendant would receive less punishment than an unattractive defendant involved in an identical offense. When, however, the crime committed may be viewed as attractiveness-related, as in a confidence game, despite being seen as possessing more potential, the attractive defendant may be regarded as relatively more dangerous, and the effects of beauty could be expected to be cancelled out or reversed. The major hypothesis, then, called for an interaction: An attractive defendant would receive more lenient treatment than an unattractive defendant when the offense was unrelated to attractiveness; when the crime was related to attractiveness, the attractive defendant would receive relatively harsh treatment.

METHOD

Subjects and Overview

Subjects were 60 male and 60 female undergraduates. After being presented with an account of a criminal case, each subject sentenced the defendant to a term of imprisonment. One-third of the subjects were led to believe that the defendant was physically attractive, another third that she was unattractive, and the remainder received no information concerning appearance. Cross-cutting the attractiveness variable, half of the subjects were presented with a written account of an attractiveness-unrelated crime, a burglary, and the rest with an attractiveness-related crime, a swindle. Subjects were randomly assigned to condition, with the restriction that an equal number of males and females appeared in each of the six cells formed by the manipulated variables.

Procedure

Upon arrival, each subject was shown to an individual room and given a booklet which contained the stimulus materials. The top sheet informed subjects that they would read a criminal case account, that they would receive biographical information about the defendant, and that after considering the materials they would be asked to answer some questions.

The case account began on the second page. Clipped to this page was a 5 × 8 inch card which contained routine demographic information and was identical in all conditions.[1] In the attractive conditions, a photograph of a rather attractive woman was affixed to the upper right-hand corner of the card;

while in the unattractive conditions, a relatively unattractive photograph was affixed. No photograph was presented in the control conditions.

Subjects then read either the account of a burglary or a swindle. The burglary account described how the defendant, Barbara Helm, had moved into a high-rise building, obtained a pass key under false pretenses, and then illegally entered the apartment of one of her neighbors. After stealing $2,200 in cash and merchandise she left town. She was apprehended when she attempted to sell some of the stolen property and subsequently was charged with breaking and entering and grand larceny. The swindle account described how Barbara Helm had ingratiated herself to a middle-aged bachelor and induced him to invest $2,200 in a non-existent corporation. She was charged with obtaining money under false pretenses and grand larceny. In both cases, the setting for the offense and the victim were described identically. The information presented left little doubt concerning the defendant's guilt.

The main dependent measure was collected on the last page of the booklet. Subjects were asked to complete the following statement by circling a number between 1 and 15: "I sentence the defendant, Barbara Helm, to ____ years of imprisonment." Subjects were asked to sentence the defendant, rather than to judge guilt versus innocence in order to provide a more sensitive dependent measure.

After sentencing had been completed, the experimenter provided a second form, which asked subjects to recall who the defendant was and to rate the seriousness of the crime. In addition, the defendant was rated on a series of 9-point bipolar adjective scales, including physically unattractive (1) to physically attractive (9), which constituted the check on the attractiveness manipulation. A post-experimental interview followed, during which subjects were debriefed.

RESULTS AND DISCUSSION

The physical attractiveness manipulation was successful: The attractive defendant received a mean rating of 7.53, while the mean for the unattractive defendant was 3.20, $F(1, 108) = 184.29$, $p < .001$. These ratings were not affected by the nature of the crime, nor was there an interaction.

The criminal cases were designed so as to meet two requirements. First, the swindle was assumed to be attractiveness-related, while the burglary was intended to be attractiveness-unrelated. No direct check on this assumption was made. However, indirect evidence is available: Since all subjects filled out the same forms, we obtained physical attractiveness ratings from control condition subjects who were not presented with a photograph. These subjects attributed greater beauty to the defendant in the swindle condition ($X = 6.65$) than in the burglary condition ($X = 5.65$), $F(1, 108) = 4.93, p < .05$. This finding offers some support for our contention that the swindle was viewed as attractiveness-related. Second, it was important that the two crimes be viewed as roughly comparable in seriousness. This was necessary to preclude alternative explanations in terms of differential seriousness. Subjects rated the seriousness of the crime on a 9-point scale extending from not at all serious (1) to extremely serious (9). The resulting responses indicated that the second requirement was met: In the swindle condition the mean seriousness rating was 5.02; in the burglary condition it was 5.07 ($F < 1$).

Table 1 presents the mean punishment assigned to the defendant, by condition. Since a preliminary analysis demonstrated there were no differences in responses between males and females, subject sex was ignored as a variable. It can be seen that our hypothesis was supported: When the offense was attractiveness-unrelated (burglary), the unattractive defendant was more severely punished than the attractive defendant; however, when the offense was attractiveness-related (swindle), the attractive defendant was treated more harshly. The overall Attractiveness × Offense interaction was statistically significant, $F(2, 108) = 4.55, p < .025$, end this interaction was significant, as well, when the control condition was excluded, $F(1, 108) = 7.02, p < .01$. Simple comparisons revealed that the unattractive burglar received significantly more punishment than the attractive burglar, $F(1, 108) = 6.60, p < .025$, while the difference in sentences assigned to the attractive and unattractive swindler was not statistically significant, $F(1, 108) = 1.39$. The attractive-swindle condition was compared with the unattractive-swindle and control-swindle conditions also, $F(1, 108) = 2.00, ns$. Thus, strictly speaking, we cannot say that for the swindle attractiveness was a great liability; there was a tendency in this direction but the conservative conclusion is that when the crime is attractiveness-related, the advantages otherwise held by good-looking defendants are lost.

Another feature of the data worth considering is that the sentences administered in the control condition are almost identical to those assigned in the unattractive condition. It appears that being unattractive did not produce discriminatory responses, per se. Rather, it seems that appearance had its effect through the attractive conditions: The beautiful burglar got off lightly, while the beautiful swindler paid somewhat, though not significantly, more. It can be recalled that in the unattractive conditions the stimulus person was seen as relatively unattractive and not merely average looking. Therefore, the absence of unattractive-control condition differences does not seem to be the result of a weak manipulation in the unattractive conditions.

Perhaps it is possible to derive a small bit of consolation from this outcome, if we speculate that only the very attractive receive special (favorable or unfavorable) treatment, and that others are treated similarly. That is a less frightening conclusion than one which would indicate that unattractiveness brings about active discrimination.

As indicated earlier, previous findings (Efran, 1974) that attractive offenders are treated leniently can be interpreted in a number of ways. The results of the present experiment support the cognitive explanation we offered. The notion that good-looking people usually tend to be treated generously because they are

TABLE 1 / Mean Sentence Assigned, in Years (n = 20 per cell)

| Offense | Defendant Condition | | |
	Attractive	Unattractive	Control
Swindle	5.45	4.35	4.35
Burglary	2.80	5.20	5.10

seen as less dangerous and more virtuous remains tenable. The argument that physical attractiveness is a positive trait and therefore has a unidirectionally favorable effect on judgments of those who have it, would have led to accurate predictions in the burglary conditions. However, this position could not account for the observed interaction. The cognitive view makes precisely that prediction.

Finally, we feel compelled to note that our laboratory situation is quite different from actual courtroom situations. Most important, perhaps, our subjects made decisions which had no consequences for the defendant, and they made those decisions by themselves, rather than arriving at judgments after discussions with others exposed to the same information. Since the courtroom is not an appropriate laboratory, it is unlikely that actual experimental tests in the real situation would ever be conducted. However, simulations constitute legitimate avenues for investigating person perception and interpersonal judgment, and there is no obvious reason to believe that these processes would not have the effects in trial proceedings that they do elsewhere.

Whether a discussion with other jurors would affect judgment is an empirical, and researchable, question. Perhaps if even 1 of 12 jurors notes that some irrelevant factor may be affecting the jury's judgment, the others would see the light. Especially now when the prospect of reducing the size of juries is being entertained, it would be important to find out whether extralegal considerations are more likely to have greater influence as the number of jurors decreases.

REFERENCES

Byrne, D., & Clore, G. L. A reinforcement model of evaluative responses. *Personality: An International Journal,* 1970, *1,* 103–128.

Dion, K. Physical attractiveness and evaluation of children's transgressions. *Journal of Personality and Social Psychology,* 1972, *24,* 207–213.

Dion, K., Berscheid, E., & Walster, E. What is beautiful is good. *Journal of Personality and Social Psychology,* 1972, *24,* 285–290.

Efran, M. G. The effect of physical appearance on the judgment of guilt, interpersonal attraction, and severity of recommended punishment in a simulated jury task. *Journal of Research in Personality,* 1974, *8,* 45–54.

Landy, D., & Aronson, E. The influence of the character of the criminal and victim on the decisions of simulated jurors. *Journal of Experimental Social Psychology,* 1969, *5,* 141–152.

Miller, A. G. Role of physical attractiveness in impression formation. *Psychonomic Science,* 1970, *19,* 241–243.

Monahan, F. *Women in crime.* New York: Washburn, 1941.

ENDNOTE

1. This information as well as copies of the case accounts referred to below, can be obtained from the first author.

This study was supported by a grant from the University of Maryland General Research Board.

CRITICAL THINKING QUESTIONS

1. This article used pictures only of females to show defendants of varying attractiveness. Would the same results be obtained if male defendants were used? In other words, do you think that attractiveness stereotypes operate in the same way for males as for females? Defend your answer.

2. As the authors of the article noted, the methodology of the study differed from real-life jury trials in several ways. For example, subjects made their decisions alone and were presented with a paper description of the person and deed, not a real-life person and crime. Design a study that would investigate the same variables studied in the article in a more natural environment.

3. Would the results of this study be generalizable to situations other than jury trials? Think of a situation in which the attractiveness of a person making a request or performing a certain action may result in his or her being treated differently as a result of his or her attractiveness. Explain your answer.

4. What implications do these findings have for the U.S. legal system? How could the effects of irrelevant factors such as attractiveness somehow be minimized in the real-world courtroom? For example, would telling the jurors beforehand about the tendency to let attractiveness influence their judgments make any difference? Why or why not?

ADDITIONAL RELATED READINGS

MacLin, O. H., MacLin, M. K., & MacLin, O. H. (2004). The effect of criminality on face attractiveness, typicality, memorability, and recognition. *North American Journal of Psychology, 6*(1), 145–154.

Wuensch, K. L., & Moore, C. H. (2004). Effects of physical attractiveness on evaluations of a male employee's allegation of sexual harassment by his female employer. *Journal of Social Psychology, 144*(2), 207–217.

ARTICLE 42 _____

In the legal systems of the United States, Canada, and many other countries, the conviction and sentencing of a defendant is supposed to be based on the admissible evidence presented in the courtroom. What is considered *admissible* usually is based on precedent and other rules concerning the appropriateness of certain types of evidence. However, there are certain factors pertaining to the defendant that, while not admissible as evidence, are impossible to conceal from the jury. For example, Article 41 demonstrated how the physical attractiveness of the defendant may play an important role in the likelihood of his or her being convicted and the severity of his or her recommended punishment.

Besides physical attractiveness, many other personal characteristics of the defendant are obvious to the jury yet should not necessarily affect the decision it makes. Race, ethnic background, and perceived intelligence are but a few of the defendant characteristics that cannot be concealed from the jury. While such factors presumably should not enter into the decision making of the jury, they certainly may.

The following article by Christine E. Bergeron and Stuart J. McKelvie examines how age may have an impact on jury decision making. This article, along with the information already presented in Articles 40 and 41, further demonstrates that many potential sources of bias enter into the criminal justice system.

Effects of Defendant Age on Severity of Punishment for Different Crimes

■ Christine E. Bergeron and Stuart J. McKelvie

Abstract. *After reading a murder or theft vignette in which the perpetrator was a 20-, 40-, or 60-year-old man, 95 undergraduates gave sentence and parole recommendations. Punishment was harsher for the murder than for the theft. For murder, participants treated the 20- and 60-year-old men less harshly than the 40-year-old man, which confirms previous archival findings. However, this inverted U-shaped function occurred for murder only. The authors discussed the results in the context of the just-desert and utilitarian rationales that guide sentencing and gave suggestions for future research.*

Key Words   crime severity, defendant age, sentencing

The judicial system should be free of any bias that would influence a judge's or a jury's decisions concern-ing verdicts and recommendations for punishment. That is, judgments should be based solely on evidential—not extralegal—factors (Mazzella & Feingold, 1994).

Evidential factors are based on legally admissible evidence and include offense severity (Ryckman, Bums, & Robbins, 1986; Zamble & Kalm, 1990) and criminal responsibility (Sinha & Kumar, 1985). Punishment should be greater for a more serious offense than for a less serious offense and for an intended (deliberate) act than for an unintended act. Sentencing follows a tariff system according to which the primary goal is retribution (Kapardis & Farrington, 1981). Under this just-desert rationale, a more culpable defendant receives a more severe punishment (Gebotys & Roberts, 1987; Steffensmeier, Ulmer, & Kramer, 1998).

Reprinted from *The Journal of Social Psychology, 144*(1), pp. 75–90, February 2004. Reprinted with permission of the Helen Dwight Reid Educational Foundation. Published by Heldref Publications, 1319 Eighteenth St., N.W., Washington, DC 20036-1802. Copyright © 2004.

However, the North American justice system allows for considerable discretion in sentencing (Wheeler, Weisburd, & Bode, 1982), which permits extralegal factors to play a role. In particular, sentencing may be guided by utilitarian rather than just-desert rationales (Gebotys, & Roberts, 1987; Steffensmeier et al., 1998). Here, such goals as deterrence, incapacitation, and rehabilitation may determine how the offender is treated (Gebotys & Roberts; Kapardis & Farrington, 1981). A heavier sentence may be given to warn others what will happen to them if they commit the same crime, for deterrence, or to keep the criminal out of public circulation, for incapacitation. On the other hand, a lighter sentence may be given if the system judges that the offender can be rehabilitated. For example, a judge may argue that an employed person is more likely to be rehabilitated than an unemployed one (Gebotys & Roberts).

Actions like this, which Canadian case law has supported (Gebotys & Roberts, 1987), may be justifiable if they are based on empirically demonstrated risk factors for reoffending. In fact, investigators have related race and gender, which are thought to predict recidivism, to processing by the criminal justice system (Wilbanks, 1988) and to judgments that the system has made under experimental conditions (Mazzella & Feingold, 1994). Generally, Caucasian and female defendants have been treated more leniently than African American and male defendants (Wilbanks).

Nevertheless, such "profiling," in which the sentencing decision is influenced by a subject variable, runs the risk that truly causal factors are overlooked and that judges' attributions may be biased (Wheeler et al., 1982). Indeed, Steffensmeier et al. (1998) stated that judges have invoked race and gender as stereotypical attributions when they attempt to reduce uncertainty in the sentencing process. Furthermore, archival (Stewart, 1980) and experimental (Mazzella & Feingold, 1994) research has shown that sentences are shorter for attractive defendants than for unattractive defendants. This is clear evidence of bias because physical attractiveness is unlikely to be related to any utilitarian goals.

Of interest here is the extralegal characteristic of defendant age, which courts in Canada and the United States have cited as a mitigating factor (Gebotys & Roberts, 1987; Kapardis & Farrington, 1981). From the just-desert perspective, the law does not list age as a mitigating factor (Silverman, Smith, Nelson, & Dembo, 1984), so any effect of it on punishment would be inequitable. However, from the utilitarian perspective, the system may see a younger person as more likely to be rehabilitated than an older person, thereby justifying more lenient treatment. If age actually predicts recidivism, this may be justifiable; if not, it may only reflect a stereotyped perception and bias against the older person (Steffensmeier et al., 1998).

Archival Research on Age

Although Steffensmeier et al. (1998) characterized research on age as "sparse," investigators have conducted both archival and experimental studies. Champion (1987) examined the conviction records of many crimes for elderly felons who were 60 years old and over and found that the sentences given and the sentences actually served were both a very small proportion of the maximum possible sentence (only .14 and .09 respectively). This suggests that the elderly are treated leniently, but Champion did not have comparative data from other age groups. However, Wilbanks (1988) examined secondary records of elderly (over 60 years old) and nonelderly (25–59 years old) offenders at various decision points in the justice system. Relative to their number in the general population, the nonelderly were more likely to be arrested and punished than the elderly, but the ratio of nonelderly to elderly was higher for incarceration and sentencing (39:1) than for arrest and conviction (26:1). This indicates more lenient treatment of the elderly at the final decision points than at the front end of the system. Similarly, once arrested, the elderly were slightly more likely to be convicted than the nonelderly, but they were slightly less likely to be sentenced to prison terms.

In an archival study of shoplifting, Cutshall and Adams (1983) examined the relationship between age (17–25 years, 26–49 years, over 50 years) and the decision to prosecute. Overall, older people were significantly less likely to be prosecuted than middle-aged but not younger people (29%, 45%, 39%, respectively), indicating an inverted U-shaped function between age and treatment. Moreover, in a study of white collar crimes (Wheeler, Weisburd, & Bode, 1982), there was also an inverted U-shaped function for decisions to incarcerate convicted offenders: 50%

of people aged around 40 years, but 42% and 32% for those around 20 years and 60 years, respectively. In contrast, there was no relationship between age and length of sentence. However, in two other studies that examined the full range of adult ages over a variety of crimes, the curvilinear function was found for both incarceration and length of sentence: treatment was more lenient for people under 21 years old and 40–49 years old than for people 21–29 years old, and most lenient of all for people over 50 years old (Steffensmeier et al., 1998). From interviews with American judges, Steffensmeier et al. offer a utilitarian account of these findings: perceptions were that the youngest people were more likely to be harmed by prison, the oldest were less blameworthy and dangerous, and the 21–29-year-olds were more of a threat and less reformable.

Experimental Research on Age

These American archival studies suggest that people over 50 years old and people under 21 years old are treated more leniently than people of middle age. However, while studies of secondary records are realistic, they suffer from the disadvantage that many variables are not controlled. That is, external validity is high, but internal validity is low (Kapardis & Farrington, 1981). For example, age effects may be confounded with race (Cutshall & Adams, 1983) or with strength of evidence or prior record (Wilbanks, 1988). The experimental method, which investigators have widely used in mock jury studies (e.g., Gerbasi, Zuckerman, & Reis, 1977), can overcome this weakness by manipulating age and keeping other variables constant.

Indeed, in one such investigation with British lay magistrates (civilians who administer the law) working in groups of three, there was no effect of age (22 years vs. 32 years) on sentencing severity (from discharge to six months of prison or committal to a higher court) for a simulated case of assault (Kapardis & Farrington, 1981). The authors speculated that the age information might not have been noticed because it was embedded in other case details, and they note that this could have been ascertained if they had included a manipulation check for the magistrates' memory for the ages. In addition, they also wonder if the difference between the ages was too small to pro-

duce an effect. However, with a wider age gap (18 years vs. 38 years) and members of the Canadian public as participants, Gebotys and Roberts (1987) also found no effect of age on sentencing for two crimes (breaking and entering; manslaughter). On the other hand, and again with the Canadian public, sentences were shorter for 17–19-year-olds than for 35–38-year-olds over four crimes that ranged in severity (Zamble & Kalm, 1990). American undergraduates have also given more lenient sentences to juveniles vs. adults over a variety of crimes (Faulkner & Steffensmeier, 1979) and to 23-year-olds vs. 53-year-olds for a swindle and a burglary (Smith & Hed, 1979). Finally, Silverman et al. (1984) presented American undergraduates, senior citizens, and law enforcement officers with a crime vignette (theft of $250) in which the perpetrator was juvenile, adult, or elderly (no ages specified in years). Punishment, which could range from none to more than 1 year in jail, was harsher for the adult than for both the juvenile and the elderly offenders. In a table footnote, Silverman et al. stated that punishment did not differ between the elderly and juvenile offenders, but in the text the investigators presented post hoc tests that showed harsher treatment of the elderly.

The Present Experiment

In general, these experiments show that younger people under 23 years old receive more lenient treatment than middle-aged people up to 53 years old, which is consistent with the archival research findings. The archival result of more lenient treatment for elderly offenders also received support, but on the basis of only a single study (Silverman et al., 1984). The major purpose of the present experiment was to gather further evidence of the effect of age on punishment, particularly for the elderly offender. Consequently, we manipulated age by including three levels (20 years, 40 years, 60 years) that cover the important ranges in the archival and experimental studies. Participants read a vignette that referred to the defendant by age, then gave sentencing recommendations.

Our second purpose was to investigate whether age had a different effect with two crimes (second-degree murder, theft) that differed in severity. In the archival studies, the curvilinear relationship occurred with less serious crimes (Cutshall & Adams, 1983; Wheeler et al., 1982) and over many (unspecified) crimes (Steffensmeier et al., 1998). In the latter case, more serious crimes such as murder were not separated out, but Steffensmeier et al. speculate that age effects are more likely for a less serious offense like shoplifting, which may be subject to "discretionary processing," than for a more serious crime like murder, which is "uniformly repugnant." Over 19 crimes, Wilbanks (1988) found relatively more lenient treatment for the elderly than the nonelderly at sentencing, but he stated that this occurred more often when the crimes were less serious. Together, these archival studies suggest that age effects are more likely with the less serious crimes than with the more serious crimes.

Experimental investigators have differentiated more and less serious crimes but have not consistently related this factor to age effects. For example, age has been significant for less serious crimes such as shoplifting, swindle, and burglary or breaking and entering (Faulkner & Steffensmeier, 1979; Smith & Hed, 1979; Zamble & Kalm, 1990) and for more serious crimes that involve drugs and robbery and assault (Faulkner & Steffensmeier; Zamble & Kalm). But, it has also not been significant for either less serious crimes, such as drunkenness, robbery or theft, and breaking and entering (Faulkner & Steffensmeier; Gebotys & Roberts, 1987; Zamble & Kalm), or more serious crimes, such as manslaughter and murder (Faulkner & Steffensmeier; Gebotys & Roberts). The only replicated finding here is that there was no effect of age for the most serious crimes, those involving death. In the present study, we compared the effects of age for the less serious crime of theft with the more serious crime of second-degree murder.

As a third purpose, we investigated the effects of age and crime severity not only on length of jail sentence, but also on a second measure of punishment, parole recommendation. This does not appear to have been done before, but it adds realism in that many criminals do not serve their full sentences. Indeed, in Section 743 of the Criminal Code of Canada (Watt & Fuerst, 1998), there is provision for the jury to make a parole recommendation. Furthermore, although participants recommended the number of years for the jail sentence and the number of years that should be served before eligibility for parole, we also calculated two ratio measures of parole severity: the parole recommendation divided by the sentence recommendation, and the parole recommendation divided by the maximum possible sentence under Canadian law. The latter is similar to the proportional statistic that Champion (1987) reported.

Lastly, because the numbers of male and female participants were not equal, we examined whether gender of judge moderated the effect of age. Previous research on this variable has shown mixed results (Abwender & Hough, 2001). In some studies (e.g., Faulkner & Steffensmeier, 1979; McKelvie, Mitchell, Arnott, & Sullivan, 1993; Riedel, 1993), gender of judge has not been significantly related to severity of punishment. In others in which gender of judge has been significant, women have usually been harsher than men (Schutte & Hosch, 1997; Wuensch, Castellow, & Moore, 1991), particularly in cases of sexual assault (Abwender & Hough, 2001). One investigator found evidence of own-gender bias: women gave longer sentences when the victim was a woman, and men gave longer sentences when the victim was a man (McKelvie, 2002).

Hypotheses

First, we hypothesized that the evidential factor of crime severity would influence the sentence and parole recommendations of the participants, with harsher punishment for murder than for theft. This hypothesis is derived directly from the just-desert rationale, but it is also consistent with the utilitarian rationale because a murderer is likely to be more of a threat to society than is a thief. For a stimulus check, we asked participants to rate the severity of the crime about which they had just read.

Second, we hypothesized that participants would rate the murder vignette as more serious than the theft vignette.

Third, because second-degree murder differs from first-degree murder in the degree to which the crime is planned and deliberate, the murder vignette indicated that the murder occurred when the defendant lost control of his emotions. However, the theft vignette indicated that the theft was planned and deliberate. For a second stimulus check, we asked participants to rate how much the defendant intended to commit the crime. Our third hypothesis was that participants would rate intention higher for theft than for murder.

Fourth, and most importantly, from the archival and experimental research, we hypothesized that the participants would treat the 20-year-old offender and the 60-year-old offender less harshly than the 40-year-old offender.

Fifth, from the statements of archival researchers (Steffensmeier et al., 1998; Wilbanks, 1988) and from results of the two experimental studies (Gebotys & Roberts, 1987; Zamble & Kalm, 1990) with crimes involving death, the present researchers hypothesized that the offender's age would affect participants' sentence judgments for theft but not for murder.

Finally, participants rated how mentally ill the criminal was. Because the vignettes contained no information about mental illness, it was not clear whether these ratings would vary as a function of crime. However, we hypothesized that participants would perceive a person who murders as more mentally ill than they would perceive one who steals.

Initially, we gave participants freedom to make sentence and parole recommendations in the range from 0 to 99 years. This freedom is not realistic in Canada because the maximum sentence under Canadian law is life imprisonment for murder and 10 years for theft. However, the common scale allowed us to investigate the effect of age and of crime severity on punishment, which provides information on the general process of judgment (Mook, 1983). In addition, to give participants the opportunity to ensure that the criminal remained in prison for the rest of his life, the maximum number of years had to be at least 80 (assuming a person would not live beyond 100 years). The maximum of 99 years, which has been used before (Hendrick & Shaffer, 1975; McKelvie et al., 1993), satisfies this requirement and also has the connotation of a permanent stay in jail. Following the unrestricted judgments, participants then made recommendations under Canadian law, which requires for second-degree murder a sentence of mandatory life imprisonment with the possibility of parole after 10 years and for theft a sentence in the range from 2 to 10 years with the possibility of parole at any time (taken from Section 745 of the Criminal Code of Canada, Watt & Fuerst, 1998).

METHOD

Participants

The participants were 95 Canadian undergraduates (58 women, 37 men, mean age = 20.9 years) who were members of a psychology department subject pool. Race was not recorded, but we observed that the vast majority were Caucasian Canadians. Although some participants' mother tongue was French, they all spoke and read English. We contacted participants by e-mail and invited them to sign up for a psychology experiment. They received 0.5% credit in a psychology course of their choice.

We randomly allocated participants to six conditions in a 2 (crime) × 3 (defendant age) design, with gender proportionally balanced. Participants were approximately 60% women and 40% men in each condition; murder with the 20-, 40-, or 60-year-old defendant; theft with the 20-, 40-, or 60-year-old defendant. Before the experiment began, participants signed an informed consent form. Later, they were debriefed by receiving a one-page written account of the results.

Materials and Procedure

We constructed second-degree murder and theft vignettes (approximately 250 words in each) that were consistent with legal texts (Carswell Thomas Commercial Publishing, 2000; Watt & Fuerst, 1998; Reader's Digest Association, 1984). The murder vignette was for the second degree because an argument over money turned violent and did not seem to be planned and deliberate. However, the theft from a jewelry store was clearly planned and deliberate.

Participants read either the theft vignette or the murder vignette in which a 20-, 40-, or 60-year-old White man had been found guilty. Participants gave recommendations for sentence and for parole (in the range of possibilities from 0 to 99 years). Then, for the theft condition, participants were also asked to make sentence and parole recommendations according to Canadian law (in the range from 2 to 10 years with parole at any time). For the murder condition, we then told participants the relevant Canadian law (mandatory life sentence) and asked them to make a parole recommendation (eligible after 10 years).

One problem in the present study is that a life sentence is by definition longer for the 20-year-old defendant than it is for the 40- or 60-year-old defendant. Because one of our ratio measures of parole severity was parole divided by maximum sentence, it was important to operationally define "life" in the same manner for all ages. Assuming a life span of 100 years, this could mean 80, 60, or 40 years, depending on whether the 20-, 40-, or 60-year-old was chosen as the baseline. Our free sentencing and free parole judgments were made on a scale from 0 to 99 years, which is closest to the 80-year definition, which implies that the 20-year-old should be taken as the baseline. However, because our major interest was in the 20- and 60-year-old conditions, we chose to take the 60-year-old person as the baseline, thereby adopting 40 years as the operational definition of a life sentence. Participants in the murder condition were told to consider 40 years as the maximum length of time for parole.

Participants then gave us three ratings on rating scales (in which all 7 points were labeled): the first item asked, "How severe do you think the crime was?" (from 1 = *not at all severe* to 7 = *very severe*); the second item asked, "Do you think that this crime was intended by the defendant?" (from 1 = *definitely no* to 7 = *definitely yes*); and the third item asked, "Do you think that the defendant has a mental illness?" (from 1 = *definitely no* to 7 = *definitely yes*). As noted in the introduction of the present article, severity served as a stimulus check to ensure that the participant perceived murder as more serious than theft. Intention served as a check that the transcript had been read carefully. In the murder vignette, it was stated that "This was a case in which anger turned into aggressive action," whereas in the theft vignette, it was stated that "This is a simple case of planned theft." These statements imply that the murder was not as deliberate as the theft. There was no information about mental illness, perhaps implying that ratings would not vary.

RESULTS

Validity Checks of the Crime Manipulation

Before analyzing the judgments, it was important to ensure that the crimes were perceived as varying in severity and that the participant perceived intention as slightly different in the two vignettes. Ratings of crime severity were significantly higher for murder than for theft (Ms = 5.9, 3.7; SDs = 1.2, 1.1, respectively), $F(1, 89)$ = 90.68, $p < .001$, and did not vary with defendant age in either condition. The standardized effect size for this difference was d = 1.96, which is much greater than Cohen's (1977) standard of .80 for "large." Ratings of intent were marginally significantly higher for theft than for murder (Ms = 5.4, 5.0; SDs = 1.1, 1.2, respectively), $F(1, 89)$ = 3.16, p = .079, but did not vary with age. Here the effect size of d = 0.37 was between small (0.20) and medium (0.50). Ratings of mental illness did not vary significantly with crime or with age.

Table 1 shows the mean scores for each kind of judgment in each condition.

The text in the following sections includes the standardized effect sizes for type of crime (murder vs. theft) and for age of defendant (40 years old vs. 20 years old, 40 years old vs. 60 years old). Because our main interest was in defendant age, these effect sizes are reported regardless of whether they were significant.

Although more participants were women than men in each condition, gender of participant was initially included in the analyses. Because it was never significant as a main effect or as an interaction, 2 × 3 (crime × defendant age) factorial analyses of variance (ANOVAs) were run without it.

Sentencing and Parole Judgments

For free sentence judgments, all three effects were significant: crime, $F(1, 89)$ = 87.12, $p < .001$; defendant age, $F(2, 89)$ = 4.53, $p < .02$; and their interaction, $F(2, 89)$ = 4.94, $p < .01$. Sentences were shorter for theft than for murder, d = 1.92. From Newman-Keuls post hoc tests with alpha set at .05, sentences were also shorter for both the 20-year-old and the 60-year-old than for the 40-year-old (ds = 0.52, 0.80, respectively). However, separate post hoc tests on age for murder and for theft showed that the differences were only significant for murder. In that case, effect sizes for the 20-year-old and the 60-year-old compared to the 40-year-old were ds = 1.01 and 1.53, respectively. For theft, they were (ds = −0.06 and −0.02 (indicating slightly lower sentences for the 40-year-old than for the 20- or 60-year-old).

TABLE 1 / Mean Sentence in Years, Standard Deviations, and Parole Recommendations in Each Condition

| | Defendant's Age in Years | | | | | |
| | 20 | | 40 | | 60 | |
Condition	M	SD	M	SD	M	SD
Free Sentence						
Murder	27.8	14.6	41.6	27.1	20.8	11.4
Theft	4.4	3.1	3.6	1.4	3.9	3.7
Both	16.1	15.8	23.2	27.2	12.4	11.9
Free Parole						
Murder	14.1	8.3	28.8	29.9	13.4	7.0
Theft	2.3	2.1	1.4	0.7	2.2	2.6
Both	8.2	8.5	15.5	25.3	7.8	7.7
Proportional Parole						
Murder	.54	.26	.58	.53	.66	.15
Theft	.52	.14	.41	.18	.52	.26
Both	.53	.21	.50	.23	.59	.22
Restricted Sentence						
Murder	—	—	—	—	—	—
Theft	4.7	2.7	3.5	1.4	3.5	2.2
Restricted Parole						
Murder	16.5	8.9	21.4	11.2	14.6	5.9
Theft	2.6	1.9	1.4	0.7	2.1	1.5
Both	9.5	9.5	11.7	12.9	8.3	7.6
Restricted Proportional Parole						
Murder	.41	.22	.53	.28	.36	.15
Theft	.26	.19	.14	.07	.21	.15
Both	.33	.22	.34	.28	.29	.16

Note: Proportional parole is free parole divided by free sentence. For free sentence, minimum is 0 years, maximum is 99 years; for restricted sentence and restricted parole for theft, minimum is 0 years, maximum is 10 years; for restricted parole for murder, minimum is 0 years, maximum is 40 years. Restricted proportional parole is restricted parole divided by legal maximum sentence. Sample size was 15 or 16 per condition.

For free parole, the effect of crime, $F(1, 89) = 38.80$, $p < .001$, and the interaction between crime and defendant age, $F(2, 89) = 3.82$, $p < .05$, were significant. The main effect of defendant age was marginally significant, $F(2, 89) = 2.99$, $p = .055$. Parole recommendations were shorter for theft than for murder ($d = 1.28$). From Newman-Keuls tests, parole recommendations were shorter for both the 20-year-old and the 60-year-old than for the 40-year-old ($ds = 0.55$, 0.58). These comparisons were also significant for murder, where effect sizes for the 20-year-old and the 60-year-old compared to the 40-year-old were $ds = 1.11$ and 1.17, respectively. For theft, the comparisons were not significant; $ds = -0.07$ and -0.06 (slightly lower parole time for the 40-year-old than for the 20- or 60-year-old).

These parole judgments may have been influenced by the prior sentence judgments. To correct for this possibility, we calculated a stricter measure of parole severity by dividing the parole by the sentence recommendations. This ratio score shows what proportion of the sentence should be served before parole is granted. In this case, only the effect of crime was significant, $F(1, 88) = 6.28$, $p < .05$. Proportional parole was shorter for theft than for murder ($d = 0.52$). Effect sizes for age were $ds = -0.13$ and -0.42 for the 40-year-old vs. the 20-year-old and for the 40-year-old vs. the 60-year-old (slightly smaller for the 40-year-old), respectively. For murder, corresponding effect sizes were $ds = 0.20$ and -0.35, respectively. For theft, they were $ds = -0.48$ and -0.51, respectively.

For restricted sentencing in the theft condition, a 1-way ANOVA for defendant age was not significant ($p > .20$). (There were no judgments for murder because life imprisonment was mandated by law.) For restricted parole judgments, the effect of crime was significant, $F(1, 89) = 136.72$, $p < .001$, and the interaction between crime and defendant age was marginally significant, $F(2, 89) = 3.03$, $p = .053$. However, these restricted parole judgments were not comparable for murder and for theft because the permitted ranges (0–40 years for murder, 0–10 years for theft) were different. To make them comparable, we calculated the scores as a proportion of the maximum possible sentences for murder (40 years) and for theft (10 years). This measure is similar to previous ratio scores defined as actual sentence divided by maximum sentence and time served divided by maximum sentence (Champion, 1987). For this measure (restricted proportional parole equals parole recommendation divided by maximum), the effect of crime, $F(1, 89) = 36.64$, $p < .001$, and the interaction between crime and defendant age, $F(2, 89) = 4.32$, $p < .05$, were significant. Restricted proportional parole was longer for murder than for theft ($d = 1.23$). Post hoc tests showed that in the murder condition, it was significantly longer for the 40-year-old than for the 60-year-old ($d = 0.95$) but not significantly longer for the 40- than for the 20-year-old (although $d = 0.64$). None of the post hoc tests for age were significant for theft, although proportional parole was slightly shorter for the 40- than

for the 20- or 60-year-old ($ds = -0.63, -0.40$, respectively). The main effect of defendant age was not significant, but effect sizes were $ds = 0.04$ and 0.28 for the 40-year-old vs. the 20- and 60-year-old, respectively.

DISCUSSION

Validity Checks: Ratings of Crime Severity, Intent, and Mental Illness

The ratings of crime severity confirmed that participants perceived the murder as more serious than the theft. Participants rated murder as strongly severe and theft as slightly-to-somewhat severe. As predicted, ratings of intent were slightly higher for theft (probably intended to very probably intended) than for murder (probably intended), which indicates that participants paid attention to the crime information. Moreover, ratings of intention did not vary with age, which is consistent with the fact that the murder and theft descriptions were identical for the 20-, 40-, and 60-year-olds, except in indicating the offender's age. Mental illness ratings did not vary with crime or with age, which is consistent with the finding that this factor was not mentioned in either vignette. Overall, the ratings indicate that the participants read and understood the vignettes. Most importantly, the crimes were perceived as varying in severity.

Effects of Crime Severity on Punishment

Free sentence, free parole, and free proportional parole judgments were harsher for murder than for theft. Under the restriction of Canadian law, the proportional parole recommendations were also longer for murder than for theft. The two ratio parole scores are a strict measure of severity of punishment because they correct for the length of sentence and indicate what proportion of the sentence (or maximum sentence) should be served. On the basis of Cohen's (1977) standards of 0.20, 0.50, and 0.80 for small, medium, and large effect sizes, respectively, three of these effects (free sentence, free parole, and restricted proportional parole) were extremely large, and one (proportional parole) was medium in size.

Overall, participants treated the murderer more severely than the thief, with a mean effect size over the six estimates of $d = 1.22$ ($SD = 0.57$), which is very large. This result supports previous findings that punishment is a function of crime seriousness. It also extends the previous findings from sentencing recommendations to parole recommendations (Faulkner & Steffensmeier, 1979; Gebotys & Roberts, 1987; Ryckman, Bums, & Robbins, 1986; Zamble & Kalm, 1990). In the present study, not only did participants recommend a longer sentence for the murderer than for the thief, they also tried to ensure that the murderer would actually spend a longer time behind bars. Theoretically, these results are consistent with the just-desert rationale according to which the punishment should fit the crime. However, they are also consistent with utilitarian rationales. That is, a murderer may be seen as less likely than a thief to be rehabilitated and so should spend longer time in jail. The murderer is also likely to be seen as more of a threat than the thief and so should be incapacitated for a longer period of time. The harsher penalty may also be seen as a warning to others.

Effects of Defendant Age

When we allowed participants to give jail terms up to 99 years, the extralegal factor of defendant age was significant as a main effect for free sentencing and was almost significant for free parole. As we had predicted, the results took the form of an inverted U-shaped function with the 20- and 60-year-olds being treated more leniently than the 40-year-old. The effect sizes for the 40- vs. 20-year-old on free sentence and on free parole were both medium, and the corresponding effect sizes for the 60- vs. 40-year-old were large and medium, respectively. However, when parole was calculated as a proportion of the sentence (proportional parole) or as a proportion of the maximum sentence under Canadian law (restricted proportional parole), the main effect of defendant age was not significant.

Although defendant age was significant or almost significant with free sentence and free parole, it interacted with crime, and this interaction also occurred with restricted proportional parole under Canadian law. On the basis of previous research and from Steffensmeier et al.'s (1998) suggestion that less serious crimes might be more subject to discretionary processing, it had been hypothesized that the effect of defendant age would be stronger for theft than for murder. However, in the present study, the opposite result was obtained. For murder, the effect sizes for the harsher treatment of the 40-year-old compared to the 20-year-old and of the 40-year-old compared to the 60-year-old were very large for free sentence and for free parole, but these effects were smaller for the two proportional parole scores. This pattern is the same that we reported earlier in the present article for the main effect of age. The greater effects of defendant age with free sentencing and free parole than with parole under Canadian law indicate that age is less likely to be a determinant of punishment under more realistic conditions.

Because only one group of experimenters (Silverman et al., 1984) in only one study has studied the elderly criminal, the primary interest in the present study was the treatment of the 60-year-old offender. We found that effect sizes were generally greater for the 60-year-old vs. the 40-year-old comparison than they were for the 20- vs. 40-year-old comparison. This result occurred for the main effect of age and for the effect of age on murder with the free sentence, free parole, and restricted proportional parole measures. This result is consistent with archival work showing more lenient treatment of people over 50 years than of people under 50, and with the more lenient treatment of an elderly person than of a nonelderly adult in the only experiment to include the oldest age group (Silverman et al.).

The present inverted U-shaped function between defendant age and severity of punishment does not support the nonsignificant results of two previous experiments (Faulkner & Steffensmeier, 1979; Gebotys & Roberts, 1987). However, in view of the mixed significant and nonsignificant experimental results with less serious crimes of those and other experiments (Faulkner & Steffensmeier; Gebotys & Roberts; Kapardis & Farrington, 1981; Silverman et al., 1984; Smith & Hed, 1979; Zamble & Kalm, 1990), the present experiment's nonsignificant effects of defendant age with theft are not surprising. Perhaps the effect of age in previous archival research with less serious crimes is due to a confounding variable. Notably, our effect sizes were all negative, indicating a trend for slightly harsher treatment of the 20- and 60-year-olds than of the 40-year-old. This intriguing finding contrasts with the more lenient treatment of the younger and older defendants convicted of murder and deserves further investigation.

As observed earlier in the present article, the clearest distinction between the effects of age on sentencing for murder and the effects of age on sentencing for theft in the present experiment occurred when participants were free to make recommendations on the scale from 0 to 99 years. Because murder is serious, participants were likely to consider a wide range of options, giving them 100 scale points to choose from. However, with the less serious crime of theft, the effective range on the scale was much narrower. People chose from 2 to 99 years for murder and only from 0 to 15 years for theft. Furthermore, over 90% of the recommendations for theft were below 10 years, meaning that participants used only 10–15 scale points. Although past researchers have found an effect of age for less serious crimes when the maximum possible sentence was 10 years (Faulkner & Steffensmeier, 1979; Smith & Hed, 1979), future researchers should avoid this restriction in range for theft by allowing people to give recommendations in months rather than in years.

Effects of Gender of Participant (Judge)

Although it was of secondary interest, we included the gender of the participant as a variable in the analyses. It was never significant, which is consistent with previous reports that sentencing recommendations do not differ between men and women (Faulkner & Steffensmeier, 1979; McKelvie et al., 1993; Riedel, 1993). In other experiments, when women were harsher, the crime was often sexual assault (Abwender & Hough, 2001). That result was not the case in the present experiment. In the experiment in which an own-gender bias occurred (McKelvie, 2002), the crime was murder, but it was a case of perceived job discrimination. Perhaps gender of judge is a factor in punishment when the crime is sex-related.

Limitations, Strengths, and Conclusion

This study was artificial in that participants did not make the initial sentencing and parole judgments

under Canadian law. In addition, participants were undergraduates, who do not represent the general population from which most jurors would be chosen. Furthermore, the fictional vignettes lacked the details of a real case (e.g., previous record of the defendant). Although participants made some judgments according to Canadian law, they may have been influenced by the prior free judgments.

At the same time, the effects with free sentencing and parole show what can happen and provide useful information on the process of judgment (Mook, 1983), and the parole recommendations were novel. Furthermore, as in other mock jury research, the experimental methodology permitted the isolation and manipulation of the independent variables, particularly defendant age. Overall, therefore, the finding that the 60- and 20-year-olds received more lenient treatment that the 40-year-old indicates that the inverted U-shaped function from archival studies is a true effect of age. The effect of age is also noteworthy because the information was embedded in the crime vignettes and was not specifically brought to the participants' attention. Because age is an extralegal factor, these results may reflect sterotypes about younger, middle-aged, and older people, in which case they demonstrate bias. Alternatively, they may reflect the phenomenon of people of different ages differing in their risk of reoffending (a utilitarian rationale), in which case they demonstrate a justifiable mitigating factor.

Future researchers on age might further examine sentence and parole judgments, which had not been differentiated before. Future researchers might also conduct the research only under the law of the land, thereby permitting participants a full range of choices for less serious crimes.

REFERENCES

Abwender, D. A., & Hough, K. (2001). Interactive effects of characteristics of defendant and mock juror on U.S. participants' judgment and sentencing recommendations. *The Journal of Social Psychology, 141,* 603–615.

Carswell Thomas Commercial Publishing. (2000). *Pocket Criminal Code 2000.* Scarborough, Ontario, Canada: Author.

Champion, D. J. (1987). Elderly felons and sentencing severity: Intergenerational variations in leniency and sentencing trends. *Criminal Justice Review, 12,* 7–14.

Cohen, J. (1977). *Statistical power analysis for the behavioral sciences* (Rev. ed.). New York: New York Academic Press.

Cutshall, C. R., & Adams, K. (1983). Responding to older offenders: Age selectivity in the processing of shoplifters. *Criminal Justice Review, 6,* 1–8.

Faulkner, G. L., & Steffensmeier, D. J. (1979). Effects of defendant's sex and age status on severity of punishment: An experimental test. *Psychological Reports, 45,* 917–918.

Gebotys, R. J., & Roberts, J. V. (1987). Public views of sentencing: The role of the offender. *Canadian Journal of Behavioural Science, 19,* 479–488.

Gerbasi, K. C., Zuckerman, M., & Reis, H. T. (1977). Justice needs a new blindfold: A review of mock jury research. *Psychological Bulletin, 84,* 323–343.

Hendrick, C., & Shaffer, D. R. (1975). Murder: Effects of number of killers and victim mutilation on simulated jurors' judgments. *Bulletin of the Psychonomic Society, 6,* 303–316.

Kapardis, A., & Farrington, D. P. (1981). An experimental study of sentencing by magistrates. *Law and Human Behavior, 5,* 107–121.

Mazzella, R., & Feingold, A. (1994). The effects of physical attractiveness, rape, socioeconomic status, and gender of defendants and victims on judgments of mock jurors: A meta-analysis. *Journal of Applied Social Psychology, 25,* 1315–1344.

McKelvie, S. J. (2002). Effects of sex of judge and sex of victim on recommended punishment of a male offender. *Psychological Reports, 91,* 533–536.

McKelvie, S. J., Mitchell, M., Arnott, R., & Sullivan, M. (1993). Effects of offenders' and victims' characteristics on severity of punishment. *Psychological Reports, 72,* 399–402.

Mook, D. G. (1983). In defense of external invalidity. *American Psychologist, 38,* 379–387.

Reader's Digest Association. (1984). *You and the law* (3rd ed.). Westmount, Montreal, Canada: Author.

Riedel, R. G., II. (1993). Effects of pretrial publicity on male and female jurors and judges in a mock rape trial. *Psychological Reports, 73,* 819–832.

Ryckman, R. M., Burns, M. J., & Robbins, M. A. (1986). Authoritarianism and sentencing strategies for low and high severity crimes. *Personality and Social Psychology Bulletin, 12,* 227–235.

Schutte, J. W., & Ilosch, H. M. (1997). Gender differences in sexual assault verdicts: A meta-analysis. *Journal of Social Behavior and Personality, 12,* 759–772.

Silverman, M., Smith, L. G., Nelson, C., & Dembo, R. (1984). The perception of the elderly criminal when compared to juvenile and adult offenders. *Journal of Applied Gerontology, 3,* 97–104.

Sinha, A. K., & Kumar, P. (1985). Antecedents of crime and suggested punishment. *The Journal of Social Psychology, 125,* 485–488.

Smith, F. D., & Hed, A. (1979). Effects of offenders' age and attractiveness on sentencing by mock juries. *Psychological Reports, 44,* 691–694.

Steffensmeier, D., Ulmer, J., & Kramer, J. (1998). The interaction of race, gender, and age in criminal sentencing: The punishment cost of being young, black, and male. *Criminology, 36,* 763–798.

Stewart, J. E., II. (1980). Defendant's attractiveness as a factor in the outcome of criminal trials: An observational study. *Journal of Applied Social Psychology, 10,* 348–361.

Watt, D., & Fuerst, M. (1998). *The 1999 annotated Tremecar's criminal code.* Scarborough, Ontario, Canada: Carswell Thomas Canada.

Wheeler, S., Weisburd, D., & Bode, N. (1982). Sentencing the white-collar offender: Rhetoric and reality. *American Sociological Review, 47,* 641–659.

Willbanks, W. (1988). Are elderly felons treated more leniently by the criminal justice system? *International Journal of Aging and Human Development, 26,* 275–288.

Wuensch, Castellow, & Moore. (1991). Effects of defendant attractiveness and type of crime on juridic judgment. *Journal of Social Behavior and Personality, 6,* 713–724.

Zamble, E., & Kalm, K. L. (1990). General and specific measures of public attitudes towards sentencing. *Canadian Journal of Behavioural Science, 22,* 327–337.

The authors thank Dr. Andrea Drumheller and lawyer Peter Turner for helpful comments and advice.

CRITICAL THINKING QUESTIONS

1. All of the *subjects* in the present study were traditional college-aged students. The results of the study were that 20- and 60-year-old defendants were treated more leniently than 40-year-old defendants. What if the *subjects* were 40-year-olds? Or 60-year-olds? Does the age of the subjects have an impact on their sentencing recommendations? Explain your reasoning.

2. The present study used two types of crimes, theft and manslaughter, as variables. For what other types of crimes may the defendant's age affect his or her possible conviction and sentencing? Be specific and defend your reasoning. Design a study to test your hypothesis.

3. Are the findings of studies such as this one, which employ simulated jury trials, relevant to the real world of jury trials? Why or why not? How might the results of such studies be of use in making real-world jury trials more impartial and fair? Explain your answers.

4. Is there an interaction between physical attractiveness and age in determining the guilt or innocence of a defendant? If so, what might it be? Design a study that would test your hypothesis.

CHAPTER INTEGRATION QUESTIONS ⎯⎯⎯⎯⎯⎯⎯⎯

1. By this time, you have undoubtedly read many of the previous chapters in this book. What other chapters and topics have particular relevance to the field of forensic psychology? Be specific in discussing how these chapters/topics may be of importance to forensic psychology.

2. What theme or themes are common to all three of the articles in this chapter? Explain.

3. "Justice is truth in action," according to Benjamin Disraeli, former British Prime Minister. What does this quotation mean to you? Based on the research presented in this chapter, how true is this quote? Explain your answer.

Chapter Fifteen

HEALTH PSYCHOLOGY

THIS FINAL CHAPTER addresses the contributions of social psychology to health issues. When we think of health, often the first thing that comes to mind is the medical or biological component of illness. But what about the behaviors that are linked to illness? Obviously, we can do many things to increase or decrease the likelihood of becoming ill. *Health psychology*, which has a long and strong connection with social psychology, is concerned with the psychosocial factors affecting the prevention, development, and treatment of physical illness.

Think of the various chapters and topics that you have read about in this book thus far. In one way or another, virtually every one of them has some implications for health psychology. For example, how we think about the social world around us (social cognition), our views of ourselves (social identity), how we form and change attitudes and the connection between attitudes and behaviors (attitudes), the impact of being subject to prejudice (prejudice), the role of supportive relationships (helping behavior), and the role of conformity in starting (or stopping) unhealthy behaviors (social influence) are all topics in social psychology that have direct implications for health.

Article 43 presents the mounting evidence that psychosocial factors, such as social isolation and anger, are major contributing factors in the occurrence of cardiovascular disease. "Research to the Heart of the Matter" discusses these risk factors along with effective interventions that may help people lead stronger and healthier lives.

We all know that stress can cause illness, but can even good events make us ill? Perhaps it is not just negative events but anything that makes us adapt and change that causes stress. From this view, getting married may be almost as stressful as getting fired from work. Article 44, "The Social Readjustment Rating Scale," is a classic article about pioneering work on how life changes in general may affect health.

Finally, Article 45 examines how the terrorist attacks of September 11, 2001, may have had a long-term impact on people. "Have There Been Lasting Effects Associated with the September 11, 2001, Terrorist Attacks among Inner-City Parents and Children?" is interesting for a number of reasons. In particular, it is one of the few studies that had data available on the subjects prior to the attack, thus allowing researchers to make a pre- and postattack comparison of subjects' behaviors and well-being.

ARTICLE 43 _____

Over the years, numerous connections have been made between personality/lifestyle factors and health. Perhaps the best-known link is that between stress and health. But what is *stress?* To a large extent, it is subjective. What is a source of stress for one person may be a neutral or even positive experience for another. Effectively, then, *stress* may be defined as physical, mental, or emotional strain or tension. It has evolved as a shortened version of the word *distress*.

Many studies have linked the amount of stress people experience with negative health consequences. Sometimes, these negative consequences are the direct result of stress—for instance, developing cardiovascular disease as a result of having elevated blood pressure. In other cases, the health problems may stem from behaviors developed in response to stress, such as smoking out of nervousness and contracting lung cancer. Thus, an important factor in determining the impact of stress on health is one's ability to cope. Someone who has developed effective coping mechanisms in response to stress is less likely to develop stress-related health problems than someone with less effective coping mechanisms.

While the sources and manifestations of stress may be unique to each individual, certain factors seem to predispose most people to health risks. For example, anger and hostility have been linked to cardiovascular disease in numerous studies. Likewise, factors such as social isolation may not only predispose individuals to disease but also impair their recovery from illness. The following article by Rebecca A. Clay examines the mounting evidence that psychosocial factors play a major role in the development of cardiovascular disease. In fact, psychosocial factors are far more malleable than, say, heredity factors, which makes the intervention strategies noted in the article particularly important.

Research to the Heart of the Matter

■ Rebecca A. Clay

The man clutching his heart and falling dead of a heart attack during a fight with his wife has been the stuff of cliché. Now psychologists are producing the science to prove the cliché true—and using that science to design interventions they hope will save lives.

"Although there's still some debate, there is increased recognition among the medical community about the importance of psychosocial factors in cardiovascular disease," says James A. Blumenthal, PhD, a professor of medical psychology at Duke University Medical Center in Durham, N.C. "There are clearly more papers on psychosocial topics being published in the more mainstream medical journals, not just in the

psychology journals. We're not just preaching to the converted anymore."

Blumenthal points to the literature review he and colleagues published in the pre-eminent cardiology journal *Circulation* in 1999 (Vol. 99, No. 16). "That the American Heart Association would afford us so much space is a testament to how important they consider psychosocial variables as potentially being," he says.

Today Blumenthal and other psychologists are producing clear evidence that psychosocial factors like hostility, anger, stress, depression and social isolation contribute to cardiovascular disease. They're showing

Reprinted from *Monitor on Psychology,* 2001, *32*(1), 42–45. Copyright © 2001 by the Amerian Psychological Association. Reprinted with permission.

that these factors influence the disease's development both directly and indirectly, through pathophysiological mechanisms and through unhealthy habits such as smoking and bad diets.

And they're beginning to come up with interventions that may help patients live longer, healthier lives.

LINKING PSYCHOSOCIAL FACTORS AND HEART DISEASE

Speculations about the link between psychosocial factors and cardiovascular disease are almost as old as medicine itself. In 1628 William Harvey first described the circulatory, system and noted that emotions affect the heart. In 1897, William Osler—often called the father of internal medicine—described the typical heart disease patient as "a keen and ambitious man, the indicator of whose engine is always at 'full speed ahead.'" In the 1950s, cardiologists Meyer Friedman, MD, and Ray Rosenman, MD, began their work connecting Type-A traits—free-floating hostility, impatience and insecurity—with cardiovascular disease.

Despite this long history, controversy lingers in the medical community. For instance, a study of 630 Army personnel published in the *New England Journal of Medicine* (Vol. 343, No. 18) last year found no link between their levels of anxiety, hostility, depression and stress and their chances of developing clogged arteries.

In recent years, anger in particular has attracted great interest from researchers. In a prospective study published in *Circulation* (Vol. 101, No. 17) last year, for instance, psychologist Janice E. Williams, PhD, explored whether angry dispositions would lead to heart disease among 12,986 white and African-American men and women aged 45 to 64 at baseline. Conducted while Williams was at the University of North Carolina in Chapel Hill, the study used a questionnaire to assess what researchers call "trait" anger—a propensity for frequent, intense, long-lasting rages. Questions included whether study participants considered themselves quick-tempered or whether they felt like hitting someone when they got angry.

During a median follow-up period of about four and a half years, Williams and her colleagues checked to see if participants had had heart attacks or other cardiovascular problems. The results were striking. Among people with normal blood pressure, those with high scores on the anger scale were three times more likely to have suffered heart attacks or sudden cardiac death than were those with low scores. The findings held true even after controlling for risk factors such as smoking, having diabetes or weighing too much.

"This and other studies have shown a positive association between anger and heart attacks or sudden cardiac death," says Williams, who now works in the Cardiovascular Health Branch at the U.S. Centers for Disease Control and Prevention. "The implication is that individuals who find themselves prone to anger might benefit from anger management training."

Other psychologists have also become fixtures in the cardiac field, sharing their expertise in psychosocial factors. One is Karen A. Matthews, PhD, a professor of psychiatry, psychology and epidemiology at the University of Pittsburgh. In a study published in the *Journal of the American Medical Association* *(JAMA)* last year (Vol. 283, No. 19), she and her colleagues examined the role that hostility—defined as a personality trait marked by cynicism, mistrust, anger and aggression—plays in predisposing young people to cardiovascular disease.

To explore the connection, Matthews and her colleagues assessed the hostility levels of 374 white and African-American men and women aged 18 to 30. A decade later, the researchers used a technique called electron-beam computed tomography to check participants' coronary arteries for calcification—an early sign of the hardening of the arteries known as atherosclerosis.

The researchers discovered that people who scored above the median on the baseline assessment of hostility were twice as likely to have coronary calcification than were those scoring below the median. These results held true even after the researchers controlled for demographic, lifestyle and physiological variables.

"Our study lets us predict really early which individuals are going to be at higher risk down the road," says Matthews. "From a prevention standpoint, that's very helpful. By identifying people early, you can design early interventions to retard further development of coronary artery disease."

Psychologists are also studying the ways psychosocial factors can exacerbate problems in people who already have heart disease. In an article in *JAMA* last year (Vol. 283, No. 14), for instance, psychologist David S. Krantz, PhD, reviewed the evidence he and other researchers have amassed demonstrating that both chronic and acute mental stress can negatively affect patients with coronary artery disease.

Krantz's own work has focused on identifying factors that trigger myocardial ischemia, which occurs when the heart doesn't get the blood supply it needs. In laboratory experiments, for example, he has provoked ischemia via such mental stresses as math exercises and harassment. He has also studied stress's impact on ischemia in everyday life by asking patients to keep detailed diaries of their activities and emotions.

"What surprises me about our findings over the years is that mental stress is about as powerful as strenuous exercise as a trigger for ischemia," says Krantz, professor and chair of the department of medical and clinical psychology at the Uniformed Services University in Bethesda, Md. "This suggests that stress management may be an appropriate addition to rehabilitation programs for patients with coronary disease."

Psychosocial factors also influence patients' recovery from heart attacks and other cardiovascular problems, researchers have found. In a study of 896 heart attack sufferers, for instance, psychologist Nancy Frasure-Smith, PhD, found that patients who were depressed were three times more likely to die in the year following their heart attack than those who were not depressed, regardless of how severe their initial heart disease was. Frasure-Smith, an associate professor of psychiatry at the McGill University School of Medicine and a senior research associate at the Montreal Heart Institute, published her study in *Psychosomatic Medicine* in 1999 (Vol. 61, No. 26).

The study also identified striking gender differences: Women were twice as likely as men to develop depression after a heart attack, with half of women and a quarter of men experiencing at least mild to moderate depression. Yet women's death rates were nonetheless the same as men's.

Social support may influence which depressed patients die, Frasure-Smith found in a study published in *Circulation* (Vol. 101, No. 16) last year. Based on interviews with 887 heart attack patients, the study found that depression's impact on survival was medi-

ated by patient's perceived social support. Depressed patients who felt they didn't get enough support from friends and family members had the highest death rates. In contrast, depressed patients who reported the most support had the same death rates as nondepressed patients.

INTERVENING FOR PATIENTS' HEALTH

Now that researchers have data suggesting causal relationships between psychosocial factors and cardiovascular disease, the next step is to test whether interventions designed to influence those factors can prevent heart disease or improve the prognosis of those who already have it.

Researchers have been working in this area for years and have developed compelling evidence that such interventions cannot only enhance patients' quality of life but also dramatically improve their physical health:

- In the Recurrent Coronary Prevention Project, for example, Friedman and his colleagues randomly assigned 1,013 heart attack patients to receive routine medical care, group counseling about cardiac risk factors or group therapy designed to modify Type-A behavior, plus counseling about risk factors. After four and a half years, patients who received the group therapy intervention had a 44 percent reduction in second heart attacks compared with the other two groups.
- In the Lifestyle Heart Trial, Dean Ornish, MD, and his colleagues assigned 28 patients to a rigorous lifestyle-modification program that included group therapy, meditation and yoga as well as exercise and a lowfat diet. At the one-year follow-up, 82 percent of these patients saw regression in their atherosclerotic lesions compared with only 42 percent of the 20 patients in a control group. Patients in the experimental group also reported reductions in the frequency, duration and severity of their angina; angina symptoms actually worsened in the control group.
- In Project New Life, Swedish psychologist Gunilla Burell, PhD, randomly assigned 261 post-bypass patients to receive routine medical care or one year of behaviorally oriented group therapy plus half a

dozen "booster" sessions in the project's second and third years. At the follow-up five to six years later, patients in the treatment group were significantly less likely to have undergone further cardiac procedures, spent time in the coronary care unit, had heart attacks or died.

Now a ground-breaking trial called Enhancing Recovery in Coronary Heart Disease is taking this research to a new level. Funded by the National Heart, Lung and Blood Institute, the ongoing eight-center trial will determine whether psychological intervention can reduce heart attack patients' chances of having another heart attack or dying.

Currently in the follow-up stage, the trial randomly assigned about 2,600 heart attack patients to receive treatment as usual or a cognitive-behavioral therapy intervention targeting social isolation and major and minor depression, whether it was related to the illness or other aspects of patients' lives. Patients began with individual therapy, then progressed to group therapy. Results should be available about a year and a half from now.

"This is a landmark study in the field of psychology," says Robert M. Carney, PhD, principal investigator of the St. Louis site and professor of medical psychology and psychiatry at the Washington University School of Medicine. "It's the first opportunity we've had to show that what psychologists do can be potentially very important to the medical outcomes of certain groups of patients. It's very exciting."

Patients aren't the only ones who need interventions, however. Psychologists are also conducting research aimed at physicians and nurses who work with cardiovascular patients. Wayne M. Sotile, PhD, for example, has devoted his career to alerting healthcare professionals about the need to pay attention to cardiac patients' psychosocial needs.

With funding from the cardiac device company Medtronic, Sotile and psychologist Samuel F. Sears Jr. recently explored the psychosocial needs of patients with implantable cardioverter defibrillators (ICDs) and also surveyed the family members, doctors and nurses who care for them. Implanted in the chest, the devices provide a lifesaving shock when patients' heart rhythms start going haywire.

The result was a manual called *Brief Psychosocial Interventions for ICD Patients & Their Families,* three audiotapes and patient materials, all designed to help health-care providers meet these patients' psychosocial needs. Since ICD patients will never get better, for example, health-care providers need to replace their usual emphasis on recovery with a new focus on coping skills.

"By choice or by default, physicians, nurses and allied health professionals are the ones who need to take responsibility for systematically and effectively addressing patients' psychosocial needs," says Sotile, director of psychological services for the Wake Forest University Cardiac Rehabilitation Program in Winston–Salem, N.C. "There aren't enough psychologists who are trained in the ins and outs of life with cardiovascular illness. It's a huge area of unmet need."

CRITICAL THINKING QUESTIONS

1. Examine a social psychology textbook to learn more about the psychosocial factors associated with disease. Based on this evidence, what factors may predispose *you* to disease later in life? What interventions can you make now to lower your risk for these factors?

2. Chapter Four of this book dealt with the issues of attitude and attitude change. What role does attitude play in the development of cardiovascular disorders? What techniques of attitude change can be used to help people adapt those behaviors or characteristics that put them at greater risk for disease? Explain your answers.

3. The article notes that social isolation is important both in contributing to cardiovascular disease and in recovering from illness. How can society help decrease the amount of social isolation that some people experience?

4. Numerous books are available dealing with stress management techniques. Review some of them and comment on whether the techniques recommended are effective in reducing cardiovascular risk factors.

ARTICLE 44 _____

Just about everyone these days accepts the idea that stress can cause illness. However, this concept was not always deemed to be true. In the past, it was commonly believed that illness was due to germs and organ pathology. There was not much focus on what was going on in a person's life that actually might be causing the illness.

A new view of the relationship between stress and illness was pioneered by the work of Hans Selye a half century ago. Selye defined *stress* as the body's physiological response to threatening events, whether physiological or psychological in nature. Thus, Selye was the first to clearly demonstrate that a purely psychological state, such as worrying too much about something, could produce a negative physiological state.

While Selye began to expand our understanding of how psychological states could produce physiological consequences, other researchers began to examine specifically what types of events might produce stress and consequently physical changes. The following classic article by Thomas H. Holmes and Richard H. Rahe represents the beginning of a line of research that tried to relate life events and health. Holmes and Rahe suggest that *stress* is the extent to which people have to readjust or change their lives in response to an outside event. Thus, a great deal of stress would be associated with a major life change, such as getting divorced, while considerably less stress would be associated with a lesser life change, such as getting a parking ticket. Furthermore, any life change, positive or negative, could produce such stress. Getting married, which involves many changes in a person's life, is a good example of how an event typically thought of as positive may nonetheless produce stress.

This article by Holmes and Rahe discusses the methodology that they used in developing their scale, which has been widely reproduced and used in many research studies. For example, several subsequent studies have found that the higher a person scores on this scale, the more likely his or her physical health will suffer.

Our understanding of the relationship between stress and health has become much more complex over the years. For example, the original Holmes and Rahe scale assumed that anyone experiencing a divorce would find that event to be extremely stressful. But isn't it possible that someone in a terribly abusive relationship might actually find that getting divorced lessens his or her stress? A critical factor may be our subjective interpretation of the events that we experience. That is, it may not be the event itself that causes stress but how we subjectively react to it. Certainly, a given event is not viewed the same by everyone who experiences it. While the Holmes and Rahe scale does not take this subjective reaction into account, it is nonetheless a good example of how the research on stress and health began.

The Social Readjustment Rating Scale[1]
■ Thomas H. Holmes and Richard H. Rahe

In previous studies [1] it has been established that a cluster of social events requiring change in ongoing life adjustment is significantly associated with the time of illness onset. Similarly, the relationship of what has been called 'life stress,' 'emotional stress,' 'object loss,' etc. and illness onset has been demonstrated by other investigations [2–13]. It has been adduced from these studies that this clustering of social or life events achieves etiologic significance as a necessary but not sufficient cause of illness and accounts in part for the time of onset of disease.

Methodologically, the interview or questionnaire technique used in these studies has yielded only the number and types of events making up the cluster. Some estimate of the magnitude of these events is now required to bring greater precision to this area of research and to provide a quantitative basis for new epidemiological studies of diseases. This report defines a method which achieves this requisite.

METHOD

A sample of convenience composed of 394 subjects completed the paper and pencil test (Table 1). (See Table 2 for characteristics of the sample.) The items were the 43 life events empirically derived from clinical experience. The following written instructions were given to each subject who completed the Social Rating Questionnaire (SRRQ).

(A) Social readjustment includes the amount and duration of change in one's accustomed pattern of life resulting from various life events. As defined, social readjustment measures the intensity and length of time necessary to accommodate to a life event, *regardless of the desirability of this event.*

(B) You are asked to rate a series of life events as to their relative degrees of necessary readjustment. In scoring, *use all of your experience* in arriving at your answer. This means personal experience where it applies as well as what you have learned to be the case for others. Some persons accommodate to change more readily than others; some persons adjust with particular ease or difficulty to only certain events. Therefore, strive to give your opinion of the average degree of readjustment necessary for each event rather than the extreme.

(C) The mechanics of rating are these: Event 1, Marriage, has been given an arbitrary value of 500. As you complete each of the remaining events think to yourself, "Is this event indicative of more or less readjustment than marriage?" "Would the readjustment take longer or shorter to accomplish?" If you decide the readjustment is more intense and protracted, then choose a *proportionately larger* number and place it in the blank directly opposite the event in the column marked "VALUES." If you decide the event represents less and shorter readjustment than marriage then indicate how much less by placing a *proportionately smaller* number in the opposite blank. (If an event requires intense readjustment over a short time span, it may approximate in value an event requiring less intense readjustment over a long period of time.) If the event is equal in social readjustment to marriage, record the number 500 opposite the event.

The order in which the items were presented is shown in Table 1.

RESULTS

The Social Readjustment Rating Scale (SRRS) is shown in Table 3. This table contains the magnitude of the life events which is derived when the mean score, divided by 10, of each item for the entire sample is calculated and arranged in rank order. That consensus is high concerning the relative order and magnitude of

Reprinted from *The Journal of Psychosomatic Research, 11*, T. H. Holmes and R. H. Rahe, "The Social Readjustment Rating Scale," pp. 213–218, Copyright 1967, with permission from Elsevier.

TABLE 1 / Social Readjustment Rating Questionnaire

Events	Values
1. Marriage	500
2. Troubles with the boss	—
3. Detention in jail or other institution	—
4. Death of spouse	—
5. Major change in sleeping habits (a lot more or a lot less sleep, or change in part of day when asleep)	—
6. Death of a close family member	—
7. Major change in eating habits (a lot more or a lot less food intake, or very different meal hours or surroundings)	—
8. Foreclosure on a mortgage or loan	—
9. Revision of personal habits (dress, manners, associations, etc.)	—
10. Death of a close friend	—
11. Minor violations of the law (e.g. traffic tickets, jay walking, disturbing the peace, etc.)	—
12. Outstanding personal achievement	—
13. Pregnancy	—
14. Major change in the health or behavior of a family member	—
15. Sexual difficulties	—
16. In-law troubles	—
17. Major change in number of family get-togethers (e.g. a lot more or a lot less than usual)	—
18. Major change in financial state (e.g. a lot worse off or a lot better off than usual)	—
19. Gaining a new family member (e.g. through birth, adoption, oldster moving in, etc.)	—
20. Change in residence	—
21. Son or daughter leaving home (e.g. marriage, attending college, etc.)	—
22. Marital separation from mate	—
23. Major change in church activities (e.g. a lot more or a lot less than usual)	—
24. Marital reconciliation with mate	—
25. Being fired from work	—
26. Divorce	—
27. Changing to a different line of work	—
28. Major change in the number of arguments with spouse (e.g. either a lot more or a lot less than usual, regarding childrearing, personal habits, etc.)	—
29. Major change in responsibilities at work (e.g. promotion, demotion, lateral transfer)	—
30. Wife beginning or ceasing work outside the home	—
31. Major change in working hours or conditions	—
32. Major change in usual type and/or amount of recreation	—
33. Taking on a mortgage greater than $10,000 (e.g. purchasing a home, business, etc.)	—
34. Taking on a mortgage or loan less than $10,000 (e.g. purchasing a car, TV, freezer, etc.)	—
35. Major personal injury or illness	—
36. Major business readjustment (e.g. merger, reorganization, bankruptcy, etc.)	—
37. Major change in social activities (e.g. clubs, dancing, movies, visiting, etc.)	—
38. Major change in living conditions (e.g. building a new home, remodeling, deterioration of home or neighborhood)	—
39. Retirement from work	—
40. Vacation	—
41. Christmas	—
42. Changing to a new school	—
43. Beginning or ceasing formal schooling	—

TABLE 2 / Pearson's Coefficient of Correlation between Discrete Groups in the Sample

Group	No. in Group		Group	No. in Group	Coefficient of Correlation
Male	179	vs.	Female	215	0-965
Single	171	vs.	Married	223	0-960
Age < 30	206	vs.	Age 30–60	137	0-958
Age < 30	206	vs.	Age > 60	51	0-923
Age 30–60	137	vs.	Age > 60	51	0-965
1st Generation	19	vs.	2nd Generation	69	0-908
1st Generation	19	vs.	3rd Generation	306	0-929
2nd Generation	69	vs.	3rd Generation	306	0-975
< College	182	vs.	4 Years of College	212	0-967
Lower class	71	vs	Middle class	323	0-928
White	363	vs.	Negro	19	0-820
White	363	vs.	Oriental	12	0-940
Protestant	241	vs.	Catholic	42	0-913
Protestant	241	vs.	Jewish	19	0-971
Protestant	241	vs.	Other religion	45	0-948
Protestant	241	vs.	No religious preference	47	0-926

the means of items is demonstrated by the high coefficients of correlation (Pearson's r) between the discrete groups contained in the sample. Table 2 reveals that all the coefficients of correlation are above 0-90 with the exception of that between white and Negro which was 0-82. Kendall's coefficient of concordance (W) for the 394 individuals was 0-477, significant at $p = < 0-0005$.

DISCUSSION

Placed in historical perspective, this research evolved from the chrysalis of Psychobiology generated by Adolph Meyer [14]. His invention of the 'life chart,' a device for organizing the medical data as a dynamic biography, provided a unique method for demonstrating his schema of the relationship of biological, psychological, and sociological phenomena to the processes of health and disease in man. The importance of many of the life events used in this research was emphasized by Meyer: ". . . changes of habitat, of school entrance, graduations or changes or failures; the various jobs, the dates of possibly important births and deaths in the family, and other fundamentally important environmental influences" [14].

More recently, in Harold G. Wolff's laboratory,[2] the concepts of Pavlov, Freud, Cannon and Skinner were incorporated in the Meyerian schema. The research resulting from this synthesis adduced powerful evidence that 'stressful' life events, by evoking psychophysiologic reactions, played an important causative role in the natural history of many diseases [15–19]. Again, many of the life events denoted 'stressful' were those enumerated by Meyers and in Table 1 of this report.

Beginning in this laboratory in 1949, the life chart device has been used systematically in over 5000 patients to study the quality and quantity of life events empirically observed to cluster at the time of disease onset. Inspection of Table 1 reveals that each item derived from this experience is unique. There are 2 categories of items: those indicative of the life style of the individual, and those indicative of occurrences involving the individual. Evolving mostly from ordinary, but some from extraordinary, social and interpersonal transactions, these events pertain to major areas of dynamic significance in the social structure of the American way of life. These include family constellation, marriage, occupation, economics, residence, group and peer relationships, education, religion, recreation and health.

During the developmental phase of this research the interview technique was used to assess the mean-

TABLE 3 / Social Readjustment Rating Scale

Rank	Life Event	Mean Value
1	Death of spouse	100
2	Divorce	73
3	Marital separation	65
4	Jail term	63
5	Death of close family member	63
6	Personal injury or illness	53
7	Marriage	50
8	Fired at work	47
9	Marital reconciliation	45
10	Retirement	45
11	Change in health of family member	44
12	Pregnancy	40
13	Sex difficulties	39
14	Gain of new family member	39
15	Business readjustment	39
16	Change in financial state	38
17	Death of close friend	37
18	Change to different line of work	36
19	Change in number of arguments with spouse	35
20	Mortgage over $10,000	31
21	Foreclosure of mortgage or loan	30
22	Change in responsibilities at work	29
23	Son or daughter leaving home	29
24	Trouble with in-laws	29
25	Outstanding personal achievement	28
26	Wife begin or stop work	26
27	Begin or end school	26
28	Change in living conditions	25
29	Revision of personal habits	24
30	Trouble with boss	23
31	Change in work hours or conditions	20
32	Change in residence	20
33	Change in schools	20
34	Change in recreation	19
35	Change in church activities	19
36	Change in social activities	18
37	Mortgage or loan less than $10,000	17
38	Change in sleeping habits	16
39	Change in number of family get-togethers	15
40	Change in eating habits	15
41	Vacation	13
42	Christmas	12
43	Minor violations of the law	11

ing of the events for the individual. As expected, the psychological significance and emotions varied widely with the patient. Also it will be noted that only some of the events are negative or 'stressful' in the conventional sense, i.e. are socially undesirable. Many are socially desirable and consonant with the American values of achievement, success, materialism, practicality, efficiency, future orientation, conformism and self-reliance.

There was identified, however, one theme common to all these life events. The occurrence of each usually evoked or was associated with some adaptive or coping behavior on the part of the involved individual. Thus, each item has been constructed to contain life events whose advent is either indicative of or requires a significant change in the ongoing life pattern of the individual. The emphasis is on change from the existing steady state and not on psychological meaning, emotion, or social desirability.

The method for assigning a magnitude to the items was developed for use in Psychophysics—the study of the psychological perception of the quality, quantity, magnitude, intensity of physical phenomena. This subjective assessment of the observer plotted against the physical dimension being perceived (length of objects, intensity of sound, brightness of light, number of objects, etc.) provides a reliable delineation of man's ability to quantify certain of his experiences [20]. In this research, the assumption was made that participants in the contemporary American way of life could utilize this innate psychological capacity for making quantitative judgments about psychosocial phenomena as well as psychophysical phenomena [21, 22]. The data generated by this investigation appear to justify the assumption. Although some of the discrete subgroups do assign a different order and magnitude to the items, it is the degree of similarity between the populations within the sample that is impressive. The high degree of consensus also suggests a universal agreement between groups and among individuals about the significance of the life events under study that transcends differences in age, sex, marital status, education, social class, generation American, religion and race.

The method used in this research, when applied to psychophysical phenomena, generates a ratio scale. A discussion of whether or not the magnitudes assigned to the items in Table 3 actually constitute a ratio scale is beyond the intent of this report [21, 22]. However, this issue will be dealt with in a subsequent report [23].

REFERENCES

1. Rahe R. H., Meyer M., Smith M., Kjaer G. and Holmes T. H. Social stress and illness onset. *J. Psychosom. Res. 8,* 35 (1964).

2. Graham D. T. and Stevenson I. Disease as response to life stress. In *The Psychological Basis of Medical Practice* (H. I. Lief, V. F. Lief, and N. R. Lief, Eds.) Harper & Row, New York (1963).

3. Greene W. A., Jr. Psychological factors and reticulo-endothelial disease—I. Preliminary observations on a group of males with lymphomas and leukemias. *Psychosom. Med. 16,* 220 (1954).

4. Greene W. A. Jr., Young L. E. and Swisher S. N. Psychological factors and reticulo-endothelial disease—II. Observations on a group of women with lymphomas and leukemias. *Psychosom. Med. 18,* 284 (1956).

5. Greene W. A., Jr. and Miller G. Psychological factors and reticulo-endothelial disease—IV. Observations on a group of children and adolescents with leukemia: an interpretation of disease development in terms of the mother-child unit. *Psychosom. Med. 20,* 124 (1958).

6. Weiss E., Dlin B., Rollin H. R., Fischer H. K. and Bepler C. R. Emotional factors in coronary occlusion. *A.M.A. Archs. Internal Med. 99,* 628 (1957).

7. Fischer H. K., Dlin B., Winters W., Hagner S. and Weiss E. Time patterns and emotional factors related to the onset of coronary occlusion. [Abstract] *Psychosom. Med. 24,* 516 (1962).

8. Kissen D. M. Specific psychological factors in pulmonary tuberculosis. *Hlth Bull. Edinburgh 14,* 44 (1956).

9. Kissen D. M. Some psychosocial aspects of pulmonary tuberculosis. *Int. J. Soc. Psychiat. 3,* 252 (1958).

10. Hawkins N. G., Davies R. and Holmes T. H. Evidence of psychosocial factors in the development of pulmonary tuberculosis. *Am. Rev. Tuberc. Pulmon. Dis. 75,* 5 (1957).

11. Smith M. Psychogenic factors in skin disease, Medical Thesis, University of Washington, Seattle (1962).

12. Rare R. H. and Holmes T. H. Social, psychologic and psychophysiologic aspects of inguinal hernia. *J. Psychosom. Res. 8,* 487 (1965).

13. Kjaer G. Some psychosomatic aspects of pregnancy with particular reference to nausea and vomiting, Medical Thesis, University of Washington, Seattle (1959).

14. Lief A. (Ed.) *The Commonsense Psychiatry of Dr. Adolf Meyer,* McGraw-Hill, New York (1948).

15. Wolff H. G., Wolf S. and Hare C. C. (Eds.) *Life Stress and Bodily Disease,* Res. Publs. Ass. Res. Nerv. Ment. Dis. Vol. 29. Williams & Wilkins, Baltimore (1950).

16. Holmes T. H., Goodell H., Wolf S. and Wolff H. G. *The Nose. An Experimental Study of Reactions Within the Nose in Human Subjects During Varying Life Experiences,* Charles C. Thomas, Springfield, Illinois (1950).

17. Wolf S. *The Stomach,* Oxford University Press, New York (1965).

18. Wolf S., Cardon P. V., Shepard E. M., and Wolff H. G. *Life Stress and Essential Hypertension,* Williams & Wilkins, Baltimore (1955).

19. Grace W. J., Wolf S. and Wolff H. G. *The Human Colon,* Paul B. Hoeber, New York (1951).

20. Stevens S. S. and Galanter E. H. Ratio scales and category scales for a dozen perceptual continua. *J. Exp. Psychol. 54,* 377 (1957).

21. Sellin T. and Wolfgang M. E. *The Measurement of Delinquency,* John Wiley, New York (1964).

22. Stevens S. S. A metric for the social consensus. *Science 151,* 530 (1966).

23. Masuda M. and Holmes T. H. This issue, p. 219.

ENDNOTES

1. This investigation was supported in part by Public Health Service Undergraduate Training in Psychiatry Grant No. 5-T2-MH-5939-13 and Undergraduate Training in Human Behavior Grant No. 5-T2-MH-7871-03 from the National Institute of Mental Health; O'Donnell Psychiatric Research Fund; and The Scottish Rite Committee for Research in Schizophrenia.

2. Harold G. Wolff, M.D. (1898–1962) was Anne Parrish Titzell, Professor of Medicine (Neurology), Cornell University Medical College and the New York Hospital.

CRITICAL THINKING QUESTIONS

1. Examine the methodology that Homes and Rahe used. For example, subjects were asked not only how stressful they found the events to be but also how stressful they thought other people typically found the events to be. Is this a problem? If so, why? If not, why not? What other issues in how Holmes and Rahe collected their data might limit the conclusions that they have drawn? Be specific in your answers.

2. Examine the items on the Social Readjustment Rating Scale (Table 3). Are any "life events" missing from the scale that you think are important stressors? If so, what are they, and why are they important? Why do you think these items were not included in the original scale?

3. The introduction to the article mentioned how the subjective perception of events may be more critical in determining stress reactions than the objective events themselves. In other words, not everyone reacts to the same situation in the same manner. Select an item from the scale, and give a concrete example of how you have seen two people react to it in very different ways.

4. According to this scale, getting married is more stressful than getting fired and hence more likely to cause physical illness. Do you accept the premise that *positive* life events, such as getting married, are just as stressful as *negative* life events, such as getting fired? Why or why not? If positive life events cause stress and hence illness, why do people seek them out in the first place? Explain your reasoning.

ADDITIONAL RELATED READINGS

Hobson, C. J., & Delunas, L. (2001). National norms and life-event frequencies for the revised Social Readjustment Rating Scale. *International Journal of Stress Management,* *8*(4), 299–314.

Scully, J. A., Tosi, H., & Banning, K. (2000). Life event checklists: Revisiting the Social Readjustment Rating Scale after 30 years. *Educational and Psychological Measurement,* *60*(6), 864–876.

ARTICLE 45 _____

Do you remember exactly where you were and what you were doing when you first heard of the terrorist attacks on September 11, 2001? For most people in the United States, and indeed the world, the destruction of the World Trade Center in New York City and the attack on the Pentagon in Arlington, Virginia, are events they will always remember. Whether we were 10 or 10,000 miles away from the horrific events of that day, few of us can say that we were not profoundly affected by them.

Given the impact of the events of 9-11, it only stands to reason that they represented a stressor in the lives of many people. Obviously, the more directly affected someone was by the attacks—such as knowing a person who was killed or injured—the more stressful the events were. But even people far removed from the events were profoundly affected. And so, the events of 9-11 were believed to be a major stressor and, as such, to have many negative effects on people's psychological well-being and physical health.

At least, that was what common sense and much media reporting reasoned. In the weeks, months, and years following the events of 9-11 (and other terrorist acts as well, such as the Madrid train bombings), commentators and experts alike took to the press and the airwaves to discuss how these events were going to affect us all. In particular, they claimed, children's sense of safety and security would be greatly diminished in the aftermath.

But do you think that all of the people who witnessed the events of 9-11 were affected in the same way? Current thinking on the impact of stress is that the subjective interpretation we make of the events is what causes stress, rather than the events per se. Thus, two people experiencing the same event could react quite differently to it, depending on their individual subjective interpretations of it.

The following article by David B. Henry, Patrick H. Tolan, and Deborah Gorman-Smith examines the possible lasting effects of the events of 9-11 on a particular population: children and parents living in U.S. inner cities. What is particularly noteworthy about this study is that in includes both pre– and post–September 11 measures of symptoms and behaviors. Many other studies on the impact of 9-11 have asked people about their symptoms and reactions *after* the fact, but those studies have no way of measuring how these people dealt with life prior to the 9-11 events. Unlike those studies, this study was able to make those comparisons.

As you will see in reading it, the authors of the study didn't exactly find what many others have taken for granted. Namely, they didn't find many differences between pre– and post–September 11 measures of parent and child anxiety, depression, and feelings of safety, at least in their population. As we continue to deal with the realities of terrorism in the twenty-first century, the results of this study are noteworthy.

Have There Been Lasting Effects Associated with the September 11, 2001, Terrorist Attacks among Inner-City Parents and Children?

■ David B. Henry, Patrick H. Tolan, and Deborah Gorman-Smith

Should mental health practitioners expect lasting post-traumatic stress symptoms in the general population after future terrorist attacks or other disasters? Serendipitous random assignment of families allowed assessment of the effects of the September 11, 2001, terrorist attacks on parent and child trauma-related symptoms and parenting. Surprisingly, there were no differences between pre– and post–September 11 groups on measures of parent and child anxiety, depression, and feelings of safety. However, levels of parental monitoring and beliefs about family were higher in the group assessed after September 11, 2001. Implications for practitioners' responses to terrorism and disaster are discussed.

How likely is it that future terrorist attacks or other publicized disasters will result in enduring mental health consequences for significant numbers in the general population? There has been widespread worry that the terrorist attacks of September 11, 2001, would amplify the anxiety and other psychopathology of children in this country who were not directly affected by the attacks (Askew & Joseph, 2001). The recent Institute of Medicine (2003) report on preparing for the psychological consequences of terrorism assumes that there will be widespread mental health problems in the wake of future terrorist attacks or other publicized disasters, especially among those already at risk because of environmental stressors. Recent reports seem to add credence to this worry (Ahern et al., 2002; Schuster et al., 2001). For example, using a version of the Posttraumatic Stress Disorder Checklist (Asmundson et al., 2000), Schuster et al. reported that 44% of adults and 37% of children included in a representative telephone survey reported one or more stress symptoms. In addition, 47% of children experienced heightened concern for their own safety or the safety of loved ones. Substantial stress reactions among adults were more prevalent among persons of non-White ethnicity. Female adults and children were more like to report stress symptoms and concerns for safety than were men. Stress symptoms were also more likely to be reported by those living closer to New York City, those with prior mental health problems, and those who watched more hours of television coverage on September 11.

The characteristics of those more affected have been interpreted as showing that the impact was greater for those already facing other stressors and limitations, such as those families living with fewer resources in more unsafe communities. Thus, it has been suggested that parents and children already under stress would experience symptoms of trauma following the terrorist attacks at levels similar to or perhaps greater than those found in the general population (Pantin, Schwartz, Prado, Feaster, & Szapocznik, 2003). In contrast, it has been suggested that the attacks would not have the same impact among those living in communities where everyday threats to safety were high.

The Institute of Medicine (2003) report acknowledged that, in most studies, the absence of baseline data prior to the terrorist attacks makes it impossible to determine the role that preexisting stressors played in posttraumatic stress reactions to the attacks themselves. It is possible that reactions to the terrorist attacks would be less intense among inner-city parents and children than among those in less distressed communities. Epstein (1983) hypothesized that stress and anxiety are naturally reduced in daily life by facing more stressful situations or repeatedly thinking about more upsetting aspects of a frightening situation. The fear and uncertainty attributed to "post-9/11" may not be new or specific to that incident for parents and children in distressed communities, who routinely are

Reprinted from *Professional Psychology: Research and Practice,* 2004, *35*(5), 542–547. Copyright © 2004 by the American Psychological Association. Reprinted with permission.

exposed to violence. For example, Gorman-Smith, Henry, and Tolan (in press) found that, in a single year, half of a sample of 13- to 15-year-old inner-city boys reported seeing someone beaten, and one fifth reported seeing someone shot or killed. When thinking about impact on children, an immediate concern is how parental fears and related parenting practices may have shifted following the September 11 attacks. It might be that children's fears and other problems, if increased, were not due to the event per se, but to increased fear and anxiety of adults caring for them. Some evidence consistent with this view can be found in the survey by Schuster et al. (2001): 75% of the adults evidenced heightened concern about their families. They reported responding to the terrorist attacks by checking on the safety of friends and family members. In this investigation, we hypothesized that heightened concern about family members would be seen in measures of beliefs about family and in measures of supervision of children.

Previous studies of the effects of the terrorist attacks also have not been able to assess the extent to which stress-related symptoms were in existence prior to September 11, 2001, and thus are not able to determine the extent to which symptoms observed were preexisting. In this study, we were able to analyze preexisting symptom levels as well as the impact of this historical event on child and parent trauma symptom levels and on parental monitoring.

Few opportunities exist to explore the effects of traumatic historical events because of the unpredictability of these events and the small likelihood that samples and assessments will be occurring prior to and after they take place. As a result, psychologists must rely on related research when asked to guide the public in responding to the psychological effects of these events.

In the course of conducting follow-up assessments for a prevention study, we had the opportunity to assess the effects of the terrorist attacks on a variety of individual and family variables. The assessments were planned prior to the attacks and used measures that did not make reference to the attacks themselves. Families were randomly assigned to assessment appointments before and after September 11, 2001. This created an opportunity to assess the effects of the attacks on measures of psychological well being, feelings of safety, and parenting practices.

On the basis of other research findings and cautions expressed by many mental health professionals, we expected those assessed before and after the terrorist attacks to differ on symptoms associated with trauma: primarily anxiety, depression, and fears for their safety. In addition, we expected that increased concerns for security might motivate parents to monitor their children more closely than would have been the case prior to the terrorist attacks.

This study reports comparisons of urban parents and children assessed in the 100 days prior to September 11, 2001, and the 100 days following September 11, 2001. Specifically, we compared the two groups on depression in both parents and children, anxiety in children, fear of harm from violence in parents and sense of safety in children, parents' beliefs about family, and supervision from both parents' and childrens' perspectives. In addition, we tested possible alternative explanations for the effects obtained, such as seasonal variation in these characteristics.

PROJECT DESCRIPTION

The data for assessing the effects of the attacks came from the eighth wave of a longitudinal prevention study (Schools and Families Educating Children; SAFEChildren). This project targeted early predictors of risk for delinquency and drug use among African American and Latino children living in economically disadvantaged neighborhoods in Chicago (Tolan, Gorman-Smith, & Henry, in press). In addition, data from previous waves of interviews were used to assess competing explanations for any differences found.

Wave 8 of the SAFEChildren assessments spanned the terrorist attacks on September 11, 2001. Approximately five sixths of the sample (84%) was assessed in the 100 days preceding September 11, and one sixth (16%) was assessed in the 100 days following September 11. To provide pretest comparisons between the groups whose Wave 8 assessments were collected before and after September 11, 2001, we used Wave 6 assessments, all of which were collected prior to September 11, 2001. Using Wave 6 assessments helped us determine whether the pre–9/11 and post–9/11 groups differed prior to September 11, 2001.

The participants in the SAFEChildren study were 47% African American and 53% Latino. Forty percent lived in single-parent households, and 44% of the primary caregivers (usually mothers) did not graduate from high school. Fifty-nine percent of participating families had incomes below $20,000 per year, 85% had a total family income below $30,000 per year, and 62% of the families had five or more people living in the household. Fifty-seven percent (57%) of the families reported having moved at least once in the previous year. The sample of children was split approximately evenly by gender, with 49% boys and 51% girls. The participating children were all in fourth grade at the time of the September 11, 2001, terrorist attacks.

Children's depression was measured using the Parent Observations of Classroom Adaptation–Revised Scale (POCA–R; Kellam, Brown, Rubin, & Ensminger, 1983). This is a brief parent-observation measure assessing various aspects of children's mental health. It has been used in several longitudinal and prevention studies with this age group in urban populations. The three-item Depression subscale had an internal consistency of .42. Children's anxiety was assessed with a single-parent report item from the service need and use portion of the POCA–R. That item was, "Do you think your child needs services because he/she is sad, worried, or upset?" The POCA Shyness subscale also contained items that might be reflective of increased anxiety. The internal consistency of the Shyness subscale was .77. Children's feelings of being safe were measured using the Sense of Safety Scale (Henry, 2000). This 10-item scale is an extension of the four-item scale used by Schwab-Stone et al. (1995). Internal consistencies of this measure ranged from .93 with second-grade children to .95 with eighth-grade children (Henry, 2000). Parental depression was assessed using the Beck Depression Inventory (BDI; Beck, Emery, Rush, & Shaw, 1979). This is a 21-item self-report measure of depressive symptoms that has been widely used in research and clinical practice with good psychometric properties and evidence of convergent validity with clinical diagnoses of depression. Parents' sense of safety was measured using the Fear of Harm Scale (Richters & Martinez, 1993). This 13-item scale assesses the respondent's fear of being the victim of violence in their homes and/or neighborhoods, the impact of such fear on their daily activities, and the measures they have taken to protect themselves from violence. In this sample, the measure had an internal consistency of .88. Parents' beliefs

about family were assessed using the Family Beliefs subscale of the Family Relationships Scales (FRS; Tolan, Gorman-Smith, Huesmann, & Zelli, 1997), which taps beliefs about the importance of family and beliefs about family purpose. The internal consistency of this scale was .87. Parental supervision of children was measured with parent and child versions of the Supervision and Rules subscale of the Parenting Practices Questionnaire (Gorman-Smith, Tolan, Zelli, & Huesmann, 1996). This scale assesses the extent to which parents set time for children to be home on weekdays and weekends. The parent and child versions of this measure had internal consistencies of .67 and .73, respectively.

The data were collected through individual interviews with the child and his or her primary caregiver. Trained interviewers conducted interviews in participants' homes or at mutually agreed on locations. Families were paid $30 for completing the interviews.

Participants were randomly assigned to interviewers in blocks of 10 interviews each. Interviewers were paid for the interviews only when the block of 10 was completed. These procedures distributed the difficulty of interviews evenly across interviewing teams and across the course of the assessment and ensured that the most hard-to-locate families would not be left for the end of the wave of assessment. The ways in which the interviewers were assigned created a natural experiment in which a random subgroup of families was interviewed shortly after the terrorist attacks and another subgroup was interviewed before the terrorist attacks. On average, the pre–September 11 group was interviewed 62.17 days prior to the attacks, and the post–September 11 group was interviewed 31.28 days after the attacks.

There were no significant differences between the pre– and post–September 11 groups on demographic characteristics. The two groups did differ significantly on both parent and child depression measured at Wave 6 of the SAFEChildren study. In Wave 6, both parents and children in the group whose Wave 8 assessments occurred after September 11, 2001 (post–9/11 group), had significantly lower scores on measures of depression than the group whose Wave 8 assessments occurred prior to September 11, 2001 (pre–9/11 group). Table 1 reports these comparisons.

Wave 8 was the wave of measurement that spanned the September 11, 2001, terrorist attacks.

TABLE 1 / Equivalence of Pre– and Post–September 11, 2001, Groups on Measures Collected at Wave 6 of the SAFEChildren Study

Variable	Pre–9/11 ($n = 281$)	Post–9/11 ($n = 53$)	Comparison
Demographics			
Family income	$15,595	$15,515	$t(330) < 1$, *ns*
Married or living as married	43.4%	47.0%	$\chi^2(1, N = 334) = 1.92$, *ns*
Gender of child (female)	53.7%	49.0%	$\chi^2(1, N = 334) < 1$, *ns*
Ethnicity (African American)	42.3%	45.1%	$\chi^2(1, N = 334) < 1$, *ns*
Assigned to intervention condition	55.9%	49.0%	$\chi^2(1, N = 334) < 1$, *ns*
Wave 6 Assessments[a]			
BDI Depression (parent)	0.23	0.16	$t(88.8^{b}) = 2.90$, $p < .01$
POCA Depression (child)	1.44	1.31	$t(70.8) = 2.63$, $p < .01$
Supervision and rules			
Parent report	1.86	1.93	$t(309) = 0.89$, *ns*
Child report	1.42	1.50	$t(61.9^{b}) = 0.62$, *ns*
Aggression	0.44	0.37	$t(317) = 1.37$, *ns*
Beliefs about family	3.60	3.70	$t(316) = 1.86$, *ns*
Fear of harm (parent)	1.63	1.67	$t(317) = 0.34$, *ns*
Sense of safety (child)	3.36	3.50	$t(329) = 1.52$, *ns*
Child needs services for anxiety	4.0%	0%	$\chi^2(N = 334) = 1.71$, *ns*

Note: BDI = Beck Depression Inventory; POCA = Parent Observations of Classroom Adaptation.
[a]The pre– and post–9/11 groups are defined by when their Wave 8 assessments occurred. All Wave 6 assessments occurred prior to September 11, 2001.
[b]Fractional degrees freedom are used in the Welch unequal variances *t* tests (Overall, Atlas, & Gibson, 1995; Zimmerman, 1996; Zimmerman & Zumbo, 1993).

Table 2 shows the comparisons between those assessed prior to and following the attacks. Approximately five sixths of the cases had been assessed prior to September 11, 2001. This created unbalanced samples whose variances were unequal on many variables. We adjusted for unequal variances by using a Welch *t*-test procedure. The Welch procedure involves adjusting both the standard error of the estimate and the degrees of freedom to compensate for inequality of variances. This procedure has been shown to provide more correct estimates and greater statistical power than either the Mann–Whitney U-test or the Student's *t* test when variances are unequal (Overall, Atlas, & Gibson, 1995; Zimmerman, 1996; Zimmerman & Zumbo, 1993).

We expected both adults and children assessed after September 11, 2001, to show symptoms such as increased anxiety, depression, and aggression and a lessening of a sense of safety in their neighborhoods. In addition, we expected more parents assessed after September 11 to report concern about symptoms of anxiety in their children.

As Table 2 shows, in Wave 8, the pre– and post–September 11 groups did not differ significantly on either parent or child depression. They did not differ on shy behavior or on parents' concerns for anxiety in their children. Comparisons also revealed no significant difference in sense of safety among children and a significant difference in the opposite of the predicted direction among parents. Parents assessed after September 11, 2001, had a higher sense of safety (lower fear of harm from violence) than did parents assessed prior to September 11. As can be seen in Table 1, parents in these groups did not differ on fear of harm when assessed approximately 9 months before at Wave 6.

TABLE 2 / Pre– and Post–September 11, 2001, Group Comparisons

Wave 8 Variable	Assessment Group		Comparison
	Pre–9/11	Post–9/11	
BDI Depression (parent)	0.24	0.17	$t(82.1^a) = 1.68$, *ns*
POCA Depression (child)	1.40	1.43	$t(332) = 0.49$, *ns*
Supervision and rules			
Child report	1.50	1.74	$t(90.5^a) = 3.13$, $p < .01$
Parent report	1.89	1.97	$t(206.2^a) = 3.29$, $p < .01$
Aggression	1.48	1.52	$t(332) = 0.93$, *ns*
Beliefs about family	3.63	3.72	$t(332) = 2.08$, $p < .05$
Fear of harm (parent)	1.51	1.27	$t(96.3^a) = 3.13$, $p < .01$
Sense of safety (child)	3.43	3.50	$t(329) = 0.87$, *ns*
Shy behavior	3.39	3.43	$t(332) = 0.76$, *ns*
Child needs services for anxiety	6.5%	5.7%	$\chi^2(1, N = 334) < 1$, *ns*

Note: BDI = Beck Depression Inventory; POCA = Parent Observations of Classroom Adaptation.
[a]Fractional degrees of freedom are used in the Welch unequal variances *t* tests (Overall, Atlas, & Gibson, 1995; Zimmerman, 1996; Zimmerman & Zumbo, 1993).

We hypothesized that after September 11, 2001, parents would monitor their children more closely than prior to September 11, 2001. Comparisons of the groups on the measure of supervision and rules revealed that this was, in fact, the case. Both child and parent reports of supervision and rules showed that those assessed after September 11, 2001, reported higher levels of parental monitoring than did those assessed prior to September 11, 2001. These same groups did not differ significantly in the previous wave of measurement.

Because the pre–9/11 group was interviewed primarily in the summer and the post–9/11 group was interviewed primarily in the fall, we investigated the possible role of seasonal variation as an alternative explanation for the effects obtained. Using Wave 6 of the assessments, we compared means of those assessed in the 100 days before and after September 11, 2000, 1 year prior to the attacks, on all variables considered in this study. The groups did not differ significantly on any measure.

DISCUSSION AND IMPLICATIONS

This study took advantage of a wave of assessment in a prevention study that spanned the 100 days before and the 100 days after September 11, 2001. Despite the use of numerous measures, there was no evidence in this investigation for increased anxiety or depression symptoms in children or parents assessed after September 11, 2001. Differences between the groups assessed before and after September 11 were found, however, which could not be attributed to pre-existing differences or seasonal variation.

A counterintuitive but significant effect was on parents' fear of harm due to violence, which was lower among those assessed after September 11, 2001, than among those assessed before that date. There was no evidence for seasonal variation in fear of harm that was due to violence, but Chicago neighborhoods had been experiencing decreasing rates of violent crime throughout the 1990s and early 2000s (Chicago Police Department, Research and Development Division, 2002). It is possible that this effect reflects such neighborhood trends.

Scores on the Family Beliefs subscale were higher in the post–September 11 group than in the pre–September 11 group. This measure taps beliefs about the purposes and importance of family. Analyses of seasonal variation did not suggest any seasonal effect for this variable. Thus, it is possible that this effect is associated with the historical events surrounding September 11, 2001.

The most pronounced effects were on parental supervision of children. Scores on both parent and child reports of parental supervision and rules were higher for the group assessed after September 11 than for the group assessed before September 11. The Supervision and Rules subscale of the Parenting Practices Scale measures the extent to which children have specified times to be home on weekends and weekdays. Both parents and their children agreed that parental rules were tightened in the months after the September 11, 2001, when concern over future terrorist incidents would have been heightened.

Thus, the two effects that might reasonably be interpreted as relating to the historical events surrounding September 11, 2001, were an increase in the level of reported beliefs about the importance and purposes of family and an increase in parental monitoring of children. Both responses appear to be reasonable, adaptive responses to these historical events.

These results differ from other reports of increased symptoms suggesting posttraumatic stress in children and adults following the terrorist attacks (e.g., Pantin et al., 2003; Schuster et al., 2001). We administered several measures that should have been sensitive to differences between the groups in symptoms of depression and anxiety, but none showed any indication that levels of anxiety or depression were higher in the post–September 11 group.

The findings that differed from those of other studies are not due to a lack of sufficient statistical power. None of the mean comparisons of the pre– and post–September 11 groups would have been significant with a larger sample size. The means on parental depression were in the opposite direction from what would have been expected if anxiety or depression had increased after September 11, 2001. We also do not feel it is likely that preexisting differences or seasonal variation accounted for the findings obtained because we conducted analyses to determine if there was evidence supporting either explanation.

One possible reason for the differences between these findings and others has to do with the amount of elapsed time between the terrorist attacks and the administration of measures. As was noted earlier, the Schuster et al. (2001) measures were administered within a week of the attacks. The measures in the Pantin et al. (2003) study were administered in October and November 2001, that is, at approximately the same time as the measures in this study were administered. Although the amount of elapsed time may have to do with differences between the results of the Schuster et al. study and this study, the same cannot be said of the Pantin et al. study. In our view, differences in elapsed time are not a likely explanation for the results obtained.

A more plausible reason for the difference between these findings and those of other studies is that other studies have used measures of PTSD that explicitly referenced the events of September 11, 2001, whereas this study analyzed measures that were administered as part of a scheduled assessment and did not make reference to the terrorist attacks. For example, the measure used by Pantin et al. (2003) assessed hyperarousal with items such as, "Since the terrorist attacks of September 11th, I have been nervous and/or startled easily." Similarly, Schuster et al.'s (2001) study explicitly referenced the day of the terrorist attacks in a survey conducted less than a week following the attacks (e.g., "Since Tuesday, how much have you been bothered by feeling very upset when something reminds you of what happened?").

The historical events surrounding September 11, 2001, appeared to have little if any lasting effect on inner-city parents' or children's levels of anxiety, depression, or feelings of safety. These findings are at variance with the mental health expectations of many following September 11, 2001, which may be summarized by quoting a news item that appeared shortly after the attacks:

> *"Personal security is going to be shaken and everybody's perspective on human life is likely to be shifted by it," said Leslie Carrick-Smith, a British psychologist and trauma expert. "Nobody is really going to feel safe because those towers were icons, symbols of world commerce and order. People realize how vulnerable they are to whoever could actually do that," he said. (Reaney, 2001)*

Similar predictions have appeared in the wake of the disaster befalling the space shuttle Columbia and the beginning of the war with Iraq. Each time, psychologists have been called on to advise the public on what mental health consequences to expect and how to prepare for them. The counsel given has been based, like the recent Institute of Medicine report (2003), either on studies of people directly affected by disaster, or on studies using measures that specifically referenced the disaster in question. Either type of study might be more likely to find effects than studies of noninvolved members of the general population or studies using content-neutral measures of psychological symptoms.

The results of this study suggest four points to consider when called upon to give advice in the wake of publicized disaster or terrorism. First, the evidence is inconclusive regarding the nature and severity of psychological consequences of terrorist attacks. Expectations that are based on studies of victims may not be applicable to those who are not directly victimized, and studies of victims and nonvictims alike suffer from a lack of measures of preexisting pathology and the near impossibility of random assignment. Second, even though the presence of other stressors may amplify the psychological effects of terrorist attacks for victims (Institute of Medicine, 2003), the same may not be true of people who are not directly victimized. Related to this is a third point, namely that those who cope with daily crime and violence in their neighborhoods may have a kind of stress inoculation (Meichenbaum, 1996) against the psychological effects of acts of terrorism. In this study, stress inoculation is one plausible explanation for the absence of symptoms of anxiety, depression, or fear of harm in the urban children and parents assessed after September 11, 2001. Fourth, barring preexisting psychological disorder, nonvictims may cope with the psychological effects of acts of terrorism in ways that are adaptive for their own adjustment and appropriate to the perceived threat facing them or their families. The increased monitoring of children found among the parents in this study may represent a kind of problem-focused coping (Folkman & Lazarus, 1988), when considered in light of the threat of future attacks that was widely believed to exist after September 11, 2001.

Overall, these results suggest that the psychological consequences of such historical tragedies, particularly among residents of distressed neighborhoods who are not directly affected by the tragedy, may be more limited in impact than many have previously predicted. Moreover, parents' natural responses to these kinds of events may be adaptive for their own adjustment and reassuring to their children.

REFERENCES

Ahern, J., Galea, S., Resnick, H., Kilpatrick, D., Bucuvalas, M., Gold, J., & Vlahov, D. (2002). Television images and psychological symptoms after the September 11 terrorist attacks. *Psychiatry, 65,* 289–300.

Askew, G. L., & Joseph, G. E. (2001). *Helping children handle anxiety related to September 11 events.* Retrieved July 22, 2004, from http://www.acf.hhs.gov/programs/cb/publications/helping.htm

Asmundson, G. J. G., Frombach, I., McQuaid, J., Pedrelli, P., Lenox, R., & Stein, M. B. (2000). Dimensionality of posttraumatic stress symptoms: A confirmatory factor analysis of DSM-IV symptom clusters and other symptom models. *Behavioral Research and Therapy, 38,* 203–214.

Beck, A. T., Emery, G., Rush, A. J., & Shaw, B. F. (1979). *Cognitive therapy of depression.* New York: Guilford Press.

Chicago Police Department, Research and Development Division. (2002, October). *Homicide in Chicago.* Chicago: Author.

Epstein, S. (1983). Natural healing processes of the mind: Graded stress inoculation as an inherent coping mechanism. In D. Meichenbaum & M. E. Jaremko (Eds.), *Stress reduction and prevention* (pp. 39–66). New York: Plenum Press.

Folkman, S., & Lazarus, R. S. (1988). Coping as a mediator of emotion. *Personality and Social Psychology Bulletin, 54,* 466–475.

Gorman-Smith, D., Henry, D. B., & Tolan, P. H. (in press). Exposure to community violence and violence perpetration: The protective effects of family functioning. *Journal of Clinical Child and Adolescent Psychology.*

Gorman-Smith, D., Tolan, P. H., Zelli, A., & Huesmann, L. R. (1996). The relation of family functioning to violence among inner-city minority youth. *Journal of Family Psychology, 10,* 115–129.

Henry, D. B. (2000). *Initial report of the Pilot Study for the Evaluation of the SAFE-TO-LEARN Demonstration Project* (Technical Report, Child Health Data Lab, Children's Memorial Hospital). Chicago, IL: Author.

Institute of Medicine. (2003). *Preparing for the psychological consequences of terrorism: A public health strategy.* Washington, DC: National Academies Press.

Kellam, S. G., Brown, C. H., Rubin, B. R., & Ensminger, M. E. (1983). Paths leading to teenage psychiatric symptoms and substance use: Developmental epidemiological studies in Woodlawn. In S. B. Guze, F. J. Earls, & J. E. Barrett (Eds.), *Childhood psychopathology and development* (pp. 17–47). Chicago: University of Chicago Press.

Meichenbaum, D. (1996). Stress inoculation training for coping with stressors. *Clinical Psychologist, 49,* 4–7.

Overall, J. E., Atlas, R. S., & Gibson, J. M. (1995). Tests that are robust against variance heterogeneity in k 2 designs with unequal cell frequencies. *Psychological Reports, 76,* 1011–1017.

Pantin, H. M., Schwartz, S. J., Prado, G., Feaster, D. J., & Szapocznik, J. (2003). Posttraumatic stress disorder symptoms in Hispanic immigrants after the September 11th attacks: Severity and relationship to previous traumatic exposure. *Hispanic Journal of Behavioral Sciences, 25,* 56–72.

Reaney, P. (2001, September 11). *Psychologists: Attacks will leave deep scars.* Retrieved July 22, 2004, from http://www.fenichel.com/yahoo-wtc.shtml

Richters, J. E., & Martinez, P. (1993). The NIMH community violence project: I. Children as victims of and witnesses to violence. *Psychiatry, 56,* 7–21.

Schuster, M. A., Stein, B. D., Jaycox, L. H., Collins, R. L., Marshall, G. N., Elliott, M. N., Zhou, A. J., Kanouse, D. E., Morrison, J. L., & Berry, S. H. (2001). A national survey of stress reactions after the September 11, 2001, terrorist attacks. *New England Journal of Medicine, 345,* 1507–1512.

Schwab-Stone, M. E., Ayers, T. S., Kasprow, W., Voyce, C., Barone, C., Shriver, T., & Weissberg, R. P. (1995). No safe haven: A study of violence exposure in an urban community. *Journal of the American Academy of Child and Adolescent Psychiatry, 34,* 1343–1352.

Tolan, P. H., Gorman-Smith, D., & Henry, D. (in press). Supporting families in a high-risk setting: Proximal effects of the SAFEChildren prevention program. *Journal of Consulting and Clinical Psychology.*

Tolan, P. H., Gorman-Smith, D., Huesmann, L. R., & Zelli, A. (1997). Assessing family processes to explain risk for antisocial behavior and depression among urban youth. *Psychological Assessment, 9,* 212–223.

Wilson, W. J. (1987). *The truly disadvantaged: The inner city, the underclass, and public policy.* Chicago: University of Chicago Press.

Zimmerman, D. W. (1996). Some properties of preliminary tests of equality of variances in the two-sample location problem. *Journal of General Psychology, 123,* 217–231.

Zimmerman, D. W., & Zumbo, B. D. (1993). Rank transformations and the power of the Student *t* test and Welch *t* test for non-normal populations with unequal variances. *Canadian Journal of Experimental Psychology, 47,* 523–539.

CRITICAL THINKING QUESTIONS

1. What do you think of the *stress inoculation* explanation presented in the "Discussion" section to explain the results of this study? Do you think that people with less stress and danger in their daily lives would be more affected by the events of major terrorist attacks? Defend your position, using concrete examples, where possible, of how people reacted differently to the events of 9-11.

2. Previous studies have found that viewers' subjective sense of well-being is negatively affected by how much news they watch. In other words, the more news a person watches, the less safe he or she feels. Do you think this is true for how people responded to the events of September 11? Why or why not? Could you test your ideas, even this far removed in time from the event? Explain.

3. Other than the issues discussed in the article, what other factors may have affected how a person responded to the events of September 11? Be sure to discuss why you think each of these factors may have had an impact.

4. On December 26, 2004, the tsunami disaster had just occurred in Southeast Asia. Considering what this article said about the response of people near to and far removed from the September 11 attacks, how might people respond to the tsunami disaster? Discuss your answer, addressing both similarities and differences.

CHAPTER INTEGRATION QUESTIONS _____

1. "That which does not kill me, makes me stronger," wrote Friedrich Nietzsche, German philosopher. Discuss this quotation in the context of the three articles in this chapter.

2. The three articles in this chapter all dealt with stress in one form or another. Integrate the findings of the articles into one or more conclusions on how stress affects people. Explain your conclusions.

3. Again, all three articles in this chapter looked at stress. What social psychological factors other than stress might have an impact on health? Explain your answers.

Author Index

Subject Index